GENERAL MOTORS
DEVILLE/FLEETWOOD/ELDORADO/SEVILLE
1990-98 REPAIR MANUAL

CHILTON'S CHILTON'S

Covers all U.S. and Canadian models of
**Cadillac DeVille, DeVille Concours, Eldorado,
Fleetwood and Seville
Front Wheel Drive Models**

by **Joseph D'Orazio,** A.S.S.
and **Eric Michael Mihalyi,** A.S.E., S.T.S., S.A.E.,

CHILTON *Automotive Books*

PUBLISHED BY **HAYNES NORTH AMERICA. Inc.**

APA
AUTOMOTIVE
PARTS &
ACCESSORIES
ASSOCIATION MEMBER

Manufactured in USA
© 2000 Haynes North America, Inc.
ISBN 0-8019-9104-8
Library of Congress Catalog Card No. 00-132513
1234567890 9876543210

Haynes Publishing Group
Sparkford Nr Yeovil
Somerset BA22 7JJ England

Haynes North America, Inc
861 Lawrence Drive
Newbury Park
California 91320 USA

ABCDE
FGH

Contents

Contents

SAFETY NOTICE

Proper service and repair procedures are vital to the safe, reliable operation of all motor vehicles, as well as the personal safety of those performing repairs. This manual outlines procedures for servicing and repairing vehicles using safe, effective methods. The procedures contain many NOTES, CAUTIONS and WARNINGS which should be followed, along with standard procedures to eliminate the possibility of personal injury or improper service which could damage the vehicle or compromise its safety.

It is important to note that repair procedures and techniques, tools and parts for servicing motor vehicles, as well as the skill and experience of the individual performing the work vary widely. It is not possible to anticipate all of the conceivable ways or conditions under which vehicles may be serviced, or to provide cautions as to all possible hazards that may result. Standard and accepted safety precautions and equipment should be used when handling toxic or flammable fluids, and safety goggles or other protection should be used during cutting, grinding, chiseling, prying, or any other process that can cause material removal or projectiles.

Some procedures require the use of tools specially designed for a specific purpose. Before substituting another tool or procedure, you must be completely satisfied that neither your personal safety, nor the performance of the vehicle will be endangered.

Although information in this manual is based on industry sources and is complete as possible at the time of publication, the possibility exists that some car manufacturers made later changes which could not be included here. While striving for total accuracy, the authors or publishers cannot assume responsibility for any errors, changes or omissions that may occur in the compilation of this data.

PART NUMBERS

Part numbers listed in this reference are not recommendations by Haynes North America, Inc. for any product brand name. They are references that can be used with interchange manuals and aftermarket supplier catalogs to locate each brand supplier's discrete part number.

SPECIAL TOOLS

Special tools are recommended by the vehicle manufacturer to perform their specific job. Use has been kept to a minimum, but where absolutely necessary, they are referred to in the text by the part number of the tool manufacturer. These tools can be purchased, under the appropriate part number, from your local dealer or regional distributor, or an equivalent tool can be purchased locally from a tool supplier or parts outlet. Before substituting any tool for the one recommended, read the SAFETY NOTICE at the top of this page.

ACKNOWLEDGMENTS

Portions of materials contained herein have been reprinted with the permission of General Motors Corporation, Service Technology Group.

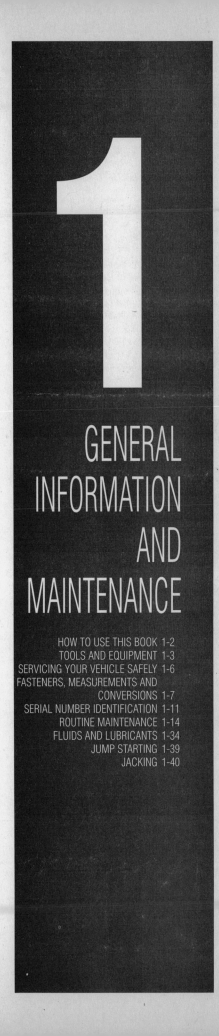

1

GENERAL INFORMATION AND MAINTENANCE

HOW TO USE THIS BOOK

Chilton's Total Car Care manual for the 1990 to 1998 Cadillac Deville, Fleetwood (front wheel drive only), Eldorado, and Seville is intended to help you learn more about the inner workings of your vehicle while saving you money on its upkeep and operation.

The beginning of the book will likely be referred to the most, since that is where you will find information for maintenance and tune-up. The other sections deal with the more complex systems of your vehicle. Operating systems from engine through brakes are covered to the extent that the average do-it-yourselfer becomes mechanically involved. This book will not explain such things as rebuilding a differential for the simple reason that the expertise required and the investment in special tools make this task uneconomical. It will, however, give you detailed instructions to help you change your own brake pads and shoes, replace spark plugs, and perform many more jobs that can save you money, give you personal satisfaction and help you avoid expensive problems.

A secondary purpose of this book is a reference for owners who want to understand their vehicle and/or their mechanics. In this case, no tools at all are required.

Where to Begin

Before removing any bolts, read through the entire procedure. This will give you the overall view of what tools and supplies will be required. There is nothing more frustrating than having to walk to the bus stop on Monday morning because you were short one bolt on Sunday afternoon. So read ahead and plan ahead. Each operation should be approached logically and all procedures thoroughly understood before attempting any work.

All sections contain adjustments, maintenance, removal and installation procedures, and in some cases, repair or overhaul procedures. When repair is not considered practical, we tell you how to remove the part and then how to install the new or rebuilt replacement. In this way, you at least save labor costs. "Backyard" repair of some components is just not practical.

Avoiding Trouble

Many procedures in this book require you to "label and disconnect . . . " a group of lines, hoses or wires. Don't be lulled into thinking you can remember where everything goes—you won't. If you hook up vacuum or fuel lines incorrectly, the vehicle may run poorly, if at all. If you hook up electrical wiring incorrectly, you may instantly learn a very expensive lesson.

You don't need to know the official or engineering name for each hose or line. A piece of masking tape on the hose and a piece on its fitting will allow you to assign your own label such as the letter A or a short name. As long as you remember your own code, the lines can be reconnected by matching similar letters or names. Do remember that tape will dissolve in gasoline or other fluids; if a component is to be washed or cleaned, use another method of identification. A permanent felt-tipped marker or a metal scribe can be very handy for marking metal parts. Remove any tape or paper labels after assembly.

Maintenance or Repair?

It's necessary to mention the difference between maintenance and repair. Maintenance includes routine inspections, adjustments, and replacement of parts which show signs of normal wear. Maintenance compensates for wear or deterioration. Repair implies that something has broken or is not working. A need for repair is often caused by lack of maintenance. Example: draining and refilling the automatic transmission fluid is maintenance recommended by the manufacturer at specific mileage intervals. Failure to do this can shorten the life of the transmission/transaxle, requiring very expensive repairs. While no maintenance program can prevent items from breaking or wearing out, a general rule can be stated: MAINTENANCE IS CHEAPER THAN REPAIR.

Two basic mechanic's rules should be mentioned here. First, whenever the left side of the vehicle or engine is referred to, it is meant to specify the driver's side. Conversely, the right side of the vehicle means the passenger's side. Second, screws and bolts are removed by turning counterclockwise, and tightened by turning clockwise unless specifically noted.

Safety is always the most important rule. Constantly be aware of the dangers involved in working on an automobile and take the proper precautions. See the information regarding SERVICING YOUR VEHICLE SAFELY and the SAFETY NOTICE on the acknowledgment page.

Avoiding the Most Common Mistakes

Pay attention to the instructions provided. There are 3 common mistakes in mechanical work:

1. Incorrect order of assembly, disassembly or adjustment. When taking something apart or putting it together, performing steps in the wrong order usually just costs you extra time; however, it CAN break something. Read the entire procedure before beginning disassembly. Perform everything in the order in which the instructions say you should, even if you can't immediately see a reason for it. When you're taking apart something that is very intricate, you might want to draw a picture of how it looks when assembled at one point in order to make sure you get everything back in its proper position. We will supply exploded views whenever possible. When making adjustments, perform them in the proper order. One adjustment possibly will affect another.

2. Overtorquing (or undertorquing). While it is more common for overtorquing to cause damage, undertorquing may allow a fastener to vibrate loose causing serious damage. Especially when dealing with aluminum parts, pay attention to torque specifications and utilize a torque wrench in assembly. If a torque figure is not available, remember that if you are using the right tool to perform the job, you will probably not have to strain yourself to get a fastener tight enough. The pitch of most threads is so slight that the tension you put on the wrench will be multiplied many times in actual force on what you are tightening. A good example of how critical torque is can be seen in the case of spark plug installation, especially where you are putting the plug into an aluminum cylinder head. Too little torque can fail to crush the gasket, causing leakage of combustion gases and consequent overheating of the plug and engine parts. Too much torque can damage the threads or distort the plug, changing the spark gap.

There are many commercial products available for ensuring that fasteners won't come loose, even if they are not torqued just right (a very common brand is Loctite®). If you're worried about getting something together tight enough to hold, but loose enough to avoid mechanical damage during assembly, one of these products might offer substantial insurance. Before choosing a threadlocking compound, read the label on the package and make sure the product is compatible with the materials, fluids, etc. involved.

3. Crossthreading. This occurs when a part such as a bolt is screwed into a nut or casting at the wrong angle and forced. Crossthreading is more likely to occur if access is difficult. It helps to clean and lubricate fasteners, then to start threading the bolt, spark plug, etc. with your fingers. If you encounter resistance, unscrew the part and start over again at a different angle until it can be inserted and turned several times without much effort. Keep in mind that many parts, especially spark plugs, have tapered threads, so that gentle turning will automatically bring the part you're threading to the proper angle. Don't put a wrench on the part until it's been tightened a couple of turns by hand. If you suddenly encounter resistance, and the part has not seated fully, don't force it. Pull it back out to make sure it's clean and threading properly.

Be sure to take your time and be patient, and always plan ahead. Allow yourself ample time to perform repairs and maintenance. You may find maintaining your car a satisfying and enjoyable experience.

TOOLS AND EQUIPMENT

▶ **See Figures 1 thru 15**

Naturally, without the proper tools and equipment it is impossible to properly service your vehicle. It would also be virtually impossible to catalog every tool that you would need to perform all of the operations in this book. Of course, It would be unwise for the amateur to rush out and buy an expensive set of tools on the theory that he/she may need one or more of them at some time.

The best approach is to proceed slowly, gathering a good quality set of those tools that are used most frequently. Don't be misled by the low cost of bargain tools. It is far better to spend a little more for better quality. Forged wrenches, 6 or 12-point sockets and fine tooth ratchets are by far preferable to their less expensive counterparts. As any good mechanic can tell you, there are few worse experiences than trying to work on a vehicle with bad tools. Your monetary savings will be far outweighed by frustration and mangled knuckles.

Begin accumulating those tools that are used most frequently: those associated with routine maintenance and tune-up. In addition to the normal assortment of screwdrivers and pliers, you should have the following tools:

• Wrenches/sockets and combination open end/box end wrenches in sizes from 1/8 –3/4 in. or 3–19mm, as well as a 13/16 in. or 5/8 in. spark plug socket (depending on plug type).

➡ **If possible, buy various length socket drive extensions. Universal-joint and wobble extensions can be extremely useful, but be careful when using them, as they can change the amount of torque applied to the socket.**

• Jackstands for support.
• Oil filter wrench.
• Spout or funnel for pouring fluids.

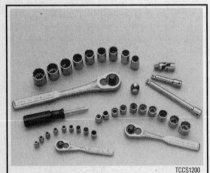

TCCS1200

Fig. 1 All but the most basic procedures will require an assortment of ratchets and sockets

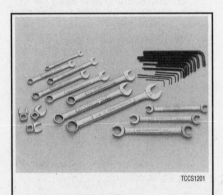

TCCS1201

Fig. 2 In addition to ratchets, a good set of wrenches and hex keys will be necessary

TCCS1202

Fig. 3 A hydraulic floor jack and a set of jackstands are essential for lifting and supporting the vehicle

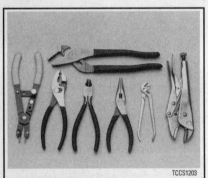

TCCS1203

Fig. 4 An assortment of pliers, grippers and cutters will be handy for old rusted parts and stripped bolt heads

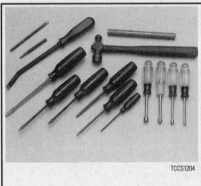

TCCS1204

Fig. 5 Various drivers, chisels and prybars are great tools to have in your toolbox

TCCS1205

Fig. 6 Many repairs will require the use of a torque wrench to assure the components are properly fastened

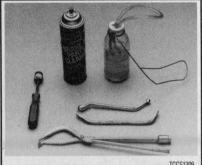

TCCS1209

Fig. 7 Although not always necessary, using specialized brake tools will save time

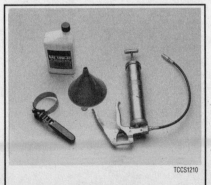

TCCS1210

Fig. 8 A few inexpensive lubrication tools will make maintenance easier

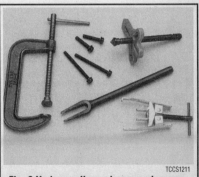

TCCS1211

Fig. 9 Various pullers, clamps and separator tools are needed for many larger, more complicated repairs

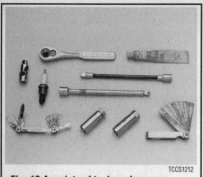

Fig. 10 A variety of tools and gauges should be used for spark plug gapping and installation

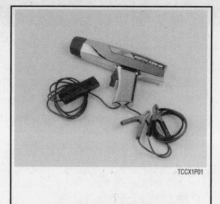

Fig. 11 Inductive type timing light

Fig. 12 A screw-in type compression gauge is recommended for compression testing

Fig. 13 A vacuum/pressure tester is necessary for many testing procedures

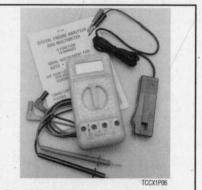

Fig. 14 Most modern automotive multimeters incorporate many helpful features

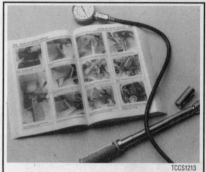

Fig. 15 Proper information is vital, so always have a Chilton Total Car Care manual handy

• Grease gun for chassis lubrication (unless your vehicle is not equipped with any grease fittings—for details, please refer to information on Fluids and Lubricants).

• Hydrometer for checking the battery (unless equipped with a sealed, maintenance-free battery).

• A container for draining oil and other fluids.

• Rags for wiping up the inevitable mess.

In addition to the above items there are several others that are not absolutely necessary, but handy to have around. These include Oil Dry® (or an equivalent oil absorbent gravel—such as cat litter) and the usual supply of lubricants, antifreeze and fluids, although these can be purchased as needed. This is a basic list for routine maintenance, but only your personal needs and desire can accurately determine your list of tools.

After performing a few projects on the vehicle, you'll be amazed at the other tools and non-tools on your workbench. Some useful household items are: a large turkey baster or siphon, empty coffee cans and ice trays (to store parts), ball of twine, electrical tape for wiring, small rolls of colored tape for tagging lines or hoses, markers and pens, a note pad, golf tees (for plugging vacuum lines), metal coat hangers or a roll of mechanic's wire (to hold things out of the way), dental pick or similar long, pointed probe, a strong magnet, and a small mirror (to see into recesses and under manifolds).

A more advanced set of tools, suitable for tune-

up work, can be drawn up easily. While the tools are slightly more sophisticated, they need not be outrageously expensive. There are several inexpensive tach/dwell meters on the market that are every bit as good for the average mechanic as a professional model. Just be sure that it goes to a least 1200–1500 rpm on the tach scale and that it works on 4, 6 and 8-cylinder engines. The key to these purchases is to make them with an eye towards adaptability and wide range. A basic list of tune-up tools could include:

• Tach/dwell meter.
• Spark plug wrench and gapping tool.
• Feeler gauges for valve adjustment.
• Timing light.

The choice of a timing light should be made carefully. A light which works on the DC current supplied by the vehicle's battery is the best choice; it should have a xenon tube for brightness. On any vehicle with an electronic ignition system, a timing light with an inductive pickup that clamps around the No. 1 spark plug cable is preferred.

In addition to these basic tools, there are several other tools and gauges you may find useful. These include:

• Compression gauge. The screw-in type is slower to use, but eliminates the possibility of a faulty reading due to escaping pressure.
• Manifold vacuum gauge.
• 12V test light.
• A combination volt/ohmmeter

• Induction Ammeter. This is used for determining whether or not there is current in a wire. These are handy for use if a wire is broken somewhere in a wiring harness.

As a final note, you will probably find a torque wrench necessary for all but the most basic work. The beam type models are perfectly adequate, although the newer click types (breakaway) are easier to use. The click type torque wrenches tend to be more expensive. Also keep in mind that all types of torque wrenches should be periodically checked and/or recalibrated. You will have to decide for yourself which better fits your pocketbook, and purpose.

Special Tools

Normally, the use of special factory tools is avoided for repair procedures, since these are not readily available for the do-it-yourself mechanic. When it is possible to perform the job with more commonly available tools, it will be pointed out, but occasionally, a special tool was designed to perform a specific function and should be used. Before substituting another tool, you should be convinced that neither your safety nor the performance of the vehicle will be compromised.

Special tools can usually be purchased from an automotive parts store or from your dealer. In some cases special tools may be available directly from the tool manufacturer.

DIAGNOSTIC TEST EQUIPMENT

Modern vehicles equipped with computer-controlled fuel, emission and ignition systems require modern electronic tools to diagnose problems. Many of these tools are designed solely for the professional mechanic and are too costly and difficult to use for the average do-it-yourselfer. However, various automotive aftermarket companies have introduced products that address the needs of the average home mechanic, providing sophisticated information at affordable cost. Consult your local auto parts store to determine what is available for your vehicle.

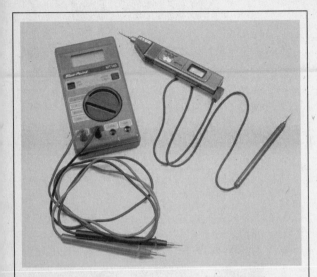

Digital multimeters come in a variety of styles and are a "must-have" for any serious home mechanic. Digital multimeters measure voltage (volts), resistance (ohms) and sometimes current (amperes). These versatile tools are used for checking all types of electrical or electronic components

Trouble code tools allow the home mechanic to extract the "fault code" number from an on-board computer that has sensed a problem (usually indicated by a Check Engine light). Armed with this code, the home mechanic can focus attention on a suspect system or component

Sensor testers perform specific checks on many of the sensors and actuators used on today's computer-controlled vehicles. These testers can check sensors both on or off the vehicle, as well as test the accompanying electrical circuits

Hand-held scanners represent the most sophisticated of all do-it-yourself diagnostic tools. These tools do more than just access computer codes like the code readers above; they provide the user with an actual interface into the vehicle's computer. Comprehensive data on specific makes and models will come with the tool, either built-in or as a separate cartridge

SERVICING YOUR VEHICLE SAFELY

▶ **See Figures 16, 17, 18 and 19**

It is virtually impossible to anticipate all of the hazards involved with automotive maintenance and service, but care and common sense will prevent most accidents.

The rules of safety for mechanics range from "don't smoke around gasoline," to "use the proper tool(s) for the job." The trick to avoiding injuries is to develop safe work habits and to take every possible precaution.

Do's

• Do keep a fire extinguisher and first aid kit handy.

• Do wear safety glasses or goggles when cutting, drilling, grinding or prying, even if you have 20–20 vision. If you wear glasses for the sake of vision, wear safety goggles over your regular glasses.

• Do shield your eyes whenever you work around the battery. Batteries contain sulfuric acid. In case of contact with the eyes or skin, flush the area with water or a mixture of water and baking soda, then seek immediate medical attention.

• Do use safety stands (jackstands) for any undervehicle service. Jacks are for raising vehicles; jackstands are for making sure the vehicle stays raised until you want it to come down. Whenever the vehicle is raised, block the wheels remaining on the ground and set the parking brake.

• Do use adequate ventilation when working with any chemicals or hazardous materials. Like carbon monoxide, the asbestos dust resulting from some brake lining wear can be hazardous in sufficient quantities.

• Do disconnect the negative battery cable when working on the electrical system. The secondary ignition system contains EXTREMELY HIGH VOLTAGE. In some cases it can even exceed 50,000 volts.

• Do follow manufacturer's directions whenever working with potentially hazardous materials. Most chemicals and fluids are poisonous if taken internally.

• Do properly maintain your tools. Loose hammerheads, mushroomed punches and chisels, frayed or poorly grounded electrical cords, excessively worn screwdrivers, spread wrenches (open end), cracked sockets, slipping ratchets, or faulty droplight sockets can cause accidents.

• Likewise, keep your tools clean; a greasy wrench can slip off a bolt head, ruining the bolt and often harming your knuckles in the process.

• Do use the proper size and type of tool for the job at hand. Do select a wrench or socket that fits the nut or bolt. The wrench or socket should sit straight, not cocked.

• Do, when possible, pull on a wrench handle rather than push on it, and adjust your stance to prevent a fall.

• Do be sure that adjustable wrenches are tightly closed on the nut or bolt and pulled so that the force is on the side of the fixed jaw.

• Do strike squarely with a hammer; avoid glancing blows.

• Do set the parking brake and block the drive wheels if the work requires a running engine.

Don'ts

• Don't run the engine in a garage or anywhere else without proper ventilation—EVER! Carbon monoxide is poisonous; it takes a long time to leave the human body and you can build up a deadly supply of it in your system by simply breathing in a little every day. You may not realize you are slowly poisoning yourself. Always use power vents, windows, fans and/or open the garage door.

• Don't work around moving parts while wearing loose clothing. Short sleeves are much safer than long, loose sleeves. Hard-toed shoes with neoprene soles protect your toes and give a better grip on slippery surfaces. Jewelry such as watches, fancy belt buckles, beads or body adornment of any kind is not safe working around a vehicle. Long hair should be tied back under a hat or cap.

• Don't use pockets for toolboxes. A fall or bump can drive a screwdriver deep into your body. Even a rag hanging from your back pocket can wrap around a spinning shaft or fan.

• Don't smoke when working around gasoline, cleaning solvent or other flammable material.

• Don't smoke when working around the battery. When the battery is being charged, it gives off explosive hydrogen gas.

• Don't use gasoline to wash your hands; there are excellent soaps available. Gasoline contains dangerous additives which can enter the body through a cut or through your pores. Gasoline also removes all the natural oils from the skin so that bone dry hands will suck up oil and grease.

• Don't service the air conditioning system unless you are equipped with the necessary tools and training. When liquid or compressed gas refrigerant is released to atmospheric pressure it will absorb heat from whatever it contacts. This will chill or freeze anything it touches.

• Don't use screwdrivers for anything other than driving screws! A screwdriver used as an prying tool can snap when you least expect it, causing injuries. At the very least, you'll ruin a good screwdriver.

• Don't use an emergency jack (that little ratchet, scissors, or pantograph jack supplied with the vehicle) for anything other than changing a flat! These jacks are only intended for emergency use out on the road; they are NOT designed as a maintenance tool. If you are serious about maintaining your vehicle yourself, invest in a hydraulic floor jack of at least a 1½ ton capacity, and at least two sturdy jackstands.

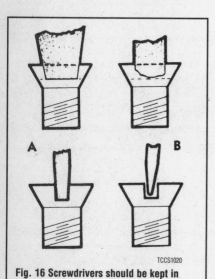

TCCS1020

Fig. 16 Screwdrivers should be kept in good condition to prevent injury or damage which could result if the blade slips from the screw

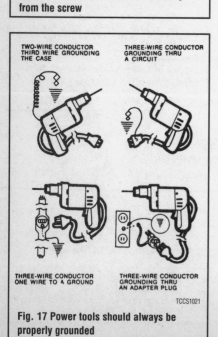

TWO-WIRE CONDUCTOR THIRD WIRE GROUNDING THE CASE

THREE-WIRE CONDUCTOR GROUNDING THRU A CIRCUIT

THREE-WIRE CONDUCTOR ONE WIRE TO A GROUND

THREE-WIRE CONDUCTOR GROUNDING THRU AN ADAPTER PLUG

TCCS1021

Fig. 17 Power tools should always be properly grounded

TCCS1022

Fig. 18 Using the correct size wrench will help prevent the possibility of rounding off a nut

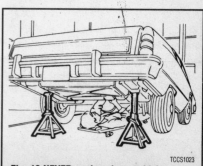

TCCS1023

Fig. 19 NEVER work under a vehicle unless it is supported using safety stands (jackstands)

FASTENERS, MEASUREMENTS AND CONVERSIONS

Bolts, Nuts and Other Threaded Retainers

▶ See Figures 20, 21, 22 and 23

Although there are a great variety of fasteners found in the modern car or truck, the most commonly used retainer is the threaded fastener (nuts, bolts, screws, studs, etc.). Most threaded retainers may be reused, provided that they are not damaged in use or during the repair. Some retainers (such as stretch bolts or torque prevailing nuts) are designed to deform when tightened or in use and should not be reinstalled.

Whenever possible, we will note any special retainers which should be replaced during a procedure. But you should always inspect the condition of a retainer when it is removed and replace any that show signs of damage. Check all threads for rust or corrosion which can increase the torque necessary to achieve the desired clamp load for which that fastener was originally selected. Additionally, be sure that the driver surface of the fastener has not been compromised by rounding or other damage. In some cases a driver surface may become only partially rounded, allowing the driver to catch in only one direction. In many of these occurrences, a fastener may be installed and tightened, but the driver would not be able to grip and loosen the fastener again. (This could lead to frustration down the line should that component ever need to be disassembled again).

If you must replace a fastener, whether due to design or damage, you must ALWAYS be sure to use the proper replacement. In all cases, a retainer of the same design, material and strength should be used. Markings on the heads of most bolts will help determine the proper strength of the fastener. The same material, thread and pitch must be selected to assure proper installation and safe operation of the vehicle afterwards.

Thread gauges are available to help measure a bolt or stud's thread. Most automotive and hardware stores keep gauges available to help you select the proper size. In a pinch, you can use another nut or bolt for a thread gauge. If the bolt you are replacing is not too badly damaged, you can select a match by finding another bolt which will thread in its place. If you find a nut which threads properly onto the damaged bolt, then use that nut to help select the replacement bolt. If however, the bolt you are replacing is so badly damaged (broken or drilled

Fig. 20 Here are a few of the most common screw/bolt driver styles

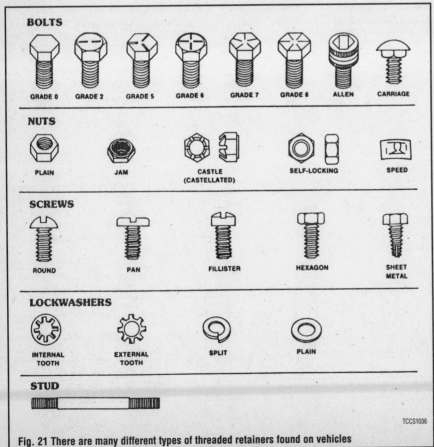

Fig. 21 There are many different types of threaded retainers found on vehicles

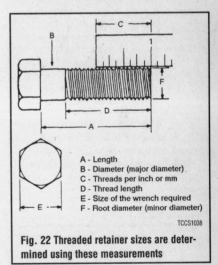

A - Length
B - Diameter (major diameter)
C - Threads per inch or mm
D - Thread length
E - Size of the wrench required
F - Root diameter (minor diameter)

Fig. 22 Threaded retainer sizes are determined using these measurements

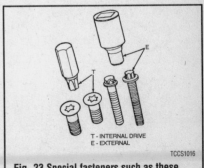

T - INTERNAL DRIVE
E - EXTERNAL

Fig. 23 Special fasteners such as these Torx® head bolts are used by manufacturers to discourage people from working on vehicles without the proper tools

out) that its threads cannot be used as a gauge, you might start by looking for another bolt (from the same assembly or a similar location on your vehicle) which will thread into the damaged bolt's mounting. If so, the other bolt can be used to select a nut; the nut can then be used to select the replacement bolt.

In all cases, be absolutely sure you have selected the proper replacement. Don't be shy, you can always ask the store clerk for help.

✳✳ WARNING

Be aware that when you find a bolt with damaged threads, you may also find the nut or drilled hole it was threaded into has also been damaged. If this is the case, you may have to drill and tap the hole, replace the nut or otherwise repair the threads. NEVER try to force a replacement bolt to fit into the damaged threads.

Torque

Torque is defined as the measurement of resistance to turning or rotating. It tends to twist a body about an axis of rotation. A common example of this would be tightening a threaded retainer such as a nut, bolt or screw. Measuring torque is one of the most common ways to help assure that a threaded retainer has been properly fastened.

When tightening a threaded fastener, torque is applied in three distinct areas, the head, the bearing surface and the clamp load. About 50 percent of the measured torque is used in overcoming bearing friction. This is the friction between the bearing surface of the bolt head, screw head or nut face and the base material or washer (the surface on which the fastener is rotating). Approximately 40 percent of the applied torque is used in overcoming thread friction. This leaves only about 10 percent of the applied torque to develop a useful clamp load (the force which holds a joint together). This means that friction can account for as much as 90 percent of the applied torque on a fastener.

TORQUE WRENCHES

▶ **See Figures 24, 25 and 26**

In most applications, a torque wrench can be used to assure proper installation of a fastener. Torque wrenches come in various designs and most automotive supply stores will carry a variety

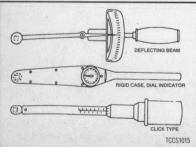

DEFLECTING BEAM

RIGID CASE, DIAL INDICATOR

CLICK TYPE

TCCS1015

Fig. 24 Various styles of torque wrenches are usually available at your local automotive supply store

	Mark	Class		Mark	Class
Hexagon head bolt	4— 5— Bolt 6— head No. 7— 8— 9— 10— 11—	4T 5T 6T 7T 8T 9T 10T 11T	Stud bolt	No mark	4T
	No mark	4T			
Hexagon flange bolt w/ washer hexagon bolt	No mark	4T		Grooved	6T
Hexagon head bolt	Two protruding lines	5T			
Hexagon flange bolt w/ washer hexagon bolt	Two protruding lines	6T	Welded bolt		
Hexagon head bolt	Three protruding lines	7T			4T
Hexagon head bolt	Four protruding lines	8T			

TCCS1240

Fig. 25 Determining bolt strength of metric fasteners—NOTE: this is a typical bolt marking system, but there is not a worldwide standard

Class	Diameter mm	Pitch mm	Specified torque					
			Hexagon head bolt			Hexagon flange bolt		
			N·m	kgf·cm	ft·lbf	N·m	kgf·cm	ft·lbf
4T	6	1	5	55	48 in.·lbf	6	60	52 in.·lbf
	8	1.25	12.5	130	9	14	145	10
	10	1.25	26	260	19	29	290	21
	12	1.25	47	480	35	53	540	39
	14	1.5	74	760	55	84	850	61
	16	1.5	115	1,150	83	—	—	—
5T	6	1	6.5	65	56 in.·lbf	7.5	75	65 in.·lbf
	8	1.25	15.5	160	12	17.5	175	13
	10	1.25	32	330	24	36	360	26
	12	1.25	59	600	43	65	670	48
	14	1.5	91	930	67	100	1,050	76
	16	1.5	140	1,400	101	—	—	—
6T	6	1	8	80	69 in.·lbf	9	90	78 in.·lbf
	8	1.25	19	195	14	21	210	15
	10	1.25	39	400	29	44	440	32
	12	1.25	71	730	53	80	810	59
	14	1.5	110	1,100	80	125	1,250	90
	16	1.5	170	1,750	127	—	—	—
7T	6	1	10.5	110	8	12	120	9
	8	1.25	25	260	19	28	290	21
	10	1.25	52	530	38	58	590	43
	12	1.25	95	970	70	105	1,050	76
	14	1.5	145	1,500	108	165	1,700	123
	16	1.5	230	2,300	166	—	—	—
8T	8	1.25	29	300	22	33	330	24
	10	1.25	61	620	45	68	690	50
	12	1.25	110	1,100	80	120	1,250	90
9T	8	1.25	34	340	25	37	380	27
	10	1.25	70	710	51	78	790	57
	12	1.25	125	1,300	94	140	1,450	105
10T	8	1.25	38	390	28	42	430	31
	10	1.25	78	800	58	88	890	64
	12	1.25	140	1,450	105	155	1,600	116
11T	8	1.25	42	430	31	47	480	35
	10	1.25	87	890	64	97	990	72
	12	1.25	155	1,600	116	175	1,800	130

TCCS1241

Fig. 26 Typical bolt torques for metric fasteners—WARNING: use only as a guide

to suit your needs. A torque wrench should be used any time we supply a specific torque value for a fastener. A torque wrench can also be used if you are following the general guidelines in the accompanying charts. Keep in mind that because there is no worldwide standardization of fasteners, the charts are a general guideline and should be used with caution. Again, the general rule of "if you are using the right tool for the job, you should not have to strain to tighten a fastener" applies here.

Beam Type

▶ See Figure 27

The beam type torque wrench is one of the most popular types. It consists of a pointer attached to the head that runs the length of the flexible beam (shaft) to a scale located near the handle. As the wrench is pulled, the beam bends and the pointer indicates the torque using the scale.

Click (Breakaway) Type

▶ See Figure 28

Another popular design of torque wrench is the click type. To use the click type wrench you pre-adjust it to a torque setting. Once the torque is reached, the wrench has a reflex signaling feature that causes a momentary breakaway of the torque wrench body, sending an impulse to the operator's hand.

Pivot Head Type

▶ See Figures 28 and 29

Some torque wrenches (usually of the click type) may be equipped with a pivot head which can allow it to be used in areas of limited access. BUT, it must be used properly. To hold a pivot head wrench, grasp the handle lightly, and as you pull on the handle, it should be floated on the pivot point. If the handle comes in contact with the yoke extension during the process of pulling, there is a very good chance the torque readings will be inaccurate because this could alter the wrench loading point. The design of the handle is usually such as to make it inconvenient to deliberately misuse the wrench.

➡ **It should be mentioned that the use of any U-joint, wobble or extension will have an effect on the torque readings, no matter what type of wrench you are using. For the most accurate readings, install the socket directly on the wrench driver. If necessary, straight extensions (which hold a socket directly under the wrench driver) will have the least effect on the torque reading. Avoid any extension that alters the length of the wrench from the handle to the head/driving point (such as a crow's foot). U-joint or wobble extensions can greatly affect the readings; avoid their use at all times.**

Rigid Case (Direct Reading)

▶ See Figure 30

A rigid case or direct reading torque wrench is equipped with a dial indicator to show torque values. One advantage of these wrenches is that they can be held at any position on the wrench without affecting accuracy. These wrenches are often preferred because they tend to be compact, easy to read and have a great degree of accuracy.

TORQUE ANGLE METERS

▶ See Figure 31

Because the frictional characteristics of each fastener or threaded hole will vary, clamp loads which are based strictly on torque will vary as well. In most applications, this variance is not significant enough to cause worry. But, in certain applications, a manufacturer's engineers may determine that more precise clamp loads are necessary (such is the case with many aluminum cylinder heads). In these cases, a torque angle method of installation would be specified. When installing fasteners which are torque angle tightened, a predetermined seating torque and standard torque wrench are usually used first to remove any compliance from the joint. The fastener is then tightened the specified additional portion of a turn measured in degrees. A torque angle gauge (mechanical protractor) is used for these applications.

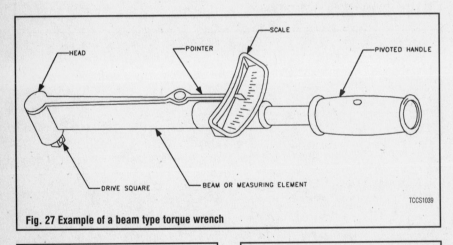

Fig. 27 Example of a beam type torque wrench

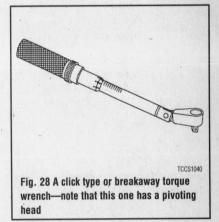

Fig. 28 A click type or breakaway torque wrench—note that this one has a pivoting head

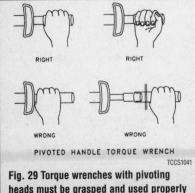

Fig. 29 Torque wrenches with pivoting heads must be grasped and used properly to prevent an incorrect reading

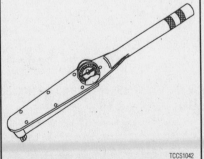

Fig. 30 The rigid case (direct reading) torque wrench uses a dial indicator to show torque

Fig. 31 Some specifications require the use of a torque angle meter (mechanical protractor)

Standard and Metric Measurements

♦ See Figure 32

Throughout this manual, specifications are given to help you determine the condition of various components on your vehicle, or to assist you in their installation. Some of the most common measurements include length (in. or cm/mm), torque (ft. lbs., inch lbs. or Nm) and pressure (psi, in. Hg, kPa or mm Hg). In most cases, we strive to provide the proper measurement as determined by the manufacturer's engineers.

Though, in some cases, that value may not be conveniently measured with what is available in your toolbox. Luckily, many of the measuring devices which are available today will have two scales so the Standard or Metric measurements may easily be taken. If any of the various measuring tools which are available to you do not contain the same scale as listed in the specifications, use the accompanying conversion factors to determine the proper value.

CONVERSION FACTORS

LENGTH–DISTANCE

Inches (in.)	x 25.4	= Millimeters (mm)	x .0394	= Inches
Feet (ft.)	x .305	= Meters (m)	x 3.281	= Feet
Miles	x 1.609	= Kilometers (km)	x .0621	= Miles

VOLUME

Cubic Inches (in3)	x 16.387	= Cubic Centimeters	x .061	= in3
IMP Pints (IMP pt.)	x .568	= Liters (L)	x 1.76	= IMP pt.
IMP Quarts (IMP qt.)	x 1.137	= Liters (L)	x .88	= IMP qt.
IMP Gallons (IMP gal.)	x 4.546	= Liters (L)	x .22	= IMP gal.
IMP Quarts (IMP qt.)	x 1.201	= US Quarts (US qt.)	x .833	= IMP qt.
IMP Gallons (IMP gal.)	x 1.201	= US Gallons (US gal.)	x .833	= IMP gal.
Fl. Ounces	x 29.573	= Milliliters	x .034	= Ounces
US Pints (US pt.)	x .473	= Liters (L)	x 2.113	= Pints
US Quarts (US qt.)	x .946	= Liters (L)	x 1.057	= Quarts
US Gallons (US gal.)	x 3.785	= Liters (L)	x .264	= Gallons

MASS–WEIGHT

Ounces (oz.)	x 28.35	= Grams (g)	x .035	= Ounces
Pounds (lb.)	x .454	= Kilograms (kg)	x 2.205	= Pounds

PRESSURE

Pounds Per Sq. In. (psi)	x 6.895	= Kilopascals (kPa)	x .145	= psi
Inches of Mercury (Hg)	x .4912	= psi	x 2.036	= Hg
Inches of Mercury (Hg)	x 3.377	= Kilopascals (kPa)	x .2961	= Hg
Inches of Water (H_2O)	x .07355	= Inches of Mercury	x 13.783	= H_2O
Inches of Water (H_2O)	x .03613	= psi	x 27.684	= H_2O
Inches of Water (H_2O)	x .248	= Kilopascals (kPa)	x 4.026	= H_2O

TORQUE

Pounds–Force Inches (in–lb)	x .113	= Newton Meters (N·m)	x 8.85	= in–lb
Pounds–Force Feet (ft–lb)	x 1.356	= Newton Meters (N·m)	x .738	= ft–lb

VELOCITY

Miles Per Hour (MPH)	x 1.609	= Kilometers Per Hour (KPH)	x .621	= MPH

POWER

Horsepower (Hp)	x .745	= Kilowatts	x 1.34	= Horsepower

FUEL CONSUMPTION*

Miles Per Gallon IMP (MPG)	x .354	= Kilometers Per Liter (Km/L)		
Kilometers Per Liter (Km/L)	x 2.352	= IMP MPG		
Miles Per Gallon US (MPG)	x .425	= Kilometers Per Liter (Km/L)		
Kilometers Per Liter (Km/L)	x 2.352	= US MPG		

*It is common to covert from miles per gallon (mpg) to liters/100 kilometers (1/100 km), where mpg (IMP) x 1/100 km = 282 and mpg (US) x 1/100 km = 235.

TEMPERATURE

Degree Fahrenheit (°F)	= (°C x 1.8) + 32
Degree Celsius (°C)	= (°F – 32) x .56

Fig. 32 Standard and metric conversion factors chart

TCCS1044

The conversion factor chart is used by taking the given specification and multiplying it by the necessary conversion factor. For instance, looking at the first line, if you have a measurement in inches such as "free-play should be 2 in." but your ruler reads only in millimeters, multiply 2 in. by the conversion factor of 25.4 to get the metric equivalent of 50.8mm. Likewise, if the specification was given only in a Metric measurement, for example in Newton Meters (Nm), then look at the center column first. If the measurement is 100 Nm, multiply it by the conversion factor of 0.738 to get 73.8 ft. lbs.

SERIAL NUMBER IDENTIFICATION

Vehicle Identification Plate

♦ See Figures 33 and 34

The Vehicle Identification Number (VIN) is stamped on a metal plate that is fastened to the left upper instrument panel and is visible through the windshield. The vehicle identification number contains 17 characters that represent codes supplying important information about your vehicle. The number is used for title and registration purposes and indicates the vehicle manufacturer, country of origin, type of restraint system, assembly line, series, body type, engine, model year, and consecutive unit number. It is important for servicing and ordering parts to be certain of the vehicle and engine identification.

A nine-character derivative of the vehicle identification number is applied to the engine and transaxle. This derivative is used for in-plant control of these assemblies and may be used by law enforcement or other officials to identify proper engine/chassis combinations. This number in a condensed form should contain the same numbers and letters as the vehicle identification number.

The eighth digit of the VIN plate will specify the engine in the vehicle. All engines have a nine-digit engine identification number.

91041P22

Fig. 34 The VIN plate can be viewed through the windshield

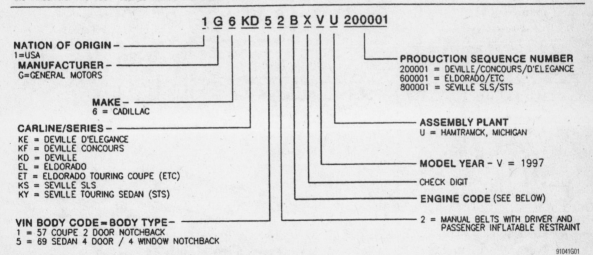

Fig. 33 Vehicle Identification Information—1997 Cadillac shown, others similar

ENGINE AND VEHICLE IDENTIFICATION

		Engine					Model Year	
Code ①	Liters (cc)	Cu. In.	Cyl.	Fuel Sys.	Engine Type	Eng. Mfg.	Code ②	Year
3	4.5 (4474)	273	8	MFI	OHV	Cadillac	L	1990
9	4.6 (4573)	279	8	SFI	DOHC	Cadillac	M	1991
B	4.9 (4917)	300	8	SFI	OHV	Cadillac	N	1992
Y	4.6 (4573)	279	8	SFI	DOHC	Cadillac	P	1993
							R	1994
							S	1995
							T	1996
							V	1997
							W	1998

DOHC - Double Overhead Camshafts

OHV - Overhead Valve

MFI - Multi-point Fuel Injection

SFI - Sequential Fuel Injection

① 8th position of VIN

② 10th position of VIN

91041CR1

Engine Number

▶ See Figures 35, 36 and 37

The engine identification code is located in the VIN at the eighth digit. All engines have a nine digit engine identification number.

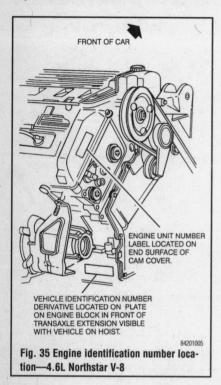

Fig. 35 Engine identification number location—4.6L Northstar V-8

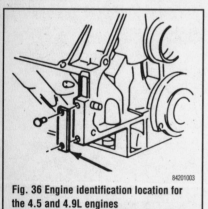

Fig. 36 Engine identification location for the 4.5 and 4.9L engines

Fig. 37 This label in the engine compartment contains emissions information among other things

Transmission/Tansaxle ID Number

▶ See Figures 38 and 39

The transmission has two identifying stampings; the transmission identification and the VIN derivative. The transmission identification number gives the transmission model, build date, and the application code. The transmission identification number is stamped on the automatic transmission case. The VIN derivative is created from the complete VIN and is stamped in two different places.

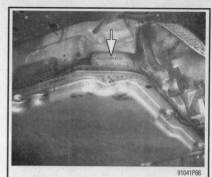

Fig. 38 The location of the transaxle stamping on the rearward corner of the box

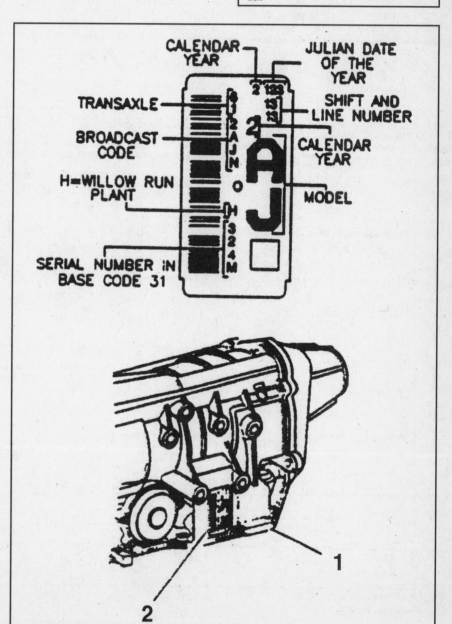

Fig. 39 The transaxle VIN derivative number (1) is stamped into the horizontal cast rib on the right-hand rear of the transaxle housing, the transaxle ID nameplate (2) is located just forward of the VIN derivative

GENERAL ENGINE SPECIFICATIONS

Year	Model	Engine Displacement Liters (cc)	No. of Cyl.	Engine Series (ID/VIN)	Engine Type	Fuel System	Net Horsepower @ rpm	Net Torque @ rpm (ft. lbs.)	Bore x Stroke (in.)	Compression Ratio	Oil Pressure @ rpm
1990	Deville	4.5 (4474)	8	3	OHV	MFI	180@4400	245@3000	3.62x3.31	9.0:1	37@1500
	Eldorado	4.5 (4474)	8	3	OHV	MFI	180@4400	245@3000	3.62x3.31	9.0:1	37@1500
	Fleetwood	4.5 (4474)	8	3	OHV	MFI	180@4400	245@3000	3.62x3.31	9.0:1	37@1500
	Seville	4.5 (4474)	8	3	OHV	MFI	180@4400	245@3000	3.62x3.31	9.0:1	37@1500
1991	Deville	4.9 (4917)	8	B	OHV	SFI	200@4100	275@3000	3.62x3.62	9.5:1	53@2000
	Eldorado	4.9 (4917)	8	B	OHV	SFI	200@4100	275@3000	3.62x3.62	9.5:1	53@2000
	Fleetwood	4.9 (4917)	8	B	OHV	SFI	200@4100	275@3000	3.62x3.62	9.5:1	53@2000
	Seville	4.9 (4917)	8	B	OHV	SFI	200@4100	275@3000	3.62x3.62	9.5:1	53@2000
1992	Deville	4.9 (4917)	8	B	OHV	SFI	200@4100	275@3000	3.62x3.62	9.5:1	53@2000
	Eldorado	4.9 (4917)	8	B	OHV	SFI	200@4100	275@3000	3.62x3.62	9.5:1	53@2000
	Fleetwood	4.9 (4917)	8	B	OHV	SFI	200@4100	275@3000	3.62x3.62	9.5:1	53@2000
	Seville	4.9 (4917)	8	B	OHV	SFI	200@4100	275@3000	3.62x3.62	9.5:1	53@2000
1993	Deville	4.9 (4917)	8	B	OHV	SFI	200@4100	275@3000	3.62x3.62	9.5:1	53@2000
	Eldorado TC	4.6 (4565)	8	9	DOHC	SFI	295@6000	290@4400	3.66x3.31	10.3:1	35@2000
	Eldorado	4.9 (4917)	8	B	OHV	SFI	200@4100	275@3000	3.62x3.62	9.5:1	53@2000
	Fleetwood	4.9 (4917)	8	B	OHV	SFI	200@4100	275@3000	3.62x3.62	9.5:1	53@2000
	Seville TS	4.6 (4565)	8	9	DOHC	SFI	295@6000	290@4400	3.66x3.31	10.3:1	35@2000
	Seville	4.9 (4917)	8	B	OHV	SFI	200@4100	275@3000	3.62x3.62	9.5:1	53@2000
1994	Deville Concours	4.6 (4565)	8	Y	DOHC	SFI	270@5600	300@4400	3.66x3.31	10.3:1	35@2000
	Deville	4.9 (4917)	8	B	OHV	SFI	200@4100	275@3000	3.62x3.62	9.5:1	53@2000
	Eldorado TC	4.6 (4565)	8	9	DOHC	SFI	295@6000	290@4400	3.66x3.31	10.3:1	35@2000
	Eldorado	4.9 (4917)	8	B	OHV	SFI	200@4100	275@3000	3.62x3.62	9.5:1	53@2000
	Eldorado	4.6 (4565)	8	Y	DOHC	SFI	270@5600	300@4400	3.66x3.31	10.3:1	35@2000
	Seville STS	4.6 (4565)	8	9	DOHC	SFI	295@6000	290@4400	3.66x3.31	10.3:1	35@2000
	Seville SLS	4.6 (4565)	8	Y	DOHC	SFI	270@5600	300@4400	3.66x3.31	10.3:1	35@2000
1995	Deville Concours	4.6 (4565)	8	Y	DOHC	SFI	275@5600	300@4000	3.66x3.31	10.3:1	35@2000
	Deville	4.9 (4917)	8	B	OHV	SFI	200@4400	275@3000	3.62x3.62	9.5:1	53@2000
	Eldorado	4.6 (4565)	8	Y	DOHC	SFI	275@5600	300@4000	3.66x3.31	10.3:1	35@2000
	Eldorado	4.6 (4565)	8	9	DOHC	SFI	300@6000	290@4400	3.66x3.31	10.3:1	35@2000
	Seville SLS	4.6 (4565)	8	Y	DOHC	SFI	275@5600	300@4000	3.66x3.31	10.3:1	35@2000
	Seville STS	4.6 (4565)	8	9	DOHC	SFI	295@6000	290@4400	3.66x3.31	10.3:1	35@2000
1996	Deville	4.6 (4565)	8	Y	DOHC	SFI	275@5600	300@4000	3.66x3.31	10.3:1	35@2000
	Deville Concours	4.6 (4565)	8	9	DOHC	SFI	300@6000	295@4400	3.66x3.31	10.3:1	35@2000
	Eldorado	4.6 (4565)	8	Y	DOHC	SFI	275@5600	300@4000	3.66x3.31	10.3:1	35@2000
	Eldorado ETC	4.6 (4565)	8	9	DOHC	SFI	300@6000	295@4400	3.66x3.31	10.3:1	35@2000
	Seville SLS	4.6 (4565)	8	Y	DOHC	SFI	275@5600	300@4000	3.66x3.31	10.3:1	35@2000
	Seville STS	4.6 (4565)	8	9	DOHC	SFI	300@6000	295@4400	3.66x3.31	10.3:1	35@2000
1997	Deville	4.6 (4565)	8	Y	DOHC	SFI	275@5600	300@4000	3.66x3.31	10.3:1	35@2000
	Deville Concours	4.6 (4565)	8	9	DOHC	SFI	300@6000	290@4400	3.66x3.31	10.3:1	35@2000
	Eldorado	4.6 (4565)	8	Y	DOHC	SFI	275@5600	300@4000	3.66x3.31	10.3:1	35@2000
	Eldorado ETC	4.6 (4565)	8	9	DOHC	SFI	300@6000	290@4400	3.66x3.31	10.3:1	35@2000
	Seville SLS	4.6 (4565)	8	Y	DOHC	SFI	275@5600	300@4000	3.66x3.31	10.3:1	35@2000
	Seville STS	4.6 (4565)	8	9	DOHC	SFI	300@6000	290@4400	3.66x3.31	10.3:1	35@2000
1998	Deville	4.6 (4565)	8	Y	DOHC	SFI	275@5600	300@4000	3.66x3.31	10.3:1	35@2000
	Deville Concours	4.6 (4565)	8	9	DOHC	SFI	300@6000	290@4400	3.66x3.31	10.3:1	35@2000
	Eldorado	4.6 (4565)	8	Y	DOHC	SFI	275@5600	300@4000	3.66x3.31	10.3:1	35@2000
	Eldorado ETC	4.6 (4565)	8	9	DOHC	SFI	300@6000	290@4400	3.66x3.31	10.3:1	35@2000
	Seville SLS	4.6 (4565)	8	Y	DOHC	SFI	275@5600	300@4000	3.66x3.31	10.3:1	35@2000
	Seville STS	4.6 (4565)	8	9	DOHC	SFI	300@6000	290@4400	3.66x3.31	10.3:1	35@2000

MFI - Multi-point Fuel Injection

SFI - Sequential Fuel Injection

91041CR2

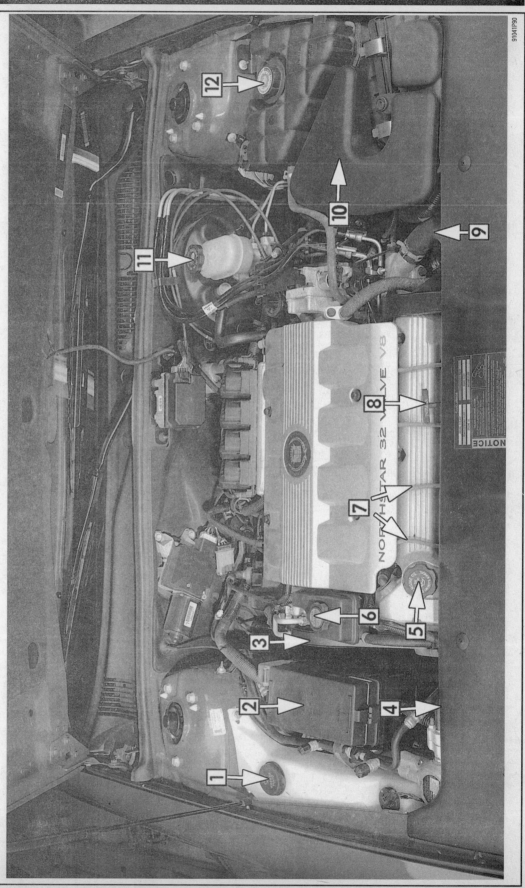

MAINTENANCE COMPONENT LOCATIONS—4.6L NORTHSTAR ENGINE

1. Washer fluid reservoir
2. Engine compartment fuse box
3. Accessory belt
4. Battery
5. Engine oil fill cap
6. Power steering fluid reservoir
7. Spark plug wires
8. Engine oil dipstick
9. Upper radiator hose
10. Air cleaner housing
11. Brake master cylinder reservoir
12. Coolant recovery tank

▶ **See Figures 40 and 41**

Proper maintenance and tune-up is the key to long and trouble-free vehicle life, and the work can yield its own rewards. Studies have shown that a properly tuned and maintained vehicle can achieve better gas mileage than an out-of-tune vehicle. As a conscientious owner and driver, set aside a Saturday morning, say once a month, to check or replace items that could cause major problems later. Keep your own personal log to jot down which services you performed, how much the parts cost you, the date, and the exact odometer reading at the time. Keep all receipts for such items as engine oil and filters, so that they may be referred to in case of related problems or to determine operating expenses. As a do-it-yourselfer, these receipts are the only proof you have that the required maintenance was performed. In case of a warranty problem, these receipts will be invaluable.

The literature provided with your vehicle when it was originally delivered includes the factory recommended maintenance schedule. If you no longer have this literature, replacement copies are usually available from the dealer. A maintenance schedule is provided in case you do not have the factory literature.

Air Cleaner

The intake air system provides clean air to the engine, optimizes airflow, and reduces unwanted induction noise. The intake air system consists of an air cleaner assembly, resonator assemblies and hoses. A flat air filter element provides maximum air filtration with minimum flow restriction. The main component of the air intake system is the air cleaner assembly. The air cleaner assembly houses the air cleaner element that removes potential engine contaminants, particularly abrasive types. The air cleaner housing and ducts are designed to allow the maximum airflow possible with a minimum of noise, and to reduce the potential for water ingestion into the engine.

If an engine maintenance procedure requires the temporary removal of the air cleaner, remove it; otherwise, never run the engine without it. The air filter should be replaced every 30,000 miles (50,000 km).

REMOVAL & INSTALLATION

▶ **See Figures 42 thru 52**

Locate the air cleaner in the engine compartment. Inspect the flexible air intake ducting for cracks and tears. If the ducting is torn it should be replaced.

The air cleaner element may be replaced easily.

1. Remove or disconnect the intake air temperature (IAT) sensor, if equipped and mounted in the air cleaner housing.
2. Loosen the intake air duct clamp and remove the air duct as necessary.
3. Disengage the fasteners securing the top of the air cleaner.

➡**Some fasteners are clips, some are screws, depending on the vehicle configuration.**

4. Carefully tilt the air filter cover back to expose the element.
5. Remove the air filter element.
6. Wipe out the housing with a clean rag.
To install:
7. Position the air filter element in the housing, make sure it seats properly.
8. Install the air cleaner cover. Connect the intake air duct and tighten the clamp.
9. Install the IAT sensor, if removed, or reconnect as necessary.
10. Install the air cleaner fasteners, and tighten as necessary.

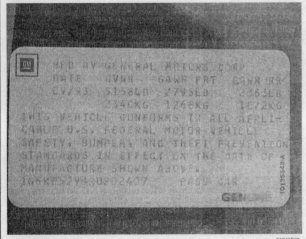

Fig. 40 This vehicle sticker gives the gross vehicle weight and body configuration, as well as the federal law compliance

Fig. 41 This sticker, located in the engine compartment, gives the serpentine belt routing, as well as other pertinent information

Fig. 42 Before any work can be done on the left side of the engine compartment, it is necessary to remove the strut rod. Remove the bolt at the radiator frame

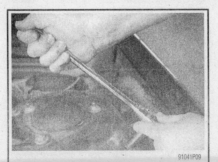

Fig. 43 Loosen the bolt on the other end of the rod at the strut housing. Now the rod can be moved out of the way, allowing access to the components

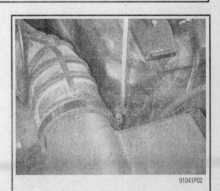

Fig. 44 Loosen the screw on the cold air intake hose clamp

Fig. 45 Slide the hose off the outlet tube of the air cleaner box

Fig. 46 Release the fasteners holding the top of the air cleaner box and remove the top of the box

Fig. 47 Grasp the air filter element and . . .

Fig. 48 . . . lift it out of the air cleaner box

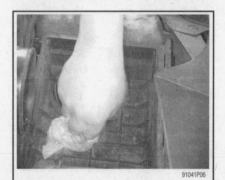

Fig. 49 Clean the filter box of any dirt and debris before replacing the element

Fig. 50 Early model air intake system

Fig. 51 Removing the center nut of the upper air cleaner housing—early model

Fuel Filter

✱✱ CAUTION

Observe all applicable safety precautions when working around fuel. Whenever servicing the fuel system, always work in a well ventilated area. Do not allow fuel spray or vapors to be exposed to a spark or open flame. Keep a dry chemical fire extinguisher near the work area. Always keep fuel in a container specifically designed for fuel storage; also, always properly seal fuel containers to avoid the possibility of fire or explosion.

The purpose of the in-line fuel filter is to provide filtration to protect the small metering orifices of the injector nozzles. The filter is located downstream of the electric fuel pump and is mounted on the underbody. The fuel filter is a one-piece construction that cannot be cleaned. If it becomes clogged, it must be replaced.

REMOVAL & INSTALLATION

▶ See Figures 53 thru 61

✱✱ CAUTION

Never smoke when working around gasoline! Avoid all sources of sparks or ignition. Gasoline vapors are EXTREMELY volatile!

✱✱ WARNING

Fuel supply lines on all vehicles equipped with fuel injected engines will remain pressurized for long periods after engine shutdown. The pressure must be relieved before servicing these fuel systems.

1. Disconnect the negative battery cable.
2. Depressurize the fuel system.
3. Remove the filter bracket retainer.
4. For plastic type fittings:
   a. Grasp the filter and one fuel line fitting. Twist the quick connect fitting ¼ turn in each direction to loosen any dirt within the fitting. Repeat for the other fuel line fitting.
   b. Squeeze the plastic retainer release tabs

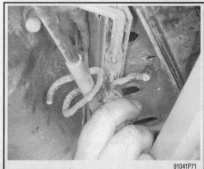

Fig. 53 There are a couple of fasteners that need to be removed to access the filter. This is one of them

Fig. 52 Removing the air cleaner—early model

Fig. 54 Some models utilize a plastic fitting on the fuel filter

Fig. 55 Twist the fuel line back and forth while holding the filter still. This will loosen any dirt caught in the connection

Fig. 56 Squeeze the tabs on the plastic line to free them from the lock

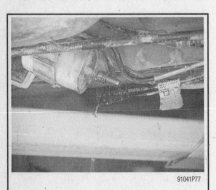

Fig. 57 Slide the hose off the front end of the filter first. It's easier to work with

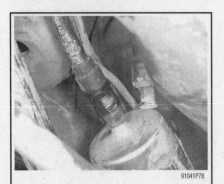

Fig. 58 Remove the other fitting in the same manner

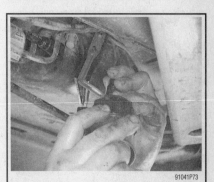

Fig. 59 After removing the fuel line from the other side, you can now slide it out of the sleeve and remove it from the vehicle

Fig. 60 The filter is typically attached to this bracket

Fig. 61 Remove the filter from this bracket before installing the new filter

and pull the connection apart. Repeat for the other fitting.

  5. For metal type fittings:

    a. Use a fuel pipe quick-connect separator J37088 or equivalent.

    This is available from your local parts store.

    b. Insert the tool into the female side of the connector, then push inward to release locking tabs. Pull the connection apart.

    This will loosen any dirt caught in the connection

To install:

  6. Remove the protective caps from the new filter and apply a few drops of clean engine oil to both tube ends of the filter and O-rings. Install the fuel filter so that the flow arrow follows the direction of fuel flow.

  7. Install the new plastic connector retainers onto the filter inlet and outlet tubes (plastic collar type fittings).

  8. Push the connectors together to cause the retaining tabs to snap into place. Once installed pull on both ends of each connection to make sure they are secure.

  9. Before installing the fitting on the filter, wipe the filter end with a clean cloth. Inspect the inside of the fitting to make sure it is free of dirt and/or obstructions

  10. Align the fitting, and filter axially and push the fitting onto the filter end. Pull on the fitting to make sure it is fully engaged.

  11. Install the fuel filter and bracket on the frame.

  12. Connect the negative battery cable.

  13. Start the engine and check for leaks.

PCV Valve

A Positive Crankcase Ventilation (PCV) system is used to consume crankcase vapors in the combustion process instead of venting them to the atmosphere. In gasoline engines, small amounts of the combustion gas leak past the piston rings into the crankcase. These crankcase blow-by gases contain undesirable hydrocarbon air pollutants. The PCV system is used to prevent these vapors from escaping into the atmosphere, while allowing proper ventilation of the crankcase to maintain good oil quality.

The PCV system should be checked at every oil change and serviced every 30,000 miles (48,000 km).

NOTE: Never operate an engine without a PCV valve or a ventilation system, for it can become damaged.

REMOVAL & INSTALLATION

▶ See Figures 62, 63 and 64

  1. Locate the PCV valve; usually located either in the valve cover or in the intake manifold.

  2. Disconnect the crankcase ventilation tube from the positive crankcase ventilation valve.

  3. Remove the PCV valve from the PCV valve grommet.

To install:

  4. Install the PCV valve into the grommet.

  5. Connect the ventilation tube to the PCV valve.

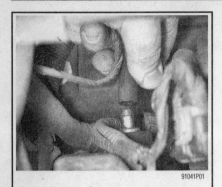

Fig. 62 Pull the vacuum line off the top of the PCV valve

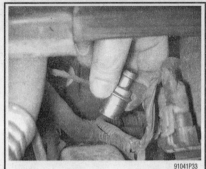

Fig. 63 A gentle twist and pull usually will remove the PCV valve from the valve cover

Fig. 64 A twist and a push will also install a new one

Evaporative Canister

To limit gasoline vapor discharge into the air when the vehicle is not operating. This system transfers fuel vapors from the fuel tank to a charcoal canister storage device. This canister absorbs fuel vapors and stores them until they can be burned in the engine. When the engine is running, the fuel vapor is purged from the carbon element by intake airflow and consumed in the normal combustion process. The EVAP purge solenoid valve allows manifold vacuum to purge the canister.

Poor idle, stalling and poor driveability can be caused by:
• Hoses split, cracked, and/or not connected properly.
• Damaged canister.
• Malfunctioning purge solenoid.

SERVICING

Servicing the evaporative canister is only necessary if it is clogged, cracked, or contains liquid fuel. If replacement is necessary, the canister must be replaced as a unit; it cannot be disassembled.

Inspect the Evaporative Emission Canister for the following conditions:
• Cracked or damaged
• Fuel leaking from canister

If either condition is found it will be necessary to replace the canister as follows.

1. Tag and detach all hoses connected to the charcoal canister.
2. Unbolt the retaining bolts and then remove the canister.
3. Install the new canister and tighten the retaining bolts.
4. Install all hoses to the canister.

Battery

PRECAUTIONS

Always use caution when working on or near the battery. Never allow a tool to bridge the gap between the negative and positive battery terminals. Also, be careful not to allow a tool to provide a ground between the positive cable/terminal and any metal component on the vehicle. Either of these conditions will cause a short circuit, leading to sparks and possible personal injury.

Do not smoke, have an open flame, or create sparks near a battery; the gases contained in the battery are very explosive and, if ignited, could cause severe injury or death.

A battery hold-down device should carefully secure all batteries, regardless of type. If this is not done, the battery terminals or casing may crack from stress applied to the battery during vehicle operation. A battery which is not secured may allow acid to leak out, making it discharge faster; such leaking corrosive acid can also eat away at components under the hood.

Always visually, inspect the battery case for cracks, leakage, and corrosion. A white corrosive substance on the battery case or on nearby components would indicate a leaking or cracked battery. If the battery is cracked, it should be replaced immediately.

GENERAL MAINTENANCE

♦ See Figure 65

A battery that is not sealed must be checked periodically for electrolyte level. You cannot add water to a sealed maintenance-free battery (though not all maintenance-free batteries are sealed); however, a sealed battery must also be checked for proper electrolyte level, as indicated by the color of the built-in hydrometer "eye."

Always keep the battery cables and terminals free of corrosion. Check these components about once a year. Refer to the removal, installation, and cleaning procedures.

Keep the top of the battery clean, as a film of dirt can help completely discharge a battery that is not

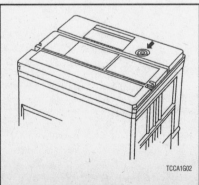

Fig. 65 A typical location for the built-in hydrometer on maintenance-free batteries

used for long periods. A solution of baking soda and water may be used for cleaning, but be careful to flush this off with clear water. DO NOT let any of the solution into the filler holes. Baking soda neutralizes battery acid and will de-activate a battery cell.

Batteries in vehicles which are not operated on a regular basis can fall victim to parasitic loads (small current drains which are constantly drawing current from the battery). Normal parasitic loads may drain a battery on a vehicle that is in storage and not used for 6–8 weeks. Vehicles that have additional accessories such as a cellular telephone, an alarm system, or other devices that increase parasitic load may discharge a battery sooner. If the vehicle is to be stored for 6–8 weeks in a secure area and the alarm system, if present, is not necessary, the negative battery cable should be disconnected at the onset of storage to protect the battery charge.

Remember that constantly discharging and recharging will shorten battery life. Take care not to allow a battery to be needlessly discharged.

BATTERY FLUID

Check the battery electrolyte level at least once a month, or more often in hot weather or during periods of extended vehicle operation. On non-sealed batteries, the level can be checked either through the case on translucent batteries or by removing the cell caps on opaque-cased types. The electrolyte level in each cell should be kept filled to the split ring inside each cell, or the line marked on the outside of the case.

If the level is low, add only distilled water through the opening until the level is correct. Each cell is separate from the others, so each must be checked and filled individually. Distilled water should be used, because the chemicals and minerals found in most drinking water are harmful to the battery and could significantly shorten its life.

If water is added in freezing weather, the vehicle should be driven several miles to allow the water to mix with the electrolyte. Otherwise, the battery could freeze.

Although some maintenance-free batteries have removable cell caps for access to the electrolyte, the electrolyte condition and level on all sealed maintenance-free batteries must be checked using the built-in hydrometer "eye." The exact type of "eye" varies among manufacturers, but most apply a sticker to the battery explaining the possible readings. When in doubt, refer to the battery manufacturer's instructions to interpret battery condition using the built-in hydrometer.

Fig. 66 On non-maintenance-free batteries, the fluid level can be checked through the case on translucent models; the cell caps must be removed on other models

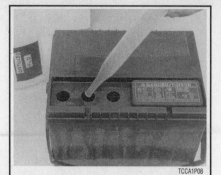

Fig. 67 If the fluid level is low, add only distilled water through the opening until the level is correct

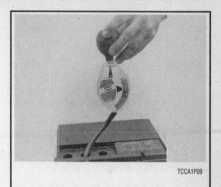

Fig. 68 Check the specific gravity of the battery's electrolyte with a hydrometer

➡Although the readings from built-in hydrometers found in sealed batteries may vary, a green eye usually indicates a properly charged battery with sufficient fluid level. A dark eye is normally an indicator of a battery with sufficient fluid, but one, which may be low in charge. Moreover, a light or yellow eye is usually an indication that electrolyte supply has dropped below the necessary level for battery (and hydrometer) operation. In this last case, sealed batteries with an insufficient electrolyte level must usually be discarded.

Checking the Specific Gravity

▶ See Figures 66, 67 and 68

A hydrometer is required to check the specific gravity on all batteries that are not maintenance-free. On batteries that are maintenance-free, observing the built-in hydrometer "eye" on the top of the battery case checks the specific gravity. Check with your battery's manufacturer for proper interpretation of its built-in hydrometer readings.

❖❖ CAUTION

Battery electrolyte contains sulfuric acid. If you should splash any on your skin or in your eyes, flush the affected area with plenty of clear water. If it gets in your eyes, or is ingested, get medical help immediately.

The fluid (sulfuric acid solution) contained in the battery cells will tell you many things about the condition of the battery. Because the cell plates must be kept submerged below the fluid level in order to operate, maintaining the fluid level is extremely important. In addition, because the specific gravity of the acid is an indication of electrical charge, testing the fluid can be an aid in determining if the battery must be replaced. A battery in a vehicle with a properly operating charging system should require little maintenance, but careful, periodic inspection should reveal problems before they leave you stranded.

As stated earlier, the specific gravity of a battery's electrolyte level can be used as an indication of battery charge. At least once a year, check the specific gravity of the battery. It should be between 1.20 and 1.26 on the gravity scale. Most auto supply stores carry a variety of inexpensive battery testing hydrometers. These can be used on any non-sealed battery to test the specific gravity in each cell.

The battery testing hydrometer has a squeeze bulb at one end and a nozzle at the other. Battery electrolyte is sucked into the hydrometer until the float is lifted from its seat. The specific gravity is then read by noting the position of the float. If gravity is low in one or more cells, the battery should be slowly charged and checked again to see if the gravity has come up. Generally, if after charging, the specific gravity between any two cells varies more than 50 points (0.50), the battery should be replaced, as it can no longer produce sufficient voltage to guarantee proper operation.

CABLES

▶ See Figures 69 thru 74

Once a year (or as necessary), the battery terminals and the cable clamps should be cleaned. Loosen the clamps and remove the cables, negative cable first. On batteries with posts on top, the use of a puller specially made for this purpose is recommended. These are inexpensive and available in most auto parts stores. Side terminal battery cables are secured with a small bolt.

Clean the cable clamps and the battery terminal with a wire brush, until all corrosion, grease, etc., is removed and the metal is shiny. It is especially important to clean the inside of the clamp thoroughly (an old knife is useful here), since a small deposit of foreign material or oxidation there will prevent a sound electrical connection and inhibit either starting or charging. Special tools are available for cleaning these parts, one type for conventional top post batteries and another type for side terminal batteries. It is also a good idea to apply some dielectric grease to the terminal, as this will aid in the prevention of corrosion.

After the clamps and terminals are clean, reinstall the cables, negative cable lasts; DO NOT hammer the clamps onto battery posts. Tighten the clamps securely, but do not distort them. Give the clamps and terminals a thin external coating of grease after installation, to retard corrosion.

Fig. 69 Loosen the battery cable retaining nut . . .

Fig. 70 . . . then, disconnect the cable from the battery

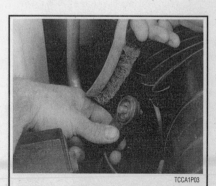

Fig. 71 A wire brush may be used to clean any corrosion or foreign material from the cable

Fig. 72 The wire brush can also be used to remove any corrosion or dirt from the battery terminal

Fig. 73 The battery terminal can also be cleaned using a solution of baking soda and water

Fig. 74 Before connecting the cables, it's a good idea to coat the terminals with a small amount of dielectric grease

Check the cables at the same time that the terminals are cleaned. If the cable insulation is cracked or broken, or if the ends are frayed, the cable should be replaced with a new cable of the same length and gauge.

CHARGING

A battery should be charged at a slow rate to keep the plates inside from getting too hot. However, if some maintenance-free batteries are allowed to discharge until they are almost "dead," they may have to be charged at a high rate to bring them back to "life." Always follow the charger manufacturer's instructions on charging the battery.

➡ Always turn the ignition "OFF" when connecting or disconnecting battery cables, battery chargers or jumper cables. Failure to do so may damage the Powertrain Control Module (PCM) or other electronic compon-ents.

REPLACEMENT

When it becomes necessary to replace the battery, select one with amperage rating equal to or greater than the battery originally installed. Deterioration and just plain aging of the battery cables, starter motor, and associated wires makes the battery's job harder in successive years. The slow increase in electrical resistance over time makes it prudent to install a new battery with a greater capacity than the old.

Belts

INSPECTION

▶ **See Figures 75, 76, 77, 78 and 79**

Inspect the belts for signs of glazing or cracking. A glazed belt will be perfectly smooth from slippage, while a good belt will have a slight texture of fabric visible. Cracks will usually start at the inner edge of the belt and run outward. All worn or damaged drive belts should be replaced immediately. It is best to replace all drive belts at one time, as a preventive maintenance measure, during this service operation.

The belts, which drive the engine accessories such as the alternator, the air pump, power steering pump, air conditioning compressor, and water pump, are of serpentine belt design. Older style belts show wear and damage readily, since their basic design was a belt with a rubber casing. As the casing wore, cracks and fibers were readily appar-

ent. Newer design, caseless belts do not show wear as readily, and many untrained people cannot distinguish between a good, serviceable belt and one that is worn to the point of failure. It is a good idea, therefore, to visually inspect the belt regularly and replace it, routinely, every two to three years.

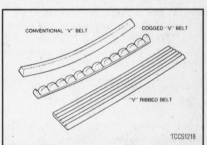

Fig. 75 There are typically 3 types of accessory drive belts found on vehicles today

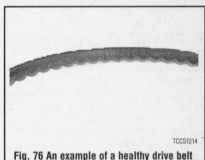

Fig. 76 An example of a healthy drive belt

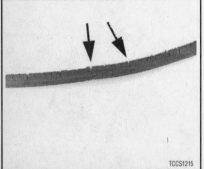

Fig. 77 Deep cracks in this belt will cause flex, building up heat that will eventually lead to belt failure

Fig. 78 The cover of this belt is worn, exposing the critical reinforcing cords to excessive wear

Fig. 79 Installing too wide a belt can result in serious belt wear and/or breakage

ADJUSTING

The newer engines employ a single serpentine belt, which drives each of the engine-mounted accessories. The belt is wider than conventional belts due to its 'Poly-V' design, similar to six narrow V-belts joined at their sides.

Newer vehicles are equipped with V-ribbed (serpentine) accessory drive belts. To ensure maximum life, the replacement belt should be of the same type as the original. An engine mounted belt automatic tensioner mechanism is designed to maintain 120 lbs. (534 N) of belt tension. A worn belt can result in slippage, which may cause a noise concern or improper accessory operation.

Automatic tensioners do not have to be removed to remove a drive belt. To remove a drive belt, rotate the tensioner away from the belt.

Serpentine Belt

On some applications, a single belt is used to drive all of the engine accessories formerly driven by multiple drive belts. The single belt is referred to a serpentine belt. All the belt driven accessories are rigidly mounted with belt tension maintained by a spring-loaded tensioner. Because of the belt tensioner, no adjustment is necessary.

Cracks on the rib side of a serpentine drive belt are considered acceptable. If the drive belt has chunks missing from the ribs, if two or more adjacent ribs have lost sections, or if the missing chunks are creating a noise, vibrations, or harshness condition, replace the drive belt.

REMOVAL & INSTALLATION

4.5L, 4.6L and 4.9L Engines

◗ See Figures 80, 81, 82, 83 and 84

1. Insert a ½ inch flex handle in the square hole in the tensioner. The tensioner has a square hole cast into it. Rotate the tensioner counter-clockwise and remove the belt from the pulleys.
   To install:
2. Following the schematic on the decal under the hood, loop the drive belt over all the pulleys except the power steering pulley.
3. With the belt installed properly on all except the power steering pulley, rotate the tensioner as described above and install the belt

Fig. 80 Insert the drive tool into the square hole on the tensioner and . . .

Fig. 81 . . . rotate the tensioner to relieve pressure on the belt

Fig. 82 Remove the belt from around one pulley, then the other ones to remove it from the engine

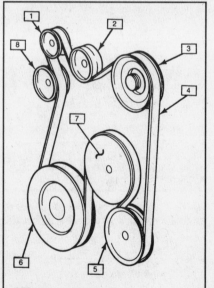

1	GENERATOR PULLEY
2	TENSIONER
3	STEERING PUMP PULLEY
4	SERPENTINE BELT
5	A/C COMPRESSOR PULLEY
6	CRANKSHAFT PULLEY
7	WATER PUMP PULLEY
8	IDLER PULLEY

Fig. 83 Serpentine belt routing and pulley identification—typical

Fig. 84 Adjusting the alternator to install the serpentine belt

on the power steering pulley. Ensure that all the V-grooves make proper contact with the pulleys.

✳✳ WARNING

Do not allow the drive belt tensioner to snap back as damage to the drive belt tensioner or personal injury could result.

Hoses

INSPECTION

◗ See Figures 85, 86, 87 and 88

Upper and lower radiator hoses, along with the heater hoses, should be checked for deterioration, leaks and loose hose clamps at least every 15,000 miles (24,000 km). It is also wise to check the hoses periodically in early spring and at the beginning of the fall or winter when you are performing other maintenance. A quick visual inspection could discover a weakened hose, which might leave you stranded if it fails.

Whenever you are checking the hoses, make sure the engine and cooling system are cold. Visually inspect for cracking, rotting or collapsed hoses, and replace as necessary. Run your hand along the length of the hose. If a weak or swollen spot is noted when squeezing the hose wall, the hose should be replaced.

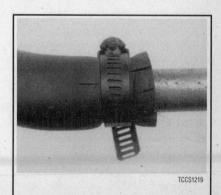

Fig. 85 The cracks developing along this hose are a result of age-related hardening

Fig. 86 A hose clamp that is too tight can cause older hoses to separate and tear on either side of the clamp

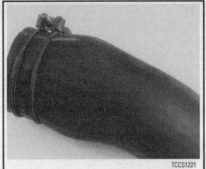

Fig. 87 A soft spongy hose (identifiable by the swollen section) will eventually burst and should be replaced

Fig. 88 Hoses are likely to deteriorate from the inside if the cooling system is not periodically flushed

REMOVAL & INSTALLATION

✳✳ CAUTION

Never open, service, or drain the radiator or cooling system when hot; serious burns can occur from the steam and hot coolant. In addition, when draining engine coolant, keep in mind that cats and dogs are attracted to ethylene glycol antifreeze and could drink any that is left in an uncovered container or in puddles on the ground. This will prove fatal in sufficient quantities. Always drain coolant into a sealable container. Coolant should be reused unless it is contaminated or is several years old.

1. Remove the radiator pressure cap.
2. Position a clean container under the radiator and/or engine draincock or plug, then open the drain and allow the cooling system to drain to an appropriate level. For some upper hoses, only a little coolant must be drained. To remove hoses positioned lower on the engine, such as a lower radiator hose, the entire cooling system must be emptied.
3. Loosen the hose clamps at each end of the hose requiring replacement. Clamps are usually either of the spring tension type (which require pliers to squeeze the tabs and loosen) or of the screw tension type (which require screw or hex drivers to loosen). Pull the clamps back on the hose away from the connection.
4. Twist, pull and slide the hose off the fitting, taking care not to damage the neck of the component from which the hose is being removed.

➡ If the hose is stuck at the connection, do not try to insert a screwdriver or other sharp tool under the hose end in an effort to free it, as the connection and/or hose may become damaged. Heater connections especially may be easily damaged by such a procedure. If the hose is to be replaced, use a single-edged razor blade or suitable cutting edge, to make a slice along the portion of the hose that is stuck on the connection, perpendicular to the end of the hose. Do not cut too deeply, damage to the connection could result. The hose can then be peeled from the connection and discarded.

5. Clean both hose mounting connections.

Inspect the condition of the hose clamps and replace them, if necessary.

To install:
6. Dip the ends of the new hose into clean engine coolant to ease installation.
7. Slide the clamps over the replacement hose, then slide the hose ends over the connections into position.
8. Position and secure the clamps at least ¼ in. (6.35mm) from the ends of the hose. Make sure they are located beyond the raised bead of the connector.
9. Close the radiator or engine drains and properly refill the cooling system with the clean drained engine coolant or a suitable mixture of ethylene glycol coolant and water. Be sure to maintain a ⁵⁰⁄₅₀ mix as a minimum in the system.
10. If available, install a pressure tester and check for leaks. If a pressure tester is not available, run the engine until normal operating temperature is reached (allowing the system to naturally pressurize), then check for leaks.

✳✳ CAUTION

If you are checking for leaks with the system at normal operating temperature, BE EXTREMELY CAREFUL not to touch any moving or hot engine parts. Once temperature has been reached, shut the engine OFF, and check for leaks around the hose fittings and connections that were removed earlier.

CV-Boots

INSPECTION

◆ See Figures 89 and 90

The CV (Constant Velocity) boots should be checked for damage each time the oil is changed and any other time the vehicle is raised for service. These boots keep water, grime, dirt and other damaging matter from entering the CV-joints. Any of these could cause early CV-joint failure that can be expensive to repair. Heavy grease thrown around the inside of the front wheel(s) and on the brake caliper/drum can be an indication of a torn boot. Thoroughly check the boots for missing clamps and tears. If the boot is damaged, it should be replaced immediately.

Fig. 89 CV-boots must be inspected periodically for damage

Fig. 90 A torn boot should be replaced immediately

Spark Plugs

◆ See Figure 91

Resistor type, tapered seat spark plugs are used. Some applications use a platinum spark plug. These are usually designated by a 'P' suffix in the part number.

Normal service is assumed to be a mixture of idling, slow speed, and high speed driving. Occasional intermittent high-speed driving is needed for good spark plug performance. It gives increased combustion heat, burning away carbon or oxides that have built up from frequent idling, or continual stop-and-go driving.

Worn or dirty spark plugs may give satisfactory operation at idling speed, but at higher RPM, they frequently fail. Faulty plugs are indicated in a number of ways: poor fuel economy, power loss, loss of speed, hard starting and generally poor engine performance.

Excessive gap wear, on plugs of low mileage, usually indicates the engine is operating at high speeds, or loads that are consistently greater than normal, or that a plug which is too hot is being used. Electrode wear may also be the result of plug overheating, caused by combustion gases leaking past the threads due to insufficient torquing of the spark plug. Excessively lean fuel mixture will also result in accelerated electrode wear.

A typical spark plug consists of a metal shell surrounding a ceramic insulator. A metal electrode extends downward through the center of the insulator and protrudes a small distance. Located at the end of the plug and attached to the side of the outer metal shell is the side electrode. The side electrode bends in at a 90° angle so that its tip is just past and parallel to the tip of the center electrode. The distance between these two electrodes (measured in thousandths of an inch or hundredths of a millimeter) is called the spark plug gap.

The spark plug does not produce a spark, but instead provides a gap across which the current can arc. The coil produces anywhere from 20,000 to 50,000 volts (depending on the type and application) which travels through the wires to the spark plugs. The current passes along the center electrode and jumps the gap to the side electrode, and in doing so, ignites the air/fuel mixture in the combustion chamber.

SPARK PLUG HEAT RANGE

▶ **See Figure 92**

Spark plug heat range is the ability of the plug to dissipate heat. The longer the insulator (or the farther it extends into the engine), the hotter the plug will operate; the shorter the insulator (the closer the electrode is to the block's cooling passages) the cooler it will operate. A plug that absorbs little heat and remains too cool will quickly accumulate deposits of oil and carbon since it is not hot enough to burn them off. This leads to plug fouling and consequently to misfiring. A plug that absorbs too much heat will have no deposits but, due to the excessive heat, the electrodes will burn away quickly and might possibly lead to preignition or other ignition problems. Preignition takes place when plug tips get so hot that they glow sufficiently to ignite the air/fuel mixture before the actual spark occurs. This early ignition will usually cause a pinging during low speeds and heavy loads.

The general rule of thumb for choosing the correct heat range when picking a spark plug is: if most of your driving is long distance, high speed travel, use a colder plug; if most of your driving is stop and go, use a hotter plug. Original equipment plugs are generally a good compromise between the 2 styles and most people never have the need to change their plugs from the factory-recommended heat range.

REMOVAL & INSTALLATION

▶ **See Figures 93 thru 98**

A set of standard spark plugs usually requires replacement after about 30,000 miles (48,000 km), depending on your style of driving. In normal operation plug gap increases about 0.001 in. (0.025mm) for every 2500 miles (4000 km). As the gap increases, the voltage requirement of the plug also increases. It

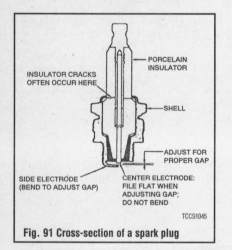

Fig. 91 Cross-section of a spark plug

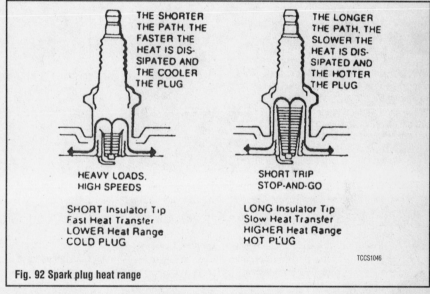

Fig. 92 Spark plug heat range

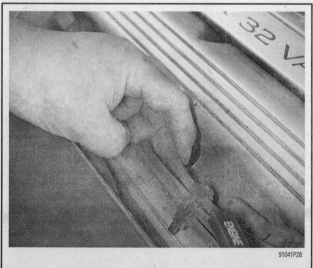

Fig. 93 Carefully disengage the plug boot from the spark plug

Fig. 94 Slide the boot off the plug and out of the access hole. Clean the area with compressed air. If air is unavailable, try using a shop vacuum

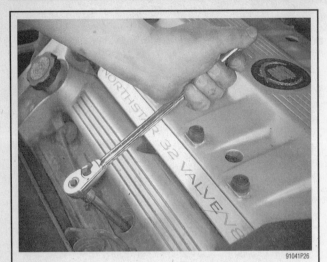

Fig. 95 Using a spark plug socket and an extension may not be enough. You may need a flex head ratchet to extract the spark plugs

Fig. 96 The plug socket should be equipped with a retaining device to hold the plug

Fig. 97 Once the spark plug has been removed, examine it for any problems, like oil fouling or cracked ceramic around the electrode

Fig. 98 Carefully torque the new spark plugs, especially when installing them into aluminum heads

requires a greater voltage to jump the wider gap and about two to three times as much voltage to fire the plug at high speeds than at idle. The improved air/fuel ratio control of modern fuel injection combined with the higher voltage output of modern ignition systems will often allow an engine to run significantly longer on a set of standard spark plugs, but keep in mind that efficiency will drop as the gap widens (along with fuel economy and power).

When you're removing spark plugs, work on one at a time. Don't start by removing the plug wires all at once, because, unless you number them, they may become mixed up. Take a minute before you begin and number the wires with tape.

1. Disconnect the negative battery cable, and if the vehicle has been run recently, allow the engine to thoroughly cool.

2. On some applications, it may be necessary to remove the air cleaner assembly.

3. Carefully twist the spark plug wire boot ½ turn to loosen it, then pull upward and remove the boot from the plug. Be sure to pull on the boot and not on the wire, otherwise the connector located inside the boot may become separated.

4. Using compressed air, blow any water or debris from the spark plug well to assure that no harmful contaminants are allowed to enter the combustion chamber when the spark plug is removed. If compressed air is not available, use a rag or a brush to clean the area.

➡Remove the spark plugs when the engine is cold, if possible, to prevent damage to the threads. If removal of the plugs is difficult, apply a few drops of penetrating oil or silicone spray to the area around the base of the plug, and allow it a few minutes to work.

5. Using a spark plug socket that is equipped with a rubber insert to properly hold the plug, turn the spark plug counterclockwise to loosen and remove the spark plug from the bore,

To install:

6. Inspect the spark plug boot for tears or damage. If a damaged boot is found, the spark plug wire must be replaced.

7. Using a wire feeler gauge, check and adjust the spark plug gap. When using a gauge, the proper size should pass between the electrodes with a slight

drag. The next larger size should not be able to pass while the next smaller size should pass freely.

8. Carefully thread the plug into the bore by hand. If resistance is felt before the plug is almost completely threaded, back the plug out and begin threading again. In small, hard to reach areas, an old spark plug wire and boot could be used as a threading tool. The boot will hold the plug while you twist the end of the wire and the wire is supple enough to twist before it would allow the plug to crossthread.

✳ WARNING

Do not use the spark plug socket to thread the plugs. Always carefully thread the plug by hand or using an old plug wire, or vacuum line, to prevent the possibility of crossthreading and damaging the cylinder head bore.

9. Carefully tighten the spark plug. These engine applications use a tapered seat plug.

10. Apply a small amount of silicone dielectric compound to the end of the spark plug. This

assures no water will enter and no corrosion will develop. It will also aid in removal of the boot when the time comes.

Use special care when reinstalling spark plug boots, to assure that the metal terminal within the boot is fully seated on the spark plug terminal and that the boot has not moved on the wire. If boot to wire movement has occurred, the boot will give a false visual impression of being fully seated. A good check to assure that boots have been properly assembled is to push sideways on the installed boots. If they have been correctly installed, a stiff boot, with only slight looseness, will be noted. If the terminal has not been properly seated on the sparkplug, only the resistance of the rubber boot will be felt when pushing sideways.

INSPECTION & GAPPING

▶ See Figures 99, 100, 101, 102 and 103

Check the plugs for deposits and wear. If they are not going to be replaced, clean the plugs thoroughly. Remember that any kind of deposit will decrease the efficiency of the plug. Plugs can be cleaned on a spark plug cleaning machine, which can sometimes be found in service stations, or you can do an acceptable job of cleaning with a stiff brush. If the plugs are cleaned, the electrodes must be filed flat. Use an ignition points file, not an emery board or the like, which will leave deposits. The electrodes must be filed perfectly flat with sharp edges; rounded edges reduce the spark plug voltage by as much as 50%.

Check spark plug gap before installation. The ground electrode (the L-shaped one connected to the body of the plug) must be parallel to the center electrode and the specified size wire gauge (please refer to the Specifications chart under the hood for details) must pass between the electrodes with a slight drag.

➡NEVER adjust the gap on a used platinum type spark plug.

Always check the gap on new plugs as they may have changed during handling. Do not use a flat feeler gauge when measuring the gap on a used plug, because the reading may be inaccurate. A round-wire type gapping tool is the best way to check the gap. The correct gauge should pass

A **normally worn** spark plug should have light tan or gray deposits on the firing tip.

A **carbon fouled** plug, identified by soft, sooty, black deposits, may indicate an improperly tuned vehicle. Check the air cleaner, ignition components and engine control system.

This spark plug has been **left in the engine too long,** as evidenced by the extreme gap- Plugs with such an extreme gap can cause misfiring and stumbling accompanied by a noticeable lack of power.

An **oil fouled** spark plug indicates an engine with worn poston rings and/or bad valve seals allowing excessive oil to enter the chamber.

A **physically damaged** spark plug may be evidence of severe detonation in that cylinder. Watch that cylinder carefully between services, as a continued detonation will not only damage the plug, but could also damage the engine.

A **bridged or almost bridged** spark plug, identified by a build-up between the electrodes caused by excessive carbon or oil build-up on the plug.

TCCA1P40

Fig. 99 Inspect the spark plug to determine engine running conditions

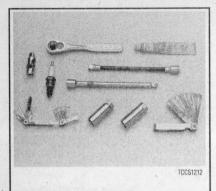

TCCS1212

Fig. 100 A variety of tools and gauges are needed for spark plug service

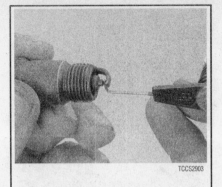

TCCS2903

Fig. 101 Checking the spark plug gap with a feeler gauge

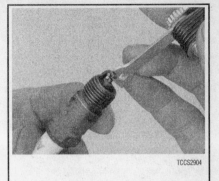

TCCS2904

Fig. 102 Adjusting the spark plug gap

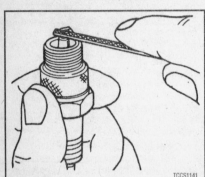

TCCS1141

Fig. 103 If the standard plug is in good condition, the electrode may be filed flat—WARNING: do not file platinum plugs

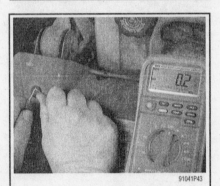

91041P43

Fig. 104 Calibrate (zeroing) the ohmmeter before using it

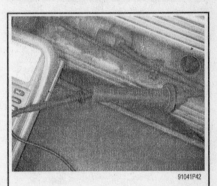

91041P42

Fig. 105 Make one connection at the spark plug end and . . .

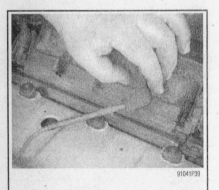

91041P39

Fig. 106 . . . one connection at the coil end to check the plug wire resistance

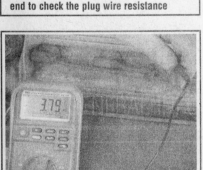

91041P41

Fig. 107 Checking the resistance of the spark plug wire

through the electrode gap with a slight drag. If you're in doubt, try one size smaller and one larger. The smaller gauge should go through easily, while the larger one shouldn't go through at all. Wire gapping tools usually have a bending tool attached. Use that to adjust the side electrode until the proper distance is obtained. Absolutely never attempt to bend the center electrode. Also, be careful not to bend the side electrode too far or too often as it may weaken and break off within the engine, requiring removal of the cylinder head to retrieve it.

Spark Plug Wires

The spark plug wiring used with electronic ignition systems is a carbon impregnated cord conductor, incased in 8mm diameter silicone rubber insulation. The silicone jacket withstands very high temperatures and provides an excellent insulator for the higher voltage of the electronic ignition system. Silicone spark plug boots form a tight seal on the plug.

When it becomes necessary to replace spark plug wires, because of age or breakage, it is recommended that you purchase a wire set for your specific engine model. These wire sets are precut to the proper length, and already have the boots installed.

The material used to construct the spark plug cables is very soft. This cable will withstand more heat and carry higher voltage, but scuffing and cutting becomes easier. The spark plug cables must be routed correctly to prevent chaffing or cutting.

TESTING

▶ See Figures 104, 105, 106 and 107

Visually inspect the spark plug wires for burns, cuts, or breaks in the insulation. Check the spark plug boots and the nipples on the distributor cap and/or coil(s). Replace any damaged wiring. If no physical damage is obvious, the wires can be checked with an ohmmeter for excessive resistance and continuity.

At every tune-up/inspection, visually check the spark plug cables for burns cuts, or breaks in the insulation. Check the boots and the nipples on the distributor cap and/or coil. Replace any damaged wiring.

Every 50,000 miles (80,000 Km) or 60 months, the resistance of the wires should be checked with an ohmmeter. Wires with excessive resistance will cause misfiring, and may make the engine difficult to start in damp weather.

To check resistance, disconnect plug wires (do only one at a time) from the spark plug and distributor cap or coil pack.

• Connect one lead of an ohmmeter to the spark plug side of the wire (make sure to contact the metal clip inside the boot).

• Attach the other lead of the ohmmeter to the distributor (coil pack) side of the wire. Again, make sure you contact the metal clip.

• Spark plug wire resistance is a function of length, the longer the wire the greater the resistance. You should replace any wire with a resistance over 7k ohms per foot.

• Spraying the secondary ignition wires with a light mist of water may help locate an intermittent problem. Ignition components will arc to ground when a secondary component is faulty.

REMOVAL & INSTALLATION

➡**To avoid confusion label, remove, and replace spark plug cables one at a time, where possible.**

Use care when removing spark plug wire boots from spark plugs. Grasp the wire by the rubber boot. Twist and pull the boot and wire from the spark plug. Never pull on the plug wire directly, or it may become separated from the connector inside the boot. Twist the boot ½ turn before trying to pull the boot off. Pull only on the boot, pulling on the wire could cause separation or breakage.

4.5L and 4.9L Engines

▶ **See Figure 108**

1. Disconnect the spark plug cables at the distributor assembly.
2. Disconnect the spark plug wires at the spark plugs.

➡**Use care when removing the spark plug boots from the spark plugs. Twist the boot ½ turn before removing and then pull on the boot only. Do not pull on the wire, as it may damage the spark plug cable.**

3. Remove the spark plug channel from the engine.
4. Remove the spark plug wire from the engine.
To install:
5. Position the spark plug wire assembly on top of the engine. Install the plug wire channel.
6. Install the spark plug wire at the spark plug. Make sure the wires are fully seated on the plugs.
7. Install the spark plug wires at the distributor assembly. Secure wires in position.

Fig. 108 Disconnecting the spark plug cable at the distributor assembly

4.6L Engine

▶ **See Figure 109**

1. Disconnect the spark plug cables at the Ignition Control Module (ICM) assembly.
2. Disconnect the spark plug wires at the spark plugs.

➡**Use care when removing the spark plug boots from the spark plugs. Twist the boot ½ turn before removing and then pull on the boot only. Do not pull on the wire, as it may damage the spark plug cable.**

3. Remove the spark plug channel from the camshaft cover and the intake manifold.
4. Remove the spark plug wire from the engine.
To install:
5. Position the spark plug wire assembly on top of the engine. Install the plug wire channel onto the front camshaft cover and intake manifold.
6. Install the spark plug wire at the spark plug. Make sure the wires are fully seated on the plugs.
7. Install the spark plug wires at the ICM assembly.

Distributor Cap and Rotor

Ignition systems have changed dramatically since these vehicles were first introduced. Most vehicles today use coil packs instead of distributors. They have no need of distributor caps or rotors. Camshaft and crankshaft sensors have replaced these items. For the most part, timing is no longer adjustable, but is being controlled by the PCM (Powertrain Control Module). However, in the interest of those vehicles that operate with a distributor cap and rotor, some basic information will be given.

INSPECTION

A physical inspection of the distributor cap and rotor should be done at the same time as the plug wires are being checked. When inspecting the distributor cap, check for obvious signs of damage, such as a broken tower, crack in the body of the cap, or external carbon tracks . When checking on the inside of the cap, use a bright light to illuminate the inner surface. Check for charred or eroded terminals, inspect for carbon tracks that go from terminal to terminal or run to the bottom of the cap. Look for a worn or damaged rotor button (center electrode). Also, take a close look at the inside terminals for metal to metal contact. Damaged or cut terminals could mean a rotor or cap that was not properly installed. It could mean that the distributor housing has worn beyond its limits and the shaft is wobbling when it rotates, or that the distributor shaft is bent.

REMOVAL & INSTALLATION

▶ **See Figure 110**

1. Disconnect the negative battery cable.

➡**Record wire placement at each wire location in order to maintain the correct firing order.**

2. Simultaneously depress and rotate the two retaining screws counterclockwise, in the cap, 180° to disengage from the distributor housing.
3. Remove the cap, this exposes the ignition rotor.
4. Remove the two hold down screws retaining

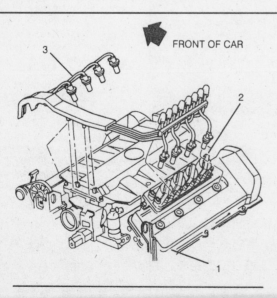

1	ENGINE
2	IGNITION CONTROL MODULE ASSEMBLY
3	SPARK PLUG WIRES

Fig. 109 Ignition Control Module (ICM) assembly and spark plug cables—4.6L engine

Fig. 110 Removing the distributor cap and coil assembly from the housing

the rotor to the distributor shaft. Note the position of the rotor before removal.

To install:

5. To install the rotor, align it to the distributor shaft. Do not put the square peg into the round hole!

➡The rotor can be mounted incorrectly. If this occurs, the engine timing will be off by 180°. Be careful to align the rotor properly, it should seat snugly and level on the distributor shaft.

6. Seat the distributor cap onto the distributor housing, making sure to align the cap properly.

7. Simultaneously depress and rotate the cap screws clockwise 180° to hold the cap in place.

Ignition Timing

Ignition timing is the measurement, in degrees of crankshaft rotation, of the point at which the spark plugs fire in each of the cylinders. It is measured in degrees before or after Top Dead Center (TDC) of the compression stroke.

Ideally, the air/fuel mixture in the cylinder will be ignited by the spark plug just as the piston passes TDC of the compression stroke. If this happens, the piston will be beginning the power stroke just as the compressed and ignited air/fuel mixture starts to expand. The expansion of the air/fuel mixture then forces the piston down on the power stroke and turns the crankshaft.

Because it takes a fraction of a second for the spark plug to ignite the mixture in the cylinder, the spark plug must fire a little before the piston reaches TDC. Otherwise, the mixture will not be completely ignited as the piston passes TDC and the full power of the explosion will not be used by the engine.

The timing measurement is given in degrees of crankshaft rotation before the piston reaches TDC (BTDC, or Before Top Dead Center). If the setting for the ignition timing is 10 BTDC, each spark plug must fire 10 degrees before each piston reaches TDC. This only holds true, however, when the engine is at idle speed.

As the engine speed increases, the pistons go faster. The spark plugs have to ignite the fuel even sooner if it is to be completely ignited when the piston reaches TDC.

The Vehicle Emission Control Information label is attached in the engine compartment. Follow all instructions on the label. However, if the label is missing or defaced, making it unreadable, use the following procedures:

ADJUSTMENT

4.5L Engine

➡Make timing adjustment with engine at normal operating temperature and the air conditioning system, if so equipped, turned off.

Set the parking brake and block the drive wheels. The vehicle should be in Neutral or Park.

Check the Service Engine light. It should not be lit.

1. With the ignition off, connect an inductive type timing light to the number one spark plug lead. Find the timing marks on the front of the engine just above and slightly to the side of the crankshaft pulley. Make sure this is clean and readable. If neces-

sary, mark the timing mark at 10° BTDC with a dot of white paint or white correction fluid. There is a slot cut on the crankshaft pulley that should be dabbed with a spot of paint to ease in setting the timing.

2. Jump pins A and B together at the ALDL connector, while not in diagnostic display.

3. Start the engine and aim the timing light at the timing mark. The line of the balancer or pulley will line up at the timing mark. If a change is necessary, loosen the distributor hold-down clamp bolt at the base of the distributor slightly. While observing the mark with the timing light, slightly rotate the distributor until the line indicates the correct timing. Tighten the hold-down bolt to 25 ft. lbs. (34Nm).

Turn off the engine and remove the timing light.

4.6L Engine

♦ See Figures 111 and 112

The basic ignition timing on the 4.6L Northstar is determined by the relationship of the crankshaft position sensors to the reluctor ring. This relationship is not adjustable and results in a base ignition timing of 10° BTDC.

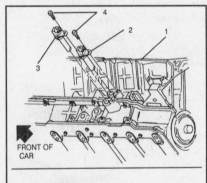

1	ENGINE
2	CRANKSHAFT POSITION "A" SENSOR
3	CRANKSHAFT POSITION "B" SENSOR
4	BOLT (10 N•m/89 LB.IN.)

84202027

Fig. 111 Crankshaft position sensor—4.6L engine

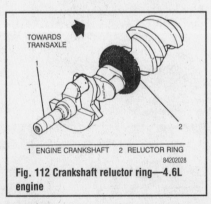

| 1 ENGINE CRANKSHAFT | 2 RELUCTOR RING |

84202028

Fig. 112 Crankshaft reluctor ring—4.6L engine

4.9L Engine

♦ See Figures 113 and 114

Timing specifications and adjustment procedure for each engine are listed on the underhood Vehicle

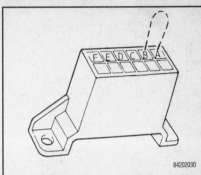

84202030

Fig. 113 Jumper pins A and B at the ALDL connector in order to set timing

Emissions Control Information (VECI) label in the engine compartment. Use specifications or procedures from the VECI, if they differ from the specifications or procedure listed in this manual.

The 4.9L engine incorporates a magnetic timing probe hole for use with special electronic timing equipment. Consult manufacturer's instructions for use of this equipment. Malfunction codes may be set during ignition timing adjustment procedure. Enter diagnostics and clear trouble codes if this occurs. Refer to trouble codes for more information.

1. Place the transmission in Park.

2. With the ignition in the **OFF** position, attach a timing light to No. 1 spark plug cable.

➡Do not pierce the wire or attempt to insert a probe between the boot and the wire. Connect the timing light power leads according to manufacturer instruction. Do not time the engine on 7 cylinders as the unburned fuel could cause damage to the catalytic converter.

3. With the engine at normal operating temperature and the air conditioning **OFF**, take off the air cleaner upper housing. The engine should be **OFF** at this time.

4. Jump pins A and B at the ALDL connector, while not in the diagnostic display. 'SET TIMING MODE' message will be displayed on the climate control Driver Information Center (CCDIC).

5. Start the engine and aim the timing light at the timing mark. If an adjustment is necessary, loosen the distributor hold-down nut using a

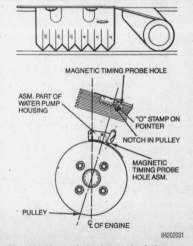

84202031

Fig. 114 Magnetic timing probe hole—4.9L engine

ENGINE TUNE-UP SPECIFICATIONS

Year	Engine Displacement Liters (cc)	Engine ID/VIN	Spark Plug Gap (in.)	Ignition Timing (deg.)	Fuel Pump (psi)	Idle Speed (rpm)	Valve Clearance	
							Intake	Exhaust
1990	4.5 (4474)	3	0.060	①	45-50	①	HYD	HYD
1991	4.9 (4917)	B	0.060	①	45-50	①	HYD	HYD
1992	4.9 (4917)	B	0.060	①	45-50	①	HYD	HYD
1993	4.6 (4593)	9	0.060	①	45-50	①	HYD	HYD
	4.9 (4917)	B	0.060	①	45-50	①	HYD	HYD
1994	4.6 (4593)	9	0.060	①	45-50	①	HYD	HYD
	4.6 (4573)	Y	0.050	①	40-50	①	HYD	HYD
	4.9 (4917)	B	0.060	①	45-50	①	HYD	HYD
1995	4.6 (4573)	9	0.050	①	40-50	①	HYD	HYD
	4.6 (4573)	Y	0.050	①	40-50	①	HYD	HYD
	4.9 (4917)	B	0.060	①	40-50	①	HYD	HYD
1996	4.6 (4573)	9	0.050	①	40-50	①	HYD	HYD
	4.6 (4573)	Y	0.050	①	40-50	①	HYD	HYD
1997	4.6 (4573)	9	0.050	①	40-50	①	HYD	HYD
	4.6 (4573)	Y	0.050	①	40-50	①	HYD	HYD
1998	4.6 (4573)	9	0.050	①	40-50	①	HYD	HYD
	4.6 (4573)	Y	0.050	①	40-50	①	HYD	HYD

NOTE: The Vehicle Emission Control Information label often reflects specification changes made during production. The label figures must be used if they differ from those in this chart.

HYD-Hydraulic

① Controlled by PCM

9104CR3

suitable distributor wrench. While observing the timing mark, rotate the distributor until the line indicates the correct timing. Set base timing at 10 degrees BTDC, at any speed less than 800 rpm.

6. Turn OFF the engine and remove the timing light.

7. Remove the jumper from the ALDL connector and install the air cleaner upper housing.

➡Remove the jumper from the ALDL connector when the procedure is complete. If the jumper remains in the ALDL connector, the engine will run at base timing and cause driveability problems

Valve Lash

ADJUSTMENT

Adjustment of the hydraulic lash adjusters or hydraulic lifters is neither possible nor necessary.

Idle Speed Adjustment

The Idle Air Control (IAC) valve assembly controls engine idle speed. The IAC valve assembly meters intake air around the throttle plate through a bypass within the IAC valve assembly and throttle body. The PCM determines the desired idle speed or bypass air and signals the IAC valve assembly through a specified duty cycle. The IAC solenoid responds by positioning the IAC valve to control the amount of bypassed air. By varying the amount of air intake, different idle speeds can be achieved. When the pintle is in, the valve is closed and a low idle

speed results. When the pintle is out, the valve is open and high idle speeds occur. The PCM monitors engine rpm and increases or decreases the IAC duty cycle in order to achieve the desired rpm. There are no external mechanical adjustments to be made.

Air Conditioning System

SYSTEM SERVICE & REPAIR

The do-it-yourselfer should not service his/her own vehicle's A/C system for many reasons, including legal concerns, personal injury, environmental damages and cost. The following are some of the reasons why you may decide not to service the A/C system of your own vehicle.

According to the U.S. Clean Air Act, it is a federal crime to service or repair (involving the refrigerant) a Motor Vehicle Air Conditioning (MVAC) system for money without being EPA certified. It is also illegal to vent R-12 and R-134a refrigerants into the atmosphere. Selling or distributing A/C system refrigerant (in a container that contains less than 20 pounds of refrigerant) to any person whom is not EPA 609 certified is also not allowed by law.

State and/or local laws may be stricter than the federal regulations, so be sure to check with your state and/or local authorities for further information. For further federal information on the legality of servicing your A/C system, call the EPA Stratospheric Ozone Hotline.

➡Federal law dictates that a fine of up to $25,000 may be levied on people convicted of venting refrigerant into the atmosphere. Additionally, the EPA may pay up to $10,000 for

information or services leading to a criminal conviction of the violation of these laws.

When servicing an A/C system you run the risk of handling or coming in contact with refrigerant, which may result in skin or eye irritation or frostbite. Although low in toxicity (due to chemical stability), inhalation of concentrated refrigerant fumes is dangerous and can result in death; cases of fatal cardiac arrhythmia have been reported in people accidentally subjected to high levels of refrigerant. Some early symptoms include loss of concentration and drowsiness.

➡Generally, the limit for exposure is lower for R-134a than it is for R-12. Exceptional care must be practiced when handling R-134a.

In addition, refrigerants can decompose at high temperatures (near gas heaters or open flame), that may result in hydrofluoric acid, hydrochloric acid, and phosgene (a fatal nerve gas).

R-12 refrigerant can damage the environment because it is a Chlorofluorocarbon (CFC), which has been proven to add to ozone layer depletion, leading to increasing levels of UV radiation. UV radiation has been linked with an increase in skin cancer, suppression of the human immune system, an increase in cataracts, damage to crops, damage to aquatic organisms, an increase in ground-level ozone, and increased global warming.

R-134a refrigerant is a greenhouse gas which, if allowed to vent into the atmosphere, will contribute to global warming (the Greenhouse Effect).

It is usually more economically feasible to have a certified MVAC automotive technician perform A/C system service on your vehicle. Some possible reasons for this are as follows:

• While it is illegal to service an A/C system without the proper equipment, the home mechanic would have to purchase an expensive refrigerant recovery/recycling machine to service his/her own vehicle.

• Since only a certified person may purchase refrigerant—according to the Clean Air Act, there are specific restrictions on selling or distributing A/C system refrigerant—it is legally impossible (unless certified) for the home mechanic to service his/her own vehicle. Procuring refrigerant in an illegal fashion exposes one to the risk of paying a $25,000 fine to the EPA.

R-12 Refrigerant Conversion

If your vehicle still uses R-12 refrigerant, one way to save A/C system costs down the road is to investigate the possibility of having your system converted to R-134a. The older R-12 systems can be easily converted to R-134a refrigerant by a certified automotive technician by installing a few new components and changing the system oil.

The cost of R-12 is steadily rising and will continue to increase, because it is no longer imported or manufactured in the United States. Therefore, it is often possible to have an R-12 system converted to R-134a and recharged for less than it would cost to just charge the system with R-12.

If you are interested in having your system converted, contact local automotive service stations for more details and information.

PREVENTIVE MAINTENANCE

♦ See Figures 115 and 116

• The easiest and most important preventive maintenance for your A/C system is to be sure that it is used on a regular basis. Running the system for five minutes each month (no matter what the season) will help ensure that the seals and all internal components remain lubricated.

➡Some newer vehicles automatically operate the A/C system compressor whenever the windshield defroster is activated. When running, the compressor lubricates the A/C system components; therefore, the A/C system would not need to be operated each month.

• In order to prevent heater core freeze-up during A/C operation, it is necessary to maintain proper antifreeze protection. Use a hand-held coolant tester

Fig. 115 A coolant tester can be used to determine the freezing and boiling levels of the coolant in your vehicle

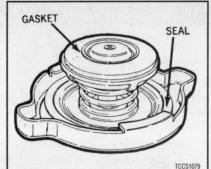

Fig. 116 To ensure efficient cooling system operation, inspect the radiator cap gasket and seal

(hydrometer) to periodically check the condition of the antifreeze in your engine's cooling system.

➡Antifreeze should not be used longer than the manufacturer specifies.

• For efficient operation of an air conditioned vehicle's cooling system, the radiator cap should have a holding pressure that meets manufacturer's specifications. A cap that fails to hold these pressures should be replaced.

• Any obstruction of or damage to the condenser configuration will restrict air flow that is essential to its efficient operation. It is, therefore, a good rule to keep this unit clean and in proper physical shape.

➡Bug screens that are mounted in front of the condenser (unless original equipment) are regarded as obstructions.

• The condensation drain tube expels any water that accumulates on the bottom of the evaporator housing into the engine compartment. If this tube is obstructed, the air conditioning performance can be restricted and condensation buildup can spill over onto the floor of the vehicle.

SYSTEM INSPECTION

♦ See Figure 117

Although the A/C system should not be serviced by the do-it-yourselfer, preventive maintenance can be practiced and A/C system inspections can be performed to help maintain the efficiency of the A/C system of the vehicle. For A/C system inspection, perform the following:

The easiest and often most important check for the air conditioning system consists of a visual inspection of the system components. Visually inspect the air conditioning system for refrigerant leaks, damaged compressor clutch, abnormal compressor drive belt tension and/or condition, plugged evaporator drain tube, blocked condenser fins, disconnected or broken wires, blown fuses, corroded connections and poor insulation.

A refrigerant leak will usually appear as an oily residue at the leakage point in the system. The oily residue soon picks up dust or dirt particles from the surrounding air and appears greasy. Through time, this will build up and appear to be a heavy dirt impregnated grease.

For a thorough visual and operational inspection, check the following:

• Check the surface of the radiator and condenser for dirt, leaves, or other material that might block air flow.

• Check for kinks in hoses and lines. Check the system for leaks.

• Make sure the drive belt is properly tensioned. When the air conditioning is operating, make sure the drive belt is free of noise or slippage.

• Make sure the blower motor operates at all appropriate positions, then check for distribution of the air from all outlets with the blower on **HIGH** or **MAX**.

➡Keep in mind that under conditions of high humidity, air discharged from the A/C vents may not feel as cold as expected, even if the system is working properly. This is because vaporized moisture in humid air retains heat more effectively than dry air, thereby making humid air more difficult to cool.

• Make sure the air passage selection lever is operating correctly. Start the engine and warm it to normal operating temperature, then make sure the temperature selection lever is operating correctly.

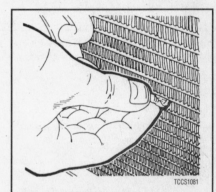

Fig. 117 Periodically remove any debris from the condenser and radiator fins

Windshield Wipers

ELEMENT (REFILL) CARE & REPLACEMENT

♦ See Figures 118 thru 127

For maximum effectiveness and longest element life, the windshield and wiper blades should be kept clean. Dirt, tree sap, road tar and so on will cause streaking, smearing and blade deterioration if left on the glass. It is advisable to wash the windshield carefully with a commercial glass cleaner at least once a month. Wipe off the rubber blades with the wet rag afterwards. Do not attempt to move wipers across the windshield by hand; damage to the motor and drive mechanism will result.

To inspect and/or replace the wiper blade elements, place the wiper switch in the **LOW** speed position and the ignition switch in the **ACC** position. When the wiper blades are approximately vertical on the windshield, turn the ignition switch to **OFF**.

Examine the wiper blade elements. If they cracked, broken or torn, they should be replaced immediately. Replacement intervals will vary with usage, although ozone deterioration usually limits element life to about one year. If the wiper pattern is smeared or streaked, or if the blade chatters across the glass, the elements should be replaced. It is easiest and most sensible to replace the elements in pairs.

If your vehicle is equipped with aftermarket blades, there are several different types of refills and your vehicle might have any kind. Aftermarket blades and arms rarely use the exact same type blade or refill as the original equipment. Here are some typical aftermarket wiper blades; not all may be available for your vehicle:

The Anco® type uses a release button that is pushed down to allow the refill to slide out of the yoke jaws. The new refill slides back into the frame and locks in place.

Some Trico® refills are removed by locating where the metal backing strip or the refill is wider. Insert a small screwdriver blade between the frame and metal backing strip. Press down to release the refill from the retaining tab.

Other types of Trico® refills have two metal tabs that are unlocked by squeezing them together. The rubber filler can then be withdrawn from the frame jaws. A new refill is installed by inserting the refill into the front frame jaws and sliding it rearward to engage the remaining frame jaws. There are usually four jaws; be certain when installing that the refill is engaged in all of them. At the end of its travel, the tabs will lock into place on the front jaws of the wiper blade frame.

Another type of refill is made from polycarbon-

ate. The refill has a simple locking device at one end which flexes downward out of the groove into which the jaws of the holder fit, allowing easy release. By sliding the new refill through all the jaws and pushing through the slight resistance when it reaches the end of its travel, the refill will lock into position.

To replace the Tridon® refill, it is necessary to remove the wiper blade. This refill has a plastic backing strip with a notch about 1 in. (25mm) from the end. Hold the blade (frame) on a hard surface so that the frame is tightly bowed. Grip the tip of the backing strip and pull up while twisting counter-clockwise. The backing strip will snap out of the retaining tab. Do this for the remaining tabs until the refill is free of the blade. The length of these

Fig. 118 Bosch® wiper blade and fit kit

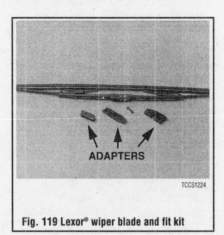

Fig. 119 Lexor® wiper blade and fit kit

Fig. 120 Pylon® wiper blade and adapter

Fig. 121 Trico® wiper blade and fit kit

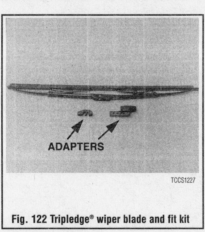

Fig. 122 Tripledge® wiper blade and fit kit

Fig. 123 To remove and install a Lexor® wiper blade refill, slip out the old insert and slide in a new one

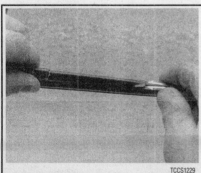

Fig. 124 On Pylon® inserts, the clip at the end has to be removed before sliding the insert off

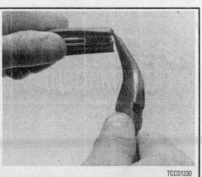

Fig. 125 On Trico® wiper blades, the tab at the end of the blade must be turned up . . .

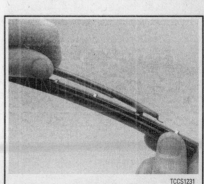

Fig. 126 . . . then, the insert can be removed. After installing the replacement insert, bend the tab back

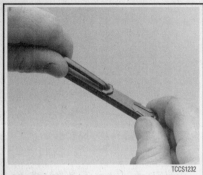

Fig. 127 The Tripledge® wiper blade insert is removed and installed using a securing clip

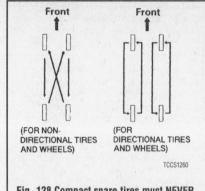

Fig. 128 Compact spare tires must NEVER be used in the rotation pattern

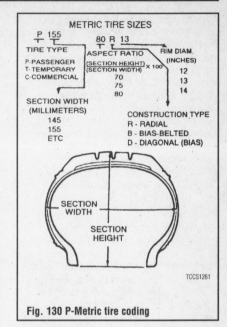

Fig. 130 P-Metric tire coding

refills is molded into the end and they should be replaced with identical types.

Regardless of the type of refill used, be sure to follow the part manufacturer's instructions closely. Make sure that all of the frame jaws are engaged as the refill is pushed into place and locked. If the metal

blade holder and frame are allowed to touch the glass during wiper operation, the glass will be scratched.

Tires and Wheels

Common sense and good driving habits will afford maximum tire life. Fast starts, sudden stops and hard cornering are hard on tires and will shorten their useful life span. Make sure that you don't overload the vehicle or run with incorrect pressure in the tires. Both of these practices will increase tread wear.

➡**For optimum tire life, keep the tires properly inflated, rotate them often and have the wheel alignment checked periodically.**

Inspect your tires frequently. Be especially careful to watch for bubbles in the tread or sidewall, deep cuts or underinflation. Replace any tires with bubbles in the sidewall. If cuts are so deep that they penetrate to the cords, discard the tire. Any cut in the sidewall of a radial tire renders it unsafe. Also, look for uneven tread wear patterns that may indicate the front end is out of alignment or that the tires are out of balance.

Most tires today have a service description branded on the side wall after the tire size. This service description consists of two parts: the load index and the speed symbol. The load index is a number usually between 75 and 115, which defines the tire's load capacity at maximum inflation. Higher numbers mean greater load capacity. The speed symbol is a letter usually between P and Z, which defines the speed capability of the tire. In the past, this letter might have been part of the tire size.

TIRE ROTATION

▶ **See Figures 128 and 129**

Tires must be rotated periodically to equalize wear patterns that vary with a tire's position on the vehicle. Tires will also wear in an uneven way as the front steering/suspension system wears to the point where the alignment should be reset.

Fig. 129 Unidirectional tires are identifiable by sidewall arrows and/or the word "rotation"

Rotating the tires will ensure maximum life for the tires as a set, so you will not have to discard a tire early due to wear on only part of the tread. Regular rotation is required to equalize wear.

When rotating "unidirectional tires," make sure that they always roll in the same direction. This means that a tire used on the left side of the vehicle must not be switched to the right side and vice-versa. Such tires should only be rotated front-to-rear or rear-to-front, while always remaining on the same side of the vehicle. These tires are marked on the sidewall as to the direction of rotation; observe the marks when reinstalling the tire(s).

Some styled or "mag" wheels may have different offsets front to rear. In these cases, the rear wheels must not be used up front and vice-versa. Furthermore, if these wheels are equipped with unidirectional tires, they cannot be rotated unless the tire is remounted for the proper direction of rotation.

➡**The compact or space-saver spare is strictly for emergency use. It must never be included in the tire rotation or placed on the vehicle for everyday use.**

TIRE DESIGN

▶ **See Figure 130**

For maximum satisfaction, tires should be used in sets of four. Mixing of different types (radial, bias-belted, fiberglass belted) must be avoided. In most cases, the vehicle manufacturer has designated a type of tire on which the vehicle will perform best. Your first choice when replacing tires

should be to use the same type of tire that the manufacturer recommends.

When radial tires are used, tire sizes and wheel diameters should be selected to maintain ground clearance and tire load capacity equivalent to the original specified tire. Radial tires should always be used in sets of four.

➡**Changing the tire size or wheel diameter from the original factory installed component could cause speedometer error and driveability concerns.**

❋❋ CAUTION

Radial tires should never be used on the front axle only.

When selecting tires, pay attention to the original size as marked on the tire. Most tires are described using an industry size code sometimes referred to as P-Metric. This allows the exact identification of the tire specifications, regardless of the manufacturer. If selecting a different tire size or brand, remember to check the installed tire for any sign of interference with the body or suspension while the vehicle is stopping, turning sharply or heavily loaded.

Snow Tires

Good radial tires can produce a big advantage in slippery weather, but in snow, a street radial tire does not have sufficient tread to provide traction and control. The small grooves of a street tire quickly pack with snow and the tire behaves like a billiard ball on a marble floor. The more open, chunky tread of a snow tire will self-clean as the tire turns, providing much better grip on snowy surfaces.

To satisfy municipalities requiring snow tires during weather emergencies, most snow tires carry either an M + S designation after the tire size stamped on the sidewall, or the designation "all-season." In general, no change in tire size is necessary when buying snow tires.

Most manufacturers strongly recommend the use of four snow tires on their vehicles for reasons of stability. If snow tires are fitted only to the drive wheels, the opposite end of the vehicle may become very unstable when braking or turning on slippery surfaces. This instability can lead to unpleasant endings if the driver can't counteract the slide in time.

Note that snow tires, whether 2 or 4, will affect vehicle handling in all non-snow situations. The stiffer, heavier snow tires will noticeably change the turning and braking characteristics of the vehicle. Once the snow tires are installed, you must re-learn the behavior of the vehicle and drive accordingly.

➡ **Consider buying extra wheels on which to mount the snow tires. Once done, the "snow wheels" can be installed and removed as needed. This eliminates the potential damage to tires or wheels from seasonal removal and installation. Even if your vehicle has styled wheels, see if inexpensive steel wheels are available. Although the look of the vehicle will change, the expensive wheels will be protected from salt, curb hits and pothole damage.**

TIRE STORAGE

If they are mounted on wheels, store the tires at proper inflation pressure. All tires should be kept in a cool, dry place. If they are stored in the garage or basement, do not let them stand on a concrete floor; set them on strips of wood, a mat or a large stack of newspaper. Keeping them away from direct moisture is of paramount importance. Tires should not be stored upright, but in a flat position.

INFLATION & INSPECTION

▶ **See Figures 131 thru 138**

The importance of proper tire inflation cannot be overemphasized. A tire employs air as part of its structure. It is designed around the supporting strength of the air at a specified pressure. For this reason, improper inflation drastically reduces the tire's ability to perform as intended. A tire will lose some air in day-to-day use; having to add a few pounds of air periodically is not necessarily a sign of a leaking tire.

Two items should be a permanent fixture in every glove compartment: an accurate tire pressure gauge and a tread depth gauge. Check the tire pressure (including the spare) regularly with a pocket type gauge. Too often, the gauge on the end of the air hose at your corner garage is not accurate because it suffers too much abuse. Always check tire pressure when the tires are cold, as pressure increases with temperature. If you must move the vehicle to check the tire inflation, do not drive more than a mile before checking. A cold tire is generally one that has not been driven for more than three hours.

A plate or sticker is normally provided somewhere in the vehicle (doorpost, hood, trunk, or trunk lid)

This shows the proper pressure for the tires. Never counteract excessive pressure build-up by bleeding off air pressure (letting some air out). This will cause the tire to run hotter and wear quicker.

Once you've maintained the correct tire pressures for several weeks, you'll be familiar with the vehicle's braking and handling personality. Slight adjustments in tire pressures can fine-tune these characteristics, but never change the cold pressure specification by more than 2 psi. A slightly softer tire pressure will give a softer ride but also yield lower fuel mileage. A slightly harder tire will give crisper dry road handling but can cause skidding on wet surfaces. Unless you're fully attuned to the vehicle, stick to the recommended inflation pressures.

All tires made since 1968 have built-in tread wear indicator bars that show up as ½ in. (13mm) wide smooth bands across the tire when ¹⁄₁₆ in. (1.5mm) of tread remains. The appearance of tread wear indicators means that the tires should be replaced. In fact, many states have laws prohibiting the use of tires with less than this amount of tread.

When replacing tires, only the size, load range, and construction as were originally installed on the vehicle are recommended.

You can check your own tread depth with an inexpensive gauge or by using a Lincoln head

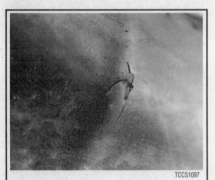

Fig. 131 Tires should be checked frequently for any sign of puncture or damage

Fig. 132 Tires with deep cuts, or cuts which bulge, should be replaced immediately

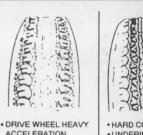

• DRIVE WHEEL HEAVY ACCELERATION
• OVERINFLATION

• HARD CORNERING
• UNDERINFLATION
• LACK OF ROTATION

Fig. 133 Examples of inflation-related tire wear patterns

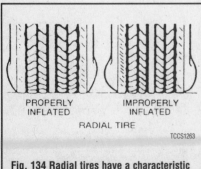

PROPERLY INFLATED   IMPROPERLY INFLATED

RADIAL TIRE

Fig. 134 Radial tires have a characteristic sidewall bulge; don't try to measure pressure by looking at the tire. Use a quality air pressure gauge

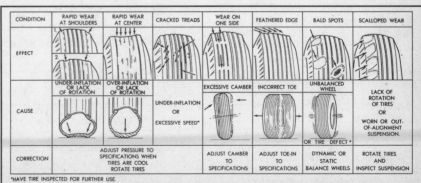

CONDITION	RAPID WEAR AT SHOULDERS	RAPID WEAR AT CENTER	CRACKED TREADS	WEAR ON ONE SIDE	FEATHERED EDGE	BALD SPOTS	SCALLOPED WEAR
EFFECT							
CAUSE	UNDER-INFLATION OR LACK OF ROTATION	OVER-INFLATION OR LACK OF ROTATION	UNDER-INFLATION OR EXCESSIVE SPEED*	EXCESSIVE CAMBER	INCORRECT TOE	UNBALANCED WHEEL OR TIRE DEFECT*	LACK OF ROTATION OF TIRES OR WORN OR OUT-OF-ALIGNMENT SUSPENSION.
CORRECTION		ADJUST PRESSURE TO SPECIFICATIONS WHEN TIRES ARE COOL ROTATE TIRES		ADJUST CAMBER TO SPECIFICATIONS	ADJUST TOE-IN TO SPECIFICATIONS	DYNAMIC OR STATIC BALANCE WHEELS	ROTATE TIRES AND INSPECT SUSPENSION

*HAVE TIRE INSPECTED FOR FURTHER USE.

Fig. 135 Common tire wear patterns and causes

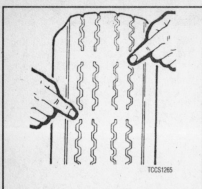

Fig. 136 Tread wear indicators will appear when the tire is worn

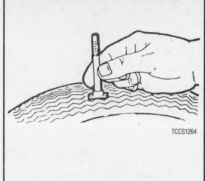

Fig. 137 Accurate tread depth indicators are inexpensive and handy

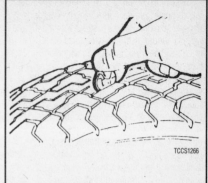

Fig. 138 A penny works well for a quick check of tread depth

penny. Slip the Lincoln penny (with Lincoln's head upside-down) into several treads grooves. If you can see the top of Lincoln's head in 2 adjacent grooves, the tire has less than 1/16 in. (1.5mm) tread left and should be replaced. You can measure snow tires in the same manner by using the "tails" side of the Lincoln penny. If you can see the top of the Lincoln memorial, it's time to replace the snow tire(s).

CARE OF SPECIAL WHEELS

If you have invested money in magnesium, aluminum alloy or sport wheels, special precautions should be taken to make sure your investment is not wasted and that your special wheels look good for the life of the vehicle.

Special wheels are easily damaged and/or scratched. Occasionally check the rims for cracking, impact damage or air leaks. If any of these are found, replace the wheel. However, in order to prevent this type of damage and the costly replacement of a special wheel, observe the following precautions:

• Use extra care not to damage the wheels during removal, installation, balancing, etc. After removal of the wheels from the vehicle, place them on a mat or other protective surface. If they are to be stored for any length of time, support them on strips of wood. Never store tires and wheels upright; the tread may develop flat spots.

• When driving, watch for hazards; it doesn't take much to crack a wheel.

• When washing, use a mild soap or non-abrasive dish detergent (keeping in mind that detergent tends to remove wax). Avoid cleansers with abrasives or the use of hard brushes. There are many cleaners and polishes for special wheels.

• If possible, remove the wheels during the winter. Salt and sand used for snow removal can severely damage the finish of a wheel.

• Make certain the recommended lug nut torque is never exceeded or the wheel may crack. Never use snow chains on special wheels; severe scratching will occur. Use a STAR pattern sequence to install and tighten the wheel nuts to a maximum of 100 ft. lbs. (140 Nm).

FLUIDS AND LUBRICANTS

Fluid Disposal

Used fluids such as engine oils, transmission fluid, antifreeze and brake fluids are hazardous wastes and must be disposed of properly. Before draining any fluids, consult with your local authorities; in many areas, waste oil, antifreeze, etc. is being accepted as a part of recycling programs. A number of service stations and auto parts stores are also accepting waste fluids for recycling.

Be sure of the recycling center's policies before draining any fluids, as many will not accept different fluids that have been mixed together.

Fuel Recommendations

The engine is designed to operate on unleaded gasoline ONLY and is essential for the proper operation of the emission control system. The use of unleaded fuel will reduce spark plug fouling, exhaust system corrosion and engine oil deterioration.

In most parts of the United States, fuel with an octane rating of 91 should be used unless otherwise specified by the vehicle manufacturer for performance reasons. Using fuels with a lower octane may decrease engine performance, increase emissions and engine wear.

In some areas, fuel consisting of a blend of alcohol may be used; this blend of gasoline and alcohol is known as gasohol. When using gasohol, never use blends exceeding 10% ethanol or 5% methanol.

➡ The use of fuel with excessive amounts of alcohol may jeopardize the new car warranties.

Oil Recommendations

▶ **See Figures 139 and 140**

Use only oil that has the API (American Petroleum Institute) designation "SJ," "SJ/CC" or "SJ/CD."

Since the viscosity (thickness) of the engine oil affects fuel economy, it is recommended to select oil with reference to the outside temperature. For satisfactory lubrication, use lower viscosity oil for colder temperatures and higher viscosity oil for warmer temperatures.

For maximum fuel economy, look for an oil that carries the words "Energy Conserving II" in the API symbol. This means that the oil contains friction-reducing additives that help reduce the amount of fuel burned to overcome engine friction.

The Society of Automotive Engineers (SAE) viscosity rating indicates an oil's ability to flow at a given temperature. The number designation indicates the thickness or "weight" of the oil. SAE 5-weight oil is thin light oil; it allows the engine to crank over easily even when it is very cold, and quickly provides lubrication for all parts of the engine. However, as the engine temperature

Fig. 139 Look for the API oil identification label when choosing your engine oil

Fig. 140 Typically, the oil cap will identify the oil viscosity the engine requires

increases, the 5-weight oil becomes too thin, resulting in metal-to-metal contact and damage to internal engine parts. Heavier SAE 50-weight oil can lubricate and protect internal engine parts even under extremely high operating temperatures. However, it would not be able to flow quickly enough to provide internal engine protection during cold weather start-up, one of the most critical periods for lubrication protection in an engine.

The answer to the temperature extreme problem is the multi-grade or multi-viscosity oil. Multi-viscosity oils carry multiple number designations, such as SAE 5W-30 oil that has the flow characteristics of the thin 5 weight oil in cold weather, providing rapid lubrication and allowing easy engine cranking. When the engine warms up, the oil acts like a straight 30 weight oil providing internal engine protection under higher temperatures.

OIL LEVEL CHECK

▶ **See Figures 141, 142, 143 and 144**

1. Make sure the vehicle is parked on level ground.

2. When checking the oil level it is best for the engine to be at normal operating temperature, although checking the oil immediately after stopping will lead to a false reading. Wait a few minutes after turning off the engine to allow the oil to drain back into the crankcase.

3. Open the hood and locate the dipstick. Pull the dipstick from its tube, wipe it clean, and then reinsert it.

4. Pull the dipstick out again and, holding it horizontally, read the oil level. The oil should be between the "FULL" and "ADD" marks on the dipstick. If the oil is below the "ADD" mark, add oil of the proper viscosity through the capped opening in the top of the cylinder head cover.

5. Replace the dipstick and check the oil level again after adding any oil. Be careful not to overfill the crankcase. Approximately 1 quart of oil will raise the level from the "ADD" mark to the "FULL" mark. Excess oil will generally be consumed at an accelerated rate.

CHANGING OIL & FILTER

▶ **See Figures 145 thru 151**

The oil is to be changed every 7,500 miles (12,500 km) or 12 months, which ever occurs first. Under normal conditions, change the filter at first oil change and then at every other oil change, unless 12 months pass between changes. We recommend that the oil filter be changed every time the oil is changed. About a quart of dirty oil remains in the old filter. For a few dollars, it is a small expense for extended engine life.

If driving under such conditions, such as: dusty areas, trailer towing, idling for long periods of time, low speed operation, or when operating with temperatures below freezing or driving short distances (under 4 miles), change the oil and filter every 3,000 miles (5,000 km) or 3 months.

1. Run the engine until it reaches normal operating temperature.

2. Usually a run to the parts store to pick up the oil and filter will get the engine hot enough.

3. Apply the parking brake and block the rear wheels.

4. Raise the vehicle and support it on jack stands. Slide a six-quart (minimum) drain pan under the oil pan drain plug.

5. Loosen the drain plug with a socket or box wrench. Push in on the plug as you turn in so no oil escapes until the plug is completely removed.

6. Remove the oil pan plug and drain the dirty oil into a catch pan. Allow the oil to drain into the pan. Be careful, if the engine is at operating temperature, the oil is hot enough to burn you.

7. Clean the drain plug and check it carefully; if the threads are stripped, replace it with a new one and a new gasket. If the gasket is cracked or damaged, replace it. Slide the oil drain pan under the oil filter.

8. Using the right size oil filter wrench, remove the oil filter by turning it counter-clockwise. Wrap a rag around it (to protect you from the hot oil), unscrew it the rest of the way, and place it in the oil catch pan.

9. Ensure that the old oil filter gasket is not stuck on the cylinder block or oil filter adapter. Using a clean rag, wipe the filter-mounting surface.

To install:

10. When installing the oil filter, spread a small amount of clean oil on the sealing gasket on the new filter and tighten the filter only hand tight. Install the oil pan plug and tighten to 20 ft. lbs. (27 Nm).

11. Make sure the plug is tight in the pan, but do not overtighten.

12. Slide the oil drain pan out from under the vehicle, and lower the vehicle to the ground.

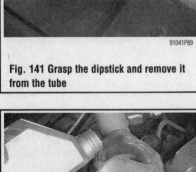

Fig. 141 Grasp the dipstick and remove it from the tube

Fig. 142 Wipe the dipstick clean and reinsert it. Pull it out again to read it

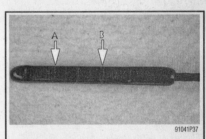

Fig. 143 When the oil registers on the add side (below the A), put in a quart. Between the A and B means the oil level is low, but not critical. The B is at the full mark; if oil is at this level, no service is necessary

Fig. 144 Using a funnel, add oil directly into the engine after removing the fill cap

Fig. 145 Make sure you use the proper size wrench for the oil pan plug. You don't want to round this nut off. GM uses 15mm or 9/16 inch and interchanges them, so have both handy

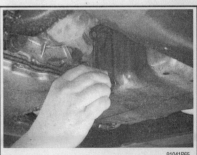

Fig. 146 The pan plug should be loosened by hand, unless it has been stripped. Loosen the plug until it is just about to come out, then . . .

Fig. 147 . . . quickly pull it away from the oil pan to avoid the hot flowing oil

Fig. 148 Use a good oil filter wrench to loosen the oil filter

Fig. 149 Grab the oil filter with a heavy cloth or shop towel so you won't be burned. Allow the oil filter to drain into the pan, before discarding it

Fig. 150 Wipe the oil filter-mounting block clean, before installing a new filter

Fig. 151 Before installing a new oil filter, lightly coat the rubber gasket with clean oil

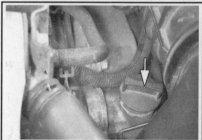

Fig. 152 The transaxle fill tube and dipstick is typically located as shown here. The cap is rather large compared to those on other vehicles

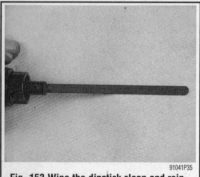

Fig. 153 Wipe the dipstick clean and reinsert it into the transaxle, remove it again and . . .

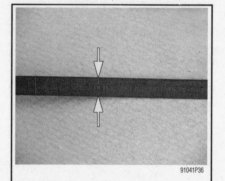

Fig. 154 . . . make sure the fluid is between the marks on the dipstick

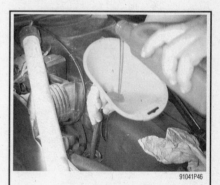

Fig. 155 Adding fluid to the transaxle is easier if the funnel has a hose on the end

13. Remove the oil filler cap from the rocker arm cover and place a funnel in the oil filler hole. Fill the crankcase with the oil specified for the engine.

14. Remove the funnel, install the oil cap, and wipe away any spilled oil.

15. Start the engine and inspect for oil leaks.

Automatic Transaxle

FLUID LEVEL CHECK

♦ **See Figures 152, 153, 154 and 155**

Check the automatic transaxle fluid level at least every 15,000 miles (24,000 km) or 12 months. The

dipstick can be found on the left (driver) side of the engine compartment. The fluid level should be checked only when the transaxle is hot (normal operating temperature). The transaxle is considered hot after about 20 miles of highway driving.

1. Start the engine, set the parking brake, and put the transaxle selector lever in the **PARK** position.

2. Move the selector lever through all the positions and return to the **PARK** position. DO NOT TURN OFF THE ENGINE DURING THE FLUID LEVEL CHECK.

3. Remove the dipstick, wipe it clean, and then reinsert it firmly. Be sure that it has been pushed all the way in. Remove the dipstick again and check the fluid level while holding it horizontally. With the engine running, the fluid level should be in the cross-hatched area.

4. If the fluid level is below the crosshatched area (engine hot), add DEXRON®III automatic transaxle fluid through the dipstick tube. This is easily done with the aid of a funnel. Check the level often as you are filling the transaxle. Be extremely careful not to overfill it. Overfilling will cause slippage, seal damage and overheating. Approximately 1 pint of ATF will raise the fluid level into the cross-hatched area.

➡**Use only DEXRON®III ATF. The use of any other fluid will cause severe damage.**

The fluid on the dipstick should always be a bright red color. If it is discolored (brown or black), or smells burnt, serious transaxle troubles, probably due to overheating, should be suspected. A qualified technician should inspect the transaxle to determine the cause of the burnt fluid.

DRAIN AND REFILL

▶ **See Figure 156**

In normal service, it should not be necessary or required to drain and refill the automatic transaxle. However, under severe operation or dusty conditions, the fluid should be changed every 36 months or 30,000 miles (48,000 km).

1. Raise the car and safely support it on jackstands.

Fig. 156 Remove the transaxle pan to drain the fluid out of the transaxle

2. Place a suitable drain pan underneath the transaxle oil pan. Loosen the oil pan mounting bolts and allow the fluid to drain until it reaches the level of the pan flange. Remove the attaching bolts, leaving one end attached so that the pan will tip and the rest of the fluid will drain.

3. Remove the oil pan and thoroughly clean it. Remove the old gasket. Make sure that the gasket mounting surfaces are clean.

4. Remove the transaxle filter screen retaining bolt and remove the screen.

5. Install a new filter screen and O-ring. Place a new gasket on the pan and install the pan to the transaxle. Tighten the transaxle pan to 15–19 ft. lbs. (20–26 Nm).

6. Remove the jackstands and lower the car to the ground. Fill the transaxle to the correct level.

Cooling System

FLUID RECOMMENDATION

▶ **See Figure 157**

When adding or changing the fluid in the system, be sure to maintain a ⁵⁰/₅₀ mixture of high quality ethylene glycol antifreeze and water in the cooling system. Use only antifreeze that is safe for use with an aluminum radiator.

Some GM Vehicles came equipped with a new silicate free anti freeze. This is called DEX-COOL®. There will be a label under the hood, in the area of the coolant bottle advising of this. DEX-COOL® was developed to last for 150,000 miles (240,000 km) or 5 years, whichever occurs first. Make sure only GM Goodwrench DEX-COOL® or equivalent is used when coolant is added or changed.

➡**DO not use a solution stronger than 70% antifreeze. Pure antifreeze will freeze at -22°C (-8°F).**

LEVEL CHECK

Check the coolant level in the recovery bottle or surge tank. The fluid level may be checked by observing the fluid level marks of the recovery tank. With the engine cold, the level should be at the FULL COLD or between the HOT and ADD level. When the engine is at normal operating temperatures, the coolant level should be at the HOT level. Only add coolant to bring the system to the proper level.

✳✳ CAUTION

Should it he necessary to remove the radiator cap, make sure that the system has had time to cool, reducing the internal pressure.

DRAIN, FLUSH AND REFILL

▶ **See Figures 158, 159, 160, 161 and 162**

The cooling system should be drained, thoroughly flushed, and refilled at least every 30,000 miles (48,000 km) or 24 months. These operations should be done with the engine cold.

Most Cadillac engines today use GM Goodwrench DEX-COOL® or HAVOLINE® DEX-COOL® coolant. Check the maintenance charts for service intervals.

1. Remove the radiator and recovery tank caps. Run the engine until the upper radiator hose gets hot. This means that the thermostat is open and the coolant is flowing through the system.

2. Turn the engine **OFF** and place a large container under the radiator. Open the drain valve at the bottom of the radiator. Open the block drain plugs to speed up the draining process, if so equipped.

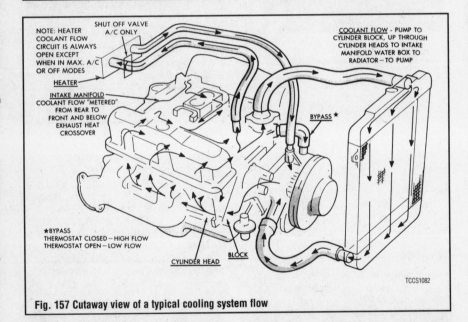

Fig. 157 Cutaway view of a typical cooling system flow

Fig. 158 The radiator drain is located on the left side of the radiator, under the lower radiator hose. It is difficult to reach, but easy to turn

Fig. 159 You may find it easier to drop the splash shield to give you more room to get access to the drain. Small pliers may be needed to turn the drain open

Fig. 160 The radiator cap gives you the warning about opening a hot cooling system. It also shows the pressure the system holds

Fig. 161 Removing the radiator cap to check the coolant level in the radiator

Fig. 162 Add coolant into the radiator

Fig. 163 The master cylinder cap informs you to use ONLY DOT 3 brake fluid. Mixing different types of brake fluid can have disastrous results

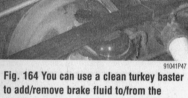

Fig. 164 You can use a clean turkey baster to add/remove brake fluid to/from the master cylinder

Fig. 165 The power steering reservoir is mounted on the pump

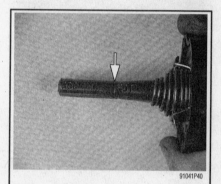

Fig. 166 The arrow shows the FULL HOT line on the dipstick

3. Close the drain valves and add water until the system is full. Run the engine until hot. Repeat the draining and filling process several times, until the liquid is nearly colorless.

4. After the last draining, fill the system with a 50/50 mixture of ethylene glycol and water. Run the engine until the system is hot and add coolant, if necessary. Replace the caps and check for any leak.

cooling system. It also shows the pressure the system holds

➡**The Northstar uses a coolant solution and GM coolant supplement (sealant) designed for use in aluminum engines. These engines use DEX-COOL® and GM coolant supplement (sealant) P/N 3634621 (or equivalent) specifically designed for use in aluminum engines. Failure to use the engine coolant supplement (sealant) and the approved coolant antifreeze could result in major engine damage. When refilling the engine cooling system, add three pellets of engine coolant supplement sealant, GM Part No. 3634621 or equivalent and coolant antifreeze meeting GM specification 1825–M.**

Master Cylinder

FLUID RECOMMENDATION

▶ **See Figure 163**

When adding or replacing the brake fluid, always use a top quality fluid, such as DOT 3. DO NOT allow the brake fluid container or master cylinder

reservoir to remain open for long periods; brake fluid absorbs moisture from the air, reducing its effectiveness and causing corrosion in the lines.

FLUID LEVEL

▶ **See Figure 164**

The master cylinder, located in the left rear section of the engine compartment, consists of an aluminum body and a reservoir with minimum fill indicators. The fluid level of the reservoirs should be kept near the top of the observation windows.

➡**Avoid spilling brake fluid on any of the vehicles painted surfaces, wiring cables or electrical connectors. Brake fluid will damage paint and electrical connections. If any fluid is spilled on the vehicle, flush the area with water to lessen the damage.**

A sudden decrease in the fluid level indicates a possible leak in the system and should be checked out immediately.

Power Steering Pump

FLUID RECOMMENDATION

▶ **See Figure 165**

When filling or replacing the fluid of the power steering pump reservoir, use power steering fluid only. Automatic transmission fluid may cause damage to the internal power steering components.

LEVEL CHECK

▶ **See Figures 166 and 167**

Power steering fluid level should be checked at least once every 12 months or 7,500 miles (12,000 km). To prevent possible overfilling, check the fluid level only when the fluid has warmed to operating temperatures and the wheels are turned straight ahead. If the level is low, fill the pump reservoir until the fluid level measures full (hot) on the reservoir dipstick.

A low fluid level usually produces a moaning sound as the wheels are turned. It also increases steering wheel effort (especially when standing still or parking).

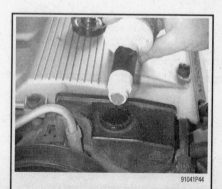

Fig. 167 Add power steering fluid directly into the reservoir

Chassis Greasing

▶ See Figures 168 and 169

Chassis greasing can be performed with a pressurized grease gun or by using a hand-operated grease gun. Wipe the grease fittings clean before greasing in order to prevent the possibility of forcing any dirt into the component. Do not over grease

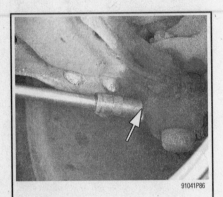

Fig. 168 The lower ball joint has a grease fitting on the side

Fig. 169 The tie rod end has a grease fitting right on the top

the components; because damage may occur to the grease seals.

Body Lubrication

HOOD LATCH AND HINGES

Clean the latch surfaces, apply clean engine oil or all-purpose lithium grease to the latch pilot

bolts, spring anchor, and hood hinges as well. Use chassis grease to lubricate all the pivot points in the latch release mechanism.

DOOR HINGES

The gas tank filler door, front door hinges, and rear trunk hinges, should be wiped clean and lubricated with multi-purpose grease spray. Use engine oil to lubricate the trunk lock mechanism and the lock bolt and striker. The door lock cylinders can be lubricated easily with a silicone spray or one of the many dry penetrating lubricants commercially available.

The door weather-strips may be lubricated using silicone type grease. Apply a thin film using a clean cloth.

PARKING BRAKE LINKAGE

Use chassis grease on the parking brake cable where it contacts the guides, links, levers, and pulleys.

Do not lubricate the parking brake cables. Lubrication can destroy the plastic coating on the cables.

JUMP STARTING

▶ See Figure 170

Whenever a vehicle is jump started, precautions must be followed in order to prevent the possibility of personal injury. Remember that batteries contain a small amount of explosive hydrogen gas that is a by-product of battery charging. Sparks should always be avoided when working around batteries, especially when attaching jumper cables. To minimize the possibility of accidental sparks, follow the procedure carefully.

✷✷ WARNING

NEVER hook up the batteries in a series circuit or the entire electrical system will go up in smoke, including the starter!

Vehicles equipped with a diesel engine may use two 12-volt batteries. If so, the batteries are con-

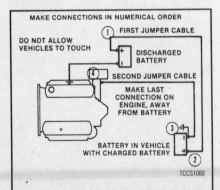

Fig. 170 Connect the jumper cables to the batteries and engine in the order shown

nected in a parallel circuit (positive terminal to positive terminal, negative terminal to negative terminal). Hooking the batteries together in a parallel circuit increases battery-cranking power without increasing total battery voltage output. Output remains at 12 volts. On the other hand, hooking two 12 volt batteries up in a series circuit (positive terminal to negative terminal, positive terminal to negative terminal) increases total battery output to 24 volts (12 volts plus 12 volts).

Precautions

• Be sure both batteries are of the same voltage.
• Be sure both batteries are of the same polarity (have the same grounded terminal).
• Be sure the vehicles are not touching.
• Be sure the vent cap holes are not obstructed.
• Do not smoke or allow sparks around the battery.
• In cold weather, check for frozen electrolyte in the battery. Do not jump-start a frozen battery.
• Do not allow electrolyte on your skin or clothing.
• Be sure the electrolyte is not frozen.

✷✷ CAUTION

Make certain that the ignition key, in the vehicle with the dead battery, is in the OFF position. Connecting cables to vehicles with on-board computers will result in computer destruction if the key is not in the OFF position. Turn the heater blower motor on the high speed setting.

Jump Starting Procedure

1. Bring the starting vehicle close (they must not touch) so that the batteries can be reached easily.
2. Turn off all accessories and both engines. Put both vehicles in Neutral or Park and set the parking brake.
3. Cover the cell caps with a rag—do not cover terminals.
4. If the terminals on the run-down battery are heavily corroded, clean them.
5. Identify the positive and negative posts on both batteries and connect the cables in the order shown.
6. Start the engine of the starting vehicle and run it at a moderate speed for a few minutes to allow the dead battery to receive an initial charge. On the dead car, switch on the blower motor to high speed, this should absorb any electrical spike created by the initial, sudden draw of the starter.
7. Try to start the car with the dead battery. Crank it for no more than 10 seconds at a time and let the starter cool for 20 seconds in between tries.
8. If it does not start in three or four tries, there is probably something else wrong.
9. Disconnect the cables in the reverse order.
10. Replace the cell covers and dispose of the rags.

✷✷ CAUTION

Be very careful to keep the jumper cables away from moving parts (cooling fan, belts, etc.) on both engines.

JACKING

▶ **See Figures 171 thru 176**

The standard jack uses slots in the frame, or bumper to raise and lower the vehicle. Do not attempt to use the jack on any portion of the vehicle other than specified by the vehicle manufacturer. The jack supplied with the car should never be used for any service operation other than tire changing. Never go under a car that is supported by a jack only. Always block the wheels when changing tires.

The service operations in this book often require that one end or the other, or both, of the car be raised and safely supported. The ideal method, of course, would be a hydraulic hoist. Since this is beyond the resource and requirement of the do-it-yourselfer, a garage or floor jack will suffice for the procedures in this guide.

Two sturdy jackstands should be acquired if you intend to work under the car at any time. An alternate method of raising the car would be drive-on ramps. These are available commercially or can be fabricated from heavy boards or steel. Be sure to block the wheels when using ramps. Never use concrete blocks to support the car. They may break if the load is not evenly distributed.

Regardless of the method of jacking or hoisting the car, there are only certain areas of the undercarriage and suspension you can safely use to support it. See the illustration in the owner's manual and make sure that only the frame areas are used. In addition, be especially careful that you do not damage the catalytic converter. Remember that various cross braces and supports on a lift can sometimes contact low hanging parts of a car.

Jacking Precautions

The following safety points cannot be overemphasized:

- Always block the opposite wheels or wheels to keep the vehicle from rolling off the jack.
- When raising the front of the vehicle, firmly apply the parking brake.
- When the drive wheels are to remain on the ground, leave the vehicle in park to help prevent it from rolling.
- Always use jackstands to support the vehicle when you are working underneath. Place the stands beneath the vehicle's jacking brackets. Before climbing underneath, rock the vehicle a bit to make sure it is firmly supported.
- Never place the jack under the radiator, engine or transmission components, severe and extensive damage will result when the jack is raised . . . Additionally, never jack under the floorpan or bodywork.

Fig. 171 The front of the vehicle can be lifted by placing a jack under the front subframe

Fig. 172 The rear of the vehicle can be lifted under the rear axle assembly

Fig. 173 Make sure to use a jackstand. Never trust a jack to hold the car up for any length of time. Place jackstands on the frame when lifting either the front or rear of the vehicle

Fig. 174 It is advisable to place a wheel chock behind the wheel on the opposite side and axle. For example, if you are lifting the passenger side rear of the vehicle, place a chock behind the driver's side

Fig. 175 This is a two-ton jackstand. If you are working on blacktop, use a plate or piece of wood to spread the load, or the jackstand may sink

Fig. 176 This is a five-ton jackstand. It too will sink into blacktop without a base. Place a ¾ inch thick piece of plywood as a base

MANUFACTURER RECOMMENDED NORMAL MAINTENANCE INTERVALS
VEHICLE MAINTENANCE INTERVAL

Miles (x1000)	5	7.5	10	15	20	22.5	25	30	35	37.5	40	45	50	52.5	55	60	100	150
km (x1000)	8	12.5	16	24	32	37.5	40	48	56	62.5	64	72	80	84.5	88	96	160	240

Component	Type of Service	5	7.5	10	15	20	22.5	25	30	35	37.5	40	45	50	52.5	55	60	100	150
Engine oil and filter	Replace	✓		✓	✓	✓		✓	✓	✓		✓	✓	✓		✓	✓		
Chassis lube	Service		✓		✓		✓		✓		✓		✓		✓		✓		
Steering & suspension	Inspect				✓				✓				✓				✓		
Tires	Rotate	✓			✓			✓		✓			✓			✓			
Air cleaner	Replace								✓								✓		
Spark plugs	Replace																	✓	
Spark plug wires	Inspect								✓								✓		
PCV valve	Replace								✓								✓		
Fuel cap & lines	Inspect								✓								✓		
Acc. drive belt	Inspect								✓								✓		
Transaxle	Service																	✓	
Brake linings & drums	Inspect				✓				✓				✓				✓		
Brake pads & rotors	Inspect				✓				✓				✓				✓		
Brake lines & hoses	Inspect				✓				✓				✓				✓		
Cooling system	Inspect				✓				✓				✓				✓		
Coolant	Replace								✓								✓		
DEX-COOL ®	Replace																		✓
Fuel Filter	Replace								✓								✓		

① Continue the maintenance schedule from 60,000 - 100,000 miles (96,000 - 160,000 km) as done for the first 60,000 miles (96,000 km)

91041C04

MANUFACTURER RECOMMENDED SEVERE MAINTENANCE INTERVALS
VEHICLE MAINTENANCE INTERVAL

Miles (x1000)	3	6	9	12	15	18	21	24	27	30	33	36	39	42	45	48 ①	100	150
km (x1000)	5	10	15	20	25	30	35	40	45	50	55	60	65	70	75	80	160	240

Component	Type of Service	3	6	9	12	15	18	21	24	27	30	33	36	39	42	45	48 ①	100	150
Engine oil and filter	Replace	✓	✓	✓	✓	✓	✓	✓	✓	✓	✓	✓	✓	✓	✓	✓	✓	✓	✓
Chassis lube	Service		✓		✓		✓		✓		✓		✓		✓		✓		
Steering & suspension	Inspect		✓		✓		✓		✓		✓		✓		✓		✓		✓
Tires	Rotate		✓		✓		✓		✓		✓		✓		✓		✓		✓
Air cleaner	Replace				✓						✓					✓			✓
Spark plugs	Replace																	✓	
Spark plug wires	Inspect										✓								✓
PCV valve	Replace				✓										✓				✓
Fuel cap & lines	Inspect					✓			✓										
Acc. drive belt	Inspect				✓										✓				✓
Transaxle	Service																	✓	
Brake linings & drums	Inspect				✓				✓				✓				✓		
Brake pads & rotors	Inspect				✓				✓				✓				✓		
Brake lines & hoses	Inspect				✓				✓				✓				✓		
Cooling system	Inspect				✓				✓				✓				✓		
Coolant	Replace										✓						✓		
DEX-COOL ®	Replace																		✓
Fuel Filter	Replace				✓						✓					✓			✓

① Continue the maintenance schedule from 48,000 - 100,000 miles (80,000 - 160,000 km) as done for the first 48,000 miles (80,000 km)

91041C05

CAPACITIES

Year	Model	Engine Displacement Liters (cc)	Engine ID/VIN	Engine Oil with Filter (qts.)	Transmission (pts.) ①	Fuel Tank (gal.)	Cooling System (qts.)
1990	Deville	4.5 (4474)	3	5.5	13.0	18.8	12.1
	Eldorado	4.5 (4474)	3	5.5	13.0	18.8	12.1
	Fleetwood	4.5 (4474)	3	5.5	13.0	18.8	12.1
	Seville	4.5 (4474)	3	5.5	13.0	18.8	12.1
1991	Deville	4.9 (4917)	B	5.5	13.0	18.0	12.0
	Eldorado	4.9 (4917)	B	5.5	13.0	18.8	12.0
	Fleetwood	4.9 (4917)	B	5.5	13.0	18.0	12.0
	Seville	4.9 (4917)	B	5.5	13.0	18.8	12.1
1992	Deville	4.9 (4917)	B	5.5	13.0	18.0	12.0
	Eldorado	4.9 (4917)	B	5.5	13.0	18.8	10.6
	Fleetwood	4.9 (4917)	B	5.5	13.0	18.0	12.0
	Seville	4.9 (4917)	B	5.5	13.0	18.8	10.6
1993	Deville	4.9 (4917)	B	5.5	13.0	18.0	12.0
	Eldorado	4.6 (4573)	9	7.5	13.0	20.0	10.6
	Eldorado	4.9 (4917)	B	5.5	13.0	20.0	10.6
	Seville STS	4.6 (4573)	9	7.5	13.0	20.0	10.6
	Seville	4.9 (4917)	B	5.5	13.0	20.0	12.5
1994	Deville Concours	4.6 (4573)	Y	7.5	13.0	20.0	12.5
	Deville	4.9 (4917)	B	5.5	13.0	20.0	10.7
	Eldorado ETC	4.6 (4573)	9	7.5	13.0	20.0	12.5
	Eldorado	4.6 (4573)	Y	7.5	13.0	20.0	12.5
	Seville STS	4.6 (4573)	9	7.5	13.0	20.0	12.5
	Seville SLS	4.6 (4573)	Y	7.5	13.0	20.0	12.5
1995	Deville Concours	4.6 (4573)	Y	7.5	16.0	18.0	12.1
	Deville	4.9 (4917)	B	5.5	16.0	18.0	12.1
	Eldorado	4.6 (4573)	Y	7.5	16.0	20.0	12.3
	Eldorado	4.6 (4573)	9	7.5	16.0	20.0	12.3
	Seville SLS	4.6 (4573)	Y	7.5	16.0	20.0	12.3
	Seville STS	4.6 (4573)	9	7.5	16.0	20.0	12.3
1996	Deville	4.6 (4573)	Y	7.5	16.0	20.0	12.3
	Deville Concours	4.6 (4573)	9	7.5	16.0	18.0	12.3
	Eldorado	4.6 (4573)	Y	7.5	16.0	20.0	12.3
	Eldorado ETC	4.6 (4573)	9	7.5	16.0	20.0	12.3
	Seville SLS	4.6 (4573)	Y	7.5	16.0	20.0	12.3
	Seville STS	4.6 (4573)	9	7.5	16.0	20.0	12.3
1997	Deville	4.6 (4573)	Y	7.5	16.0	20.0	12.3
	Deville Concours	4.6 (4573)	9	7.5	16.0	18.0	12.3
	Eldorado	4.6 (4573)	Y	7.5	16.0	20.0	12.3
	Eldorado ETC	4.6 (4573)	9	7.5	16.0	20.0	12.3
	Seville SLS	4.6 (4573)	Y	7.5	16.0	20.0	12.3
	Seville STS	4.6 (4573)	9	7.5	16.0	20.0	12.3
1998	Deville	4.6 (4573)	Y	7.5	16.0	20.0	12.3
	Deville Concours	4.6 (4573)	9	7.5	16.0	18.0	12.3
	Eldorado	4.6 (4573)	Y	7.5	16.0	20.0	12.3
	Eldorado ETC	4.6 (4573)	9	7.5	16.0	20.0	12.3
	Seville SLS	4.6 (4573)	Y	7.5	16.0	20.0	12.3
	Seville STS	4.6 (4573)	9	7.5	16.0	20.0	12.3

① Including Bottom pan and side cover

91041CR6

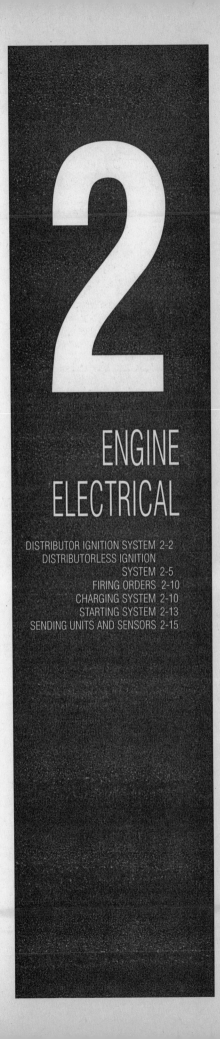

2

ENGINE
ELECTRICAL

DISTRIBUTOR IGNITION SYSTEM

➡For information on understanding electricity and troubleshooting electrical circuits, please refer to Section 6 of this manual.

General Information

The ignition system used on these engines is a High-Energy Ignition (HEI) system with Electronic Spark Timing (EST). The High-Energy Ignition (HEI) system controls fuel combustion by providing a spark to ignite the air/fuel mixture at the appropriate time.

The ignition circuit consists of the battery, the distributor, the ignition switch, the spark plugs, and the primary and secondary wiring.

The spark plug wires used with the HEI system are composed of four major components:

An 8 mm silicone jacket for high temperature protection. This outer jacket also provides excellent insulation for the high voltage produced in the HEI system.

A reinforced fiberglass braid for strength.

Inner core insulation is composed of Ethylene Propylene Diene Monomer (EPDM) for strength and voltage insulation.

A composite High Temperature (CHT) core composed of aramid fibers impregnated with conductive latex and wrapped with conductive silicone.

Diagnosis and Testing

VISUAL INSPECTION

On of the most important steps in the diagnosis of a problem is a visual underhood inspection. This can often fix a problem. Inspect all vacuum hoses for pinches, cuts, or disconnections. Inspect all wiring in the engine compartment for good, tight connections. Inspect all wiring for burned of chaffed spots, pinches, or contact with sharp edges or hot exhaust manifolds. These quick tests take only a few minutes but can save you valuable time, and help you repair the problem.

1. Inspect all vacuum hoses for being pinched, cut or disconnected. Be sure to inspect hoses that are difficult to see such as beneath the upper intake, generator, etc.

2. Check for proper ground connections, ground eyelets connected to ground points and star washer installation, if applicable.

3. Check both battery positive junction blocks for loose retainer nuts.

4. Inspect other wiring in the engine compartment, bad connections, burned or chaffed spots, pinched wires or harnesses contacting sharp edges or hot exhaust manifolds.

5. Check for blown or missing fuses; or relays missing or installed in the wrong locations.

6. Inspect plug wires for proper routing, connection, cuts, or visible signs of arcing to ground.

COMPONENT TESTING

Hall Effect Switch

4.5L ENGINE

♦ See Figure 1

1. Detach the wiring connectors at the distributor cap.

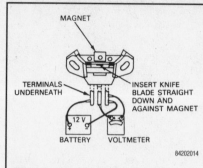

Fig. 1 Testing the Hall Effect switch—4.5L engine

2. Turn the four screws and remove the cap and coil assembly from the distributor lower housing.

3. Inspect the interior and exterior of the cap for signs of tracking. If tracking is present, replace the cap.

4. Connect a 12-volt source and ground, and a voltmeter to the switch as shown. Be careful to observe the polarity shown in the illustration or damage to the Hall Effect switch may occur.

5. Without the blade in the switch, the voltmeter should read less than 0.5 volts. If not, the Hall Effect switch is defective.

6. With the blade in the switch, the voltmeter should read within 0.5 volts of battery voltage. If not, the switch is defective.

4.9L ENGINE

♦ See Figure 2

The distributor must be removed from the engine in order to perform this procedure. Refer to the distributor removal procedure.

1. Detach the wiring connectors at the distributor cap.

2. Turn the four screws and remove the cap and coil assembly from the distributor lower housing.

3. Inspect the interior and exterior of the cap for signs of tracking. If tracking is present, replace the cap. Connect a 12-volt source and ground to the distributor base 3 wire connector, as illustrated.

4. Attach the voltmeter positive test lead to terminal E of the five-wire distributor harness connector. Attach the negative test lead to terminal D of the five-wire distributor harness connector.

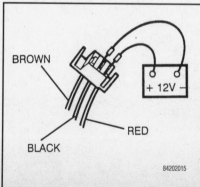

Fig. 2 Attaching 12-volt battery and ground to the distributor base 3-wire connector

5. Rotate the distributor shaft and observe the blade passing through the Hall switch. Note readings on voltmeter during the shaft rotation.

6. Without the blade in the switch, the voltmeter should read less than 0.5 volts. If not, the Hall switch or harness is bad.

7. With the blade in the switch, the voltmeter should read within 0.5 volts of battery voltage. If not, the switch or harness is bad.

8. Check the harness and retest. If the problem still exists, replace the switch.

Pick-Up Coil

♦ See Figure 3

1. Disconnect the negative battery cable.

2. Detach the wiring connectors at the distributor cap.

3. Turn the four screws and remove the cap and coil assembly from the distributor lower housing.

4. Remove the retainers and the rotor assembly from the shaft.

5. Remove the pick-up coil leads from the module.

6. Connect an ohmmeter as shown in Test 1 and Test 2 of the illustration.

7. Observe the ohmmeter while flexing leads by hand. This will check for intermittent shorts (test 1) or intermittent opens (test 2). Compare the obtained reading with the desired results:

- Test 1—should read infinite at all times
- Test 2—should read steady at one value within 500–1500-ohm range.

8. If test results are not as specified, replace the pick-up coil.

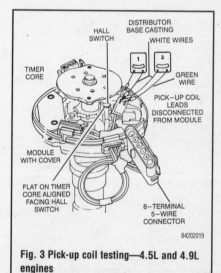

Fig. 3 Pick-up coil testing—4.5L and 4.9L engines

Ignition Coil

The ignition coil is contained in the distributor cap and connects through a center contact to the rotor.

The capacitor, if equipped, is part of the coil wire harness assembly. The capacitor is used only for radio noise suppression.

TESTING

Ignition Coil

◆ See Figures 4 and 5

1. Detach the wiring connectors at the distributor cap. If necessary, label the position of each wire prior to disconnecting it.

2. Turn the four screws and remove the cap and coil assembly from the distributor lower housing.

3. Inspect the interior and exterior of the cap for signs of tracking. If tracking is present, replace the cap.

4. Connect an ohmmeter across the coil terminals, which are the outermost terminals located in the recessed boss of the cap.

5. If the reading is not at 0, or nearly 0, replace the coil.

6. Connect the test leads of an ohmmeter to the coil center contact, located in the center of the cap. Attach the other test lead to the center terminal of the 3-wire connector, located on the cap. Make sure to set the ohmmeter to the highest setting.

7. If the reading is infinite, replace the ignition coil.

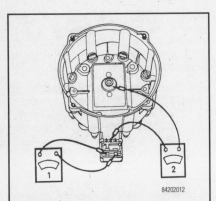

Fig. 4 Testing the ignition coil in the distributor cap—4.5L and 4.9L engines

Fig. 5 Removing the distributor cap and coil assembly from the housing

➡ If no problems are found, then the coil may still be faulty, but will have to be checked on a scope.

REMOVAL & INSTALLATION

◆ See Figures 6 and 7

1. Disconnect the negative battery cable.

2. Detach the wiring connectors at the distributor cap. Remove the cap from the distributor housing.

3. Remove the coil cover attaching screws on the top of the cap. Remove the cover from the cap.

4. Remove the ignition coil attaching screws and lift the coil with leads, from the cap.

5. Inspect the cap for signs of carbon tracking on the inside of the cap, below the coil.

6. Remove the ignition coil arc seal. Clean with soft cloth and inspect cap for defects, replace cap as required.

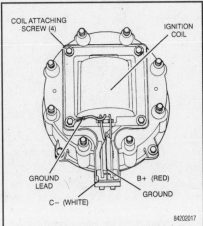

Fig. 6 Ignition coil attaching screws—4.5L and 4.9L engines

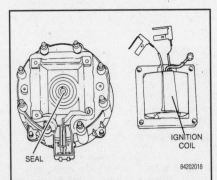

Fig. 7 Ignition coil removed from cap—4.5L and 4.9L engines

Ignition Module

The HEI module, acting as an electronic ON/OFF switch controls the current flow in the primary winding of the ignition coil. This switching action induces a high voltage in the ignition coil secondary winding which is directed through the rotor and secondary leads to fire the spark plugs.

REMOVAL & INSTALLATION

➡ It is not necessary to remove the distributor from the car.

1. Remove the distributor cap.

2. Remove the rotor.

3. Remove the module attaching screws, and then carefully lift the stamped sheet metal shield and the module up and out of the distributor.

4. Disconnect the leads from the module. Be careful and observe the color code on the leads as this must not be interchanged.

➡ Do not wipe the grease from the module for the distributor base if the same module is to be replaced. If a new module is to be installed, a package of silicone grease will be included with it. Spread the grease on the metal face of the module and on the distributor base where the module seats. This grease is necessary for module cooling.

To install:

5. Connect the leads to the module. Maintain the color code observed in the procedure for removal.

6. Install the module shield and module to the distributor using the attaching screws.

7. Install the rotor and the distributor cap.

Distributor

✳✳ CAUTION

The HEI coil secondary voltage output capabilities can exceed 40,000 volts. Avoid body contact with the HEI high voltage secondary components when the engine is running, or personal injury may result.

The High-Energy Ignition (HEI) distributor with Electronic Spark Control (ESC) combines all necessary ignition components in one contained unit. The system includes:

• An integral ignition coil assembly
• A magnetic pick-up coil and pole piece assembly
• A Hall Effect switch
• A solid state ignition module
• An RFI-suppression capacitor and primary winding harness
• A distributor cap and rotor

All spark timing changes in the HEI (ESC) distributor are performed electronically by the Powertrain Control Module (PCM). The PCM monitors information from various engine sensors, computes the desired spark timing, and signals the distributor to change the timing accordingly. A back up spark advance system is programmed into the ignition module in case of PCM failure. No vacuum or mechanical advance is used.

• When making compression checks, disconnect the ignition switch feed wire at the distributor. When detaching this connector, do NOT use a screwdriver or tool to release the locking tabs, as it may break.

• No periodic lubrication is required. Engine oil lubricates the lower bushing and an oil filled reservoir provides lubrication for the upper bushing.

• The tachometer (TACH) terminal is next to the

ignition switch (BAT) connector on the distributor cap.

➡**The tachometer terminal must never be allowed to touch ground, as damage to the module and/or ignition coil can result. Some tachometers currently in use may not be compatible with the HEI system used. Consult the manufacturer of the tachometer if a question arises.**

• Dwell adjustment is controlled by the PCM can not be adjusted.

• The material used to construct the spark plug cables is very soft. This cable will withstand more heat and carry higher voltage, but scuffing and cutting becomes easier. The spark plug cables must be routed correctly to prevent chaffing or cutting. When removing a spark plug wire from a plug, twist the boot on the spark plug and pull on the boot.

REMOVAL & INSTALLATION

♦ **See Figures 8, 9 and 10**

During the distributor removal and installation, it is very important that the engine crankshaft not be rotated. If rotated, the reference marks made during

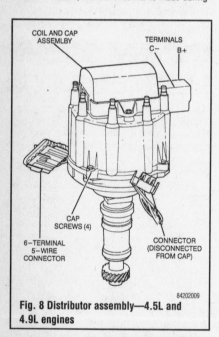

Fig. 8 Distributor assembly—4.5L and 4.9L engines

Labels: COIL AND CAP ASSEMLBY; TERMINALS C− B+; CAP SCREWS (4); 6−TERMINAL 5−WIRE CONNECTOR; CONNECTOR (DISCONNECTED FROM CAP)

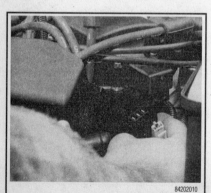

Fig. 9 Detach wire connectors at the distributor cap

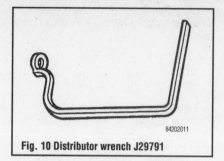

Fig. 10 Distributor wrench J29791

removal will have to be disregarded. If the engine is accidentally rotated, the timing will be disturbed. If this is the case, make sure to follow the appropriate distributor installation procedure.

1. Disconnect the negative battery cable.
2. Label and disconnect all wires leading from the distributor cap.
3. Remove the four bolts from the distributor cap and move the cap out of the way. Note the position of the distributor cap prior to removal.

➡**Location of the cap doghouse must be in the same area on reinstallation for sufficient clearance for adjustment.**

4. Detach the six terminal connector from the distributor, if not already done.
5. Using a distributor wrench, remove the distributor hold-down nut and clamp.
6. Matchmark the rotor-to-distributor body and the distributor body-to-engine positions. Pull the distributor upward until the rotor just stops turning counterclockwise and again note the position of the rotor. Remove the distributor from the engine.

➡**A thrust washer is used between the distributor drive gear and the crankcase. This washer may stick to the bottom of the distributor as it is removed from the engine. Before replacing the distributor, verify that the thrust washer is located in the crankcase at the bottom of the distributor bore.**

INSTALLATION

Timing Not Disturbed

➡**Before installing, visually inspect the distributor. The drive gear should be free of nicks, cracks, and excessive wear. The distributor drive shaft should move freely, without binding. If equipped with an O-ring, it should fit tightly and be free of cuts.**

1. To install the distributor, rotate the distributor shaft until the rotor aligns with the second mark, when the shaft stopped moving. Lubricate the drive gear with clean engine oil and install the distributor into the engine. As the distributor is installed, the rotor should rotate to the first alignment mark; this will ensure proper timing. If the marks do not align properly, remove the distributor and reinstall. Be sure to install the thrust washer on the distributor shaft prior to installation.
2. Install the hold-down clamp and distributor clamp nut. Tighten the nut until the distributor can just be moved with a little effort.
3. Connect the six terminal harness. Install the distributor cap and secure with the four retainer bolts.

4. Connect the coil harness and the ignition switch battery feed wire at the distributor cap.
5. Connect the negative battery cable.
6. Adjust the ignition timing. Once the timing has been adjusted, tighten the distributor hold-down nut to 20 ft. lbs. (25 Nm).

Timing Disturbed

If the engine was accidentally cranked after the distributor was removed, the following procedure can be used for distributor installation.

1. Remove the No. 1 spark plug.
2. Place your finger over No. 1 spark plug hole and crank the engine slowly until compression is felt.
3. Continue cranking slowly until the timing mark on the crankshaft pulley aligns with the 0 degrees on the engine timing indicator. At this point, No. 1 piston is at the TDC of its compression stroke.
4. Position the distributor in the block but do not allow it to engage with the drive gear.
5. Rotate the distributor shaft until the rotor points between No. 1 and No. 8 spark plug towers on the distributor cap. Install the distributor into the engine. If correctly installed, the rotor will point toward the No. 1 tower in the distributor cap when it is fully installed in the engine.

➡**If installed correctly, the rotor should point toward the No. 1 spark plug tower in the distributor cap. If this is not the case, remove the distributor and reinstall until correct rotor positioning is achieved.**

6. Install the hold-down clamp and tighten the nut until it is snug, do not tighten at this time.
7. Connect the ignition feed wire.
8. Install the distributor cap and spark plug wires.
9. Check the engine timing and adjust as required. Once the timing is set to specifications, tighten the distributor hold-down nut to 20 ft. lbs. (25 Nm).

➡**Malfunction trouble codes must be cleared after removal or adjustment of the distributor. Refer to clearing trouble codes for the proper procedure.**

10. Installation is the reverse of the removal procedure.

Crankshaft Position Sensor

The magnetic pick-up assembly, located inside the distributor, contains a permanent magnet, a pole piece with internal teeth, and a pick-up coil. A toothed timer core, attached to the distributor main shaft, rotates inside the pole piece. As the teeth of the timer core align with the teeth on the pole piece, a varying current is induced in the pick-up coil. The induced current flow is converted by the HEI module, into a distributor reference pulse.

Camshaft Position Sensor

A Hall Effect Switch positioned in the distributor housing, serves as a cam position sensor for the sequential port fuel injection system. The Hall Effect senses the opening point of the intake valve on the number one cylinder and provides that information to the Powertrain Control Module (PCM). Fuel injection is sequenced relative to the engine firing order once No. 1 intake stroke is determined.

DISTRIBUTORLESS IGNITION SYSTEM

General Information

▶ See Figure 11

The 4.6L Northstar ignition control system does not use a conventional distributor or a single ignition coil. In this ignition system, both ends of the four ignition coils are connected to a spark plug. Each coil is connected with spark plugs on companion cylinders, i.e. 1–4, 2–5, 6–7, 3–8. One cylinder is on its compression stroke when the other one is on its exhaust stroke.

The 4.6L Northstar ignition control system controls the fuel combustion by providing a spark to ignite the compressed air/fuel mixture in each cylinder at the correct time.

The PCM controls spark advance and fuel injection for all driving conditions. The PCM monitors input signals from the following components as part of its ignition control function, to determine the required ignition timing:
- Ignition Control Module (ICM)
- Engine Coolant Temperature (ECT) sensor

- Transaxle Range (TR) switch
- Throttle Position (TP) sensor
- Vehicle Speed Sensor (VSS)
- Knock sensor

Diagnosis and Testing

The secondary ignition check tests for faulty spark plugs, plug wires, or IC Module/Coils. This test requires the J 26792 (or equivalent) spark tester (ST-125).

Ensure that a good DVM contact is made when measuring spark plug resistance. When manufactured, the normal resistance for he spark plug is 900–2500 ohms but resistance growth up to 10K ohms is considered normal.

1. The spark tester presents a more difficult load on the secondary ignition than a normal spark plug. If a miss, stumble, or hesitation is being caused by a spark plug not firing, the spark tester should also not fire.

2. Check the suspected spark plug wire resis-

tance to ground and resistance end to end. If the wire is shorted to ground or measures more than 15k ohms, replace the wire and retest.

3. Remove the suspected spark plug and perform a physical inspection. Look for cracks, chips, splits, or other abnormalities. If any occur, replace the plug. Measure the resistance; if out of spec, replace the plug.

4. If the no spark condition follows the suspected coil, that coil is faulty. This test could also be performed by substituting a known good coil for the one causing the no spark condition. Otherwise, the ignition module is the cause of the no spark condition.

Ignition System Diagnostics

▶ See Figures 12 thru 21

1. For diagnosis of the ignition system components on the 4.6L engine, refer to the following diagnostic charts. Use of special tools for the test procedures listed may be required. The tool numbers will be given, when applicable.

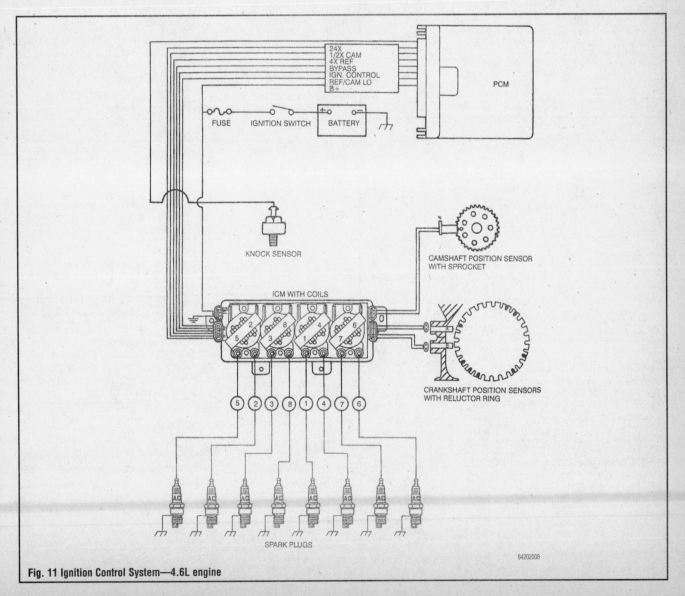

Fig. 11 Ignition Control System—4.6L engine

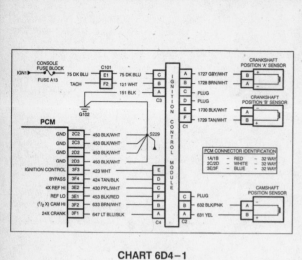

CHART 6D4-1

IGNITION SYSTEM CHECK

CIRCUIT DESCRIPTION:

The Ignition System Check provides a means of testing ignition system performance and references other charts in this section for specific ignition system conditions. This chart requires J 35616 jumper kit.

NOTES ON FAULT TREE:

1. This procedure reduces spark advance. Engine rpm should drop as spark is retarded.
2. This procedure grounds the BYPASS circuit and causes the ignition to operate in MODULE MODE. This will also cause Code 23 to set.

84202034

Fig. 12 Ignition System Diagnostics—4.6L Engine

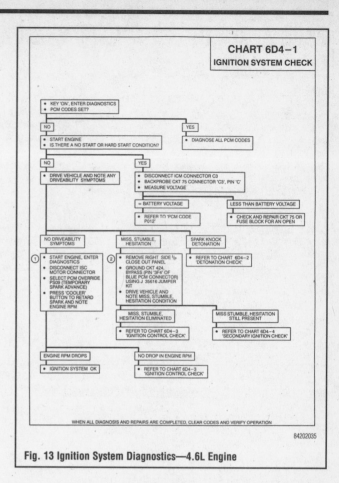

Fig. 13 Ignition System Diagnostics—4.6L Engine

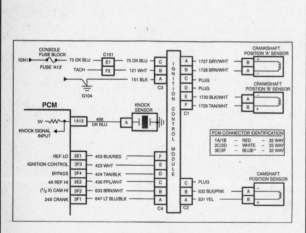

CHART 6D4-2

DETONATION CHECK

CIRCUIT DESCRIPTION:

The Detonation Check test for proper knock sensor operation. Possible causes of detonation include knock sensor, wiring, or PCM faults, poor fuel quality or engine mechanical conditions. This chart requires J 39200 voltmeter and J 35616 jumper kit.

NOTES ON FAULT TREE:

1. Tapping on engine block simulates the noise created by detonation.
2. The knock sensor produces an AC voltage proportional in amplitude to the 'loudness' of the knock condition.
3. The PCM uses the knock sensor information to estimate the octane level of the fuel being used. The PCM selects a spark calibration for either 87, 90 or 93 octane. Early production vehicles have this octane value set to 0.
4. Fuel with an octane level below 87 may cause detonation even with a properly operating engine. Engine mechanical problems such as low oil pressure, worn rod or main bearings or valve train problems may cause a knock condition.

84202036

Fig. 14 Ignition System Diagnostics—4.6L Engine

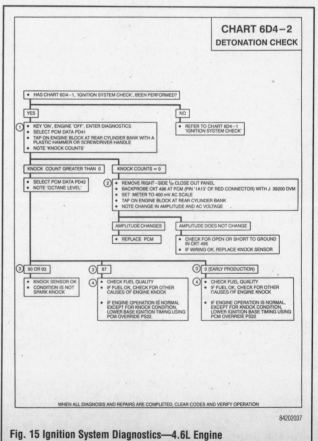

Fig. 15 Ignition System Diagnostics—4.6L Engine

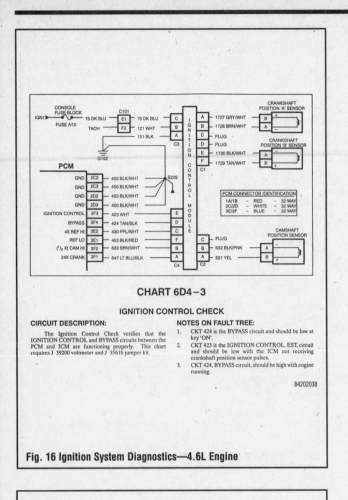

CHART 6D4-3

IGNITION CONTROL CHECK

CIRCUIT DESCRIPTION:

The Ignition Control Check verifies that the IGNITION CONTROL and BYPASS circuits between the PCM and ICM are functioning properly. This chart requires J 39200 voltmeter and J 35616 jumper kit.

NOTES ON FAULT TREE:

1. CKT 424 is the BYPASS circuit and should be low at key 'ON'.
2. CKT 423 is the IGNITION CONTROL, EST, circuit and should be low with the ICM not receiving crankshaft position sensor pulses.
3. CKT 424, BYPASS circuit, should be high with engine running.

84202038

Fig. 16 Ignition System Diagnostics—4.6L Engine

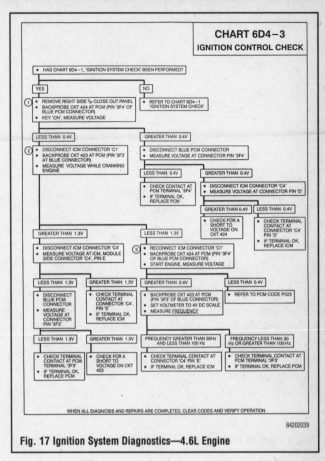

Fig. 17 Ignition System Diagnostics—4.6L Engine

84202039

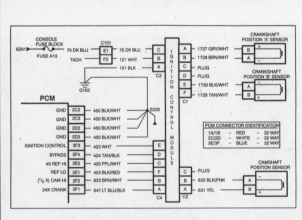

CHART 6D4-4

SECONDARY IGNITION CHECK

CIRCUIT DESCRIPTION:

The Secondary Ignition Check tests for faulty spark plugs, plug wires or ICM/coils. This chart requires J 26792 spark tester (ST-125).

NOTES ON FAULT TREE:

1. After performing the power balance test, if 1 cylinder or non-companion cylinders had no RPM change use Page 1 of 3. If 2 companion cylinders had no RPM change, use Page 2 of 3. Otherwise use Page 3 of 3.

2. J 26792 spark tester (ST-125) presents a more difficult load on the secondary ignition than a normal spark plug. If a miss, stumble or hesitation is being caused by a spark plug not firing, the spark tester should also not fire.

3. The companion spark plug shares the same ignition coil with the spark plug being tested (1-4, 2-5, 6-7, 3-8).

4. A suspected ignition system 'miss' may actually be a fuel system problem.

5. If the no spark condition follows the suspected coil, that coil is faulty. Otherwise, the ignition module is the cause of no spark. This test cold also be performed by substituting a known good coil for the one causing the no spark condition.

6. If no spark condition follows the suspected coil, that coil is faulty. This test could also be performed by substituting a known good coil for the one causing the no spark condition.

84202040

Fig. 18 Ignition System Diagnostics—4.6L Engine

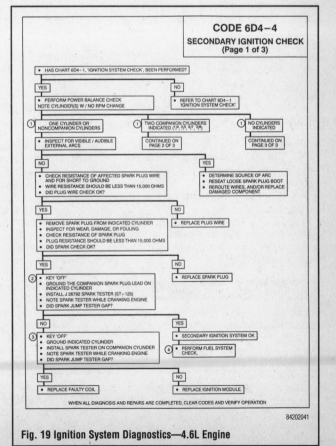

Fig. 19 Ignition System Diagnostics—4.6L Engine

84202041

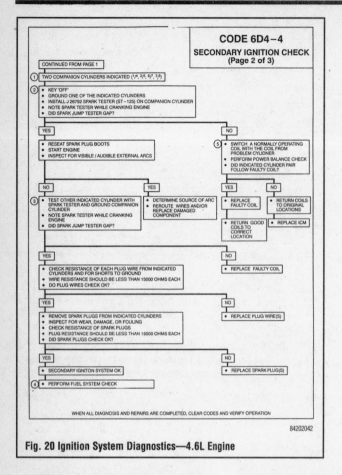

Fig. 20 Ignition System Diagnostics—4.6L Engine

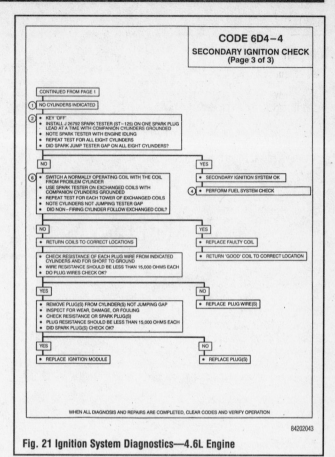

Fig. 21 Ignition System Diagnostics—4.6L Engine

• When performing electrical tests on circuits that use solid state control module, such as the Powertrain Control Module (PCM), use a 10 mega-ohm or higher impedance digital multimeter, J-34029-A or equivalent.

• When measuring the resistance with a digital multimeter, the vehicle battery should be disconnected. This will prevent incorrect readings.

• Diodes and solid state components in a circuit can cause an ohmmeter to give a false reading. To find out if a component is affecting a measurement, take a reading once, reverse the test leads and then take a second reading. If the readings differ, the solid state component is affecting the measurement.

• Never pierce a high-tension lead or boot for any testing purpose.

• The material used to construct the spark plug cables is very soft. This cable will withstand more heat and carry higher voltage, but scuffing and cutting becomes easier.

Ignition Coil Pack

Each end of the secondary winding of an ignition coil is attached to a spark plug. Each cylinder is paired with the cylinder that is opposite it (1–4, 2–5, 6–7, 3–8). These cylinders are referred to as "companion" cylinders since they are on top dead center at the same time.

When the coil discharges, both plugs fire at the same time to complete the series circuit. The cylinder on the compression stroke is said to be the "event" cylinder and the one on the exhaust stroke

is said to be the "waste" cylinder. The cylinder on the exhaust stroke requires very little of the available energy to fire the spark plug. The remaining energy will be used as required by the cylinder on the compression stroke. The same process is repeated when the cylinders reverse roles. This method of ignition is called a "waste spark" ignition system.

The Ignition coil design is improved, with saturation time and primary current flow increased. This redesign of the system allows higher secondary voltage to be available from the ignition coils—greater than 40kv. (40,000 volts) at any engine RPM. Secondary voltage requirements are very high with an open spark plug or spark plug wire. The ignition coil has enough reserve energy to fire the plug that is still connected, at idle, but the coil may not fire the spark plug under high engine load. A more noticeable misfire may be evident under load, both spark plugs may then be misfiring. Running for an extended period like this will burn out the coil.

This ignition control system has several advantages over a mechanical distributor ignition system:
1. No moving parts to wear out
2. No mechanical load on the engine
3. Eliminate of mechanical timing adjustment
4. Improved high engine speed performance

The Northstar ignition control system is composed of the following components:
• Two crankshaft position sensors
• Crankshaft reluctor ring
• Camshaft position sensor
• Ignition control module

• 4 separate ignition coils
• 8 spark plug wires and conduit
• 8 spark plugs
• Knock sensor
• Powertrain Control Module (PCM)

Four separate coils are mounted to the module assembly. Each coil provides the spark for 2 spark plugs simultaneously. Each coil can be replaced separately.

TESTING

Before beginning the electrical testing of the coil pack, it is a good idea to perform some preliminary checks, these checks should also include a visual inspection of the circuits involved. These checks should include:

• Check PCM grounds, make sure they are clean, tight, and in their proper location.

• Check vacuum hoses for splits, kinks, and proper connections, as show on the Vehicle Emission Control Information label, and check thoroughly for any type of restriction.

• Check the air intake ducts for collapsed or damaged areas.

• Check air leaks at throttle body mounting area. Mass Air Flow (MAF) sensor and intake manifold sealing surfaces.

• Check the ignition wires for cracking, hardness, proper routing, and carbon tracking.

• Check the wiring for proper connection, pinches, and cuts. Check the insulation for evidence of rubbing against metal and wearing through, causing a short to ground.

REMOVAL & INSTALLATION

4.6L Engines

▶ See Figures 22 thru 27

1. Remove the spark plug wires for corresponding ignition coils at the ignition control module assembly.
2. Remove the ignition coil retaining bolts (2 per coil).
3. Remove the coil from the IC module assembly.

To install:

4. Install the ignition coil to the IC module assembly with the 2 retaining bolts, tighten to 30 inch lbs. (3.5 Nm).
5. Install the spark plug wires at the IC module assembly.

Ignition Module

The Ignition Control Module (ICM) on the 4.6L engine is located on the top of the rear camshaft cover. The ICM performs several functions:

- It monitors the ON-OFF pulses produced by the 2 crankshaft and one camshaft position sensors
- It creates a camshaft reference signal sent to the PCM to ignition control
- It creates a camshaft reference signal sent to the PCM for fuel injection control
- It provides a ground reference to the PCM
- It provides a means for the PCM to control spark advance

The ICM is not repairable. When the module is replaced, the remaining components must be transferred to the new module

REMOVAL & INSTALLATION

4.6L Engine

1. Remove the spark plug wires at the ignition control module assembly.
2. Remove the four electrical connectors at the ignition control module.
3. Remove the four bolts (4 and 8) retaining the IC module assembly to the rear camshaft cover.
4. Remove the IC module assembly from the vehicle.
5. Remove the ignition coils from the IC module assembly (1, 2, 3, and 7).
6. Remove the IC module from the assembly bracket.

To install:

7. Installation is the reversal of the removal procedure.

Crankshaft Position Sensor

For procedures on the position sensors, please refer to electronic engine controls.

The 2 crankshaft sensors are located on the front of the engine block, between cylinder Numbers 4 and 6. Crankshaft position A sensor is located on the upper crankcase and crankshaft position B sensor is located in the lower crankcase. Both sensors

extend into the crankcase and are sealed into the engine block with O-rings. The crankshaft position sensors are not adjustable.

The magnetic crankshaft position sensors operate similar to the pick-up coil in a distributor. When a piece of steel, called the reluctor, is repeatedly moved over the sensor, a voltage will be created that appears to go ON-OFF-ON-OFF-ON-OFF. This ON-OFF signal is also the signal that a set of breaker points in a distributor would generate as the distributor shaft turned and the points open and closed.

Reluctor Ring

The reluctor ring is cast onto the crankshaft between the No. 3 and No. 4 main bearing journals. The reluctor ring has 24 evenly spaced notches or air gaps and additional 8 unevenly spaced notches for 32 notches. As the crankshaft makes one revolution, both A and B sensors will produce 32 ON-OFF pulses per revolution. In addition, the "A" sensor is positioned 27 degrees of crankshaft revolution before the B sensor. This creates a unique pattern of ON-OFF pulses sent to the ignition control module so that it can recognize crankshaft position.

Camshaft Position Sensor

For procedures on the position sensors, please refer to electronic engine controls.

The camshaft position sensor is located on the rear cylinder bank in front of the exhaust camshaft. The camshaft position sensor extends into the rear

Fig. 22 Unplug the coil assembly connectors for the control and . . .

Fig. 23 . . . for the trailing side

Fig. 24 Remove the coil pack retaining bolts

Fig. 25 It is easier to unbolt the entire assembly before removing the individual spark plug wires. Make sure they are tagged before disassembly

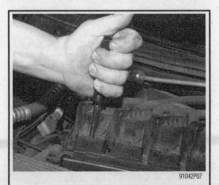

Fig. 26 Remove the screws that hold the coil in place

Fig. 27 Lift up the individual coil that needs to be replaced and remove it from the rest of the coil pack

cylinder head and is sealed with an O-ring. The camshaft position sensor is not adjustable.

As the rear cylinder bank exhaust camshaft turns, a steel pin on its drive sprocket passes over the magnetic camshaft position sensor. This creates an ON-OFF-ON-OFF signal sent to the ignition control module similar to the crankshaft position sensor. The camshaft position sensor produces one ON-OFF pulse for every one revolution of the camshaft or every 2 revolutions of the crankshaft. This allows the ignition control module to recognize the position of the camshaft.

FIRING ORDERS

▶ See Figures 28 and 29

➡To avoid confusion, remove and tag the spark plug wires one at a time, for replacement.

If a distributor is not keyed for installation with only one orientation, it could have been removed previously and rewired. The resultant wiring would hold the correct firing order, but could change the relative placement of the plug towers in relation to the engine. For this reason it is imperative that you label all wires before disconnecting any of them. Also, before removal, compare the current wiring with the accompanying illustrations. If the current wiring does not match, make notes in your book to reflect how your engine is wired.

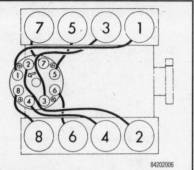

Fig. 28 4.5L and 4.9L Engines
Engine Firing Order: 1-8-4-3-6-5-7-2
Distributor Rotation: Counterclockwise

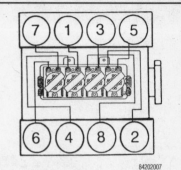

Fig. 29 4.6L Engine
Engine Firing Order: 1-2-7-3-4-5-6-8
Distributorless Ignition System

CHARGING SYSTEM

Alternator Precautions

To prevent damage to the alternator and regulator, the following precautionary measures must be taken when working with the electrical system.

• Never reverse the battery connections. Always check the battery polarity visually. This is to be done before any connections are made to ensure that all of the connections correspond to the battery ground polarity of the vehicle.

• Booster batteries must be connected properly. Make sure the positive cable of the booster battery is connected to the positive terminal of the battery that is getting the boost.

• Disconnect the battery cables before using a fast charger; the charger has a tendency to force current though the diodes in the opposite direction for which they were designed.

• Make sure the ignition switch is "OFF" when connecting or disconnecting any electrical component, especially when equipped with an on-board computer control system.

• NEVER attempt to polarize an alternator.

• Never disconnect the voltage regulator while the engine is running, unless directed to do so for testing purposes.

• Disconnect the battery if any welding is to be done on the vehicle.

• Do not short one terminal to another or short any terminal to ground from the alternator.

Alternator

TESTING

Voltage Test

1. Make sure the engine is **OFF**, and turn the headlights on for 15–20 seconds to remove any surface charge from the battery.

2. Using a DVOM set to volts DC, probe across the battery terminals.
3. Measure the battery voltage.
4. Write down the voltage reading and proceed to the next test.

No-Load Test

1. Connect a tachometer to the engine.

✳✳ CAUTION

Ensure that the transmission is in PARK and the emergency brake is set. Blocking a wheel is optional and an added safety measure.

2. Turn off all electrical loads (radio, blower motor, wipers, etc.)
3. Start the engine and increase engine speed to approximately 1500 rpm.
4. Measure the voltage reading at the battery with the engine holding a steady 1500 rpm. Voltage should have raised at least 0.5 volts, but no more than 2.5 volts.
5. If the voltage does not go up more than 0.5 volts, the alternator is not charging. If the voltage goes up more than 2.5 volts, the alternator is overcharging.

➡Usually under and overcharging is caused by a defective alternator, or its related parts (regulator), and replacement will fix the problem; however, faulty wiring and other problems can cause the charging system to malfunction. Further testing, which is not covered by this book, will reveal the exact component failure. Many automotive parts stores have alternator bench testers available for use by customers. An alternator bench test is the most definitive way to determine the condition of your alternator.

6. If the voltage is within specifications, proceed to the next test.

Load Test

1. With the engine running, turn on the blower motor and the high beams (or other electrical accessories to place a load on the charging system).
2. Increase and hold engine speed to 2000 rpm.
3. Measure the voltage reading at the battery.
4. The voltage should increase at least 0.5 volts from the voltage test. If the voltage does not meet specifications, the charging system is malfunctioning.

➡Usually under and overcharging is caused by a defective alternator, or its related parts (regulator), and replacement will fix the problem; however, faulty wiring and other problems can cause the charging system to malfunction. Further testing, which is not covered by this book, will reveal the exact component failure. Many automotive parts stores have alternator bench testers available for use by customers. An alternator bench test is the most definitive way to determine the condition of your alternator.

REMOVAL & INSTALLATION

4.6L Engine Except Seville

▶ See Figures 30 thru 41

1. Disconnect the negative battery cable.
2. Remove the cover from the headlamps and radiator shroud.
3. Remove the air cleaner, if necessary.
4. Disconnect the left engine torque strut from the radiator support.
5. Disconnect the upper trans oil cooler line from the trans cooler.
6. Remove the right cooling fan and the left cooling fan.
7. Remove the serpentine belt from the generator pulley.

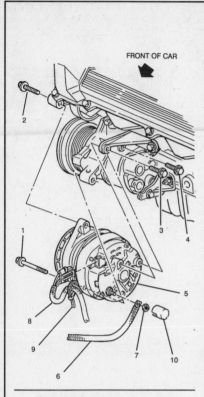

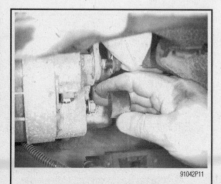

1. BOLT – FRONT LOWER
2. BOLT – FRONT UPPER
3. BOLT – REAR
4. BOLT – REAR
5. GENERATOR
6. BATTERY CHARGING CABLE
7. OUTPUT STUD NUT 20 N•m (15 LBS. FT.)
8. HARNESS CONNECTOR
9. WIRE TIE STRAP
10. CAP

NOTE: BOLTS 1, 2, 3 AND 4 TORQUE IN ORDER
SHOWN TO AVOID BREAKAGE 47 N•m (36 LBS. FT.)

84203017

Fig. 30 Alternator mounting—4.6L North-star engine

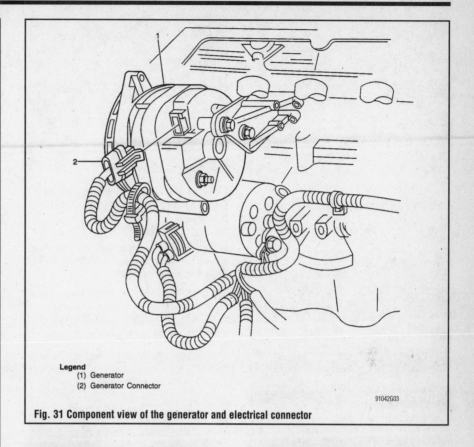

Legend
(1) Generator
(2) Generator Connector

91042G03

Fig. 31 Component view of the generator and electrical connector

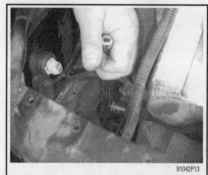

91042P13

Fig. 32 Remove the top retaining bolt for the alternator

91042P09

Fig. 33 Loosen the lower mounting bolt

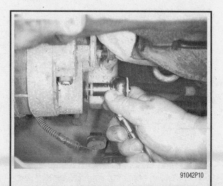

91042P11

Fig. 34 Remove the protective cap to gain access to the electrical connectors

91042P10

Fig. 35 Removing the retaining nut that holds the battery cable to the alternator

91042P12

Fig. 36 Back the bolt on the rear of the alternator out as far as possible and the unit can be removed from the mounting

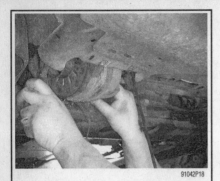

Fig. 37 Pull the lower mounting bolt from the generator

Fig. 38 With the cable removed, attempt to bring the alternator through the allotted opening

Fig. 39 Rotate the generator, if it aids the removal

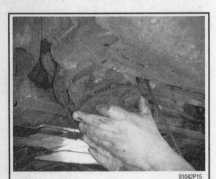

Fig. 40 Rotating the generator nose down . . .

Fig. 41 . . . seemed to be the only way to extract it from the mounting

8. Remove the bolt from the front top of the generator, and the bolt from the lower front of the generator.

9. Detach the harness connector and output cable from the generator.

➡The bolt nearest the exhaust manifold cannot be removed from the bracket but can be backed out to allow for removal of the generator.

10. Removal the A/C splash shield from the cradle, and the access panel from the bottom side of the radiator support.

11. Disconnect the engine harness from the cradle.

➡The generator can be moved out away from the engine and removed from the bottom side of the engine compartment.

12. Connect the negative battery cable.

To install:

13. Install the generator to mounting with the two bolts to the rear of the generator. Hand tighten the bolts.

14. Connect the engine harness clip to the cradle.

15. Install the access panel to the lower radiator support. Install the A/C splash shield to the cradle.

16. Attach the harness connector and output cable to the generator.

17. Tighten the rear mounting bolts to 36 ft. lbs. (47 Nm). The output cable to 15 ft. lbs. (20 Nm).

18. Install the bolt to the lower front of the generator and tighten to 36 ft. lbs. (47 Nm). Install the bolt to the top front of the generator and tighten to 36 ft. lbs. (47 Nm).

19. Rotate the drive belt tensioner and install the drive belt around the generator pulley. Inspect for correct alignment of the belt with all the accessory pulleys.

20. Install the left cooling fan, and then the right.

21. Attach the upper trans oil cooler line to the trans cooler.

22. Install the left engine torque strut.

23. If the air cleaner was removed, install it now.

24. Replace the cover from the headlamps and radiator shroud.

25. Connect the negative battery cable.

Seville With 4.6L Engine

▶ **See Figure 42**

On some models, the generator is water-cooled. When this is the case, the repair procedure is as follows:

1. Disconnect the negative battery cable.
2. Remove the accessory drive belt.
3. Drain and recycle the engine coolant.
4. Remove the radiator.

➡If your vehicle is equipped with air conditioning, refer to the information regarding the implications of servicing your A/C system yourself. Only an MVAC-trained, EPA-certified, automotive technician should service the A/C system or its components.

5. Remove the A/C condenser.
6. Raise and safely support the vehicle securely.
7. Disconnect the coolant inlet and outlet hoses from the generator.
8. Detach the electrical connections from the generator. The regulator, the battery output, and the heated windshield (if equipped) will need to be unplugged.
9. Remove the generator fasteners from the generator.
10. Remove the generator from the vehicle.

To install:

11. Attach the generator to the engine and tighten the fasteners to 37 ft. lbs. (50 Nm).
12. Attach the electrical connections for the regulator, battery output, and the heated windshield.
13. Tighten the battery output cable to 15 ft. lbs. (20 Nm).
14. Reconnect the coolant inlet and outlet hoses to the generator.
15. Lower the vehicle.
16. Install the A/C condenser.
17. Install the radiator.
18. Install the accessory drive belt.

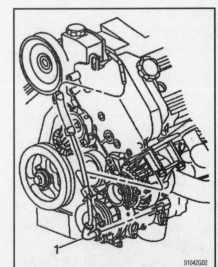

Fig. 42 This shows the coolant outlet hose being removed, signified by the "1" in the diagram

4.5L and 4.9L Engines

▶ **See Figures 43 and 44**

1. Disconnect the negative battery cable.
2. Remove the generator harness connector and battery charging wire on the back of the generator. Heated windshield 3-phase connector and clip if equipped.
3. Release the tension from the drive belt land remove the belt from the generator pulley. Do not remove the belt from any other component pulleys.
4. Remove the volts, ABS ground strap, and generator from the vehicle.

To install:

5. Install the generator and ground strap to the mounting bracket with bolts tightened to 20 ft. lbs. (27 Nm).
6. Raise the drive belt tensioner. Position the drive belt over the generator pulley and release the tensioner.
7. Attach the generator harness connector and battery-charging wire to the generator output stud. Do not route the battery charging wire to rest against the cruise control servo. Tighten to 15 ft. lbs. (20 Nm). Do not overtighten.
8. Connect the negative battery cable.

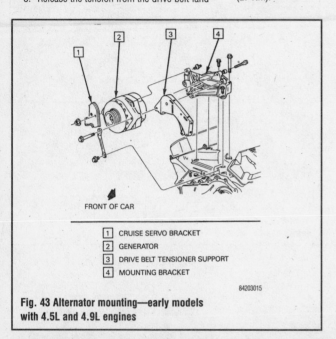

1	CRUISE SERVO BRACKET
2	GENERATOR
3	DRIVE BELT TENSIONER SUPPORT
4	MOUNTING BRACKET

84203015

Fig. 43 Alternator mounting—early models with 4.5L and 4.9L engines

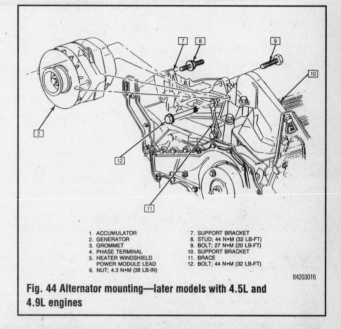

1. ACCUMULATOR
2. GENERATOR
3. GROMMET
4. PHASE TERMINAL
5. HEATER WINDSHIELD POWER MODULE LEAD
6. NUT; 4.3 N•M (38 LB-IN)
7. SUPPORT BRACKET
8. STUD; 44 N•M (32 LB-FT)
9. BOLT; 27 N•M (20 LB-FT)
10. SUPPORT BRACKET
11. BRACE
12. BOLT; 44 N•M (32 LB-FT)

84203016

Fig. 44 Alternator mounting—later models with 4.5L and 4.9L engines

STARTING SYSTEM

Starter

TESTING

Voltage Drop Test

▶ **See Figure 45**

➡ **The battery must be in good condition and fully charged prior to performing this test.**

1. Disable the ignition system by unplugging the coil pack. Verify that the vehicle will not start.
2. Connect a voltmeter between the positive terminal of the battery and the starter **B+** circuit.
3. Turn the ignition key to the **START** position and note the voltage on the meter.
4. If voltage reads 0.5 volts or more, there is high resistance in the starter cables or the cable ground, repair as necessary. If the voltage reading is ok proceed to the next step.
5. Connect a voltmeter between the positive terminal of the battery and the starter **M** circuit.
6. Turn the ignition key to the **START** position and note the voltage on the meter.
7. If voltage reads 0.5 volts or more, there is high resistance in the starter. Repair or replace the starter as necessary.

➡ **Many automotive parts stores have starter bench testers available for use by customers.**

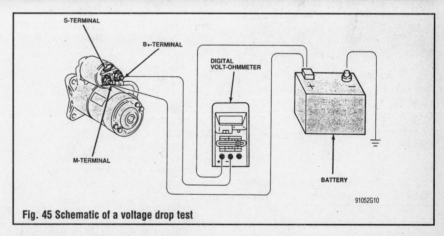

Fig. 45 Schematic of a voltage drop test

A starter bench test is the most definitive way to determine the condition of your starter.

REMOVAL & INSTALLATION

4.6L Engine

▶ **See Figures 46, 47 and 48**

1. Disconnect the negative battery cable.
2. Disconnect the positive battery cable.

➡ **In order to get to the starter assembly the intake manifold must be removed. Refer to** the procedure for removing the intake manifold.

3. Reposition the front bank spark plug wires.
4. Remove the air intake duct from the throttle body.
5. Detach the electrical connectors for the intake manifold, Throttle Position (TP) sensor, and Idle Speed Control (ISC) motor, Evaporative Emission (EVAP) Control solenoid and Cruise Control Servo.
6. Disconnect the vacuum hoses at the brake vacuum booster, fuel pipe bundle and to the body.

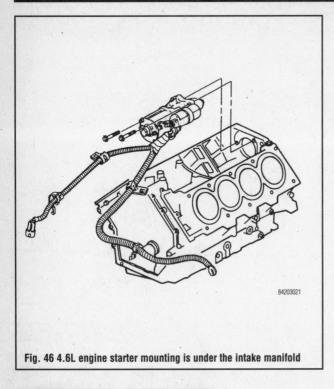

Fig. 46 4.6L engine starter mounting is under the intake manifold

Fig. 47 This is where (and how) the starter motor is mounted in the engine valley on the 4.6L engine. The arrows show the 2 mounting bolts

Fig. 48 This is the battery connection to the solenoid. Make sure it is clean and tight

7. Disconnect the PCV hoses at the intake manifold.

8. Unhook the accelerator cable at the throttle body and position it out of the way.

9. Relieve the fuel system pressure. Disconnect the fuel pipe quick connects at the fuel pipe bundle in the engine compartment.

10. Remove the EVAP solenoid bracket at the rear (or right) cam cover.

11. Reposition the transaxle range control cable away from the cruise control servo.

12. Disconnect the coolant hoses at the throttle body and to the coolant reservoir and plug the hoses. Wrap a shop towel around the hoses when disconnecting to avoid spillage.

13. Remove the four intake manifold bolts and lift the intake manifold with the throttle body out of the engine compartment.

14. Unbolt the solenoid 'S' terminal nut and bat-tery cable nut. Remove the starter motor mounting bolts, and lift the starter motor out of the manifold cavity.

To install:

➡Before installing the starter motor to the engine, tighten inner nuts on the solenoid terminals to be sure they are secure in the cap. Tighten the inner nuts on the battery terminal and motor terminal to 71 inch lbs. (8 Nm). If the nuts are not properly tightened, the starter may fail later due to the terminal or cap damage.

15. Install the solenoid switch lead, and tighten the nut to 22 inch lbs. (2.5 Nm).

16. Install the battery cable nut and tighten to 71 inch lbs. (8 Nm).

17. Install the starter motor and tighten the mounting bolts to 22 ft. lbs. (30 Nm).

18. Install the intake manifold with the throttle body onto the engine and install the four bolts. The four intake manifold bolts must be tightend in a specific sequence to 71 inch lbs. (8 Nm), then an additional 120°.

19. Connect the coolant hoses at the throttle body and at the coolant reservoir. Add coolant as needed.

20. Position the transaxle range control cable to the cruise control bracket.

21. Fasten the EVAP solenoid bracket to the rear cam cover.

22. Reconnect the fuel pipes quick connects at the fuel pipe bundle in the engine compartment.

23. Hook the accelerator cable up at the throttle body.

24. Connect the vacuum hoses at the brake vac-uum booster, fuel pipe bundle and to the body. Install the PCV hose at the intake manifold.

25. Install the electrical connectors for the intake manifold, the TP sensor ISC motor, EVAP solenoid and the cruise control servo.

26. Install the air intake duct to the throttle body.

27. Reposition the front bank spark plug wires.

28. Connect the negative battery cable.

29. Connect the positive battery cable.

4.5L and 4.9L Engines

▶ See Figures 49, 50 and 51

1. Disconnect the negative battery cable.

2. Raise and safely support the vehicle securely on jackstands.

3. Remove the starter motor shield.

4. Remove the exhaust front and rear pipe assembly.

5. Remove the flexplate inspection cover.

6. Disconnect the solenoid 'S' terminal nut and battery cable nut.

7. Unbolt the starter motor mounting bolts, and remove the starter motor.

To install:

8. Install the starter motor, and tighten to 32 ft. lbs. (43 Nm).

9. Install the solenoid 'S' terminal nut. Tighten the nut to 35 inch lbs. (4 Nm).

10. Install the battery cable nut and tighten to 12 ft. lbs. (15 Nm).

11. Install the flexplate inspection cover, the front and rear exhaust pipe assembly and the starter motor shield.

12. Lower the vehicle.

13. Connect the negative battery cable.

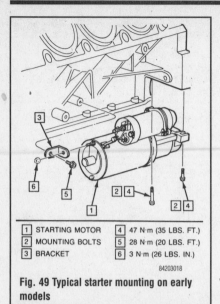

1	STARTING MOTOR	4	47 N·m (35 LBS. FT.)
2	MOUNTING BOLTS	5	28 N·m (20 LBS. FT.)
3	BRACKET	6	3 N·m (26 LBS. IN.)

84203018

Fig. 49 Typical starter mounting on early models

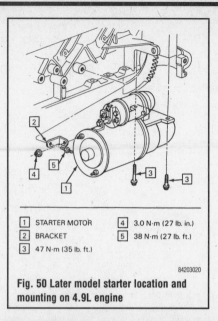

1	STARTER MOTOR	4	3.0 N·m (27 lb. in.)
2	BRACKET	5	38 N·m (27 lb. ft.)
3	47 N·m (35 lb. ft.)		

84203020

Fig. 50 Later model starter location and mounting on 4.9L engine

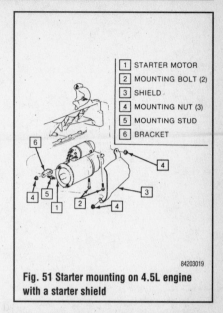

1	STARTER MOTOR
2	MOUNTING BOLT (2)
3	SHIELD
4	MOUNTING NUT (3)
5	MOUNTING STUD
6	BRACKET

84203019

Fig. 51 Starter mounting on 4.5L engine with a starter shield

SENDING UNITS AND SENSORS

➡This section describes the operating principles of sending units, warning lights and gauges. Sensors, which provide information to the Powertrain Control Module (PCM), are covered under electronic engine controls.

Instrument panels contain a number of indicating devices (gauges and warning lights). These devices are composed of two separate components. One is the sending unit, mounted on the engine or other remote part of the vehicle, and the other is the actual gauge or light in the instrument panel.

Several types of sending units exist, however most can be characterized as being either a pressure type or a resistance type. Pressure type sending units convert liquid pressure into an electrical signal that is sent to the gauge. Resistance type sending units are most often used to measure temperature and use variable resistance to control the current flow back to the indicating device. Both types of sending units are connected in series by a wire to the battery (through the ignition switch). When the ignition is turned **ON**, current flows from the battery through the indicating device and on to the sending unit.

Coolant Temperature Sensor

⁂ CAUTION

Never open, service, or drain the radiator or cooling system when hot; serious burns can occur from the steam and hot coolant. In addition, when draining engine coolant, keep in mind that cats and dogs are attracted to ethylene glycol antifreeze and could drink any that is left in an uncovered container or in puddles on the ground. This will prove fatal in sufficient quantities. Always drain coolant into a sealable con-

tainer. Coolant should be reused unless it is contaminated or is several years old.

TESTING

The coolant temperature sensor is a thermistor, (a resistor which changes value based on temperature) mounted in the engine coolant stream. Low coolant temperature produces a high resistance (100,000 ohms at -40°F -40°C), while high temperature causes low resistance (70 ohms at 266°F/130°C).

The PCM supplies a 5 volt signal to the ECT sensor through a resistor in the PCM and monitors the terminal voltage. Since this forms a series circuit to ground through the ECT sensor, high sensor resistance (low temperature) will result in high PCM terminal voltage. When the ECT sensors resistance is low (high temperature), the terminal voltage will be drawn lower. This terminal voltage indicates engine coolant temperature to the PCM.

REMOVAL & INSTALLATION

4.5L And 4.9L Engines

⧫ See Figure 52

1. Properly relieve the cooling system pressure.
2. Make sure ignition is in the OFF position.
3. Detach the electrical connector to the coolant temperature sensor.
4. Remove sensor carefully.
   To install:
5. Coat threads of sensor with proper type sealant.
6. Install sensor to engine and tighten to 15 ft. lbs. (20 Nm).
7. Attach electrical connector to sensor.
8. Check coolants level and refill if necessary.

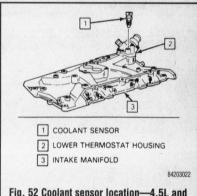

1	COOLANT SENSOR
2	LOWER THERMOSTAT HOUSING
3	INTAKE MANIFOLD

84203022

Fig. 52 Coolant sensor location—4.5L and 4.9L engines

4.6L Engine

⧫ See Figure 53

1. Let the cooling system cool before removing the sensor.
2. Partially drain the cooling system
3. Disconnect the throttle control cable from the cruise control servo bracket.
4. Remove the cruise control servo and bracket.
5. Detach the coolant sensor electrical connector.
6. Remove the coolant sensor from the manifold.
   To install:
7. Apply a non-hardening sealer to the sensor threads and install the sensor in the manifold. Tighten the sensor to 106 inch lbs. (12 Nm).
8. Attach the coolant sensor electrical connector.
9. Install the cruise control servo and bracket.
10. Connect the throttle control cable to the cruise control servo bracket.
11. Fill the cooling system

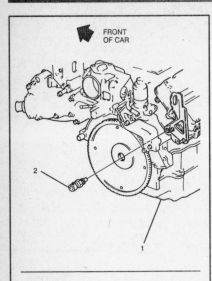

1 ENGINE
2 ENGINE COOLANT TEMPERATURE SENSOR
   (12 N•m/106 lb. in.)

84203023

Fig. 53 Coolant sensor location—4.6L Northstar engine

Oil Pressure Switch

REMOVAL & INSTALLATION

4.5L And 4.9L Engines

♦ See Figure 54

1. Disconnect the locking collar from the switch.
2. Remove the electrical connector.
3. Remove oil pressure switch.
To install:
4. Make sure fittings are properly aligned to allow sensor installation.

1 ECM HARNESS – CONNECTOR TO OIL
   PRESSURE SWITCH
2 OIL PRESSURE SWITCH
3 OIL FILTER

84203024

Fig. 54 Oil pressure switch location—4.5L and 4.9L engines

5. Wrap Teflon tape or apply Thread lock to threads on sensor.
6. Install new oil pressure switch.
7. Reattach electrical connector and locking collar onto switch.
8. Start engine check for leaks.

4.6L Engine

♦ See Figure 55

1. Raise and safely support the vehicle.
2. Remove the electrical connector from the switch.
3. Remove oil pressure switch at the oil filter adapter.
To install:
4. Install the oil pressure switch at the oil filter adapter and tighten to 106 inch lbs. (12 Nm).
5. Install the electrical connector to the switch.
6. Lower the vehicle and check for leaks.

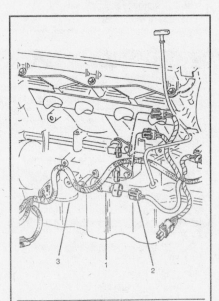

1 OIL PRESSURE SWITCH 12 N•m (106 lb. in.)
2 OIL PRESSURE SWITCH HARNESS CONNECTOR
3 OIL FILTER ADAPTER

84203025

Fig. 55 Oil pressure switch location—4.6L Northstar engine

Electric Fan Switch

REMOVAL & INSTALLATION

✳✳ CAUTION

An electric fan under the hood can start up even when the engine is not running and can injure you. Keep hands, clothing, and tools away from any underhood electric fan.

✳✳ CAUTION

To help avoid personal injury or damage to the vehicle, a bent, cracked, or damaged fan blade or housing should always be replaced.

Deville, Deville Concours, and Eldorado

1. Remove the upper filler panel.
2. Remove the air cleaner.
3. Remove the left engine torque strut.
4. Disconnect the upper radiator hose.
5. Disconnect the upper oil cooler line from the radiator.
6. Detach the cooling fan electrical connectors, unbolt the fans, and remove them.
To install:
7. Install the cooling fans and tighten the bolts to 89 inch lbs. (10 Nm).
8. Attach the cooling fan electrical connectors.
9. Connect the upper oil cooler line to the radiator.
10. Reattach the upper radiator hose.
11. Install the left engine torque strut.
12. Install the air cleaner.
13. Install the upper filler panel.

Seville

1. Remove the hood latch bracket.
2. Drain and recycle the engine coolant.
3. Remove the headlamps.
4. Remove the condenser mounting bolts.
5. Remove the radiator brackets.
6. Disconnect the upper engine oil cooler hose from the radiator.
7. Remove the air cleaner.
8. Disconnect the lower radiator hose from the radiator.
9. Tilt the radiator forward.
10. Detach the electrical connectors from the cooling fans.
11. Disconnect the generator inlet cooler hose from the radiator.
12. Remove the cooling fan assembly from the radiator.
13. Remove the radiator.
To install:
14. Install the cooling fan assembly to the radiator.
15. Install the radiator to the vehicle.
16. Connect the generator inlet cooler line to the radiator.
17. Attach the electrical connectors to the cooling fans.
18. Connect the lower radiator hose to the engine.
19. Install the air cleaner.
20. Connect the upper engine oil cooler hose to the radiator.
21. Install the radiator brackets.
22. Install the condenser mounting bolts, and tighten to 10 ft. lbs. (13 Nm).
23. Install the hood latch bracket.
24. Install the headlamps.
25. Fill the cooling system.

Troubleshooting Basic Starting System Problems

Problem	Cause	Solution
Starter motor rotates engine slowly	• Battery charge low or battery defective	• Charge or replace battery
	• Defective circuit between battery and starter motor	• Clean and tighten, or replace cables
	• Low load current	• Bench-test starter motor. Inspect for worn brushes and weak brush springs.
	• High load current	• Bench-test starter motor. Check engine for friction, drag or coolant in cylinders. Check ring gear-to-pinion gear clearance.
Starter motor will not rotate engine	• Battery charge low or battery defective	• Charge or replace battery
	• Faulty solenoid	• Check solenoid ground. Repair or replace as necessary.
	• Damaged drive pinion gear or ring gear	• Replace damaged gear(s)
	• Starter motor engagement weak	• Bench-test starter motor
	• Starter motor rotates slowly with high load current	• Inspect drive yoke pull-down and point gap, check for worn end bushings, check ring gear clearance
	• Engine seized	• Repair engine
Starter motor drive will not engage (solenoid known to be good)	• Defective contact point assembly	• Repair or replace contact point assembly
	• Inadequate contact point assembly ground	• Repair connection at ground screw
	• Defective hold-in coil	• Replace field winding assembly
Starter motor drive will not disengage	• Starter motor loose on flywheel housing	• Tighten mounting bolts
	• Worn drive end busing	• Replace bushing
	• Damaged ring gear teeth	• Replace ring gear or driveplate
	• Drive yoke return spring broken or missing	• Replace spring
Starter motor drive disengages prematurely	• Weak drive assembly thrust spring	• Replace drive mechanism
	• Hold-in coil defective	• Replace field winding assembly
Low load current	• Worn brushes	• Replace brushes
	• Weak brush springs	• Replace springs

TCCS2C01

Troubleshooting Basic Charging System Problems

Problem	Cause	Solution
Noisy alternator	• Loose mountings • Loose drive pulley • Worn bearings • Brush noise • Internal circuits shorted (High pitched whine)	• Tighten mounting bolts • Tighten pulley • Replace alternator • Replace alternator • Replace alternator
Squeal when starting engine or accelerating	• Glazed or loose belt	• Replace or adjust belt
Indicator light remains on or ammeter indicates discharge (engine running)	• Broken belt • Broken or disconnected wires • Internal alternator problems • Defective voltage regulator	• Install belt • Repair or connect wiring • Replace alternator • Replace voltage regulator/alternator
Car light bulbs continually burn out—battery needs water continually	• Alternator/regulator overcharging	• Replace voltage regulator/alternator
Car lights flare on acceleration	• Battery low • Internal alternator/regulator problems	• Charge or replace battery • Replace alternator/regulator
Low voltage output (alternator light flickers continually or ammeter needle wanders)	• Loose or worn belt • Dirty or corroded connections • Internal alternator/regulator problems	• Replace or adjust belt • Clean or replace connections • Replace alternator/regulator

TCCS2C02

3

ENGINE AND ENGINE OVERHAUL

ENGINE MECHANICAL

Engine

REMOVAL & INSTALLATION

In the process of removing the engine, you will come across a number of steps which call for the removal of a separate component or system, such as "disconnect the exhaust system" or "remove the radiator." In most instances, a detailed removal procedure can be found elsewhere in this manual.

It is virtually impossible to list each individual wire and hose which must be disconnected, simply because so many different model and engine combinations have been manufactured. Careful observation and common sense are the best possible approaches to any repair procedure.

Removal and installation of the engine can be made easier if you follow these basic points:

- If you have to drain any of the fluids, use a suitable container.
- Before disconnecting them, always tag any wires or hoses. In addition, tag the components they came from.
- Because there are so many bolts and fasteners involved, store, and label the retainers from components separately in muffin pans, jars, or coffee cans. This will prevent confusion during installation.
- After unbolting the transmission or transaxle, always make sure it is properly supported.
- If it is necessary to disconnect the air conditioning system, have this service performed by a qualified technician using a recovery/recycling station. If the system does not have to be disconnected, unbolt the compressor and set it aside.
- When unbolting the engine mounts, always make sure the engine is properly supported. When removing the engine, make sure that any lifting devices are properly attached to the engine. It is recommended that if your engine is supplied with lifting hooks, your lifting apparatus be attached to them.
- Lift the engine from its compartment slowly, checking that no hoses, wires, or other components are still connected.
- After the engine is clear of the compartment, place it on an engine stand or workbench.
- After the engine has been removed, you can perform a partial or full teardown of the engine using the procedures outlined in this manual.

4.5L and 4.9L Engines

1. Disconnect the negative battery cable.
2. Drain and recycle the engine coolant.
3. Remove the air cleaner. Matchmark the hood to the support brackets and remove the hood.

➡️**If your vehicle is equipped with air conditioning, refer to the information regarding the implications of servicing your A/C system yourself. Only a MVAC-trained, EPA-certified, automotive technician should service the A/C system or its components.**

4. If equipped with air conditioning, perform the following procedures:

a. Remove the hose strap from the right-strut tower.

b. Remove the accumulator from its bracket and position it aside.

c. Remove the canister hoses from the accumulator bracket.

d. Remove the accumulator bracket from the wheelhouse.

5. Remove the cooling fans, the accessory drive belt, the radiator and heater hoses.

6. Label and detach the electrical connectors from the following items:

a. Oil pressure switch
b. Coolant temperature sensor
c. Distributor
d. EGR solenoid
e. Engine temperature switch

7. Label and disconnect the cables from the following items:

a. Accelerator
b. Cruise control linkage
c. Transaxle Throttle Valve (TV) cable

8. If equipped with cruise control, remove the diaphragm with the bracket attached and move it aside.

9. Remove the vacuum supply hose and the exhaust crossover pipe.

10. Disconnect the oil cooler lines from the oil filter adapter, the oil line cooler bracket from the transaxle and position them aside.

11. Remove the air cleaner mounting bracket.

12. Properly relieve the fuel system pressure.

13. Disconnect the fuel lines from the throttle body. Remove the fuel lines bracket from the transaxle and secure the fuel lines aside.

14. Remove the small vacuum line from the brake booster.

15. Label and detach the AIR solenoid electrical and hose connections. Remove the AIR valves with the bracket.

16. Label and detach the electrical connectors from the following:

a. Idle Speed Control (ISC) motor
b. Throttle Position Switch (TPS)
c. Fuel injectors
d. Manifold Air Temperature (MAT) sensor
e. Oxygen sensor
f. Electric Fuel Evaporation (EFE) grid
g. Alternator bracket

17. Remove the power steering pump hose strap and the stud-headed bolt from in front of the right cylinder head.

18. Remove the AIR pipe clip located near the No. 2 spark plug, if equipped.

19. Remove the power steering pump and belt tensioner with bracket attached; wire them aside.

20. Raise and safely support the vehicle.

21. Label and detach the electrical connectors from the starter and the ground wire from the cylinder block.

22. Remove the two flywheel covers. Remove the starter-to-engine bolts and the starter. Matchmark the flywheel-to-torque converter location. Remove the three flywheel-to-torque converter bolts and slide the converter back into the bell housing.

23. If equipped with air conditioning, perform the following procedures:

a. Remove the compressor lower dust shield.

b. Remove the right front wheel/tire assembly and outer wheelhouse plastic shield.

c. Remove the compressor-to-bracket bolts and lower the compressor from the engine. Do not disconnect the refrigerant lines.

24. Remove the lower radiator hose.

25. From the lower right front of the Engine and cradle, remove the driveline vibration damper with the brackets, if equipped, and the engine-to-transaxle bracket bolts. Pull the alternator wire with the plastic cover down and aside.

26. Remove the exhaust pipe-to-manifold bolts with the springs attached and the AIR pipe-to-converter bracket from the exhaust manifold stud.

➡️**Be careful not to lose the springs when detaching the exhaust pipe.**

27. Remove the lower right side bell housing-to-engine bolt. Lower the vehicle.

28. Using a vertical Engine hoist, attach it to the Engine and support it.

29. Remove the upper bell housing-to-engine bolts and left front Engine mount bracket-to-engine bolts. Remove the Engine from the vehicle.

To install:

30. Raise the transaxle with a separate jack to engage the engine.

31. Install the engine into the vehicle, using a suitable Engine hoist. Engage the dowels on the block with the transaxle case.

32. Install the transaxle bell housing-to-engine mounting bolts.

33. Lower and remove the floor jack assembly from the transaxle.

34. Lower the engine, making sure it is seated on the mount properly.

35. Remove the engine hoist. Raise and safely support the vehicle.

36. Lower the right hand transaxle bell housing-to-engine bolt. Support the engine.

37. Install the left front engine mount bracket-to-engine bolts and the flexplate-to-converter bolts.

38. Replace the flexplate covers.

39. Install the starter motor and connect the electrical wires to the starter.

40. Connect the AIR pipe-to-converter bracket to the exhaust manifold stud.

41. Install the exhaust pipe to manifold bolts and springs.

42. Connect the alternator and install the plastic cover. Install the right front engine-to-transaxle bracket and tighten the bolts to 30 ft. lbs. (41 Nm).

43. Install the lower radiator hose and replace the air conditioning compressor mounting bolts.

44. Install the air conditioning compressor lower dust shield and the outer wheel house plastic shield.

45. Install the right front tire and wheel assembly.

46. Lower the vehicle.

47. Install the power steering pump and the belt tensioner. Replace the stud headed bolt.

48. Install the power steering hose strap to the stud headed bolt in front of the cylinder head.

49. Connect the electrical connectors to the following:

a. Idle Speed Control (ISC) motor
b. Throttle Position Switch (TPS)

   c. Fuel injectors
   d. Manifold Air Temperature (MAT) sensor
   e. Oxygen sensor
   f. Electric Fuel Evaporator (EFE) grid
   g. Alternator bracket

50. Replace the air valve and bracket. Connect the air solenoid electrical and hose connections.

51. Connect the vacuum line to the brake booster.

52. Connect the fuel lines at the throttle body and replace the fuel line bracket at the transaxle.

53. Replace the air cleaner mounting bracket and connect the oil cooler lines to the oil filter adapter.

54. Connect the oil cooler line bracket at the transaxle. Replace the exhaust crossover pipe.

55. Replace the cruise control diaphragm and connect the vacuum line.

56. Connect the accelerator, cruise control and the transaxle throttle valve cables to the throttle lever.

57. Connect the wire connectors to the following:
   a. Oil pressure switch
   b. Coolant temperature sensor
   c. Distributor
   d. EGR solenoid
   e. Engine temperature switch

58. Replace the accessory drive belt, heater hoses, and upper radiator hose.

59. Install the cooling fans and connect the air conditioning accumulator bracket.

60. Install the air conditioning accumulator and connect the wires and hoses.

61. Install the hood assembly and replace the air cleaner.

62. Refill the Engine coolant. Connect the negative battery cable.

63. Start the engine, allow it to reach normal operating temperatures and check for leaks.

4.6L Engine

1. Disconnect the negative battery cable.
2. Remove the air cleaner inlet duct.
3. Matchmark the hood hinge-to-hood and remove the hood.
4. Drain the coolant from the radiator.
5. Remove the left and right torque struts. Install the left front strut bolt back into the bracket.
6. Disconnect the radiator hoses at the water crossover. Remove both cooling fans from the engine.
7. Remove the serpentine accessory drive belt.
8. Detach the cruise control servo connections and the ISC motor electrical connector.
9. Disconnect the throttle cable from the throttle body cam. Disconnect the shift cable from the park/neutral switch. Remove the cable bracket at the transaxle.
10. Remove the park/neutral switch and disconnect the power brake vacuum hose.
11. At the rear of the right head, disconnect the cylinder head temperature switch.
12. Remove the bellhousing bolts.
13. Remove the ignition coils and remove the spark plug wires.
14. Raise and safely support the vehicle.
15. Remove the oil pan-to-transmission brace. Remove the torque converter splash shield and the four converter-to-flywheel bolts.

16. Disconnect the oil cooler lines from the oil filter adapter.
17. Remove the A/C compressor mounting bolts and detach the electrical connectors. Move compressor out of way.
18. Detach the electrical connectors from the left side of the engine and move the harness from behind the exhaust manifold.
19. Remove the two nuts that secure the motor mount to the engine cradle front crossmember.
20. Remove the exhaust Y-pipe and remove the right front wheel.
21. Remove the crankcase to transmission bracket at the transmission tail shaft. Disconnect the knock sensor.
22. Remove the bolt from the transmission to the cylinder head brace at the cylinder head.
23. Lower the vehicle. Disconnect the fuel inlet and fuel return lines using special tool J37088 or equivalent.
24. Detach the injector harness connector and the hoses from the coolant reservoir. Remove the reservoir.
25. Disconnect the cam position sensor. Disconnect the heater hoses from the water pipes at the front of the right cylinder head.
26. Disconnect the battery cable from the junction block and remove the retainer at the cylinder head.
27. Disconnect the starter cable from the junction block.
28. Disconnect the power steering pump pressure and return lines at the pump. Return power steering line retainer from the right front of the crankcase.
29. Disconnect the rear oxygen sensor.
30. Remove the three screws securing the wiring harness retainer to right cam cover and position harness out of the way.
31. Connect an engine-lifting device to the engine using the support hooks at left and right rear of engine. The torque strut bracket at the left front of the engine should be used as a third lifting hook.
32. Carefully remove the engine from the vehicle.

To install:

33. Lower the engine into the vehicle. Remove the lifting device.
34. Install the 4 bell housing bolts and tighten to 75 ft. lbs. (100 Nm).
35. Raise and safely support the vehicle.
36. Install 2 nuts to the motor mount at the front cradle crossmember. Do not fully tighten.
37. Install bolt to the cylinder head for transmission brace. Do not fully tighten.
38. Install the transmission to crankcase bracket with the 4 bolts. Do not fully tighten the bolts.
39. Tighten the motor mount to cradle crossmember bolts to 30 ft. lbs. (40 Nm). Tighten the transmission brace bolt and transmission to crankcase bolts to 45 ft. lbs. (60 Nm).
40. Install the right front wheel and connect the knock sensor.
41. Install the exhaust Y-pipe.
42. Install the 4 torque converter to flywheel bolts and tighten to 45 ft. lbs. (60 Nm).
43. Install the converter splash shield and install the transmission to oil pan brace. Tighten the bolt to 35 ft. lbs. (50 Nm).
44. Position the A/C compressor in place and install the mounting bolts.

45. Route the electrical harness along the left side of the engine and connect the connectors.
46. Connect the oil cooler lines to the oil filter adapter.
47. Lower the vehicle.
48. Secure the wiring harness to the right cam cover with the 3 screws.
49. Connect the rear oxygen sensor and connect the cam position sensor.
50. Connect the power steering hoses to the pump and secure the return line to the crankcase.
51. Connect the heater hoses to the water pipes.
52. Connect the starter and battery cables at the junction box. Secure battery cable with retainer.
53. Connect and install the coolant reservoir.
54. Install coils and secure with 4 screws.
55. Install the serpentine drive belt and connect the injector harness to the FIS harness.
56. Connect the fuel line connectors. Connect the cylinder head temperature switch to the rear of the right head.
57. Connect the power brake vacuum line.
58. Install the park/neutral switch and shift cable. Adjust switch if necessary.
59. Install the cruise servo and connect the ISC motor.
60. Connect the throttle cable and install both cooling fans.
61. Connect the radiator hoses to the water crossover.
62. Install the torque struts and adjust the preload to zero.
63. Connect the negative battery cable.
64. Refill the engine with coolant. Install the hood and install the air cleaner.
65. Start the engine and check for oil, coolant, or transaxle leaks.

Powertrain Assembly

REMOVAL & INSTALLATION

4.6L Engine

➡**For some engine service, it may be most economical to remove the entire powertrain and cradle out the bottom of the body and to utilize the cradle as an engine stand.**

1. Disconnect the negative battery cable.
2. Remove the air cleaner inlet duct.
3. Remove the left and right torque struts. Install the left front strut bolt back into the bracket.
4. Disconnect the radiator hoses at the water crossover.
5. Remove both cooling fans from the engine.
6. Have a MVAC certified tech recover the A/C system refrigerant.
7. Disconnect the cruise control servo connections.
8. Disconnect the throttle cable from the throttle body cam. Disconnect the shift cable from the park/neutral switch. Remove the cable bracket at the transaxle.
9. Remove the park/neutral switch and disconnect the power brake vacuum hose.
10. Disconnect the fuel inlet and fuel return lines using special tool J37088 or equivalent.
11. Remove the fuel line retainer at the transaxle case.

12. Disconnect the hoses from the coolant reservoir. Remove the reservoir.

13. Disconnect the heater hoses from the front of the right cylinder head.

14. Disconnect the battery cable from the junction block and remove the retainer at the cylinder head.

15. Disconnect the starter cable from the junction block.

16. Disconnect the power steering pump pressure and return lines at the pump. Return power steering line retainer from the right front of the crankcase.

17. Detach the engine harness connectors at the PCM.

18. From under the hood, remove the wiring harness retainer screws at the cowl and pull the engine harness through.

19. Disconnect the refrigerant high temperature switch.

20. Open the relay cover and remove the fan control relays from the relay center.

21. To remove the engine harness connector on the left wheelhouse, remove 1 screw holding the connector halves together and separate. The engine portion of the harness will be removed with the engine.

22. Remove the serpentine accessory drive belt.

23. Raise and safely support the vehicle.

24. Remove both front wheels.

25. Remove both front drive axles.

26. Disconnect the oil cooler lines at the oil filter adapter.

27. Remove the exhaust Y-pipe.

28. Disconnect the coupling between the steering rack and the column.

29. Disconnect the speed sensitive steering solenoid.

30. Disconnect the power steering switch.

31. Remove the A/C manifold from the rear of the A/C compressor.

32. Separate the traction control controller from the engine cradle and wire controller into position to stay with the body.

33. Move the powertrain dolly such as J 36295 into position and lower the vehicle onto the table.

34. Remove the six engine cradle mounting bolts and remove the powertrain assembly by lifting the vehicle or lowering the table.

To install:

35. With the powertrain on the dolly such as J 36295, move into approximate position under the vehicle that is raised on a hoist.

36. Lower the vehicle onto the powertrain.

37. Align the engine cradle to the body and install the six engine cradle mounting bolts. tighten the bolts to 75 ft. lbs. (100 Nm).

38. Raise the vehicle and remove the dolly.

39. Install both front drive axles.

40. Connect the oil cooler lines at the oil filter adapter.

41. Install the exhaust Y-pipe.

42. Connect the coupling between the steering rack and the column.

43. Connect the speed sensitive steering solenoid.

44. Connect the power steering switch.

45. Install the A/C manifold to the rear of the A/C compressor.

46. Position the traction control controller to the engine cradle.

47. Lower the vehicle.

48. Pull the engine wiring harness through the cowl and install the 2 retaining screws.

49. Connect the engine harness connectors at the PCM.

50. Connect the refrigerant high temperature switch.

51. Open the relay cover and install the fan control relays to the relay center.

52. Position the engine harness connector on the left wheelhouse, install the 1 screw holding the connector halves together.

53. Connect the power steering pump pressure and return lines at the pump. Install the power steering line retainer to the right front of the crankcase.

54. Connect the battery and starter cables to the junction block and install the retainer at the cylinder head.

55. Connect the heater hoses to the front of the right cylinder head.

56. Connect the hoses and install the coolant reservoir.

57. Connect the fuel inlet and fuel return lines.

58. Connect the power brake vacuum hose.

59. Install the park/neutral switch.

60. Connect the throttle cable to the throttle body cam.

61. Connect the cruise control servo.

62. Install both cooling fans.

63. Connect the radiator hoses at the water crossover.

64. Add engine coolant.

65. Install the right and left torque struts and tighten the retaining bolts as follows:

➡It is important during installation that the engine torque struts are not preloaded in their installed position. Adjustment is provided at the point the strut fastens to the core support bracket. Make sure this bolt is loose during assembly. Tighten to 45 ft. lbs. (60 Nm) as the final step of assembly.

   a. Torque strut bracket to cylinder head (M10) bolt: 35 ft. lbs. (50 Nm).

   b. Torque strut bracket to cylinder head (M10) stud: 35 ft. lbs. (50 Nm).

   c. Torque strut bracket to water manifold (M8) bolts: 20 ft. lbs. (25 Nm).

   d. Torque strut bracket to cylinder head (M10) bolt: 35 ft. lbs. (50 Nm).

   e. Torque strut to core support bracket bolt 45 ft. lbs. (60 Nm) (see note above).

66. Connect the negative battery cable.

67. Charge the A/C system.

68. Install the air cleaner.

Rocker Arms and Valve Covers

REMOVAL & INSTALLATION

4.5L and 4.9L Engines

▸ See Figures 1 and 2

RIGHT

1. Disconnect the negative battery cable. Remove the air cleaner and the AIR management valve with bracket, move the assembly aside.

2. From the throttle body, remove the Manifold Absolute Pressure (MAP) hose.

3. Remove the right side spark plug wires and conduit.

4. Remove the fuel vapor canister pipe bracket from the valve cover stud.

5. Drain the cooling system to a level below the thermostat housing. Remove the heater hose from the thermostat housing and move it aside.

6. Remove the brake booster vacuum hose from the intake manifold.

7. Remove the rocker arm cover-to-cylinder screws, the cover, and the gasket/seals. Discard them.

8. Remove the rocker arm pivot-to-rocker arm support bolts, the pivots, and the rocker arms.

9. If necessary, remove the rocker arm support-to-cylinder head nuts/bolts and the support.

10. Clean the gasket mounting surfaces. Inspect the parts for wear and/or damage and replace the parts, if necessary.

To install:

11. Lubricate the parts with clean Engine oil, use a new gasket and coat both sides with RTV sealant, install RTV sealant between the intake manifold-to-cylinder head mating surfaces.

12. Install the rocker arms and pivots to the rocker arm support. Tighten the pivot bolts to 22 ft. lbs. (30 Nm).

13. Install the rocker arm support and place each pushrod into the rocker arm seat.

14. Install the rocker arm support retaining nuts, tighten to 37 ft. lbs. (50 Nm).

15. Install the rocker arm support retaining bolts, tighten to 7 ft. lbs. (9 Nm).

16. Install the rocker arm cover seals and place the molded seal into the groove in the rocker arm cover.

17. Install the rocker arm cover and tighten the mounting screws to 8 ft. lbs. (11 Nm).

18. Connect the brake booster vacuum hose and the EECS pipe bracket.

19. Install the spark plug wires and conduit. Connect the MAP hose to the throttle body.

20. Install the air management and bracket assembly.

21. Replace the heater hose and air cleaner assembly.

22. Connect the negative battery cable. Start the Engine and check for leaks.

LEFT

1. Disconnect the negative battery cable. Remove the air cleaner, the PCV valve, the throttle return spring and the serpentine drive belt.

2. Loosen the lower power steering pump bracket nuts.

3. Remove the power steering pump, the belt tensioner, the bracket-to-engine bolts, and the bracket. Move the power steering pump assembly toward the front of the vehicle; do not disconnect the pressure hoses.

4. Remove the left side spark plug wires and conduit.

5. Remove the rocker arm cover-to-cylinder screws, the cover, and the gasket/seals. Discard them.

6. Remove the rocker arm pivot-to-rocker arm support bolts, the pivots, and the rocker arms.

7. If necessary, remove the rocker arm support-to-cylinder head nuts/bolts and the support.

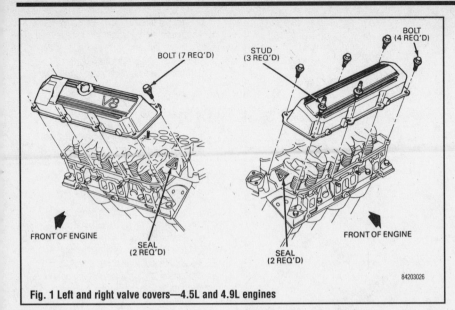

Fig. 1 Left and right valve covers—4.5L and 4.9L engines

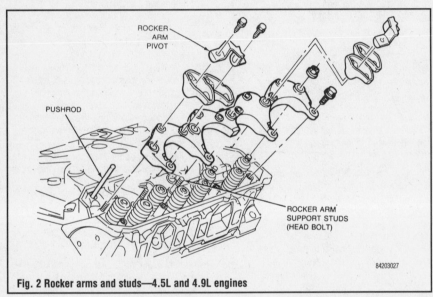

Fig. 2 Rocker arms and studs—4.5L and 4.9L engines

8. Clean the gasket mounting surfaces. Inspect the parts for wear and/or damage and replace the parts, if necessary.

To install:

9. Lubricate the parts with clean engine oil, use a new gasket, coat both sides with RTV sealant, install RTV sealant between the intake manifold-to-cylinder head mating surfaces.

10. Install the rocker arms and pivots to the rocker arm support. Tighten the pivot bolts to 22 ft. lbs. (30 Nm).

11. Install the rocker arm support and place each pushrod into the rocker arm seat.

12. Install the rocker arm support retaining nuts, tighten to 37 ft. lbs. (50 Nm).

13. Install the rocker arm support retaining bolts, tighten to 7 ft. lbs. (9 Nm).

14. Install the rocker arm cover seals and place the molded seal into the groove in the rocker arm cover.

15. Install the rocker arm cover and tighten the mounting screws to 8 ft. lbs. (11 Nm).

16. Install the spark plug wires and conduit.

17. Install the power steering pump, belt ten-

sioner and bracket assembly. Replace the accessory drive belt.

18. Install the throttle return spring and the PCV valve.

19. Install the air cleaner and connect the negative battery cable.

20. Start the engine and check for leaks.

Camshaft Cover

REMOVAL & INSTALLATION

4.6L Engine

LEFT SIDE

▶ **See Figures 3 and 4**

1. Disconnect the negative battery cable.
2. Partially drain the coolant from the radiator.
3. Disconnect the upper radiator hose at the water crossover.
4. Disconnect the spark plug wires.
5. Remove the right side fan.
6. Disconnect the battery cable at the alternator, disconnect the cable harness at the cam cover, and move it out of the way.
7. Disconnect the PCV fresh air tube from the cam cover.
8. Remove the right and left torque struts.
9. Disconnect the water pump drive belt.
10. Remove the water pump pulley with tool J 38825 or equivalent.
11. Remove the camshaft seal retainer screws and remove the seal.
12. Disconnect the battery cable retainer at the front of the cam cover.
13. Remove the cam cover screws and remove the cam cover by moving the cam drive end of the cover up and then pivot the entire cover around the water pump drive shaft. Continue moving the cover upward and pivoting so that the edge of the cover closely follows the left edge of the intake manifold cover.

To install:

14. Install spark plug and cam cover seals.
15. Insert the intake cam through the hole in the cam cover and using your fingers guide the cam cover up over the edge of the cylinder head.

✳✳ WARNING

Use care to prevent the exposed section of the cam cover seal from being damaged by the edge of the cylinder head casting.

16. Work the cover into position by allowing the top edge of the cover to follow the left side edge of the intake manifold.
17. Install the cam cover screws and tighten to 7 ft. lbs. (10 Nm).
18. Connect the battery cable retainer to the front of the cam cover.

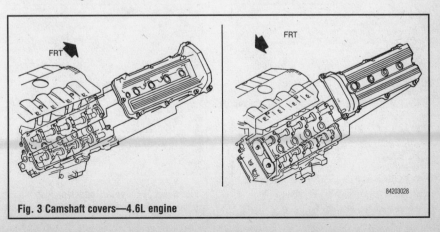

Fig. 3 Camshaft covers—4.6L engine

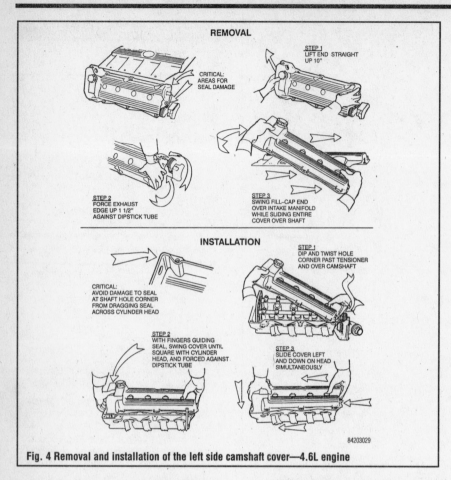

REMOVAL

STEP 1
LIFT END STRAIGHT
UP 10"

CRITICAL:
AREAS FOR
SEAL DAMAGE

STEP 2
FORCE EXHAUST
EDGE UP 1 1/2"
AGAINST DIPSTICK TUBE

STEP 3
SWING FILL-CAP END
OVER INTAKE MANIFOLD
WHILE SLIDING ENTIRE
COVER OVER SHAFT

INSTALLATION

STEP 1
DIP AND TWIST HOLE
CORNER PAST TENSIONER
AND OVER CAMSHAFT

CRITICAL:
AVOID DAMAGE TO SEAL
AT SHAFT HOLE CORNER
FROM DRAGGING SEAL
ACROSS CYLINDER HEAD

STEP 2
WITH FINGERS GUIDING
SEAL, SWING COVER UNTIL
SQUARE WITH CYLINDER
HEAD, AND FORCED AGAINST
DIPSTICK TUBE

STEP 3
SLIDE COVER LEFT
AND DOWN ON HEAD
SIMULTANEOUSLY

84203029

Fig. 4 Removal and installation of the left side camshaft cover—4.6L engine

19. Connect the battery cable at the alternator.
20. Lubricate the seal lips and install the camshaft seal to the end of the intake cam. Seal the screw threads with sealer.
21. Install the water pump pulley with tool J 38825 or equivalent.
22. Install the water pump drive belt.
23. Install the right and left torque struts and tighten the retaining bolts as follows:

➡It is important during installation that the engine torque struts are not preloaded in their installed position. Adjustment is provided at the point the strut fastens to the core support bracket. Make sure this bolt is loose during assembly. Tighten to 45 ft. lbs. (60 Nm) as the final step of assembly.

  a. Torque strut bracket to cylinder head (M10) bolt: 35 ft. lbs. (50 Nm).
  b. Torque strut bracket to cylinder head (M10) stud: 35 ft. lbs. (50 Nm).
  c. Torque strut bracket to water manifold (M8) bolts: 20 ft. lbs. (25 Nm).
  d. Torque strut bracket to cylinder head (M10) bolt: 35 ft. lbs. (50 Nm).
  e. Torque strut to core support bracket bolt 45 ft. lbs.: (60 Nm) (see the preceding note).
24. Connect the PCV fresh air tube to the cam cover.
25. Install the right side fan.
26. Connect the spark plug wires.
27. Connect the PCV fresh air tube to the cam cover.
28. Install the right side fan.

29. Connect the spark plug wires.
30. Connect the upper radiator hose to the water crossover.
31. Fill the radiator with coolant.
32. Connect the negative battery cable.

RIGHT SIDE

◗ See Figures 3, and 5 thru 12

1. Disconnect the negative battery cable.
2. Raise and support the vehicle safely and disconnect the exhaust 'Y' pipe at the converter. Position the converter out of the way.
3. Lower the vehicle.
4. Remove the tower-to-tower brace.
5. Detach the 4 DIS wiring connectors and mounting bolts.
6. Remove the DIS and the spark plug wires on the right bank. Tag wires for installation.
7. Disconnect the PCV valve.
8. Remove the purge canister solenoid from the rear of the cover.
9. Remove the 3 screws retaining wiring harness to the cover.
10. Remove the cam cover screws.
11. Safely support the front of the engine cradle and remove the 2 mounting screws at the front of the cradle.
12. Remove the right and left torque struts.
13. Lower the engine cradle (or raise the vehicle) to provide clearance at the rear of the engine compartment.
14. Remove the cam cover and discard the seal if damaged.
To install:
15. Install spark plug and cam cover seals.
16. Install the cam cover and tighten the screws to 7 ft. lbs. (10 Nm).
17. Raise the engine cradle into position and install and tight the 2 mounting bolts to 75 ft. lbs. (100 Nm).
18. Install the right and left torque struts and tighten the retaining bolts as follows:

➡It is important during installation that the engine torque struts are not preloaded in their installed position. Adjustment is provided at the point the strut fastens to the core support bracket. Make sure this bolt is loose during assembly. Tighten to 45 ft. lbs. (60 Nm) as the final step of assembly.

  a. Torque strut bracket to cylinder head (M10) bolt: 35 ft. lbs. (50 Nm).

91043P55

Fig. 5 A special pulley removing tool such as this one is necessary to remove the pulley from the camshaft

91043P59

Fig. 6 Install the pulley removing tool onto the water pump belt drive pulley and . . .

91043P58

Fig. 7 . . . tighten the forcing screw while stabilizing the holding nut to remove it from the camshaft

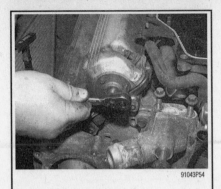

Fig. 8 Remove the front and . . .

Fig. 9 . . . the top camshaft cover retaining bolts

Fig. 10 Lift the cover up and forward to remove it from the engine

Fig. 11 Remove the camshaft cover gasket along with . . .

Fig. 12 . . . the spark plug O-rings and replace with new ones before reinstalling the cover onto the engine

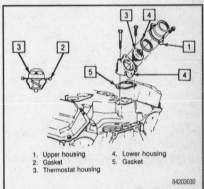

1. Upper housing
2. Gasket
3. Thermostat housing
4. Lower housing
5. Gasket

Fig. 13 Thermostat installation—4.5L and 4.9L engines

b. Torque strut bracket to cylinder head (M10) stud: 35 ft. lbs. (50 Nm).

c. Torque strut bracket to water manifold (M8) bolts: 20 ft. lbs. (25 Nm).

d. Torque strut bracket to cylinder head (M10) bolt: 35 ft. lbs. (50 Nm).

e. Torque strut to core support bracket bolt 45 ft. lbs.: (60 Nm) (see the preceding note).

19. Install the 3 screws retaining wiring harness to the cover.

20. Install the purge canister solenoid to the rear of the cover.

21. Connect the PCV valve.

22. Install the DIS (4 bolts) and the spark plug wires on the right bank.

23. Connect the 4 DIS wiring connectors.

24. Install the tower-to-tower brace.

25. Raise and support the vehicle safely and connect the exhaust 'Y' pipe to the converter. Tighten the bolts to 20 ft. lbs. (25 Nm).

26. Connect the negative battery cable.

Thermostat

✷✷ CAUTION

Never open, service, or drain the radiator or cooling system when hot; serious burns can occur from the steam and hot coolant. In addition, when draining engine coolant, keep in mind that cats and dogs are attracted to ethylene glycol antifreeze and could drink any that is left in an uncovered container or in puddles on the ground. This will prove fatal in sufficient quantities. Always drain coolant into a sealable container. Coolant should be reused unless it is contaminated or is several years old.

REMOVAL & INSTALLATION

4.5L And 4.9L Engines

◆ See Figure 13

1. Drain the coolant to a level below the thermostat housing.

2. It may be necessary to remove the upper air filter assembly on some models.

3. Remove the 2 bolts securing the upper thermostat housing to the lower housing.

4. Remove the upper thermostat housing.

5. Remove the thermostat and O-ring from the lower housing.

To install:

6. Install the thermostat and a new O-ring to the lower housing.

7. Install the upper thermostat housing to the lower housing. Tighten the thermostat housing bolts to 20 ft. lbs. (27 Nm).

8. Refill the cooling system using a 50/50 mixture of water and ethylene glycol antifreeze.

9. Start the engine and check for coolant leaks. Allow the engine to come to normal operating temperature. Recheck for coolant leaks.

4.6L Engine

◆ See Figures 14 thru 19

1. Drain the coolant to a level below the thermostat housing.

2. On some vehicles, access is easier if the front-end beauty panel and the air cleaner are removed.

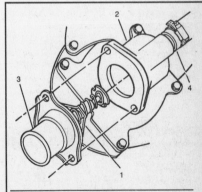

1	THERMOSTAT
2	THERMOSTAT HOUSING
3	COOLANT PUMP INLET
4	THERMOSTAT BY-PASS HOSE

Fig. 14 Thermostat installation—4.6L engine

Fig. 15 Loosen the upper radiator hose clamp at the thermostat housing

Fig. 16 Remove the upper radiator hose clamp from the thermostat housing

Fig. 17 Remove the thermostat housing retaining bolts and . . .

Fig. 18 . . . remove the thermostat housing from the engine

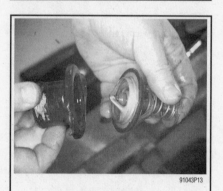

Fig. 19 Separate the thermostat from the housing

3. Remove the 2 bolts securing the thermostat housing to the intake manifold.

4. Remove the thermostat housing.

5. Remove the thermostat and O-ring from the housing.

To install:

6. Install the thermostat and new O-ring to the housing.

7. Install the thermostat housing to the intake manifold. Tighten the thermostat housing bolts to 18 ft. lbs. (25 Nm).

8. Refill the cooling system using a 50/50 mixture of water and ethylene glycol antifreeze.

9. Install the air cleaner and beauty panel, if removed.

10. Start the engine and check for coolant leaks. Allow the engine to come to normal operating temperature. Recheck for coolant leaks.

Intake Manifold

REMOVAL & INSTALLATION

4.5L and 4.9L Engines

▸ See Figures 20 and 21

1. Disconnect the negative battery cable.
2. Properly relieve the fuel system pressure.
3. Drain and recycle the engine coolant.
4. Remove the coolant reservoir. Disconnect the upper radiator hose from the thermostat housing.
5. Remove the air cleaner and the serpentine drive belt. Label and disconnect the spark plug wires from the spark plugs.

6. Remove the cross brace.

7. Remove the power steering pump and tensioner bracket assembly and reposition them toward the front of engine.

8. Remove the alternator and bracket.

9. Remove the cruise control servo with the bracket and the throttle valve cables and position them aside.

10. Detach the wire connections and reposition:

a. Distributor
b. Oil pressure switch
c. Coolant temperature sensor
d. EGR solenoid
e. ISC motor
f. Throttle position switch
g. If equipped, electric EFE grid
h. Injectors
i. MAT sensor

11. If equipped, disconnect the MAP hoses. Remove the upper radiator hose and the heater hose. Remove the air-conditioning hose bracket.

12. Disconnect the spark plug wire protectors and reposition the cap.

13. Mark the distributor rotor position and remove the distributor.

➡**Do not crank or in any other way rotate the crankshaft with the distributor removed.**

14. Disconnect the fuel and vacuum lines from the throttle body. Disconnect the vacuum supply solenoid and lines.

15. Remove the valve covers. Remove the rocker arms and pushrods.

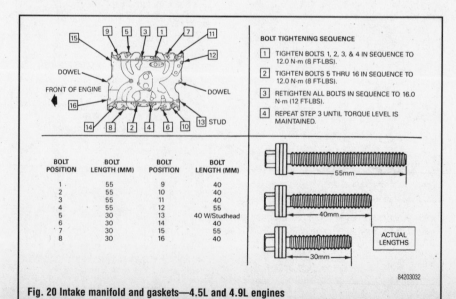

BOLT TIGHTENING SEQUENCE

1. TIGHTEN BOLTS 1, 2, 3, & 4 IN SEQUENCE TO 12.0 N·m (8 FT-LBS).
2. TIGHTEN BOLTS 5 THRU 16 IN SEQUENCE TO 12.0 N·m (8 FT-LBS).
3. RETIGHTEN ALL BOLTS IN SEQUENCE TO 16.0 N·m (12 FT-LBS).
4. REPEAT STEP 3 UNTIL TORQUE LEVEL IS MAINTAINED.

BOLT POSITION	BOLT LENGTH (MM)	BOLT POSITION	BOLT LENGTH (MM)
1	55	9	40
2	55	10	40
3	55	11	40
4	55	12	55
5	30	13	40 W/Studhead
6	30	14	40
7	30	15	55
8	30	16	40

ACTUAL LENGTHS — 55mm — 40mm — 30mm

Fig. 20 Intake manifold and gaskets—4.5L and 4.9L engines

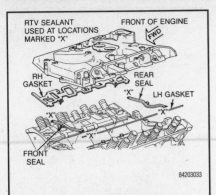

Fig. 21 Intake manifold bolt tightening sequence—4.5L and 4.9L engines

➡ Pushrods should be marked or retained in sequence so they may be reinstalled in their original positions.

16. Remove the right front and rear lift brackets. Remove the intake manifold bolts and remove the intake manifold, gaskets, and seals. Discard the gaskets and seals.

17. Clean the sealing surfaces of the intake manifold, cylinder head, and cylinder block.

To install:

18. Install new end seals. Use RTV at the 4 corners where the end seals will meet the side gaskets.

19. Install the new intake to cylinder head gaskets. Use RTV at the 4 corners of end seals.

20. Tighten the intake manifold bolts by performing the following:

a. Tighten bolts 1, 2, 3, and 4, in sequence, to 8 ft. lbs. (12 Nm).

b. Tighten bolts 5 through 16, in sequence, to 8 ft. lbs. (12 Nm).

c. Retighten all bolts, in sequence, to 12 ft. lbs. (16 Nm).

21. Install the pushrods and rocker arm assemblies.

22. Install the valve and rocker arm assemblies.

23. Install the valve covers. Install the vacuum supply solenoid and lines. Install the fuel and vacuum lines to the throttle body.

24. Install the distributor in its original position. Install the distributor cap and wire protectors.

25. Install the air-conditioning hose bracket.

26. Install the upper radiator hose and heater hose. If equipped, connect the MAP hoses.

27. Connect following wire connectors:

a. Distributor
b. Oil pressure switch
c. Coolant temperature sensor
d. EGR solenoid
e. ISC motor
f. Throttle position switch
g. If equipped, the electric EFE grid
h. Injectors
i. MAT sensor

28. Install cruise control servo and throttle valve cables.

29. Install the alternator bracket and alternator.

30. Install the power steering pump and tensioner assembly. Install the power steering line brace to the right side cylinder head.

31. Install the serpentine drive belt. Install the coolant reservoir.

32. Install the cross brace.

33. Fill the cooling system.

34. Install the air cleaner assembly.

35. Connect the negative battery cable.

36. Start the engine and check for coolant, oil, or fuel leaks. Allow the engine to come to normal operating temperature and recheck for leaks.

4.6L Engine

▶ **See Figures 22 thru 31**

1. Disconnect the negative battery cable.

2. Properly relieve the fuel system pressure.

3. Drain and recycle the engine coolant.

4. Remove the intake duct from the throttle body.

5. Disconnect the coolant hoses at the throttle body.

6. Detach the 2 electrical connectors at the intake manifold. Also the TP sensor, ISC motor, EVAP solenoid and cruise control servo.

7. Disconnect the vacuum hoses at the brake vacuum booster, and the fuel pipe bundle to the body.

8. Disconnect the PCV valve at the intake manifold.

9. Disconnect the accelerator cable at the throttle body and position it out of the way.

10. Detach the fuel pipe quick connects at the fuel pipe bundle in the engine compartment.

11. Remove the EVAP solenoid bracket at the rear cam cover.

12. Reposition the transaxle range control cable away from the cruise control servo.

13. Remove the 4 intake manifold bolts and lift

Fig. 22 Remove the appearance cover to gain access to the intake manifold

Fig. 23 Detach the vacuum connection from the throttle body

Fig. 24 Detach the throttle cable from the throttle body

Fig. 25 Remove the fuel line from the intake manifold

Fig. 26 Remove the intake manifold retaining bolts and . . .

Fig. 27 . . . lift the intake from the engine

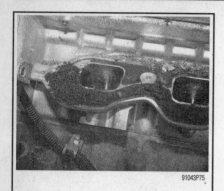

Fig. 28 Thoroughly clean the intake manifold mounting surfaces

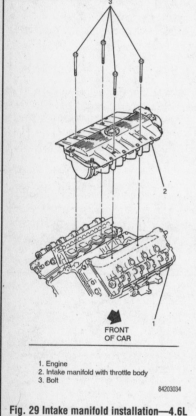

1. Engine
2. Intake manifold with throttle body
3. Bolt

84203034

Fig. 29 Intake manifold installation—4.6L engine

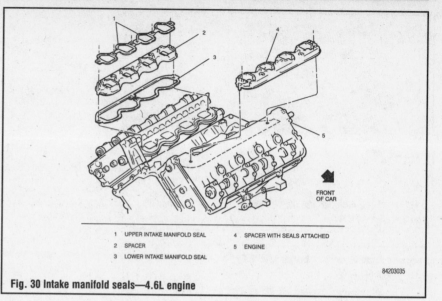

1 UPPER INTAKE MANIFOLD SEAL   4 SPACER WITH SEALS ATTACHED
2 SPACER   5 ENGINE
3 LOWER INTAKE MANIFOLD SEAL

84203035

Fig. 30 Intake manifold seals—4.6L engine

○ TORQUE (4) INTAKE MANIFOLD BOLTS IN
  SEQUENCE ABOVE TO 8 N•m (71 LB. IN.)
  THEN AN ADDITIONAL 120o (1/3 TURN).

◇ TORQUE (12) INTAKE MANIFOLD COVER
  BOLTS IN SEQUENCE ABOVE TO 12 N•m
  (106 LB. IN.).

1   INTAKE MANIFOLD
2   THROTTLE BODY
INTAKE MANIFOLD BOLTS
INTAKE MANIFOLD COVER BOLTS

84203036

Fig. 31 Intake manifold torque sequence—4.6L engine

the intake manifold with the throttle body out of the engine compartment.

14. Remove the intake manifold seals and spacers at the cylinder heads.

15. Remove the fuel pipe retainer at the ISC bracket.

16. Remove the 4 throttle body bolts and remove the throttle body from the intake manifold.

To install:

17. It is important to use a NEW throttle body seal on the throttle body coated with petroleum jelly.

Do not reuse the old throttle body seal because it may not seat properly. Do not

use any type of silicone lubricant on the seal or damage could result.

18. Install the throttle body with the 4 bolts to the intake manifold and tighten to 106 inch lbs. (12 Nm).

19. Install the fuel pipe retainer at the ISC bracket.

20. Install the intake manifold seals and spacers at the cylinder heads.

21. Install the intake manifold and throttle body with the 4 intake manifold bolts and tighten to the torque and sequence in the illustration.

22. Connect the coolant hoses at the throttle body and coolant reservoir and add coolant as necessary.

23. Position the transaxle range control cable away at the cruise control servo bracket.

24. Install the EVAP solenoid bracket at the rear cam cover.

25. Connect the fuel pipe quick connects at the fuel pipe bundle in the engine compartment.

26. Connect the accelerator cable at the throttle body.

27. Connect the vacuum hoses at the brake vacuum booster, fuel pipe bundle and to body.

28. Connect the PCV valve at the intake manifold.

29. Connect the 2 electrical connectors at the intake manifold. Also the TP sensor, ISC motor, EVAP solenoid and cruise control servo.

30. Install the intake duct to the throttle body.

31. Connect the negative battery cable.

Exhaust Manifold

REMOVAL & INSTALLATION

4.5L and 4.9L Engines

RIGHT

▶ **See Figures 32, 33, 34 and 35**

1. Disconnect the negative battery cable. Remove the air cleaner.

2. Remove the exhaust crossover pipe. Disconnect the oxygen and coolant temperature sensors.

3. Remove the catalytic converter-to-AIR pipe clip bolt. Remove the upper manifold-to-cylinder head bolts. Raise and safely support the vehicle.

4. Disconnect the converter air pipe bracket from the stud and remove the converter-to-manifold exhaust pipe.

5. Support the engine cradle with screw jacks and remove the rear cradle bolts. Loosen the front cradle bolts and slightly lower the Engine cradle.

6. Remove the remaining exhaust manifold-to-cylinder head bolts, the AIR pipe, and the manifold.

7. Clean the gasket mounting surfaces.

To install:

8. Install the exhaust manifold and replace the

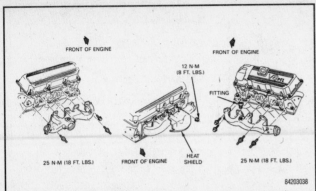

Fig. 32 Exhaust manifold installation—Fleetwood and Deville with the 4.5L engine

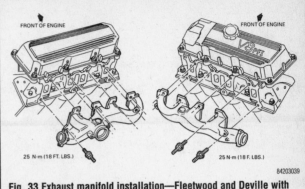

Fig. 33 Exhaust manifold installation—Fleetwood and Deville with the 4.9L engine

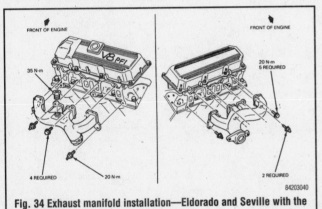

Fig. 34 Exhaust manifold installation—Eldorado and Seville with the 4.5L engine

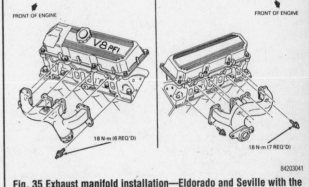

Fig. 35 Exhaust manifold installation—Eldorado and Seville with the 4.9L engine

AIR pipe. Tighten the manifold mounting bolts to 16–18 ft. lbs. (21–24 Nm).

9. Install the manifold-to-converter exhaust pipe and replace the converter air pipe bracket to the stud.

10. Raise the Engine cradle and install the rear cradle bolts. Tighten to 75 ft. lbs. (102 Nm).

11. Lower the vehicle. Replace the upper manifold-to-cylinder head bolts.

12. Replace the converter air pipe to AIR pipe clip bolt.

13. Connect the coolant temperature and oxygen sensor connectors. Replace the exhaust crossover pipe.

14. Replace the air cleaner and connect the negative battery cable.

15. Start the Engine and check for leaks.

LEFT

1. Disconnect the negative battery cable. Remove the cooling fan(s) and the exhaust crossover pipe.

2. Remove the serpentine drive belt and the AIR pump pivot bolt.

3. Remove the belt tensioner and the power steering pump brace.

4. Remove the exhaust manifold-to-cylinder head bolts, the AIR pipe, and the manifold.

To install:

5. Clean the gasket mounting surfaces.

6. Install the manifold, AIR pipe and exhaust manifold-to-cylinder head bolts. Tighten to 16–18 ft. lbs. (21–24 Nm).

7. Install the belt tensioner and the power steering pump brace.

8. Install the AIR pump pivot bolt and the serpentine drive belt.

9. Install both cooling fans and the exhaust crossover pipe.

10. Connect the negative battery cable.

4.6L Engine

▶ See Figure 36

LEFT

1. Disconnect the negative battery cable.

2. Remove the radiator cover panel. Remove the air cleaner assembly.

3. Disconnect the left and right engine torque struts and position out of the way.

4. Remove the engine cooling fans.

5. Install engine support fixture J 28467-A.

6. Raise and safely support the vehicle.

7. Remove the 2 nuts securing the motor mount to the engine cradle.

8. Remove the 2 bolts securing the motor mount bracket to the crankcase.

9. Remove the 2 bolts securing the motor mount bracket to the cylinder head.

10. Remove the 2 nuts securing the motor mount to the mount bracket.

11. Disconnect the Y-pipe from the front of the catalytic converter and position the converter out of the way.

12. Lower the vehicle.

13. Raise the engine by adjusting the engine support fixture.

14. Remove the motor mount and bracket.

15. Raise and safely support the vehicle.

16. Remove the rear alternator bracket.

17. Remove the 2 bolts at the manifold outlet flange.

18. Disconnect the oxygen sensor.

19. Remove the exhaust manifold from the cylinder head and remove the manifold.

20. Remove the gasket. Remove the oxygen sensor from the manifold.

To install:

21. Position the exhaust manifold by inserting the outlet pipe partially into the exhaust crossover pipe and moving the manifold into position.

22. Install the gasket to the manifold. Insert 2 screws to hold the gasket in place.

23. Tighten the manifold bolts to 20 ft. lbs. (24 Nm).

24. Coat the oxygen sensor threads with Hi temperature anti-seize compound and install the sensor. Tighten sensor nut to 30 ft. lbs. (40 Nm).

25. Connect the oxygen sensor connector. Install the rear alternator bracket. Tighten the crankcase bolts to 40 ft. lbs. (60 Nm) and the alternator bolts to 25 ft. lbs. (30 Nm).

26. Install 2 new bolts at the manifold outlet flange and tighten to 25 ft. lbs. (30 Nm).

27. Position the motor mount and bracket.

28. Loosely install the 2 nuts securing the mount to the bracket.

29. Lower the vehicle.

30. Loosely install the 2 screws securing the mount bracket at the cylinder head.

31. Lower the engine into the installed position guiding the motor mount studs in the cradle holes.

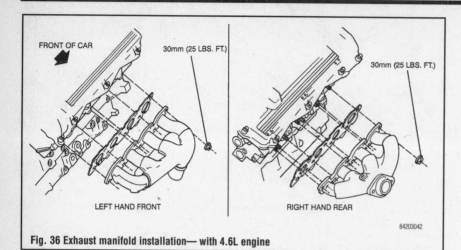

Fig. 36 Exhaust manifold installation— with 4.6L engine

(In figure: FRONT OF CAR; 30mm (25 LBS. FT.); LEFT HAND FRONT; 30mm (25 LBS. FT.); RIGHT HAND REAR; 84203042)

32. Raise the vehicle.

33. Loosely install the 2 nuts to the bottom of the motor mount.

34. Loosely install the 2 bolts securing the mount bracket to the crankcase.

35. Tighten the fasteners in the above steps to 25 ft. lbs. (30 Nm).

36. Install the 2 bolts at the converter to exhaust Y-pipe and tighten to 20 ft. lbs. (25 Nm).

37. Lower the vehicle.

38. Remove the engine support fixture J 28467-A.

39. Install the engine cooling fans.

40. Install the air cleaner assembly.

41. Connect the left and right engine torque struts and adjust and tighten.

42. Install the radiator trim panel.

43. Connect the negative battery cable.

RIGHT

1. Disconnect the negative battery cable.

2. Disconnect the rear oxygen sensor at the rear of the right cam cover. Disconnect the harness clip.

3. Raise and safely support the vehicle.

4. Disconnect the Y-pipe from the front of the catalytic converter.

5. Disconnect the suspension position sensor at lower control arm from both sides.

6. Disconnect the intermediate shaft from the steering gear.

7. Place a support below the rear cross member of the engine cradle and remove the 4 cradle to body bolts.

8. Lower the rear of the engine cradle and disconnect the Y-pipe from the exhaust crossover and from the manifold.

9. Remove the manifold nuts and remove the manifold.

10. Remove the gasket from the manifold. Replace if damaged. Remove the oxygen sensor from the manifold as necessary.

To install:

11. Coat the oxygen sensor threads with hi-temperature anti-seize compound. Tighten sensor to 30 ft. lbs. (40 Nm).

12. Install the gasket, manifold, and nuts. Tighten nuts to 25 ft. lbs. (30 Nm).

13. Install the exhaust Y-pipe and install 4 new bolts. Tighten the M10 bolts to 35 ft. lbs. (50 Nm) and the M8 bolts to 25 ft. lbs. (30 Nm).

14. Raise the engine cradle into position and tighten the bolts to 75 ft. lbs. (100 Nm).

15. Connect the intermediate shaft to the steering gear and tighten to 35 ft. lbs. (50 Nm).

16. Connect the exhaust Y-pipe to the catalytic converter and tighten 2 new bolts to 35 ft. lbs. (50 Nm).

17. Connect the suspension position sensors to the lower control arms.

18. Lower the vehicle and connect the oxygen sensor. Install the harness retainer.

19. Connect the negative battery cable.

Radiator

REMOVAL & INSTALLATION

4.5L and 4.9L Engines

1. Disconnect the negative battery cable.

2. Drain cooling system.

3. Remove the plastic radiator support cover.

4. Remove right and left cooling fans. On Eldorado and Seville, remove rear-cooling fan.

5. Disconnect coolant reservoir hose at filler neck.

6. Remove upper and lower radiator hoses from radiator.

7. Remove engine oil cooler lines and transaxle oil cooler lines from the radiator.

8. Remove the radiator top support.

9. Remove radiator from car, lifting radiator straight up and out.

To install:

10. Install radiator in vehicle.

11. Install radiator top support. Tighten radiator support retaining bolts to 18 ft. lbs. (25 Nm).

12. Connect transaxle oil cooler lines at radiator. Tighten to 20 ft. lbs. (27 Nm).

13. Connect oil cooler lines at radiator. Tighten to 13 ft. lbs. (18 Nm).

14. Install upper and lower radiator hoses to radiator securing hose clamps.

15. Connect coolant reservoir hose at filler neck.

16. Install cooling fan(s) and plastic radiator support cover.

17. Fill cooling system.

18. Connect negative battery cable.

19. Start the engine and check for leaks. Check transaxle fluids level and add, as necessary. Allow engine to come to normal operating temperature and check again for leaks.

4.6L Engine

▶ See Figures 37 thru 44

1. Disconnect the negative battery cable.

2. Drain the radiator coolant.

3. Disable the SIR (air bag) system.

4. Relocate the Forward Discriminating Sensor out of the way.

Fig. 37 Remove the Forward Discriminating Sensor retaining bolts and . . .

(91043P37)

Fig. 38 . . . position it out of the way

(91043P39)

Fig. 39 Disconnect the right and left engine support torque struts

(91043P48)

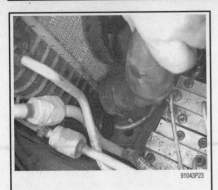

Fig. 40 Remove the radiator hoses from radiator

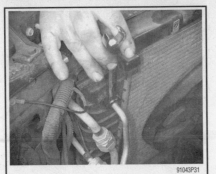

Fig. 41 Remove the transaxle cooler lines from the radiator side tank

Fig. 42 Remove the radiator support bolts from the top and . . .

Fig. 43 . . . the sides of the radiator

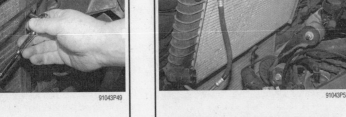

Fig. 44 Lift the radiator up and remove it from the engine compartment

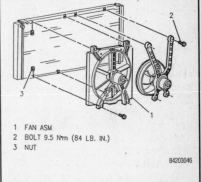

1	FAN ASM
2	BOLT 9.5 N·m (84 LB. IN.)
3	NUT

Fig. 45 Cooling fans—Deville, and Fleetwood

5. Disconnect the right and left engine support torque struts.

6. Remove the air cleaner assembly.

7. Remove the cooling fans.

8. Disconnect the upper and lower coolant hoses.

9. Disconnect the engine oil cooler lines from the right radiator end tank.

10. Disconnect the transaxle oil cooler lines from the left radiator end tank.

11. Remove the radiator top support retainers and lift the radiator up and out of the vehicle.

To install:

12. Position the radiator in the vehicle and tighten the radiator support retaining bolts to 5 ft. lbs. (7 Nm).

13. Connect the transaxle oil cooler lines to the left radiator end tank.

14. Connect the engine oil cooler lines to the right radiator end tank.

15. Connect the right and left engine support torque struts.

16. Connect the upper and lower coolant hoses.

17. Install the cooling fans.

18. Install the air cleaner assembly.

19. Reinstall the Forward Discriminating Sensor.

20. Enable the SIR (air bag) system.

21. Fill the radiator with coolant.

22. Connect the negative battery cable.

Engine Fan

REMOVAL & INSTALLATION

4.5L and 4.9L Engines

DEVILLE AND FLEETWOOD

▶ See Figure 45

➡ If your vehicle is equipped with air conditioning, refer to the information regarding the implications of servicing your A/C system yourself. Only a MVAC-trained, EPA-certified, automotive technician should service the A/C system or its components.

1. Disconnect the negative battery cable.

2. Raise and safely support the vehicle.

3. Detach the electrical connectors from the rear of the fan assemblies.

4. Remove the fan-to-lower radiator cradle bolts.

5. Lower the vehicle.

6. For the right fan removal, remove the air conditioning accumulator to gain working clearance.

7. Remove the air cleaner intake duct.

8. Remove the upper fan-to-radiator panel bolts and the upper radiator panel.

9. Remove the cooling fan assemblies.

To install:

10. Install the cooling fan(s). Replace the mounting bolts.

11. Replace the air cleaner intake duct.

12. Install the air conditioning accumulator, if removed.

13. Raise and safely support the vehicle.

14. Replace the fan-to-lower radiator cradle mounting bolts.

15. Connect the electrical connectors. Lower the vehicle.

16. Connect the negative battery cable.

FRONT FAN—ELDORADO AND SEVILLE

▶ See Figures 46 and 47

1. Disconnect the negative battery cable.

2. Remove the radiator cover panel.

3. Detach the electrical connector.

4. Remove the right headlight bracket.

5. Remove the fan-retaining bolts and remove the fan from the vehicle.

To install:

6. Install the fan to vehicle. Tighten to 88 inch lbs. (10 Nm).

7. Connect the electrical connector.

8. Install the right headlight bracket.

9. Install the radiator cover panel.

10. Connect negative battery cable.

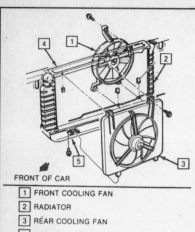

Fig. 46 Cooling fans—Eldorado and Seville with 4.5L engine

1. FRONT COOLING FAN
2. RADIATOR
3. REAR COOLING FAN
4. RADIATOR UPPER MOUNTING PANEL
5. LOWER RADIATOR CRADLE

84203047

REAR FAN—ELDORADO AND SEVILLE

1. Disconnect the negative battery cable.
2. Detach the fan electrical connector.
3. Remove the upper engine-to-radiator support torque strut and oil cooler line bracket from the fan.
4. Remove the fan-retaining bolts and remove the fan from the vehicle.

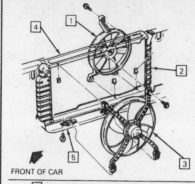

Fig. 47 Cooling fans—Eldorado and Seville with 4.9L engine

1. FRONT COOLING RAN
2. RADIATOR
3. REAR COOLING FAN
5. RADIATOR UPPER MOUNTING PANEL
6. RADIATOR SUPPORT LOWER TIE BAR

84203048

To install:

5. Install the fan in vehicle. Tighten bolts to 97 inch lbs. (11 Nm).
6. Connect the electrical connector.
7. Connect the upper engine-to-radiator support torque strut and oil cooler line bracket to the fan.

8. Tighten the torque strut-to-radiator mounting bolts to 17 ft. lbs. (23 Nm).
9. Connect the negative battery cable.

4.6L Engine

♦ See Figures 48 thru 53

1. Disconnect the negative battery cable.
2. Remove the beauty panel assembly.
3. Remove the left side engine torque support strut.
4. Position the upper radiator hose out of the way.
5. Detach the fan electrical connector.
6. Remove the retaining bolts and remove the fan(s).

To install:

7. Install the fan(s) to vehicle. Tighten the retaining bolts to 88 inch lbs. (10 Nm).
8. Connect the fan electrical connector.
9. Reposition the upper radiator hose and install the left side engine torque strut.
10. Install the beauty panel assembly and connect the negative battery cable.

TESTING

1. Check the fuse or circuit breaker for power to the cooling fan motor.
2. Remove the connector(s) at the cooling fan motor(s). Connect a jumper wire and apply battery voltage to the positive terminal of the cooling fan motor.

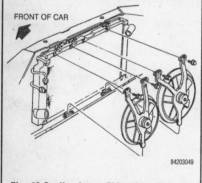

Fig. 48 Cooling fans—Eldorado and Seville with 4.6L engine

FRONT OF CAR

84203049

Fig. 49 The fan is held by two bolts at the top

91043P27

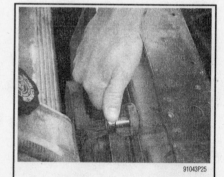

Fig. 50 Remove the bolts at the top of the fan

91043P25

Fig. 51 Detach the electrical connector from the fan

91043P29

Fig. 52 Grasp the fan and . . .

91043P28

Fig. 53 . . . lift it up to remove it from the engine

91043P35

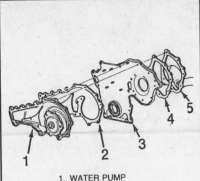

1. WATER PUMP
   ASSEMBLY
2. WATER PUMP GASKET
3. FRONT COVER
4. WATER PUMP INLET
   GASKET
5. WATER PUMP INLET

84203050

Fig. 54 Water pump assembly—4.5L and 4.9L engines

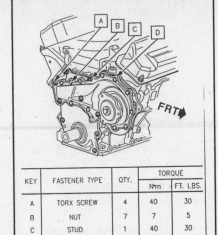

KEY	FASTENER TYPE	QTY.	TORQUE	
			N•m	FT. LBS.
A	TORX SCREW	4	40	30
B	NUT	7	7	5
C	STUD	1	40	30
D	HEX SCREW	7	7	5

84203051

Fig. 55 Water pump fasteners and torque—Deville and Fleetwood

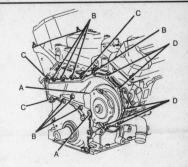

KEY	FASTENER TYPE	QTY.	TORQUE	
			N•m	FT. LBS.
A	TORX SCREW	2	40	30
B	NUT	7	7	5
C	HEX SCREW	3	40	30
D	HEX SCREW	5	7	5

84203052

Fig. 56 Water pump fasteners and torque—Eldorado and Seville with 4.5L and 4.9L engines

3. Using an ohmmeter, check for continuity in the cooling fan motor.

➡Remove the cooling fan connector at the fan motor before performing continuity checks. Perform continuity check of the motor windings only. The cooling fan control circuit is connected electrically to the PCM through the cooling fan relay center. Ohmmeter battery voltage must not be applied to the PCM.

4. Ensure proper continuity of cooling fan motor ground circuit at chassis ground connector.

Water Pump

✳✳ CAUTION

Never open, service, or drain the radiator or cooling system when hot; serious burns can occur from the steam and hot coolant. In addition, when draining engine coolant, keep in mind that cats and dogs are attracted to ethylene glycol antifreeze and could drink any that is left in an uncovered container or in puddles on the ground. This will prove fatal in sufficient quantities. Always drain coolant into a sealable container. Coolant should be reused unless it is contaminated or is several years old.

REMOVAL & INSTALLATION

4.5L and 4.9L Engines

▶ **See Figures 54, 55 and 56**

1. Disconnect the negative battery cable.
2. Drain and recycle the engine coolant.
3. Remove the air filter assembly. Disconnect and remove the coolant recovery tank.
4. Disconnect and remove the cross brace.
5. Remove the water pump pulley bolts.
6. Remove the serpentine drive belt and the water pump pulley.

7. Remove the water pump-to-engine bolts and the pump.

To install:

8. Clean the gasket mounting surfaces.
9. Place a new gasket over the water pump studs.
10. Install the water pump. Tighten the water pump bolts as follows:
   a. Water pump-to-engine Torx® bolts to 30 ft. lbs. (40 Nm)
   b. Water pump-to-engine stud nuts to 5 ft. lbs. (7 Nm)
   c. Hex head bolts to 30 ft. lbs. (40 Nm)
   d. Remaining hex head bolts to 5 ft. lbs. (7 Nm).
11. Install the water pump pulley. Install the water pump pulley bolts finger-tight.
12. Install the serpentine drive belt.
13. Tighten the water pump pulley bolts to 22 ft. lbs. (30 Nm).
14. Install the cross brace.
15. Install and connect the coolant recovery tank. Install the air filter assembly.
16. Connect the negative battery cable.
17. Fill cooling system and check for leaks. Start the engine and allow it to come to normal operating temperature. Recheck for leaks. Top-up the coolant.

➡**Because the engine block and radiator are aluminum, make sure the antifreeze solution is approved for use in cooling systems with a high aluminum content. GM recommends the use of a supplement/sealant 3634621 or equivalent, specifically designed for use in aluminum engines to protect the engine from damage.**

4.6L Engine

▶ **See Figures 57 thru 64**

1. Disconnect the negative battery cable.
2. Drain and recycle the engine coolant.
3. Remove the air cleaner assembly.
4. Remove the water pump pulley bolts.
5. Remove the water pump drive belt and the water pump pulley.
6. Remove the water pump-to-engine bolts and the pump.

To install:

7. Clean the gasket mounting surfaces.
8. Place a new gasket over the water pump studs.
9. Install the water pump and tighten the housing bolts to 5 ft. lbs. (7 Nm).
10. Install the water pump pulley. Install the water pump pulley bolts finger tight.

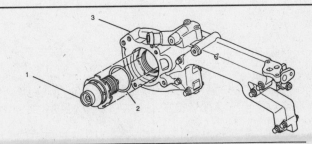

1	WATER PUMP ASM.
2	O-RING SEAL
3	WATER PUMP HOUSING ASM.

84203053

Fig. 57 Water pump assembly—4.6L engine

Fig. 58 Remove the water pump belt shield

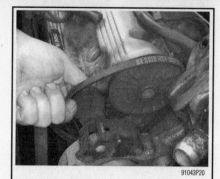

Fig. 59 Loosen the water pump belt adjuster and . . .

Fig. 60 . . . remove the belt from around the water pump

Fig. 61 Remove the water pump adjuster pulley retaining bolt and . . .

Fig. 62 . . . remove the pulley from the water pump

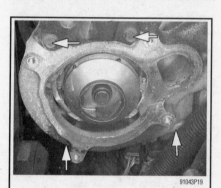

Fig. 63 Remove the water pump retaining bolts

Fig. 64 Remove the water pump from the engine and thoroughly clean the mounting surfaces

11. Install the drive belt.
12. Tighten the water pump pulley bolts to 22 ft. lbs. (30 Nm).
13. Install the air cleaner assembly.
14. Connect the negative battery cable.
15. Fill cooling system and check for leaks. Start the engine and allow it to come to normal operating temperature. Recheck for leaks. Top-up the coolant.

➡Because the engine block and radiator are aluminum, make sure the antifreeze solution is approved for use in cooling systems with a high aluminum content. GM recommends the use of a supplement/sealant 3634621 or equivalent, specifically designed for use in aluminum engines to protect the engine from damage.

Cylinder Head

REMOVAL & INSTALLATION

4.5L and 4.9L Engines

◆ See Figure 65

RIGHT SIDE

1. Disconnect the negative battery cable. Drain the engine coolant.
2. Remove rocker arm covers.
3. Remove the lower intake and right side exhaust manifolds.
4. Remove engine lift bracket and oil dipstick tube.

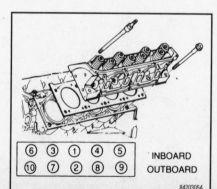

Fig. 65 Cylinder head torque sequence—4.5L and 4.9L engines

5. Reposition AIR bracket.
6. Remove 10 cylinder head bolts.
7. Remove cylinder head.

To install:

➡Clean sealing surfaces of cylinder head, block and liners. Clean cylinder head bolt holes with an appropriate tap. Ensure that bolt holes are free of shavings, oil and coolant.

8. Install new head gasket over dowels on cylinder block with either side facing up.
9. Install cylinder head.
10. Apply an appropriate lubricant to the threads of the head bolts. Install cylinder head bolts finger-tight.
11. Tighten cylinder head bolts, in sequence, to 38 ft. lbs. (50 Nm).
12. Tighten cylinder head bolts, in sequence, to 68 ft. lbs. (90 Nm).
13. Tighten No. 1, 3 and 4 cylinder head bolts to 90 ft. lbs. (120 Nm).
14. Install engine lift bracket and AIR bracket.
15. Install lower intake and right side exhaust manifolds.
16. Install rocker arm covers.
17. Fill cooling system.
18. Connect negative battery cable.
19. Start engine and check for coolant, oil and fuel leaks. Allow engine to come to normal operating temperature and recheck for leaks.

LEFT SIDE

1. Disconnect the negative battery cable.
2. Drain the cooling system.
3. Remove the rocker arm covers.

4. Remove the intake manifold-to-engine bolts and intake manifold.

5. Disconnect the exhaust manifold crossover pipe, the exhaust pipe-to-exhaust manifold bolts, the exhaust manifold-to-cylinder head bolts and the exhaust manifold.

6. Remove the engine lifting bracket and the dipstick tube.

7. Remove the AIR bracket-to-engine bolts and move the bracket aside.

8. Remove the cylinder head-to-engine bolts and the cylinder head.

To install:

9. Clean the gasket mounting surfaces.

10. Install new head gasket over dowels on cylinder block with either side facing up.

11. Install cylinder head.

12. Apply a suitable lubricant to the cylinder head bolt threads.

13. Install cylinder head bolts finger-tight.

14. Tighten bolts, in sequence, to 38 ft. lbs. (50 Nm).

15. Tighten cylinder head bolts, in sequence, to 68 ft. lbs. (90 Nm).

16. Tighten No. 1, 3 and 4 cylinder head bolts to 90 ft. lbs. (120 Nm).

17. Install AIR bracket. Install dipstick tube and engine lift bracket.

18. Install exhaust manifold. Install lower intake manifold.

19. Install rocker arm covers.

20. Fill cooling system.

21. Connect negative battery cable.

22. Start engine and check for coolant, oil and fuel leaks. Allow engine to come to normal operating temperature and recheck for leaks.

4.6L Engine

▶ **See Figure 66**

➡Because of the bulk and complexity of the 4.6L engine, cylinder head removal may best be accomplished with the engine out of the vehicle. For this procedure it may be most economical to remove the entire powertrain and cradle out the bottom of the body and to utilize the cradle as an engine stand.

1. Remove the powertrain assembly.

2. Remove the intake manifold, camshaft covers, harmonic balancer, front cover and oil pump.

3. Remove the chain tensioner from the timing chain for the cylinder head being removed.

4. Remove the cam sprockets from the head being removed. The timing chain remains in the chain case.

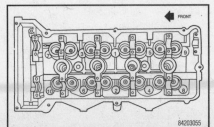

Fig. 66 4.6L cylinder head tightening sequence

5. Removing the timing chain guides. Access to the retaining screws is through the plugs at the front of the cylinder head.

6. Remove the water crossover.

7. Remove the exhaust manifold.

8. Remove the cylinder head bolts.

9. Remove the cylinder head and gasket.

✳✳ WARNING

With the camshafts remaining in the cylinder head some valves will be open at all times. Do not rest the cylinder head on a flat service with the cylinder face down, or valve damage will result.

To install:

10. Clean the gasket services and combustion chamber.

✳✳ WARNING

When cleaning aluminum gasket services, use only plastic or wood scrapers and/or an appropriate chemical dissolving agent to avoid damaging the sealing surfaces.

11. Using a new cylinder head gasket, install the cylinder head and the 10 M11 and 3 M6 head bolts. Lube the washer and the underside of the bolt head with engine oil prior to installation. Tighten the 10 M11 bolts in sequence to 22 ft. lbs. (30 Nm) plus 90°, plus an additional 90° for a total of 180°. Tighten the 3 M6 bolts to 10 ft. lbs. (12 Nm).

12. Install the camshafts.

13. Set the camshaft timing.

14. Install the camshaft guide bolt access hole plugs in the cylinder heads. The plugs should be seated and snug.

15. Install the intake manifold, camshaft covers, harmonic balancer, front cover and oil pump.

16. Install the water crossover.

17. Install the exhaust manifold.

18. Install the powertrain assembly.

Oil Pan

REMOVAL & INSTALLATION

4.5L and 4.9L Engines

▶ **See Figure 67**

1. Disconnect the negative battery cable. Raise and safely support the vehicle. Drain the crankcase.

2. Remove the 2 torque converter/flywheel covers from the lower side of the transaxle.

3. On the Eldorado and Seville, remove the exhaust crossunder pipe and reposition.

4. Remove the oil pan-to-engine bolts and the oil pan.

To install:

5. Clean the gasket mounting surfaces.

➡Apply a ¼ inch bead of RTV at the rear main bearing cap and front cover to block joints.

6. Install the oil pan and oil pan-to-engine bolts. Tighten to 14 ft. lbs. (18 Nm).

7. Install the exhaust crossunder pipe.

8. Install the 2 torque converter/flywheel covers.

9. Lower the vehicle.

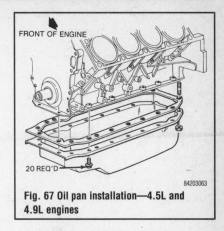

Fig. 67 Oil pan installation—4.5L and 4.9L engines

10. Fill the crankcase.

11. Connect the negative battery cable.

4.6L Engine

▶ **See Figures 68 and 69**

1. Remove the engine assembly and place it on a stand.

2. Drain the engine oil.

3. Remove the 13 oil pan bolts and remove the oil pan.

➡The oil pan gasket is reusable unless damaged. Do not remove the gasket from the oil pan groove unless replacement is required.

To install:

4. Install a new oil pan seal, if required by starting the seal into the pan groove and working the seal into the groove in both directions.

✳✳ WARNING

Once the seal is exposed to oil, it will expand and no longer stay in the groove without wrinkles. If this happens, replace with a new seal.

5. Position the oil pan to the crankcase and install the 13 retaining bolts. Tighten the bolts to 9 ft. lbs. (10 Nm) in the sequence shown.

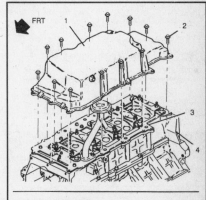

1	OIL PAN
2	OIL PAN BOLT
3	OIL MANIFOLD
4	LOWER CRANKCASE

Fig. 68 Oil pan installation—4.6L engine

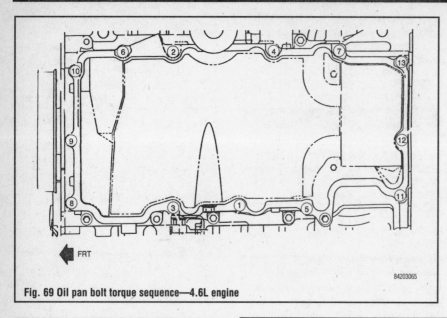

Fig. 69 Oil pan bolt torque sequence—4.6L engine

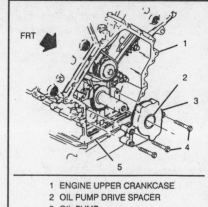

1 ENGINE UPPER CRANKCASE
2 OIL PUMP DRIVE SPACER
3 OIL PUMP
4 BOLT (3)
5 LOWER CRANKCASE

Fig. 71 Oil pump installation—4.6L engine

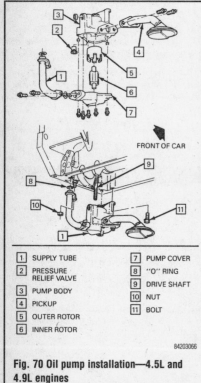

1	SUPPLY TUBE	7	PUMP COVER
2	PRESSURE RELIEF VALVE	8	"O" RING
3	PUMP BODY	9	DRIVE SHAFT
4	PICKUP	10	NUT
5	OUTER ROTOR	11	BOLT
6	INNER ROTOR		

Fig. 70 Oil pump installation—4.5L and 4.9L engines

6. Install the engine assembly and fill the crankcase with oil.

Oil Pump

REMOVAL & INSTALLATION

4.5L and 4.9L Engines

▶ See Figure 70

1. Raise and safely support the vehicle securely.
2. Remove the oil pan following the procedures outlined earlier in this chapter.

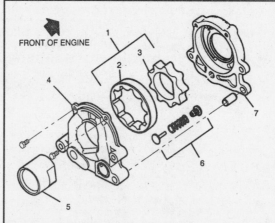

1 GEROTOR ASSEMBLY
2 OUTER GEAR
3 INNER GEAR
4 HOUSING
5 DRIVE SPACER
6 RELIEF VALVE
7 COVER

Fig. 72 Oil pump and components—4.6L engine

3. Remove the two screws and one nut securing the oil pump to the engine.

✳✳ CAUTION

The EPA warns that prolonged contact with used engine oil may cause a number of skin disorders, including cancer! You should make every effort to minimize your exposure to used engine oil. Protective gloves should be worn when changing the oil. Wash your hands and any other exposed skin areas as soon as possible after exposure to used engine oil. Soap and water, or waterless hand cleaner should be used.

To install:
4. Installation is the reversal of the removal procedure.

4.6L Engine

▶ See Figures 71 and 72

1. Remove the front cover.
2. Remove the three (3) oil pump mounting bolts.
3. Remove the pump and drive spacer.

To install:
4. Installation is the reversal of the removal procedure.

Crankshaft Damper

REMOVAL & INSTALLATION

4.5L Engine

▶ See Figures 73 and 74

1. Disconnect the negative battery cable.
2. Remove the serpentine belt.
3. Raise and safely support the vehicle securely.
4. Remove the right front wheel and tire.
5. Remove the right front air deflector.
6. Support the body of the car and the right side of the engine cradle.
7. Remove the right side cradle body bolts and lower the right side of the cradle.
8. Remove the crankshaft damper bolt and washer.
9. Install a puller and remove the damper.

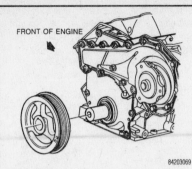

Fig. 73 Crankshaft and damper—4.5L and 4.9L engines

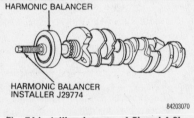

Fig. 74 Installing damper—4.5L and 4.9L engines

To install:

10. Lubricate the bore of the hub and seal with EP lubricant.

11. Position the damper on the crankshaft lining up the key slot in the hub with the key on the crankshaft.

12. Use installer J 29774 or equivalent, and bottom the hub out on the crankshaft.

13. Install the crankshaft damper bolt and washer and tighten to 60 ft. lbs. (80 Nm).

14. Raise the right side of the cradle.

➡ **Position the ball joint to the steering knuckle while raising.**

15. Support the body of the car and the right side of the engine cradle.

16. Install the right side engine cradle body bolts.

17. Install the right front air deflector.

18. Install the right front wheel and tire.

19. Lower the vehicle.

20. Connect the negative battery cable.

4.9L Engine

▶ **See Figures 73 and 74**

1. Disconnect the negative battery cable.

2. Remove the serpentine belt.

3. Raise and safely support the vehicle securely.

4. Remove the right front wheel and tire.

5. Remove the right front air deflector.

6. Loosen and reposition the heater by-pass line.

7. Remove the crankshaft damper bolt and washer.

8. Install a puller and remove the damper.

To install:

9. Lubricate the bore of the hub and seal with EP lubricant.

10. Position the damper on the crankshaft lining up the key slot in the hub with the key on the crankshaft.

11. Use installer J 29774 or equivalent, and bottom the hub out on the crankshaft.

12. Install the crankshaft damper bolt and washer and tighten to 70 ft. lbs. (95 Nm).

13. Install the right front air deflector.

14. Install the right front wheel and tire.

15. Lower the vehicle.

16. Connect the negative battery cable.

4.6L Engine

▶ **See Figures 75, 76 and 77**

1. Disconnect the negative battery cable.

2. Release tension from the accessory drive belt.

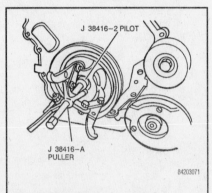

Fig. 75 Removing the harmonic balancer—4.6L engine

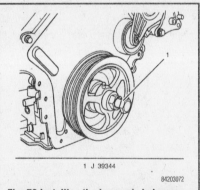

Fig. 76 Installing the harmonic balancer—4.6L engine

3. Raise and safely support the vehicle, remove the right front wheel.

4. Remove the splash shields from the wheelhouse and remove the brace between the oil pan and the transmission case.

5. Support the engine cradle and remove the 3 bolts from the right side of the cradle.

6. Disconnect the RSS sensor from the right lower control arm.

7. Install the flywheel holder tool J 39411 or equivalent and remove the balancer bolt.

8. Lower the engine cradle enough for clearance of puller tool.

9. Install pilot tool J39344-2 into the end of the crankshaft.

10. Remove the harmonic balancer using puller tool J38416 or equivalent.

To install:

11. Position the balancer to the crankshaft and using tool J39344 or equivalent, install the balancer.

12. Clean the balancer bolts threads and apply oil to the threads. Tighten the balancer bolt to 105 ft. lbs. (145 Nm); plus 120 degrees.

13. Raise the engine cradle into place and install the 3 bolts. Tighten the 3 bolts to 75 ft. lbs. (100 Nm).

14. Reconnect the suspension position sensors to the lower control arms.

15. Remove the flywheel holder tool and install the oil pan-to-transmission brace. Tighten the 4 bolts to 35 ft. lbs. (50 Nm).

16. Install the wheelhouse splash shields and the right front wheel.

17. Lower the vehicle and install the accessory drive belt.

18. Connect the negative battery cable.

Timing Chain Cover and Seal

REMOVAL & INSTALLATION

4.5L and 4.9L Engines

▶ **See Figures 78 and 79**

1. Disconnect the negative battery cable.

2. Remove the serpentine belt.

3. Raise and safely support the vehicle.

4. Remove the right front tire. Remove the right front air deflector.

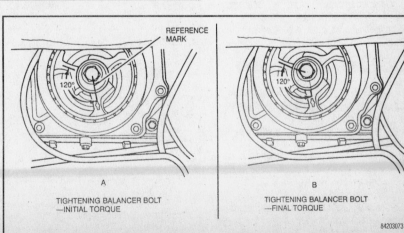

Fig. 77 Tightening the harmonic balancer bolt—4.6L engine

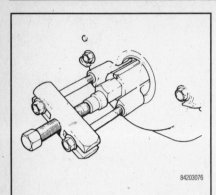

Fig. 78 Front cover oil seal removal—4.5L and 4.9L engines

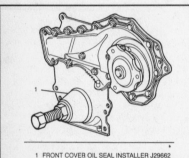

1 FRONT COVER OIL SEAL INSTALLER J29662

Fig. 79 Front cover oil seal installation— 4.5L and 4.9L engines

5. Loosen and reposition the heater bypass line.

6. Remove the crankshaft pulley-to-crankshaft pulley bolt. Attach a wheel puller to the crankshaft pulley. Using a pilot between the crankshaft and the center bolt, press the crankshaft pulley from the crankshaft. Remove the Woodruff® key from the crankshaft.

7. Using a small prybar, pry the oil seal from the timing case cover, and discard it.

To install:

8. Clean the oil seal mounting surface. Lubricate the new seal with engine oil.

9. Using a hammer and the oil seal installation tool, drive the new seal into the timing case cover until it seats.

10. Lubricate the bore of the hub and the inside diameter of the seal with EP lubricant to prevent seizure to the crankshaft and provide lubrication to the oil seal lip.

11. Position the damper onto the crankshaft, lining up the key slot in the hub with the key on the crankshaft.

12. Position the installer on end of the crankshaft. Position the thrust bearing with the inner race forward, then the washer. The installer nut is last. Install the damper on the crankshaft by tightening the installer nut.

13. The hub will bottom out on the crankshaft. Tighten the installer nut to 65 ft. lbs. (90 Nm) to ensure the balancer and timing gear are fully seated. Remove the installer and reinstall the bolt/washer into the crankshaft. Tighten to 65 ft. lbs. (90 Nm).

14. Install the heater bypass line.

15. Install the right front air deflector. Install the right front tire.

16. Install the serpentine belt.

17. Connect the negative battery cable.

4.6L Engine

▶ See Figures 80 and 81

1. Disconnect the negative battery cable.

2. Remove the harmonic balancer as described below:

a. Release tension from the accessory drive belt.

b. Raise and safely support the vehicle, remove the right front wheel.

c. Remove the splash shields from the wheelhouse and remove the brace between the oil pan and the transmission case.

d. Install the flywheel holder tool J 39411 or equivalent, and remove the balancer bolt.

e. Support the engine cradle and remove the 3 bolts from the right side of the cradle.

f. Disconnect the RSS sensor from the right lower control arm.

g. Lower the engine cradle enough for clearance of puller tool.

h. Install pilot tool J 39344–2 into the end of the crankshaft.

i. Remove the harmonic balancer using puller tool J 38416 or equivalent.

3. Using a small prybar, pry the oil seal out of the bore. Use caution not to damage the bore. Discard the old oil seal.

To install:

4. Clean the oil seal mounting surface. Lubricate the new seal with engine oil.

5. Install the new seal to the front cover, using

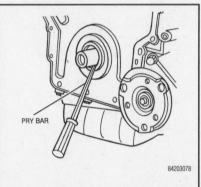

PRY BAR

Fig. 80 Front cover oil seal removal—4.6L engine

seal installer tool J 38818 and harmonic balancer installation tool J 39344, or equivalents.

6. Install the harmonic balancer as described below:

a. Position the balancer to the crankshaft and using tool J 39344 or equivalent, install the balancer.

b. Clean the balancer bolt threads and apply oil to the threads. Tighten the balancer bolt to 105 ft. lbs. (145 Nm), plus 120 degrees.

c. Raise the engine cradle into place and install the 3 bolts. Tighten the 3 bolts to 75 ft. lbs. (100 Nm).

d. Reconnect the suspension position sensors to the lower control arms.

e. Remove the flywheel holder tool and install the oil pan-to-transmission brace. Tighten the 4 bolts to 35 ft. lbs. (50 Nm).

f. Install the wheelhouse splash shields and the right front wheel.

g. Lower the vehicle and install the accessory drive belt.

h. Remove any excess RTV that is squeezed out of the sealing area.

7. Connect the negative battery cable.

Timing Chain and Gears

REMOVAL & INSTALLATION

4.5L and 4.9L Engines

▶ See Figure 82

1. Disconnect the negative battery cable. Remove the front cover.

2. Remove the oil slinger from the crankshaft. Rotate the engine to align the sprocket timing marks; the No. 1 cylinder will be on the TDC of its compression stroke.

3. From the camshaft, remove the camshaft thrust button and screw. Discard the camshaft thrust button. Slide the camshaft sprocket, the crankshaft sprocket and timing chain from the engine as an assembly.

To install:

4. Clean the gasket mounting surfaces. Inspect the parts for wear and/or damage; if necessary, replace the parts.

5. Install the timing chain and sprockets by performing the following:

a. Assemble the timing chain on the camshaft sprocket and crankshaft sprockets.

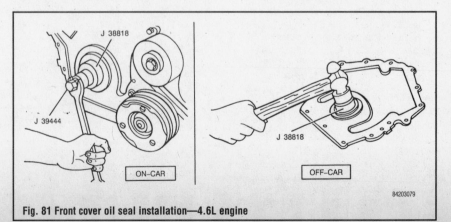

J 38818

J 39444

ON-CAR

J 38818

OFF–CAR

Fig. 81 Front cover oil seal installation—4.6L engine

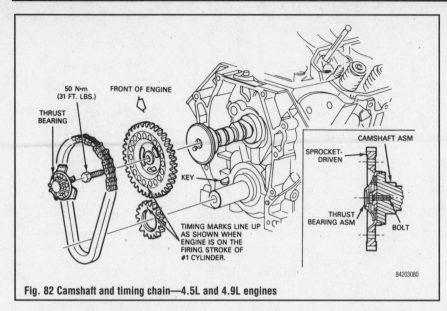

Fig. 82 Camshaft and timing chain—4.5L and 4.9L engines

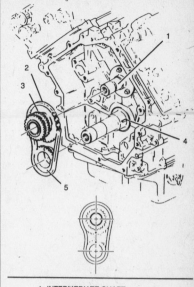

1 INTERMEDIATE SHAFT
2 PRIMARY CHAIN
3 INTERMEDIATE SHAFT SPROCKET
4 CRANKSHAFT SPROCKET KEY
5 SPROCKET

Fig. 83 Primary timing chain—4.6L engine

b. Align the timing marks on the sprockets; they must face each other.

c. Align the dowel pin in the camshaft with the index hole in the sprocket.

d. Slide the assembly onto the camshaft and crankshaft. Install the camshaft sprocket-to-camshaft bolts. Tighten the camshaft sprocket-to-camshaft sprocket bolt to 37 ft. lbs. (50 Nm).

6. Install the new thrust button and install the oil slinger to the crankshaft.

7. Install the front cover. Connect the negative battery cable.

8. Refill the cooling system. Start the engine, allow it to reach normal operating temperatures and check for leaks.

4.6L Engine

CAMSHAFT PRIMARY DRIVE CHAIN

▶ See Figure 83

1. Remove the engine assembly and put it on an engine stand or remove the powertrain assembly.

2. Remove the serpentine drive belt, idler pulley and belt tensioner, if not done previously.

3. Remove the front cover and oil pump.

4. Remove the cam covers.

5. Remove the three timing chain tensioners.

6. Remove the camshaft sprocket bolt from all four camshafts and remove the sprockets.

7. Remove the secondary drive chains from around the intermediate shaft sprocket.

8. Remove the one bolt holding the intermediate shaft sprocket and slide the gears and the primary drive chain off the crankshaft and intermediate shaft.

➡The intermediate shaft need not be removed unless wear is evident.

To install:

9. Retime the camshafts.

10. Install the oil pump.

11. Install the cam covers.

12. Install the serpentine drive belt, idler pulley, and belt tensioner.

13. Install the engine assembly or the powertrain assembly.

CAMSHAFT SECONDARY DRIVE CHAIN

▶ See Figure 84

1. Remove the front cover.

2. Remove the left side cam covers.

3. Remove the left side secondary chain tensioner.

4. Remove the left side chain guide. Access the upper chain guide mounting bolt through the hole in the cylinder head covered with the plastic plug.

5. Remove the left side cam sprocket bolts and sprockets.

6. Remove the secondary drive chain.

7. Repeat Steps 2 through 6 if the right side chain is being replaced.

To install:

8. Retime the camshafts.

9. Install the front cover.

10. Install the cam cover(s).

SETTING CAMSHAFT TIMING

4.6L Engine

▶ See Figures 85, 85 and 87

Setting camshaft timing is necessary whenever the cam drive system has been disturbed such that the relationship between any chain and sprocket has been lost. Correct timing exist when the crank sprocket and the intermediate shaft sprocket have their timing marks aligned and all 4 camshaft drive pins are perpendicular (90°) to the cylinder head surface.

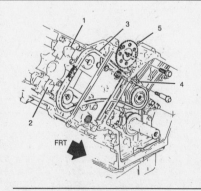
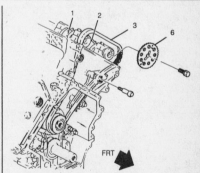

1 INTAKE CAMSHAFT
2 EXHAUST CAMSHAFT
3 SECONDARY CAM DRIVE CHAIN
4 CHAIN GUIDE

5 RH SPROCKET – INSTALL CAM PIN IN RE SLOT FOR EXHAUST POSITION; RI SLOT FOR INTAKE POSITION
6 LH SPROCKET – INSTALL CAM PIN IN LE SLOT FOR EXHAUST POSITION; LI SLOT FOR INTAKE POSITION

Fig. 84 Secondary timing chain—4.6L engine

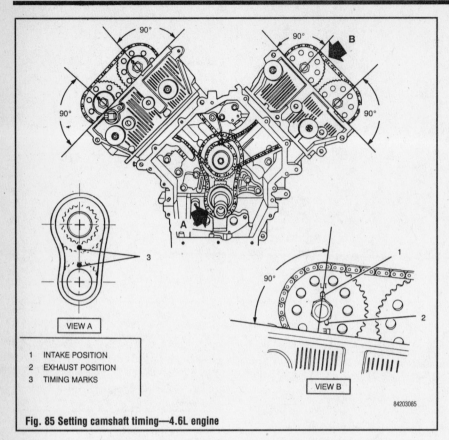

VIEW A

1	INTAKE POSITION
2	EXHAUST POSITION
3	TIMING MARKS

VIEW B

84203085

Fig. 85 Setting camshaft timing—4.6L engine

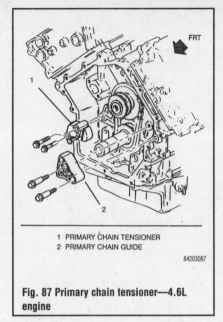

1	PRIMARY CHAIN TENSIONER
2	PRIMARY CHAIN GUIDE

84203087

Fig. 87 Primary chain tensioner—4.6L engine

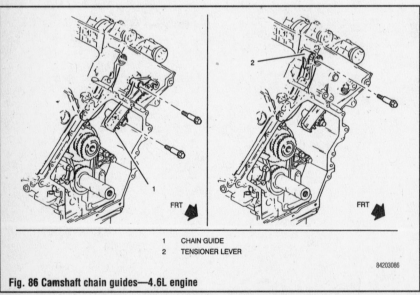

1	CHAIN GUIDE
2	TENSIONER LEVER

84203086

Fig. 86 Camshaft chain guides—4.6L engine

1. To allow access the following components must be removed:
   a. Both cam covers.
   b. Front cover
   c. The three chain tensioners. The tensioners may be in their installed positions but must be fully retracted.
   d. The oil pump.
2. The primary and secondary chain guides should be reinstalled if previously removed.
3. Rotate the crankshaft until the sprocket drive key is at approximately the 1 o'clock position. Use J 39946 to rotate the crankshaft.
4. Install the crankshaft and intermediate shaft sprockets to the primary drive chain with their timing marks adjacent to each other.
5. Install the crank and intermediate sprockets over their respective shafts.
6. Rotate the crankshaft as necessary to engage the crankshaft key in the sprocket without changing the relationship of the timing marks to each other. Use J 39946 to rotate the crankshaft.

7. Install the intermediate sprocket retainer bolt and tighten to 45 ft. lbs. (60 Nm).
8. Install the primary chain tensioner or release tensioner shoe. Tighten the two tensioner mounting bolts to 20 ft. lbs. (25 Nm).
9. Install flywheel holder J 39411 to lock the crankshaft in this position. If the engine is on a stand, an alternate method should be devised.
10. Route the secondary drive chain for the right side cylinder head over the inner row of the intermediate shaft teeth.
11. Route the secondary drive chain over the chain guide and install the exhaust cam sprocket to the chain such that the camshaft drive pin engages the sprocket notch RE (right head exhaust). There should be no slack in the lower section of the chain and the cam drive pin must be perpendicular to the cylinder head face.

➡The RE cam sprocket must contain the cam position sensor pick-up.

12. Install the intake cam sprocket into the chain so that the sprocket notch RI (right head intake) engages the camshaft drive pin remains perpendicular to the cylinder head face. A hex is cast into the camshafts behind the lobes for cylinder No. 1 (or No. 2, LH) so that an open-end wrench may be used to provide minor repositioning of the cams.
13. Loosely install the exhaust cam sprocket retainer bolt.
14. Loosely install the intake cam sprocket retainer bolt.
15. Install the chain tensioner or release tension on the shoe and tighten the tensioner mounting bolts to 20 ft. lbs. (25 Nm).
16. Tighten the cam sprocket bolts to 90 ft lbs. (120 Nm).
17. Route the secondary drive chain for the left side cylinder head over the inner row of the intermediate shaft teeth and repeat Steps 11 through 16 for left side cams. Left side cam sprockets are identified LI (left intake) and LE (left exhaust).

➡The RE cam sprocket must contain the cam position sensor pick-up.

Camshaft, Bearings and Lifters

REMOVAL & INSTALLATION

4.5L and 4.9L Engines

➡Valve lifters and pushrods should be kept in order so they can be reinstalled in their original position. Some engines will have both standard size 0.010 inch (0.25 mm) and oversize valve lifters as original equipment. The oversize lifters are etched with an O on their sides; the cylinder block will also be marked with an O if the oversize lifter is used.

1. Remove the intake manifold and gasket.
2. Remove the valve covers, rocker arm assemblies and pushrods.
3. If the lifters are coated with varnish, apply carburetor cleaning solvent to the lifter body. The solvent should dissolve the varnish in about 10 minutes.
4. Remove the lifters. A special tool for removing lifters is available, and is helpful for this procedure.

To install:

➡New lifters must be primed before installation, as dry lifters will seize when the engine is started. Submerge the lifters in SAE 10 oil, which is very thin. Carefully insert the end of a ⅛ inch (3 mm) drift into the lifter and push down on the plunger. Hold the plunger down while the lifter is still submerged; do not pump the plunger. Release the plunger. The lifter is now primed.

5. Coat the bottoms of the lifters, and the rollers with Molykote® or an equivalent molybdenum-disulfide lubricant before installation. Install the lifters and pushrods into the engine in their original order.
6. Install the intake manifold gaskets and manifold.
7. Position the rocker arms, pivots and bolts on the cylinder head. Position and install the rockers and rocker shaft.
8. Install the valve covers, connect the spark plug wires, and install the air cleaner assembly.

➡An additive containing EP lube, such as EOS, should always be added to crankcase oil for break-in when new lifters or a new camshaft is installed. This additive is generally available in automotive parts stores.

4.6L Engine

1. Remove the camshaft cover.
2. Remove the camshafts for the head being worked on.
3. Remove the valve lifters in order, and store on their camshaft face so that the residual oil is retained.

➡Retain the lifters in order so that they can be reinstalled in their original bores.

To install:
4. Install the valve lifters in their original bores.
5. Install the camshafts.
6. Install the camshaft cover.

Rear Main Seal

REMOVAL & INSTALLATION

4.5L and 4.9L Engines

▶ **See Figures 88 and 89**

➡To perform this procedure, use a Seal Removal tool J-26868 or equivalent, and a Seal Installer tool J-34604 or equivalent.

1. Remove the transaxle.
2. Unbolt and remove the flexplate from the rear end of the crankshaft.
3. Using a Seal Removal tool J-26868 or equivalent, remove the old seal. Thoroughly clean the seal bore of any leftover seal material with a clean rag.
4. Lubricate the lip of a new seal with wheel bearing grease. Position it over the crankshaft and into the seal bore with the spring facing inside the engine.
5. Using a Seal Installer tool J-34604 or equivalent, press the seal into place. The seal must be square (this is the purpose of the installer) and flush with the block to 1 mm indented.
6. To complete the installation, reverse the removal procedures. Tighten the flexplate-to-crankshaft bolts to 37 ft. lbs. (52 Nm). Refill the crankshaft. Operate the engine and check for leaks.

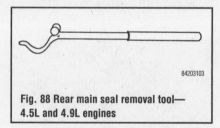

Fig. 88 Rear main seal removal tool—4.5L and 4.9L engines

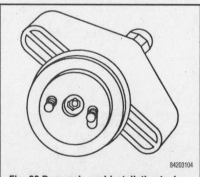

Fig. 89 Rear main seal installation tool—4.5L and 4.9L engines

4.6L Engine

▶ **See Figures 90 and 91**

1. Remove the transaxle assembly.
2. Remove the flexplate.

3. Use a suitable prying tool between the seal lips and the crankshaft and remove the seal.

✳✳ WARNING

Use extreme care to avoid damage to the crankshaft sealing surface. NOTE: The preferred method for removing the seal is by drilling a ⅛ inch hole in the metal seal body and removing with a body dent puller (slide hammer).

To install:
4. Place a small amount of RTV sealant at the crankshaft split line across the end of the upper/lower crankshaft seal.

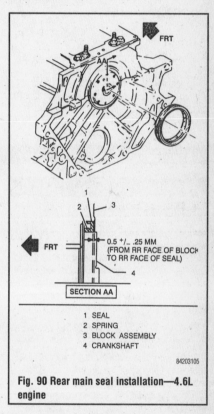

SECTION AA

1 SEAL
2 SPRING
3 BLOCK ASSEMBLY
4 CRANKSHAFT

0.5 +/_ .25 MM
(FROM RR FACE OF BLOCK TO RR FACE OF SEAL)

Fig. 90 Rear main seal installation—4.6L engine

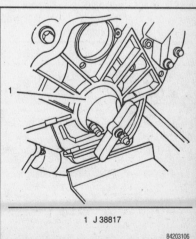

1 J 38817

Fig. 91 Installing the rear main seal—4.6L engine

5. Lubricate the rear main seal sealing lips with engine oil and slide the seal over the arbor of the seal installer J 38817. The greater spring faces in.

6. Thread the seal installer J 38818 into the crankshaft flange and install the seal by turning the handle until it bottoms against the crankcase.

7. Install the flywheel.

8. Install the transaxle assembly.

Flywheel/Flexplate

REMOVAL & INSTALLATION

4.5L, 4.6L and 4.9L Engines

▸ See Figures 92 and 93

1. Remove the transaxle.

2. Remove the 6 bolts (4.5L and 4.9L engines) or 8 bolts (4.6L engine) attaching the flywheel to the crankshaft flange. Remove the flywheel.

3. Inspect the flywheel for cracks, and inspect the ring gear for burrs or worn teeth. Replace the flywheel if any damage is apparent. Remove burrs with a mill file.

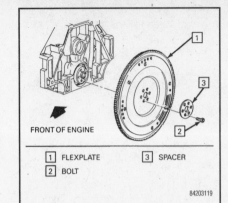

| 1 | FLEXPLATE | 3 | SPACER |
| 2 | BOLT | | |

84203119

Fig. 92 Flywheel/flexplate installation— 4.5L and 4.9L engines

4. Install the flywheel. The flywheel will only attach to the crankshaft in one position, as the bolt holes are unevenly spaced. Install the bolts and tighten to 70 ft. lbs. (95 Nm) for the 4.5L and 4.9L engines, and 11 ft. lbs. (15 Nm) plus an additional 50° turn for the 4.6L engine.

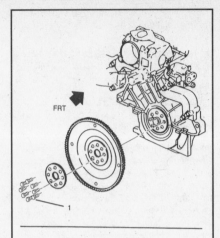

1 15 N•m +50° (11 lbs. ft. +50°)

84203120

Fig. 93 Flywheel/flexplate installation— 4.6L engine

EXHAUST SYSTEM

Inspection

▸ See Figures 94 thru 100

➡Safety glasses should be worn at all times when working on or near the exhaust system. Older exhaust systems will almost always be covered with loose rust particles which will shower you when disturbed. These particles are more than a nuisance and could injure your eye.

✳✳ CAUTION

DO NOT perform exhaust repairs or inspection with the engine or exhaust hot. Allow the system to cool completely before attempting any work. Exhaust systems are noted for sharp edges, flaking metal and rusted bolts. Gloves and eye protection are required. A healthy supply of penetrating oil and rags is highly recommended.

Your vehicle must be raised and supported safely to inspect the exhaust system properly. By placing 4 safety stands under the vehicle for support should provide enough room for you to slide

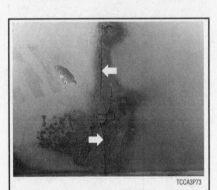

TCCA3P73

Fig. 94 Cracks in the muffler are a guaranteed leak

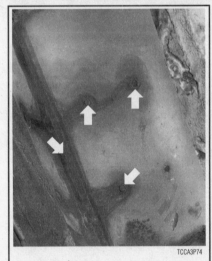

TCCA3P74

Fig. 95 Check the muffler for rotted spot welds and seams

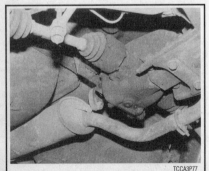

TCCA3P77

Fig. 96 Make sure the exhaust components are not contacting the body or suspension

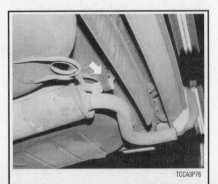

TCCA3P78

Fig. 97 Check for overstretched or torn exhaust hangers

TCCA3P75

Fig. 98 Example of a badly deteriorated exhaust pipe

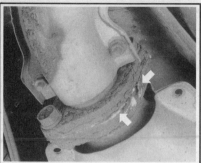

Fig. 99 Inspect flanges for gaskets that have deteriorated and need replacement

Fig. 100 Some systems, like this one, use large O-rings (doughnuts) in between the flanges

under the vehicle and inspect the system completely. Start the inspection at the exhaust manifold or turbocharger pipe where the header pipe is attached and work your way to the back of the vehicle. On dual exhaust systems, remember to inspect both sides of the vehicle. Check the complete exhaust system for open seams, holes loose connections, or other deterioration which could permit exhaust fumes to seep into the passenger compartment. Inspect all mounting brackets and hangers for deterioration, some models may have rubber O-rings that can be overstretched and non-supportive. These components will need to be replaced if found. It has always been a practice to use a pointed tool to poke up into the exhaust system where the deterioration spots are to see whether or not they crumble. Some models may have heat shield covering certain parts of the exhaust system , it will be necessary to remove these shields to have the exhaust visible for inspection also.

REPLACEMENT

▶ **See Figure 101**

There are basically two types of exhaust systems. One is the flange type where the component ends are attached with bolts and a gasket in-between.

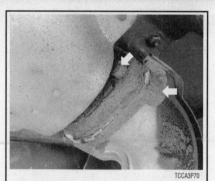

Fig. 101 Nuts and bolts will be extremely difficult to remove when deteriorated with rust

The other exhaust system is the slip joint type. These components slip into one another using clamps to retain them together.

✴✴ CAUTION

Allow the exhaust system to cool sufficiently before spraying a solvent exhaust fasteners. Some solvents are highly flammable and could ignite when sprayed on hot exhaust components.

Before removing any component of the exhaust system, ALWAYS squirt a liquid rust dissolving agent onto the fasteners for ease of removal. A lot of knuckle skin will be saved by following this rule. It may even be wise to spray the fasteners and allow them to sit overnight.

Flange Type

▶ **See Figure 102**

✴✴ CAUTION

Do NOT perform exhaust repairs or inspection with the engine or exhaust hot. Allow the system to cool completely before attempting any work. Exhaust systems are

Fig. 102 Example of a flange type exhaust system joint

noted for sharp edges, flaking metal and rusted bolts. Gloves and eye protection are required. A healthy supply of penetrating oil and rags is highly recommended. Never spray liquid rust dissolving agent onto a hot exhaust component.

Before removing any component on a flange type system, ALWAYS squirt a liquid rust dissolving agent onto the fasteners for ease of removal. Start by unbolting the exhaust piece at both ends (if required). When unbolting the headpipe from the manifold, make sure that the bolts are free before trying to remove them. if you snap a stud in the exhaust manifold, the stud will have to be removed with a bolt extractor, which often means removal of the manifold itself. Next, disconnect the component from the mounting; slight twisting and turning may be required to remove the component completely from the vehicle. You may need to tap on the component with a rubber mallet to loosen the component. If all else fails, use a hacksaw to separate the parts. An oxy-acetylene cutting torch may be faster but the sparks are DANGEROUS near the fuel tank, and at the very least, accidents could happen, resulting in damage to the under-car parts, not to mention yourself.

Slip Joint Type

▶ **See Figure 103**

Before removing any component on the slip joint type exhaust system, ALWAYS squirt a liquid rust dissolving agent onto the fasteners for ease of removal. Start by unbolting the exhaust piece at both ends (if required). When unbolting the headpipe from the manifold, make sure that the bolts are free before trying to remove them. if you snap a stud in the exhaust manifold, the stud will have to be removed with a bolt extractor, which often means removal of the manifold itself. Next, remove the mounting U-bolts from around the exhaust pipe you are extracting from the vehicle. Don't be surprised if the U-bolts break while removing the nuts. Loosen the exhaust pipe from any mounting brackets retaining it to the floor pan and separate the components.

Fig. 103 Example of a common slip joint type system

ENGINE RECONDITIONING

Determining Engine Condition

Anything that generates heat and/or friction will eventually burn or wear out (for example, a light bulb generates heat, therefore its life span is limited). With this in mind, a running engine generates tremendous amounts of both; friction is encountered by the moving and rotating parts inside the engine and heat is created by friction and combustion of the fuel. However, the engine has systems designed to help reduce the effects of heat and friction and provide added longevity. The oiling system reduces the amount of friction encountered by the moving parts inside the engine, while the cooling system reduces heat created by friction and combustion. If either system is not maintained, a breakdown will be inevitable. Therefore, you can see how regular maintenance can affect the service life of your vehicle. If you do not drain, flush, and refill your cooling system at the proper intervals, deposits will begin to accumulate in the radiator, thereby reducing the amount of heat it can extract from the coolant. The same applies to your oil and filter; if it is not changed often enough it becomes laden with contaminates and is unable to properly lubricate the engine. This increases friction and wear.

There are a number of methods for evaluating the condition of your engine. A compression test can reveal the condition of your pistons, piston rings, cylinder bores, head gasket(s), valves, and valve seats. An oil pressure test can warn you of possible engine bearing, or oil pump failures. Excessive oil consumption, evidence of oil in the engine air intake area and/or bluish smoke from the tailpipe may indicate worn piston rings, worn valve guides, and/or valve seals. Generally, an engine that uses no more than one quart of oil every 1000 miles is in good condition. Engines that use one quart of oil or more in less than 1000 miles should first be checked for oil leaks. If any oil leaks are present, have them fixed before determining how much oil is consumed by the engine, especially if blue smoke is not visible at the tailpipe.

COMPRESSION TEST

▶ **See Figure 104**

A noticeable lack of engine power, excessive oil consumption, and/or poor fuel mileage measured over an extended period are all indicators of internal engine wear. Worn piston rings, scored or worn cylinder bores, blown head gaskets, sticking or burnt valves, and worn valve seats are all possible culprits. A check of the compression of each cylinder will help locate the problem.

➡**A screw-in type compression gauge is more accurate than the type you simply hold against the spark plug hole. Although it takes slightly longer to use, it is worth the effort to obtain a more accurate reading.**

1. Make sure that the proper amount and viscosity of engine oil is in the crankcase, then ensure the battery is fully charged.
2. Warm-up the engine to normal operating temperature, then shut the engine **OFF**.
3. Disable the ignition system.

4. Label and disconnect all of the spark plug wires from the plugs.
5. Thoroughly clean the cylinder head area around the spark plug ports, then remove the spark plugs.
6. Set the throttle plate to the fully open (wide-open throttle) position. You can block the accelerator linkage open for this, or you can have an assistant fully depress the accelerator pedal.
7. Install a screw-in type compression gauge into the No. 1 spark plug hole until the fitting is snug.

✳✳ WARNING

Be careful not to crossthread the spark plug hole.

8. According to the tool manufacturer's instructions, connect a remote starting switch to the starting circuit.
9. With the ignition switch in the **OFF** position, use the remote starting switch to crank the engine through at least five compression strokes (approximately 5 seconds of cranking) and record the highest reading on the gauge.
10. Repeat the test on each cylinder, cranking the engine approximately the same number of compression strokes and/or time as the first.
11. Compare the highest readings from each cylinder to that of the others. The indicated compression pressures are considered within specifications if the lowest reading cylinder is within 75 percent of the pressure recorded for the highest reading cylinder. For example, if your highest reading cylinder pressure was 150 psi (1034 kPa), then 75 percent of that would be 113 psi (779 kPa). Therefore, the lowest reading cylinder should be no less than 113 psi (779 kPa).
12. If a cylinder exhibits an unusually low compression reading, pour a tablespoon of clean engine oil into the cylinder through the spark plug hole and repeat the compression test. If the compression rises after adding oil, it means that the cylinder's piston rings and/or cylinder bore are damaged or worn. If the pressure remains low, the valves may not be seating properly (a valve job is needed), or the head gasket may be blown near that cylinder. If compression in any two adjacent cylinders is low, and if the addition of oil doesn't help raise compression, there is leakage past the head gasket. Oil

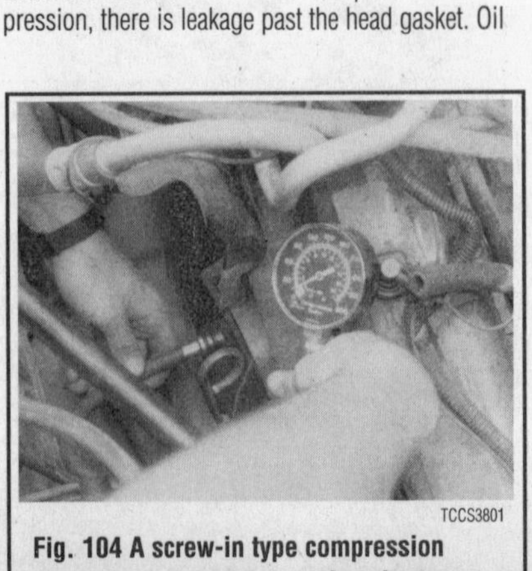

TCCS3801

Fig. 104 A screw-in type compression gauge is more accurate and easier to use without an assistant

and coolant in the combustion chamber, combined with blue or constant white smoke from the tailpipe, are symptoms of this problem. However, don't be alarmed by the normal white smoke emitted from the tailpipe during engine warm-up or from cold weather driving. There may be evidence of water droplets on the engine dipstick and/or oil droplets in the cooling system if a head gasket is blown.

OIL PRESSURE TEST

Check for proper oil pressure at the sending unit passage with an externally mounted mechanical oil pressure gauge (as opposed to relying on a factory installed dash-mounted gauge). A tachometer may also be needed, as some specifications may require running the engine at a specific rpm.

1. With the engine cold, locate and remove the oil pressure sending unit.
2. Following the manufacturer's instructions, connect a mechanical oil pressure gauge and, if necessary, a tachometer to the engine.
3. Start the engine and allow it to idle.
4. Check the oil pressure reading when cold and record the number. You may need to run the engine at a specified rpm, so check the specifications.
5. Run the engine until normal operating temperature is reached (upper radiator hose will feel warm).
6. Check the oil pressure reading again with the engine hot and record the number. Turn the engine **OFF**.
7. Compare your hot oil pressure reading to that given in the chart. If the reading is low, check the cold pressure reading against the chart. If the cold pressure is well above the specification, and the hot reading was lower than the specification, you may have the wrong viscosity oil in the engine. Change the oil, making sure to use the proper grade and quantity, then repeat the test.

Low oil pressure readings could be attributed to internal component wear, pump related problems, a low oil level, or oil viscosity that is too low. High oil pressure readings could be caused by an overfilled crankcase, too high of an oil viscosity or a faulty pressure relief valve.

Buy or Rebuild?

Now that you have determined that your engine is worn out, you must make some decisions. The question of whether or not an engine is worth rebuilding is largely a subjective matter and one of personal worth. Is the engine a popular one, or is it an obsolete model? Are parts available? Will it get acceptable gas mileage once it is rebuilt? Is the car it's being put into worth keeping? Would it be less expensive to buy a new engine, have your engine rebuilt by a pro, rebuild it yourself or buy a used engine from a salvage yard? On the other hand, would it be simpler and less expensive to buy another car? If you have considered all these matters and more, and have still decided to rebuild the engine, then it is time to decide how you will rebuild it.

➡**The editors at Chilton feel that most engine machining should be performed by a profes-**

sional machine shop. Don't think of it as wasting money, rather, as an assurance that the job has been done right the first time. There are many expensive and specialized tools required to perform such tasks as boring and honing an engine block or having a valve job done on a cylinder head. Even inspecting the parts requires expensive micrometers and gauges to properly measure wear and clearances. In addition, a machine shop can deliver to you clean, and ready to assemble parts, saving you time and aggravation. Your maximum savings will come from performing the removal, disassembly, assembly and installation of the engine and purchasing or renting only the tools required to perform the above tasks. Depending on the particular circumstances, you may save 40 to 60 percent of the cost doing these yourself.

A complete rebuild or overhaul of an engine involves replacing all of the moving parts (pistons, rods, crankshaft, camshaft, etc.) with new ones and machining the non-moving wearing surfaces of the block and heads. Unfortunately, this may not be cost effective. For instance, your crankshaft may have been damaged or worn, but it can be machined undersize for a minimal fee.

So, as you can see, you can replace everything inside the engine, but, it is wiser to replace only those parts which are really needed, and, if possible, repair the more expensive ones. Later we will break the engine down into its two main components: the cylinder head and the engine block. We will discuss each component, and the recommended parts to replace during a rebuild on each.

Engine Overhaul Tips

Most engine overhaul procedures are fairly standard. In addition to specific parts replacement procedures and specifications for your individual engine, this section is also a guide to acceptable rebuilding procedures. Examples of standard rebuilding practice are given and should be used along with specific details concerning your particular engine.

Competent and accurate machine shop services will ensure maximum performance, reliability and engine life. In most instances it is more profitable for the do-it-yourself mechanic to remove, clean and inspect the component, buy the necessary parts and deliver these to a shop for actual machine work.

Much of the assembly work (crankshaft, bearings, piston rods, and other components) is well within the scope of the do-it-yourself mechanic's tools and abilities. You will have to decide for yourself the depth of involvement you desire in an engine repair or rebuild.

TOOLS

The tools required for an engine overhaul or parts replacement will depend on the depth of your involvement. With a few exceptions, they will be the tools found in a mechanic's tool. More in-depth work will require some or all of the following:

- A dial indicator (reading in thousandths) mounted on a universal base
- Micrometers and telescope gauges
- Jaw and screw-type pullers
- Scraper
- Valve spring compressor
- Ring groove cleaner
- Piston ring expander and compressor
- Ridge reamer
- Cylinder hone or glaze breaker
- Plastigage®
- Engine stand

The use of most of these tools is illustrated in this section. Many can be rented for a one-time use from a local parts jobber or tool supply house specializing in automotive work.

Occasionally, the use of special tools is called for. See the information on Special Tools and the Safety Notice in the front of this book before substituting another tool.

OVERHAUL TIPS

Aluminum has become extremely popular for use in engines, due to its low weight. Observe the following precautions when handling aluminum parts:

- Never hot tank aluminum parts (the caustic hot tank solution will eat the aluminum.
- Remove all aluminum parts (identification tag, etc.) from engine parts prior to the tanking.
- Always coat threads lightly with engine oil or anti-seize compounds before installation, to prevent seizure.
- Never overtighten bolts or spark plugs especially in aluminum threads.

When assembling the engine, any parts that will be exposed to frictional contact must be prelubed to provide lubrication at initial start-up. Any product

specifically formulated for this purpose can be used, but engine oil is not recommended as a pre-lube in most cases.

When semi-permanent (locked, but removable) installation of bolts or nuts is desired, threads should be cleaned and coated with Loctite® or another similar, commercial non-hardening sealant.

CLEANING

▶ See Figures 105, 106, 107 and 108

Before the engine and its components are inspected, they must be thoroughly cleaned. You will need to remove any engine varnish, oil sludge and/or carbon deposits from all of the components to insure an accurate inspection. A crack in the engine block or cylinder head can easily become overlooked if hidden by a layer of sludge or carbon.

Most of the cleaning process can be carried out with common hand tools and readily available solvents or solutions. Carbon deposits can be chipped away using a hammer and a hard wooden chisel. Old gasket material and varnish or sludge can usually be removed using a scraper and/or cleaning solvent. Extremely stubborn deposits may require the use of a power drill with a wire brush. If using a wire brush, use extreme care around any critical machined surfaces (such as the gasket surfaces, bearing saddles, cylinder bores, etc.). Use of a wire brush is NOT RECOMMENDED on any aluminum components. Always follow any safety recommendations given by the manufacturer of the tool and/or solvent. You should always wear eye protection during any cleaning process involving scraping, chipping, or spraying of solvents.

An alternative to the mess and hassle of cleaning the parts yourself is to drop them off at a local garage or machine shop. They will, more than likely, have the necessary equipment to properly clean all of the parts for a nominal fee.

✳✳ CAUTION

Always wear eye protection during any cleaning process involving scraping, chipping, or spraying of solvents.

Remove any oil galley plugs, freeze plugs and/or pressed-in bearings and carefully wash and degrease all of the engine components including the fasteners and bolts. Small parts such as the valves, springs, etc., should be placed in a metal basket and allowed to soak. Use pipe cleaner type brushes, and clean all

TCCS3132

Fig. 105 Use a gasket scraper to remove the old gasket material from the mating surfaces

TCCS3211

Fig. 106 Use a ring expander tool to remove the piston rings

TCCS3208

Fig. 107 Clean the piston ring grooves using a ring groove cleaner tool, or . . .

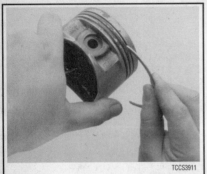

Fig. 108 . . . use a piece of an old ring to clean the grooves. Be careful, the ring can be quite sharp

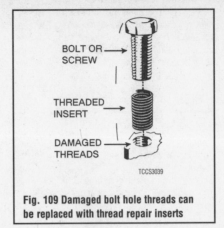

Fig. 109 Damaged bolt hole threads can be replaced with thread repair inserts

Fig. 110 Standard thread repair insert (left), and spark plug thread insert

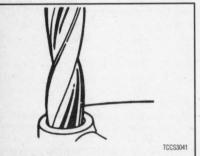

Fig. 111 Drill out the damaged threads with the specified size bit. Be sure to drill completely through the hole or to the bottom of a blind hole

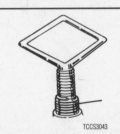

Fig. 112 Using the kit, tap the hole in order to receive the thread insert. Keep the tap well oiled and back it out frequently to avoid clogging the threads

Fig. 113 Screw the insert onto the installer tool until the tang engages the slot. Thread the insert into the hole until it is ¼–½ turn below the top surface, then remove the tool and break off the tang using a punch

passageways in the components. Use a ring expander and remove the rings from the pistons. Clean the piston ring grooves with a special tool or a piece of broken ring. Scrape the carbon off of the top of the piston. You should never use a wire brush on the pistons. After preparing all of the piston assemblies in this manner, wash and degrease them again.

✳✳ WARNING

Use extreme care when cleaning around the cylinder head valve seats. A mistake or slip may cost you a new seat.

When cleaning the cylinder head, remove carbon from the combustion chamber with the valves installed. This will avoid damaging the valve seats.

REPAIRING DAMAGED THREADS

♦ **See Figures 109, 110, 111, 112 and 113**

Several methods of repairing damaged threads are available. Heli-Coil® (shown here), Keenserts®, and Microdot® are among the most widely used. All involve basically the same principle—drilling out stripped threads, tapping the hole and installing a prewound insert—making welding, plugging and oversize fasteners unnecessary.

Two types of thread repair inserts are usually supplied: a standard type for most inch coarse, inch fine, metric course and metric fine thread sizes and a spark lug type to fit most spark plug port sizes. Consult the individual tool manufacturer's catalog to determine exact applications. Typical thread repair kits will contain a selection of prewound threaded

inserts, a tap (corresponding to the outside diameter threads of the insert) and an installation tool. Spark plug inserts usually differ because they require a tap equipped with pilot threads and a combined reamer/tap section. Most manufacturers also supply blister-packed thread repair inserts separately in addition to a master kit containing a variety of taps and inserts plus installation tools.

Before attempting to repair a threaded hole, remove any snapped, broken or damaged bolts or studs. Penetrating oil can be used to free frozen threads. The offending item can usually be removed with locking pliers or using a screw/stud extractor. After the hole is clear, the thread can be repaired, as shown in the series of accompanying illustrations and in the kit manufacturer's instructions.

Engine Preparation

To properly rebuild an engine, you must first remove it from the vehicle, then disassemble and diagnose it. Ideally you should place your engine on an engine stand. This affords you the best access to the engine components. Follow the manufacturer's directions for using the stand with your particular engine. Remove the flywheel or flexplate before installing the engine to the stand.

Now that you have the engine on a stand, and assuming that you have drained the oil and coolant from the engine, it's time to strip it of all but the necessary components. Before you start disassembling the engine, you may want to take a moment to draw some pictures, or fabricate some labels or containers to mark the locations of various components and the bolts and/or studs which fasten them.

Modern day engines use a lot of little brackets and clips which hold wiring harnesses and such, and these holders are often mounted on studs and/or bolts that can be easily mixed up. The manufacturer spent a lot of time and money designing your vehicle, and they would not have wasted any of it by haphazardly placing brackets, clips or fasteners on the vehicle. If it's present when you disassemble it, put it back when you assemble, you will regret not remembering that little bracket which holds a wire harness out of the path of a rotating part.

You should begin by unbolting any accessories still attached to the engine, such as the water pump, power steering pump, alternator, etc. Then, unfasten any manifolds (intake or exhaust) which were not removed during the engine removal procedure. Finally, remove any covers remaining on the engine such as the rocker arm, front, or timing cover and oil pan. Some front covers may require the vibration damper and/or crank pulley to be removed beforehand. The idea is to reduce the engine to the bare necessities (cylinder head(s), valve train, engine block, crankshaft, pistons and connecting rods), plus any other 'in block' components such as oil pumps, balance shafts and auxiliary shafts.

Finally, remove the cylinder head(s) from the engine block and carefully place on a bench. Disassembly instructions for each component follow later.

Cylinder Head

There are two basic types of cylinder heads used on today's automobiles: the Overhead Valve (OHV) and the Overhead Camshaft (OHC). The latter can also be broken down into two subgroups: the Single

Overhead Camshaft (SOHC) and the Dual Overhead Camshaft (DOHC). Generally, if there is only a single camshaft on a head, it is just referred to as an OHC head. In addition, an engine with an OHV cylinder head is also known as a pushrod engine.

Most cylinder heads these days are made of an aluminum alloy due to its light weight, durability, and heat transfer qualities. However, cast iron was the material of choice in the past, and is still used on many vehicles today. Whether made from aluminum or iron, all cylinder heads have valves and seats. Some use two valves per cylinder, while the more hi-tech engines will utilize a multi-valve configuration using 3, 4 and even 5 valves per cylinder. When the valve contacts the seat, it does so on precision-machined surfaces, which seals the combustion chamber. All cylinder heads have a valve guide for each valve. The guide centers the valve to the seat and allows it to move up and down within it. The clearance between the valve and guide can be critical. Too much clearance and the engine may consume oil, lose vacuum, and/or damage the seat. Too little, and the valve can stick in the guide causing the engine to run poorly if at all, and possibly causing severe damage. The last components all cylinder heads have are valve springs. The spring holds the valve against its seat. It also returns the valve to this position when the valve has been opened by the valve train or camshaft. The spring is fastened to the valve by a retainer and valve locks (sometimes called keepers). Aluminum heads will also have a valve spring shim to keep the spring from wearing away the aluminum.

An ideal method of rebuilding the cylinder head would involve replacing all of the valves, guides,

seats, springs, etc. with new ones. However, depending on how the engine was maintained, often this is not necessary. A major cause of valve, guide, and seat wear is an improperly tuned engine. An engine that is running too rich will often wash the lubricating oil out of the guide with gasoline, causing it to wear rapidly. Conversely, an engine, which is running too lean, will place higher combustion temperatures on the valves and seats allowing them to wear or even burn. Springs fall victim to the driving habits of the individual. A driver who often runs the engine rpm to the redline will wear out or break the springs faster then one that stays well below it. Unfortunately, mileage takes it tolls on all of the parts. Generally, the valves, guides, springs and seats in a cylinder head can be machined and re-used, saving you money. However, if a valve is burnt, it may be wise to replace all of the valves, since they were all operating in the same environment. The same goes for any other component on the cylinder head. Think of it as an insurance policy against future problems related to that component.

Unfortunately, the only way to find out which components need replacing is to disassemble and carefully check each piece. After the cylinder head(s) are disassembled, thoroughly clean all of the components.

DISASSEMBLY

4.5L and 4.9L Engines

♦ See Figures 114, 115, 116, 117, 118, 119

Before disassembling the cylinder head, you may want to fabricate some containers to hold the

various parts, as some of them can be quite small (such as keepers) and easily lost. Also keeping yourself and the components organized will aid in assembly and reduce confusion. Where possible, try to maintain a components original location; this is especially important if there is not going to be any machine work performed on the components.

1. If you haven't already removed the rocker arms and/or shafts, do so now.

2. Position the head so that the springs are easily accessed.

3. Use a valve spring compressor tool, and relieve spring tension from the retainer.

➡**Due to engine varnish, the retainer may stick to the valve locks. A gentle tap with a hammer may help to break it loose.**

4. Remove the valve locks from the valve tip and/or retainer. A small magnet may help in removing the locks.

5. Lift the valve spring, tool and all, off of the valve stem.

6. If equipped, remove the valve seal. If the seal is difficult to remove with the valve in place, try removing the valve first, then the seal. Follow the steps below for valve removal.

7. Position the head to allow access for withdrawing the valve.

➡**Cylinder heads that have seen a lot of miles and/or abuse may have mushroomed the valve lock grove and/or tip, causing difficulty in removal of the valve. If this has happened, use a metal file to carefully remove the high spots**

TCCS3137

Fig. 114 When removing an OHV valve spring, use a compressor tool to relieve the tension from the retainer

TCCS3138

Fig. 115 A small magnet will help in removal of the valve locks

TCCS3139

Fig. 116 Be careful not to lose the small valve locks (keepers)

TCCS3140

Fig. 117 Remove the valve seal from the valve stem—O-ring type seal shown

TCCS3252

Fig. 118 Removing an umbrella/positive type seal

TCCS3141

Fig. 119 Invert the cylinder head and withdraw the valve from the valve guide bore

around the lock grooves and/or tip. Only file it enough to allow removal.

8. Remove the valve from the cylinder head.

9. If equipped, remove the valve spring shim. A small magnetic tool or screwdriver will aid in removal.

10. Repeat Steps 3 though 9 until all of the valves have been removed.

4.6L Engine

◆ See Figures 120 and 121

Whether it is a single or dual overhead camshaft cylinder head, the disassembly procedure is rela-

tively unchanged. One aspect to pay attention to is careful labeling of the parts on the dual camshaft cylinder head. There will be an intake camshaft and followers as well as an exhaust camshaft and followers and they must be labeled as such. In some cases, the components are identical and could easily be installed incorrectly. DO NOT MIX THEM UP! Determining which is which is very simple; the intake camshaft and components are on the same side of the head as was the intake manifold. Conversely, the exhaust camshaft and components are on the same side of the head as was the exhaust manifold.

ROCKER ARM TYPE CAMSHAFT FOLLOWERS

◆ See Figures 122 thru 130

Most cylinder heads with rocker arm-type camshaft followers are easily disassembled using a standard valve spring compressor. However, certain models may not have enough open space around the spring for the standard tool and may require you to use a C-clamp style compressor tool instead.

1. If not already removed, remove the rocker arms and/or shafts and the camshaft. If applicable, also remove the hydraulic lash adjusters. Mark their positions for assembly.

2. Position the cylinder head to allow access to the valve spring.

3. Use a valve spring compressor tool to relieve the spring tension from the retainer.

➡Due to engine varnish, the retainer may stick to the valve locks. A gentle tap with a hammer may help to break it loose.

TCCA3P54

Fig. 120 Exploded view of a valve, seal, spring, retainer and locks from an OHC cylinder head

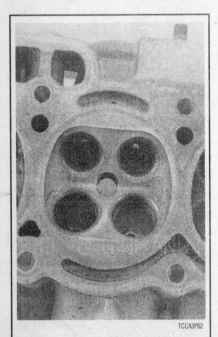

TCCA3P62

Fig. 121 Example of a multi-valve cylinder head. Note how it has 2 intake and 2 exhaust valve ports

TCCA3P53

Fig. 122 Example of the shaft mounted rocker arms on some OHC heads

TCCA3P61

Fig. 123 Another example of the rocker arm type OHC head. This model uses a follower under the camshaft

TCCA3P60

Fig. 124 Before the camshaft can be removed, all of the followers must first be removed . . .

TCCA3P59

Fig. 125 . . . then the camshaft can be removed by sliding it out (shown), or unbolting a bearing cap (not shown)

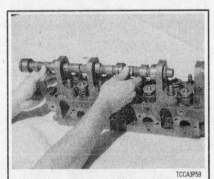

TCCA3P57

Fig. 126 Compress the valve spring . . .

TCCA3P58

Fig. 127 . . . then remove the valve locks from the valve stem and spring retainer

Fig. 128 Remove the valve spring and retainer from the cylinder head

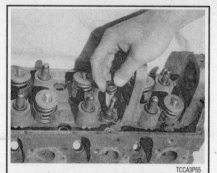

Fig. 129 Remove the valve seal from the guide. Some gentle prying or pliers may help to remove stubborn ones

Fig. 130 All aluminum and some cast iron heads will have these valve spring shims. Remove all of them as well

4. Remove the valve locks from the valve tip and/or retainer. A small magnet may help in removing the small locks.

5. Lift the valve spring, tool and all, off of the valve stem.

6. If equipped, remove the valve seal. If the seal is difficult to remove with the valve in place, try removing the valve first, then the seal. Follow the steps below for valve removal.

7. Position the head to allow access for withdrawing the valve.

➡Cylinder heads that have seen a lot of miles and/or abuse may have mushroomed the valve lock grove and/or tip, causing difficulty in removal of the valve. If this has happened, use a metal file to carefully remove the high spots around the lock grooves and/or tip. Only file it enough to allow removal.

8. Remove the valve from the cylinder head.

9. If equipped, remove the valve spring shim. A small magnetic tool or screwdriver will aid in removal.

10. Repeat Steps 3 though 9 until all of the valves have been removed.

INSPECTION

Now that all of the cylinder head components are clean, it's time to inspect them for wear and/or damage. To accurately inspect them, you will need some specialized tools:

• A 0–1 in. micrometer for the valves

• A dial indicator or inside diameter gauge for the valve guides
• A spring pressure test gauge

If you do not have access to the proper tools, you may want to bring the components to a shop that does.

Valves

◆ **See Figures 131 and 132**

The first things to inspect are the valve heads. Look closely at the head, margin, and face for any cracks, excessive wear, or burning. The margin is the best place to look for burning. It should have a squared edge with an even width all around the diameter. When a valve burns, the margin will look melted and the edges rounded. Also, inspect the valve head for any signs of tulipping. This will show as a lifting of the edges or dishing in the center of the head and will usually not occur to all of the valves. All of the heads should look the same, any that seem dished more than others are probably bad. Next, inspect the valve lock grooves and valve tips. Check for any burrs around the lock grooves, especially if you had to file them to remove the valve. Valve tips should appear flat, although slight rounding with high mileage engines is normal. Slightly worn valve tips will need to be machined flat. Last, measure the valve stem diameter with the micrometer. Measure the area that rides within the guide, especially towards the tip where most of the wear occurs. Take several measurements along its length and compare them to each other. Wear

should be even along the length with little to no taper. If no minimum diameter is given in the specifications, then the stem should not read more than 0.001 in. (0.025 mm) below the unworn area of the valve stem. Any valves that fail these inspections should be replaced.

Springs, Retainers and Valve Locks

◆ **See Figures 133 and 134**

The first thing to check is the most obvious, broken springs. Next, check the free length and squareness of each spring. If applicable, insure to distinguish between intake and exhaust springs. Use a ruler and/or carpenters square to measure the length. A carpenter's square should be used to check the springs for squareness. If a spring pressure test gauge is available, check each spring rating and compare to the specification chart. Check the readings against the specifications given. Any springs that fail these inspections should be replaced.

The spring retainers rarely need replacing, however they should still be checked as a precaution. Inspect the spring mating surface and the valve lock retention areas for any signs of excessive wear. Also, check for any signs of cracking. Replace any retainers that are questionable.

Valve locks should be inspected for excessive wear on the outside contact area as well as on the inner notched surface. Any locks which appear worn or broken and its respective valve should be replaced.

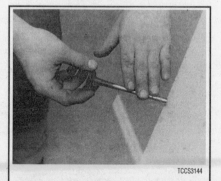

Fig. 131 Valve stems may be rolled on a flat surface to check for bends

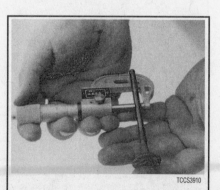

Fig. 132 Use a micrometer to check the valve stem diameter

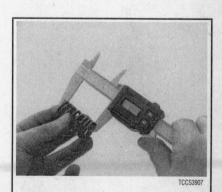

Fig. 133 Use a caliper to check the valve spring free-length

Fig. 134 Check the valve spring for squareness on a flat surface; a carpenter's square can be used

Cylinder Head

There are several things to check on the cylinder head: valve guides, seats, cylinder head surface flatness, cracks, and physical damage.

VALVE GUIDES

▶ See Figure 135

Now that you know the valves are good, you can use them to check the guides, although a new valve, if available, is preferred. Before you measure anything, look at the guides carefully and inspect them for any cracks, chips, or breakage. Also, if the guide is a removable style (as in most aluminum heads), check them for any looseness or evidence of movement. All of the guides should appear to be at the same height from the spring seat. If any seem lower (or higher) from another, the guide has moved. Mount a dial indicator onto the spring side of the cylinder head. Lightly oil the valve stem and insert it into the cylinder head. Position the dial indicator against the valve stem near the tip and zero the gauge. Grasp the valve stem, wiggle towards and away from the dial indicator, and observe the readings. Mount the dial indicator 90 degrees from the initial point, zero the gauge, and again take a reading. Compare the two readings for an out of round condition. Check the readings against the specifications given. An Inside Diameter (I.D.) gauge designed for valve guides will give you an accurate valve guide bore measurement. If the I.D. gauge is used, compare the readings with the specifications given. Any guides that fail these inspections should be replaced or machined.

VALVE SEATS

A visual inspection of the valve seats should show a slightly worn and pitted surface where the valve face contacts the seat. Inspect the seat carefully for severe pitting or cracks. In addition, a seat that is badly worn will be recessed into the cylinder head. A severely worn or recessed seat may need to be replaced. All cracked seats must be replaced. A seat concentricity gauge, if available, should be used to check the seat run-out. If run-out exceeds a specification the seat must be machined (if no specification is given use 0.002 in. or 0.051 mm).

CYLINDER HEAD SURFACE FLATNESS

▶ See Figures 136 and 137

After you have cleaned the gasket surface of the cylinder head of any old gasket material, check the head for flatness.

Place a straightedge across the gasket surface. Using feeler gauges, determine the clearance at the center of the straightedge and across the cylinder head at several points. Check along the centerline and diagonally on the head surface. If the warpage exceeds 0.003 in. (0.076 mm) within a 6.0 in. (15.2 cm) span, or 0.006 in. (0.152 mm) over the total length of the head, the cylinder head must be resurfaced. After resurfacing the heads of a V-type engine, the intake manifold flange surface should be checked, and if necessary, milled proportionally to allow for the change in its mounting position.

CRACKS AND PHYSICAL DAMAGE

Generally, cracks are limited to the combustion chamber, however, it is not uncommon for the head to crack in a spark plug hole, port, outside of the head or in the valve spring/rocker arm area. The first area to inspect is always the hottest: the exhaust seat/port area.

A visual inspection should be performed, but just because you don't see a crack does not mean it is not there. Some more reliable methods for inspecting for cracks include Magnaflux®, a magnetic process or Zyglo®, a dye penetrant. Magnaflux® is used only on ferrous metal (cast iron) heads. Zyglo® uses a spray on fluorescent mixture along with a black light to reveal the cracks. It is strongly recommended to have your cylinder head checked professionally for cracks, especially if the engine was known to have overheated and/or leaked or consumed coolant. Contact a local shop for availability and pricing of these services.

Physical damage is usually very evident. For example, a broken mounting ear from dropping the head or a bent or broken stud and/or bolt. All of these defects should be fixed or, if not repairable, the head should be replaced.

Camshaft and Followers

Inspect the camshaft(s) and followers as described earlier.

REFINISHING & REPAIRING

Many of the procedures given for refinishing and repairing the cylinder head components must be performed by a machine shop. Certain steps, if the inspected part is not worn, can be performed yourself inexpensively. However, you spent a lot of time and effort so far, why risk trying to save a couple bucks if you might have to do it all over again?

Valves

Any valves that were not replaced should be refaced and the tips ground flat. Unless you have access to a valve grinding machine, this should be done by a machine shop. If the valves are in extremely good condition, as well as the valve seats and guides, they may be lapped in without performing machine work.

It is a recommended practice to lap the valves even after machine work has been performed and/or new valves have been purchased. This insures a positive seal between the valve and seat.

LAPPING THE VALVES

➡Before lapping the valves to the seats, read the rest of the cylinder head section to insure that any related parts are in acceptable enough condition to continue.

➡Before any valve seat machining and/or lapping can be performed, the guides must be within factory recommended specifications.

1. Invert the cylinder head.
2. Lightly lubricate the valve stems and insert them into the cylinder head in their numbered order.
3. Raise the valve from the seat and apply a small amount of fine lapping compound to the seat.
4. Moisten the suction head of a hand-lapping tool and attach it to the head of the valve.
5. Rotate the tool between the palms of both hands, changing the position of the valve on the

Fig. 135 A dial gauge may be used to check valve stem-to-guide clearance; read the gauge while moving the valve stem

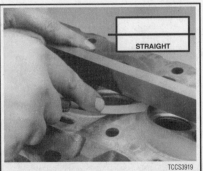

Fig. 136 Check the head for flatness across the center of the head surface using a straightedge and feeler gauge

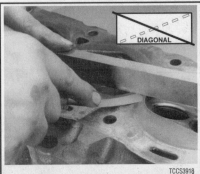

Fig. 137 Checks should also be made along both diagonals of the head surface

ENGINE AND ENGINE OVERHAUL

ENGINE AND ENGINE OVERHAUL 3-33

valve seat and lifting the tool often to prevent grooving.

6. Lap the valve until a smooth, polished circle is evident on the valve and seat.

7. Remove the tool and the valve. Wipe away all traces of the grinding compound and store the valve to maintain its lapped location.

※※ WARNING

Do not get the valves out of order after they have been lapped. They must be put back with the same valve seat with which they were lapped.

Springs, Retainers and Valve Locks

There is no repair or refinishing possible with the springs, retainers and valve locks. If they are found to be worn or defective, they must be replaced with new (or known good) parts.

Cylinder Head

Most refinishing procedures dealing with the cylinder head must be performed by a machine shop. Read below and review your inspection data to determine whether or not machining is necessary.

VALVE GUIDE

➡**If any machining or replacements are made to the valve guides, the seats must be machined.**

Unless the valve guides need machining or replacing, the only service to perform is to thoroughly clean them of any dirt or oil residue.

There are only two types of valve guides used on automobile engines: the replaceable-type (all aluminum heads) and the cast-in integral-type (most cast iron heads). There are four recommended methods for repairing worn guides.

- Knurling
- Inserts
- Reaming oversize
- Replacing

Knurling is a process in which metal is displaced and raised, thereby reducing clearance, giving a true center, and providing oil control. It is the least expensive way of repairing the valve guides. However, it is not necessarily the best, and in some cases, a knurled valve guide will not stand up for more than a short time. It requires a special knurlizer and precision reaming tools to obtain proper clearances. It would not be cost effective to purchase these tools, unless you plan to rebuild several of the same type cylinder head.

Installing a guide insert involves machining the guide to accept a bronze insert. One style is the coil-type, which is installed into a threaded guide. Another is the thin-walled insert where the guide is reamed oversize to accept a split-sleeve insert. After the insert is installed, a special tool is then run through the guide to expand the insert, locking it to the guide. The insert is then reamed to the standard size for proper valve clearance.

Reaming for oversize valves restores normal clearances and provides a true valve seat. Most cast-in type guides can be reamed to accept an valve with an oversize stem. The cost factor for this can become quite high as you will need to purchase the reamer and new, oversize stem valves for all

guides which were reamed. Oversize are generally 0.003 to 0.030 in. (0.076 to 0.762 mm), with 0.015 in. (0.381 mm) being the most common.

To replace cast-in type valve guides, they must be drilled out, then reamed to accept replacement guides. This must be done on a fixture which will allow centering and leveling off of the original valve seat or guide, otherwise a serious guide-to-seat misalignment may occur making it impossible to properly machine the seat.

Replaceable-type guides are pressed into the cylinder head. A hammer and a stepped drift or punch may be used to install and remove the guides. Before removing the guides, measure the protrusion on the spring side of the head and record it for installation. Use the stepped drift to hammer out the old guide from the combustion chamber side of the head. When installing, determine whether or not the guide also seals a water jacket in the head, and if it does, use the recommended sealing agent. If there is no water jacket, grease the valve guide and its bore. Use the stepped drift, and hammer the new guide into the cylinder head from the spring side of the cylinder head. A stack of washers the same thickness as the measured protrusion may help the installation process.

VALVE SEATS

➡**Before any valve seat machining can be performed, the guides must be within factory recommended specifications.**

➡**If any machining or replacements were made to the valve guides, the seats must be machined.**

If the seats are in good condition, the valves can be lapped to the seats, and the cylinder head assembled. See the procedure on lapping valves for instructions.

If the valve seats are worn, cracked or damaged, they must be serviced by a machine shop. The valve seat must be perfectly centered to the valve guide, which requires very accurate machining.

CYLINDER HEAD SURFACE

If the cylinder head is warped, it must be machined flat. If the warpage is extremely severe, the head may need to be replaced. In some instances, it may be possible to straighten a warped head enough to allow machining. In either case, contact a professional machine shop for service.

➡**Any OHC cylinder head that shows excessive warpage should have the camshaft bearing journals align bored after the cylinder head has been resurfaced.**

※※ WARNING

Failure to align bore the camshaft bearing journals could result in severe engine damage including but not limited to: valve and piston damage, connecting rod damage, camshaft and/or crankshaft breakage.

CRACKS AND PHYSICAL DAMAGE

Certain cracks can be repaired in both cast iron and aluminum heads. For cast iron, a tapered threaded insert is installed along the length of the crack. Aluminum can also use the tapered inserts,

however welding is the preferred method. Some physical damage can be repaired through brazing or welding. Contact a machine shop to get expert advice for your particular dilemma.

ASSEMBLY

The first step for any assembly job is to have a clean area in which to work. Next, thoroughly clean all of the parts and components that are to be assembled. Finally, place all of the components onto a suitable work space and, if necessary, arrange the parts to their respective positions.

4.5L and 4.9L Engines

1. Lightly lubricate the valve stems and insert all of the valves into the cylinder head. If possible, maintain their original locations.

2. If equipped, install any valve spring shims, which were removed.

3. If equipped, install the new valve seals, keeping the following in mind:
   - If the valve seal presses over the guide, lightly lubricate the outer guide surfaces.
   - If the seal is an O-ring type, it is installed just after compressing the spring but before the valve locks.

4. Place the valve spring and retainer over the stem.

5. Position the spring compressor tool and compress the spring.

6. Assemble the valve locks to the stem.

7. Relieve the spring pressure slowly and insure that neither valve lock becomes dislodged by the retainer.

8. Remove the spring compressor tool.

9. Repeat Steps 2 through 8 until all of the springs have been installed.

4.6L Engine

ROCKER ARM TYPE CAMSHAFT FOLLOWERS

1. Lightly lubricate the valve stems and insert all of the valves into the cylinder head. If possible, maintain their original locations.

2. If equipped, install any valve spring shims, which were removed.

3. If equipped, install the new valve seals, keeping the following in mind:
   - If the valve seal presses over the guide, lightly lubricate the outer guide surfaces.
   - If the seal is an O-ring type, it is installed just after compressing the spring but before the valve locks.

4. Place the valve spring and retainer over the stem.

5. Position the spring compressor tool and compress the spring.

6. Assemble the valve locks to the stem.

7. Relieve the spring pressure slowly and insure that neither valve lock becomes dislodged by the retainer.

8. Remove the spring compressor tool.

9. Repeat Steps 2 through 8 until all of the springs have been installed.

10. Install the camshaft(s), rockers, shafts and any other components that were removed for disassembly.

Engine Block

GENERAL INFORMATION

A thorough overhaul or rebuild of an engine block would include replacing the pistons, rings, bearings, timing belt/chain assembly and oil pump. For OHV engines also include a new camshaft and lifters. The block would then have the cylinders bored and honed oversize (or if using removable cylinder sleeves, new sleeves installed) and the crankshaft would be cut undersize to provide new wearing surfaces and perfect clearances. However, your particular engine may not have everything worn out. What if only the piston rings have worn out and the clearances on everything else are still within factory specifications? Well, you could just replace the rings and put it back together, but this would be a very rare example. Chances are, if one component in your engine is worn, other components are sure to follow, and soon. At the very least, you should always replace the rings, bearings and oil pump. This is what is commonly called a "freshen up."

Cylinder Ridge Removal

Because the top piston ring does not travel to the very top of the cylinder, a ridge is built up between the end of the travel and the top of the cylinder bore.

Pushing the piston and connecting rod assembly past the ridge can be difficult, and damage to the piston ring lands could occur. If the ridge is not removed before installing a new piston or not removed at all, piston ring breakage and piston damage may occur.

➡ **It is always recommended that you remove any cylinder ridges before removing the piston and connecting rod assemblies. If you know that new pistons are going to be installed and the engine block will be bored oversize, you may be able to forego this step. However, some ridges may actually prevent the assemblies from being removed, necessitating its removal.**

There are several different types of ridge reamers on the market, none of which are inexpensive. Unless a great deal of engine rebuilding is anticipated, borrow or rent a reamer.

1. Turn the crankshaft until the piston is at the bottom of its travel.
2. Cover the head of the piston with a rag.
3. Follow the tool manufacturer instructions and cut away the ridge, exercising extreme care to avoid cutting too deeply.
4. Remove the ridge reamer, the rag and as many of the cuttings as possible. Continue until all of the cylinder ridges have been removed.

DISASSEMBLY

▸ **See Figures 138 and 139**

The engine disassembly instructions following assume that you have the engine mounted on an engine stand. If not, it is easiest to disassemble the engine on a bench or the floor with it resting on the bell housing or transmission-mounting surface. You must be able to access the connecting rod fasteners

and turn the crankshaft during disassembly. Also, all engine covers (timing, front, side, oil pan, whatever) should have already been removed. Engines, which are seized or locked up, may not be able to be completely disassembled, and a core (salvage yard) engine should be purchased.

4.5L and 4.9L Engines

If not done during the cylinder head removal, remove the pushrods and lifters, keeping them in order for assembly. Remove the timing gears and/or timing chain assembly, then remove the oil pump drive assembly, and withdraw the camshaft from the engine block. Remove the oil pick-up and pump assembly. If equipped, remove any balance or auxiliary shafts. If necessary, remove the cylinder ridge from the top of the bore. See the cylinder ridge removal procedure.

4.6L Engine

If not done during the cylinder head removal, remove the timing chain/belt and/or gear/sprocket assembly. Remove the oil pick-up and pump assembly and, if necessary, the pump drive. If equipped, remove any balance or auxiliary shafts. If necessary, remove the cylinder ridge from the top of the bore. See the cylinder ridge removal procedure.

All Engines

Rotate the engine over so that the crankshaft is exposed. Use a number punch or scribe and mark each connecting rod with its respective cylinder number. The cylinder closest to the front of the engine is always number 1. However, depending on the engine placement, the front of the engine could either be the flywheel or damper/pulley end. Generally, the front of the engine faces the front of the vehicle. Use a number punch or scribe and also mark the main bearing caps from front to rear with the front most cap being number 1 (if there are five caps, mark them 1 through 5, front to rear).

✳✳ WARNING

Take special care when pushing the connecting rod up from the crankshaft because the sharp threads of the rod bolts/studs will score the crankshaft journal. Insure that special plastic caps are installed over them, or cut two pieces of rubber hose to do the same.

Fig. 138 Place rubber hose over the connecting rod studs to protect the crankshaft and cylinder bores from damage

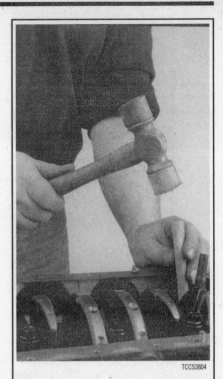

Fig. 139 Carefully tap the piston out of the bore using a wooden dowel

Again, rotate the engine, this time to position the number one cylinder bore (head surface) up. Turn the crankshaft until the number one piston is at the bottom of its travel, this should allow the maximum access to its connecting rod. Remove the number one connecting rods fasteners and cap and place two lengths of rubber hose over the rod bolts/studs to protect the crankshaft from damage. Using a sturdy wooden dowel and a hammer, push the connecting rod up about 1 in. (25 mm) from the crankshaft and remove the upper bearing insert. Continue pushing or tapping the connecting rod up until the piston rings are out of the cylinder bore. Remove the piston and rod by hand, put the upper half of the bearing insert back into the rod, install the cap with its bearing insert installed, and hand-tighten the cap fasteners. If the parts are kept in order in this manner, they will not get lost and you will be able to tell which bearings came form what cylinder if any problems are discovered and diagnosis is necessary. Remove all the other piston assemblies in the same manner. On V-style engines, remove all of the pistons from one bank, then reposition the engine with the other cylinder bank head surface up, and remove the piston assemblies of that bank.

The only remaining component in the engine block should now be the crankshaft. Loosen the main bearing caps evenly until the fasteners can be turned by hand, then remove them and the caps. Remove the crankshaft from the engine block. Thoroughly clean all of the components.

INSPECTION

Now that the engine block and all of its components are clean, it's time to inspect them for wear and/or damage. To accurately inspect them, you will need some specialized tools:

- Two or three separate micrometers to measure the pistons and crankshaft journals
  - A dial indicator
  - Telescoping gauges for the cylinder bores
  - A rod alignment fixture to check for bent connecting rods

If you do not have access to the proper tools, you may want to bring the components to a shop that does.

Generally, you should not expect cracks in the engine block or its components unless it was known to leak, consume, or mix engine fluids, it was severely overheated, or there was evidence of bad bearings and/or crankshaft damage. A visual inspection should be performed on all of the components, but just because you don't see a crack does not mean it is not there. Some more reliable methods for inspecting for cracks include Magnaflux®, a magnetic process or Zyglo®, a dye penetrant. Magnaflux® is used only on ferrous metal (cast iron). Zyglo® uses a spray on fluorescent mixture along with a black light to reveal the cracks. It is strongly recommended to have your engine block checked professionally for cracks, especially if the engine was known to have overheated and/or leaked or consumed coolant. Contact a local shop for availability and pricing of these services.

Engine Block

ENGINE BLOCK BEARING ALIGNMENT

Remove the main bearing caps and, if still installed, the main bearing inserts. Inspect all of the main bearing saddles and caps for damage, burrs, or high spots. If damage is found, and it is caused from a spun main bearing, the block will need to be align-bored or, if severe enough, replacement. Any burrs or high spots should be carefully removed with a metal file.

Place a straightedge on the bearing saddles, in the engine block, along the centerline of the crankshaft. If any clearance exists between the straightedge and the saddles, the block must be align-bored.

Align-boring consists of machining the main bearing saddles and caps by means of a flycutter that runs through the bearing saddles.

DECK FLATNESS

The top of the engine block where the cylinder head mounts is called the deck. Insure that the deck surface is clean of dirt, carbon deposits, and old gasket material. Place a straightedge across the surface of the deck along its centerline and, using feeler gauges, check the clearance along several points. Repeat the checking procedure with the straightedge placed along both diagonals of the deck surface. If the reading exceeds 0.003 in. (0.076 mm) within a 6.0 in. (15.2 cm) span, or 0.006 in. (0.152 mm) over the total length of the deck, it must be machined.

CYLINDER BORES

◆ See Figure 140

The cylinder bores house the pistons and are slightly larger than the pistons themselves. A common piston-to-bore clearance is 0.0015–0.0025 in. (0.0381 mm–0.0635mm). Inspect and measure the cylinder bores. The bore should be checked for out-of-roundness, taper and size. The results of this

TCCS3209

Fig. 140 Use a telescoping gauge to measure the cylinder bore diameter—take several readings within the same bore

inspection will determine whether the cylinder can be used in its existing size and condition, or a rebore to the next oversize is required (or in the case of removable sleeves, have replacements installed).

The amount of cylinder wall wear is always greater at the top of the cylinder than at the bottom. This wear is known as taper. Any cylinder that has a taper of 0.0012 in. (0.305 mm) or more, must be rebored. Measurements are taken at a number of positions in each cylinder: at the top, middle and bottom and at two points at each position; that is, at a point 90 degrees from the crankshaft centerline, as well as a point parallel to the crankshaft centerline. The measurements are made with either a special dial indicator or a telescopic gauge and micrometer. If the necessary precision tools to check the bore are not available, take the block to a machine shop and have them mike it. Also if you don't have the tools to check the cylinder bores, chances are you will not have the necessary devices to check the pistons, connecting rods and crankshaft. Take these components with you and save yourself an extra trip.

For our procedures, we will use a telescopic gauge and a micrometer. You will need one of each, with a measuring range which covers your cylinder bore size.

1. Position the telescopic gauge in the cylinder bore, loosen the gauges lock and allow it to expand.

➡**Your first two readings will be at the top of the cylinder bore, then proceed to the middle and finally the bottom, making a total of six measurements.**

2. Hold the gauge square in the bore, 90 degrees from the crankshaft centerline, and gently tighten the lock. Tilt the gauge back to remove it from the bore.

3. Measure the gauge with the micrometer and record the reading.

4. Again, hold the gauge square in the bore, this time parallel to the crankshaft centerline, and gently tighten the lock. Again, you will tilt the gauge back to remove it from the bore.

5. Measure the gauge with the micrometer and record this reading. The difference between these two readings is the out-of-round measurement of the cylinder.

6. Repeat steps 1 through 5, each time going to the next lower position, until you reach the bottom of the cylinder. Then go to the next cylinder, and continue until all of the cylinders have been measured.

The difference between these measurements will tell you all about the wear in your cylinders. The measurements which were taken 90 degrees from the crankshaft centerline will always reflect the most wear. That is because at this position is where the engine power presses the piston against the cylinder bore the hardest. This is known as thrust wear. Take your top, 90 degree measurement and compare it to your bottom, 90 degree measurement. The difference between them is the taper. When you measure your pistons, you will compare these readings to your piston sizes and determine piston-to-wall clearance.

Crankshaft

Inspect the crankshaft for visible signs of wear or damage. All of the journals should be perfectly round and smooth. Slight scores are normal for a used crankshaft, but you should hardly feel them with your fingernail. When measuring the crankshaft with a micrometer, you will take readings at the front and rear of each journal, then turn the micrometer 90 degrees and take two more readings, front and rear. The difference between the front-to-rear readings is the journal taper and the first-to-90 degree reading is the out-of-round measurement. Generally, there should be no taper or out-of-roundness found, however, up to 0.0005 in. (0.0127 mm) for either can be overlooked. In addition, the readings should fall within the factory specifications for journal diameters.

If the crankshaft journals fall within specifications, it is recommended that it be polished before being returned to service. Polishing the crankshaft insures that any minor burrs or high spots are smoothed, thereby reducing the chance of scoring the new bearings.

Pistons and Connecting Rods

PISTONS

◆ See Figure 141

The piston should be visually inspected for any signs of cracking or burning (caused by hot spots or detonation), and scuffing or excessive wear on the skirts. The wrist pin attaches the piston to the connecting rod. The piston should move freely on the wrist pin, both sliding and pivoting. Grasp the connecting rod securely, or mount it in a vise, and try to rock the piston back and forth along the cen-

TCCS3210

Fig. 141 Measure the piston's outer diameter, perpendicular to the wrist pin, with a micrometer

terline of the wrist pin. There should not be any excessive play evident between the piston and the pin. If there are C-clips retaining the pin in the piston then you have wrist pin bushings in the rods. There should not be any excessive play between the wrist pin and the rod bushing. Normal clearance for the wrist pin is approx. 0.001–0.002 in. (0.025 mm–0.051mm).

Use a micrometer and measure the diameter of the piston, perpendicular to the wrist pin, on the skirt. Compare the reading to its original cylinder measurement obtained earlier. The difference between the two readings is the piston-to-wall clearance. If the clearance is within specifications, the piston may be used as is. If the piston is out of specification, but the bore is not, you will need a new piston. If both are out of specification, you will need the cylinder rebored and oversize pistons installed. Generally if two or more pistons/bores are out of specification, it is best to rebore the entire block and purchase a complete set of oversize pistons.

CONNECTING ROD

You should have the connecting rod checked for straightness at a machine shop. If the connecting rod is bent, it will unevenly wear the bearing and piston, as well as place greater stress on these components. Any bent or twisted connecting rods must be replaced. If the rods are straight and the wrist pin clearance is within specifications, then only the bearing end of the rod need be checked. Place the connecting rod into a vice, with the bearing inserts in place, install the cap to the rod and tighten the fasteners to specifications. Use a telescoping gauge and carefully measure the inside diameter of the bearings. Compare this reading to the rods original crankshaft journal diameter measurement. The difference is the oil clearance. If the oil clearance is not within specifications, install new bearings in the rod and take another measurement. If the clearance is still out of specifications, and the crankshaft is not, the rod will need to be reconditioned by a machine shop.

➥You can also use Plastigage® to check the bearing clearances. The assembling procedures have complete instructions on its use.

Camshaft

Inspect the camshaft and lifters/followers.

Bearings

All of the engine bearings should be visually inspected for wear and/or damage. The bearing should look evenly worn all around with no deep scores or pits. If the bearing is severely worn, scored, pitted or heat blued, then the bearing, and the components that use it, should be brought to a machine shop for inspection. Full-circle bearings (used on most camshafts, auxiliary shafts, balance shafts, etc.) require specialized tools for removal and installation, and should be brought to a machine shop for service.

Oil Pump

➥The oil pump is responsible for providing constant lubrication to the whole engine and so it is recommended that a new oil pump be installed when rebuilding the engine.

Completely disassemble the oil pump and thoroughly clean all of the components. Inspect the oil pump gears and housing for wear and/or damage. Insure that the pressure relief valve operates properly and there is no binding or sticking due to varnish or debris. If all of the parts are in proper working condition, lubricate the gears and relief valve, and assemble the pump.

REFINISHING

◗ See Figure 142

Almost all engine block refinishing must be performed by a machine shop. If the cylinders are not to be rebored, then the cylinder glaze can be removed with a ball hone. When removing cylinder glaze with a ball hone, use a light or penetrating type oil to lubricate the hone. Do not allow the hone to run dry as this may cause excessive scoring of the cylinder bores and wear on the hone. If new pistons are required, they will need to be installed to the connecting rods. This should be performed by a machine shop as the pistons must be installed in the correct relationship to the rod or engine damage can occur.

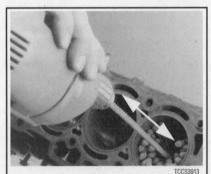

Fig. 142 Use a ball type cylinder hone to remove any glaze and provide a new surface for seating the piston rings

Pistons and Connecting Rods

◗ See Figure 143

Only pistons with the wrist pin retained by C-clips are serviceable by the home-mechanic. Press fit pistons require special presses and/or heaters to remove/install the connecting rod and should only be performed by a machine shop.

Fig. 143 Most pistons are marked to indicate positioning in the engine (usually a mark means the side facing the front)

All pistons will have a mark indicating the direction to the front of the engine and the must be installed into the engine in that manner. Usually it is a notch or arrow on the top of the piston, or it may be the letter F cast or stamped into the piston.

ASSEMBLY

Before you begin assembling the engine, first give yourself a clean, dirt free work area. Next, clean every engine component again. The key to a good assembly is cleanliness.

Mount the engine block into the engine stand and wash it one last time using water and detergent (dishwashing detergent works well). While washing it, scrub the cylinder bores with a soft bristle brush and thoroughly clean all of the oil passages. Completely dry the engine and spray the entire assembly down with an anti-rust solution such as WD-40® or similar product. Take a clean lint-free rag and wipe up any excess anti-rust solution from the bores, bearing saddles, etc. Repeat the final cleaning process on the crankshaft. Replace any freeze or oil galley plugs which were removed during disassembly.

Crankshaft

◗ See Figures 144, 145, 146 and 147

1. Remove the main bearing inserts from the block and bearing caps.
2. If the crankshaft main bearing journals have been refinished to a definite undersize, install the correct undersize bearing. Be sure that the bearing inserts and bearing bores are clean. Foreign material under inserts will distort bearing and cause failure.
3. Place the upper main bearing inserts in bores with tang in slot.

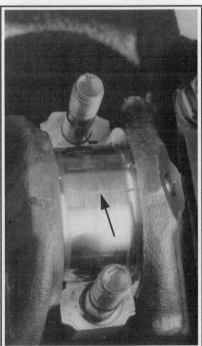

Fig. 144 Apply a strip of gauging material to the bearing journal, then install and torque the cap

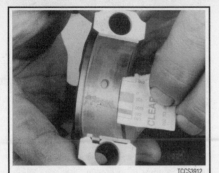

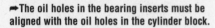

Fig. 145 After the cap is removed again, use the scale supplied with the gauging material to check the clearance

Fig. 146 A dial gauge may be used to check crankshaft end-play

Fig. 147 Carefully pry the crankshaft back and forth while reading the dial gauge for end-play

➡The oil holes in the bearing inserts must be aligned with the oil holes in the cylinder block.

4. Install the lower main bearing inserts in bearing caps.

5. Clean the mating surfaces of block and rear main bearing cap.

6. Carefully lower the crankshaft into place. Be careful not to damage bearing surfaces.

7. Check the clearance of each main bearing by using the following procedure:

a. Place a piece of Plastigage® or its equivalent, on bearing surface across full width of bearing cap and about 1/4 in. off center.

b. Install caps and tighten bolts to specifications. Do not turn crankshaft while Plastigage® is in place.

c. Remove the cap. Using the supplied Plastigage® scale, check width of Plastigage® at widest point to get maximum clearance. Difference between readings is taper of journal.

d. If clearance exceeds specified limits, try a 0.001 in. or 0.002 in. undersize bearing in combination with the standard bearing. Bearing clearance must be within specified limits. If standard and 0.002 in. undersize bearing does not bring clearance within desired limits, refinish crankshaft journal, then install undersize bearings.

8. After the bearings have been fitted, apply a light coat of engine oil to the journals and bearings. Install the rear main bearing cap. Install all bearing caps except the thrust bearing cap. Be sure that main bearing caps are installed in original locations. Tighten the bearing cap bolts to specifications.

9. Install the thrust bearing cap with bolts finger-tight.

10. Install the rear main seal.

11. Pry the crankshaft forward against the thrust surface of upper half of bearing.

12. Hold the crankshaft forward and pry the thrust bearing cap to the rear. This aligns the thrust surfaces of both halves of the bearing.

13. Retain the forward pressure on the crankshaft. Tighten the cap bolts to specifications.

14. Measure the crankshaft end-play as follows:

a. Mount a dial gauge to the engine block and position the tip of the gauge to read from the crankshaft end.

b. Carefully pry the crankshaft toward the rear of the engine and hold it there while you zero the gauge.

c. Carefully pry the crankshaft toward the front of the engine and read the gauge.

d. Confirm that the reading is within specifications. If not, install a new thrust bearing and repeat the procedure. If the reading is still out of specifications with a new bearing, have a machine shop inspect the thrust surfaces of the crankshaft, and if possible, repair it.

15. Rotate the crankshaft to position the first rod journal to the bottom of its stroke.

Pistons and Connecting Rods

▶ **See Figures 148, 149, 150 and 151**

1. Before installing the piston/connecting rod assembly, oil the pistons, piston rings and the cylinder walls with light engine oil. Install connecting rod bolt protectors or rubber hose onto the connecting rod bolts/studs. Also perform the following:

a. Select the proper ring set for the size cylinder bore.

b. Position the ring in the bore in which it is going to be used.

c. Push the ring down into the bore area where normal ring wear is not encountered.

d. Use the head of the piston to position the ring in the bore so that the ring is square with the cylinder wall. Use caution to avoid damage to the ring or cylinder bore.

e. Measure the gap between the ends of the ring with a feeler gauge. Ring gap in a worn cylinder is normally greater than specification. If the ring gap is greater than the specified limits, try an oversize ring set.

f. Check the ring side clearance of the compression rings with a feeler gauge inserted between the ring and its lower land according to specification. The gauge should slide freely around the entire ring circumference without binding. Any wear that occurs will form a step at the inner portion of the lower land. If the lower lands have high steps, the piston should be replaced.

2. Unless new pistons are installed, be sure to install the pistons in the cylinders from which they were removed. The numbers on the connecting rod and bearing cap must be on the same side when installed in the cylinder bore. If a connecting rod is ever transposed from one engine or cylinder to another, new bearings should be fitted and the connecting rod should be numbered to correspond with the new cylinder number. The notch on the piston head goes toward the front of the engine.

Fig. 148 Checking the piston ring-to-ring groove side clearance using the ring and a feeler gauge

Fig. 149 The notch on the side of the bearing cap matches the tang on the bearing insert

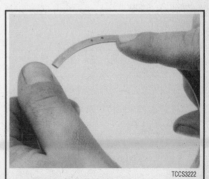

Fig. 150 Most rings are marked to show which side of the ring should face up when installed to the piston

Fig. 151 Install the piston and rod assembly into the block using a ring compressor and the handle of a hammer

3. Install all of the rod bearing inserts into the rods and caps.

4. Install the rings to the pistons. Install the oil control ring first, then the second compression ring and finally the top compression ring. Use a piston ring expander tool to aid in installation and to help reduce the chance of breakage.

5. Make sure the ring gaps are properly spaced around the circumference of the piston. Fit a piston ring compressor around the piston and slide the piston and connecting rod assembly down into the cylinder bore, pushing it in with the wooden hammer handle. Push the piston down until it is only slightly below the top of the cylinder bore. Guide the connecting rod onto the crankshaft bearing journal carefully, to avoid damaging the crankshaft.

6. Check the bearing clearance of all the rod bearings, fitting them to the crankshaft bearing journals. Follow the procedure in the crankshaft installation above.

7. After the bearings have been fitted, apply a light coating of assembly oil to the journals and bearings.

8. Turn the crankshaft until the appropriate bearing journal is at the bottom of its stroke, then push the piston assembly all the way down until the connecting rod bearing seats on the crankshaft journal. Be careful not to allow the bearing cap screws to strike the crankshaft bearing journals and damage them.

9. After the piston and connecting rod assemblies have been installed, check the connecting rod side clearance on each crankshaft journal.

10. Prime and install the oil pump and the oil pump intake tube.

4.5L and 4.9L Engines

CAMSHAFT, LIFTERS AND TIMING ASSEMBLY

1. Install the camshaft.
2. Install the lifters/followers into their bores.
3. Install the timing gears/chain assembly.

CYLINDER HEAD (S)

1. Install the cylinder head(s) using new gaskets.
2. Assemble the rest of the valve train (pushrods and rocker arms and/or shafts).

4.6L Engine

CYLINDER HEAD (S)

1. Install the cylinder head(s) using new gaskets.
2. Install the timing sprockets/gears and the belt/chain assemblies.

Engine Covers and Components

Install the timing cover(s) and oil pan. Refer to your notes and drawings made prior to disassembly and install all of the components that were removed. Install the engine into the vehicle.

Engine Start-Up And Break-In

STARTING THE ENGINE

Now that the engine is installed and every wire and hose is properly connected, go back and double check that all coolant and vacuum hoses are connected. Check that your oil drain plug is installed and properly tightened. If not already done, install a new oil filter onto the engine. Fill the crankcase with the proper amount and grade of engine oil. Fill the cooling system with a 50/50 mixture of coolant/water.

1. Connect the vehicle battery.
2. Start the engine. Keep your eye on your oil pressure indicator; if it does not indicate oil pressure within 10 seconds of starting, turn the vehicle off.

✹ WARNING

Damage to the engine can result if it is allowed to run with no oil pressure. Check the engine oil level to make sure that it is full. Check for any leaks and if found, repair the leaks before continuing. If there is still no indication of oil pressure, you may need to prime the system.

3. Confirm that there are no fluid leaks (oil or other).

4. Allow the engine to reach normal operating temperature (the upper radiator hose will be hot to the touch).

5. At this point, you can perform any necessary checks or adjustments, such as checking the ignition timing.

6. Install any remaining components or body panels that were removed.

BREAKING IT IN

Make the first miles on the new engine, easy ones. Vary the speed but do not accelerate hard. Most importantly, do not lug the engine, and avoid sustained high speeds until at least 100 miles. Check the engine oil and coolant levels frequently. Expect the engine to use a little oil until the rings seat. Change the oil and filter at 500 miles, 1500 miles, then every 3000 miles past that.

KEEP IT MAINTAINED

Now that you have just gone through all of that hard work, keep yourself from doing it all over again by thoroughly maintaining it. Not that you may not have maintained it before, heck you could have had one to two hundred thousand miles on it before doing this. However, you may have bought the vehicle used, and the previous owner did not keep up on maintenance. Which is why you just went through all of that hard work. See?

4.5L ENGINE MECHANICAL SPECIFICATIONS

Description	English Specification	Metric Specification
General Information		
Engine Type	90° OHV V-8	
Displacement	273 CID	4.5 Liter
Horsepower	200 @ 4400rpm	
Bore	3.623 in.	92 mm
Stroke	3.307 in.	84 mm
Compression Ratio	9.5:1	
Firing Order	1-8-4-3-6-5-7-2	
Valves		
Stem/Guide Clearance		
Intake	0.001 - 0.003 in.	0.03 - 0.07 mm
Exhaust	0.002 - 0.004 in.	0.05 - 0.10 mm
Worn Limits	0.005 in.	0.12 mm
Head Diameter		
Intake	1.77 in.	45 mm
Exhaust	1.50 in.	38 mm
Face Angle	44°	
Seat Angle	45°	
Stem Diameter		
Intake	0.3420 - 0.3413 in.	8.687 - 8.669 mm
Exhaust	0.3401 - 0.3408 in.	8.638 - 8.656 mm
Camshaft		
Timing Chain		
Type	Silent Chain	
Adjustment	None	
Number of Links	44	
Pitch	0.50 in.	12.7 mm
Width		16.2 mm
Bearing Clearance		
Number	5	
New Limit	0.0018 - 0.0037 in.	0.045 - 0.095 mm
Worn Limits	0.004 in.	0.10 mm
Out-of-Round	0.0009 in.	0.022 mm
Valve Timing		
Intake Opens	20° BTDC	
Intake Closes	257° ATDC	
Exhaust Opens	244° BTDC	
Exhaust Closes	29° ATDC	
Valve Lift		
Intake	0.384 in.	9.75 mm
Exhaust	0.396	10.06 mm
Valve Lift		
Duration		
Intake	277°	
Exhaust	273°	
Valve Overlap	49°	
Connecting Rods		
Bearing clearance	0.005 - 0.028 in.	0.012 - 0.071 mm
Lower End Diameter	2.052 in.	52.144 mm
Center/Center Length	5.51 in.	140 mm
End Play of Rods	0.008 - 0.020 in.	0.20 - 0.50 mm
Piston Rings		
Groove Clearance		
Compression	0.0016 - 0.0037 in.	0.04 - .095 mm
Oil Rings	None - Side Sealing	
Ring Gap		
Compression	0.015 - 0.024in.	0.30 - 0.55 mm
Oil Rings	0.010 - 0.050in.	0.25 - 1.27 mm
Piston Pins		
Pin/Piston Clearance	0.0002 - 0.0004 in.	0.005 - 0.010 mm
Pin Length	2.64 in.	67 mm
Pin Diameter	0.8661 - 0.8656 in.	21.998 - 21.985 mm
Pistons & Cylinders		
Bore Out-of-Round	0.0008 in.	0.020 mm
Skirt-to-Bore	0.0010 - 0.0018 in.	0.025 - 0.045 mm

91043CR1

4.5L ENGINE MECHANICAL SPECIFICATIONS

Description	English Specification	Metric Specification
Crank & Bearings		
Clearance		
#1	0.0008 - 0.0031 in.	0.020 - 0.079 mm
#2,3,4,5	0.0016 - 0.0039 in.	0.040 - 0.100 mm
Journal Length		
#1	0.984 in.	24.99 mm
#2	1.023 in.	25.98 mm
#3	1.096 in.	27.86 mm
#4	1.023 in.	25.98 mm
#5	1.495 in.	37.98 mm
Crankpin Diameter	1.927 in.	48.9575 mm
Crank End Play	0.0010 - 0.007 in.	0.026 - 0.177 mm

4.6L ENGINE MECHANICAL SPECIFICATIONS

Description	English Specification	Metric Specification
General Information		
Engine Type	DOHC 4 Valve	
Displacement	279 CID	4.6 Liter
Horsepower L37	295 @ 6000rpm	
LD8	270 @ 5600rpm	
Torque L37	290 ft.lbs. @ 4400rpm	
LD8	300 ft.lbs. @ 4400rpm	
Bore	3.66 in.	93 mm
Stroke	3.31 in.	84 mm
Compression Ratio	10.3:1	
Firing Order	1-2-7-3-4-5-6-8	
Cylinder Head		
Material	Aluminum	
Combustion Chamber Volume		51.8 cc
Valves		
Face Angle	45°	
Seat Angle	46°	
Valve Seat Width		
Intake	0.030 in.	0.762 mm
Exhaust	0.035 in.	0.900 mm
Stem Clearance		
Intake	0.001 - 0.003 in.	0.028 - 0.068 mm
Exhaust	0.002 - 0.004 in.	0.05 - 0.10 mm
Valve Springs		
L37 Free Length	1.575 in.	40 mm
Lbs to Valve closed	53 lb @ 1.19 in.	236 N @ 30.3 mm
Lbs to Valve open	109 lb @ 0.823 in.	485 N @ 20.9
Installed Height	1.19 in.	30.3 mm
LD8 Free Length	1.591 in.	40.4 mm
Lbs to Valve closed	46 lb @ 1.19 in.	205 N @ 30.3 mm
Lbs to Valve open	92 lb @ 0.854 in.	409 N @ 21.7 mm
Installed Height	1.19 in.	30.3 mm
Valve Lifters		
Type	Direct Acting Hydraulic	
Diameter	1.297 - 1.298 in.	32.959 - 32.975 mm
Clearance	0.001 - 0.003 in.	0.025 - 0.0666 mm
Camshaft		
Primary Drive Chain		
Type	Endless Chain	
Adjustment	Hydraulic, Automatic	
Pitch	0.315 in.	8 mm
Width	Single Row	

91043CR2

4.6L ENGINE MECHANICAL SPECIFICATIONS

Description	English Specification	Metric Specification
Camshaft (cont'd)		
Secondary Chain		
Type	Endless Chain	
Adjustment	Direct Acting Hydraulic	
Pitch		
Width	0.315 in.	8 mm
Bearing Journal Diameter	1.061 - 1.062 in.	26.948 - 26.972 mm
Bearing Bore Diameter	1.064 in.	27.023 mm
Bearing Clearance	0.002 - 0.003 in.	0.051 - 0.076 mm
Out-of-Round	0.0009 in.	0.022 mm
Valve Timing L37		
Intake Opens	13° BTDC	
Intake Closes	73° ABDC	
Exhaust Opens	51° BBDC	
Exhaust Closes	13° ATDC	
Valve Lift L37		
Intake	0.370 in.	9.4 mm
Exhaust	0.339 in.	8.6 mm
Duration L37		
Intake	266°	
Exhaust	244°	
Valve Overlap	26°	
Valve Timing LD8		
Intake Opens	9°	
Intake Closes	55° ABDC	
Exhaust Opens	51° BBDC	
Exhaust Closes	13° ATDC	
Valve Lift LD8		
Intake	0.339 in.	8.6 mm
Exhaust	0.339 in.	8.6 mm
Duration LD8		
Intake	244°	
Exhaust	244°	
Valve Overlap	22°	
Connecting Rods		
Bearing clearance	0.001 - 0.003 in.	0.025 - 0.076 mm
Lower End Diameter	2.249 in.	57.144 mm
Piston Hole Diameter	0.8662 - 0.866 in	22.002 - 22.008 mm
Center/Center Length	5.94 in.	151 mm
End Play of Rods	0.008 - 0.020 in.	0.20 - 0.50 mm
Piston Rings		
Top Compression Ring		
Side Clearance	0.0016 - 0.0037 in.	0.040 - 0.095 mm
Groove Clearance	0.002 - 0.004 in.	0.040 - 0.095 mm
Ring Gap	0.010 - 0.016 in.	0.25 - 0.40 mm
Second Compression Ring		
Side Clearance	0.0016 - 0.0037 in.	0.040 - 0.095 mm
Groove Clearance	0.002 - 0.004 in.	0.040 - 0.095 mm
Ring Gap	0.014 - 0.020 in.	0.35 - 0.50 mm
Oil Rings		
Side Clearance	None – Side Sealing	
Ring Gap	0.010 - 0.030 in.	0.25 - 0.76 mm
Pistons		
Piston Material	Aluminum	
Piston Diameter	3.6597 - 3.6603 in.	92.957 - 92.972 mm
Piston Pin Diameter	0.865 - 0.866 in.	21.995 - 22.000 mm
Piston Pin Bore Diameter	0.8662 - 0.8665 in.	22.002 - 22.08 mm
Crank and Bearings		
Bearing Clearance	0.0006 - 0.002 in.	0.015 - 0.055 mm
Bearing Clearance Worn	0.0025 in.	0.0635 mm
Main Bearing Journal		
Diameter	2.5335 - 2.5337 in.	64.352 - 64346 mm
Out-of-Round	0.00016 in.	0.004 mm
Taper	0.00016 in.	0.004 mm
Length # 1	0.969 in.	24.6 mm

4.6L ENGINE MECHANICAL SPECIFICATIONS

Description	English Specification	Metric Specification
Main Bearing Journal (cont'd)		
Length # 2	0.969 in.	24.6 mm
Length # 3	0.992 in.	25.2 mm
Length # 4	0.969 in.	24.6 mm
Length # 5	0.969 in.	24.6 mm
Crank End Play	0.002 - 0.019 in.	0.05 - 0.5 mm
End Play - Worn	0.020 in.	0.5 mm

4.9L ENGINE MECHANICAL SPECIFICATIONS

Description	English Specification	Metric Specification
General Information		
Engine Type	90° OHV V 8	
Displacement	300 CID	4.9 Liter
Horsepower	200@4400rpm	
Torque	275 ft @ 3000rpm	
Bore	3.623 in.	92 mm
Stroke	3.623 in.	92 mm
Compression Ratio	9.5:1	
Firing Order	1-8-4-3-6-5-7-2	
Valves		
Stem/Guide Clearance		
Intake	0.001 - 0.003 in.	0.03 - 0.07 mm
Exhaust	0.002 - 0.004 in.	0.05 - 0.10 mm
Worn Limits	0.005 in.	0.12 mm
Head Diameter		
Intake	1.77 in.	45 mm
Exhaust	1.50 in.	38 mm
Face Angle	44°	
Seat Angle	45°	
Stem Diameter		
Intake	0.3420 - 0.3413 in.	8.687 - 8.699 mm
Exhaust	0.3401 - 0.3408 in.	8.639 - 8.656 mm
Camshaft		
Timing Chain		
Type	Silent Chain	
Adjustment	None	
Number of Links	44	
Pitch	0.50 in.	12.7 mm
Width		16.2 mm
Bearing Clearance		
Number	5	
New Limit	0.0018 - 0.0037 in.	0.045 - 0.095 mm
Worn Limit	0.004 in.	0.10 mm
Out-of-Round	0.0009 in.	0.022 mm
Valve Timing		
Intake Opens	21° BTDC	
Intake Closes	77° ABDC	
Exhaust Opens	65° BBDC	
Exhaust Closes	29° ATDC	
Valve Lift		
Intake	0.384 in.	9.75 mm
Exhaust	0.396	10.06 mm
Duration		
Intake	278°	
Exhaust	274°	
Valve Overlap	49°	
Connecting Rods		
Bearing/Shaft Clearance	0.0005 - 0.0028 in.	0.012 - 0.071 mm
Worn Limits	0.0035 in.	0.090 mm
Lower End Diameter	2.052 - 2.053 in.	52.132 - 52.150
End Play	0.008 - 0.020 in.	0.20 - 0.50 mm

91043CR3

91043CR4

4.9L ENGINE MECHANICAL SPECIFICATIONS

Description	English Specification	Metric Specification
Piston Rings		
Groove Clearance		
Compression	0.0016 - 0.0037 in.	0.04 - .095 mm
Oil Rings	None - Side Sealing	
Ring Gap		
Compression	0.012 - 0.022 in.	0.30 - 0.55 mm
Oil Rings	0.0004 - 0.020 in.	0.10 - 0.50 mm
Piston Pins		
Pin/Piston Clearance	0.0003 - 0.0007 in.	0.008 - 0.019 mm
Pin Length	2.48 in.	63 mm
Pin Diameter	0.8661 - 0.8659 in.	21.998 - 21.993 mm
Pistons & Cylinders		
Bore Out-of-Round	0.0008 in.	0.020 mm
Skirt-to-Bore	0.0004 - 0.0020 in.	0.010 - 0.050 mm
Crank & Bearings		
Clearance		
#1	0.0008 - 0.0031 in.	0.020 - 0.079 mm
#2,3,4,5	0.0016 - 0.0039 in.	0.040 - 0.100 mm
Journal Length		
#1	0.984 in.	24.99 mm
#2	1.023 in.	25.98 mm
#3	1.098 in.	27.88 mm
#4	1.023 in.	25.98 mm
#5	1.495 in.	37.98 mm
Crankpin Diameter	1.927 - 1.928 in.	48.945 - 48.970 mm
Crank End Play	0.0010 - 0.008 in.	0.026 - 0.206 mm

91043CR5

4.5L ENGINE TORQUE SPECIFICATIONS

Components	English	Metric
Connecting rod bolts	24 ft. lbs.	32 Nm
Coolant temperature sensor	22 ft. lbs.	30 Nm
Crankshaft pulley-to-hub bolt	18 ft. lbs.	25 Nm
Cylinder head bolts	65 ft. lbs. ①	90 Nm
Damper to crankshaft bolt	15 ft. lbs.	20 Nm
EGR valve mounting screws	18 ft. lbs.	25 Nm
Exhaust manifold bolts	70 ft. lbs.	95 Nm
Flywheel to crankshaft	15 ft. lbs.	20 Nm
Front cover screws	15 ft. lbs. ①	
Intake manifold bolts	85 ft. lbs.	115 Nm
Main bearing cap bolts	11 ft. lbs.	15 Nm
Oil pan bolts	22 ft. lbs.	30 Nm
Oil pan drain plug	11 ft. lbs.	15 Nm
Oil pan nuts	15 ft. lbs.	20 Nm
Oil pan studs	8 ft. lbs.	10 Nm
Rocker cover screws & studs	11 ft. lbs.	15 Nm
Spark plugs	37 ft. lbs.	50 Nm
Timing sprocket to camshaft bolt	5 ft. lbs.	7 Nm
Timing tab to water pump nuts		

4.6L ENGINE TORQUE SPECIFICATIONS

Components	English	Metric
Coolant drain plug (in block)	71 inch lbs.	8 Nm
Main bearing bolt	①	
Cylinder head bolt	①	
Harmonic balancer bolt	44 ft. lbs. + 120°	60 Nm
Flywheel retaining bolts	11 ft. lbs. + 50°	15 Nm
Connecting Rod Bolt	18 ft. lbs. + 90°	25 Nm
Oil pan bolts	89 inch lbs.	10 Nm
Oil pan drain plug	15 ft. lbs.	20 Nm
Front cover retainers	89 inch lbs.	10 Nm
Belt tensioner retaining bolts	37 ft. lbs.	50 Nm
Idler pulley retaining bolt	37 ft. lbs.	50 Nm
Water manifold plug	18 ft. lbs.	25 Nm
Water pump housing bolts (to head)	18 ft. lbs.	25 Nm
Water pump housing bolts (to block)	18 ft. lbs.	25 Nm
Water outlet to cylinder head bolts	18 ft. lbs.	25 Nm

91043CR6

4.9L ENGINE TORQUE SPECIFICATIONS

Components	English	Metric
Connecting rod bolts	25 ft. lbs.	35 Nm
Coolant temperature sensor	15 ft. lbs.	20 Nm
Cylinder head bolts	①	
Damper to crankshaft bolt	70 ft. lbs.	95 Nm
EGR valve mounting screws	20 ft. lbs.	25 Nm
Exhaust manifold bolts	16 ft. lbs.	20 Nm
Flywheel to crankshaft bolts	70 ft. lbs.	95 Nm
Front cover screws		
Lower 4	17 ft. lbs	25 Nm
Upper 4	30 ft. lbs.	40 Nm
Intake manifold bolts	①	
Main bearing cap bolts	85 ft. lbs.	115 Nm
Oil pan bolts	14 ft. lbs.	20 Nm
Oil pan drain plug	22 ft. lbs.	30 Nm
Oil pan studs	15 ft. lbs.	20 Nm
Rocker cover screws	8 ft. lbs.	10 Nm
Spark plug	23 ft. lbs.	30 Nm
Timing sprocket to camshaft bolt	36 ft. lbs.	50 Nm

① Refer to the procedure

91043CR7

4

DRIVEABILITY AND EMISSIONS CONTROLS

EMISSION CONTROLS

The following is a list of the abbreviations used and their meaning.
- ALDL: Assembly Line Data Link
- AIR: Air Injection Reaction
- BCM: Body Computer Module
- CCDIC: Climate Control Driver Information Center
- CCV: Canister Control Valve
- CO: Carbon Monoxide
- DLC: Data Link Connector
- DTC: Diagnostic Trouble Code
- EAC: Electric Air Control Valve
- EAS: Electric Air Switching Valve
- ECCP: Electronic Climate Control
- ECM: Engine Control Module
- ECT: Electric Air Control Valve with Relief Tube
- ECTS: Engine Coolant Temperature Sensor
- EDV: Electric Divert Valve
- EEC: Electronic Climate Control
- EGR: Exhaust Gas Recirculation
- ESC: Electronic Spark Control
- EVAP: Evaporative Emission System
- FDC: Fuel Data Center
- HC: Hydrocarbon
- HEI: High Energy Ignition
- IAC: Idle Air Control Valve
- IAT: Intake Air Temperature Sensor
- MAP: Manifold Absolute Pressure Sensor
- NOx: Oxides of Nitrogen
- PCM: Powertrain Control Module (previously called PCM)
- PCV: Positive Crankcase Ventilation
- PROM: Programmable Read Only Memory
- SES: Service Engine Soon Light
- SFI: Sequential Multiport Fuel Injection
- TPS: Throttle Position Switch
- TVV: Thermal Vacuum Valve
- VSS: Vehicle Speed Sensor
- WOT: Wide-Open Throttle

Crankcase Ventilation System

A Positive Crankcase Ventilation (PCV) system is used to consume crankcase vapors in the combustion process instead of venting them to the atmosphere. In gasoline engines, a small amount of combustion gases leak past the piston rings into the crankcase. These crankcase blow-by gases contain undesirable hydrocarbon air pollutants. The PCV system is used to prevent these vapors from escaping into the atmosphere, while allowing proper ventilation of the crankcase to maintain good oil quality. Fresh air from the air cleaner is pulled into the crankcase, mixed with blow-by gases and then purged through the Positive Crankcase Ventilation (PCV) valve into the intake manifold.

OPERATION

▶ See Figures 1, 2 and 3

The primary control is through the PCV valve, which meters the flow rate dependent on intake manifold vacuum.

When intake manifold vacuum is high, during deceleration, low speed driving or idle, the PCV valve controls a low flow rate. This is because dur-

ing these modes of operation, the crankcase gas levels, including cylinder blow-by, are low.

When intake manifold vacuum is low, such as during acceleration or high load operation, the PCV valve controls flow to a higher rate to accommodate increased engine crankcase gases.

Under full throttle operation or abnormal conditions, such as a worn or damaged engine, or during high speed light load operation, the system allows excess blow-by gases to flow through the fresh air tube into the inlet duct to be combined with incoming air from the air cleaner.

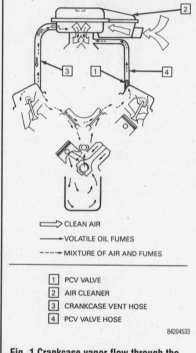

CLEAN AIR
VOLATILE OIL FUMES
MIXTURE OF AIR AND FUMES

1	PCV VALVE
2	AIR CLEANER
3	CRANKCASE VENT HOSE
4	PCV VALVE HOSE

84204533

Fig. 1 Crankcase vapor flow through the PCV system—4.9L engine shown

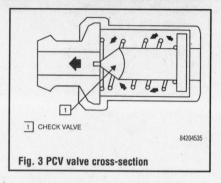

| 1 | CHECK VALVE |

84204535

Fig. 3 PCV valve cross-section

A plugged PCV valve or hose may cause the following conditions:
- Rough idle
- Stalling or slow idle speed
- Oil leaks
- Oil in the air cleaner
- Sludge in the engine

A leaking valve or hose could cause the following conditions:
- Erratic idle speed
- Rough idle
- Stalling

PCV SYSTEM TESTING

▶ See Figures 4 and 5

If an engine is idling rough, check for a clogged PCV valve or plugged hose. Replace system components as required.

1. Remove the PCV valve from the rocker cover.
2. Run the engine at idle.
3. Place your thumb over the end of the valve to check for vacuum. If there is no vacuum at the valve, check for plugged hoses, intake manifold port, or PCV valve. Replace plugged or deteriorated hoses.
4. Turn the engine OFF and remove the PCV valve. Shake the valve and listen for the rattle of the check needle inside the valve. If the valve does not rattle, replace it.

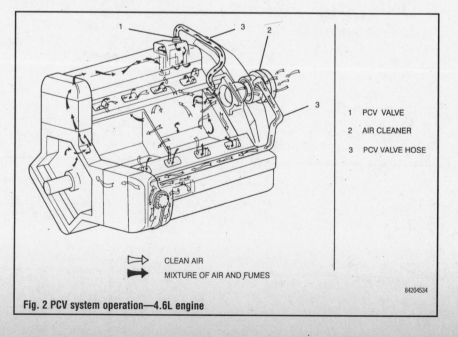

CLEAN AIR
MIXTURE OF AIR AND FUMES

1	PCV VALVE
2	AIR CLEANER
3	PCV VALVE HOSE

84204534

Fig. 2 PCV system operation—4.6L engine

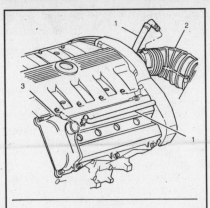

1 PCV FRESH AIR TUBE
2 AIR CLEANER
3 GROMMET

84204536

Fig. 4 PCV hose, air cleaner and grommet on left cam cover—4.6L engine

TCCS4P05

Fig. 5 Check the PCV valve for vacuum at idle

REMOVAL & INSTALLATION

1. Locate the PCV valve on the valve cover or in the intake manifold.
2. Grasp the PCV valve firmly and pull it out of the rubber grommet.
3. Once free of the grommet, disconnect it from the vacuum line.

To install:

4. Inspect the rubber grommet. Replace if necessary.
5. Installation is the reversal of the removal procedure.

Evaporative Emission Controls

The Evaporative Emission Control (EVAP) System helps to reduce evaporated hydrocarbons (fuel) that enter the atmosphere. The most important component f this system is the EVAP charcoal canister The EVAP canister draws the evaporated fuel from the fuel tank and stores it. When several conditions are met, the PCM commands the EVAP solenoid to open and allow engine vacuum to draw stored fuel from the EVAP canister into the throttle body. This is called purging the canister. Once the evaporated fuel enters the throttle body, it is burned in the combustion process.

OPERATION

▶ **See Figures 6 and 7**

The Evaporative Emission Control (EEC) or (EVAP) system stores fuel vapor generated by the vehicle and regulates its consumption during nor-

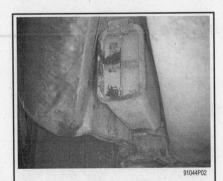

91044P02

Fig. 6 The charcoal canister is typically located under the rear of the car

mal driving operation. The main purpose of the EEC system is to prevent fuel vapor from dispelling into the atmosphere.

The EEC routine is controlled by the PCM via the electronic solenoid.

Should the EVAP solenoid fail closed, electrically or mechanically, the canister charcoal bed could become saturated allowing vapors to escape to the atmosphere. The vapors should not enter the passenger compartment because of the rear-mounted canister.

Charcoal Canister

▶ **See Figure 8**

The canister is filled with activated carbon that stores vapor transferred from the fuel tank. The tank also stores the vapor that is emitted from the engine's induction system while the engine is not running. When the engine is running, the stored vapor is purged from the carbon storage device by the intake airflow and then consumed in the normal combustion process.

The 3 ports coming off the canister are identified as:

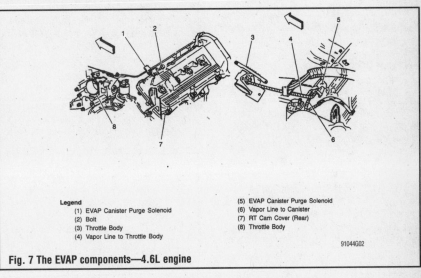

Legend
(1) EVAP Canister Purge Solenoid
(2) Bolt
(3) Throttle Body
(4) Vapor Line to Throttle Body
(5) EVAP Canister Purge Solenoid
(6) Vapor Line to Canister
(7) RT Cam Cover (Rear)
(8) Throttle Body

91044G02

Fig. 7 The EVAP components—4.6L engine

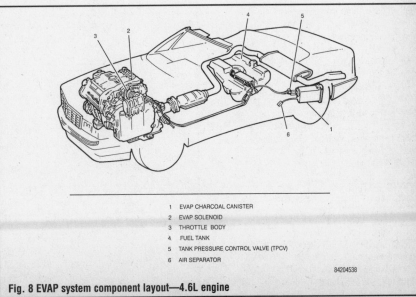

1 EVAP CHARCOAL CANISTER
2 EVAP SOLENOID
3 THROTTLE BODY
4 FUEL TANK
5 TANK PRESSURE CONTROL VALVE (TPCV)
6 AIR SEPARATOR

84204538

Fig. 8 EVAP system component layout—4.6L engine

1. Fuel vapor port (from fuel tank)
2. EEC port (purge line to throttle body)
3. Atmospheric port (from fresh air source via the body mounted vent hose)

EVAP Canister Purge Valve

The EVAP Canister purge valve controls engine vacuum to the canister. Under the appropriate conditions., the PCM commands the purge valve open. This allows engine vacuum to draw fresh air into the canister through the EVAP Vent Valve. The fuel vapors exit the canister and are consumed during the normal combustion process.

EVAP Canister Vent Valve

The EVAP Canister Vent Valve is used for certain EVAP system performance tests performed by the PCM. The PCM can close the vent that effectively seals the system. The PCM can then evaluate pressure changes within the system by monitoring the Fuel Tank Pressure Sensor signal.

Fuel Tank

Fuel vapor generated inside the fuel tank is released to the canister for containment.

Fuel Tank Pressure Sensor

The Fuel Tank Pressure Sensor is used for certain EVAP system performance tests performed by the PCM. The Fuel Tank Pressure sensor contains a diaphragm that changes resistance based on pressure. When EVAP system pressure is low (during purge) sensor output voltage is low. When the system pressure is high, sensor output voltage is high. The PCM monitors pressure changes within the system using the Fuel Tank Pressure Sensor signal. This information can be used to detect leads within the system or to verify the operation of the system components.

The PCM operates a solenoid valve that purges the canister with ported vacuum at the throttle body. Under cold engine operation 'OPEN LOOP' or idle conditions the solenoid is de-energized by the PCM, this does not allow vacuum to the canister through the normally closed solenoid.

The canister will be enabled, the PCM will energize the solenoid when:
• Coolant temperature is above 80°C
• Closed loop has been achieved for at least 30 seconds
• Throttle switch open
• Vehicle speed greater than 10 mph
When the solenoid is closed (is not receiving voltage or has a stuck plunger) the canister will not purge to the intake manifold. This will prevent the canister from purging vapors and could result in a saturated canister.

COMPONENT TESTING

Late Model Vehicles

During specific operating conditions, the PCM performs various tests on the evaporative emission system. The system tests consist of the following series of events. After ensuring that the EVAP purge

solenoid valve duty cycle has dropped to 0%, indicating that the valve is closed, the PCM commands the EVAP canister vent solenoid valve closed, sealing the system. The PCM monitors the accumulation of vapor pressure within the fuel tank via the fuel tank pressure sensor. The EVAP test is aborted if the vapor pressure is too high. If any vapor pressure is measured, it will be used later to compensate a pressure reading during the small leak detection test. If a vacuum is measured which exceeds a calculated limit during vapor accumulation, DTC P0440 will set. The EVAP canister purge solenoid valve is then opened. Simultaneously, the Vent solenoid is opened. If the vapor pressure does not bleed off or bleeds off too slowly, DTC P0440 is set. Once the EVAP purge solenoid valve reaches its position for the remainder of the diagnostic test, the Vent solenoid will be closed again. This causes vacuum to be applied to the entire EVAP system. The PCM monitors the vacuum level within the system. If the desired vacuum level can not be achieved, or if the vacuum level is reached but it took too much time, DTC P0455 will set. Once the desired vacuum level is reached, the purge solenoid is closed, sealing the system, The PCM continues to monitor the fuel tank pressure sensor signal, measuring the rate of vacuum decay. If the system holds vacuum, as it should, the vent solenoid is opened and the test is completed. In.addition to the system tests, the PCM monitors the circuit integrity of the purge solenoid (DTC P0443), the vent solenoid (DTC P0446), and the fuel tank pressure sensor (DTC P0450).

Early Model Vehicles

1. Attach a clean length of hose to the fuel tank vapor line connection on the canister and attempt to blow through the purge control valve. It should be

difficult or impossible to blow through the valve. If air passes easily, the valve is stuck open and should be replaced.

2. Connect a hand-held vacuum pump to the top vacuum line fitting of the purge control valve. Apply a vacuum of 15 in. Hg (51 kPa) to the purge valve diaphragm. If the vacuum reading is less than 10 inches after 10 seconds, the diaphragm is leaking and the TPCV must be replaced. If the diaphragm holds vacuum, try to blow through the hose connected to the lower tube while vacuum is still being applied. An increase flow of air should be observed. If not, replace the TPCV.

3. Attach a hose to the lower port of the canister and attempt to blow through it. Air should pass through and into the canister. If not, replace the canister.

4. Detach the electrical connector at the canister purge solenoid. Attach a hose to the upper port on the canister and attempt to blow air through it. Air should not pass through into the canister. If air passes, replace the purge solenoid.

5. Measure the resistance of the purge control solenoid. The resistance should be greater than 20 ohms and less than 100 ohms. If the solenoid resistance is not in this range, replace the solenoid.

6. Reattach all purge hoses and the solenoid electrical connector.

DIAGNOSTIC AIDS

▶ **See Figure 9**

Check for the following conditions.
• Faulty fuel cap.
• Damaged, pinched, or blocked EVAP purge line.

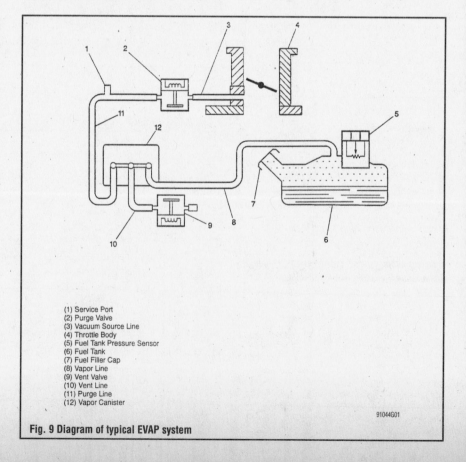

(1) Service Port
(2) Purge Valve
(3) Vacuum Source Line
(4) Throttle Body
(5) Fuel Tank Pressure Sensor
(6) Fuel Tank
(7) Fuel Filler Cap
(8) Vapor Line
(9) Vent Valve
(10) Vent Line
(11) Purge Line
(12) Vapor Canister

91044G01

Fig. 9 Diagram of typical EVAP system

- Damaged EVAP vent hose.
- Damaged, pinched, or blocked fuel tank vapor line.
- EVAP canister purge valve problem (non-electrical).
- EVAP vent solenoid problem (non-electrical).
- Damaged EVAP canister.
- Leaking fuel sender assembly O-ring.
- Leaking fuel tank or fuel filler neck.

Exhaust Gas Recirculation System

OPERATION

The Exhaust Gas Recirculation (EGR) system is used in an automotive engine to decrease the emission levels of oxides of nitrogen (NOx). NOx defines a group of chemical compounds containing nitrogen and varying amounts of oxygen that can have harmful environmental effects in large quantities.

NOx forms during the combustion process in amounts that is dependent on the concentration of oxygen in the combustion chamber and the duration that the combustion process temperatures exceed 1500°F. Decreased NOx levels are accomplished by reducing the peak combustion temperature through dilution of the incoming air/fuel charge with exhaust. During combustion, exhaust gas (largely non-reactive carbon dioxide and water vapor) acts to absorb a portion of the combustion energy, resulting in lower temperatures throughout the combustion process yielding lower amounts of NOx.

Desired amounts of EGR depend upon geometry of the combustion chamber and the operating condition of the engine. Extensive laboratory and vehicle tests are used to determine optimal EGR rates for all operating conditions. Too little EGR can yield high NOx, while too much EGR can disrupt combustion events.

COMPONENT TESTING

Early Model Engines

▶ See Figures 10, 11, 12 and 13

The EGR valve is opened by vacuum to allow exhaust gases to flow into the intake manifold. The exhaust gas then moves with the air/fuel mixture into the combustion chamber. The Powertrain Control Module (PCM) controls the vacuum to the EGR valve with a solenoid valve. A constant 12 volts is supplied to the positive terminal on the EGR valve. The vacuum supply to the EGR valve is regulated by the PCM controlling the EGR solenoid ground. The percentage that the PCM grounds the EGR solenoid is called the duty cycle. The duty cycle is the time the solenoid is on divided by the time it is off. A de-energized solenoid allows vacuum to pass to the EGR valve. A duty cycle of 100 percent will turn the EGR full off since the solenoid will be energized and not allow vacuum to pass to the valve. The EGR pulse width is regulated by the PCM depending on engine load conditions. When the engine is cold, within specified load range and above a specified rpm, the PCM sends 100 percent duty cycle to the solenoid and blocks vacuum to the EGR valve. When the engine is warm, the PCM sends a duty cycle to the solenoid to allow EGR.

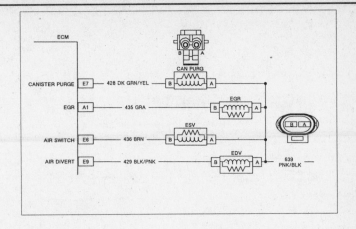

PFI CHART C-7

EGR DIAGNOSIS

Before Staring

- Check 10 amp fuse (# 3) in underhood relay center.
- Measure EGR solenoid resistance – should be 20 - 100 ohms.

The 4.5L DLPFI engine uses a positive backpressure EGR valve which limits EGR flow with low exhaust backpressure (idle, decel, etc.). It is very important that exhaust tubes which decrease backpressure (pull air through) are not hooked to the vehicle when diagnosing the EGR system.

VACUUM TEST

1. Connect a vacuum gage to the source side of the EGR solenoid. Start the engine, manifold vacuum should be present. If it is not, repair leaks or obstruction between the EGR solenoid and throttle body.

2. Connect a vacuum gage to the EGR valve vacuum supply. There should be no vacuum with the engine idling. If there is, follow Chart C-7

3. With the gage hooked to the EGR valve vacuum supply, disconnect the EGR solenoid connector. There should be more than 8 inches of vacuum available. If not, repair leak or obstruction in EGR valve vacuum hose.

84204007

Fig. 10 Exhaust Gas Recirculation (EGR) system check—4.5L engine

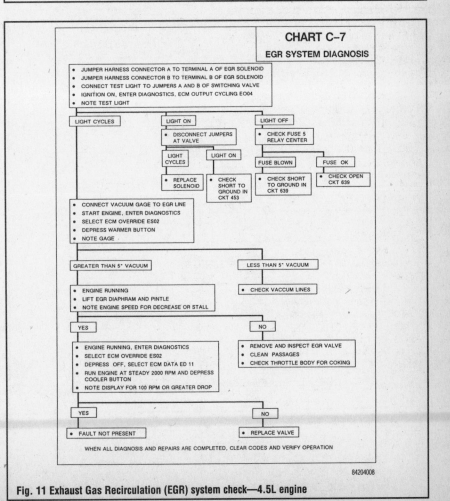

84204008

Fig. 11 Exhaust Gas Recirculation (EGR) system check—4.5L engine

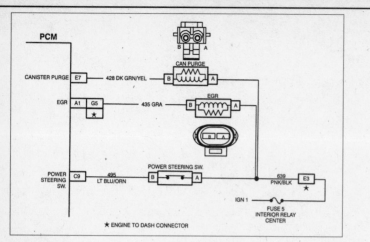

PFI CHART C-7

EGR DIAGNOSIS

Before Staring

- Check 10 amp fuse (#5) in underhood relay center.
- Measure EGR solenoid resistance – should be 20 – 100 ohms.

The 4.9L DLPFI engine uses a positive backpressure EGR valve which limits EGR flow with low exhaust backpressure (idle, decel, etc.). It is very important that exhaust tubes which decrease backpressure (pull air through) are **not** hooked to the vehicle when diagnosing the EGR system.

VACUUM TEST

1. Connect a vacuum gage to the source side of the EGR solenoid. Start the engine, manifold vacuum should be present. If it is not, repair leaks or obstruction between the EGR solenoid and throttle body.

2. Connect a vacuum gage to the EGR valve vacuum supply. There should be no vacuum with the engine idling. If there is, follow Chart C-7.

3. With the gage hooked to the EGR valve vacuum supply, disconnect the EGR solenoid connector. There should be more than 15 inches of vacuum available. If not, repair leak or obstruction in EGR valve vacuum hose.

84204005

Fig. 12 Exhaust Gas Recirculation (EGR) system check—4.9L engine

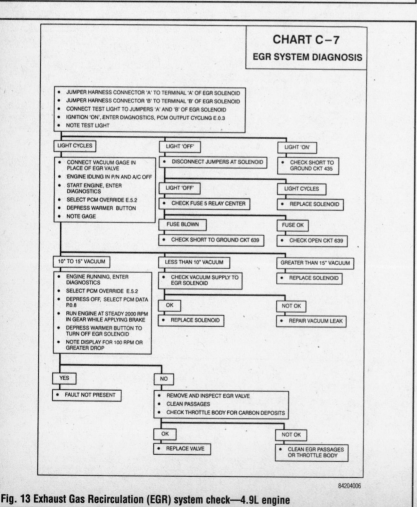

84204006

Fig. 13 Exhaust Gas Recirculation (EGR) system check—4.9L engine

These engine use a positive backpressure EGR valve, which requires exhaust backpressure (proportional to engine flow) to open and allow exhaust gas to flow into the intake manifold.

The PCM uses the following sensors to control the EGR solenoid:

- Coolant Temperature (CTS)
- Throttle Position (TPS)
- Manifold Pressure (MAP)
- Manifold Air Temperature (MAT)
- Throttle Switch (ISC)
- RPM data from the distributor reference pulses
- Vehicle Speed Sensor (VSS)

Too much EGR flow tends to weaken combustion, causing the engine to run roughly or stall. With too much EGR flow at idle, cruise speed or cold operation, any of the following conditions may occur:

- Engine stalls after cold start
- Engine stalls at idle after deceleration
- Car surges during cruise
- Rough idle

If the EGR valve should stay open due to a stuck open valve, the engine may not run.

Too little or no EGR flow allows combustion temperatures to get too high during acceleration and load conditions. Any of the following conditions may occur:

- Spark knock
- Emission test failure

Later Model Engines

▶ See Figures 14, 15, 16, 17 and 18

The Northstar 4.6L engine uses a computer controlled EGR valve to precisely regulate the amount of EGR delivered to the engine for all operating conditions. Exhaust gases are routed to the engine through a corrugated semi-flexible feed pipe (EGR valve pipe) which connects the crossover exhaust pipe to the crossover water pump housing.

In the crossover water pump housing, exhaust gases are precisely metered by the PCM controlled EGR valve, then cooled by the engine coolant and finally routed to the front and rear cylinder heads. A potential drawback with EGR is that with certain driving schedules, deposits can accumulate when hot exhaust gases are cooled. The Northstar system uses the crossover water pump housing as a cross-flow heat exchanger to cool exhaust gases in large easily cleaned passages to virtually eliminate any concern with deposit accumulation during the service life of the engine. This is done by having the cooling passages reduce EGR gasses below their deposit forming temperature prior to routing these gasses into the cylinder distribution channels.

In each cylinder bank, exhaust gases travel under the intake manifold along an irregular shaped sandwich passage made up of the aluminum alloy cylinder head and a non-metallic distribution plate. Engine vacuum acts to draw exhaust gases through outlets in the distribution plate where mixing with the incoming fuel/air charges for each cylinder occurs. Although the openings look small, the EGR valve pintle is the flow limiter in the system.

The EGR valve regulates the amount of exhaust gas fed to the engine. This mixture is dependent upon the height of the pintle above the orifice in the base of the valve. The EGR system is comprised of the following subassemblies:

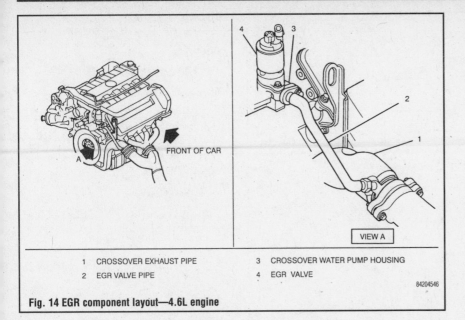

Fig. 14 EGR component layout—4.6L engine

1	CROSSOVER EXHAUST PIPE	3	CROSSOVER WATER PUMP HOUSING
2	EGR VALVE PIPE	4	EGR VALVE

84204546

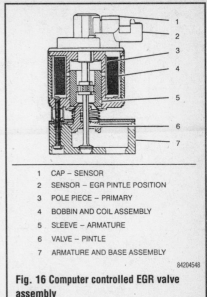

1	CAP – SENSOR
2	SENSOR – EGR PINTLE POSITION
3	POLE PIECE – PRIMARY
4	BOBBIN AND COIL ASSEMBLY
5	SLEEVE – ARMATURE
6	VALVE – PINTLE
7	ARMATURE AND BASE ASSEMBLY

84204548

Fig. 16 Computer controlled EGR valve assembly

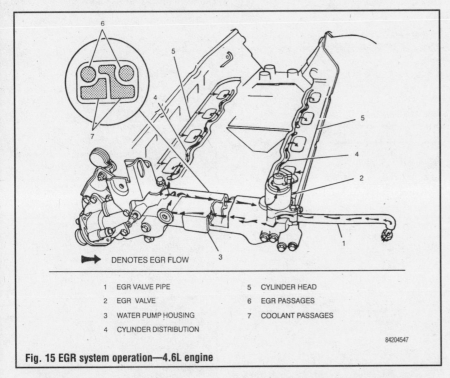

DENOTES EGR FLOW

1	EGR VALVE PIPE	5	CYLINDER HEAD
2	EGR VALVE	6	EGR PASSAGES
3	WATER PUMP HOUSING	7	COOLANT PASSAGES
4	CYLINDER DISTRIBUTION		

84204547

Fig. 15 EGR system operation—4.6L engine

- Bobbin and Coil (Solenoid) assembly
- Armature Assembly
- Base

The bobbin and coil (solenoid) assembly consists of one solenoid that is encapsulated to maximize reliability, seal coils from the environment and prevent movement of the coils and terminal. Inside the solenoid (bobbin and coil) assembly, is an armature assembly, consisting of a pintle and valve assembly, two seals, retaining washer, a seal spring, and armature spring and a bearing. The valve pintle shaft is sealed from the exhaust chamber by a bearing. In addition, an armature shield, held in place by a compression spring, deflects exhaust gas from the shaft and the armature. The base adapter and base plate make up the base assembly.

As mentioned above, the PCM controlled EGR valve regulates the amount of exhaust gas fed to the engine. This device offers more precise EGR flow metering than a backpressure or digital type valve and superior emission control and driveability. The PCM monitors the following sensors to control the linear EGR valve:

- Coolant Temperature (CT) sensor
- Throttle position (TP) sensor
- Manifold Pressure (MAP) sensor
- Throttle Switch (TS)
- RPM data
- Vehicle Speed Sensor (VSS)

Output messages are then sent to the EGR system indicating the proper amount of exhaust gas recirculation necessary to lower combustion temperatures. The solenoid assembly is energized by 12 volt current that enters the valve through an electrical connector, then flows through the solenoid assembly to the PCM, and creates an electromagnetic field. This field causes the armature assembly to be pulled upward, lifting the pintle a variable amount off the base. The exhaust gas then flows from the exhaust manifold (through the orifice) to the cylinder distribution channels. The height of the pintle is read by the pintle position sensor, and the PCM closes the loop on the desired position versus the actual position read. Then, until the actual pintle position equals the desired pintle position, the PCM changes the pulse width modulated command to the solenoid. This results in improved flow accuracy. The EGR valve is unique in that the PCM continuously monitors pintle height and continuously corrects it in order to obtain accurate flow in a closed loop system. When the solenoid is de-energized, (PCM breaks the circuit), the pintle is sealed against the orifice, blocking exhaust flow to the cylinder distribution channels.

To regulate EGR flow to the engine, the PCM controls the solenoid to directly vary the pintle position relative to the closed valve position. The EGR valve contains a potentiometer type position sensor that provides a voltage proportional to pintle position. Pintle position is used by the PCM for closed-loop control of the valve pintle position to follow commanded position, for diagnostics, and to correct fuel spark for EGR.

Too much EGR flow tends to weaken combustion, causing the engine to run roughly or stall. With too much EGR flow at idle, cruise speed or cold operation, any of the following conditions may occur:

- Engine stalls after cold start
- Engine stalls at idle after deceleration
- Car surges during cruise

If the EGR valve should stay open due to a stuck open valve, the engine may not run.

Too little or no EGR flow allows combustion temperatures to get too high during acceleration and load conditions. Any of the following conditions may occur:

- Spark knock
- Emission test failure

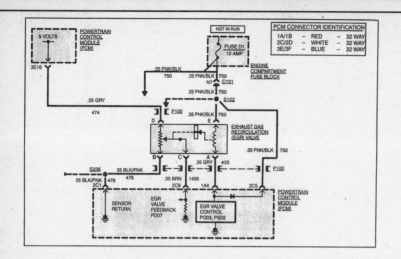

CHART 6E-C-1

EXHAUST GAS RECIRCULATION (EGR) SYSTEM CHECK

CIRCUIT DESCRIPTION:

This procedure tests the EGR system's ability to functionally regulate the amount of exhaust gas fed to the engine.

NOTES ON FAULT TREE:

1. Checking if by using PCM overrides the EGR valve can be shut off (less than 103 counts).
2. Checking if by using PCM overrides the EGR valve can return to full on (greater then 200 counts).

3. Checking CKT 750 and fuse 'D1' for an open.
4. Checking if EGR valve is open circuited.
5. Checking if CKT 435 is open.
6. Checking if PCM is open internally or if CKT 435 is shorted to voltage.
7. EGR valve control circuits are OK. Checking to see if the EGR valve can respond correctly to the signal being sent to it from the PCM.

84204003

Fig. 17 Exhaust Gas Recirculation (EGR) system check—4.6L engine

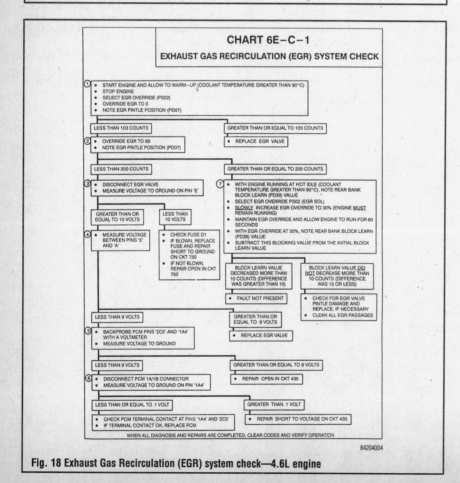

CHART 6E-C-1

EXHAUST GAS RECIRCULATION (EGR) SYSTEM CHECK

84204004

Fig. 18 Exhaust Gas Recirculation (EGR) system check—4.6L engine

REMOVAL & INSTALLATION

EGR Valve

4.5L AND 4.9L ENGINES

▶ See Figures 19, 20, 21 and 22

1. Disconnect the negative battery terminal.
2. Remove the air cleaner assembly.
3. Remove the vacuum valve at the EGR valve.
4. Remove the 2 EGR valve mounting bolts and the EGR valve from the engine.
5. Inspect the EGR passages in the intake manifold for deposits and clean as necessary.

To install:

6. Install the cleaned or replacement EGR valve onto the intake manifold using new gasket. Tighten the 2 mounting bolts to 14 ft. lbs. (18 Nm).
7. Install the vacuum hose to the valve.
8. Install the air cleaner assembly and connect the negative battery terminal.

4.6L ENGINE

▶ See Figures 23, 24, 25 and 26

1. Detach the electrical connector from the solenoid.
2. Remove the fuel line bracket nut (if equipped).
3. Lift the fuel line bracket off the stud (if equipped).
4. Push the fuel line bracket away from the EGR valve base (if equipped).

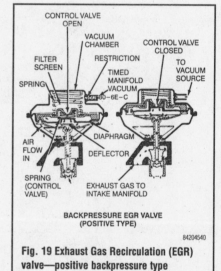

84204540

Fig. 19 Exhaust Gas Recirculation (EGR) valve—positive backpressure type

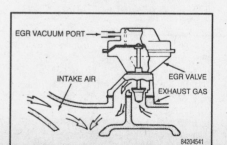

84204541

Fig. 20 Typical exhaust gas recirculation flow

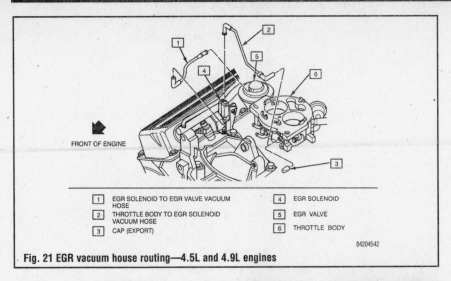

FRONT OF ENGINE

1	EGR SOLENOID TO EGR VALVE VACUUM HOSE
2	THROTTLE BODY TO EGR SOLENOID VACUUM HOSE
3	CAP (EXPORT)
4	EGR SOLENOID
5	EGR VALVE
6	THROTTLE BODY

84204542

Fig. 21 EGR vacuum house routing—4.5L and 4.9L engines

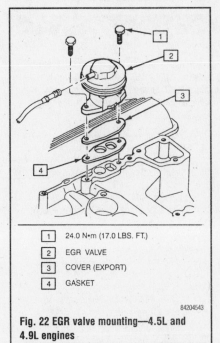

1	24.0 N•m (17.0 LBS. FT.)
2	EGR VALVE
3	COVER (EXPORT)
4	GASKET

84204543

Fig. 22 EGR valve mounting—4.5L and 4.9L engines

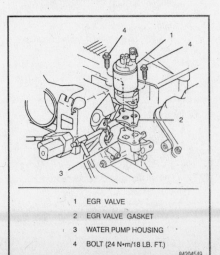

1	EGR VALVE
2	EGR VALVE GASKET
3	WATER PUMP HOUSING
4	BOLT (24 N•m/18 LB. FT.)

84204549

Fig. 23 EGR valve mounting—4.6L engine

91044P12

Fig. 24 Unplug the connector from the EGR valve

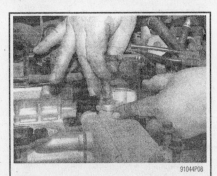

91044P08

Fig. 25 Remove the EGR-to-intake manifold retaining bolts

91044P09

Fig. 26 Removing the EGR valve and inspecting the mounting gasket

5. Remove the mounting nuts and/or volts from the base (if equipped).

6. Pull the EGR valve off its mounting base.

a. Inspect the EGR passages in the crossover water pump housing for deposits.

b. Clean the EGR passages as needed.

7. Clean the mounting surface for the EGR.

To install:

8. Install the cleaned or replacement EGR valve using a new gasket.

9. Tighten the mounting nuts and/or bolts to 18 ft. lbs. (24 Nm).

10. Place the fuel line bracket onto the EGR valve stud (if equipped).

a. Tighten the bracket nut to 14 ft. lbs. (19 Nm).

11. Attach the electrical connector.

EGR Valve Pipe

▶ **See Figure 27**

➡ **It may be necessary to remove the crossover exhaust pipe in order to facilitate EGR valve pipe removal from the engine.**

1. Remove the pipe mounting bolt at water pump bracket.

2. Raise and safely support the vehicle.

3. Remove the crossover exhaust pipe, if required.

4. Remove the pipe-mounting nut at the crossover exhaust pipe. Remove the EGR valve pipe from the vehicle.

To install:

5. Install the EGR valve pipe. Install the nut at the crossover exhaust pipe and tighten to 44 ft. lbs. (60 Nm). Install the crossover-exhaust pipe and related components, if removed.

6. Lower the vehicle. Install the bolts at the water pump housing and tighten to 18 ft. lbs. (24 Nm).

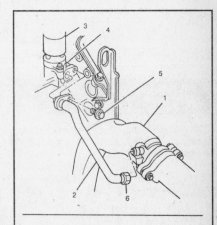

1	CROSSOVER EXHAUST PIPE
2	EGR VALVE PIPE
3	EGR VALVE
4	WATER PUMP HOUSING
5	BOLT (24 N•m/18 LB. FT.)
6	NUT (60 N•m/44 LB. FT.)

84204550

Fig. 27 EGR valve pipe mounting—4.6L engine

EGR Control Solenoid

♦ **See Figure 28**

1. Disconnect the negative battery cable.
2. Remove the air cleaner assembly.
3. Detach the electrical connector and the vacuum hoses at the EGR solenoid.
4. Remove the solenoid and nut from the engine.

To install:

5. Installation is the reverse of the removal procedure.

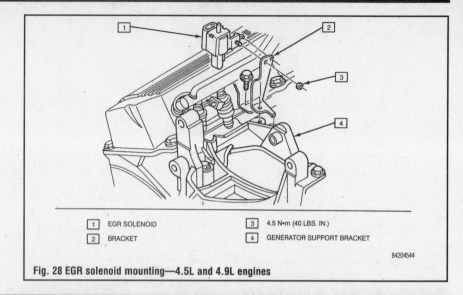

1	EGR SOLENOID	3	4.5 N·m (40 LBS. IN.)
2	BRACKET	4	GENERATOR SUPPORT BRACKET

84204544

Fig. 28 EGR solenoid mounting—4.5L and 4.9L engines

ELECTRONIC ENGINE CONTROLS

➡ When the term **Powertrain Control Module (PCM) is used, it will refer to the engine control computer regardless that it may be called a Powertrain Control Module (PCM) or Engine Control Module (ECM).**

The PCM is designed to maintain exhaust emission levels to Federal or California standards, while providing excellent driveability and fuel efficiency. Review the component sections and wiring diagrams to determine which systems are controlled by each specific control module. The control module monitors numerous engine and vehicle functions and controls the following operations.

- Fuel control
- Ignition control (IC)
- Knock Sensor (KS) system
- Automatic Transaxle shift functions
- Cruise Control Enable
- Generator
- Evaporative Emission (EVAP) Purge
- A/C Clutch Control
- Cooling Fan Control

Powertrain Control Module (PCM)

The PCM constantly monitors the input information, processes this information from various sensors, and generates output commands to the various systems that affect vehicle performance.

The PCM monitors engine operations and environmental conditions (ambient temperature, barometric pressure, etc.) needed to calculate the fuel delivery time (pulse width/injector on-time) of the fuel injector. The fuel pulse may be modified by the PCM to account for special operating conditions, such as cranking, cold starting, altitude, acceleration, and deceleration.

The ability of the PCM to recognize and adjust for vehicle variations (engine transmission, vehicle weight, axle ratio, etc.) is provided by a removable calibration unit , referred to as a PROM (Programmable Read Only Memory) that is programmed to tailor the PCM for the particular vehicle. There is a specific PCM/PROM combination for each specific

vehicle, and the combinations are not interchangeable with those of other vehicles.

The PCM also performs the diagnostic function of the system. It can recognize operational problems, alert the driver through the SERVICE ENGINE SOON light, and store a code or codes, which identify the problem areas to aid the technician in making repairs.

OPERATION

The Powertrain Control Module (PCM) performs many functions on your vehicle. The module accepts information from various engine sensors and computes the required fuel flow rate necessary to maintain the correct amount of air/fuel ratio throughout the entire engine operational range.

Based on the information that is received and programmed into the PCM's memory, the PCM generates output signals to control relays, actuators and solenoids. The PCM also sends out a command to the fuel injectors that meters the appropriate quantity of fuel. The module automatically senses and compensates for any changes in altitude when driving your vehicle.

REMOVAL & INSTALLATION

Later Model Vehicles

This powertrain has very complex components with equally complex operating characteristics. Therefore, it is essential that the Powertrain diagnostic procedures given be used for diagnosis before any repairs are made. While the PCM may appear to be the source of a problem, it may be operating properly based on the incorrect inputs it receives.

➡ **To prevent internal PCM damage, the ignition must be in the OFF (Lock) position when disconnecting or reconnecting power to the PCM, as when the battery cables, PCM connectors, or fuses are connected or disconnected. The ignition switch supplies power to the PCM in all key positions except LOCK. The**

key must be in the LOCK position for a minimum of 30 seconds prior to disconnecting power to the PCM. This is to allow the PCM to store the Transaxle fluid life, transaxle shift adapts and Throttle Position Learned value into the EEPROM.

Service of the PCM will consist of replacement of the PCM and flashing the EPROM. When flashing the EPROM, also refer to the latest service publications for updated programming procedures and information.

The service PCM will not contain data. The EPROM must be flashed after the service PCM is installed.

1. Record the Transaxle Fluid and Engine Oil Life Indexes.
2. Disconnect the negative battery cable.
3. Detach the IAT sensor connector.
4. Remove the gusset (brace) from between the LH fender and t he radiator core support by removing the 5 attaching bolts.
5. Loosen the Intake Air duct clamp at the MAF sensor.
6. Remove the Intake Air duct/air cleaner assembly.
7. Remove the air cleaner assembly.
8. Lift the air inlet assembly onto the radiator core support area by pulling firmly straight up.
9. Open the air inlet housing to gain aces to the PCM.
10. Loosen the connector attaching bolts.
11. Detach both PCM connectors.

To install:

- If installing a replacement PCM the KS module will have to be transferred from the original PCM to the replacement PCM.
- If installing a replacement, the PCM isolators will have to be transferred to the replacement PCM.

12. Slide the PCM isolators onto the PCM.
13. Install the PCM connectors and tighten the screws to 71 inch lbs. (8 Nm).
14. Close and latch the air inlet housing.
15. Install the air inlet housing by inserting the outboard locating pin into the inside fender alignment hole.

16. Press the air inlet housing firmly down to engage the bottom locating pins.

17. Ensure that the locating pin grommets are present and properly positioned in the bottom of the air cleaner assembly.

18. Install the intake air duct/air cleaner assembly onto the air inlet housing.

19. Install the intake air duct to the MAF sensor and tighten the clamp.

20. Attach the IAT sensor connector.

21. Install the gusset (brace) between the LH fender and the radiator core support. Tighten the attaching bolts to 18 ft. lbs. (24 Nm).

22. Disconnect the negative battery cable.

Early Model Vehicles

▶ See Figures 29, 30 and 31

1. Disconnect the negative battery cable.

2. Remove the glove box assembly, if necessary. Remove the right lower dash panel and kick panel to gain access to the PCM.

3. Detach the connectors from the PCM.

4. Remove the PCM mounting hardware and remove the PCM from the passenger compartment.

5. Remove the PROM access cover from the old PCM. Using 2 fingers, push both retaining tabs back away from the PROM at the same time. Grasp the PROM at both ends and lift the up out of the PROM socket.

To install:

6. Install the old PROM into the socket of the PCM. The small notches in the PROM must align with the small notches in the socket on the PCM. Press on the ends of the PROM unit until the retaining clips snap into the ends of the PROM. Press the clips into the sides of the PROM until they snap into place. Do not press on the middle of the PROM; only on the ends.

7. Install the PROM accessories cover.

8. Install the PCM and mounting hardware into the passenger compartment of the vehicle. Secure the PCM in place.

9. Reattach the harness connectors at the PCM.

10. Install the kick panel and glove box, as required.

11. Reconnect the negative battery cable.

Oxygen Sensor

OPERATION

▶ See Figure 32

The oxygen (O2) sensor is a device that produces an electrical voltage when exposed to the oxygen present in the exhaust gases. The sensor is mounted in the exhaust system, usually in the manifold or a boss located on the down pipe before the catalyst. Most of the oxygen sensors used on the sophisticated systems of today are heated internally for faster reaction when the engine is started cold. The oxygen sensor produces a voltage between zero and one volt. When there is a large amount of oxygen present (lean mixture), the sensor produces a low voltage (less than 0.4v). When there is a lesser amount present (rich mixture) it produces a higher voltage (0.6 –1.0v). The stoichiometric or correct air to fuel ratio will cause the voltage to fluctuate between 0.4 and 0.6v. By monitoring the oxygen content and converting it to electrical voltage, the sensor acts as a rich-lean switch. The voltage is transmitted to the PCM.

Some models have two or more sensors, before the catalyst and after. This is done for a catalyst efficiency monitor that is a part of the OBD-II engine controls that are on all models from the 1996 model year on. The sensor before the catalyst measures the exhaust emissions right out of the engine, and sends the signal to the PCM about the state of the mixture as previously talked about. The second sensor reports the difference in the emissions after the exhaust gases have gone through the catalyst. This sensor reports to the PCM the amount of emissions reduction the catalyst is performing.

The oxygen sensor will not work until a predetermined temperature is reached, until this time the PCM is running in OPEN LOOP operation. OPEN LOOP means that the PCM has not yet begun to correct the air-to-fuel ratio by reading the oxygen sensor. After the engine comes to operating temperature, the PCM will monitor the oxygen sensor and correct the air/fuel ratio from the readings of the sensor. This is known as CLOSED LOOP operation.

A heated oxygen sensor (O2 S) has a heating element that keeps the sensor at proper operating temperature during all operating modes. Maintaining correct sensor temperature at all times allows the system to enter CLOSED LOOP operation sooner.

In CLOSED LOOP operation the PCM monitors the sensor input (along with other inputs) and adjusts the injector pulse width accordingly. During OPEN LOOP operation, the PCM ignores the sensor input and adjusts the injector pulse to a preprogrammed value based on other inputs.

TESTING

Single Wire Sensor

This type oxygen sensor is found on the earlier model vehicles. Later years went to a heated O2 sensor because it would react quicker, allowing the PCM to switch into closed loop operation faster.

1. Visually inspect the pigtail for proper routing and connection.

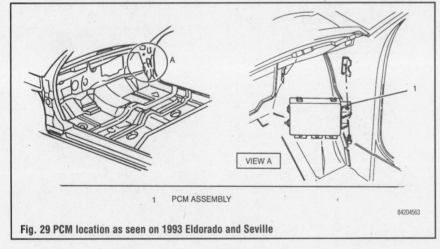

1 PCM ASSEMBLY

VIEW A

84204563

Fig. 29 PCM location as seen on 1993 Eldorado and Seville

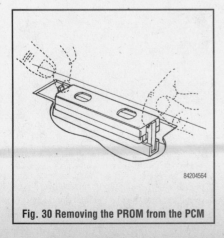

84204564

Fig. 30 Removing the PROM from the PCM

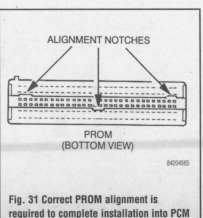

ALIGNMENT NOTCHES

PROM
(BOTTOM VIEW)

84204565

Fig. 31 Correct PROM alignment is required to complete installation into PCM

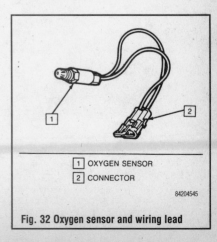

1 OXYGEN SENSOR
2 CONNECTOR

84204545

Fig. 32 Oxygen sensor and wiring lead

2. Check for an adequate air supply, and a clean unclogged air filter.

3. Poor PCM to engine block grounds.

4. Fuel Injectors; faulty or sticky fuel injectors can cause a false reading or false DTC indicating an O2 sensor problem.

5. Fuel pressure; the system will go lean if pressure is too low. The PCM can compensate for some decrease. Likewise, the system will go rich if pressure is too high. The PCM can compensate for some increase. However, if fuel pressure is not in spec, a DTC may be set.

6. Vacuum leaks. Check for disconnected or damaged vacuum hoses and for vacuum leaks at the intake manifold, throttle body, EGR system, and crankcase ventilation system.

7. Exhaust leaks. An exhaust leak may cause outside air to enter the exhaust gas stream going past the O2 sensor, causing the system to appear lean. Check for exhaust leaks that may cause a false lean condition.

8. Fuel contamination; Water, even in small amounts, can be delivered to the fuel injectors. The water passing through the system can cause a lean exhaust. Excessive alcohol in the fuel can also cause this condition.

9. Check the EVAP canister for fuel saturation. If the canister is full of fuel, check the canister control and hoses.

10. Check for a leaking fuel pressure regulator diaphragm by checking the vacuum line to the regulator for the presence of fuel.

11. An intermittent TP sensor output will cause the system to go rich due to a false indication of engine acceleration.

12. A faulty Manifold Absolute Pressure (MAP) Sensor can affect O2 operation.

13. Connect a DVOM between the signal wire and ground. With the engine at normal operating temperature and the engine running (1200 to 1500) RPM, the O2 sensor should be generating a fluctuating signal between zero and 1 volt. If the reading stays above or below .5 volts and does not fluctuate, the sensor could be bad. If the sensor is slow in switching, or acts lazy in changing its voltage reading, it could be bad.

14. If the sensor is operating within specifications, check the circuits to the PCM for continuity.

15. If the sensor and circuits are functional, the PCM may be bad.

Heated Oxygen Sensor

▶ **See Figure 33**

1. Visually check the connector. Make sure it is clean tight and secure. The sensor pigtail may be routed incorrectly and contacting the exhaust system.

2. Poor PCM to engine block grounds.

3. Fuel Injectors; faulty or sticky fuel injectors can cause a false reading or false DTC indicating an O2 sensor problem.

4. Fuel pressure; the system will go lean if pressure is too low. The PCM can compensate for some decrease. Likewise, the system will go rich if pressure is too high. The PCM can compensate for some increase. However, if fuel pressure is not in spec, a DTC may be set.

5. Vacuum leaks. Check for disconnected or damaged vacuum hoses and for vacuum leaks at the intake manifold, throttle body, EGR system, and crankcase ventilation system.

6. Exhaust leaks. An exhaust leak may cause

outside air to enter the exhaust gas stream going past the O2 sensor, causing the system to appear lean. Check for exhaust leaks that may cause a false lean condition.

7. MAF sensor; disconnect the MAF sensor and see if the condition is corrected. A faulty MAF sensor can give a false reading (lean or rich) to the O2 sensor.

8. Fuel contamination; Water, even in small amounts, can be delivered to the fuel injectors. The water passing through the system can cause a lean exhaust. Excessive alcohol in the fuel can also cause this condition.

9. Check the EVAP canister for fuel saturation. If the canister is full of fuel, check the canister control and hoses.

10. Check for a leaking fuel pressure regulator diaphragm by checking the vacuum line to the regulator for the presence of fuel.

11. An intermittent TP sensor output will cause the system to go rich due to a false indication of engine acceleration.

12. An internally shorted Heated Oxygen Sensor will indicate voltage output of over 1 volt.

13. If the sensor and circuits are functioning properly, the PCM may be faulty.

REMOVAL & INSTALLATION

▶ **See Figures 34, 35, 36 and 37**

The oxygen sensor uses a permanently attached pigtail and connector. This pigtail should not be removed from the oxygen sensor. Damage or removal of the pigtail connector could effect the

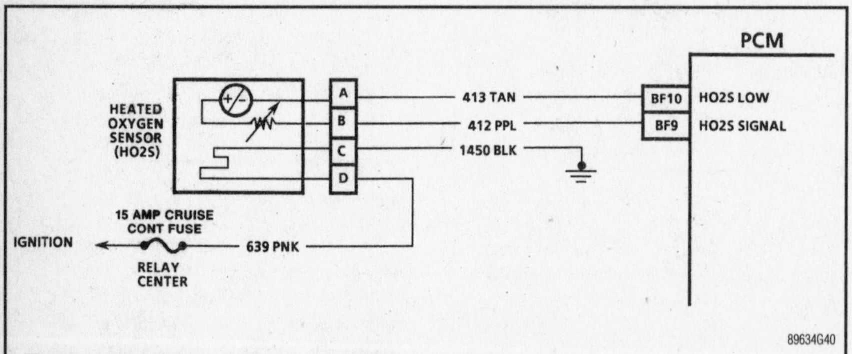

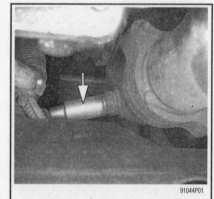

Fig. 34 Location of the rear O2 sensor

Fig. 33 Typical Heated Oxygen Sensor (HO2S) schematic—4 wire

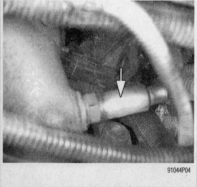

Fig. 35 Location of the the front O2 sensor

Fig. 36 Use a wrench or special socket to loosen the O2 sensor

Fig. 37 When replacing or reinstalling an oxygen sensor, be sure to lube the threads sufficiently

proper operation of the oxygen sensor. Use caution when handling the oxygen sensor. The in-line electrical connector and louvered end must be kept free of grease, dirt, or other contaminants. Also, avoid using cleaner solvent of any type. Do not drop or roughly handle the oxygen sensor. It is not recommended to clean or wire brush an oxygen sensor when in question, it is recommended that a new oxygen sensor be used.

➡**The oxygen sensor may be difficult to remove when the engine temperature is below 120°F (48°C). Excessive force may damage the threads in the exhaust manifold of exhaust pipe.**

1. Start the engine and let it warm up to 120°F (48°C), stop the engine and disconnect the negative battery cable.
2. Detach the electrical connector from the oxygen sensor.
3. Using a special, oxygen sensor socket, remove the oxygen sensor from the exhaust manifold or exhaust pipe.

➡**A special anti-seize compound is used on the oxygen sensor threads. The compound consists of liquid graphite and glass beads. The graphite will burn away, but the glass beads will remain, making the sensor easier to remove. New or service sensors will already have the compound applied to the threads. If an oxygen sensor is removed from the engine and if for any reason, it is to be reinstalled, the threads must have this anti-seize compound applied before installation.**

4. Coat the threads of the oxygen sensor with anti-seize compound 5613695 or equivalent.
5. Install the sensor and tighten it to 30 ft. lbs. (40 Nm).
6. Reattach the electrical connector to the sensor and the negative battery cable.

Idle Air Control Valve

The purpose of the Idle Air Control (IAC) system is to control engine idle speeds while preventing stalls due to changes in engine load.

OPERATION

The throttle blade, when closed allows a small amount of air into the intake manifold. The IAC system controls idle speed by allowing a controlled amount of air to bypass the throttle blade via a passage in the IAC valve. The IAC valve consists of a rotating shutter that is held in a neutral position by opposing springs within the valve assembly (equal to a slightly elevated idle). Switched B+ is provided the drive unit within the IAC valve. The PCM controls the valve via two control circuits, one to drive the valve open and the other to drive the valve closed. The PCM pulse Width Modulates both control circuits simultaneously. The ration of the frequency between two PWM signals determines the direction and amount that the drive unit rotates the shutter within the valve. As the shutter closes, bypass airflow is reduced and idle speed decreases. To increase idle speed, the PCM commands the shutter open, allowing more air to bypass the throttle plates.

TESTING

Preliminary tests for an IAC related problem include checking for the following conditions:
- Poor connection at PCM or IAC motor. Inspect the harness connectors for backed out terminals, improper mating, broken locks, improperly formed or damaged terminals, and poor terminal to wire connection.
- Inspect the wire harness for damage, including; proper routing, broken insulation, rub through, or broken wires.
- A restricted air intake system. Check for a possible collapsed air intake duct, restricted air filter element, or foreign objects blocking the air intake system.
- Check the throttle body for objects blocking the IAC passage or throttle bore, excessive deposits in the IAC passage and on the IAC pintle, and excessive deposits in the throttle bore and on the throttle plate. Check for a sticking throttle plate. Also inspect the IAC passage for deposits or objects which will not allow the IAC pintle to fully extend.
- Check for a condition that causes a vacuum leak, such as disconnected or damaged hoses, leaks at the EGR valve or EGR pipe to intake manifold, leaks at the throttle body, faulty or incorrectly installed PCV valve, leaks at the intake manifold, a brake booster hose that leaks or is disconnected, or a faulty component that uses engine vacuum to operate.
1. If a scan tool is available, connect it to the system, and start the engine.
2. Turn all accessories **OFF** (A/C, Heater, Rear Defroster, etc.).
3. Using the scan tool, command RPM up to 1500, down to 650, and then up to 1500 while monitoring Engine Speed on the scan tool. If the IAC valve follows these commands and holds the commanded engine speed, then it is good.
4. If a scan tool is unavailable, then try the following test procedure:
5. Unplug the IAC connector and check resistance between the IAC terminals. Resistance between terminals A & B and terminals C & D should be 40– to 80 ohms. If resistance is not within specification, the IAC valve should be replaced.
6. Check the resistance between the IAC terminals A to C, A to D, B to C and B to D. Resistance should be infinite. If not the IAC is faulty.
7. If the resistances are within specifications, check the IAC circuits for continuity back to the PCM. If the valve and circuits are functional, the PCM may be faulty.
8. If intermittent poor driveability or idle symptoms are resolved by detaching the IAC, carefully re-check connections and the IAC valve terminal resistance or replace the IAC.

REMOVAL & INSTALLATION

4.5L and 4.9L Engines

1. Disconnect the negative battery cable.
2. Detach the electric connector from the harness connection.
3. Remove the retaining screws attaching the ISC motor to the throttle body and remove the ISC motor.
4. Remove the harness from the ISC motor.

➡**The ISC motor is calibrated at the factory. It is a nonservicable unit. Do not attempt to disassemble it. Do not immerse the ISC motor in any type of cleaning solvent and always remove it prior to cleaning or servicing the throttle body. Immersing in cleaner will damage the ISC unit.**

5. Installation is the reverse of the removal procedure. After the ISC motor is installed, perform Minimum Air, Throttle Position Sensor (TPS), and Idle Learn adjustments.

4.6L Engine

1. Disconnect the air intake duct.
2. Remove the cruise control servo and bracket.
3. Detach the ISC electrical connector.
4. Remove the ISC motor.
To install:
5. Install the ISC motor and tighten the retaining nuts to 53 inch lbs. (6 Nm).
6. Attach the ISC electrical connector.
7. Install the cruise control servo and bracket.
8. Connect the air intake duct.
9. Perform the ISC check as outlined.
10. Perform the TP Sensor/Idle Learn procedure.

Coolant Temperature Sensor

OPERATION

The engine coolant temperature sensor is a thermistor (a resistor which changes value based on temperature) mounted in the engine coolant stream. Low coolant temperature produces a high resistance (100,000 ohms{100K ohms} at -40°C/-40°F) While high temperature causes low resistance (70 ohms at 130°C/266°F).

The PCM supplies a 5 volt signal to the engine coolant temperature sensor through a resistor in the PCM and measures the voltage. The voltage will be high when the engine is cold, and low when the engine is hot. By measuring the voltage, the PCM calculates the engine coolant temperature. The scan tool displays engine coolant temperature in degrees. After engine start-up, the temperature should rise steadily to about 90°C (194°F) then stabilize when ht thermostat open. If the engine has not been run for several hours (overnight), the engine coolant temperature and intake air temperature displays should be close to each other.

Engine coolant temperature affects most systems the PCM controls.

TESTING

▶ **See Figure 38**

1. Detach the electrical connector.
2. Attach an ohmmeter to the sensor terminals and then measure the resistance and compare with the accompanying chart on a cold engine. Measure the coolant temperature in the radiator or overflow bottle.
   a. Compare the resistance and temperature on the chart.

DIAGNOSTIC AID

TEMPERATURE VS. RESISTANCE VALUES (APPROXIMATE)

°C	°F	OHMS
100	212	177
90	194	241
80	176	332
70	158	467
60	140	667
50	122	973
45	113	1188
40	104	1459
35	95	1802
30	86	2238
25	77	2796
20	68	3520
15	59	4450
10	50	5670
5	41	7280
0	32	9420
-5	23	12300
-10	14	16180
-15	5	21450
-20	-4	28680
-30	-22	52700
-40	-40	100700

89634G47

Fig. 38 Engine Coolant Temperature (ECT) and Intake Air Temperature (IAT) Sensor Resistance Values vs. Temperature Readings

3. Tape an automotive thermometer tightly to the upper radiator hose. Start and run the engine to normal operating temperature, comparing the temperature on the thermometer to the resistance reading on the ohmmeter. The readings should coincide with the chart.

4. If the sensor is not in specification, replace it.

Sensor Removed From Vehicle

1. Remove the ECT from the vehicle.
2. Immerse the tip of the sensor in a container of icy water (0°C/32°F), as measured with a calibrated thermometer.
3. Attach an Ohmmeter to the sensor connector. The Ohms value should read approximately 9400 to 9500 Ohms.
4. Using the thermometer readings, compare the resistance of the sensor to the temperature of the water.
5. Repeat the test at two other temperature readings, heating the water as necessary.
6. Refer to the resistance value chart; if the sensor is not within specification, replace it.

REMOVAL & INSTALLATION

➡ Use care when handling the ECT sensor. Damage to the coolant sensor will affect the operation of the fuel control system.

➡ The engine coolant temperature sensor is located on the intake manifold water jacket or near the thermostat housing. On the 4.6L engine, the coolant temperature sensor is located on the rear cylinder head, at the cruise control servo bracket. It is necessary to drain

coolant from the cooling system to a level below the sensor, prior to sensor removal.

1. Disconnect the negative battery cable.
2. Drain the coolant level below the height of the ECT and recycle the engine coolant.
3. Detach the electrical connector at the sensor.
4. Remove any obstruction to access the ECT.
5. Using a deep well socket, remove the sensor.
To install:
6. Coat the threads of the new sensor and install it in the engine. Tighten to 15 ft. lbs. (20 Nm).
7. Install the electrical connector.
8. Refill the system with coolant.
9. Connect the negative battery cable.

Intake Air Temperature Sensor

OPERATION

The Intake Air Temperature (IAT) sensor is a thermistor, which changes value based on the temperature of air entering the engine. Low temperature produces a high resistance (100,000 ohms{100K ohms} at -40°C/-40°F), while high temperature causes low resistance (70 ohms at 130°C/266°F). The PCM supplies a 5 volt signal to the sensor through a resistor in the PCM and measures the voltage the voltage will be high when the incoming air is cold, and low when the air is hot. By measuring the voltage, the PCM calculates the incoming air temperature.

The IAT sensor signal is used to adjust spark timing according to incoming air density. The scan tool displays temperature of the air entering the engine, which should read close to ambient air temperature when the engine is cold, and rise as underhood temperature increases. If the engine has not been run for several hours (overnight) the IAT sensor temperature and engine coolant temperature should read close to each other.

TESTING

1. Access the IAT; if necessary, remove it from the vehicle.
2. Connect a digital ohmmeter to the terminals of the IAT.
3. On a cold engine, compare the resistance of the sensor to the temperature of the ambient air.
4. With the DVOM connected to the IAT sensor, and a thermometer at the sensor end, heat the sensor slightly, with a blow dryer or similar tool. Watch as the temperature goes up and the resistance goes down. Check the temperature against resistance on the chart.
5. Allow the sensor to cool, then repeat the test.
6. If the sensor does not meet specs, it should be replaced.

REMOVAL & INSTALLATION

4.6L Engine

1. Disconnect the negative battery cable.
2. Remove the intake manifold cover.
3. Remove the Intake Air Temperature (IAT) sensor from the fuel rail.

To install:
4. Installation is the reverse of the removal procedure. Tighten the intake manifold cover bolts to 106 inch lbs. (12 Nm).

4.9L Engine

▶ **See Figure 39**

The Intake Air Temperature sensor (IAT) is the same sensor as the Manifold Air Temperature (MAT) Sensor, the name has been changed. It operates in the same manner and performs the same function.

➡ When servicing the MAT sensor, be careful not to damage the tip of the sensor. Damage to the MAT sensor tip will affect proper operation of the fuel injection system.

1. Disconnect the negative battery cable.
2. Detach the electrical connector to the MAT sensor.
3. Unscrew the MAT sensor from the intake manifold.
To install:
4. Installation is the reverse order of the removal procedure. Prior to installing the sensor, coat threads with a nonhardening sealant.

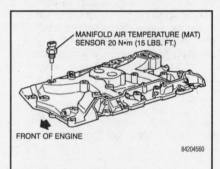

MANIFOLD AIR TEMPERATURE (MAT) SENSOR 20 N•m (15 LBS. FT.)

FRONT OF ENGINE

84204560

Fig. 39 Intake Air Temperature (IAT) sensor—4.9L engine shown

Mass Airflow Sensor

OPERATION

The Mass Air Flow (MAF) sensor measures the amount of air that is ingested by the engine. Direct measurement of air entering the engine is more accurate than calculating airflow from other sensor inputs.

The MAF sensor has a switched battery feed, a ground, a signal circuit and a signal return circuit. The MAF sensor used on this vehicle is a hot film type and is used to measure airflow rate. The MAF output voltage is a function of the power required to keep the airflow sensing elements at a fixed temperature above airflow sensing elements at a fixed temperature above ambient temperature. Air flowing through the sensor cools the sensing elements. The amount of cooling is proportional to the amount of airflow. As airflow increases, a greater amount of current is required to maintain the hot film at a constant temperature. The MAF sensor converts the changes in current draw to a voltage signal read by the PCM. The PCM calculates airflow based on this signal.

TESTING

The scan tool reads the MAF value and displays it in grams per second (gm/s). Values should change rather quickly on acceleration, but values should remain stable at any given RPM. When the PCM detects a malfunction in the MAF sensor circuit, a DTC will set.

1. Visually check the connector and make sure it is secure, clean, and tight.

2. Bring the engine to normal operating conditions, lightly tap on the MAF sensor (with a suitable tool), and wiggle the wires at the connector, watch for a change in the idle speed. A common problem is MAF sensor wire damage.

3. Backprobe the sensor connector using a DVOM set to the Hertz scale. Attach the leads to A and B while simulating driving conditions by blowing air across the wire in the sensor. There should be a frequency swing from air crossing the wire in the sensor. A normal flow signal will be close to 1200 Hertz. If the frequency does not register, or is not proportional to the airflow across the sensing wire, then the sensor is faulty.

4. Check for battery positive (source voltage) on terminal C and ground on terminal B. If voltage or ground do not register, check the circuits to the PCM for continuity.

5. If voltage checks are good at the electrical connector and a driveability problem still exists, it may be the MAF sensor.

6. If the sensor and circuits are functional, the PCM may be at fault.

REMOVAL & INSTALLATION

4.6L Engine

1. Remove the intake air duct
2. Detach the MAF sensor electrical connector
3. Remove the 3 MAF sensor mounting screws and remove the sensor.
   To install:
4. Installation is the reversal of the removal procedure.

Manifold Air Pressure Sensor

OPERATION

The Manifold Absolute Pressure (MAP) sensor measures the changes in the intake manifold pressure, which result from engine load and speed changes. The pressure measured by the MAP sensor is the difference between barometric pressure (outside air) and manifold pressure (vacuum). A closed throttle engine coastdown would produce a relatively low MAP value (approximately 20–35 kPa), while wide-open throttle would produce a high value (100 kPa). This high value is produced when the pressure inside the manifold is the same as outside the manifold, and 100% of outside air (or 100 kPa) is being measured. This MAP output is the opposite of what you would measure on a vacuum gauge. The use of this sensor also allows the PCM to adjust automatically for different altitude.

The PCM sends a 5 volt reference signal to the MAP sensor. As the MAP changes, the electrical resistance of the sensor also changes. By monitoring the sensor output voltage, the PCM can determine the manifold pressure. A higher pressure, lower vacuum (high voltage) requires more fuel, while a lower pressure, higher vacuum (low voltage) requires less fuel. The PCM uses the MAP sensor to control fuel delivery and ignition timing. A failure in the MAP sensor circuit should set a Code.

TESTING

▶ **See Figure 40**

The MAP sensor voltage reading is the opposite of a vacuum gauge reading. When manifold pressure is high, the MAP sensor value is high, and vacuum is low.

1. Using the accompanying chart as a guide, determine the height above sea level and the comparative voltage range.

2. Now, backprobe the MAP connector between terminals A and B.

3. Key On, Engine Off, the voltage reading

obtained should coincide with the chart; voltage and altitude should match.

4. Now apply 34 kPa (10" Hg) vacuum to the MAP sensor, it should cause the voltage to be 1.5 to 2.1 volts less than the voltage at Step 1. Upon applying vacuum to the sensor, the change in voltage should be instantaneous. A slow voltage change indicates a faulty sensor.

5. Check the voltage between terminal C and ground, you should read reference voltage (about 5 volts).

6. If the reference voltage is right, and the sensor voltage is not within specs, replace the sensor.

7. If the sensor and the circuits are functional, the PCM may be faulty.

8. Be sure to test the vacuum hose for leaks or restrictions. This source must supply vacuum to the MAP sensor only.

REMOVAL & INSTALLATION

1. Remove the intake manifold top cover.
2. Disconnect the crankcase breather tube from the throttle body.
3. Remove the MAP sensor from the intake manifold.
4. Detach the MAP sensor electrical connector.
5. Inspect the MAP sensor grommet for wear or damage and replace as needed.
   To install:
6. Installation is the reversal of the removal procedure.

Throttle Position Sensor

OPERATION

The Throttle Position (TP) Sensor is a potentiometer that provides a voltage signal that changes relative to the throttle blade angle. It is connected to the throttle shaft on the throttle body. By monitoring the voltage on the signal line, the PCM calculates throttle position. As the throttle blade angle is changed (accelerator pedal moved), the TP sensor signal also changes. At a closed throttle position, the output of the TP sensor is low. As the throttle

Altitude—Meters	Altitude—Feet	Pressure—kPa	Voltage Range
Below 305	Below 1000	100–98	3.8–5.5V
305–610	1000–2000	98–95	3.6–5.3V
610–914	2000–3000	95–92	3.5–5.1V
914–1219	3000–4000	92–89	3.3–5.0V
1219–1524	4000–5000	89–86	3.2–4.8V
1524–1829	5000–6000	86–83	3.0–4.6V
1829–2133	6000–7000	83–80	2.9–4.5V
2133–2438	7000–8000	80–77	2.8–4.3V
2438–2743	8000–9000	77–74	2.6–4.2V
2743–3948	9000–10,000	74–71	2.5–4.0V

89634G61

Fig. 40 MAP sensor specifications—note how altitude and pressure affect the voltage readings

blade opens the TP sensor voltage increases so that at Wide-Open Throttle (WOT), The TP sensor voltage should be above 4 volts. The PCM calculates fuel delivery based on throttle blade angle (driver demand).

TESTING

A broken or loose TP sensor may cause intermittent bursts of fuel from and injector and unstable idle because the PCM thinks the throttle is moving. A hard failure in the TP sensor 5 volts reference or signal circuits should set a DTC. A hard fault in the ground circuit will also set a DTC. Once a DTC is set, the PCM will use an artificial flow for throttle position and some vehicle performance will return. A high idle may result when there is a hard fault in the system.

1. Visually check the connector for cracks, or looseness, and that the connector is corrosion free.
2. With the key ON, engine OFF, measure the voltage at Terminal B., the voltage should read about .5 volts.
3. Operate the throttle smoothly to wide-open throttle (WOT), the voltage reading should follow the lever action, but not exceed 5 volts. If it does, or the voltage reading jumps, then replace the sensor.
4. Check terminal A for a proper ground signal.
5. Check terminal C for a 5 volt reference signal. If the signals are correct, the sensor is faulty.
6. If the signals are not correct, check the circuits for continuity.
7. If the circuits are not faulty, the PCM may be at fault.

REMOVAL & INSTALLATION

4.5 And 4.9L Engines

1. Remove the air cleaner.
2. Remove the TP sensor connector.
3. Unscrew the 2 TP sensor attaching screws and retainers, and remove the TP sensor.
   To install:
4. With the throttle valve in the normal closed idle position, install the TP sensor on the throttle body assembly.
5. Install 2 TP sensor attaching screws with retainers. Do not tighten the screw until the TP sensor is adjusted.
6. Install the TP Sensor connector. Adjust the TP Sensor and perform the idle learn procedure.
7. To Perform the TP sensor adjustment.
   a. Disable the generator by grounding the green harness connector plug adjacent to the generator.
   b. Start the engine, enter diagnostics, and select PCM override PS103 'ISC Actuator'.
   c. Press the 'COOLER' button on the CCP to retract the ISC Actuator. This action will disengage the A/C compressor and command the EGR 'OFF'. The Climate control center display will change from '50 to 00'. The ISC Actuator will slowly retract (about 20 seconds) to a fully retracted position. Verify that the throttle lever is resting on the minimum idle speed screw. With the ISC Actuator plunger fully retracted, disconnect the ISC harness.
   d. Select the PCM data PD01, 'TP Sensor', while still in PCM override PS03. Note the throttle position (in degrees) displayed on PCM parameter PD01.

e. (-0.5° to + 0.5°)—No TP sensor adjustment required. Reattach the ISC Actuator harness and disconnect the grounding wire at the generator.
f. TP Sensor (-10.0° to -0.6°) or TP Sensor (+ 0.6° to + 90.0°)—TP Sensor adjustment required.
8. With the engine **OFF** and the ignition **ON**, reenter diagnostics and select PCM override PS03 'ISC Actuator'. Press the 'COOLER' button to retract the ISC Actuator the minimum air setting.
   a. Loosen the TP sensor screws just enough to permit the sensor to be rotated. Open the throttle slightly and allow the throttle lever to

snap shut against the minimum air screw. Adjust the TP sensor so the parameter display is 0°. Tighten the TP sensor mounting screws with the sensor in the adjusted position. Recheck the parameter to be sure the TP sensor parameter is (-0.5° to + 0.5).
9. Install the air cleaner.

4.6L Engine

▶ See Figures 41 and 42

1. Disconnect the negative battery cable.
2. Remove the throttle body assembly.
3. Remove the TP sensor electrical connector from the TP sensor.

Fig. 41 Detach the TP sensor

Fig. 42 The TP sensor is retained to the throttle body by two bolts

4. Remove the TP sensor mounting bolts from the TP sensor.

5. Remove the TP sensor from the throttle body.

6. Discard the O-ring.

To install:

7. Install the new O-ring onto the TP sensor.

8. Install the TP sensor onto the throttle body.

   a. Tighten the TP sensor screws to 20 inch lbs. (2.3 Nm).

9. Install the TP sensor electrical connector to the sensor.

10. Install the throttle body assembly.

11. Connect the negative battery cable.

Camshaft Position Sensor

OPERATION

The Camshaft Position (CMP) sensor works in conjunction with a single tooth reluctor wheel on the Bank 2 intake camshaft. The PCM pulls up the CMP sensor signal circuit to 12 volts and monitors this voltage. As the reluctor wheel tooth rotates past the sensor, the sensor's internal circuitry pulls the signal circuit to ground, creating a square wave signal used by the PCM. The reluctor wheel tooth covers 180 degrees of the camshaft circumference. This causes the CMP signal voltage to transition once per crankshaft revolution. This signal, when combined with the CKP sensor signal, enables the PCM to determine exactly which cylinder is on a firing strike. The PCM can then properly synchronize the ignition system, fuel injectors and knock control. Note that as long as the CKP signal is available, the engine can start even if there is no CMP sensor signal. The PCM will default to non-sequential fuel injector operation.

TESTING

The PCM also monitors the CKP sensor system for malfunctions. The following DTC will indicate that the PCM has detected a CMP system problem. DTC PO335.

For any test that requires probing the PCM harness connector or a component harness connector, use the connector test adapter kit (J 35616-A). Using this kit will prevent damage to the harness connector terminals.

1. Check for the following conditions:

   a. Poor connections at the PCM or at the component.—Inspect the harness connectors for backed out terminals, improper mating,

broken locks, improperly formed or damaged terminals, and poor terminal to wire connection

   b. Misrouted harness.— Inspect the harness to ensure that it is not routed too close to high voltage wires such as spark plug leads, or too close to high current devices such as the alternator, motors, solenoids etc.

   c. Damaged harness.—Inspect the wiring harness for damage. If the harness appears to be OK, observe the scan tool while moving related connectors and wiring harnesses. A change in the display may help to locate the fault.

   d. If the sensor signal is only affected when the harness is moved at a component, and there is no problem with the harness or connections, the component may be faulty.

2. Check the sensor for proper installation.—A sensor that is loose or not fully seated (causing an excessive air gap between the sensor and the reluctor wheel) may cause a DTC to set.

REMOVAL & INSTALLATION

1. Disconnect the wiring harness from the Camshaft Position (CMP) Sensor.

2. Remove the A/C Low Pressure ling bracket.

3. Remove the fastening bolt for the CMP sensor.

4. Remove the CMP sensor and the O-ring seal from the camshaft cover.

To install:

5. Thoroughly clean the mating surfaces of the CMP sensor and the camshaft cover.

6. Install the CMP sensor with a new O ring seal, into the camshaft cover.

7. Install the fastening bolt for the CMP sensor.

8. Install the A/C Low Pressure line bracket.

9. Attach the wiring harness to the CMP sensor. Be sure to route the cable correctly.

Crankshaft Position Sensor

OPERATION

The Crankshaft Position (CKP) sensor works in conjunction with a 58 tooth reluctor wheel on the crankshaft. The PCM pulls up the CKP sensor signal circuit to 12 volts and monitors this voltage. As each reluctor wheel tooth rotates past the sensor, the sensor's internal circuitry pulls the signal circuit to ground, creating a square wave signal used

by the PCM. The reluctor wheel teeth are 6 degrees apart. Having only 58 teeth leaves a 12 degree span that I s uncut. This creates a signature pattern that enables the PCM to determine crankshaft position. The PCM can determine which two cylinders are approaching top dead center based on the signal is used to determine which of the two cylinders I on a firing stroke. The PCM can then properly synchronize the ignition system, Fuel injectors and knock control. This sensor is also used to detect misfire.

The PCM also monitors the CKP sensor system for malfunctions. The following DTC's will indicate that the PCM has detected a CKP system problem.

TESTING

Diagnostic Aids — check for:

- Incorrect harness routing.
- An intermittent may be caused by a poor connection, rubbed through wire insulation or a wire broken inside the insulation.
- Check for a poor connection or damaged harness: Inspect the PCM harness connectors for backed out terminals, improper mating, broken locks, improperly formed or damaged terminals, poor terminal to wire connections and damaged harnesses.
- If the sensor signal is only affected when the harness is moved at a component, and there is no problem with the harness or connections, the component may be faulty.
- Check the sensor for proper installation.—A sensor that is loose or not fully seated (causing an excessive air gap between the sensor and the reluctor wheel) may cause a DTC to set.

REMOVAL & INSTALLATION

1. Disconnect the wiring harness from the Crankshaft Position (CKP) sensor.

2. Remove the fastening bolt for the CKP sensor.

3. Remove the CKP sensor and the O-ring seal from the engine block.

To install:

4. Thoroughly clean the mating surfaces of the CKP sensor and the engine bock.

5. Install the CKP sensor with a new O-ring seal, into the engine block.

6. Install he fastening bolt for the CKP sensor

7. Attach the wiring harness to the CKP sensor. Be sure to route the cable correctly

ELECTRONIC ENGINE CONTROL COMPONENT LOCATIONS—4.6L NORTHSTAR ENGINE

1. Camshaft Position (CMP) Sensor
2. Evaporative emissions purge solenoid
3. Manifold Absolute Pressure (MAP) sensor
4. Crankshaft Position (CKP) sensor (located on front of engine block)
5. Evaporative emissions test port
6. Engine Coolant Temperature (ECT) sensor
7. Exhaust Gas Recirculation (EGR) valve
8. Idle Air Control (IAC) valve
9. Intake Air Temperature (IAT) sensor
10. Throttle Position (TP) sensor
11. Powertrain Control Module (PCM)

91044PE1

TROUBLE CODES

General Information

Since the PCM is programmed to recognize the presence and value of electrical inputs, it will also note the lack of a signal or a radical change in values. It will, for example, react to the loss of signal from the vehicle speed sensor or note that engine coolant temperature has risen beyond acceptable (programmed) limits. Once a fault is recognized, a numeric code is assigned and held in memory. The dashboard warning lamp: CHECK ENGINE or SERVICE ENGINE SOON (SES), will illuminate to advise the operator that the system has detected a fault. This lamp is also known as the Malfunction Indicator Lamp (MIL).

More than one code may be stored. Keep in mind not every engine uses every code. Additionally, the same code may carry different meanings relative to each engine or engine family.

In the event of an computer control module failure, the system will default to a pre-programmed set of values. These are compromise values, which allow the engine to operate, although possibly at reduced efficiency. This is variously known as the default, limp-in or back-up mode. Driveability is almost always affected when the PCM enters this mode.

SCAN TOOLS

▶ See Figure 43

On 1990–95 models, the stored codes may be read with only the use of a small jumper wire, however the use of a hand-held scan tool such as GM's TECH-1• or equivalent is recommended. On all 1996–98 models, an OBD-II compliant scan tool must be used. There are many manufacturers of these tools; a purchaser must be certain that the tool is proper for the intended use. If you own a scan type tool, it probably came with comprehensive instructions on proper use. Be sure to follow the instructions that came with your unit if they differ from what is given here; this is a general guide with useful information included.

The scan tool allows any stored codes to be read from the PCM memory. The tool also allows the operator to view the data being sent to the computer control module while the engine is running. This ability has obvious diagnostic advantages; the use

TCCS4P12

Fig. 43 Some inexpensive scan tools, such as the Auto Xray®, can interface with GM vehicles

of the scan tool is frequently required for component testing. The scan tool makes collecting information easier; an operator familiar with the system must correctly interpret the data.

An example of the usefulness of the scan tool may be seen in the case of a temperature sensor, which has changed its electrical characteristics. The PCM is reacting to an apparently warmer engine (causing a driveability problem), but the sensor's voltage has not changed enough to set a fault code. Connecting the scan tool, the voltage signal being sent to the PCM may be viewed; comparison to normal values or a known good vehicle reveals the problem quickly.

ELECTRICAL TOOLS

The most commonly required electrical diagnostic tool is the digital multimeter, allowing voltage, ohmage (resistance) and amperage to be read by one instrument. The multimeter must be a high-impedance unit, with 10 megohms of impedance in the voltmeter. This type of meter will not place an additional load on the circuit it is testing; this is extremely important in low voltage circuits. The multimeter must be of high quality in all respects. It should be handled carefully and protected from impact or damage. Replace batteries frequently in the unit.

Other necessary tools include an unpowered test light, a quality tachometer with an inductive (clip-on) pick up, and the proper tools for releasing GM's Metri-Pack, Weather Pack and Micro-Pack terminals as necessary. The Micro-Pack connectors are used at the PCM electrical connector. A vacuum pump/gauge may also be required for checking sensors, solenoids and valves.

Diagnosis and Testing

Diagnosis of a driveablility and/or emissions problems requires attention to detail and following the diagnostic procedures in the correct order. Resist the temptation to perform any repairs before performing the preliminary diagnostic steps. In many cases this will shorten diagnostic time and often cure the problem without electronic testing.

The proper troubleshooting procedure for these vehicles is as follows:

VISUAL/PHYSICAL INSPECTION

This is possibly the most critical step of diagnosis and should be performed immediately after retrieving any codes. A detailed examination of connectors, wiring and vacuum hoses can often lead to a repair without further diagnosis. Performance of this step relies on the skill of the technician performing it; a careful inspector will check the undersides of hoses as well as the integrity of hard-to-reach hoses blocked by the air cleaner or other component. Wiring should be checked carefully for any sign of strain, burning, crimping, or terminal pull-out from a connector. Checking connectors at components or in harnesses is required; usually, pushing them together will reveal a loose fit.

INTERMITTENTS

If a fault occurs intermittently, such as a loose connector pin breaking contact as the vehicle hits a bump, the PCM will note the fault as it occurs and energize the dash warning lamp. If the problem self-corrects, as with the terminal pin again making contact, the dash lamp will extinguish after 10 seconds but a code will remain stored in the computer control module's memory.

When an unexpected code appears during diagnostics, it may have been set during an intermittent failure that self-corrected; the codes are still useful in diagnosis and should not be discounted.

CIRCUIT/COMPONENT REPAIR

The fault codes and the scan tool data will lead to diagnosis and checking of a particular circuit. It is important to note that the fault code indicates a fault or loss of signal in an PCM-controlled system, not necessarily in the specific component.

Refer to the appropriate Diagnostic Code chart to determine the codes meaning. The component may then be tested following the appropriate component test procedures found in this section. If the component is OK, check the wiring for shorts or opens. Further diagnoses should be left to an experienced driveability technician.

If a code indicates the PCM to be faulty and the PCM is replaced, but does not correct the problem, one of the following may be the reason:
- There is a problem with the PCM terminal connections: The terminals may have to be removed from the connector in order to check them properly.
- The PCM or PROM is not correct for the application: The incorrect PCM or PROM may cause a malfunction and may or may not set a code.
- The problem is intermittent: This means that the problem is not present at the time the system is being checked. In this case, make a careful physical inspection of all portions of the system involved.
- Shorted solenoid, relay coils or harness: Solenoids and relays are turned on and off by the PCM using internal electronic switches called drivers. Each driver is part of a group of four called Quad-Drivers. A shorted solenoid, relay coil or harness may cause an PCM to fail, and a replacement PCM to fail when it is installed. Use a short tester, J34696, BT 8405, or equivalent, as a fast, accurate means of checking for a short circuit.
- The Programmable Read Only Memory (PROM) may be faulty: Although the PROM rarely fails, it operates as part of the PCM. Therefore, it could be the cause of the problem. Substitute a known good PROM.
- The replacement PCM may be faulty: After the PCM is replaced, the system should be rechecked for proper operation. If the diagnostic code again indicates the PCM is the problem, substitute a known good PCM. Although this is a very rare condition, it could happen.

Reading Codes

OBD-I SYSTEMS

▶ **See Figures 44, 45 and 46**

Listings of the trouble codes for the various engine control systems covered in this manual are located in this section. Remember that a code only points to the faulty circuit NOT necessarily to a faulty component. Loose, damaged or corroded connections may contribute to a fault code on a circuit when the sensor or component is operating properly. Be sure that the components are faulty before replacing them, especially the expensive ones.

The Assembly Line Diagnostic Link (ALDL) connector or Data Link Connector (DLC) may be located under the dash and sometimes covered with a plastic cover labeled DIAGNOSTIC CONNECTOR.

1. On all 1990–95 models the diagnostic trouble codes can be read by grounding test terminal **B**. The terminal is most easily grounded by connecting it to terminal **A** (internal ECM ground). This is the terminal to the right of terminal B on the top row of the ALDL connector.

2. Once the terminals have been connected, the ignition switch must be moved to the **ON** position with the engine not running.

3. The Service Engine Soon or Check Engine light should be flashing. If it isn't, turn the ignition **OFF** and remove the jumper wire. Turn the ignition **ON** and confirm that light is now on. If it is not, replace the bulb and try again. If the bulb still will not light, or if it does not flash with the test terminal grounded, the system should be diagnosed by an experienced driveability technician. If the light is OK, proceed as follows.

4. The code(s) stored in memory may be read through counting the flashes of the dashboard warning lamp. The dash warning lamp should begin to flash Code 12. The code will display as one flash, a pause and two flashes. Code 12 is not a fault code. It is used as a system acknowledgment or handshake code; its presence indicates that the PCM can communicate as requested. Code 12 is used to begin every diagnostic sequence. Some vehicles also use Code 12 after all diagnostic codes have been sent.

5. After Code 12 has been transmitted 3 times, the fault codes, if any, will each be transmitted 3 times. The codes are stored and transmitted in numeric order from lowest to highest.

➡ **The order of codes in the memory does not indicate the order of occurrence.**

6. If there are no codes stored, but a driveability or emissions problem is evident, the system should be diagnosed by an experienced driveability technician.

7. If one or more codes are stored, record them. Refer to the applicable Diagnostic Code chart in this section.

8. Switch the ignition **OFF** when finished with code retrieval or scan tool readings.

➡ **After making repairs, clear the trouble codes and operate the vehicle to see if it will reset, indicating further problems.**

ECM DIAGNOSTIC CODES

CODE	DESCRIPTION	TELLTALE STATUS	CODE	DESCRIPTION	TELLTALE STATUS
E12	No Distributor Signal	Ⓐ	E49	A. I. R. Control Problem	Ⓐ
E13	Oxygen Sensor Not Ready	Ⓐ	E52	ECM Memory Reset	Ⓒ
E14	Shorted Coolant Sensor Circuit	Ⓐ	E53	Distributor Signal Interrupt	Ⓒ
E15	Open Coolant Sensor Circuit	Ⓐ	E55	TPS Misadjusted	Ⓐ
E16	Generator Voltage Out Of Range	Ⓑ	E58	PASS Control Problem	Ⓐ
E19	Shorted Fuel Pump Circuit	Ⓑ	E60	Cruise–Transmission Not In Drive	Ⓒ
E20	Open Fuel Pump Circuit	Ⓑ	E61	Cruise–Vent Solenoid Problem	Ⓒ
E21	Shorted TPS Circuit	Ⓐ	E62	Cruise–Vacuum Solenoid Problem	Ⓒ
E22	Open TPS Circuit	Ⓐ	E63	Cruise–Vehicle Speed vs Set Speed Out Of Range	Ⓒ
E23	EST Signal Problem	Ⓐ	E64	Cruise–Vehicle Acceleration Out Of Range	Ⓒ
E24	VSS Circuit Problem	Ⓐ			
E26	Shorted Throttle Switch Circuit	Ⓐ	E65	Cruise–Servo Position Sensor Failure	Ⓒ
E27	Open Throttle Switch Circuit	Ⓐ			
E28	Shorted 3rd Or 4th Gear Switch	Ⓐ	E66	Cruise–Engine RPM Out Of Range	Ⓒ
E30	ISC RPM Out Of Range	Ⓐ	E67	Cruise–Switch Shorted During Enable	Ⓐ
E31	Shorted MAP Sensor Circuit	Ⓐ			
E32	Open MAP Sensor Circuit	Ⓐ	E68	Cruise Control Command Problem	Ⓐ
E34	MAP Sensor Signal Out Of Range	Ⓐ	E74	MAT Signal Interrupt	Ⓐ
E37	Shorted MAT Sensor Circuit	Ⓐ	E75	VSS Signal Interrupt	Ⓐ
E38	Open MAT Sensor Circuit	Ⓐ	E85	Throttle Body Service Required	Ⓐ
E39	VCC Engagement Problem	Ⓐ	E90	VCC Brake Switch Input Problem	Ⓑ
E40	Power Steering Pressure Switch Problem	Ⓐ	E91	Park Neutral Switch Problem	Ⓑ
E41	Cam Sensor Circuit Problem	Ⓐ	E92	Heated W/S Request Problem	Ⓒ
E44	Oxygen Sensor Signal Lean	Ⓐ	E96	Torque Converter Overstress	Ⓑ
E45	Oxygen Sensor Signal Rich	Ⓐ	E97	P/N To D/R Engagement Problem	Ⓒ
E47	BCM–ECM Data Problem	Ⓐ	E98	P/N To D/R ISC Engaged Problem	Ⓒ
E48	EGR Control Problem	Ⓐ	E99	Cruise Servo Apply Problem	Ⓒ

TELLTALE STATUS

Ⓐ "SERVICE ENGINE SOON" Light ON.
Ⓑ "SERVICE VEHICLE SOON" Light ON.
Ⓒ NO TELLTALE ON.

84204010

Fig. 44 Diagnostic trouble codes—4.5L engine

PCM DIAGNOSTIC CODES

CODE	DESCRIPTION	TELLTALE STATUS	CODE	DESCRIPTION	TELLTALE STATUS
E012	No Distributor Signal	A	E048	EGR Control Problem	A
E013	Right Oxygen Sensor Not Read	A,P	E051	MEM–CAL Error	A
E014	Shorted Coolant Sensor Circuit	A	E052	PCM Memory Reset	C
E015	Open Coolant Sensor Circuit	A	E053	Distributor Signal Interrupt	C
E016	Voltage Out Of Range [ALL SOL.]	B	E055	TPS Misadjusted	C
E017	Left Oxygen Sensor Not Ready	A	E058	PASS Control Problem	A
E019	Shorted Fuel Pump Circuit	B	E060	Cruise–Transmission Not In Drive [C/C]	C
E020	Open Fuel Pump Circuit	B	E061	Cruise–Vent Solenoid Problem [C/C]	C
E021	Shorted TPS Circuit [VCC]	A	E062	Cruise–Vacuum Solenoid Problem [C/C]	C
E022	Open TPS Circuit [VCC]	A	E063	Cruise–Speed vs Set Speed [C/C]	C
E023	EST Signal Problem [EGR]	A	E064	Cruise–Vehicle Acceleration [C/C]	C
E024	VSS Circuit Problem [C/C, VCC]	A,Q	E065	Cruise–S P S Failure [C/C]	C
E026	Shorted Throttle Switch Circuit [EGR]	A	E066	Cruise–RPM Out Of Range [C/C]	C
E027	Open Throttle Switch Circuit [EGR]	A	E067	Cruise–Switch Shorted At Enable [C/C]	C
E030	ISC RPM Out Of Range	A	E068	Cruise Command Problem [C/C]	C,Q
E031	Shorted MAP Sensor Circuit	A	E070	Intermittent TPS	C
E032	Open MAP Sensor Circuit	A	E071	Intermittent MAP	C
E034	MAP Sensor Signal Out Of Range	A	E073	Intermittent Coolant Sensor	C
E037	Shorted MAT Sensor Circuit	A	E074	Intermittent MAT	C
E038	Open MAT Sensor Circuit	A	E075	Intermittent VSS	C
E039	VCC Engagement Problem [VCC]	A,F	E080	Fuel System Rich	A
E040	Power Steering Pressure Switch	A	E085	Throttle Body Service Required	A
E041	Cam Sensor Circuit Problem	A	E090	VCC Brake Switch Input Problem [C/C]	B
E042	Left Oxygen Sensor Lean	A,P	E091	PRNDL Switch Problem [C/C]	B
E043	Left Oxygen Sensor Rich	A,P	E092	Heated Windshield Problem	B
E044	Right Oxygen Sensor Signal Lean	A,P	E096	Torque Converter Overstress	A
E045	Right Oxygen Sensor Signal Rich	A,P	E097	High RPM P/N to D/R Shift	C
E046	Right To Left Bank Fueling Problem	A	E098	High RPM P/N To D/R Shift Under ISC	C
E047	BCM–PCM Data Problem	A	E099	Cruise Servo Apply Problem [C/C]	C

TELLTALE STATUS

A = "SERVICE ENGINE SOON" Light ON.
B = "SERVICE CAR SOON" Message On DIC.
C = NO TELLTALE or Message.
F = DISENGAGES VCC FOR IGNITION CYCLE

P = ENABLES CANISTER PURGE
Q = DISABLES CRUISE FOR IGNITION CYCLE
[ ] = BRACKETED SYSTEMS ARE DISABLED WHEN CODE IS CURRENT

DIAGNOSTICS – BASIC OPERATION

- ENTER DIAGNOSTICS BY SIMULTANEOUSLY PRESSING ECCP OFF AND WARMER BUTTONS UNTIL ALL DISPLAYS ARE LIT.
- DIAGNOSTIC CODE LEVEL DISPLAYS PCM CODES FOLLOWED BY BCM and SIR CODES.
- TO PROCEED TO THE DESIRED LEVEL, PRESS AND RELEASE THE INDICATED BUTTON.
- PRESS OFF TO RETURN TO THE NEXT SELECTION IN THE PREVIOUS LEVEL.
- EXIT DIAGNOSTICS BY PRESSING RESET ON THE DRIVER INFORMATION CENTER.

84204277

Fig. 45 Diagnostic trouble codes—4.9L engine

PCM DIAGNOSTIC CODES

CODE	DESCRIPTION	TELLTALE STATUS	CODE	DESCRIPTION	TELLTALE STATUS
P012	No 4X Reference Signal From Ignition Control Module	A	P059	Open Transaxle Temperature Sensor Circuit	B
P013	Rear Heated Oxygen Sensor Not Ready	A	P060	Cruise Control – Transaxle Not In Drive [Cruise]	C
P014	Shorted Engine Coolant Temperature Sensor	A	P061	Cruise Control – Vent Solenoid Problem [Cruise]	C
P015	Open Engine Coolant Temperature Sensor	A	P062	Cruise Control – Vacuum Solenoid Problem [Cruise]	C
P016	Generator Voltage Out Of Range [EVAP, EGR, CRUISE, TCC, Transaxle Pressure Control, Long Term Fuel Trim]	B	P063	Set vs Vehicle Speed Difference [Cruise]	C
P017	Front Heated Oxygen Sensor Not Ready	A	P064	Vehicle Acceleration Too High [Cruise]	C
P019	Shorted Fuel Pump Circuit	B	P065	Cruise Control Servo Position Sensor Failure [Cruise]	C
P020	Open Fuel Pump Circuit	B	P066	Cruise Control – Engine RPM Too High [Cruise]	C
P021	Shorted Throttle Position (TP) Sensor [TCC, Transaxle Pressure Control]	A	P067	Set/Coast Or Resume/Accel Input Shorted [Cruise]	C
P022	Open Throttle Position (TP) Sensor [TCC, EGR]	A	P068	Cruise Control Servo Position Out Of Range [Cruise]	C
P023	Ignition Control Circuit Problem [Ignition Control]	A	P069	Traction Control Active While In Cruise [Cruise]	C
P024	Vehicle Speed Sensor Circuit Problem [TCC]	A	P070	Intermittent Throttle Position (TP) Sensor	C
P025	24X Reference Signal Low	B	P071	Intermittent Manifold Absolute Pressure (MAP) Sensor	C
P026	Shorted Throttle Position (TP) Switch Circuit [EGR]	A	P073	Intermittent Engine Coolant Temperature Sensor	C
P027	Open Throttle Position (TP) Switch Circuit [EGR]	A	P074	Intermittent Intake Air Temperature (IAT) Sensor	C
P028	Transaxle Pressure Switch/Circuit Problem	A	P075	Vehicle Speed Sensor Signal Interrupt [TCC]	C
P029	Transaxle Shift 'B' Solenoid Problem [1st, 3rd, 4th Gear]	A	P076	Transaxle Pressure Control Solenoid Circuit Malfunction [Trans. Pressure Control]	A
P030	Idle Speed Control (ISC) RPM Out Of Range	A	P080	TP Sensor/Idle Learn Not Complete	A
P031	Shorted Manifold Absolute Pressure (MAP) Sensor [Long Term Fuel Trim]	A	P081	CAM To 4X Reference Correlation Problem	C
P032	Open Manifold Absolute Pressure (MAP) Sensor [Long Term Fuel Trim]	A	P083	24X Reference Signal High	A
P033	Extended Travel Brake Switch Input Circuit Problem [Cruise]	B	P085	Idle Throttle Angle Too High	A
P034	Manifold Absolute Pressure (MAP) Signal Too High [Long Term Fuel Trim]	A	P086	Undefined Gear Ratio [Trans. Pressure Control]	A
P035	Ignition Ground Voltage Out of Range	C	P088	Torque Converter Clutch (TCC) Not Disengaging [Trans. Adapts]	A
P036	Exhaust Gas Recirculation (EGR) Valve Pintle Position Out Of Range [EGR]	A	P089	Long Shift and Maximum Adapt [Trans. Pressure Control]	A
P037	Shorted Intake Air Temperature (IAT) Sensor	A	P090	TCC Brake Switch Input Circuit Problem [Cruise]	E
P038	Open Intake Air Temperature (IAT) Sensor	A	P091	Transaxle Range Switch Problem [Cruise]	B
P039	Torque Converter Clutch (TCC) Engagement Problem [4th Gear, TCC for Ignition Cycle]	A	P092	Heated Windshield Request Problem	A
P040	Power Steering Pressure Switch Open	A	P093	Traction Control System PWM Link Failure	A
P041	No Cam Reference Signal From Ignition Control Module	A	P094	Transaxle Shift 'A' Solenoid Problem [1st, 3rd, 4th Gear]	A
P042	Front Heated Oxygen Sensor Lean Exhaust Signal	A	P095	Engine Stall Detected	C
P043	Front Heated Oxygen Sensor Rich Exhaust Signal	A	P096	Torque Converter Overstress	A
P044	Rear Heated Oxygen Sensor Lean Exhaust Signal	A	P097	P/N To D/R At High Throttle Angle	E
P045	Rear Heated Oxygen Sensor Rich Exhaust Signal	A	P099	Cruise Control Servo Applied Not In Cruise	E
P046	Left To Right Bank Fueling Difference	A	P102	Shorted Brake Booster Vacuum (BBV) Sensor [EVAP, Solenoid, EGR, Cruise, TCC, Lt Fuel Trim, Transaxle Adapts]	B
P047	PCM/BCM Data Link Problem	B	P103	Open Brake Booster Vacuum (BBV) Sensor [EVAP, EGR, Cruise, TCC, Lt Fuel Trim, Transaxle Adapts]	B
P048	Exhaust Gas Recirculation (EGR) System Malfunction [EGR]	A	P105	Brake Booster Vacuum (BBV) Too Low	B
P051	PROM Checksum Mismatch	A	P106	Stop Lamp Switch Input Circuit Problem	E
P052	PCM Keep Alive Memory Reset	C	P107	PCM/BCM Data Link Problem	B
P053	4X Reference Signal Interrupt From Ignition Control Module	C	P108	PROM Checksum Mismatch	A
P055	Closed Throttle Angle Out–Of–Range [TP Sensor Learn]	A	P109	PCM Keep Alive Memory Reset	C
P056	Transaxle Input Speed Sensor Circuit Problem	A	P110	Generator L–Terminal Circuit Problem	F
P057	Shorted Transaxle Temperature Sensor Circuit	B	P112	Total EEPROM Failure	A
P058	PASS–Key® Fuel Enable Problem [PASS–Key® Fuel Inhibit]	D	P117	Shift 'A'/Shift 'B' Circuit Output Open Or Shorted	C
			P131	Active Knock Sensor Failure	A
			P132	Knock Sensor Circuitry Failure	A
			P137	Loss Of ABS/TCS Data	E

TELLTALE STATUS

A = 'SERVICE ENGINE SOON' Malfunction Indicator Lamp (MIL) ON.
B = 'SERVICE VEHICLE SOON' message On DIC.
C = No telltale or message.
D = 'THEFT SYSTEM PROBLEM – CAR MAY NOT RESTART' message.
E = 'REDUCED ENGINE POWER' message.
F = 'BATTERY NO CHARGE' message.
[ ] = BRACKETED SYSTEMS ARE DISABLED WHEN CODE IS CURRENT

84204442

Fig. 46 Diagnostic trouble codes—4.6L engine

OBD-II Systems

♦ See Figures 47 thru 54

All 1996–98 models, an OBD-II compliant scan tool must be used to retrieve the trouble codes. Follow the scan tool manufacturer's instructions on how to connect the scan tool to the vehicle and how to retrieve the codes.

91144P39

Fig. 47 The OBD-II connector is located under the driver's side of the instrument panel

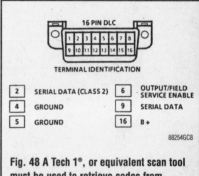

88254GC8

Fig. 48 A Tech 1®, or equivalent scan tool must be used to retrieve codes from 1996–98 models with the 16-pin DLC connector

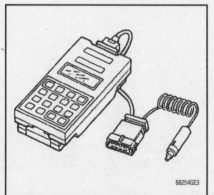

88254GE3

Fig. 49 If retrieving codes using a scan tool such as GM's TECH-1®, make sure to follow all of the manufacturer's directions carefully

DTC	Description
P0101	Mass Air Flow (MAF) System Performance
P0102	Mass Air Flow (MAF) Sensor Circuit Low Frequency
P0103	Mass Air Flow (MAF) Sensor Circuit High Frequency
P0105	MAP Sensor Circuit Insufficient Activity
P0106	Manifold Absolute Pressure (MAP) System Performance
P0107	Manifold Absolute Pressure (MAP) Sensor Circuit Low Voltage
P0108	Manifold Absolute Pressure (MAP) Sensor Circuit High Voltage
P0111	Intake Air Temperature (IAT) Sensor Circuit Performance
P0112	Intake Air Temperature (IAT) Sensor Circuit Low Voltage
P0113	Intake Air Temperature (IAT) Sensor Circuit High Voltage
P0116	Engine Coolant Temperature (ECT) Sensor Circuit Performance
P0117	Engine Coolant Temperature (ECT) Sensor Low Voltage
P0118	Engine Coolant Temperature (ECT) Sensor High Voltage

91044G09

Fig. 50 OBD II trouble codes (1 of 5)

DTC	Description
P0120	Throttle Position (TP) System Performance
P0121	Throttle Position (TP) Sensor Circuit Insufficient Activity
P0122	Throttle Position (TP) Sensor Circuit Low Voltage
P0123	Throttle Position (TP) Sensor Circuit High Voltage
P0125	Engine Coolant Temperature (ECT) Excessive Time To Closed Loop Fuel Control
P0131	Heated Oxygen Sensor (HO2S) Circuit Low Voltage Bank 1 Sensor 1 (Rear Bank)
P0132	Heated Oxygen Sensor (HO2S) Circuit High Voltage Bank 1 Sensor 1 (Rear Bank)
P0133	Heated Oxygen Sensor (HO2S) Slow Response Bank 1 Sensor 1 (Rear Bank)
P0134	Heated Oxygen Sensor (HO2S) Circuit Insufficient Activity Bank 1 Sensor 1 (Rear Bank)
P0135	Heated Oxygen Sensor (HO2S) Heater Circuit Bank 1 Sensor 1 (Rear Bank)
P0143	Heated Oxygen Sensor (HO2S) Circuit Low Voltage Bank 1 Sensor 3 (Post–Converter)
P0144	Heated Oxygen Sensor (HO2S) Circuit High Voltage Bank 1 Sensor 3 (Post–Converter)
P0146	Heated Oxygen Sensor (HO2S) Circuit Insufficient Activity Bank 1 Sensor 3 (Post–Converter)
P0147	Heated Oxygen Sensor (HO2S) Heater Circuit Bank 1 Sensor 3 (Post–Converter)
P0151	Heated Oxygen Sensor (HO2S) Circuit Low Voltage Bank 2 Sensor 1 (Front Bank)
P0152	Heated Oxygen Sensor (HO2S) Circuit High Voltage Bank 2 Sensor 1 (Front Bank)
P0153	Heated Oxygen Sensor (HO2S) Slow Response Bank 2 Sensor 1 (Front Bank)
P0154	Heated Oxygen Sensor (HO2S) Circuit Insufficient Activity Bank 2 Sensor 1 (Front Bank)
P0155	Heated Oxygen Sensor (HO2S) Heater Circuit Bank 2 Sensor 1 (Front Bank)
P0171	Fuel Trim System Lean Bank 1
P0172	Fuel Trim System Rich Bank 1
P0174	Fuel Trim System Lean Bank 2
P0175	Fuel Trim System Rich Bank 2
P0201	Injector #1 Control Circuit
P0202	Injector #2 Control Circuit
P0203	Injector #3 Control Circuit
P0204	Injector #4 Control Circuit
P0205	Injector #5 Control Circuit
P0206	Injector #6 Control Circuit
P0207	Injector #7 Control Circuit
P0208	Injector #8 Control Circuit
P0231	Fuel Pump Feedback Circuit Low Voltage

91044G10

Fig. 51 OBD II trouble codes (2 of 5)

DTC	Description
P0232	Fuel Pump Feedback Circuit High Voltage
P0300	Engine Misfire Detected (MIL will flash during misfire catalyst damage)
P0322	Ignition Control (IC) Module 4x Reference Circuit No Frequency
P0325	Knock Sensor Module Circuit
P0326	Knock Sensor Excessive Spark Retard
P0327	Knock Sensor Circuit Low Voltage
P0340	Ignition Control (IC) Module Cam Reference Circuit No Frequency
P0371	Ignition Control (IC) Module 24x Reference Circuit Too Many Pulses
P0372	Ignition Control (IC) Module 24x Reference Circuit Missing Pulses
P0401	Exhaust Gas Recirculation (EGR) System
P0404	EGR System Performance
P0405	EGR Sensor Circuit Voltage Out of Range
P0420	Three Way Catalyst Low Efficiency
P0440	Evaporative System
P0442	EVAP System Small Leak Detected
P0446	EVAP Canister Vent Blocked
P0452	EVAP Fuel Tank Pressure Sensor Circuit Low Voltage
P0453	EVAP Fuel Tank Pressure Sensor High Voltage
P0461	Fuel level Sensor Circuit Performance
P0462	Fuel level Sensor Circuit Low Voltage
P0463	Fuel level Sensor Circuit High Voltage
P0506	Idle Speed Low
P0507	Idle Speed High
P0532	A/C Pressure Sensor Circuit Low Voltage
P0533	A/C Pressure Sensor Circuit High Voltage
P0550	Power Steering Pressure (PSP) Switch Circuit Low Voltage
P0560	System Voltage Low
P0563	System Voltage High
P0601	PCM Memory
P0602	PCM Not Programmed
P0603	PCM Memory Reset
P0606	PCM Internal Communication Interrupted
P1106	Manifold Absolute Pressure (MAP) Sensor Circuit Intermittent High Voltage
P1107	Manifold Absolute Pressure (MAP) Sensor Circuit Intermittent Low Voltage
P1108	BARO To MAP Signal Circuit Comparison Too High

91044G11

Fig. 52 OBD II trouble codes (3 of 5)

DTC	Description
P1111	Intake Air Temperature (IAT) Sensor Circuit Intermittent High Voltage
P1112	Intake Air Temperature (IAT) Sensor Circuit Intermittent Low Voltage
P1114	Engine Coolant Temperature (ECT) Sensor Circuit Intermittent Low Voltage
P1115	Engine Coolant Temperature (ECT) Sensor Circuit Intermittent High Voltage
P1121	Throttle Position (TP) Sensor Circuit Intermittent High Voltage
P1122	Throttle Position (TP) Sensor Circuit Intermittent Low Voltage
P1133	Heated Oxygen Sensor (HO2S) Insufficient Switching Bank 1 Sensor 1 (Rear Bank)
P1134	Heated Oxygen Sensor (HO2S) Transition Time Ratio Bank 1 Sensor 1 (Rear Bank)
P1153	Heated Oxygen Sensor (HO2S) Insufficient Switching Bank 2 Sensor 1 (Front Bank)
P1154	Heated Oxygen Sensor (HO2S) Transition Time Ratio Bank 2 Sensor 1 (Front Bank)
P1189	Engine Oil Pressure Switch Circuit
P1258	Engine Metal Over Temperature Protection
P1320	Ignition Control (IC) Module 4x Reference Circuit Intermittent No Pulses
P1323	Ignition Control (IC) Module 24x Reference Circuit Low Frequency
P1350	Ignition Control System
P1370	Ignition Control (IC) Module 4x Reference Too Many Pulses
P1371	Ignition Control (IC) Module 4x Reference Too Few Pulses
P1375	Ignition Control (IC) Module 24x Reference High Voltage
P1376	Ignition Ground Circuit
P1377	Ignition Control (IC) Module Cam Pulse To 4x Reference Pulse Comparison
P1380	EBTCM DTC Detected — Rough Data Unusable
P1381	Misfire Detected — No EBTCM/PCM Serial Data
P1404	Exhaust Gas Recirculation (EGR) Valve Pintle Stuck Open
P1441	Evaporative System Flow During Non–Purge
P1508	Idle Air Control (IAC) System — Low RPM
P1509	Idle Air Control (IAC) System — High RPM
P1520	Park/Neutral Position Switch Circuit
P1524	Throttle Position (TP) Sensor Learned Closed Throttle Angle Degrees Out-Of-Range
P1527	Trans Range/Pressure Switch Comparison
P1554	Cruise Engaged Circuit High Voltage
P1560	Cruise Control–System — Transaxle Not In Drive
P1564	Cruise Control–System — Vehicle Acceleration Too High
P1566	Cruise Control–System — Engine RPM Too High
P1567	Cruise Control — ABCS Active
P1570	Cruise Control–System — Traction Control Active

91044G12

Fig. 53 OBD II trouble codes (4of 5)

DTC	Description
P1571	Traction Control System — PWM Circuit No Frequency
P1574	EBTCM System — Stop Lamp Switch Circuit High Voltage
P1575	Extended Travel Brake Switch Circuit High Voltage
P1579	Park/Neutral To Drive/Reverse At High Throttle Angle
P1599	Engine Stall Or Near Stall Detected
P1602	Loss Of EBTCM Serial Data
P1603	Loss Of SDM Serial Data
P1604	Loss Of IPC Serial Data
P1605	Loss Of HVAC Serial Data
P1610	Loss of PZM Serial Data
P1611	Loss of CVRTD Serial Data
P1612	Loss Of IPM Serial Data
P1613	Loss Of DIM Serial Data
P1614	Loss Of RIM Serial Data
P1615	Loss Of VTD Serial Data
P1617	Engine Oil Level Switch Circuit
P1621	PCM Memory Performance
P1626	Theft Deterrent System — Fuel Enable Circuit
P1630	Theft Deterrent — PCM in Learn Mode
P1631	Theft Deterrent — Password Incorrect
P1632	Theft Deterrent — Fuel Disabled
P1633	Ignition Supplement Power Circuit Low Voltage
P1634	Ignition 1 Power Circuit Low Voltage
P1637	Generator L Terminal Circuit
P1638	Generator F Terminal Circuit
P1640	Driver 1 — Input High Voltage
P1641	Malfunction Indicator Lamp (MIL) Control Circuit
P1642	Vehicle Speed Output Circuit
P1644	Delivered Torque Output Circuit
P1645	EVAP Solenoid Output Circuit
P1646	EVAP Vent Valve Output Circuit
P1650	Driver 2 — Input High Voltage
P1652	Lift/Dive Circuit
P1654	Cruise Disable Output Circuit
P1660	Cooling Fan Control Circuits

91044G13

Fig. 54 OBD II trouble codes (5 of 5)

Clearing Codes

Stored fault codes may be erased from memory at any time by removing power from the PCM for at least 30 seconds. It may be necessary to clear stored codes during diagnosis to check for any recurrence during a test drive, but the stored codes must be written down when retrieved. The codes may still be required for subsequent trouble-shooting. Whenever a repair is complete, the stored codes must be erased and the vehicle test driven to confirm correct operation and repair.

✳✳ WARNING

The ignition switch must be OFF any time power is disconnected or restored to the PCM. Severe damage may result if this precaution is not observed.

Depending on the electrical distribution of the particular vehicle, power to the PCM may be disconnected by removing the PCM fuse in the fuse-box, disconnecting the in-line fuse holder near the positive battery terminal or disconnecting the PCM power lead at the battery terminal. Disconnecting the negative battery cable to clear codes is not recommended as this will also clear other memory data in the vehicle such as radio presets.

VACUUM DIAGRAMS

▶ **See Figures 55 thru 62**

Following are vacuum diagrams for most of the engine and emissions package combinations covered by this manual. Because vacuum circuits will vary based on various engine and vehicle options, always refer first to the vehicle emission control information label, if present. Should the label be missing, or should vehicle be equipped with a different engine from the vehicle's original equipment, refer to the diagrams below for the same or similar configuration.

If you wish to obtain a replacement emissions label, most manufacturers make the labels available for purchase. The labels can usually be ordered from a local dealer.

➡ The following is an assortment of vehicle emission control information labels. If the label on your vehicle differs from what is listed here, always follow what is on your underhood sticker, as it is most likely the accurate label for your particular engine application.

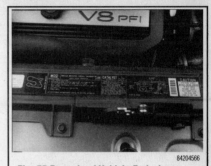

Fig. 55 Example of Vehicle Emissions Control Information (VECI) label in the engine compartment

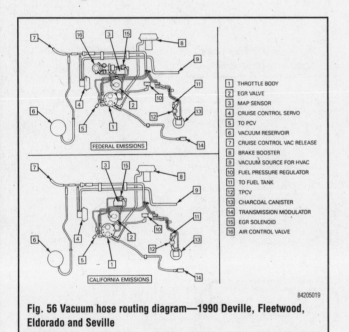

1	THROTTLE BODY
2	EGR VALVE
3	MAP SENSOR
4	CRUISE CONTROL SERVO
5	TO PCV
6	VACUUM RESERVOIR
7	CRUISE CONTROL VAC RELEASE
8	BRAKE BOOSTER
9	VACUUM SOURCE FOR HVAC
10	FUEL PRESSURE REGULATOR
11	TO FUEL TANK
12	TPCV
13	CHARCOAL CANISTER
14	TRANSMISSION MODULATOR
15	EGR SOLENOID
16	AIR CONTROL VALVE

Fig. 56 Vacuum hose routing diagram—1990 Deville, Fleetwood, Eldorado and Seville

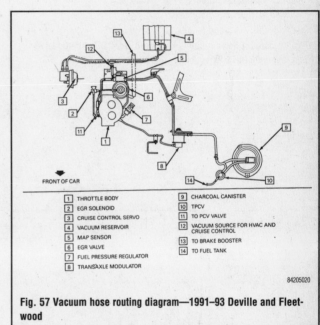

1	THROTTLE BODY	9	CHARCOAL CANISTER
2	EGR SOLENOID	10	TPCV
3	CRUISE CONTROL SERVO	11	TO PCV VALVE
4	VACUUM RESERVOIR	12	VACUUM SOURCE FOR HVAC AND CRUISE CONTROL
5	MAP SENSOR	13	TO BRAKE BOOSTER
6	EGR VALVE	14	TO FUEL TANK
7	FUEL PRESSURE REGULATOR		
8	TRANSAXLE MODULATOR		

Fig. 57 Vacuum hose routing diagram—1991–93 Deville and Fleetwood

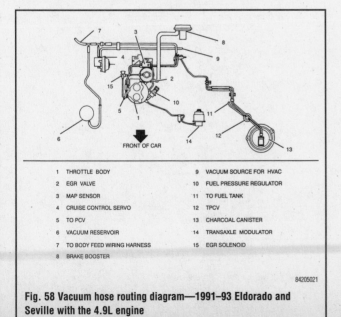

1	THROTTLE BODY	9	VACUUM SOURCE FOR HVAC
2	EGR VALVE	10	FUEL PRESSURE REGULATOR
3	MAP SENSOR	11	TO FUEL TANK
4	CRUISE CONTROL SERVO	12	TPCV
5	TO PCV	13	CHARCOAL CANISTER
6	VACUUM RESERVOIR	14	TRANSAXLE MODULATOR
7	TO BODY FEED WIRING HARNESS	15	EGR SOLENOID
8	BRAKE BOOSTER		

Fig. 58 Vacuum hose routing diagram—1991–93 Eldorado and Seville with the 4.9L engine

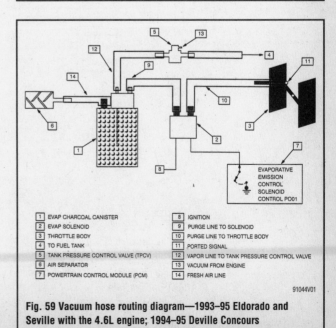

1	EVAP CHARCOAL CANISTER	8	IGNITION
2	EVAP SOLENOID	9	PURGE LINE TO SOLENOID
3	THROTTLE BODY	10	PURGE LINE TO THROTTLE BODY
4	TO FUEL TANK	11	PORTED SIGNAL
5	TANK PRESSURE CONTROL VALVE (TPCV)	12	VAPOR LINE TO TANK PRESSURE CONTROL VALVE
6	AIR SEPARATOR	13	VACUUM FROM ENGINE
7	POWERTRAIN CONTROL MODULE (PCM)	14	FRESH AIR LINE

Fig. 59 Vacuum hose routing diagram—1993–95 Eldorado and Seville with the 4.6L engine; 1994–95 Deville Concours

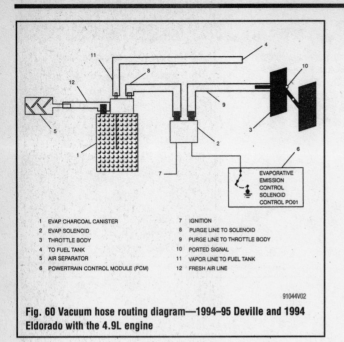

1 EVAP CHARCOAL CANISTER	7 IGNITION
2 EVAP SOLENOID	8 PURGE LINE TO SOLENOID
3 THROTTLE BODY	9 PURGE LINE TO THROTTLE BODY
4 TO FUEL TANK	10 PORTED SIGNAL
5 AIR SEPARATOR	11 VAPOR LINE TO FUEL TANK
6 POWERTRAIN CONTROL MODULE (PCM)	12 FRESH AIR LINE

91044V02

Fig. 60 Vacuum hose routing diagram—1994–95 Deville and 1994 Eldorado with the 4.9L engine

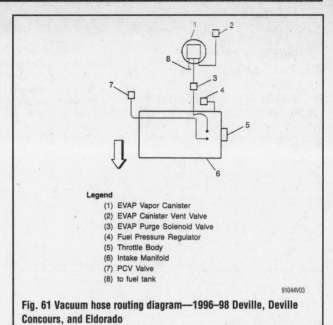

Legend
(1) EVAP Vapor Canister
(2) EVAP Canister Vent Valve
(3) EVAP Purge Solenoid Valve
(4) Fuel Pressure Regulator
(5) Throttle Body
(6) Intake Manifold
(7) PCV Valve
(8) to fuel tank

91044V03

Fig. 61 Vacuum hose routing diagram—1996–98 Deville, Deville Concours, and Eldorado

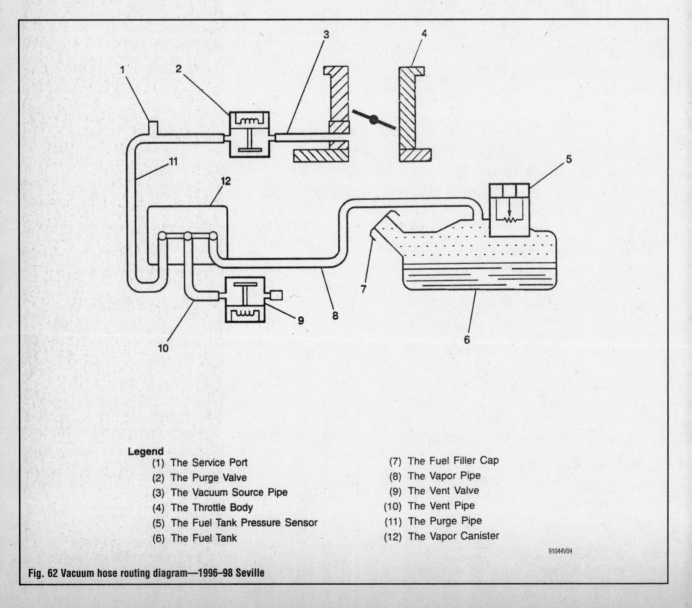

Legend
(1) The Service Port
(2) The Purge Valve
(3) The Vacuum Source Pipe
(4) The Throttle Body
(5) The Fuel Tank Pressure Sensor
(6) The Fuel Tank

(7) The Fuel Filler Cap
(8) The Vapor Pipe
(9) The Vent Valve
(10) The Vent Pipe
(11) The Purge Pipe
(12) The Vapor Canister

91044V04

Fig. 62 Vacuum hose routing diagram—1996–98 Seville

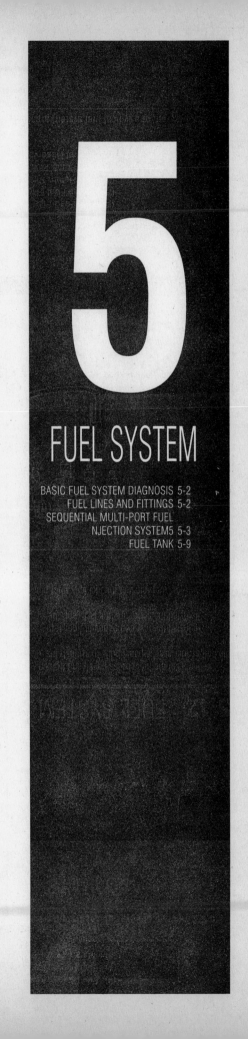

5
FUEL SYSTEM

BASIC FUEL SYSTEM DIAGNOSIS

When there is a problem starting or driving a vehicle, two of the most important checks involve the ignition and the fuel systems. The questions most mechanics attempt to answer first, "is there spark?" and "is there fuel?" will often lead to solving most basic problems. For ignition system diagnosis and testing, please refer to the information on engine electrical components and ignition systems found earlier in this manual. If the ignition system checks out (there is spark), then you must determine if the fuel system is operating properly (is there fuel?).

✳✳ CAUTION

While servicing the fuel system, fuel vapors can collect in enclosed areas such as a trunk. To reduce the risk of fire and increased exposure to vapors:

- Use forced air ventilation such as a fan.
- Plug or cap any fuel system openings in order to reduce fuel vapor formation.
- Clean up any spilled fuel immediately.

- Avoid sparks and any source of ignition.
- Use signs and any necessary warning to alert others in the work area that fuel system work is in process.

✳✳ CAUTION

Always wear safety goggles when working with fuel in order to protect the eyes from fuel splash.

FUEL LINES AND FITTINGS

Nylon fuel lines are designed to perform the same function as the steel or rubber fuel lines they replace. Nylon lines are constructed to withstand maximum fuel system pressure, exposure to fuel additives, and changes in temperature.

The fuel feed, return, vacuum and EVAP lines are assembled as a harness. Retaining clips hold the lines together and provide a means for attaching the lines to the vehicle. Sections of the lines that are exposed to chafing, high temperature or vibration are protected with heat resistant rubber hose and/or coextruded conduit.

Nylon lines are somewhat flexible and can be formed around gradual turns under the vehicle. However, if forced into sharp bends, nylon lines will kink and restrict fuel flow. In addition, once exposed to fuel, nylon lines may become stiffer and more likely to kink if bent too far. Special care should be taken when working on a vehicle with nylon fuel lines.

✳✳ CAUTION

To reduce the risk of fire and personal injury when working on nylon fuel lines.

- Always cover a nylon fuel line with a wet towel before using a torch in the vicinity. Also, never expose the vehicle to temperatures higher than 239°F (115°C) for more than one hour or more than 194°F (90°C) for any extended period.

Take care not to nick or scratch the nylon fuel lines. If they become damaged, they must be replaced.

Quick-Connect Fittings

▶ See Figures 1 and 2

Some early model vehicles do not have quick-connect fuel line fittings. On these vehicles, just make sure to use a back-up wrench on the fuel lines when disconnecting them.

➡ **If your vehicle is equipped with metal quick-connect fittings, a special tool (J 37088A) or equivalent will be required to service the fittings.**

1. Properly relieve the fuel system pressure.
2. If equipped, slide the dust cover back to access the fuel line fitting.

Grasp both ends of the fitting, Twist the female connector ¼ turn in each direction to loosen any dirt within the fittings. Using compressed air, blow out the dirt from the quick-connect fittings.

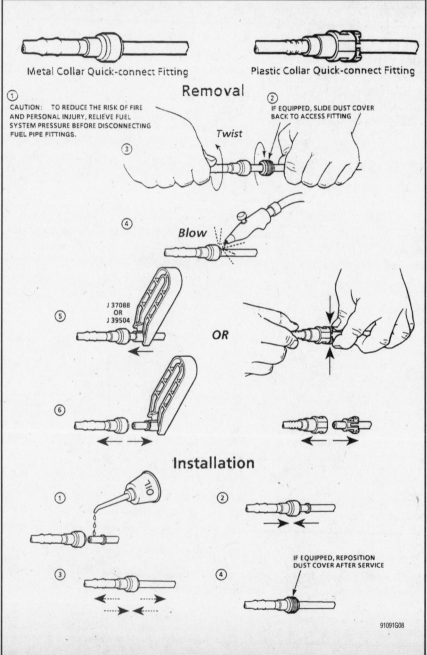

Fig. 1 Disconnecting procedure for quick-connect fuel fittings

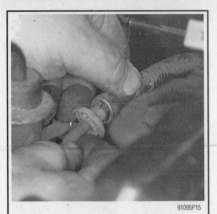

Fig. 2 Inserting the special tool to release the quick-connect fitting

91095P15

Safety glasses are recommended when trying to clean debris from an enclosed area with compressed air.

3. If the fittings are metal, choose the correct size-releasing tool, insert it into the female connector, and then push inward to release the locking tabs. Pull the connector apart.

4. It may be necessary to remove rust or burrs from the male end of a quick-connect fitting. If this is the case, use an emery cloth to clean the tube by rotating the cloth in a radial motion.

5. Using a clean shop towel, wipe off the male ends of the tube.

6. For the plastic type fittings, which are hand releasable, squeeze the plastic retainer release tabs, then pull the connection apart.

To install:

7. Make sure the connectors are clean

To reduce the chance of injury, apply a few drops of lubricant (clean engine oil), to the male end of the tube before reconnecting the fittings.

8. Push the connectors together until you can hear an audible click, indicating they have locked.

9. Once installed, pull on both ends of the connections to make sure they are secure.

10. If equipped, slide the fuel fitting dust cover back into place.

11. After all lines are connected, crank the engine for a few seconds (if the engine starts, turn it off) and then check for fuel leaks.

➡If nylon fuel feed or return lines become kinked, and cannot be straightened, they must be replaced. Do not attempt to repair sections of nylon fuel lines. If damaged, replace the line.

SEQUENTIAL MULTI-PORT FUEL INJECTION SYSTEM

Observe all applicable safety precautions when working around fuel. Whenever servicing the fuel system, always work in a well-ventilated area. Do not allow fuel spray or vapors to be exposed to a spark or open flame. Keep a dry chemical fire extinguisher near the work area. Always keep fuel in a container specifically designed for fuel storage; also, always properly seal fuel containers to avoid the possibility of fire or explosion.

The PCM controls the fuel injectors based on information it receives from several information sensors. Each injector is fired individually in engine firing order, which is called Sequential Multiport Fuel Injection. This allows precise fuel metering to each cylinder and improves driveability under all driving conditions.

The PCM has several operating modes for fuel control, depending on the information it receives from the sensors.

When the key is first turned ON, the PCM will turn on the fuel pump relay for approximately two seconds. The fuel pump runs and builds up pressure in the fuel system. The PCM then monitors the MAF, IAT, ECT, and TP sensor signal to determine the required injector pulse width for starting.

If the engine is flooded with fuel during starting and will not start, Clear Flood Mode can be manually selected. To select Clear Flood Mode, push the accelerator to Wide Open Throttle (WOT). With this signal, the PCM will completely turn Off the injectors and will maintain this as long as it sees a WOT condition with engine speed below 1000 RPM.

General Information

The fuel supply is stored in the fuel tank. An electric fuel pump attached to the fuel sender assembly (inside the fuel tank) pumps fuel through an in-line filter to the throttle body unit or fuel rail. The pump is designed to provide fuel at a pressure

above the regulated pressure needed by the throttle body unit or fuel rail. Unused fuel is returned to the fuel tank by a separate pipe.

Unleaded fuel must be used with all gasoline engines for proper emission control system operation. Using unleaded fuel will also decrease spark plug fouling and extend engine oil life. Leaded fuel can damage the emission control system, and its use can result in loss of emission warranty coverage.

The function of the fuel and air control system is to manage fuel and air delivery to each cylinder to optimize the performance and driveability of the engine under all driving conditions. The fuel supply is stored in a High Density Polyethylene (HDPE) fuel tank (in late models) located behind the rear wheels. The fuel sender allows retrieval of fuel from the tank and provides information on fuel level.

An electric fuel pump, contained in the modular fuel sender, pumps fuel through nylon lines and an in-line fuel filter to the fuel rail. The pump is designed to provide fuel at a pressure above the regulated pressure needed by the injectors Fuel is then distributed through the fuel rail to six injectors inside the intake manifold. Fuel pressure is controlled by a pressure regulator mounted on the fuel rail. The fuel system is re-circulating; this means that excess fuel that is not injected into the cylinders is sent back to the fuel tank by a separate nylon line. This removes air and vapors from the fuel as well as keeping he fuel cool during hot weather operation. Each fuel injector is located directly above the two intake valves of each cylinder. The accelerator pedal in the passenger compartment is linked to the throttle valve in the throttle body by cable. The throttle body regulates airflow from the air cleaner into the intake manifold, which then distributes this air to the two intake valves of each cylinder. This allows the driver to control the airflow into the engine, which then controls the power output of the engine.

Unleaded fuel must be used with all gasoline engines for proper emission control system operation. Using unleaded fuel will also minimize spark plug fouling and extend engine oil life. Leaded fuel can damage the emission control system, and its

use can result in loss of emission warranty coverage.

The Northstar engine is fueled by eight individual injectors, one for each cylinder, that are controlled by the PCM. The PCM controls each injector by energizing the injector coil for a brief period generally once every other engine revolution. The length of this brief period, or pulse, is carefully calculated by the PCM to deliver the correct amount of fuel for proper driveability and emissions control. The length of time the injector is energized is called the pulse width and is measured in milliseconds (thousandths of a second).

While the engine is running, the PCM is constantly monitoring its inputs and recalculating the appropriate pulse width for each injector. The pulse width calculation is based on the injector flow rate (mass or fuel the energized injector will pass per unit of time), the desired air /fuel ratio, and actual air mass in short term and long term fuel trim. The calculated pulse is timed to occur as the intake valves of each cylinder are closing to attain the largest duration and most vaporization.

Fueling during crank is slightly different than during engine run. As the engine begins to turn, a prime pulse may be injected to speed starting. As soon as the PCM can determine where in the firing order the engine is, it begins pulsing injectors. The pulse width during crank is based on coolant temperature and barometric pressure.

The Northstar fueling system has several automatic adjustments to compensate for differences in fuel system hardware, driving conditions, fuel used, and vehicle aging. The basis for fuel control is the pulse width calculation described above. Included in this calculation are an adjustment for battery voltage, short-term fuel trim, and long term fuel trim. The battery voltage adjustment is necessary since changes in voltage across the injector affect injector flow rate. Short term and long term fuel trims are fine and gross adjustments to pulse width designed to maximize driveability and emissions control. These fuel trims are based on feedback from oxygen sensors in the exhaust stream and are only used when the fuel control system is in closed loop.

Under certain stringent conditions, the fueling system will not energize injectors, individually or in groups, for a period of time. This is referred to as fuel shut-off. Fuel shut-off is used to improve traction, save fuel, improve starting, and to protect the vehicle under certain extreme or abusive conditions.

Relieving Fuel System Pressure

1. Disconnect the negative battery terminal to avoid possible fuel discharge if an accidental attempt is made to start the engine.
2. Loosen the fuel filler cap to relieve tank vapor pressure.
3. Attach a fuel gauge (J 34730) or equivalent to the fuel pressure connection. Wrap a shop towel around the fitting while connecting the gauge to avoid spillage.
4. Install the bleed hose into an approved container and open the valve to bleed the system pressure. Fuel connections are now safe for servicing.
5. Drain any fuel remaining in the gauge into an approved container.

Throttle Body

REMOVAL & INSTALLATION

4.5 and 4.9L Engines

▶ **See Figures 3, 4 and 5**

1. Properly relieve the fuel system pressure.
2. Disconnect the negative battery cable.
3. Raise the hood, install fender covers, and remove the air cleaner assembly.

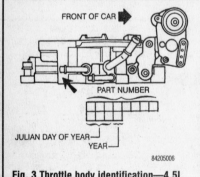

Fig. 3 Throttle body identification—4.5L and 4.9L engines

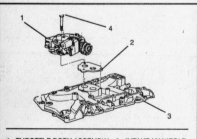

| 1 | THROTTLE BODY ASSEMBLY | 3 | INTAKE MANIFOLD |
| 2 | THROTTLE BODY GASKET | 4 | 19 N•m (14 LBS. FT.) |

Fig. 4 Throttle body assembly—4.5L and 4.9L engines

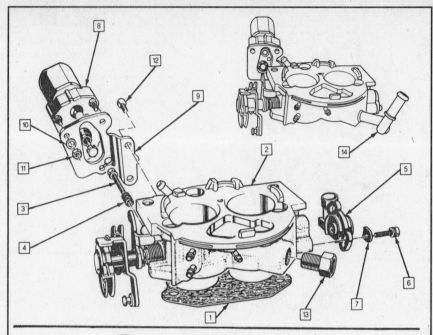

1	THROTTLE BODY GASKET
2	THROTTLE BODY ASSEMBLY
3	MINIMUM AIR (IDLE SPEED) SCREW
4	MINIMUM AIR SPRING
5	THROTTLE POSITION SENSOR (TPS)
6	TPS ATTACHING SCREW
7	TPS ATTACHING SCREW RETAINER
8	IDLE SPEED CONTROL MOTOR (ISC)
9	ISC ASSEMBLY BRACKET
10	ISC ASSEMBLY LOCKWASHER
11	ISC ASSEMBLY NUT
12	ISC BRACKET MOUNTING SCREW
13	BRAKE BOOSTER VACUUM PIPE FITTING (DESIGN 1)
14	BRAKE BOOSTER VACUUM PIPE FITTING (DESIGN 2)

Fig. 5 Throttle Body Unit—4.5L and 4.9L engines

4. Detach the electrical connectors for the idle speed control motor, the throttle position sensor, fuel injectors, EFE, and any other component necessary in order to remove the throttle body.
5. Remove the throttle return spring, cruise control, throttle linkage and downshift cable.
6. Disconnect all necessary vacuum lines, the fuel inlet line, fuel return line, brake booster line, MAP sensor hose and the AIR hose. Be sure to use a back-up wrench on all metal lines.
7. Remove the PCV, EVAP, and/or EGR hoses from the front of the throttle body.
8. Remove the 3 throttle body mounting screws and remove the throttle body and gasket.
9. The installation is the reverse order of the removal procedure.
10. Tighten the throttle body retaining bolts to 14 ft. lbs. (19 Nm). Always use new gaskets and O-rings.
11. Make certain cruise and shift cables do not hold the throttle above the idle stop. Reset the IAC by depressing the accelerator slightly, run engine for 3–4 seconds and turn ignition **OFF** for 10 seconds.

4.6L Engine

▶ **See Figures 6, 7, 8, 9 and 10**

1. Disconnect the negative battery cable.
2. Disconnect the vacuum manifold at the throttle body and the vacuum hoses at the cruise control servo.
3. Disconnect the cruise control cable at the servo. The cable can be removed at the servo without removing the plastic retainer.
4. Remove the cruise control servo and bracket at the throttle body.
5. Disconnect the cruise control cable at the throttle body.
6. Disconnect the TP sensor at the throttle body.
7. Disconnect the fuel pipe retainer at the ISC bracket.
8. Remove the throttle body from the intake manifold.
9. Remove the ISC motor and bracket from the throttle body.
   To install:
10. Install the ISC motor and bracket to the throttle body.

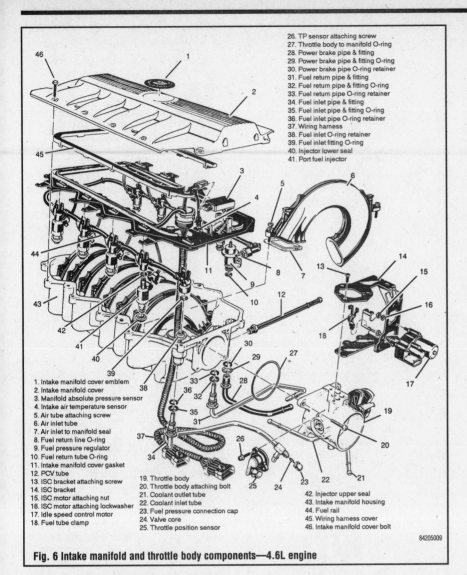

26. TP sensor attaching screw
27. Throttle body to manifold O-ring
28. Power brake pipe & fitting
29. Power brake pipe & fitting O-ring
30. Power brake pipe O-ring retainer
31. Fuel return pipe & fitting
32. Fuel return pipe & fitting O-ring
33. Fuel return pipe O-ring retainer
34. Fuel inlet pipe & fitting
35. Fuel inlet pipe & fitting O-ring
36. Fuel inlet pipe O-ring retainer
37. Wiring harness
38. Fuel inlet O-ring retainer
39. Fuel inlet fitting O-ring
40. Injector lower seal
41. Port fuel injector

1. Intake manifold cover emblem
2. Intake manifold cover
3. Manifold absolute pressure sensor
4. Intake air temperature sensor
5. Air tube attaching screw
6. Air inlet tube
7. Air inlet to manifold seal
8. Fuel return line O-ring
9. Fuel pressure regulator
10. Fuel return tube O-ring
11. Intake manifold cover gasket
12. PCV tube
13. ISC bracket attaching screw
14. ISC bracket
15. ISC motor attaching nut
16. ISC motor attaching lockwasher
17. Idle speed control motor
18. Fuel tube clamp

19. Throttle body
20. Throttle body attaching bolt
21. Coolant outlet tube
22. Coolant inlet tube
23. Fuel pressure connection cap
24. Valve core
25. Throttle position sensor

42. Injector upper seal
43. Intake manifold housing
44. Fuel rail
45. Wiring harness cover
46. Intake manifold cover bolt

84205009

Fig. 6 Intake manifold and throttle body components—4.6L engine

11. Position a NEW throttle body O-ring seal on the throttle body with petroleum jelly.

➡**Do not reuse the old throttle body O-ring seal. The seal swells when exposed to fuel and oil and will not seat properly.**

12. Install the throttle body to the intake manifold and tighten to 106 inch lbs. (12 Nm).

13. Connect the fuel pipe retainer to the ISC bracket.

14. Connect the TP sensor to the throttle body and tighten the retaining bolts to 106 inch lbs. (12 Nm).

15. Connect the cruise control cable to the throttle body.

16. Connect the cruise control servo and bracket to the throttle body and tighten the retaining bolts to 106 inch lbs. (12 Nm).

17. Connect the cruise control cable at the servo.

18. Connect the vacuum manifold to the throttle body and the vacuum hoses to the cruise control servo.

19. Install the intake manifold along with throttle body.

20. Perform the TP Sensor/Idle Learn procedure.

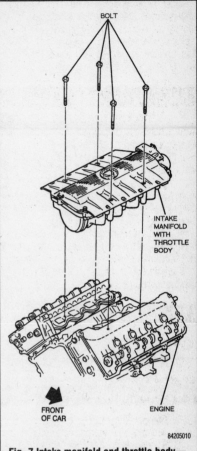

Fig. 7 Intake manifold and throttle body—4.6L engine

84205010

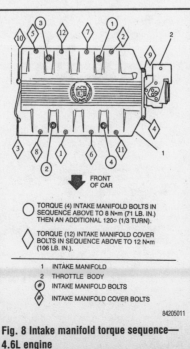

FRONT OF CAR

TORQUE (4) INTAKE MANIFOLD BOLTS IN SEQUENCE ABOVE TO 8 N•m (71 LB. IN.) THEN AN ADDITIONAL 120o (1/3 TURN).

TORQUE (12) INTAKE MANIFOLD COVER BOLTS IN SEQUENCE ABOVE TO 12 N•m (106 LB. IN.).

1   INTAKE MANIFOLD
2   THROTTLE BODY
(#) INTAKE MANIFOLD BOLTS
(#) INTAKE MANIFOLD COVER BOLTS

84205011

Fig. 8 Intake manifold torque sequence—4.6L engine

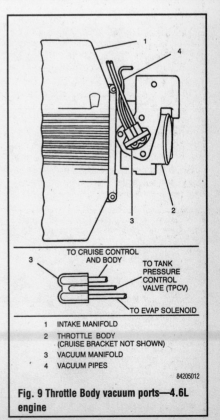

TO CRUISE CONTROL AND BODY
TO TANK PRESSURE CONTROL VALVE (TPCV)
TO EVAP SOLENOID

1   INTAKE MANIFOLD
2   THROTTLE BODY (CRUISE BRACKET NOT SHOWN)
3   VACUUM MANIFOLD
4   VACUUM PIPES

84205012

Fig. 9 Throttle Body vacuum ports—4.6L engine

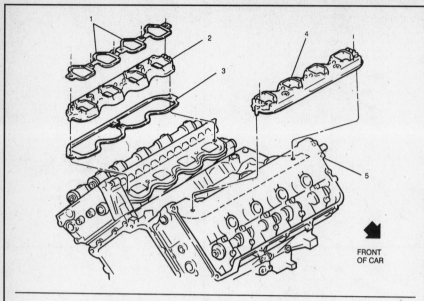

1 UPPER INTAKE MANIFOLD SEAL
2 SPACER
3 LOWER INTAKE MANIFOLD SEAL
4 SPACER WITH SEALS ATTACHED
5 ENGINE

FRONT OF CAR

84205013

Fig. 10 Intake manifold seals—4.6L engine

Fuel Injector(s)

♦ See Figures 11 and 12

The fuel injector is a solenoid device controlled by the PCM that meters pressurized fuel to a single cylinder. When the PCM energizes the injector coil, a normally closed bail valve opens, allowing fuel to flow past a director plate to the injector outlet. The director plate has holes that control the fuel flow, generating a dual conical spray pattern of finely atomized fuel at the injector outlet. Fuel from the outlet is directed at both intake valves, causing it to become further vaporized before entering the combustion chamber.

Fuel injectors will cause various driveability conditions if they will not open, are stuck open, leaking or have a low coil resistance.

Fuel system deposits can cause various driveability problems. Deposits usually occur during hot soaks. Poor fuel quality or driving patterns such as short trips followed by long cool down periods can cause injector deposits. This occurs when the fuel

remaining in the injector tip evaporates and leaves deposits. Leaking injectors can increase injector deposits. Deposits on fuel injectors affect their spray pattern, which in turn could cause reduced power, unstable idle, hard starts, and poor fuel economy.

91095P10

Fig. 11 A typical ported fuel injector with its two O-rings and retaining clip

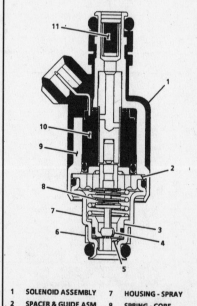

1 SOLENOID ASSEMBLY
2 SPACER & GUIDE ASM
3 CORE SEAT
4 VALVE - BALL
5 PLATE - DIRECTOR
6 BACKUP - O-RING
7 HOUSING - SPRAY
8 SPRING - CORE
9 HOUSING - SOLENOID
10 SOLENOID
11 FILTER - FUEL INLET

91095G06

Fig. 12 A schematic of a typical ported fuel injector

TESTING

The easiest way to test the operation of the fuel injectors is to listen for a clicking sound coming from the injectors while the engine is running. This is accomplished using a mechanic's stethoscope, or a long screwdriver. Place the end of the stethoscope or the screwdriver (tip end, not handle) onto the body of the injector. Place the ear pieces of the stethoscope in your ears, or if using a screwdriver, place your ear on top of the handle. An audible clicking noise should be heard; this is the solenoid operating. If the injector makes this noise, the injector driver circuit and computer are operating as designed. Continue testing all the injectors this way.

✳✳ CAUTION

Be extremely careful while working on an operating engine, make sure you have no dangling jewelry, extremely loose clothes, power tool cords or other items that might get caught in a moving part of the engine.

All Injectors Clicking

If all the injectors are clicking, but you have determined that the fuel system is the cause of your driveability problem, continue diagnostics. Make sure that you have checked fuel pump pressure as outlined earlier in this section. An easy way to determine a weak or unproductive cylinder is a cylinder drop test. This is accomplished by removing one spark plug wire at a time, and seeing which cylinder causes the least difference in the idle. The one that causes the least change is the weak cylinder.

If the injectors were all clicking and the ignition system is functioning properly, remove the injector of the suspect cylinder and bench test it. This is accomplished by checking for a spray pattern from the injector itself. Install a fuel supply line to the injector (or rail if the injector is left attached to the rail) and momentarily apply 12 volts DC and a ground to the injector itself; a visible fuel spray should appear. If no spray is achieved, replace the injector and check the running condition of the engine.

One or More Injectors Are Not Clicking

♦ See Figures 13, 14, 15 and 16

If one or more injectors are found to be not operating, testing the injector driver circuit and computer can be accomplished using a "noid" light. First, with the engine not running and the ignition key in the **OFF** position, remove the connector from the injector you plan to test, then plug the "noid" light tool into the injector connector. Start the engine and the "noid" light should flash, signaling that the injector driver circuit is working. If the "noid" light flashes, but the injector does not click when plugged in, test the injector's resistance. resistance should be between 11–18 ohms.

If the "noid" light does not flash, the injector driver circuit is faulty. Disconnect the negative battery cable. Unplug the "noid" light from the injector connector and also unplug the PCM. Check the harness between the appropriate pins on the harness side of the PCM connector and the injector connector. Resistance should be less than 5.0 ohms; if not,

Fig. 13 Unplug the fuel injector connector

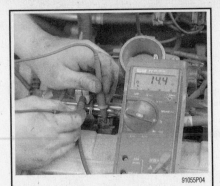

Fig. 14 Probe the two terminals of a fuel injector to check its resistance

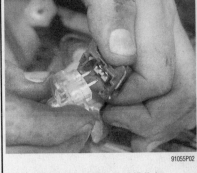

Fig. 15 Plug the correct "noid" light directly into the injector harness connector

Fig. 16 If the correct "noid" light flashes while the engine is running, the injector driver circuit inside the PCM is working

repair the circuit. If resistance is within specifications, the injector driver inside the PCM is faulty and replacement of the PCM will be necessary.

REMOVAL & INSTALLATION

4.5L and 4.9L Engines

▶ See Figures 17 and 18

1. Disconnect the negative battery cable.
2. Properly relieve the fuel system pressure.
3. Raise the hood, install fender covers, and remove the air cleaner assembly.
4. Remove the fuel rail assembly. With the fuel rail inverted, detach the electrical connector to each injector by pushing in on the connector clip while

pulling the connector body away from the injector. Spread open the clip slightly and slide the clip away from the fuel rail.

5. Remove the injector by twisting back and forth.
6. Disassemble the injector O-ring seals from the injector and discard.

To install:

7. Lubricate the new injector O-ring seals with petroleum based grease and install it on the injector assembly.
8. Install a new injector clip on the injector assembly.
9. Install the fuel injector assembly into the fuel rail socket as follows:
   a. Push in to engage the retainer clip with the fuel rail cup.

b. The electrical connectors should be facing the engine front for injectors 1 through 4. The electrical connectors should be facing the engine rear for injectors 5 through 8.

10. Attach the electrical connector to the injector assembly.
11. Install the fuel rail assembly.
12. Energize the fuel pump and check for leaks.
13. Perform the Idle Learn procedure.

4.6L Engine

▶ See Figures 6, 19, 20 and 21

1. Remove the fuel pump relay in the engine compartment micro relay center.
2. Relieve the fuel system pressure.

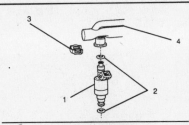

1	INJECTOR ASSEMBLY
2	SEAL-O-RING-INJECTOR
3	CLIP-INJECTOR RETAINER
4	FUEL RAIL

84205014

Fig. 17 Injector assembly and retainer— 4.5L and 4.9L engines

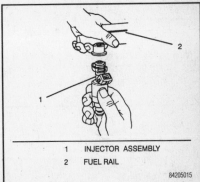

1	INJECTOR ASSEMBLY
2	FUEL RAIL

84205015

Fig. 18 Installing the injector assembly— 4.5L and 4.9L engines

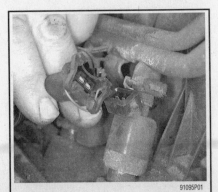

Fig. 19 Unplug the injector harness from the injector

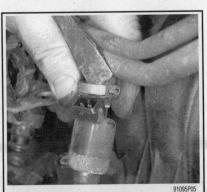

Fig. 20 Using a small pry tool, pry the injector lock from the injector

Fig. 21 Gently pull the injector from the rail. A slight twisting motion may help ease removal

3. Remove the intake manifold top cover.

4. Detach the 2 intake manifold electrical connectors.

5. Remove the fuel rail along with the injectors out of the intake manifold.

6. Remove the injectors from the fuel rail.

To install:

7. Install the injectors to the fuel rail.

8. Install the fuel rail along with the injectors into the intake manifold housing.

9. Install the intake manifold top cover and tighten the retaining bolts to 106 inch lbs. (12 Nm).

10. Attach the 2 intake manifold electrical connectors.

11. Install the fuel pump relay in the engine compartment micro relay center.

Fuel Rail Assembly

The fuel rail consists of four parts:
- The pipe that carries fuel to each injector
- The fuel pressure regulator
- The fuel pressure test port
- Six individual fuel injectors

The fuel rail is mounted on the intake manifold and distributes fuel to each cylinder through the individual injectors.

Fuel is delivered from the pump through the fuel feed line to the inlet port of the fuel rail pipe. From the fuel feed inlet, fuel is directed to the rail pipe to the fuel pressure regulator. Fuel in excess of injector needs flows back through the pressure regulator assembly to the outlet port of the fuel rail. Fuel then flows through the fuel return line to the fuel tank to begin the cycle again.

REMOVAL & INSTALLATION

▶ **See Figures 22 and 23**

When servicing the fuel rail assembly, precautions must be taken to prevent dirt and other contaminants from entering the fuel passages. It is

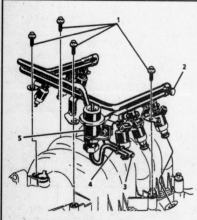

1	**BOLTS 15 N·m (11 lb. ft.)**
2	**FUEL PRESSURE CONNECTION**
3	**FUEL FEED**
4	**FUEL RETURN**
5	**FUEL PRESSURE REGULATOR**

91095G08

Fig. 22 The fuel rail assembly and fuel pressure regulator mounting

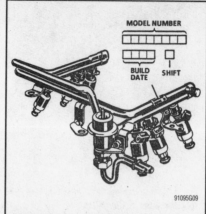

91095G09

Fig. 23 Note the fuel rail identification plate

recommended that fittings are capped and holes plugged during servicing.

1. Bleed the fuel pressure from the fuel system.

2. Clean the fuel rail assembly and connections. Use a spray type cleaner. Never immerse the fuel rail or components in a liquid solvent.

3. Remove the fuel feed and return pipes from the fuel rail.

4. Remove the vacuum line from the pressure regulator.

5. Detach the injector electrical connectors.

6. Remove the fuel rail hold-down bolts.

7. Pull on the fuel rail with equal force on both sides of the rail to remove it.

To install:

8. O-rings must be replaced on all components that are replaced.

9. Lightly oil the injector O-rings with clean motor oil.

10. Place the rail assembly on the manifold and seat the injectors by hand.

11. Tighten the fuel rail hold down bolts to 22 ft. lb. (30 Nm)

12. Install the fuel feed and returns by pushing the pipes onto the fuel rail tubes.

13. Reattach the fuel injector electrical connectors, and plug in the vacuum line to the pressure regulator.

Fuel Pressure Regulator

REMOVAL & INSTALLATION

▶ **See Figure 24**

4.5L and 4.9L Engines

1. Disconnect the negative battery cable. Remove the air cleaner upper housing assembly.

2. Relieve the fuel system pressure.

3. Disconnect the fuel return line from rear rail attachment.

4. Remove the pressure regulator-to-rail bracket mounting screws.

5. Remove the pressure regulator and fuel return line as an assembly, from the fuel rail.

6. Disconnect the fuel return line from the pressure regulator. Cover all openings with masking tape to prevent dirt entry.

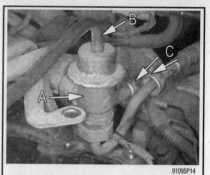

91095P14

Fig. 24 View of the fuel pressure regulator (A), vacuum hose (B), and fuel/return lines with quick connect fittings (C)

To install:

7. Prior to assembling the pressure regulator to the fuel return line and rail assembly, lubricate the new O-ring seals with petroleum base grease.

8. Place the O-ring on the fuel return line and assemble the pressure regulator to it.

9. Place a new O-ring seal on the pressure regulator and install the regulator and fuel return line assembly to the fuel rail.

10. Secure the pressure regulator in place with retaining screws. Tighten the retaining screws to 9 ft. lbs. (12 Nm).

11. Connect the fuel return line at the rear of the rail assembly, use a backup wrench on the inlet fitting to prevent turning.

12. Connect the negative battery cable.

13. Turn the ignition switch **ON** and **OFF** to allow fuel pressure back into system. Check for leaks.

14. Install the air cleaner assembly. Perform an idle learn procedure.

4.6L Engine—Early Model

▶ **See Figure 6**

1. Remove the fuel pump relay in the engine compartment micro relay center.

2. Relieve the fuel system pressure.

3. Remove the intake manifold top cover.

4. Lift the fuel rail along with the injectors out of the intake manifold housing enough to remove the pressure regulator from the rail.

5. Disconnect the vacuum line from the regulator.

6. Remove the pressure regulator from the fuel rail.

To install:

7. Install the pressure regulator to the fuel rail.

8. Install the fuel rail along with the injectors into the intake manifold housing.

9. Install the intake manifold top cover and tighten to 106 inch lbs. (12 Nm).

10. Install the fuel pump relay in the engine compartment micro relay center.

11. Reconnect the vacuum line from the regulator.

4.6L Engine—Late Model

➡**Do not use compressed air to test or clean a fuel pressure regulator. Excessive air pressure can damage the fuel pressure regulator. Do not immerse the fuel pressure regulator in a cleaning solvent in order to prevent damage to the regulator.**

1. Remove the Intake Manifold top cover.
2. Relieve fuel system pressure.
3. Disconnect the fuel pressure regulator vacuum hose from the fuel pressure regulator
4. Clean any dirt from the fuel pressure regulator retaining ring.
5. Remove the retaining ring.
6. Catch any spilled fuel using a shop towel.
7. Lift and twist the fuel pressure regulator from the fuel rail socket.
8. Cover the fuel pressure regulator housing to prevent contamination from entering the fuel system.
9. Clean the fuel pressure regulator filter screen with gasoline and a soft brush.

To install:

➡ **When servicing the fuel pressure regulator, insure that the O-ring backup, large O-ring, filter screen, and small O-ring are properly placed on the regulator.**

10. Install new O-rings on the fuel pressure regulator, if a new fuel pressure regulator is not being installed.
   a. Install the regulator seal O-ring (small O-ring).
   b. Install the regulator filter.
   c. Install the regulator seal O-ring.
   d. Install the O-ring back-up.
11. Insert the regulator into the fuel rail socket

using a turning motion to properly seat the O-rings.
12. Install the retaining ring on the fuel pressure regulator.
13. Position the vacuum port on the fuel pressure regulator in the original position.
14. Connect the vacuum hose to the fuel pressure regulator.
15. Connect the negative battery cable.
16. Turn the ignition switch **ON** for 2 seconds.
17. Turn the ignition switch **OFF** for 10 seconds.
18. Turn the ignition switch **ON**.
19. Check for fuel leaks.
20. Install the Intake Manifold top cover.

FUEL TANK

Tank Assembly

REMOVAL & INSTALLATION

Early Model Fleetwood, Deville, Eldorado and Seville

1. Disconnect the negative battery cable and relieve the fuel system pressure.
2. Drain the fuel tank.
3. Remove the fuel filler door assembly and disconnect the screw retaining the filler pipe-to-body bracket.
4. Raise the vehicle and support with jackstands.
5. Detach the tank level sender lead connector.
6. Support the tank with a transmission jack or equivalent. Remove the two tank retaining straps.
7. Lower the tank far enough to disconnect the ground lead and fuel hoses from the pump assembly.
8. Remove the tank from the vehicle slowly to ensure all connections and hoses have been disconnected.

To install:
9. Using a new fuel pump O-ring gasket, install the pump/sender assembly into the tank.

❄ CAUTION

Do not twist the strainer when installing the pump/sender assembly. Make sure the strainer does not block the full travel of the float arm.

10. Place the tank on the jack.
11. Position the tank sound insulators in their original positions and raise the tank far enough to attach the electrical and hose connectors.
12. Raise the tank to the proper position and loosely install the retaining straps. Make sure the tank is in the proper position before tightening the retaining straps.
13. Tighten the straps to 26 ft. lbs. (35 Nm).
14. Connect the grounding strap and negative battery cable.
15. With the engine OFF, turn the ignition key to the ON position and check for fuel leaks at the tank.

Later Models

1. Disconnect the negative battery cable.
2. Relieve the fuel system pressure.

3. Raise the vehicle and support with jackstands.
4. Drain the fuel tank.
5. Detach the fuel feed and return quick-connect fittings at the fuel tank as follows:
   a. Grasp both ends of one fuel pipe connection and twist ¼ turn in each direction to loosen the dirt in the connection.
   b. If compressed air is available, blow out the dirt within the connection.
   c. Squeeze the plastic tabs of the male end connector, then pull the connection apart.
   d. Repeat for the fuel return pipefitting.

❄❄ WARNING

If the nylon fuel or feed lines become kinked or damaged in any way they must be replaced. Do not try to straighten.

6. Detach the fuel sender electrical connector.
7. With the aid of an assistant, support the tank and remove the fuel tank strap retaining nuts and bolts and place the tank in a suitable work area..

To install:
8. With the aid of an assistant, position and support the tank and install the fuel tank straps and retaining nuts and bolts. Tighten to 26 ft. lbs. (34 Nm).
9. Install the vapor pipe.
10. Attach the fuel sender electrical connector.
11. Attach the fuel feed and return quick-connect fittings at the fuel tank as follows:
   a. Apply a few drops of clean engine oil to the male connector pipe ends.

❄❄ CAUTION

Applying a few drops of clean engine oil to the male connector pipe ends will ensure proper reconnecting and prevent a possible fuel leak.

   b. Push the connectors together to cause the retaining tabs to snap into place.
   c. Once installed, pull on both ends of each connection to make sure they are secure.
   d. Lower the car.
   e. Turn the ignition switch to the **ON** position for 2 seconds, then turn to **OFF** for 5 seconds. Again turn to **ON** and check for leaks.

Electric Fuel Pump

The fuel pump is a high-pressure electric pump mounted in the fuel tank. The impeller serves as a vapor separator and precharges the high-pressure assembly. Fuel is pumped at a positive pressure through an in-line fuel filter to the fuel rail assembly. A pressure regulator maintains a preset pressure in the fuel line to the injectors. Excess fuel is returned to the fuel tank through the fuel return line. The electric fuel pump is connected in parallel to the PCM and is activated by the PCM when the ignition is turned on and the engine is cranking or operating. If the engine stalls or if the starter is not engaged, the fuel pumps will stop in about one second.

REMOVAL & INSTALLATION

4.5L and 4.9L Engines

▶ **See Figures 25 and 26**

1. Disconnect the negative battery cable.
2. Relieve the fuel system pressure.
3. Raise and safely support the vehicle with jackstands.
4. Safely drain and remove the fuel tank assembly.
5. Turn the fuel pump cam lock ring counterclockwise and lift the assembly out of the tank.
6. Remove the fuel pump from the level sensor unit as follows:
   a. Pull the pump up into the attaching hose or pulsator while pulling outward away from the bottom support.
   b. Take care to prevent damage to the rubber insulator and strainer during removal.
   c. When the pump assembly is clear of the bottom support, pull the pump out of the rubber connector for removal.

To install:
7. Replace any attaching hoses or rubber sound insulator that show signs of deterioration.
8. Push the fuel pump into the attaching hoses and install the pump/sensor assembly into the tank. Always use a new O-ring seal. Be careful not to fold over or twist the strainer when installing the sensor unit. Also, make sure the strainer does not block full travel of the float arm.
9. Install the cam lock and turn clockwise to lock.
10. Install the fuel tank.

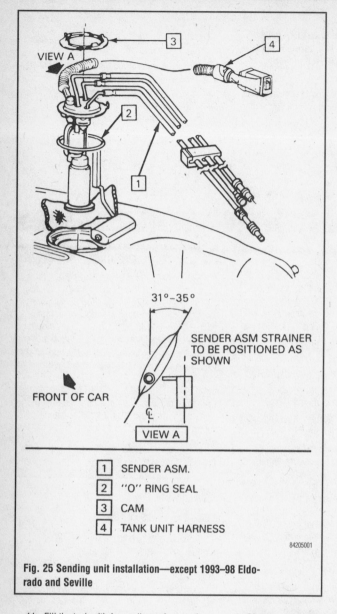

VIEW A

31°–35°

SENDER ASM STRAINER
TO BE POSITIONED AS
SHOWN

FRONT OF CAR

VIEW A

1	SENDER ASM.
2	"O" RING SEAL
3	CAM
4	TANK UNIT HARNESS

84205001

**Fig. 25 Sending unit installation—except 1993–98 Eldo-
rado and Seville**

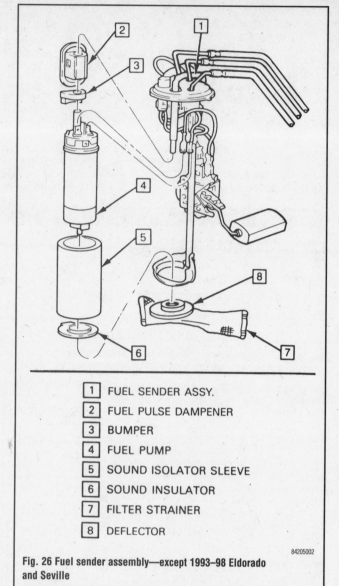

1	FUEL SENDER ASSY.
2	FUEL PULSE DAMPENER
3	BUMPER
4	FUEL PUMP
5	SOUND ISOLATOR SLEEVE
6	SOUND INSULATOR
7	FILTER STRAINER
8	DEFLECTOR

84205002

**Fig. 26 Fuel sender assembly—except 1993–98 Eldorado
and Seville**

11. Fill the tank with four gallons of gas and
check for fuel leaks.

4.6L Engine

♦ **See Figure 27**

The fuel pump used in this system is part of the
fuel sender assembly.

Special tools needed for the repair. J 34730-1A
or equivalent, fuel pressure gauge. J 39765 Fuel
sender lock nut wrench, or equivalent.

➡**Do not handle the fuel sender assembly by
the fuel pipes. The amount of leverage generated by handling the fuel pipes could damage
the joints.**

※※ **CAUTION**

**Drain the fuel tank to no more than ¾ of a
tank before removing the fuel sender retaining ring or fuel sender access panel in order
to avoid possible fuel spillage.**

➡**Always replace the fuel sender O-ring when
reinstalling the fuel sender assembly.**

1. Relieve the fuel system fuel pressure.
2. Disconnect the negative battery cable.
3. Determine if the fuel tank must be dropped
to access the pump/sender, or if it is accessible
through the rear compartment. If it is accessible
through the rear compartment, use the following
procedure.
4. Drain the fuel tank to at least ¾ of a tank, if
full.
5. If it is not accessible, safely drain and
remove the fuel tank.
6. Remove the spare tire cover, the jack, and
the spare tire.

➡**Remove the rear compartment floor trim to
avoid damage from fuel spillage.**

7. Remove the rear compartment floor trim.
8. Remove the bolts from the fuel sender
access panel.
9. Detach the quick-connect fittings at the fuel
sender assembly.

10. Detach the electrical connector at the modular fuel sender.
11. Detach the electrical connector at the fuel
tank pressure sensor.
12. Remove the fuel sender retaining ring using
the J 39765 (or equivalent) Fuel Sender Spanner
Wrench.

➡**When removing the modular fuel sender
assembly from the fuel tank, the reservoir
bucket on the fuel sender assembly must be
tipped slightly during removal in order to avoid
damage to the float. Place any remaining fuel
into an approved container once the modular
fuel sender assembly is removed from the fuel
tank.**

※※ **WARNING**

**The modular fuel sender assembly will
spring-up when the locking ring is removed.**

13. Pull the modular fuel sender straight up
while pumping the fuel from the reservoir.

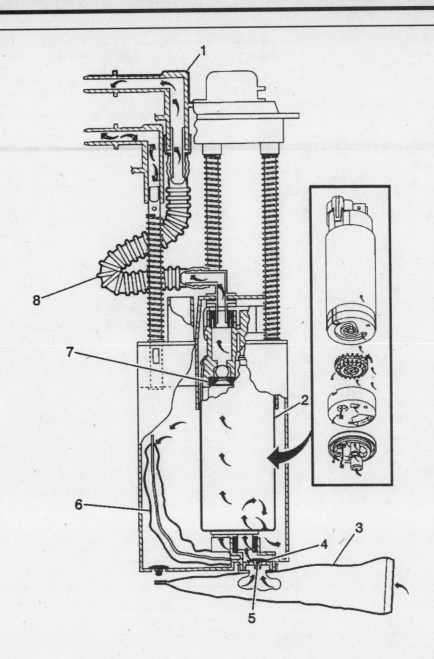

Legend

(1) Fuel Feed
(2) Fuel Pump
(3) External Strainer
(4) Secondary Umbrella Valve

(5) Fuel Flow from External Strainer
(6) Fuel Pump Strainer
(7) Check Valve
(8) Convoluted Fuel Tube (Flex Pipe)

91045G04

Fig. 27 Diagram of a modular fuel sender depicting the typical fuel flow

14. Clean and inspect the fuel sender assembly O-ring sealing surfaces.

To install:

15. Position the new fuel sender assembly O-ring on the fuel tank.

➡**Care should be taken not to fold over or twist the fuel pump strainer when installing the fuel sender assembly, as this will restrict fuel flow.**

16. Ensure that the fuel pump strainer does not block full travel of the float arm.

17. Reinstall the fuel sender assembly and the fuel sender assembly retainer cam using the fuel sender spanner wrench.

18. Install the quick-connect fittings at the fuel sender assembly.

19. Attach the electrical connector at the fuel tank pressure sensor.

20. Attach the electrical connector at the fuel sender assembly.

21. Connect the negative battery cable.

22. Inspect for leaks.

    a. Turn the ignition switch **ON** for 2 seconds.

    b. Turn the ignition switch **OFF** for 10 seconds.

    c. Turn the ignition switch **ON** and check for leaks.

23. Reinstall the fuel access panel, and tighten the fuel sender access panel bolts to 18 inch lbs. (2 Nm).

24. Reinstall the rear compartment floor trim.

25. Reinstall the spare tire, the jack, and the spare tire cover.

26. Add fuel and reinstall the fuel tank filler pipe cap.

TESTING

▶ **See Figure 28**

When the ignition switch is turned **ON**, the PCM will turn **ON** the in-tank fuel pump. The fuel pump is located inside the modular fuel sender. The fuel pump is not serviceable separate from the sender.

The in-tank fuel pump will remain **ON** as long as long as the t engine is cranking or running and the PCM is receiving reference pulses. If there are no reference pulses. The PCM will turn the in-tank fuel pump **OFF** 2 seconds after the ignition switch is turned **ON** or 2 seconds after the engine stops running.

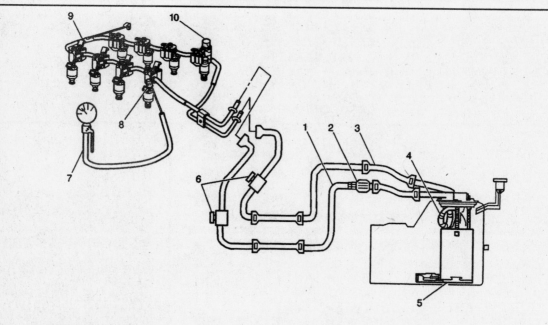

Legend

(1) Fuel Feed Pipe
(2) In-Line Fuel Filter
(3) Fuel Return Pipe
(4) Fuel Pump Flex Pipe
(5) Integral Reservoir

(6) Fuel Pipe Shut-off Adapters
(7) Fuel Pressure Gauge
(8) Fuel Pressure Connection
(9) Fuel Rail
(10) Fuel Pressure Regulator

91045G05

Fig. 28 Diagram of a typical fuel system pressure test

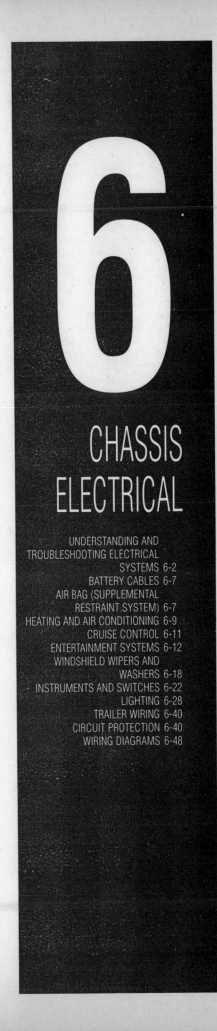

6

CHASSIS ELECTRICAL

UNDERSTANDING AND TROUBLESHOOTING ELECTRICAL SYSTEMS

Basic Electrical Theory

♦ **See Figure 1**

For any 12 volt, negative ground, electrical system to operate, the electricity must travel in a complete circuit. This simply means that current (power) from the positive (+) terminal of the battery must eventually return to the negative (-) terminal of the battery. Along the way, this current will travel through wires, fuses, switches, and components. If, for any reason, the flow of current through the circuit is interrupted, the component fed by that circuit will cease to function properly.

Perhaps the easiest way to visualize a circuit is to think of connecting a light bulb (with two wires attached to it) to the battery—one wire attached to the negative (-) terminal of the battery and the other wire to the positive (+) terminal. With the two wires touching the battery terminals, the circuit would be complete and the light bulb would illuminate. Electricity would follow a path from the battery to the bulb and back to the battery. It's easy to see that with longer wires on our light bulb, it could be mounted anywhere. Further, one wire could be fitted with a switch so that the light could be turned on and off.

The normal automotive circuit differs from this simple example in two ways. First, instead of having a return wire from the bulb to the battery, the current travels through the frame of the vehicle. Since the negative (-) battery cable is attached to the frame (made of electrically conductive metal), the frame of the vehicle can serve as a ground wire to complete the circuit. Secondly, most automotive circuits contain multiple components that receive power from a single circuit. This lessens the amount of wire needed to power components on the vehicle.

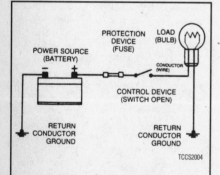

Fig. 1 This example illustrates a simple circuit. When the switch is closed, power from the positive (+) battery terminal flows through the fuse and the switch, and then to the light bulb. The light illuminates and the circuit is completed through the ground wire back to the negative (-) battery terminal. In reality, the two ground points shown in the illustration are attached to the metal frame of the vehicle, which completes the circuit back to the battery

HOW DOES ELECTRICITY WORK: THE WATER ANALOGY

Electricity is the flow of electrons—the subatomic particles that constitute the outer shell of an atom. Electrons spin in an orbit around the center core of an atom. The center core is comprised of protons (positive charge) and neutrons (neutral charge). Electrons have a negative charge and balance out the positive charge of the protons. When an outside force causes the number of electrons to unbalance the charge of the protons, the electrons will split off the atom and look for another atom to balance out. If this imbalance is kept up, electrons will continue to move and an electrical flow will exist.

Many people have been taught electrical theory using an analogy with water. In a comparison with water flowing through a pipe, the electrons would be the water and the wire is the pipe.

The flow of electricity can be measured much like the flow of water through a pipe. The unit of measurement used is amperes, frequently abbreviated as amps (a). You can compare amperage to the volume of water flowing through a pipe. When connected to a circuit, an ammeter will measure the actual amount of current flowing through the circuit. When relatively few electrons flow through a circuit, the amperage is low. When many electrons flow, the amperage is high.

Water pressure is measured in units such as pounds per square inch (psi); The electrical pressure is measured in units called volts (v). When a voltmeter is connected to a circuit, it is measuring the electrical pressure.

The actual flow of electricity depends not only on voltage and amperage, but also on the resistance of the circuit. The higher the resistance, the higher the force necessary to push the current through the circuit. The standard unit for measuring resistance is an ohm. Resistance in a circuit varies depending on the amount and type of components used in the circuit. The main factors that determine resistance are:

• Material—some materials have more resistance than others. Those with high resistance are said to be insulators. Rubber materials (or rubber-like plastics) are some of the most common insulators used in vehicles as they have a very high resistance to electricity. Very low resistance materials are said to be conductors. Copper wire is among the best conductors. Silver is actually a superior conductor to copper and is used in some relay contacts, but its high cost prohibits its use as common wiring. Most automotive wiring is made of copper.

• Size—the larger the wire size being used, the less resistance the wire will have. This is why components that use large amounts of electricity usually have large wires supplying current to them.

• Length—for a given thickness of wire, the longer the wire, the greater the resistance. The shorter the wire, the less the resistance. When determining the proper wire for a circuit, both size and length must be considered to design a circuit that can handle the current needs of the component.

• Temperature—with many materials, the higher the temperature, the greater the resistance (positive temperature coefficient). Some materials exhibit the opposite trait of lower resistance with

higher temperatures (negative temperature coefficient). These principles are used in many of the sensors on the engine.

OHM'S LAW

There is a direct relationship between current, voltage, and resistance. The relationship between current, voltage, and resistance can be summed up by a statement known as Ohm's law.

Voltage (E) is equal to amperage (I) times resistance ®: $E = I \times R$

Other forms of the formula are $R = E/I$ and $= E/R$

In each of these formulas, E is the voltage in volts, I is the current in amps and R is the resistance in ohms. The basic point to remember is that as the resistance of a circuit goes up, the amount of current that flows in the circuit will go down, if voltage remains the same.

The amount of work that the electricity can perform is expressed as power. The unit of power is the watt (w). The relationship between power, voltage, and current is expressed as:

Power (w) is equal to amperage (I) times voltage (E): $W = I \times E$

This is only true for direct current (DC) circuits; The alternating current formula is a tad different, but since the electrical circuits in most vehicles are DC type, we need not get into AC circuit theory.

Electrical Components

POWER SOURCE

Power is supplied to the vehicle by two devices: The battery and the alternator. The battery supplies electrical power during starting or during periods when the current demand of the vehicle's electrical system exceeds the output capacity of the alternator. The alternator supplies electrical current when the engine is running. The alternator does not just supply the current needs of the vehicle, but it recharges the battery.

The Battery

In most modern vehicles, the battery is a lead/acid electrochemical device consisting of six 2 volt subsections (cells) connected in series, so that the unit is capable of producing approximately 12 volts of electrical pressure. Each subsection consists of a series of positive and negative plates held a short distance apart in a solution of sulfuric acid and water.

The two types of plates are of dissimilar metals. This sets up a chemical reaction, and it is this reaction that produces current flow from the battery when its positive and negative terminals are connected to an electrical load. The power removed from the battery is replaced by the alternator, restoring the battery to its original chemical state.

The Alternator

On some vehicles, there isn't an alternator, but a generator. The difference is that an alternator supplies alternating current, which is then changed to direct current for use on the vehicle, while a generator produces direct current. Alternators tend to be more efficient and that is why they are used.

Alternators and generators are devices that consist of coils of wires wound together making big electromagnets. One group of coils spins within another set and the interaction of the magnetic fields causes a current to flow. This current is then drawn off the coils and fed into the vehicles electrical system.

GROUND

Two types of grounds are used in automotive electric circuits. Direct ground components are grounded to the frame through their mounting points. All other components use some sort of ground wire that is attached to the frame or chassis of the vehicle. The electrical current runs through the chassis of the vehicle and returns to the battery through the ground (-) cable; if you look, you'll see that the battery ground cable connects between the battery and the frame or chassis of the vehicle.

➡It should be noted that a good percentage of electrical problems can be traced to bad grounds.

PROTECTIVE DEVICES

▶ See Figure 2

It is possible for large surges of current to pass through the electrical system of your vehicle. If this surge of current were to reach the load in the circuit, the surge could burn it out or severely damage it. It can also overload the wiring, causing the harness to get hot and melt the insulation. To prevent this, fuses, circuit breakers, and/or fusible links are connected into the supply wires of the electrical system. These items are nothing more than a built-in weak spot in the system. When abnormal

amounts of current flows through the system, these protective devices work as follows to protect the circuit:

• Fuse—when an excessive electrical current passes through a fuse, the fuse "blows" (the conductor melts) and opens the circuit, preventing the passage of current.

• Circuit Breaker—a circuit breaker is basically a self-repairing fuse. It will open the circuit in the same fashion as a fuse, but when the surge subsides, the circuit breaker can be reset and does not need replacement.

• Fusible Link—a fusible link (fuse link or main link) is a short length of special, high temperature insulated wire that acts as a fuse. When an excessive electrical current passes through a fusible link, the thin gauge wire inside the link melts, creating an intentional open to protect the circuit. To repair the circuit, the link must be replaced. Some newer type fusible links are housed in plug-in modules, which are simply replaced like a fuse, while older type fusible links must be cut and spliced if they melt. Since this link is very early in the electrical path, it's the first place to look if nothing on the vehicle works, yet the battery seems to be charged and is properly connected.

❋❋ CAUTION

Always replace fuses, circuit breakers, and fusible links with identically rated components. Under no circumstances should a component of higher or lower amperage rating be substituted.

SWITCHES & RELAYS

▶ See Figures 3 and 4

Switches are used in electrical circuits to control the passage of current. The most common use is to open and close circuits between the battery and the various electric devices in the system. Switches are rated according to the amount of amperage they can handle. If a sufficient amperage rated switch is not used in a circuit, the switch could overload and cause damage.

Some electrical components, which require a large amount of current to operate use a special switch, called a relay. Since these circuits carry a large amount of current, the thickness of the wire in the circuit is also greater. If this large wire were

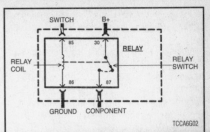

TCCA6G02

Fig. 4 Relays are composed of a coil and a switch. These two components are linked together so that when one operates, the other operates at the same time. The large wires in the circuit are connected from the battery to one side of the relay switch (B+) and from the opposite side of the relay switch to the load (component). Smaller wires are connected from the relay coil to the control switch for the circuit and from the opposite side of the relay coil to ground

connected from the load to the control switch, the switch would have to carry the high amperage load. The dash or fairing would be twice as large to accommodate the increased size of the wiring harness. To prevent these problems, a relay is used.

Relays are composed of a coil and a set of contacts. When the coil has a current passed though it, a magnetic field is formed and this field causes the contacts to move together, completing the circuit. Most relays are normally open, preventing current from passing through the circuit, but they can take any electrical form depending on the job they are intended to do. Relays can be considered "remote control switches." They allow a smaller current to operate devices that require higher amperages. When a small current operates the coil, a larger current is allowed to pass by the contacts. Some common circuits, which may use relays, are the horn, headlights, starter, electric fuel pump and other high draw circuits.

LOAD

Every electrical circuit must include a "load" (something to use the electricity coming from the source). Without this load, the battery would attempt to deliver its entire power supply from one pole to another. This is called a "short circuit." All this electricity would take a short cut to ground and cause a great amount of damage to other components in the circuit by developing a tremendous amount of heat. This condition could develop sufficient heat to melt the insulation on all the surrounding wires and reduce a multiple wire cable to a lump of plastic and copper.

WIRING & HARNESSES

The average vehicle contains meters and meters of wiring, with hundreds of individual connections. To protect the many wires from damage and to keep them from becoming a confusing tangle, they are organized into bundles, enclosed in plastic or taped together and called wiring harnesses. Different harnesses serve different parts of the vehicle. Individ-

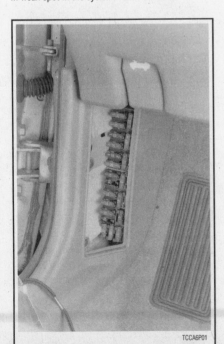

TCCA6P01

Fig. 2 Most vehicles use one or more fuse panels. This one is located on the driver's side kick panel

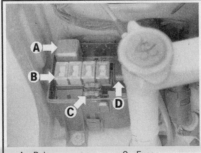

A. Relay   C. Fuse
B. Fusible link   D. Flasher

TCCA6P02

Fig. 3 The underhood fuse and relay panel usually contains fuses, relays, flashers, and fusible links

ual wires are color coded to help trace them through a harness where sections are hidden from view.

Automotive wiring or circuit conductors can be either single strand wire, multi-strand wire or printed circuitry. Single strand wire has a solid metal core. It is usually used inside such components as alternators, motors, relays, and other devices. Multi-strand wire has a core made of many small strands of wire twisted together into a single conductor. Most of the wiring in an automotive electrical system is either made up of multi-strand wire, as a single conductor or grouped together in a harness. All wiring is color coded on the insulator, either as a solid color or as a colored wire with an identification stripe. A printed circuit is a thin film of copper or other conductor that is printed on an insulator backing. Occasionally, a printed circuit is sandwiched between two sheets of plastic for more protection and flexibility. A complete printed circuit, consisting of conductors, insulating material, and connectors for lamps or other components is called a printed circuit board. Printed circuitry is used in place of individual wires or harnesses in places where space is limited, such as behind instrument panels.

Since automotive electrical systems are very sensitive to changes in resistance, the selection of properly sized wires is critical when systems are repaired. A loose or corroded connection or a replacement wire that is too small for the circuit will add extra resistance and an additional voltage drop to the circuit.

The wire gauge number is an expression of the cross-section area of the conductor. Vehicles from countries that use the metric system will typically describe the wire size as its cross-sectional area in square millimeters. In this method, the larger the wire, the greater the number. Another common system for expressing wire size is the American Wire Gauge (AWG) system. As gauge number increases, area decreases and the wire becomes smaller. An 18 gauge wire is smaller than a 4 gauge wire. A wire with a higher gauge number will carry less current than a wire with a lower gauge number. Gauge wire size refers to the size of the strands of the conductor, not the size of the complete wire with insulator. It is possible, therefore, to have two wires of the same gauge with different diameters because one may have thicker insulation than the other.

It is essential to understand how a circuit works before trying to figure out why it doesn't. An electrical schematic shows the electrical current paths when a circuit is operating properly. Schematics break the entire electrical system down into individual circuits. In a schematic, usually no attempt is made to represent wiring and components as they physically appear on the vehicle; switches and other components are shown as simply as possible. Face views of harness connectors show the cavity or terminal locations in all multi-pin connectors to help locate test points.

CONNECTORS

▶ **See Figures 5 and 6**

Three types of connectors are commonly used in automotive applications—weatherproof, molded and hard shell.

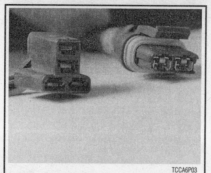

Fig. 5 Hard shell (left) and weatherproof (right) connectors have replaceable terminals

Fig. 6 Weatherproof connectors are most commonly used in the engine compartment or wherever the connector is exposed to the elements

• Weatherproof—these connectors are most commonly used where the connector is exposed to the elements. Terminals are protected against moisture and dirt by sealing rings, which provide a weather tight seal. All repairs require the use of a special terminal and the tool required to service it. Unlike standard blade type terminals, these weatherproof terminals cannot be straightened once they are bent. Make certain that the connectors are properly seated and all of the sealing rings are in place when connecting leads.

• Molded—these connectors require complete replacement of the connector if found to be defective. This means splicing a new connector assembly into the harness. All splices should be soldered to insure proper contact. Use care when probing the connections or replacing terminals in them, as it is possible to create a short circuit between opposite terminals. If this happens to the wrong terminal pair, it is possible to damage certain components. Always use jumper wires between connectors for circuit checking and NEVER probe through weatherproof seals.

• Hard Shell—unlike molded connectors, the terminal contacts in hard-shell connectors can be replaced. Replacement usually involves the use of a special terminal removal tool that depresses the locking tangs (barbs) on the connector terminal and allows the connector to be removed from the rear of the shell. The connector shell should be replaced if it shows any evidence of burning, melting, cracks, or breaks. Replace individual terminals that are burnt, corroded, distorted, or loose.

Test Equipment

Pinpointing the exact cause of trouble in an electrical circuit is most times accomplished by the use of special test equipment. The following describes different types of commonly used test equipment and briefly explains how to use them in diagnosis. In addition to the information covered below, the tool manufacturer's instructions booklet (provided with the tester) should be read and clearly understood before attempting any test procedures.

JUMPER WIRES

✷✷ CAUTION

Never use jumper wires made from a thinner gauge wire than the circuit being tested. If the jumper wire is of too small a gauge, it may overheat and possibly melt. Never use jumpers to bypass high resistance loads in a circuit. Bypassing resistances, in effect, creates a short circuit. This may, in turn, cause damages and fires. Jumper wires should only be used to bypass lengths of wire or to simulate switches.

Jumper wires are simple, yet extremely valuable, pieces of test equipment. They are test wires, which are used to bypass sections of a circuit. Although jumper wires can be purchased, they are usually fabricated from lengths of standard automotive wire and whatever types of connector (alligator clip, spade connector or pin connector) that is required for the particular application being tested. In cramped, hard-to-reach areas, it is advisable to have insulated boots over the jumper wire terminals in order to prevent accidental grounding. It is also advisable to include a standard automotive fuse in any jumper wire. This is commonly referred to as a "fused jumper." By inserting an in-line fuse holder between a set of test leads, a fused jumper wire can be used for bypassing open circuits. Use a 5 amp fuse to provide protection against voltage spikes.

Jumper wires are used primarily to locate open electrical circuits, on either the ground (-) side of the circuit or on the power (+) side. If an electrical component fails to operate, connect the jumper wire between the component and a good ground. If the component operates only with the jumper installed, the ground circuit is open. If the ground circuit is good, but the component does not operate, the circuit between the power feed and component may be open. By moving the jumper wire successively back from the component toward the power source, you can isolate the area of the circuit where the open is located. When the component stops functioning, or the power is cut off, the open is in the segment of wire between the jumper and the point previously tested.

You can sometimes connect the jumper wire directly from the battery to the "hot" terminal of the component, but first make sure the component uses 12 volts in operation. Some electrical components, such as fuel injectors or sensors, are designed to operate on about 4 to 5 volts, and running 12 volts directly to these components will cause damage.

TEST LIGHTS

▶ See Figure 7

The test light is used to check circuits and components while electrical current is flowing through them. It is used for voltage and ground tests. To use a 12 volt test light, connect the ground clip to a good ground and probe wherever necessary with the pick. The test light will illuminate when voltage is detected. This does not necessarily mean that 12 volts (or any particular amount of voltage) is present; it only means that some voltage is present. It is advisable before using the test light to touch its ground clip and probe across the battery posts or terminals to make sure the light is operating properly.

❊❊ WARNING

Do not use a test light to probe electronic ignition, spark plug, or coil wires. Never use a pick-type test light to probe wiring on computer controlled systems unless specifically instructed to do so. Any wire insulation that is pierced by the test light probe should be taped and sealed with silicone after testing.

Like the jumper wire, the 12 volt test light is used to isolate opens in circuits. However, whereas the jumper wire is used to bypass the open to operate the load, the 12 volt test light is used to locate the presence of voltage in a circuit. If the test light illuminates, there is power up to that point in the circuit; if the test light does not illuminate, there is an open circuit (no power). Move the test light in successive steps back toward the power source until the light in the handle illuminates. The open is between the probe and a point, which was previously probed.

The self-powered test light is similar in design to the 12 volt test light, but contains a 1.5 volt penlight battery in the handle. It is most often used in place of a multimeter to check for open or short circuits when power is isolated from the circuit (continuity test).

The battery in a self-powered test light does not provide much current. A weak battery may not provide enough power to illuminate the test light even when a complete circuit is made (especially if there is high resistance in the circuit). Always make sure that the test battery is strong. To check the battery, briefly touch the ground clip to the probe; if the light glows brightly, the battery is strong enough for testing.

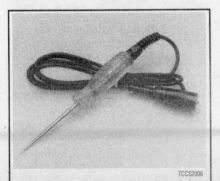

Fig. 7 A 12 volt test light is used to detect the presence of voltage in a circuit

TCCS2006

▶A self-powered test light should not be used on any computer-controlled system or component. The small amount of electricity transmitted by the test light is enough to damage many electronic automotive components.

MULTIMETERS

Multimeters are an extremely useful tool for troubleshooting electrical problems. They can be purchased in either analog or digital form and have a price range to suit any budget. A multimeter is a voltmeter, ammeter and ohmmeter (along with other features) combined into one instrument. It is often used when testing solid state circuits because of its high input impedance (usually 10 megaohms or more). A brief description of the multimeter main test functions follows:

• Voltmeter—the voltmeter is used to measure voltage at any point in a circuit, or to measure the voltage drop across any part of a circuit. Voltmeters usually have various scales and a selector switch to allow the reading of different voltage ranges. The voltmeter has a positive and a negative lead. To avoid damage to the meter, always connect the negative lead to the negative (-) side of the circuit (to ground or nearest the ground side of the circuit) and connect the positive lead to the positive (+) side of the circuit (to the power source or the nearest power source). Note that the negative voltmeter lead will always be black and that the positive voltmeter will always be some color other than black (usually red).

• Ohmmeter—the ohmmeter is designed to read resistance (measured in ohms) in a circuit or component. Most ohmmeters will have a selector switch which permits the measurement of different ranges of resistance (usually the selector switch allows the multiplication of the meter reading by 10, 100, 1,000 and 10,000). Some ohmmeters are "auto-ranging" which means the meter itself will determine which scale to use. Since the meters are powered by an internal battery, the ohmmeter can be used like a self-powered test light. When the ohmmeter is connected, current from the ohmmeter flows through the circuit or component being tested. Since the ohmmeter's internal resistance and voltage are known values, the amount of current flow through the meter depends on the resistance of the circuit or component being tested. The ohmmeter can also be used to perform a continuity test for suspected open circuits. In using the meter for making continuity checks, do not be concerned with the actual resistance readings. Zero resistance, or any ohm reading, indicates continuity in the circuit. Infinite resistance indicates an opening in the circuit. A high resistance reading where there should be none indicates a problem in the circuit. Checks for short circuits are made in the same manner as checks for open circuits, except that the circuit must be isolated from both power and normal ground. Infinite resistance indicates no continuity, while zero resistance indicates a dead short.

❊❊ WARNING

Never use an ohmmeter to check the resistance of a component or wire while there is voltage applied to the circuit.

• Ammeter—an ammeter measures the amount of current flowing through a circuit in units called amperes or amps. At normal operating voltage, most circuits have a characteristic amount of amperes, called "current draw" which can be measured using an ammeter. By referring to a specified current draw rating, then measuring the amperes and comparing the two values, one can determine what is happening within the circuit to aid in diagnosis. An open circuit, for example, will not allow any current to flow, so the ammeter reading will be zero. A damaged component or circuit will have an increased current draw, so the reading will be high. The ammeter is always connected in series with the circuit being tested. All of the current that normally flows through the circuit must also flow through the ammeter; if there is any other path for the current to follow, the ammeter reading will not be accurate. The ammeter itself has very little resistance to current flow and, therefore, will not affect the circuit, but it will measure current draw only when the circuit is closed and electricity is flowing. Excessive current draw can blow fuses and drain the battery, while a reduced current draw can cause motors to run slowly, lights to dim and other components to not operate properly.

Troubleshooting Electrical Systems

When diagnosing a specific problem, organized troubleshooting is a must. The complexity of modern automotive vehicle demands that you approach any problem in a logical organized manner. There are certain troubleshooting techniques, however, which are standard:

• Establish when the problem occurs. Does the problem appear only under certain conditions? Were there any noises, odors, or other unusual symptoms? Isolate the problem area. To do this, make some simple tests and observations, then eliminate the systems that are working properly. Check for obvious problems, such as broken wires and loose or dirty connections. Always check the obvious before assuming something complicated is the cause.

• Test for problems systematically to determine the cause once the problem area is isolated. Are all the components functioning properly? Is their power going to electrical switches and motors. Performing careful, systematic checks will often turn up most causes on the first inspection, without wasting time checking components that have little or no relationship to the problem.

• Test all repairs after the work is done to make sure that the problem is fixed. Some causes can be traced to more than one component, so a careful verification of repair work is important in order to pick up additional malfunctions that may cause a problem to reappear or a different problem to arise. A blown fuse, for example, is a simple problem that may require more than another fuse to repair. If you don't look for a problem that caused a fuse to blow, a shorted wire (for example) may go undetected.

Experience has shown that most problems tend to be the result of a fairly simple and obvious cause, such as loose or corroded connectors, bad grounds or damaged wire insulation, which causes a short. This makes careful visual inspection of components during testing essential to quick and accurate troubleshooting.

Testing

OPEN CIRCUITS

▶ See Figure 8

This test already assumes the existence of an open in the circuit and it is used to help locate the open portion.

1. Isolate the circuit from power and ground.
2. Connect the self-powered test light or ohmmeter ground clip to the ground side of the circuit and probe sections of the circuit sequentially.
3. If the light is out or there is infinite resistance, the open is between the probe and the circuit ground.
4. If the light is on or the meter shows continuity, the open is between the probe and the end of the circuit toward the power source.

SHORT CIRCUITS

➡Never use a self-powered test light to perform checks for opens or shorts when power is applied to the circuit under test. The test light can be damaged by outside power.

1. Isolate the circuit from power and ground.
2. Connect the self-powered test light or ohmmeter ground clip to a good ground. Then probe any easy-to-reach point in the circuit.
3. If the light comes on or there is continuity, there is a short somewhere in the circuit.

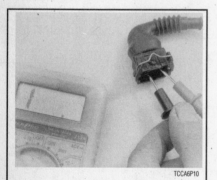

TCCA6P10

Fig. 8 The infinite reading on this multimeter indicates that the circuit is open

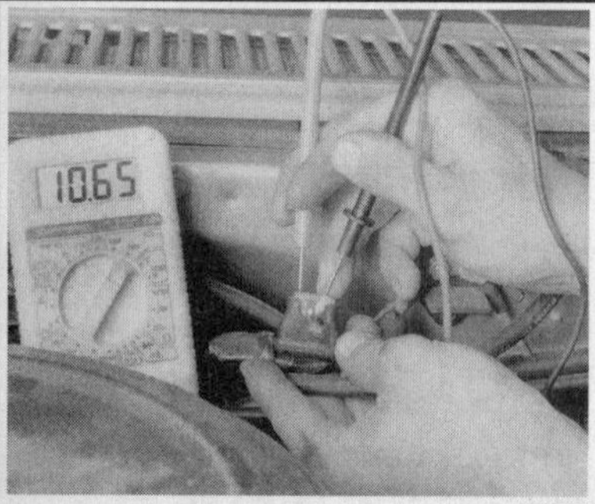

4. To isolate the short, probe a test point at either end of the isolated circuit (the light should be on or the meter should indicate continuity).
5. Leave the test light probe engaged and sequentially open connectors or switches, remove parts, etc. until the light goes out or continuity is broken.
6. When the light goes out, the short is between the last two circuit components that were opened.

VOLTAGE

This test determines voltage available from the battery. It should be the first step in any electrical troubleshooting procedure after visual inspection. Many electrical problems, especially on computer controlled systems, can be caused by a low state of charge in the battery. Excessive corrosion at the battery cable terminals can cause poor contact that will prevent proper charging and full battery current flow.

1. Set the voltmeter selector switch to the 20V position.
2. Connect the multimeter negative lead to the battery's negative (-) post or terminal and the positive lead to the battery's positive (+) post or terminal.
3. Turn the ignition switch **ON** to provide a load.
4. A well charged battery should register over 12 volts. If the meter reads below 11.5 volts, the battery power may be insufficient to operate the electrical system properly.

VOLTAGE DROP

▶ See Figure 9

When current flows through a load, the voltage beyond the load drops. This voltage drop is due to the resistance created by the load and also by small resistances created by corrosion at the connectors and damaged insulation on the wires. The maximum allowable voltage drop under load is critical, especially if there is more than one load in the circuit, since all voltage drops are cumulative.

1. Set the voltmeter selector switch to the 20 volt position.
2. Connect the multimeter negative lead to a good ground.
3. Operate the circuit and check the voltage prior to the first component (load).

TCCA6P07

Fig. 9 This voltage drop test revealed high resistance (low voltage) in the circuit

4. There should be little or no voltage drop in the circuit prior to the first component. If a voltage drop exists, the wire or connectors in the circuit are suspect.
5. While operating the first component in the circuit, probe the groundside of the component with the positive meter lead and observe the voltage readings. A small voltage drop should be noticed. This voltage drop is caused by the resistance of the component.
6. Repeat the test for each component (load) down the circuit.
7. If a large voltage drop is noticed, the preceding component, wire or connector is suspect.

RESISTANCE

▶ See Figures 10 and 11

❊❊ **WARNING**

Never use an ohmmeter with power applied to the circuit. The ohmmeter is designed to operate on its own power supply. The normal 12 volt electrical system voltage could damage the meter!

1. Isolate the circuit from the power source of the vehicle.
2. Ensure that the ignition key is **OFF** when disconnecting any components or the battery.
3. Where necessary, also isolate at least one side of the circuit to be checked, in order to avoid reading parallel resistances. Parallel circuit resistances will always give a lower reading than the actual resistance of either of the branches.
4. Connect the meter leads to both sides of the circuit (wire or component) and read the actual measured ohms on the meter scale. Make sure the selector switch is set to the proper ohm scale for the circuit being tested, to avoid misreading the ohmmeter test value.

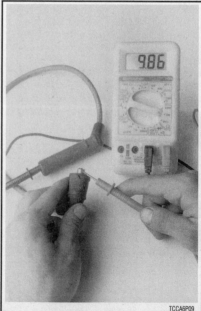

TCCA6P09

Fig. 11 Spark plug wires can be checked for excessive resistance using an ohmmeter

TCCA6P08

Fig. 10 Checking the resistance of a coolant temperature sensor with an ohmmeter. Reading is 1.04 kilohms

Wire and Connector Repair

Almost anyone can replace damaged wires, as long as the proper tools and parts are available. Wire and terminals are available to fit almost any need. Even the specialized weatherproof, molded and hard shell connectors are now available from aftermarket suppliers.

Be sure the ends of all the wires are fitted with the proper terminal hardware and connectors. Wrapping a wire around a stud is never a permanent solution and will only cause trouble later. Replace wires one at a time to avoid confusion. Always route wires the same as the factory.

➡️If connector repair is necessary, only attempt it if you have the proper tools. Weatherproof and hard shell connectors require special tools to release the pins inside the connector. Attempting to repair these connectors with conventional hand tools will damage them.

BATTERY CABLES

Disconnecting the Cables

When working on any electrical component on the vehicle, it is always a good idea to disconnect the negative (-) battery cable. This will prevent potential damage to many sensitive electrical components such as the Powertrain Control Module (PCM), radio, alternator, etc.

➡️Any time you disengage the battery cables, it is recommended that you disconnect the negative (-) battery cable first. This will prevent your accidentally grounding the positive (+) terminal to the body of the vehicle when disconnecting it, thereby preventing damage to the above mentioned components.

Before you disconnect the cable(s), first turn the ignition to the **OFF** position. This will prevent a draw on the battery which could cause arcing (electricity trying to ground itself to the body of a vehicle, just like a spark plug jumping the gap) and,

of course, damaging some components such as the alternator diodes.

When the battery cable(s) are reconnected (negative cable last), be sure to check that your lights, windshield wipers and other electrically operated safety components are all working correctly. If your vehicle contains an Electronically Tuned Radio (ETR), don't forget to also reset your radio stations. Ditto for the clock.

AIR BAG (SUPPLEMENTAL RESTRAINT SYSTEM)

General Information

General Motors calls their air bag system a Supplemental Inflatable Restraint (SIR). Most other manufacturers refer to it as a Supplemental Restraint System (SRS). SRS is also widely accepted as the industry standard nomenclature for the system. This manual may use SIR or SRS when referring to the air bag system.

SERVICE PRECAUTIONS

The Sensing Diagnostic Module (SDM) maintains a reserve energy supply with sufficient voltage to cause a deployment for up to ten minutes after the ignition switch is turned **OFF**, the battery is disconnected or the fuse powering the SDM is removed. Many of the service procedures require removal of the inflator module fuse and disconnection of the deployment loops to avoid an accidental deployment.

✳✳ CAUTION

Proper operation of the Supplemental Inflatable Restraint (SIR) sensing system requires that any repairs to the vehicle structure return the vehicle structure to the original production configuration. Not properly repairing the vehicle structure could cause non-deployment of the air bag in a frontal collision or deployment of the air bag for conditions less severe than intended.

✳✳ CAUTION

During service procedures, be very careful when handling a Sensing and Diagnostic Module (SDM). Never strike or jar the SDM. Never power up the SIR system when the SDM is not rigidly attached to the vehicle. All SDM and mounting bracket fasteners

must be carefully tightened and the arrow must be pointed toward the front of the vehicle to ensure proper operation of the SIR system. The SDM could be activated when powered while not rigidly attached to the vehicle, which could cause deployment and result in personal injury.

DISARMING THE SYSTEM

▶ **See Figures 12 and 13**

1. Turn the steering wheel to the straight ahead position.
2. Turn the ignition to the **LOCK** and remove the key.
3. Remove the SIR fuse from the engine compartment fuse block.
4. Remove the left side I/P sound insulator.
5. Detach the connector position assurance (CPA) and the driver yellow 2-way connector located at the base of the steering column.
6. Detach the Connector Position Assurance (CPA) and the passenger yellow 2-way connector located near the base of the steering column.

Fig. 12 Remove the underside panel to expose the wiring harness

Fig. 13 Detach the CPA and the yellow connector to disable the air bag

➡️With the SIR fuse removed and the ignition switch in the RUN position, the AIR BAG warning lamp illuminates. This is normal operation and does not indicate a SIR system malfunction.

ARMING THE SYSTEM

▶ **See Figures 14 thru 22**

1. Turn the ignition to the **LOCK** and remove the key.
2. Connect the Connector Position Assurance (CPA) and the passenger yellow 2-way connector pigtail through the trap door in the I/P compartment.
3. Connect the connector position assurance (CPA) and the driver yellow 2-way connector located at the base of the steering column.
4. Install the left side I/P sound insulator.
5. Install the SIR fuse to the engine compartment fuse block.
6. Staying well away from both air bags, turn the ignition switch to the **RUN** position. Verify that the AIR BAG warning lamp flashes seven times and then stays off. If the AIR BAG warning lamp does not operate as described, the system will have to be diagnosed.

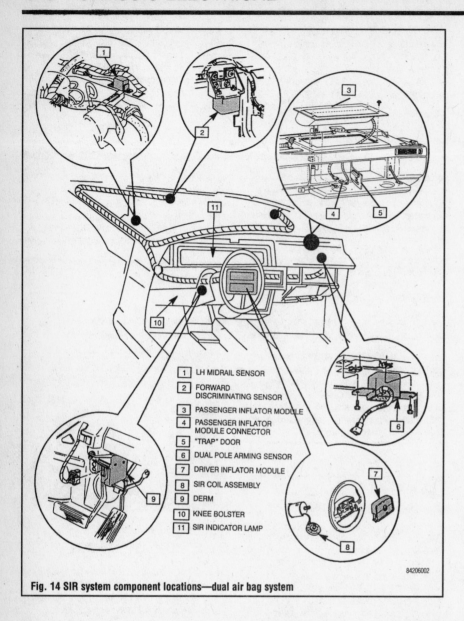

1 LH MIDRAIL SENSOR
2 FORWARD DISCRIMINATING SENSOR
3 PASSENGER INFLATOR MODULE
4 PASSENGER INFLATOR MODULE CONNECTOR
5 "TRAP" DOOR
6 DUAL POLE ARMING SENSOR
7 DRIVER INFLATOR MODULE
8 SIR COIL ASSEMBLY
9 DERM
10 KNEE BOLSTER
11 SIR INDICATOR LAMP

84206002

Fig. 14 SIR system component locations—dual air bag system

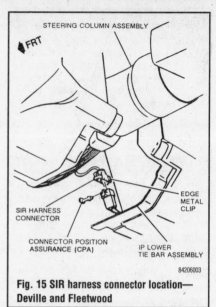

84206003

Fig. 15 SIR harness connector location— Deville and Fleetwood

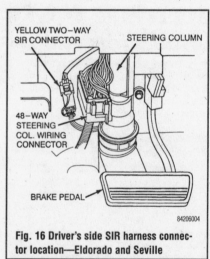

84206004

Fig. 16 Driver's side SIR harness connector location—Eldorado and Seville

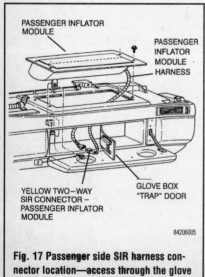

84206005

Fig. 17 Passenger side SIR harness connector location—access through the glove box

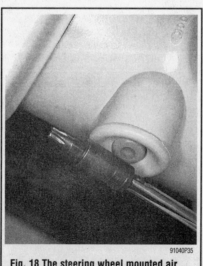

91040P35

Fig. 18 The steering wheel mounted air bag requires a Torx® style socket

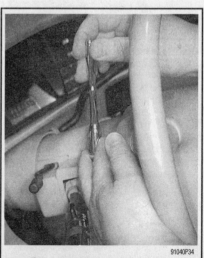

91040P34

Fig. 19 Loosen the bolts from the back side of the steering wheel

Fig. 20 After loosening the 4 screws, the air bag lifts out of the center of the steering wheel

91040P36

91040P38

Fig. 21 Removing the connector lock

91040P39

Fig. 22 Unplugging the connector for the air bag

HEATING AND AIR CONDITIONING

➡If your vehicle is equipped with air conditioning, refer to the information regarding the implications of servicing your A/C system yourself. Only an MVAC-trained, EPA-certified, automotive technician should service the A/C system or its components.

Blower Motor

Blower Motor location can change from year to year. It can change with the trim level of the vehicle. A vehicle that has front and rear climate controls may be configured differently than a vehicle that has front controls only. The following are two different repair procedures. One is given because the blower motor is located and accessed in the engine compartment, the other is given because the blower motor is mounted inside the vehicle.

REMOVAL & INSTALLATION

Engine Compartment Procedure

1. Disconnect the negative battery cable.
2. Remove the cowl cross-tower brace.
3. With a utility knife, cut the rubber insulator at the guide lines and remove the metal patch plate beneath.
4. Remove the blower motor electrical connector, cooling hose and mounting screws.
5. Disengage the blower motor from the case.

To install:

➡Failure to maintain a 25 mm clearance (about an inch) between the spark plug wires and the HVAC blower motor may result in improper operation or failure of the blower motor.

6. Install the blower motor fan assembly.
7. Connect the blower motor electrical connector, cooling hose and mounting screws.
8. Install the patch plate and the seal insulator patch.
9. Replace the cowl cross-tower brace (two nuts each side).
10. Connect the negative battery cable.

Passenger Compartment Procedure

1. Disconnect the negative battery cable.
2. Remove the right hand instrument panel insulator.
3. Detach the blower motor electrical connector.
4. Remove the right hand body hinge pillar trim panel by pulling it away from the from body hinge pillar.
5. Remove the bolts/screws holding the blower motor cover and remove the cover.
   a. Remove two bolts/screws, allowing the third bolt (nearest the right hand rear corner) of the module to remain in place.
   b. While supporting the blower motor, remove the third bolt.
   c. Remove the isolator from the blower motor flange, if necessary.

To install:

➡The impeller is part of a blower motor service kit. The kit is preassembled and balanced. Therefore, do not attempt to separate the impeller from the blower motor.

6. Install the motor.
   a. Position the isolator on the blower motor flange.
   b. Align the motor with the opening in the bottom of the module and carefully move the motor up and into position.
7. Install the bolts/screws and tighten them to 17 inch lbs. (1.9 Nm).
8. Install the right hand body hinge pillar trim panel by pressing it into position until retainers snap into place.
9. Connect the blower motor electrical connector.
10. Install the right hand instrument panel insulator.
11. Connect the negative battery cable.

Eldorado and Seville

▶ See Figure 23

1. Disconnect the negative battery cable.
2. Remove 2 nuts from each side and remove the cowl cross-tower brace.

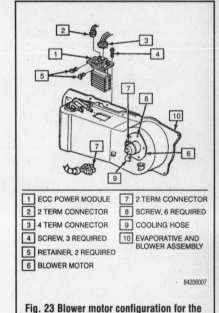

1	ECC POWER MODULE	7	2 TERM CONNECTOR
2	2 TERM CONNECTOR	8	SCREW, 6 REQUIRED
3	4 TERM CONNECTOR	9	COOLING HOSE
4	SCREW, 3 REQUIRED	10	EVAPORATIVE AND BLOWER ASSEMBLY
5	RETAINER, 2 REQUIRED		
6	BLOWER MOTOR		

84206007

Fig. 23 Blower motor configuration for the Eldorado and Seville

3. Remove the 2 cowl relay center bracket mounting nuts and position the cowl relay center aside.
4. Detach the wiring connector and the cooling tube from the blower motor and remove the blower motor mounting screws.
5. Remove the MAP sensor mounting bracket and position aside.
6. Tilt the blower motor in the case and remove the fan from the blower motor.
7. Remove the blower motor from the case.
8. Remove the fan from the case.

To install:

9. Install the fan into the case.
10. Position the blower motor into the case, then install the fan onto the blower motor.
11. Install the MAP sensor-mounting bracket.
12. Install the blower motor mounting screws and connect the cooling hose and wiring connector.
13. Position the cowl relay center and install the cowl relay center bracket nuts.

Heater Core

The heater core is the main component of the heater system. The heater core is located inside of the heater and evaporator module. Engine coolant is pumped into the heater core from the engine whenever the engine is operating. The heater core fins transfer the heat from the engine coolant to the air passing over the heater core. The heater core has specific inlet and outlet tubes. The placement of the heater hoses should be noted prior to servicing the heater core or the heater hoses.

REMOVAL & INSTALLATION

Deville and Fleetwood

1. Disconnect the negative battery cable.
2. Drain and recycle the engine coolant.

✳✳ CAUTION

Never open, service, or drain the radiator or cooling system when hot; serious burns can occur from the steam and hot coolant. In addition, when draining engine coolant, keep in mind that cats and dogs are attracted to ethylene glycol antifreeze and could drink any that is left in an uncovered container or in puddles on the ground. This will prove fatal in sufficient quantities. Always drain coolant into a sealable container. Coolant should be reused unless it is contaminated or is several years old.

3. Disconnect the heater core hoses using tool J-37097 or equivalent.
4. Remove the right side sound insulator and the glove box module.
5. Remove the programmer shield, if equipped, and disconnect the air mix valve link.
6. Detach the programmer vacuum and electrical connectors.
7. Remove the heater core cover, leaving the programmer attached.
8. Remove the heater core retaining screws and the heater core.

To install:

9. Position the heater core and secure with the retaining screws.
10. Install the heater core cover.
11. Connect the programmer vacuum and electrical connectors.
12. Connect the air mix valve link and, if equipped, install the programmer shield.
13. Connect the heater core hoses.
14. Connect the negative battery cable and fill the cooling system.
15. Adjust the air mix valve as follows:
    a. Set the temperature on the heater and A/C control panel to 90°F (32°C). Allow 1–2 minutes for the programmer arm to travel to the maximum heat position.
    b. Unsnap the threaded rod from the plastic retainer on the programmer output arm.
    c. Check the air mix valve for free travel. Push the valve to the maximum A/C position and check for binding.
    d. Preload the air mix valve in the maximum heat position by pulling the threaded rod to ensure the valve is sealing. The programmer out-

put arm should be in the maximum heat position.
    e. Snap the threaded rod into the plastic retainer on the programmer arm. Avoid moving the programmer arm or air mix valve.
    f. Set the temperature on the control panel to 60°F (16°C). Verify that the programmer arm and the air mix valve travel to the maximum cold position.
16. Install the right side sound insulator and the glove box module.

Eldorado and Seville

1. Disconnect the negative battery cable.
2. Drain and recycle the engine coolant.
3. Remove the glove box unit and right side lower sound insulator.
4. Remove the programmer as follows:
    a. Remove the 2 PCM bracket screws. Position the PCM aside to gain access to the rear programmer mounting screw.
    b. Disconnect the threaded rod from the programmer.
    c. Remove the vacuum connector retaining nut.
    d. Detach the vacuum and wiring connectors from the programmer.
    e. Remove the 3 screws and the programmer.
5. On early model vehicles, proceed as follows:
    a. Detach the wiring connectors from the BCM and PCM and remove the mounting brackets.
6. Remove the heater core cover.
7. Disconnect the heater hoses from the heater core.
8. Remove the 2 heater core retaining screws and remove the heater core.

To install:

9. Install the heater core to the heater case and secure with the 2 screws.
10. Connect the heater hoses to the heater core.
11. Install the heater core cover.
12. On early model vehicles, proceed as follows:
    a. Install the PCM mounting bracket and PCM. Connect the wiring connectors to the PCM.
    b. Install the BCM mounting bracket and BCM. Connect the wiring connectors to the BCM.
13. Install the programmer as follows:
    a. Install the programmer in the vehicle and connect the vacuum and wiring connectors.
    b. Install the vacuum connector retaining nut.
    c. Connect the threaded rod to the programmer.
    d. Return the PCM to its original position and secure with the 2 bracket screws.
14. Connect the negative battery cable and fill the cooling system.
15. Adjust the air mix valve as follows:
    a. Set the temperature on the heater and A/C control panel to 90°F (32°C). Allow 1–2 minutes for the programmer arm to travel to the maximum heat position.
    b. Unsnap the threaded rod from the plastic retainer on the programmer output arm.
    c. Check the air mix valve for free travel. Push the valve to the maximum A/C position and check for binding.

    d. Preload the air mix valve in the maximum heat position by pulling the threaded rod to ensure the valve is sealing. The programmer output arm should be in the maximum heat position.
    e. Snap the threaded rod into the plastic retainer on the programmer arm. Avoid moving the programmer arm or air mix valve.
    f. Set the temperature on the control panel to 60°F (16°C). Verify that the programmer arm and the air mix valve travel to the maximum cold position.
16. Install the right side lower sound insulator and the glove box unit.

Air Conditioning Components

Repair or service of air conditioning components is not covered by this manual, because of the risk of personal injury or death, and because of the legal ramifications of servicing these components without the proper EPA certification and experience. Cost, personal injury or death, environmental damage, and legal considerations (such as the fact that it is a federal crime to vent refrigerant into the atmosphere), dictate that the A/C components on your vehicle should be serviced only by a Motor Vehicle Air Conditioning (MVAC) trained, and EPA certified automotive technician.

➡**If the A/C system of your vehicle uses R-12 refrigerant and is in need of recharging, the A/C system can be converted over to R-134a refrigerant (less environmentally harmful and expensive). Refer to the information on R-12 to R-134a conversions, and for additional considerations dealing with the A/C system of your vehicle.**

Control Panel

REMOVAL & INSTALLATION

Deville and Fleetwood

▶ **See Figures 24 and 25**

1. Disconnect the negative battery cable.
2. Remove the right and left sound insulators and snap out the upper steering column filler panel.
3. Remove the lower steering column filler panel.
4. Remove the screws from the tops of the trim plates and remove the left and right trim plates.

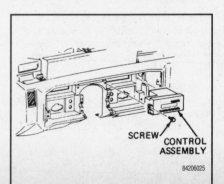

SCREW CONTROL ASSEMBLY

84206025

Fig. 24 Typical climate control panel

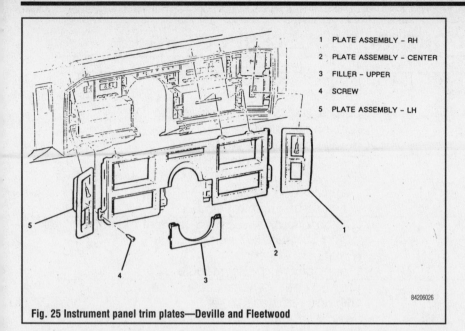

Fig. 25 Instrument panel trim plates—Deville and Fleetwood

1 PLATE ASSEMBLY – RH
2 PLATE ASSEMBLY – CENTER
3 FILLER – UPPER
4 SCREW
5 PLATE ASSEMBLY – LH

84206026

To install:

5. Connect the wiring connectors and position the control panel in the dash. Install the retaining screws.

6. Install the center trim plate and secure with the screws.

7. Connect the negative battery cable.

The climate control panel is contained within the instrument cluster on 1992–93 Eldorado and Seville.

LATE MODELS

1. Remove the instrument panel center trim plate.
2. Remove the console trim plate.
3. Remove the control assembly and the radio.
4. Remove the control assembly bracket fasteners.
5. Detach the electrical connectors from the control assembly and radio.
6. Remove the control assembly retaining nuts.
7. Remove the control assembly from the bracket.

To install:

8. Installation is the reversal of the removal procedure.

5. Remove the screws at the bottom of the center trim plate and remove the trim plate.

6. Remove the screws and pull out the climate control panel. Detach the wiring connectors and remove the panel.

To install:

7. Connect the wiring connectors and position the climate control panel in the dash. Install the retaining screws.

8. Install the trim plates with the retaining screws.

9. Install the steering column filler panel(s) and the left and right sound insulators, if removed.

10. Connect the negative battery cable.

Eldorado and Seville

EARLY MODELS

▶ **See Figure 26**

1. Disconnect the negative battery cable.
2. Remove the instrument panel center trim plate.
3. Remove the control panel retaining screws and pull out the control panel.
4. Detach the wiring connector and remove the control panel.

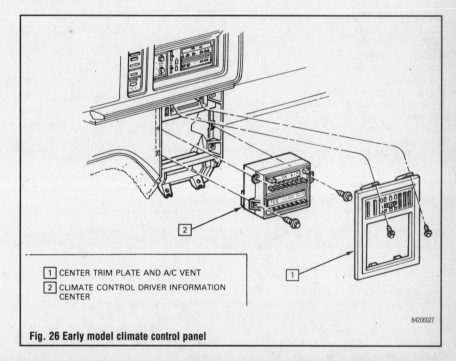

1 CENTER TRIM PLATE AND A/C VENT
2 CLIMATE CONTROL DRIVER INFORMATION CENTER

84206027

Fig. 26 Early model climate control panel

CRUISE CONTROL

▶ **See Figure 27**

Cruise control is a speed control system that maintains a desired vehicle speed under normal driving conditions. However, steep grades up or down may cause variations in the selected speeds.

The main parts of the cruise control system are the functional control switches, cruise control module assembly, vehicle speed sensor, cruise control release switch, and stoplamp switch assemblies. The cruise control system uses a cruise control module assembly to obtain the desired vehicle cruise operation. Two important components in the module assembly help to do this. The first is an electronic controller and the second is an electric

stepper motor. The electric stepper motor moves a band and the throttle linkage, in response to the electronic controller, to maintain the desired cruise speeds. The cruise control module assembly contains a low speed limit that will prevent system engagement below a minimum speed of 25 mph (40 km/h).

With cruise control, you can maintain a speed of about of 25 mph (40 km/h) or more without keeping your foot on the accelerator. This can help on long trips. The cruise control does not work at speeds below 25 mph (40 km/h). When you apply your brakes or turn off the switch, the cruise control shuts off.

❊❊ CAUTION

Do not use the cruise control on slippery roads, winding roads or in traffic of heavy or varying volume. When you are traveling down a steeply graded hill, the cruise control should be disengaged by depressing the brake pedal lightly. The automatic transmission can then be shifted into a lower gear range to help control the vehicle speed. Failure to follow these CAUTIONS could possibly cause you to lose control of the vehicle and result in damage to the vehicle and personal injury.

CRUISE CONTROL TROUBLESHOOTING

Problem	Possible Cause
Will not hold proper speed	Incorrect cable adjustment Binding throttle linkage Leaking vacuum servo diaphragm Leaking vacuum tank Faulty vacuum or vent valve Faulty stepper motor Faulty transducer Faulty speed sensor Faulty cruise control module
Cruise intermittently cuts out	Clutch or brake switch adjustment too tight Short or open in the cruise control circuit Faulty transducer Faulty cruise control module
Vehicle surges	Kinked speedometer cable or casing Binding throttle linkage Faulty speed sensor Faulty cruise control module
Cruise control inoperative	Blown fuse Short or open in the cruise control circuit Faulty brake or clutch switch Leaking vacuum circuit Faulty cruise control switch Faulty stepper motor Faulty transducer Faulty speed sensor Faulty cruise control module

Note: Use this chart as a guide. Not all systems will use the components listed.

TCCA6C01

Fig. 27 Note: Use this chart as a guide. Not all systems will use the components listed

ENTERTAINMENT SYSTEMS

There are two standard radio assemblies used in vehicle applications. Both radio assemblies have electronic memory for pre-selected station function. The radio assemblies also have integral controls, AM stereo, AM/FM stereo, preset equalization, cassette and speed compensated volume in later models.

These systems also have auto Dolby B and auto equalization (CrO2) wherever applicable.

Both radios consist of a radio assembly mounted in the instrument panel assembly and a radio receiver located in the rear compartment next to the radio power antenna assembly motor.

An electrically operated telescoping antenna assembly is standard. The radio power antenna assembly extends fully when the radio assembly is in use.

Radio Receiver/Tape Player/CD

Optional radios include the double DIN radio assemblies featuring ETR (electronically tuned receiver) tuning, vacuum fluorescent display, AM stereo and FM stereo, seek and scan tuning, preset equalization, speed compensated volume and digital clock display. Two radios are available.

• AM/FM Stereo and Clock and Tape Player Radio Assembly with equalizer.

• AM/FM Stereo and Clock and Tape Player and Compact Disc Player Radio Assembly with equalizer.

• Both radios use six speakers: two speakers and two tweeters mounted in the front side doors and two in the rear shelf of the vehicle.

REMOVAL & INSTALLATION

1990–93 Deville and Fleetwood

▶ See Figures 28, 29, 30 and 31

1. Disconnect the negative battery cable.
2. Remove the radio trim plate.
3. Remove the ashtray.
4. Remove one screw from the rear radio support bracket and 2 screws from the front of the radio.
5. Detach the radio wiring connectors and antenna lead.

6. Remove the nuts from the brackets and remove the brackets. On 1992–93 vehicles, remove the 5 push-on clips.

To install:

7. Installation is the reverse of the removal procedure.

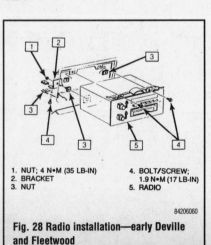

1. NUT; 4 N•M (35 LB-IN)
2. BRACKET
3. NUT
4. BOLT/SCREW; 1.9 N•M (17 LB-IN)
5. RADIO

84206060

Fig. 28 Radio installation—early Deville and Fleetwood

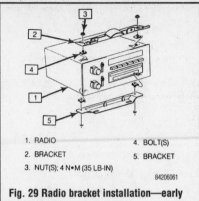

1. RADIO
2. BRACKET
3. NUT(S); 4 N•M (35 LB-IN)
4. BOLT(S)
5. BRACKET

84206061

Fig. 29 Radio bracket installation—early model Deville and Fleetwood

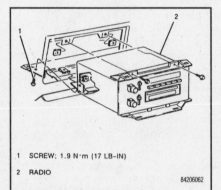

1. SCREW; 1.9 N·m (17 LB-IN)
2. RADIO

84206062

Fig. 30 Radio installation—late model Deville and Fleetwood

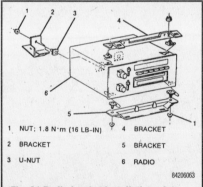

1. NUT; 1.8 N·m (16 LB-IN)
2. BRACKET
3. U-NUT
4. BRACKET
5. BRACKET
6. RADIO

84206063

Fig. 31 Radio bracket installation—late model Deville and Fleetwood

1990–91 Eldorado and Seville

▶ See Figures 32 and 33

1. Disconnect the negative battery cable.
2. Carefully pop out the radio trim plate.
3. Twist the left-hand A/C vent to remove.
4. Remove the instrument panel trim plate retaining screws and remove the trim plate.
5. Loosen the lower mounting nuts under the radio.
6. Slide the radio forward and detach the wiring connectors and antenna lead. Remove the radio.
   To install:
7. Installation is the reverse of the removal procedure.

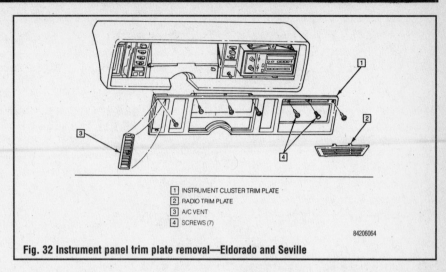

1. INSTRUMENT CLUSTER TRIM PLATE
2. RADIO TRIM PLATE
3. A/C VENT
4. SCREWS (7)

84206064

Fig. 32 Instrument panel trim plate removal—Eldorado and Seville

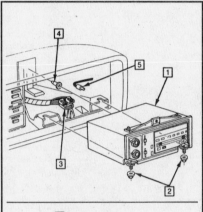

1. RADIO ASSEMBLY
2. NUTS (2)
3. RADIO CONNECTORS
4. PLASTIC ALIGNMENT PIN
5. ANTENNA LEAD-IN

84206065

Fig. 33 Radio removal—Eldorado and Seville

1992–98 Eldorado and Seville and 1994–98 Deville

RADIO CONTROL HEAD WITH CONSOLE SHIFT

▶ See Figure 34

1. Disconnect the negative battery cable.
2. Remove the radio trim plate.
3. Remove the console trim plate; it pulls up first from the upper edge.
4. Remove the nuts from the bottom of the control head.
5. Twist the control head so the right side exits first from the dash to clear the connectors on the left side.
6. Detach the wiring connectors and remove the radio control head.
   To install:
7. Installation is the reverse of the removal procedure.

RADIO CONTROL HEAD WITH COLUMN SHIFT

▶ See Figures 35, 36, 37 and 38

1. Disconnect the negative battery cable.
2. Remove the radio trim plate.

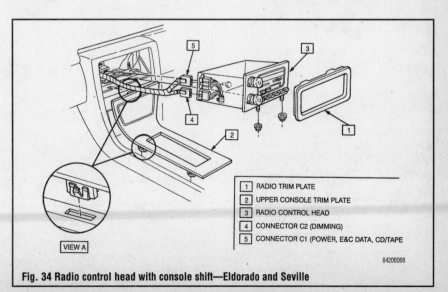

1. RADIO TRIM PLATE
2. UPPER CONSOLE TRIM PLATE
3. RADIO CONTROL HEAD
4. CONNECTOR C2 (DIMMING)
5. CONNECTOR C1 (POWER, E&C DATA, CD/TAPE)

VIEW A

84206066

Fig. 34 Radio control head with console shift—Eldorado and Seville

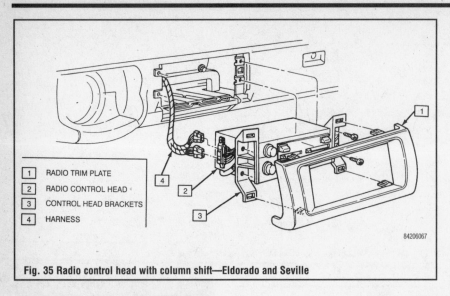

1. RADIO TRIM PLATE
2. RADIO CONTROL HEAD
3. CONTROL HEAD BRACKETS
4. HARNESS

84206067

Fig. 35 Radio control head with column shift—Eldorado and Seville

91046P24

Fig. 36 Remove the radio trim plate

91046P25

Fig. 37 Remove the fasteners and pop the radio out of the instrument panel

91046P27

Fig. 38 Unplug the connectors from the rear of the unit and don't forget the antenna coupling

3. Remove the 4 screws from the side brackets.
4. Pull out the control head and detach the wiring connectors. Remove the radio control head.
   To install:
5. The installation is the reverse of removal.

Remote Radio Receiver

REMOVAL & INSTALLATION

1992–98 Eldorado and Seville

▶ See Figures 39 and 40

1. Disconnect the negative battery cable.
2. Open the trunk.
3. On 1992 vehicles, remove the close out panel from the trunk electronics bay. On 1993–98 vehicles, remove the right hand trunk trim.
4. Detach the wiring connectors and antenna lead.

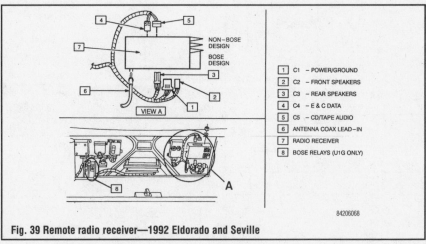

NON–BOSE DESIGN
BOSE DESIGN

VIEW A

1. C1 – POWER/GROUND
2. C2 – FRONT SPEAKERS
3. C3 – REAR SPEAKERS
4. C4 – E & C DATA
5. C5 – CD/TAPE AUDIO
6. ANTENNA COAX LEAD–IN
7. RADIO RECEIVER
8. BOSE RELAYS (U1G ONLY)

84206068

Fig. 39 Remote radio receiver—1992 Eldorado and Seville

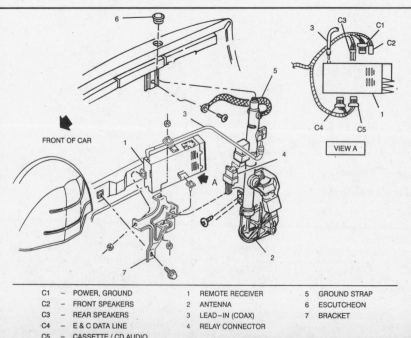

FRONT OF CAR

VIEW A

C1	–	POWER, GROUND	1	REMOTE RECEIVER	5	GROUND STRAP
C2	–	FRONT SPEAKERS	2	ANTENNA	6	ESCUTCHEON
C3	–	REAR SPEAKERS	3	LEAD–IN (COAX)	7	BRACKET
C4	–	E & C DATA LINE	4	RELAY CONNECTOR		
C5	–	CASSETTE / CD AUDIO				

84206069

Fig. 40 Remote radio receiver—1993–98 Eldorado and Seville

5. Remove the receiver attaching nuts and remove the receiver.

To install:

6. Installation is the reverse of the removal procedure.

Speakers

REMOVAL & INSTALLATION

1990–93 Deville and Fleetwood

STANDARD FRONT SPEAKER

▶ **See Figure 41**

1. Disconnect the negative battery cable.
2. Remove the 3 screws from the defroster grille.
3. Remove the 4 A/C outlets, then remove the 4 screws from behind the outlets.
4. Remove the instrument panel upper trim pad.
5. Remove the aspirator tube and wiring connector from the in-vehicle temperature sensor.
6. Remove the 2 mounting screws from the speaker flange and pull out the speaker assembly. Detach the wiring connector and remove the speaker.
7. The installation is the reverse of removal.

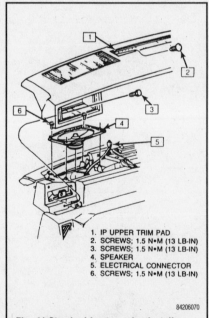

1. IP UPPER TRIM PAD
2. SCREWS; 1.5 N•M (13 LB-IN)
3. SCREWS; 1.5 N•M (13 LB-IN)
4. SPEAKER
5. ELECTRICAL CONNECTOR
6. SCREWS; 1.5 N•M (13 LB-IN)

84206070

Fig. 41 Standard front speaker installation—Deville and Fleetwood

DELCO/BOSE® FRONT SPEAKER ENCLOSURE

▶ **See Figure 42**

1. Raise the door glass to the full-up position, then disconnect the negative battery cable.
2. Remove the door panel.
3. Remove the speaker enclosure retaining screws.
4. Detach the wiring connector and remove the speaker.

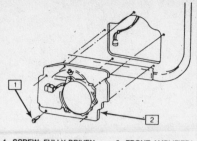

1. SCREW; FULLY DRIVEN, SEATED AND NOT STRIPPED
2. FRONT AMPLIFIER/ SPEAKER UNIT

84206071

Fig. 42 Delco/Bose® front speaker installation—Deville and Fleetwood

To install:

5. Installation is the reverse of the removal procedure.

STANDARD REAR SHELF SPEAKERS

▶ **See Figure 43**

1. Disconnect the negative battery cable.
2. Remove the 2 screws from the seat belt covers.
3. Remove the 2 bolts from the rear headrest and remove the rear headrest.
4. Remove the rear window shelf.
5. Remove the 4 screws from the speaker.
6. Detach the wiring connector and remove the speaker.
7. Installation is the reverse of the removal procedure.

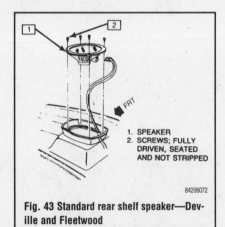

1. SPEAKER
2. SCREWS; FULLY DRIVEN, SEATED AND NOT STRIPPED

84206072

Fig. 43 Standard rear shelf speaker—Deville and Fleetwood

DELCO/BOSE® REAR SPEAKER ENCLOSURE

▶ **See Figure 44**

1. Disconnect the negative battery cable.
2. Remove the rear seat-to-back window trim panel.
3. Remove the upper enclosure housing.
4. Remove the screws from the speaker grille.
5. Detach the wiring connectors from the speaker and remove the speaker.

To install:

6. Installation is the reversal of the removal procedure.

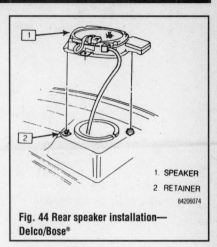

1. SPEAKER
2. RETAINER

84206074

Fig. 44 Rear speaker installation—Delco/Bose®

1994–98 Deville

STANDARD FRONT INSTRUMENT PANEL SPEAKER

▶ **See Figure 45**

1. Disconnect the negative battery cable.
2. Remove the instrument panel compartment screws and compartment.
3. Remove the 3 screws from the defroster grille.
4. Remove the 4 A/C outlets, then remove the 4 screws from behind the outlets.
5. Remove the 2 screws from inside the instrument panel compartment.
6. Remove the instrument panel upper trim pad.
7. Remove the aspirator tube and wiring connector from the in-vehicle temperature sensor.
8. Remove the 2 mounting screws from the speaker flange and pull out the speaker assembly. Detach the wiring connector and remove the speaker.

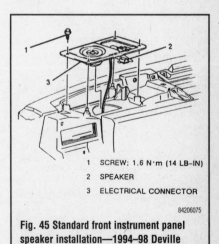

1. SCREW; 1.6 N·m (14 LB-IN)
2. SPEAKER
3. ELECTRICAL CONNECTOR

84206075

Fig. 45 Standard front instrument panel speaker installation—1994–98 Deville

To install:

9. The installation is the reverse of removal.

STANDARD FRONT DOOR SPEAKER

▶ **See Figures 46, 47 and 48**

1. Disconnect the negative battery cable.
2. Remove the door panel.

Fig. 46 Removing the speaker mounting screws

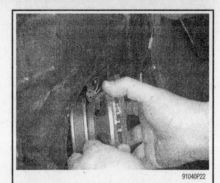

Fig. 47 Remove the speaker from the door and . . .

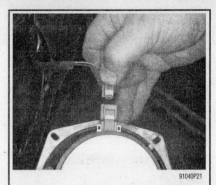

Fig. 48 . . . unplug the connector from the speaker

3. Remove the speaker-to-housing retaining screws and remove the speaker.

4. Detach the speaker wiring connector.

To install:

5. The installation is the reverse of removal.

1990–91 Eldorado and Seville

STANDARD FRONT DOOR SPEAKER

▶ See Figure 49

1. Disconnect the negative battery cable.
2. Remove the door panel.
3. Remove the speaker mounting screws and detach the wiring connector.
4. Remove the speaker.

To install:

5. Installation is the reverse of the removal procedure.

DELCO/BOSE® FRONT DOOR SPEAKER

▶ See Figures 50 and 51

1. Disconnect the negative battery cable.
2. Remove the door panel.
3. Detach the speaker wiring connector.
4. Remove the screws retaining the speaker enclosure to the door panel through the metal support strip and remove the speaker enclosure.
5. Carefully peel back the carpet from the enclosure lip.
6. Remove the screws retaining the rear enclosure cover.
7. Remove the screws retaining the speaker and detach the speaker wiring connector.
8. Remove the speaker.

To install:

9. Installation is the reverse of the removal procedure.

REAR SPEAKERS

▶ See Figures 52 and 53

1. Disconnect the negative battery cable.
2. Open the trunk.
3. Remove the 2 plastic speed nuts attaching the speaker enclosure, then swing the enclosure down. The other side is held up by the flange only.
4. Remove the speaker bracket spring clip, then swing the bracket down. The other side is held up by the flange only.
5. Detach the speaker wiring connector.
6. If equipped with the standard speakers, lift the speaker out of the bracket.

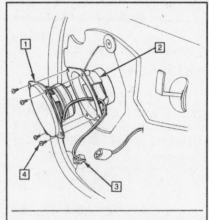

1	FRONT SPEAKER (NON-BOSE)
2	SPEAKER FLANGE
3	SPEAKER CONNECTORS
4	RETAINING SCREWS (2)

Fig. 49 Standard front door speaker installation—Eldorado and Seville

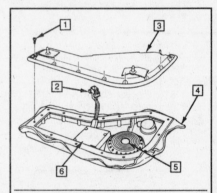

1	RETAINING SCREWS (12)
2	SPEAKER CONNECTOR
3	BOSE ENCLOSURE COVER
4	ENCLOSURE CARPET TRIM COVER
5	SPEAKER
6	BOSE AMPLIFIER

Fig. 51 Delco/Bose® front door speaker removal—Eldorado and Seville

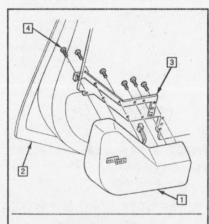

1	BOSE SPEAKER ENCLOSURE
2	DOOR TRIM PANEL
3	REINFORCEMENT BRACKET
4	SCREWS (6)

Fig. 50 Delco/Bose® front door speaker enclosure removal—Eldorado and Seville

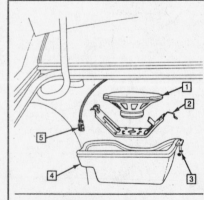

1	NON-BOSE SPEAKER
2	SPEAKER RETAINER
3	SPEED NUTS
4	SPEAKER ENCLOSURE
5	SPEAKER CONNECTOR

Fig. 52 Standard rear speaker removal—Eldorado and Seville

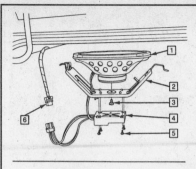

1. BOSE SPEAKER
2. SPEAKER RETAINER
3. SPEAKER SCREW TO MAGNET (1)
4. BOSE AMPLIFIER
5. AMPLIFIER SCREWS (4)
6. BOSE CONNECTOR

84206081

Fig. 53 Rear speaker removal— Eldorado and Seville with Delco/Bose®

7. If equipped with Delco/Bose® speakers, remove the screws accessed through the bottom of the amplifier. Remove the screw through the bracket into the speaker magnet and remove the speaker.

To install:

8. Installation is the reverse of the removal procedure.

1992–98 Eldorado and Seville

FRONT DOOR SPEAKER

◆ **See Figures 54, 55, 56 and 57**

1. Disconnect the negative battery cable.
2. Remove the door panel.
3. Detach the speaker wiring connector.
4. Remove the screws to release the speaker unit.
5. If equipped with standard speakers, remove the retaining screws and detach the wiring connector.
6. Remove the speaker.

7. If equipped with Delco/Bose® speakers, remove the amplifier cover and gasket and remove the amplifier. Detach the wiring connector and remove the speaker.

To install:

8. Installation is the reverse of the removal procedure.

REAR SPEAKER

◆ **See Figures 58 and 59**

1. Disconnect the negative battery cable.
2. Remove the rear seat cushion, seat back, and quarter trim panel.
3. Remove the rear shelf trim panel.
4. Detach the wiring connector and pry the speaker from the retaining clips.

To install:

5. Installation is the reverse of the removal procedure.

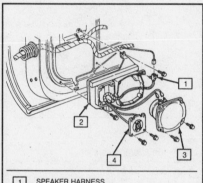

1. SPEAKER HARNESS
2. SPEAKER HOUSING
3. SPEAKER – WOOFER
4. SPEAKER – TWEETER (ELDORADO TOURING COUPE ONLY)

84206082

Fig. 54 Standard front speaker installation—Eldorado

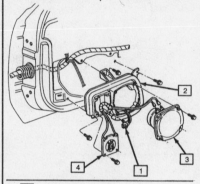

1. SPEAKER HARNESS
2. SPEAKER HOUSING
3. SPEAKER – WOOFER
4. SPEAKER – TWEETER (SEVILLE TOURING SEDAN ONLY)

84206083

Fig. 55 Standard front speaker installation—Seville

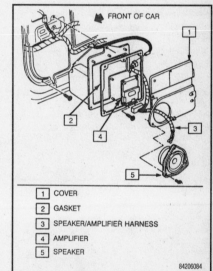

1. COVER
2. GASKET
3. SPEAKER/AMPLIFIER HARNESS
4. AMPLIFIER
5. SPEAKER

84206084

Fig. 56 Front speaker installation—Eldorado with Delco/Bose®

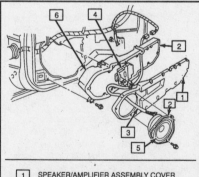

1. SPEAKER/AMPLIFIER ASSEMBLY COVER
2. GASKET
3. SPEAKER/AMPLIFIER HARNESS
4. AMPLIFIER
5. SPEAKER
6. SPEAKER/AMPLIFIER ASSEMBLY

84206085

Fig. 57 Front speaker installation—Seville with Delco/Bose®

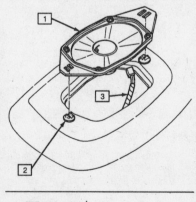

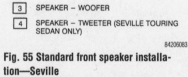

1. SPEAKER
2. CLIP
3. SPEAKER HARNESS

84206086

Fig. 58 Standard rear speaker installation—Eldorado and Seville

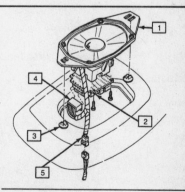

1. SPEAKER ASSEMBLY
2. AMPLIFIER
3. CLIP
4. AMPLIFIER HARNESS
5. SPEAKER/AMPLIFIER ASSEMBLY HARNESS

84206087

Fig. 59 Delco/Bose® Rear speaker installation—Eldorado and Seville

WINDSHIELD WIPERS AND WASHERS

Windshield Wiper Blade and Arm

REMOVAL & INSTALLATION

Deville and Fleetwood

▶ **See Figures 60, 61 and 62**

1. Raise the hood as needed for access to the wiper arms.
2. Operate the wipers and turn the ignition **OFF** when the wipers are at the mid-wipe position.
3. Lift the wiper arm from the windshield.
4. On 1990 vehicles, pull the retaining latch and remove the arm from the transmission shaft.
5. On 1991–up vehicles, disengage the retaining latch using a suitable tool and remove the arm from the transmission shaft.

To install:

6. Install the wiper arm onto the transmission shaft.
7. Push the retaining latch in and return the arm assembly to the windshield.
8. Park the wipers. If adjustment is necessary, proceed as follows:
   a. Remove the right wiper arm.
   b. Open the small door to access the wiper linkage; refer to the illustration for details.
   c. Loosen, but do not remove the transmission linkage adjustment nuts.

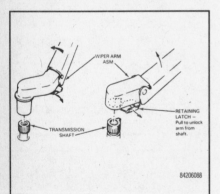

Fig. 60 Wiper arm attachment—1990 Deville and Fleetwood

84206088

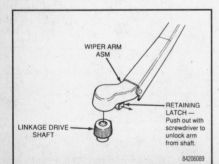

Fig. 61 Wiper arm attachment—1991–93 Deville and Fleetwood

84206089

1	AIR INLET SCREEN ASSEMBLY
2	NOZZLE HOSE ASSEMBLY
3	DRIVE LINK ADJUSTMENT ACCESS DOOR
4	NOZZLE (2)
5	PARK RAMP (2)
6	NOZZLE SPRAY PATTERN
7	WIPE PATTERN
8	RESERVOIR HOSE ASSEMBLY
9	NUT (2) – 5 N·M (44 LB. IN.)
10	WASHER RESERVOIR
11	LOW FLUID LEVEL SENSOR
12	WASHER PUMP
13	SCREW – 5 N·M (44 LB. IN.)

84206090

Fig. 62 Washer reservoir, washer pump and wipe pattern—Deville and Fleetwood

---

d. Rotate the left arm and blade assembly to slightly below the blade stops.
e. On 1990 vehicles, tighten the transmission adjustment screws to 64 inch lbs. (7 Nm). On 1991 vehicles, tighten the transmission linkage adjustment nuts to 44 inch lbs. (5 Nm). On 1992–up vehicles, tighten the transmission linkage adjustment nuts to 71 inch lbs. (8 Nm).
f. Position the right wiper arm and blade assembly below the blade stops, then install the arm onto the transmission shaft.
g. Lift both arm and blade assemblies over the stops.
h. Check the wiper pattern and park position with the windshield wet and the wipers operating at low speed. Dimension A in figure '84206090' should be 1¹¹/₁₆ from the top of the driver's blade assembly on the outwipe to the edge of the glass.

Eldorado and Seville— Early Models

▶ **See Figures 63, 64 and 65**

1. Operate the wipers and turn the ignition **OFF** when the wipers are at the mid-wipe position.
2. Detach the hose on the wiper arm from the hose connector.
3. Lift the wiper arm from the windshield and pull the retaining latch.
4. Remove the arm from the transmission shaft.

To install:

5. Install the arm on the transmission shaft.
6. Push the retaining latch in and return the arm to the windshield.

7. Attach the hose on the wiper arm to the hose connector.
8. Park the wipers. If adjustment is necessary, proceed as follows:
   a. Raise the hood and remove the wiper arms.
   b. Open the transmission adjustment window on the left side of the cowl vent screen.
   c. Loosen, but do not remove the transmission drive link-to-motor crank arm attaching screws.
   d. Position the left arm and blade assembly to the transmission shaft. Align the slot in the arm to the key-way and push the arm down. Engage the slide latch.
   e. Rotate the left arm assembly to a position one inch below the ramp stop.
   f. Tighten the attaching screws on the transmission link-to-motor crank arm to 4 ft. lbs. (6 Nm).
   g. While the left arm assembly is still below the ramp stop, position the right arm and blade assembly to the transmission shaft approximately one inch below the ramp stop. Push the arm down and engage the slide latch.
   h. Close the adjustment window and place the arm assemblies on the ramp stop on the vent screen.
   i. Check the wiper pattern and park position as shown in Figures '84206094' and '84206095'. The outwipe dimensions are determined with the wipers operating at low speed on wet glass.

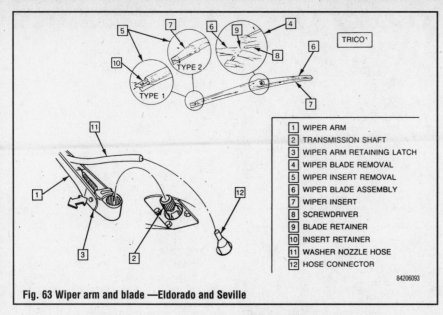

1	WIPER ARM
2	TRANSMISSION SHAFT
3	WIPER ARM RETAINING LATCH
4	WIPER BLADE REMOVAL
5	WIPER INSERT REMOVAL
6	WIPER BLADE ASSEMBLY
7	WIPER INSERT
8	SCREWDRIVER
9	BLADE RETAINER
10	INSERT RETAINER
11	WASHER NOZZLE HOSE
12	HOSE CONNECTOR

Fig. 63 Wiper arm and blade —Eldorado and Seville

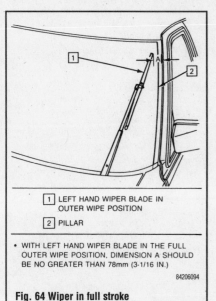

1	LEFT HAND WIPER BLADE IN OUTER WIPE POSITION
2	PILLAR

• WITH LEFT HAND WIPER BLADE IN THE FULL OUTER WIPE POSITION, DIMENSION A SHOULD BE NO GREATER THAN 78mm (3-1/16 IN.)

Fig. 64 Wiper in full stroke

Eldorado and Seville—Late Models

▶ **See Figures 66 thru 74**

1. Turn the ignition **ON**, place the wipers in the park position. Turn the ignition **OFF**.

2. Detach the washer hose from the hose connector.

3. Remove the protective cap.

4. Lift the wiper arm and insert a suitable pin or pop rivet completely through the 2 holes located next to the pivot of the arm.

5. Remove the wiper arm retaining nut.

6. Lift the arm from the shaft using a rocking motion.

➡**If the arm will not lift off the shaft using a rocking motion, use a battery terminal remover or similar tool to aid removal. Clean the knurls of the shaft with a suitable wire brush.**

To install:

7. Connect the washer hose.

8. Install the wiper arm (without the blade) one inch below the park ramp.

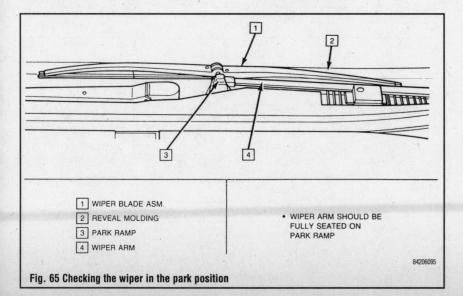

1	WIPER BLADE ASM.
2	REVEAL MOLDING
3	PARK RAMP
4	WIPER ARM

• WIPER ARM SHOULD BE FULLY SEATED ON PARK RAMP

Fig. 65 Checking the wiper in the park position

9. Remove the pivot prevention pin from the wiper arm.

10. Install a new wiper arm retaining nut.

11. Lift the wiper arm over the park ramp and install the wiper blade.

12. Tighten the nut to 15–19 ft. lbs. (20–26 Nm).

13. Operate the wipers and check for correct wipe pattern. The left-hand blade tip should wipe from 1¾₆ to 3¾₆ from the inner edge of the windshield molding. The right-hand blade should overlap the left-hand wipe pattern.

14. Install the protective cap.

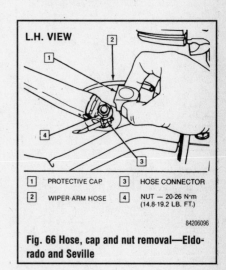

1	PROTECTIVE CAP	3	HOSE CONNECTOR
2	WIPER ARM HOSE	4	NUT — 20-26 N·m (14.8-19.2 LB. FT.)

Fig. 66 Hose, cap and nut removal—Eldorado and Seville

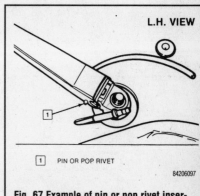

1	PIN OR POP RIVET

Fig. 67 Example of pin or pop rivet insertion —Eldorado and Seville

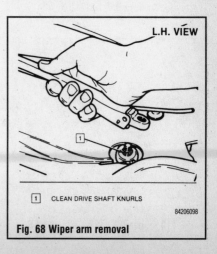

1	CLEAN DRIVE SHAFT KNURLS

Fig. 68 Wiper arm removal

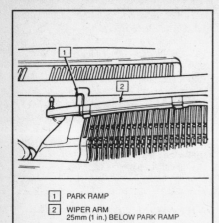

1 PARK RAMP

2 WIPER ARM
25mm (1 in.) BELOW PARK RAMP

84206099

Fig. 69 Wiper arm installation, park position—Eldorado and Seville

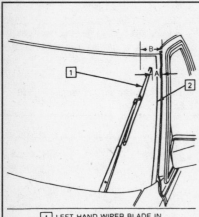

1 LEFT HAND WIPER BLADE IN OUTER WIPE POSITION

2 PILLAR

* WITH LEFT HAND WIPER BLADE IN THE FULL OUTER WIPE POSITION, DIMENSION "A" SHOULD BE NO LESS THAN 35mm (1-3/16 IN.) DIMENSION "B" SHOULD BE NO GREATER THAN 80mm (3-3/16 IN.) FROM THE INNER EDGE OF THE WINDSHIELD MOLDING

84206100

Fig. 70 Checking the wiper arm in full stroke position—Eldorado and Seville

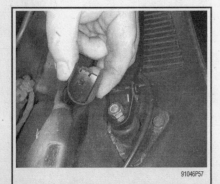

91046P57

Fig. 71 Remove the cap covering the nut

91046P56

Fig. 72 Loosen the retaining nut

91046P55

Fig. 73 Disconnect the washer hose, if equipped

91046P53

Fig. 74 Pull the wiper arm off the stud

Windshield Wiper Motor

REMOVAL & INSTALLATION

Deville and Fleetwood

♦ See Figures 75 and 76

1. On 1991–98 vehicles, disconnect the washer hoses.
2. Remove the wiper arm and blade assemblies.
3. Remove the cowl screen.
4. Disconnect the motor drive link from the motor crank arm by loosening the nuts.
5. Detach the wiring connectors.
6. Remove the wiper motor mounting bolts and remove the wiper motor, guiding the crank arm through the hole.

To install:

7. Guide the wiper motor crank arm through the hole and position the wiper motor. Install the mounting bolts and tighten to 80 inch lbs. (9 Nm).
8. Attach the wiring connectors.
9. Attach the motor drive link to the motor crank arm and tighten the nuts.
10. Install the cowl screen.
11. Install the wiper arm and blade assemblies.
12. Connect the washer hoses.

Eldorado and Seville

1. On 1992–98 vehicles, remove the A/C pipe shroud.
2. Remove the wiper arms.
3. On 1990–91 vehicles, remove the windshield reveal molding.
4. Remove the cowl vent.
5. Disconnect the wiper arm drive link from the wiper motor.
6. Detach the wiring connectors.
7. On 1992–98 vehicles, remove the A/C pipe shroud bracket from the wheelwell.
8. Remove the wiper motor mounting bolts and remove the wiper motor.

To install:

9. Position the wiper motor and install the mounting bolts. Tighten to 80 inch lbs. (9 Nm).
10. On 1992–98 vehicles, install the A/C pipe shroud bracket to the wheelwell.

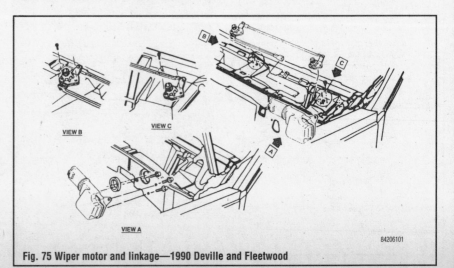

VIEW B

VIEW C

VIEW A

84206101

Fig. 75 Wiper motor and linkage—1990 Deville and Fleetwood

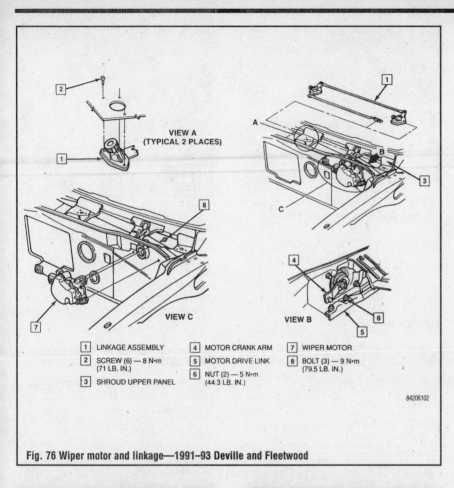

Fig. 76 Wiper motor and linkage—1991–93 Deville and Fleetwood

1	LINKAGE ASSEMBLY	4	MOTOR CRANK ARM	7	WIPER MOTOR
2	SCREW (6) — 8 N·m (71 LB. IN.)	5	MOTOR DRIVE LINK	8	BOLT (3) — 9 N·m (79.5 LB. IN.)
3	SHROUD UPPER PANEL	6	NUT (2) — 5 N·m (44.3 LB. IN.)		

84206102

11. Attach the wiring connectors.

12. Connect the wiper arm drive link to the wiper motor.

13. Install the cowl vent.

14. On 1990–91 vehicles, install the windshield reveal molding.

15. Install the wiper arms.

16. On 1992–98 vehicles, install the A/C pipe shroud.

Windshield Washer Pump

REMOVAL & INSTALLATION

Deville and Fleetwood

⏵ See Figures 77 thru 85

1. Disconnect the negative battery cable.

2. Drain or remove the washer solvent.

3. Remove the headlamp access cover.

4. Remove the radiator support brace.

5. Remove the relay center and position it out of the way.

6. Detach the electrical connectors and the washer hose.

7. Unscrew the two screws and remove the solvent container.

8. Disengage the washer pump from the solvent container.

To install:

9. Installation is the reversal of the removal procedure.

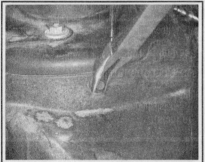

91046P61

Fig. 77 Pull the plastic pins holding the cover in place

91046P62

Fig. 78 Remove the cover

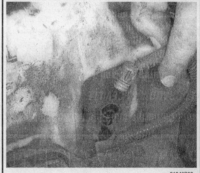

91046P63

Fig. 79 Unplug the washer pump

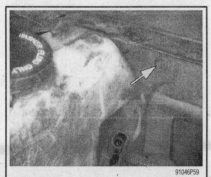

91046P59

Fig. 80 Remove the reservoir retaining screws

91046P64

Fig. 81 Unplug the water level sensor

91046P68

Fig. 82 Lift the solvent tank up gently and support it with one hand

Fig. 83 Disconnect the washer hose

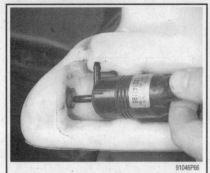

Fig. 84 Extract the washer pump from the solvent tank, by pulling gently out of the seal

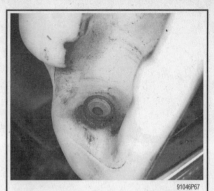

Fig. 85 Examine the seal and the seat for damage before installing a new pump

Eldorado and Seville

1. Disconnect the negative battery cable.
2. On 1992–98 Eldorado and Seville, proceed as follows:
    a. Remove the headlamp access cover.

b. Remove the radiator support-to-wheelwell brace.
c. Remove the relay center and position aside.
3. Use a syringe or similar tool to remove the washer fluid from the reservoir.

4. Detach the wiring connectors and washer hose.
5. Remove the mounting screws/nuts and remove the reservoir.
6. Installation is the reverse of the removal procedure.

INSTRUMENTS AND SWITCHES

➡ **Electrostatic Discharge (ESD) can damage many solid-state electrical components. ESD susceptible components may or may not be labeled with the ESD symbol. Handle all electrical components carefully.**

Instrument Cluster

The instrument cluster is centered above the steering column in the instrument panel and is removable from the rear of the panel (toward the steering wheel). The cluster contains instruments that provide the driver with information on vehicle performance.

REMOVAL & INSTALLATION

➡ **When an instrument cluster is replaced the law requires either the odometer reading of the replacement unit be set to register the original mileage or that a label be installed on the driver's door frame to show the previous odometer reading and the date of replacement.**

Deville and Fleetwood

▶ **See Figures 86 thru 97**

1. Disconnect the negative battery cable.
2. Remove the upper trim pad as follows:
    a. Carefully pry out the A/C outlets.
    b. Remove one screw from behind each outlet and 3 screws through the defroster outlet.
    c. Remove the glove box module retaining screws. Detach the wiring connectors from the switches and light and remove the glove box module.
    d. Remove 2 screws working through the glove box opening.
    e. Detach the in-vehicle temperature sensor electrical connector and aspirator tube.
    f. If equipped, remove the solar sensor from the trim pad.
    g. Remove the upper trim pad.
3. Remove the 2 screws and the plate.
4. Remove the instrument cluster attaching screws.
5. Label and detach the wiring connectors.

6. Remove the shift indicator cable clip and remove the instrument cluster.
To install:
7. Position the instrument cluster and attach the electrical connectors.
8. Install the attaching screws and tighten to 13 inch lbs. (1.5 Nm).
9. Install the plate with the 2 screws.
10. Install the upper trim pad in the reverse order of removal.
11. Install the shift indicator cable clip and adjust the shift indicator as follows:
    a. Position and release the shift lever in the **N** gate notch.
    b. Move the clip on the edge of the shift bowl to center the pointer on **N**.
    c. Push the clip onto the bowl. Make sure the cable rests on the bowl, not on the column jacket. Make sure the clip is tight on the bowl and does not slip.
    d. Move the shift lever through all positions and then back to **N** to check adjustment. Make sure the pointer covers a portion of each graphic.

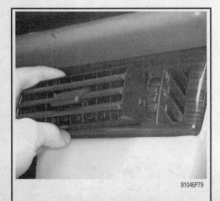

Fig. 86 Pry and squeeze the A/C vent . . .

Fig. 87 . . . to extract it from the dash

Fig. 88 Removing the vent exposes the screw

Fig. 89 Unplug the speaker . . .

Fig. 90 . . . and the electrical connectors before trying to remove the trim pad

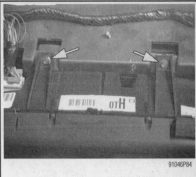

Fig. 91 Remove the center mounting screws

Fig. 92 Unfasten the screw, and detach the electrical connector on the left side . . .

Fig. 93 . . . and the right side

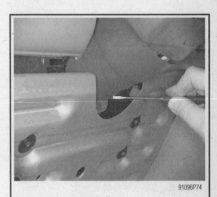

Fig. 94 Don't forget to disconnect the small cable for the PRNDL indicator

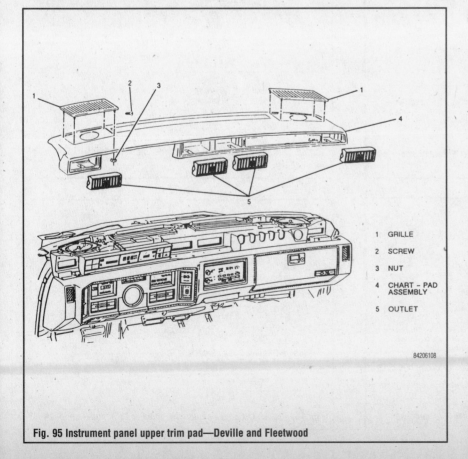

1 GRILLE
2 SCREW
3 NUT
4 CHART – PAD ASSEMBLY
5 OUTLET

Fig. 95 Instrument panel upper trim pad—Deville and Fleetwood

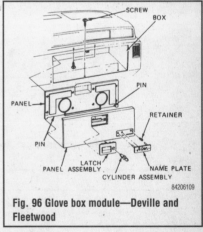

Fig. 96 Glove box module—Deville and Fleetwood

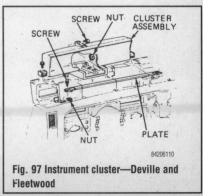

Fig. 97 Instrument cluster—Deville and Fleetwood

1990–91 Eldorado and Seville

♦ See Figures 98 and 99

1. Disconnect the negative battery cable.
2. Remove the instrument cluster trim plate as follows:
    a. Remove the left side A/C vent.
    b. Remove the radio trim plate.
    c. Remove the retaining screws and the trim plate.
3. Remove the screws and the filter lens.
4. Remove the 2 screws and the telltale warning lamp lens.
5. Remove the trip odometer reset button.
6. Remove the 2 instrument cluster retaining screws and remove the cluster.

To install:

7. Align the instrument cluster with the electrical connectors and push the cluster into the instrument panel. Install the 2 retaining screws.
8. Install the trip odometer reset button.
9. Install the telltale warning lamp lens and the filter lens.

10. Install the instrument cluster trim plate in the reverse order of removal.
11. Connect the negative battery cable.

1992–98 Eldorado and Seville

♦ See Figures 100, 101 and 102

1. Disconnect the negative battery cable.
2. Pull fuses A5-IPC (Ignition) and B5-IPC (Battery) from the rear compartment fuse panel and fuse A3-IGN1 from the engine compartment fuse panel.
3. Remove the instrument panel upper trim panel as follows:
    a. Use a small flat-bladed tool to pry up the defroster grille.
    b. Remove the Sunload and Headlamp Auto Control sensors from the defroster grille.
    c. Remove the 3 screws retaining the upper trim panel through the defroster grille opening.
    d. Remove the A/C vents from the front of the instrument panel by releasing the tab on each side from the inside vent and pulling out.
    e. Working through the vent openings,

remove the screws retaining the upper trim panel.
    f. Remove the upper trim panel.
4. Detach the 2 electrical connectors on top of the instrument cluster.
5. Remove the 4 cluster-to-instrument panel retaining screws.
6. Raise the cluster. If equipped with digital cluster, remove the 2 screws securing the PRNDL mechanism.
7. Remove the instrument cluster.

To install:

8. Position the cluster to the instrument panel. Make sure the analog needles are positioned at zero.
9. If equipped with digital cluster, install the 2 screws securing the PRNDL mechanism.
10. Install the 4 cluster-to-instrument panel retaining screws.
11. Attach the electrical connectors to the top of the cluster.
12. Install the instrument panel upper trim panel in the reverse order of removal.
13. Install the fuses in the fuse panel.
14. Connect the negative battery cable.

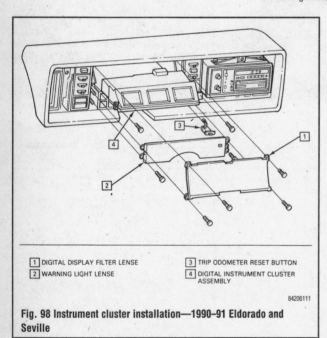

1 DIGITAL DISPLAY FILTER LENSE	3 TRIP ODOMETER RESET BUTTON
2 WARNING LIGHT LENSE	4 DIGITAL INSTRUMENT CLUSTER ASSEMBLY

84206111

Fig. 98 Instrument cluster installation—1990–91 Eldorado and Seville

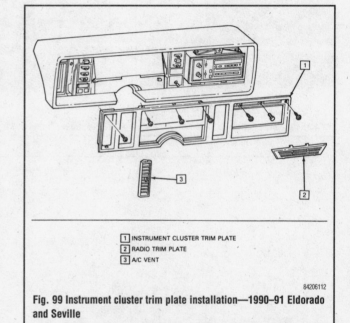

1 INSTRUMENT CLUSTER TRIM PLATE
2 RADIO TRIM PLATE
3 A/C VENT

84206112

Fig. 99 Instrument cluster trim plate installation—1990–91 Eldorado and Seville

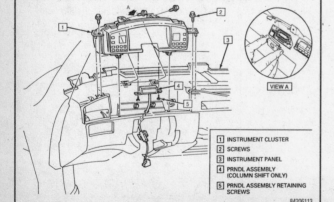

1 INSTRUMENT CLUSTER
2 SCREWS
3 INSTRUMENT PANEL
4 PRNDL ASSEMBLY (COLUMN SHIFT ONLY)
5 PRNDL ASSEMBLY RETAINING SCREWS

84206113

Fig. 100 Instrument cluster installation—1992–98 Eldorado and Seville

1 INSTRUMENT PANEL UPPER TRIM PANEL	5 INSTRUMENT PANEL CARRIER
2 SCREWS	6 SUNLOAD SENSOR
3 WINDSHIELD DEFROSTER GRILLE	7 HEADLAMP AUTO CONTROL AMBIENT LIGHT SENSOR
4 SCREWS	8 SMALL FLAT-BLADED TOOL

84206114

Fig. 101 Instrument panel upper trim panel installation—1992–98 Eldorado and Seville

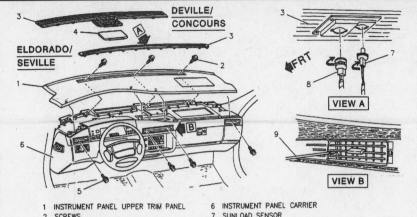

1. INSTRUMENT PANEL UPPER TRIM PANEL
2. SCREWS
3. WINDSHIELD DEFROSTER GRILLE
4. SPEAKER COVER
5. SCREWS
6. INSTRUMENT PANEL CARRIER
7. SUNLOAD SENSOR
8. HEADLAMP AUTO CONTROL AMBIENT LIGHT SENSOR
9. SMALL FLAT—BLADED TOOL

91046G07

Fig. 102 Instrument panel upper trim panel mounting—1992–98 Seville and Eldorado

Gauges

REMOVAL & INSTALLATION

Deville and Fleetwood

▶ **See Figures 103, 104 and 105**

1. Disconnect the negative battery cable.
2. Remove the upper trim pad as follows:
   a. Carefully pry out the A/C outlets.
   b. Remove one screw from behind each outlet and 3 screws through the defroster outlet.
   c. Remove the glove box module retaining screws. Detach the wiring connectors from the switches and light and remove the glove box module.
   d. Remove 2 screws working through the glove box opening.
   e. Detach the in-vehicle temperature sensor electrical connector and aspirator tube.
   f. If equipped, remove the solar sensor from the trim pad.
   g. Remove the upper trim pad.
3. Remove the 2 screws and the plate.
4. Remove the instrument cluster attaching screws.
5. Label and detach the wiring connectors.
6. Remove the shift indicator cable clip and remove the instrument cluster.
   To install:
7. Position the instrument cluster and attach the electrical connectors.
8. Install the attaching screws and tighten to 13 inch lbs. (1.5 Nm).
9. Install the plate with the 2 screws.
10. Install the upper trim pad in the reverse order of removal.
11. Install the shift indicator cable clip and adjust the shift indicator as follows:
    a. Position and release the shift lever in the **N** gate notch.

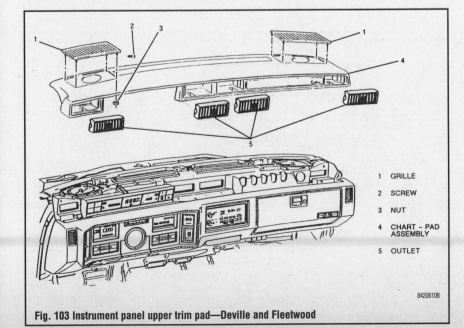

1	GRILLE
2	SCREW
3	NUT
4	CHART - PAD ASSEMBLY
5	OUTLET

84206108

Fig. 103 Instrument panel upper trim pad—Deville and Fleetwood

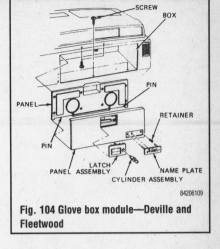

84206109

Fig. 104 Glove box module—Deville and Fleetwood

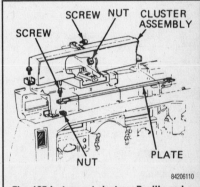

84206110

Fig. 105 Instrument cluster—Deville and Fleetwood

b. Move the clip on the edge of the shift bowl to center the pointer on **N**.
c. Push the clip onto the bowl. Make sure the cable rests on the bowl, not on the column jacket. Make sure the clip is tight on the bowl and does not slip.
d. Move the shift lever through all positions and then back to
to check adjustment. Make sure the pointer covers a portion of each graphic.

Eldorado and Seville

1990–91 MODELS

▶ **See Figures 106 and 107**

1. Disconnect the negative battery cable.
2. Remove the instrument cluster trim plate as follows:
   a. Remove the left side A/C vent.
   b. Remove the radio trim plate.
   c. Remove the retaining screws and the trim plate.
3. Remove the screws and the filter lens.
4. Remove the 2 screws and the telltale warning lamp lens.
5. Remove the trip odometer reset button.
6. Remove the 2 instrument cluster retaining screws and remove the cluster.
   To install:
7. Align the instrument cluster with the electrical connectors and push the cluster into the instrument panel. Install the 2 retaining screws.

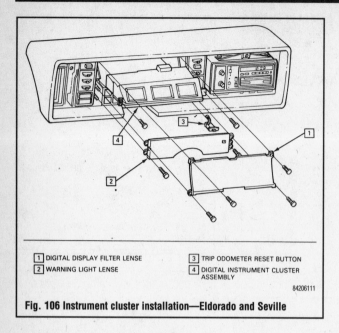

DIGITAL DISPLAY FILTER LENSE 3 TRIP ODOMETER RESET BUTTON
2 WARNING LIGHT LENSE 4 DIGITAL INSTRUMENT CLUSTER ASSEMBLY

84206111

Fig. 106 Instrument cluster installation—Eldorado and Seville

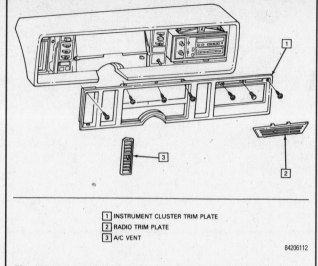

1 INSTRUMENT CLUSTER TRIM PLATE
2 RADIO TRIM PLATE
3 A/C VENT

84206112

Fig. 107 Instrument cluster trim plate installation—Eldorado and Seville

8. Install the trip odometer reset button.
9. Install the telltale warning lamp lens and the filter lens.
10. Install the instrument cluster trim plate in the reverse order of removal.
11. Connect the negative battery cable.

1992–98 MODELS

▶ See Figures 108 and 109

1. Disconnect the negative battery cable.
2. Pull fuses A5-IPC (Ignition) and B5-IPC (Battery) from the rear compartment fuse panel and fuse A3-IGN1 from the engine compartment fuse panel.
3. Remove the instrument panel upper trim panel as follows:
   a. Use a small flat-bladed tool to pry up the defroster grille.
   b. Remove the Sunload and Headlamp Auto Control sensors from the defroster grille.
   c. Remove the 3 screws retaining the upper trim panel through the defroster grille opening.
   d. Remove the A/C vents from the front of the instrument panel by releasing the tab on each side from the inside vent and pulling out.
   e. Working through the vent openings, remove the 4 screws retaining the upper trim panel.
   f. Remove the upper trim panel.
4. Detach the 2 electrical connectors on top of the instrument cluster.
5. Remove the 4 cluster-to-instrument panel retaining screws.
6. Raise the cluster. If equipped with digital cluster, remove the 2 screws securing the PRNDL mechanism.
7. Remove the instrument cluster.
   To install:
8. Position the cluster to the instrument panel. Make sure the analog needles are positioned at zero.
9. If equipped with digital cluster, install the 2 screws securing the PRNDL mechanism.
10. Install the 4 cluster-to-instrument panel retaining screws.
11. Attach the electrical connectors to the top of the cluster.

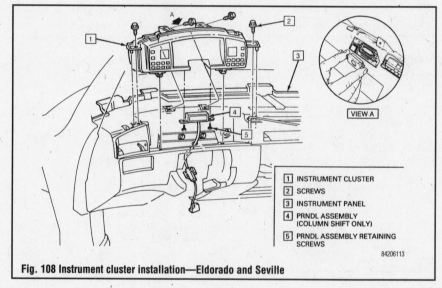

1 INSTRUMENT CLUSTER
2 SCREWS
3 INSTRUMENT PANEL
4 PRNDL ASSEMBLY (COLUMN SHIFT ONLY)
5 PRNDL ASSEMBLY RETAINING SCREWS

84206113

Fig. 108 Instrument cluster installation—Eldorado and Seville

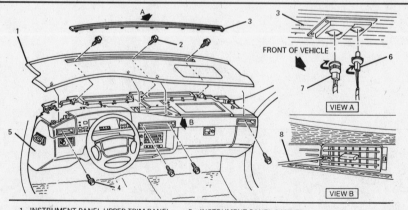

1 INSTRUMENT PANEL UPPER TRIM PANEL
2 SCREWS
3 WINDSHIELD DEFROSTER GRILLE
4 SCREWS
5 INSTRUMENT PANEL CARRIER
6 SUNLOAD SENSOR
7 HEADLAMP AUTO CONTROL AMBIENT LIGHT SENSOR
8 SMALL FLAT-BLADED TOOL

84206114

Fig. 109 Instrument panel upper trim panel installation—Eldorado and Seville

12. Install the instrument panel upper trim panel in the reverse order of removal.
13. Install the fuses in the fuse panel.
14. Connect the negative battery cable.
15. If necessary, adjust the shift indicator.

Windshield Wiper Switch

REMOVAL & INSTALLATION

Eldorado and Seville

▶ **See Figure 110**

➡**Windshield wiper control is a function of the Combination Switch on all other vehicles.**

1. Disconnect the negative battery cable.
2. Make sure all switches on the switch module are **OFF**.
3. Remove the instrument cluster trim plate as follows:
   a. Remove the left side A/C vent.
   b. Remove the radio trim plate.
   c. Remove the retaining screws and the trim plate.
4. Remove the 2 retaining screws and pull the switch module out of the electrical connectors in the instrument cluster.
5. Installation is the reverse of the removal procedure.

Headlight Switch

REMOVAL & INSTALLATION

Deville and Fleetwood

▶ **See Figures 111 thru 116**

1. Disconnect the negative battery cable.
2. Remove the instrument panel trim plates as follows:
   a. On 1990–91 vehicles, remove the right and left sound insulators and snap out the upper steering column filler panel.
   b. Remove the lower steering column filler panel.
   c. Remove the screws from the tops of the trim plates and remove the left and right trim plates.
   d. Unscrew the screws at the bottom of the center trim plate and remove the trim plate.
3. Remove the switch retaining screws and detach the electrical connector.
4. Remove the knob and bezel from the switch.

To install:
5. Installation is the reverse of the removal procedure. Tighten the switch screws to 13 inch lbs. (1.5 Nm).

Eldorado and Seville

1990–91 MODELS

▶ **See Figure 117**

1. Disconnect the negative battery cable.
2. Make sure all switches on the switch module are **OFF**.
3. Remove the instrument cluster trim plate as follows:
   a. Remove the left side A/C vent.
   b. Remove the radio trim plate.
   c. Remove the retaining screws and the trim plate.
4. Remove the 2 retaining screws and pull the switch module out of the electrical connectors in the instrument cluster.

To install:
5. Installation is the reverse of the removal procedure.

1992–98 MODELS

▶ **See Figure 118**

1. Disconnect the negative battery cable.
2. Firmly pull outward on the headlight switch knob to remove the switch module from the instrument panel.
3. Detach the electrical connector and remove the switch.

To install:
4. The installation is the reverse of removal.

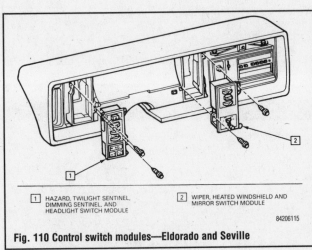

Fig. 110 Control switch modules—Eldorado and Seville

1 HAZARD, TWILIGHT SENTINEL, DIMMING SENTINEL, AND HEADLIGHT SWITCH MODULE	2 WIPER, HEATED WINDSHIELD AND MIRROR SWITCH MODULE

84206115

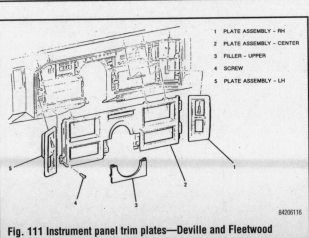

1 PLATE ASSEMBLY – RH
2 PLATE ASSEMBLY – CENTER
3 FILLER – UPPER
4 SCREW
5 PLATE ASSEMBLY – LH

84206116

Fig. 111 Instrument panel trim plates—Deville and Fleetwood

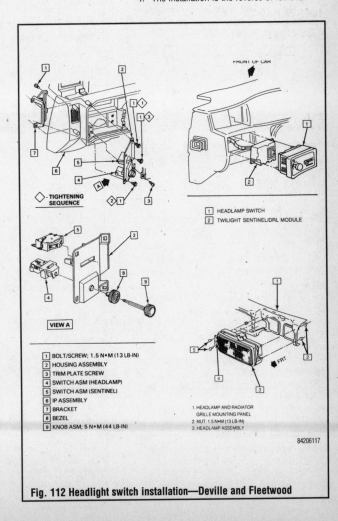

◇ - TIGHTENING SEQUENCE

VIEW A

1 BOLT/SCREW; 1.5 N•M (13 LB-IN)
2 HOUSING ASSEMBLY
3 TRIM PLATE SCREW
4 SWITCH ASM (HEADLAMP)
5 SWITCH ASM (SENTINEL)
6 IP ASSEMBLY
7 BRACKET
8 BEZEL
9 KNOB ASM; 5 N•M (44 LB-IN)

1 HEADLAMP SWITCH	2 TWILIGHT SENTINEL/DRL MODULE

1. HEADLAMP AND RADIATOR GRILLE MOUNTING PANEL
2. NUT; 1.5 N•M (13 LB-IN)
3. HEADLAMP ASSEMBLY

84206117

Fig. 112 Headlight switch installation—Deville and Fleetwood

Fig. 113 Pop out the headlight switch module

Fig. 114 Detach the electrical connector from the back of the module

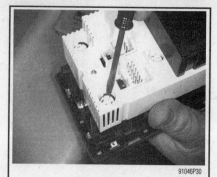

Fig. 115 A small screwdriver and a simple twist . . .

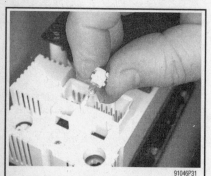

Fig. 116 . . . will allow the replacement of the small bulb that illuminates the switch assembly

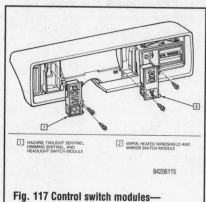

1 HAZARD, TWILIGHT SENTINEL, DIMMING SENTINEL, AND HEADLIGHT SWITCH MODULE

2 WIPER, HEATED WINDSHIELD AND MIRROR SWITCH MODULE

84206115

Fig. 117 Control switch modules— 1990–91 Eldorado and Seville

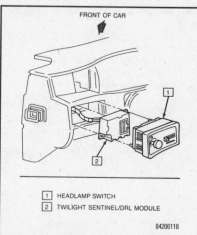

FRONT OF CAR

1 HEADLAMP SWITCH
2 TWILIGHT SENTINEL/DRL MODULE

84206118

Fig. 118 Headlight switch—1992–93 Eldorado and Seville

LIGHTING

Headlights

REMOVAL & INSTALLATION

1990 Models

▶ See Figure 119

1. Make sure the headlight switch is **OFF**.
2. Remove the front cornering/side marker lamps.
3. Remove the 2 rear headlight assembly nuts.
4. Detach the wiring connectors from the headlight bulbs.
5. Remove the 2 screws through the grille and remove the headlight assembly.
6. Detach the lamp monitor connections from the headlight assembly.
7. If necessary, remove the headlight bulbs.
To install:
8. Install the bulbs in the headlight assembly.
9. Connect the lamp monitor connections.
10. Position the headlight assembly and install the 2 screws through the grille. Tighten to 13 inch lbs. (1.5 Nm).

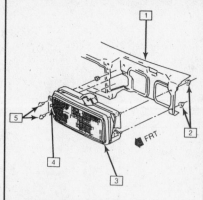

1. HEADLAMP AND RADIATOR GRILLE MOUNTING PANEL
2. NUT: 1.5 N•M (13 LB-IN)
3. HEADLAMP ASSEMBLY
4. GUIDE PIN HOLE
5. BOLT/SCREW: 1.5 N•M (13 LB-IN)

84206119

Fig. 119 Headlight installation—1990 Deville and Fleetwood

11. Attach the wiring connectors to the headlight bulbs.
12. Install the 2 headlight assembly nuts and tighten to 13 inch lbs. (1.5 Nm).
13. Install the front cornering/side marker lamps.
14. Check the headlight aim.

1991–98 Models

▶ See Figures 120, 121, 122 and 123

1. Make sure the headlight switch is **OFF**.
2. Remove the thumbscrews.
3. Pull out the headlight assembly and detach the wiring connectors from the headlight bulbs.
4. If necessary, remove the bulbs from the headlight assembly.
5. Disconnect the lamp monitor fiber optic cable.
To install:
6. Connect the lamp monitor fiber optic cable.
7. Install the bulbs in the headlight assembly.
8. Attach the wiring connectors to the headlight bulbs.
9. Position the headlight assembly and install the thumbscrews.
10. Check the headlight aim.

Fig. 120 Lift this cover to service the lamp

Fig. 121 It is difficult to extricate the bulb from the housing, but it can be done. This shows the two-finger method. A slight twist and the bulb/socket assembly is removed

Fig. 122 The halogen bulb assembly is very compact. This one is a right angle application

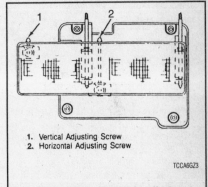

Fig. 123 Unplug the bulb/socket and replace the entire assembly

AIMING THE HEADLIGHTS

◆ **See Figures 124, 125, 126 and 127**

The headlights must be properly aimed to provide the best, safest road illumination. The lights should be checked for proper aim and adjusted as necessary. Certain state and local authorities have requirements for headlight aiming; these should be checked before adjustment is made.

✳✳ CAUTION

About once a year, when the headlights are replaced or any time front end work is per-

formed on your vehicle, the headlight should be accurately aimed by a reputable repair shop using the proper equipment. Headlights not properly aimed can make it virtually impossible to see and may blind other drivers on the road, possibly causing an accident. Note that the following procedure is a temporary fix, until you can take your vehicle to a repair shop for a proper adjustment.

Headlight adjustment may be temporarily made using a wall, as described below, or on the rear of another vehicle. When adjusted, the lights should

not glare in oncoming car or truck windshields, nor should they illuminate the passenger compartment of vehicles driving in front of you. These adjustments are rough and should always be fine-tuned by a repair shop that is equipped with headlight aiming tools. Improper adjustments may be both dangerous and illegal.

For most of the vehicles covered by this manual, horizontal and vertical aiming of each sealed beam unit is provided by two adjusting screws which move the retaining ring and adjusting plate against the tension of a coil spring. There is no adjustment for focus; this is done during headlight manufacturing.

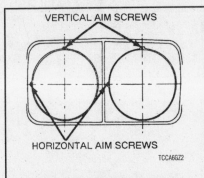

Fig. 124 Dual headlight adjustment screw locations—one side shown here (other side should be mirror image)

1. Vertical Adjusting Screw
2. Horizontal Adjusting Screw

Fig. 125 Example of headlight adjustment screw location for composite headlamps

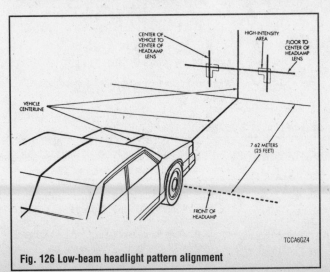

Fig. 126 Low-beam headlight pattern alignment

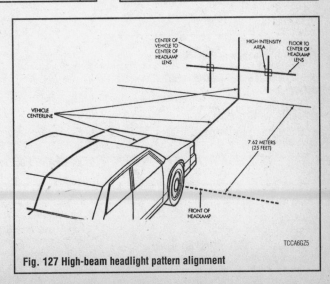

Fig. 127 High-beam headlight pattern alignment

➡Because the composite headlight assembly is bolted into position, no adjustment should be necessary or possible. Some applications, however, may be bolted to an adjuster plate or may be retained by adjusting screws. If so, follow this procedure when adjusting the lights, BUT always have the adjustment checked by a reputable shop.

Before removing the headlight bulb or disturbing the headlamp in any way, note the current settings in order to ease headlight adjustment upon reassembly. If the high or low beam setting of the old lamp still works, this can be done using the wall of a garage or a building:

1. Park the vehicle on a level surface, with the fuel tank about ½ full and with the vehicle empty of all extra cargo (unless normally carried). The vehicle should be facing a wall that is no less than 6 feet (1.8m) high and 12 feet (3.7m) wide. The front of the vehicle should be about 25 feet from the wall.

2. If aiming is to be performed outdoors, it is advisable to wait until dusk in order to properly see the headlight beams on the wall. If done in a garage, darken the area around the wall as much as possible by closing shades or hanging cloth over the windows.

3. Turn the headlights **ON** and mark the wall at the center of each light's low beam, then switch on the bright lights and mark the center of each light's high beam. A short length of masking tape that is visible from the front of the vehicle may be used. Although marking all four positions is advisable, marking one position from each light should be sufficient.

4. If neither beam on one side is working, and if another like-sized vehicle is available, park the second one in the exact spot where the vehicle was and mark the beams using the same-side light. Then switch the vehicles so the one to be aimed is back in the original spot. It must be parked no closer to or farther away from the wall than the second vehicle.

5. Perform any necessary repairs, but make sure the vehicle is not moved, or is returned to the exact spot from which the lights were marked. Turn the headlights **ON** and adjust the beams to match the marks on the wall.

6. Have the headlight adjustment checked as soon as possible by a reputable repairs shop.

Signal and Marker Lights

REMOVAL & INSTALLATION

Front Turn Signal and Parking Lights

DEVILLE AND FLEETWOOD— EARLY MODELS

▶ See Figures 128 and 129

1. Disconnect the lamp monitor fiber optic cable.
2. Remove the retaining nut, then pry the inner release tab upward, and push the assembly forward.
3. Remove the bulb and socket from the lamp assembly.
4. If replacing the bulb, remove the bulb from the socket.

To install:

5. Installation is the reverse of the removal procedure. Tighten the nut to 13 inch lbs. (1.5 Nm).

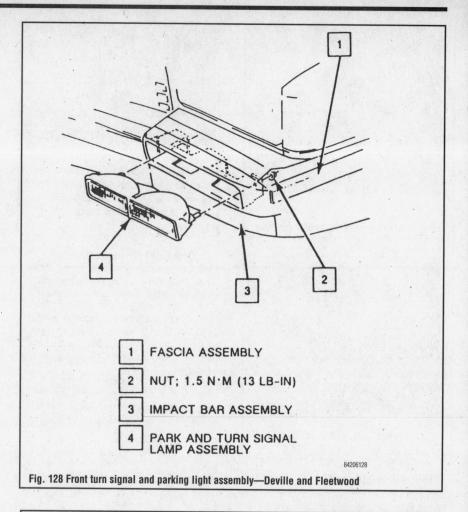

1	FASCIA ASSEMBLY
2	NUT; 1.5 N·M (13 LB-IN)
3	IMPACT BAR ASSEMBLY
4	PARK AND TURN SIGNAL LAMP ASSEMBLY

84206128

Fig. 128 Front turn signal and parking light assembly—Deville and Fleetwood

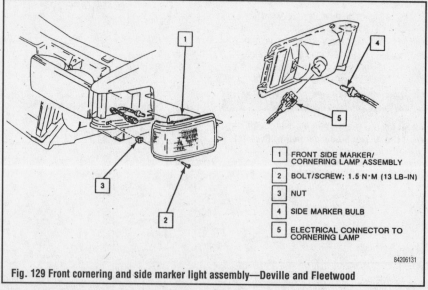

1	FRONT SIDE MARKER/ CORNERING LAMP ASSEMBLY
2	BOLT/SCREW; 1.5 N·M (13 LB-IN)
3	NUT
4	SIDE MARKER BULB
5	ELECTRICAL CONNECTOR TO CORNERING LAMP

84206131

Fig. 129 Front cornering and side marker light assembly—Deville and Fleetwood

DEVILLE AND FLEETWOOD— LATE MODELS

▶ See Figures 130, 131, 132, 133 and 134

1. Remove the screw retaining the lamp assembly.
2. Remove the lamp.
3. Remove the sockets and the bulbs from the lamp as necessary.

To install:

4. Install the sockets and bulbs to the lamp assembly.
5. Secure the lamp to the vehicle, using the retaining screw. Tighten the screws to 13 inch lbs. (1.5 Nm).
6. Align the cornering lamp with the headlamp leaving only 5/64 inch (2 mm) between them.

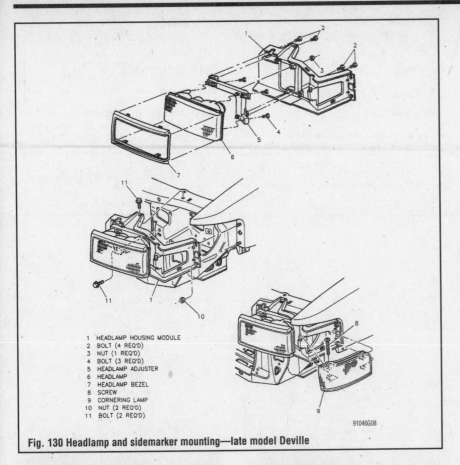

Fig. 130 Headlamp and sidemarker mounting—late model Deville

```
1   HEADLAMP HOUSING MODULE
2   BOLT (4 REQ'D)
3   NUT (1 REQ'D)
4   BOLT (3 REQ'D)
5   HEADLAMP ADJUSTER
6   HEADLAMP
7   HEADLAMP BEZEL
8   SCREW
9   CORNERING LAMP
10  NUT (2 REQ'D)
11  BOLT (2 REQ'D)
```

91046G08

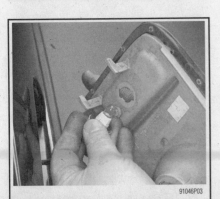

Fig. 131 Remove the retainer, and pull the front of the lamp assembly out first, then slightly forward to disengage the tabs

91046P01

Fig. 132 Detach the electrical connector on the back of the lamp assembly

91046P02

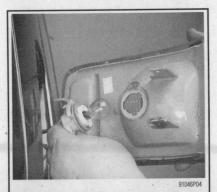

Fig. 133 Removing the sidemarker bulb requires a simple twist of the socket

91046P03

Fig. 134 To remove the turn signal bulb also requires a simple twist

91046P04

ELDORADO AND SEVILLE

▶ See Figures 135 and 136

1. On Eldorado, remove the upper filler panel.
2. Remove the bolt on Eldorado or the clip on Seville that retains the lamp assembly.
3. Remove the lamp assembly.
4. Remove the socket and bulb from the lamp assembly.

To install:

5. Installation is the reverse of the removal procedure.

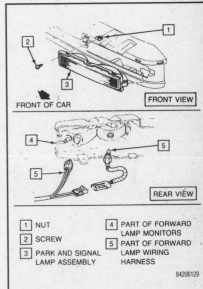

FRONT OF CAR

FRONT VIEW

REAR VIEW

```
1   NUT                       4   PART OF FORWARD
2   SCREW                         LAMP MONITORS
3   PARK AND SIGNAL           5   PART OF FORWARD
    LAMP ASSEMBLY                 LAMP WIRING
                                  HARNESS
```

84206129

Fig. 135 Front turn signal and parking light assembly—1990–91 Eldorado and Seville

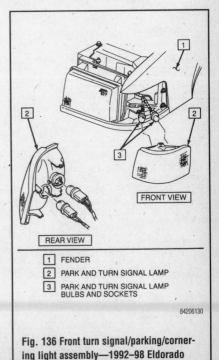

FRONT VIEW

REAR VIEW

```
1   FENDER
2   PARK AND TURN SIGNAL LAMP
3   PARK AND TURN SIGNAL LAMP
    BULBS AND SOCKETS
```

84206130

Fig. 136 Front turn signal/parking/cornering light assembly—1992–98 Eldorado and Seville

Front Cornering and Side Marker Lights

ELDORADO AND SEVILLE

▶ See Figures 138 and 139

➡The following procedure is for the front side marker light. The cornering light on these vehicles is part of the front turn signal and parking light assembly.

1. Remove the lamp assembly retaining screws and remove the lamp assembly from the bumper fascia.
2. Remove the socket and bulb from the lamp assembly.

To install:
3. Installation is the reverse of the removal procedure.

Side Marker Light

DEVILLE AND FLEETWOOD

▶ See Figure 140

1. Remove the inner trunk panel.
2. Remove the bulb and socket assembly and remove the bulb from the socket.
3. Remove the lamp assembly retaining nuts and remove the rear side marker lamp assembly.

To install:
4. Installation is the reverse of the removal procedure.

1992–98 ELDORADO

▶ See Figure 140

1. Remove the lamp assembly retaining screws.
2. Remove the socket from the lamp assembly and remove the bulb from the socket.
3. Remove the lamp assembly.

To install:
4. Installation is the reverse of the removal procedure.

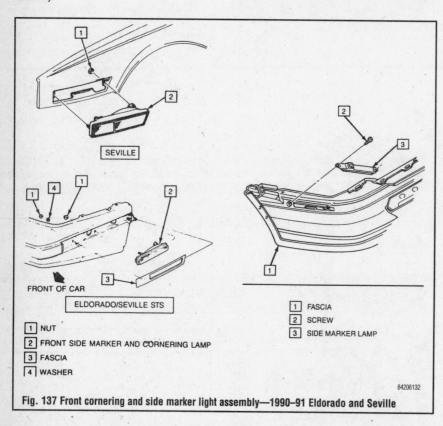

1	NUT
2	FRONT SIDE MARKER AND CORNERING LAMP
3	FASCIA
4	WASHER

84206132

Fig. 137 Front cornering and side marker light assembly—1990–91 Eldorado and Seville

1	FASCIA
2	SCREW
3	SIDE MARKER LAMP

Fig. 139 Rear side marker light assembly—Deville and Fleetwood

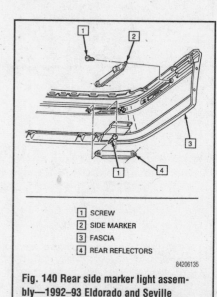

1	SCREW
2	SIDE MARKER
3	FASCIA
4	REAR REFLECTORS

84206135

Fig. 140 Rear side marker light assembly—1992–93 Eldorado and Seville

Rear Turn Signal, Brake, and Parking Lights

DEVILLE AND FLEETWOOD

▶ See Figures 141 thru 146

1. Remove the retaining screws and the bezel.
2. Remove the lamp assembly.
3. Remove the socket from the lamp assembly and remove the bulb from the socket.
4. Disconnect the lamp monitor fiber optic cable and remove the lamp assembly.

To install:
5. Installation is the reverse of the removal procedure. Tighten the screws to 13 inch lbs. (1.5 Nm).

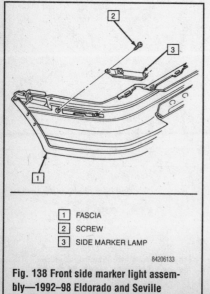

1	FASCIA
2	SCREW
3	SIDE MARKER LAMP

84206133

Fig. 138 Front side marker light assembly—1992–98 Eldorado and Seville

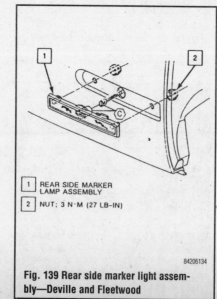

1	REAR SIDE MARKER LAMP ASSEMBLY
2	NUT; 3 N·M (27 LB-IN)

84206134

Fig. 139 Rear side marker light assembly—Deville and Fleetwood

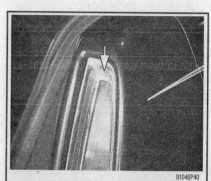

91046P40

Fig. 141 Location of the retaining screw on the taillamp assembly—late model Deville

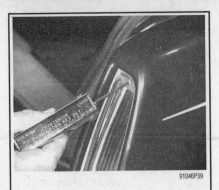

Fig. 142 A Torx® driver is necessary to remove the screw

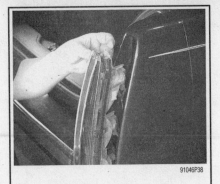

Fig. 143 Pull the lamp assembly gently away from the body cavity

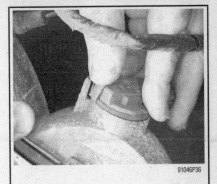

Fig. 144 Depress the tab and give a slight twist . . .

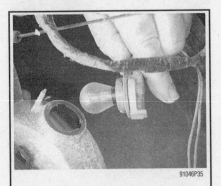

Fig. 145 . . . to facilitate removal of the socket/bulb from the tail light assembly

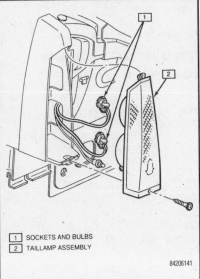

| 1 | SOCKETS AND BULBS |
| 2 | TAILLAMP ASSEMBLY |

84206141

Fig. 147 Rear turn signal, brake and parking light assembly—early model Eldorado

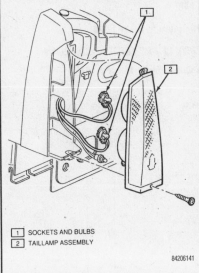

1	NUT
2	TAILLAMP ASSEMBLY
3	FILLER PANEL EXTENSION
4	SIDE MARKER BULB
5	CONNECTOR

84206144

Fig. 148 Rear turn signal, brake and parking light assembly—late model Eldorado

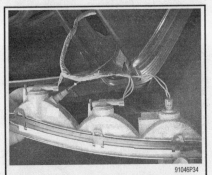

Fig. 146 The reverse, taillamp, and brake bulbs are all accessible on the taillamp assembly

1990–91 ELDORADO

▶ See Figure 147

1. Remove the lamp assembly retaining screw.
2. Pull the bottom of the lamp assembly out and down.
3. Remove the bulb sockets from the lamp and remove the bulbs from the sockets.
4. If equipped, detach the fiber optic connector.
5. Remove the lamp assembly.

To install:

6. Installation is the reverse of the removal procedure.

1992–98 ELDORADO

▶ See Figure 148

1. Remove the rear compartment trim.
2. Remove the lamp assembly retaining nuts.
3. Remove the bulb sockets from the lamp assembly and remove the bulbs from the sockets.
4. Remove the lamp assembly.

To install:

5. Installation is the reverse of the removal procedure.

1990–91 SEVILLE

▶ See Figures 149 and 150

1. Open the trunk lid and remove the rear compartment trim to gain access to the lamp assembly retaining nuts.
2. Remove the retaining nuts and pull the lamp assembly out.
3. Remove the bulb sockets and detach the fiber optic connector.
4. Remove the bulbs from the sockets.
5. Remove the lamp assembly.

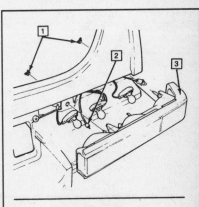

1	WING NUTS
2	FIBER OPTIC CONDUCTOR
3	COMBINATION LAMP ASSEMBLY

84206142

Fig. 149 Rear turn signal, brake and parking light assembly—early model Seville

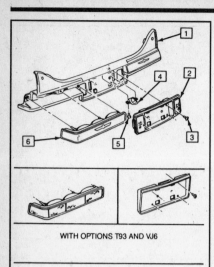

WITH OPTIONS T93 AND VJ6

1	REAR END FINISH PANEL
2	LICENSE PLATE POCKET
3	SCREW
4	LAMP ASSEMBLY
5	SCREW
6	TAIL LAMP

84206143

Fig. 150 Rear turn signal, brake and parking light assembly and license plate pocket—1991 Seville

To install:
6. Installation is the reverse of the removal procedure.

1992–98 SEVILLE

▶ **See Figures 151 and 152**

1. Open the trunk lid.
2. Remove the rear compartment trim to gain access to the quarter mounted lamp assembly retaining nuts.
3. Remove the lamp assembly-to-quarter panel nuts and the lamps assembly-to-trunk lid nuts and push pins.
4. Remove the bulb sockets from the lamp assemblies and remove the bulbs from the sockets.
5. Remove the lamp assemblies.

To install:
6. Installation is the reverse of the removal procedure.

High-mount Brake Light

DEVILLE AND FLEETWOOD SEDAN

▶ **See Figures 153 and 154**

1. Pry up the carpet trimmed cover from the center high mounted stop lamp.
2. Remove the retaining screw.
3. Pull the stoplamp toward the front of the vehicle and up to disengage the retainers

4. Unplug the electrical connectors.
5. Remove the stop lamp.
To install:
6. Attach the stop lamp to the assembly.
7. Plug in the electrical connectors.
8. Engage the stop lamp to the retaining holes in the rear shelf panel.
9. Tighten the retaining screw to 18 inch lbs. (2 Nm).
10. Install the center high mounted stop lamp cover.

DEVILLE AND FLEETWOOD COUPE

1. Remove the 2 screws from the base of the assembly.

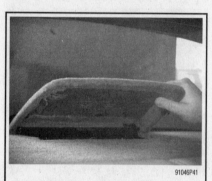

91046P41

Fig. 153 Lift the carpet trimmed cover

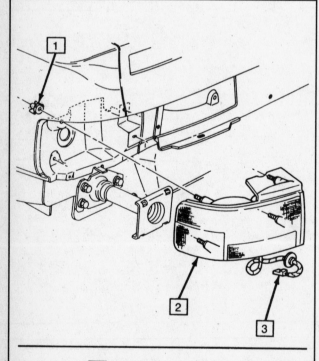

1	NUT
2	TAIL LAMP ASSEMBLY
3	CONNECTOR

84206145

Fig. 151 Quarter mounted rear turn signal, brake and parking light

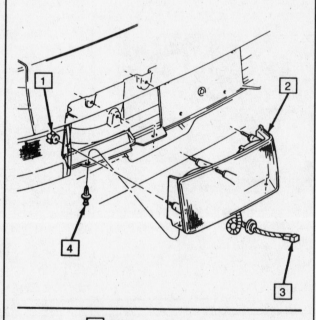

1	NUT
2	TAIL LAMP ASSEMBLY
3	CONNECTOR
4	PUSH PIN

84206146

Fig. 152 Trunk lid mounted rear turn signal, brake and parking light

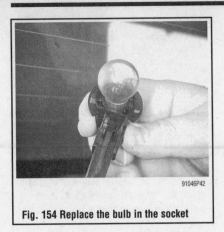

Fig. 154 Replace the bulb in the socket

2. Remove the bulb and socket assembly and remove the bulb.
3. Remove the lamp assembly.
To install:
4. Installation is the reverse of the removal procedure.

ELDORADO AND SEVILLE—EARLY MODELS

▶ **See Figure 155**

1. Remove the 2 lamp assembly retaining screws.
2. Detach the wiring connector and remove the lamp assembly.
3. Remove the bulb from the lamp assembly.
To install:
4. Installation is the reverse of the removal procedure.

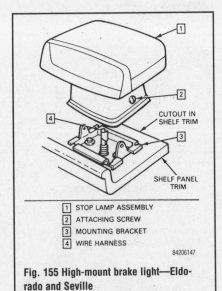

1	STOP LAMP ASSEMBLY
2	ATTACHING SCREW
3	MOUNTING BRACKET
4	WIRE HARNESS

Fig. 155 High-mount brake light—Eldorado and Seville

ELDORADO—LATE MODEL

▶ **See Figure 156**

1. Pry up the carpet trimmed cover from the lamp assembly.
2. Pull the lamp assembly toward the front of the vehicle and up to disengage the retainers.
3. Detach the wiring connectors and remove the lamp assembly.

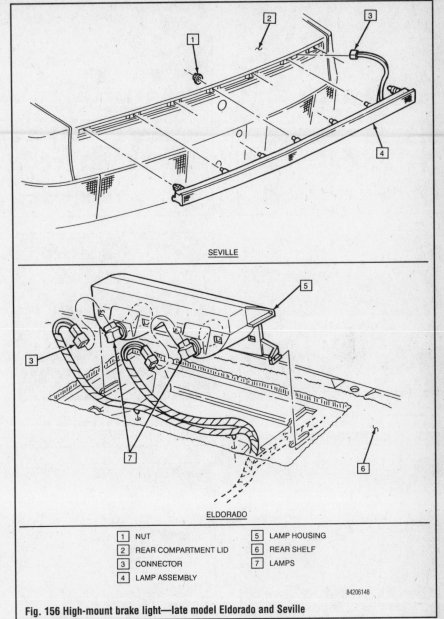

1	NUT	5	LAMP HOUSING
2	REAR COMPARTMENT LID	6	REAR SHELF
3	CONNECTOR	7	LAMPS
4	LAMP ASSEMBLY		

Fig. 156 High-mount brake light—late model Eldorado and Seville

To install:
4. Installation is the reverse of the removal procedure.

SEVILLE—LATE MODEL

1. Open the trunk lid.
2. Remove the trunk lid carpet trim.
3. Remove the lamp assembly retaining nuts.
4. Detach the wiring connector and remove the lamp assembly.
To install:
5. Installation is the reverse of the removal procedure.

Dome Light

▶ **See Figures 157, 158, 159 and 160**

1. Using a small flat bladed tool, remove the lamp cover.

2. Carefully pull the bulb down out of the receptacle, one side at a time.
To install:
3. Snap a new bulb into the holders.
4. Install the cover by snapping it in and pushing it to the seat.

License Plate Lights

▶ **See Figures 161 thru 166**

1. Open the rear compartment lid.
2. Remove the rear compartment lid trim.
3. Pull back on the rear compartment trim panel.
4. Unplug the lamp connector from the rear compartment lid wiring harness.
5. Press the grommet out of the rear compartment lid.
6. Remove the nuts retaining the lamp assembly to the rear compartment lid.
7. Remove the bulb.

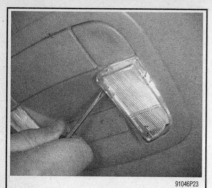

Fig. 157 Use a small tool to pry off the lamp cover

Fig. 158 Remove the bulb one side at a time

Fig. 159 Install the new bulb by snapping it into the holder. Handle the bulb carefully; it will heat up quickly and could burn you

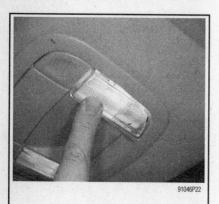

Fig. 160 Snap the cover back into place

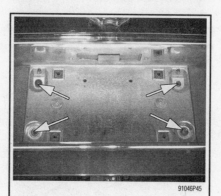

Fig. 161 Remove these four screws on the outside

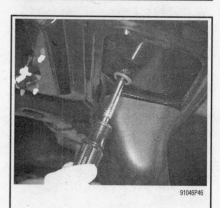

Fig. 162 Remove the inside fasteners

Fig. 163 Carefully disengage the assembly from the compartment. The bulbs are accessible from the rear

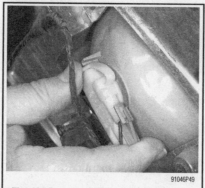

Fig. 164 Squeeze the tab and twist the socket

Fig. 165 Pull the socket assembly out to change the bulb

To install:
8. Installation is the reversal of the removal procedure.

Fog/Driving Lights

REMOVAL & INSTALLATION

Eldorado

1. Unplug the fog lamp socket connector.
2. Remove the two lamps to bracket bolts (Eldorado) or nuts (STS).

➡️It may be necessary to loosen the mounting bracket bolts to remove the lamp.

3. Remove the fog lamp
To install:
4. Connect the fog lamp to the vehicle.
5. Install the two lamps to bracket bolts (Eldorado) or nuts (STS).
6. Plug in the fog lamp socket connector.

Seville

1. Remove the front air deflector.
2. Detach the fog lamp connector from the fog lamp.

Fig. 166 The back-up and license plate bulbs are housed in this assembly

3. Remove the nuts retaining the fog lamp to the fog lamp bracket.

4. Remove the fog lamp.

➡ **If the fog lamp bracket requires replacement, remove the front bumper fascia.**

5. Remove the nuts retaining the fog lamp.

6. Remove the fog lamp bracket

To install:

7. Install the fog lamp bracket.

8. Install the nuts to retain the fog lamp bracket to the front impact bar.

9. Tighten the fog lamp bracket mounting nuts to 80 inch lbs. (9 Nm).

Instrument Cluster Bulbs
Anti-Lock 194
Brake 194
Coolant Temp 194
Fasten Belts 194
Inflatable Restraint 194
Charge 194
Service Vehicle Soon 194
Service Engine Soon 194
Oil 194
Stop Engine Temp 194
Turn Signal 194
PRNDL Illumination 161
Cluster Illumination 161
Fuel Data Center Illumination 194
High Beam 161
Right Information Center Bulbs
Service Air Cond PC168
Trunk PC168
Left Information Center Bulbs
Washer Fluid PC161
Security PC194
Interior Bulbs
Ash Tray 1445
Center High-Mounted Stop Lamp
  2 Door 1156
Center High-Mounted Stop Lamp
  4 Door 1141
Courtesy - Rear Sail Panel 562
Reading - Rear Sail Panel 561

Door Courtesy Lights 562
Door Warning Lights 168
Courtesy/Maplight with Astro Roof 562
Courtesy/Maplight without Astro
Roof 906
Vanity Mirrors - Front 124
Vanity Mirrors - Rear 74
Cruise Control Switch
  Illumination 194
Cruise Control Switch
  "ON" Indicator 161
Cruise Control Switch
  "Engaged" Indicator 161
IP Compartment 194
Illuminated Entry - Door Key 194
Exterior Bulbs
Backup 3057
Cornering 881
Headlamps
  High Beam 9005
  Low Beam 9006
License 194
Luggage Compartment 1003
Parking - Front 194NA
Parking - Rear 194
Park/Turn - Front 2057NA
Side Marker - Front 194
Side Marker - Rear 194
Tail Stop Turn 3057
Underhood 1003

84206154

Light bulb application chart—1990 Deville and Fleetwood

Instrument Cluster Bulbs
Antilock 194
Brake 194
Coolant Temp 194
Fasten Belts 194
Inflatable Restraint 194
Charge 194
Service Vehicle Soon 194
Service Engine Soon 194
Oil 194
Stop Engine Temp 194
Turn Signal 194
PRNDL Illumination 161
Cluster Illumination 161
Fuel Data Center Illumination 194
High Beam 161
Right Information Center Bulbs
Service Air Cond PC168
Trunk PC168
Left Information Center Bulbs
Washer Fluid PC161
Security PC194
Interior Bulbs
Ash Tray 1445
Center High-Mounted Stoplamp 2 Door 1156
Center High-Mounted Stoplamp 4 Door 1141
Courtesy - Rear Sail Panel 562

Reading - Rear Sail Panel 561
Door Courtesy Lights 12864
Door Warning Lights 12864
Courtesy/Map Light with Astro Roof 562
Courtesy/Map Light without Astro Roof 906
Vanity Mirrors - Front 124
Vanity Mirrors - Rear 74
Cruise Control Switch Illumination 194
Cruise Control Switch ON" Indicator 161
Cruise Control Switch "Engaged" Indicator 161
IP Compartment 194
Illuminated Entry - Door Key 194
Exterior Bulbs
Backup 3057
Cornering 881
Headlamps
  High Beam 9005
  Low Beam 9006
License 194
Luggage Compartment 93
Parking - Front 194NA
Parking - Rear 194
  Park/Turn - Front 2057NA
Side Marker - Front 194
Side Marker - Rear T24
Tail Stop Turn 3057
Underhood 561

84206155

Light bulb application chart—1991–93 Deville and Fleetwood

BULB	TRADE #
ASHTRAY ILLUMINATION	161
BACKUP LAMP	1156
CCDIC ILLUMINATION	74
CENTER HIGH MOUNT STOPLAMP	1156
CORNERING LAMP	880H
COURTESY LAMPS	
–FLOOR LH	168
–FLOOR RH	89
–DOOR COURTESY (WHT)	563
–DOOR WARNING (RED)	168(K)
	214-2(E)
–REAR COURTESY READ	562
CRUISE CONTROL ILLUM.	194
DOME LAMP	
–WITHOUT SUNROOF	906
–WITH SUNROOF	562
GLOVE BOX ILLUMINATION	194
HEADLAMP	9004H
HEADLAMP SWITCH ILLUMINATION	74/194
ILLUM. ENTRY LOCK CYLINDER	192
INSTRUMENT PANEL TELTALLES	74 194
INSTRUMENT PANEL ILLUMINATION	194
LICENSE PANEL ILLUMINATION	194
MIRROR CONTROL SWITCH ILLUM.	194
PARK/STOP-TURN LAMPS	
–DOUBLE FILAMENT	2057NA
–SINGLE FILAMENT	1156
SIDE MARKER LAMP	194NA
TRIP RESET BUTTON ILLUM.	74
TRUNK ILLUMINATION	1003
UNDERHOOD LAMP	93
VANITY MIRROR ILLUM.	124
WINDS. WIPER SWITCH ILLUM.	194

84206156

Light bulb application chart—1990 Eldorado and Seville

BULB	TRADE #	TO ACCESS BULB
ASHTRAY ILLUMINATION	161	REMOVE FRONT CONSOLE (SEE SECTION 8C)
BACKUP LAMP	2057	REMOVE LICENSE PLATE ASSEMBLY (SEE SECTION 10)
CCDIC ILLUMINATION	74	REMOVE CCDIC (SEE SECTION 8C)
CENTER HIGH MOUNT STOPLAMP (CHMSL)	1156	REMOVE CHMSL (SEE SECTION 10)
CORNERING LAMP	880H	REACH BEHIND BUMPER
COURTESY LAMPS		
– FLOOR – LH	168	PULL FROM SOCKET IN LOWER SOUND INSULATOR
– FLOOR – RH	89	(SEE SECTION 8C)
– DOOR COURTESY (WHT)	563	REMOVE LENS FROM BRACKET
	214-2(E)	
– DOOR WARNING (RED)	168(K)	REMOVE LENS AND BRACKET
	214-2(E)	
– REAR COURTESY/READ	212-2(E)	REMOVE LENS FROM BRACKET
	562	
DOME LAMP		
– WITHOUT SUNROOF	906	REMOVE LENS FROM BRACKET
– WITH SUNROOF	562	REMOVE LENS FROM BRACKET
	212-2(E)	
GLOVE BOX ILLUMINATION	194	REMOVE GLOVE BOX DOOR INNER PANEL (SEE SECTION 8C)
HEADLAMP	9004(H)	REMOVE HEADLAMP ASSEMBLY (SEE SECTION 10)
HEADLAMP INDICATOR	194	REMOVE LEFT SWITCH POD (SEE SECTION 8C)
ILLUMINATION ENTRY LOCK CYLINDER	192	REMOVE DOOR LOCK CYLINDER (SEE SECTION 10)
INSTRUMENT PANEL TELLTALES	76/161	REMOVE INSTRUMENT PANEL CLUSTER (SEE SECTION 8C)
LICENSE PLATE ILLUMINATION	194	REMOVE LICENSE PLATE ASSEMBLY (SEE SECTION 10)
LIGHTS OFF INDICATOR	194	REMOVE LEFT SWITCH POD (SEE SECTION 8C)
MIRROR CONTROL SWITCH ILLUMINATION	194	REMOVE RIGHT SWITCH POD (SEE SECTION 8C)
PARK INDICATOR	194	REMOVE LEFT SWITCH POD (SEE SECTION 8C)
PARK/STOP/TURN LAMP	2057NA	REMOVE LAMP ASSEMBLY (SEE SECTION 10)
PRNDL ILLUMINATION	103	REMOVE FRONT CONSOLE (SEE SECTION 8C)
SIDE MARKER LAMP	194	REACH BEHIND BUMPER
TRIP RESET BUTTON ILLUMINATION	76	REMOVE INSTRUMENT PANEL CLUSTER (SEE SECTION 8C)
TRUNK ILLUMINATION	1004	OPEN TRUNK LID
UNDERHOOD LAMP	93	RAISE HOOD
VANITY MIRROR ILLUMINATION	7065	REMOVE LENS FROM BRACKET
WINDSHIELD WIPER SWITCH ILLUMINATION	194	REMOVE RIGHT SWITCH POD (SEE SECTION 8C)

84206157

Light bulb application chart—1991 Eldorado and Seville

BULB	TRADE #	TO ACCESS BULB
ASHTRAY ILLUMINATION	1445	REMOVE FRONT CONSOLE/ASHTRAY
BACKUP LAMP	2057	REMOVE LICENSE PLATE ASSEMBLY (SEE SECTION 10)
CENTER HIGH MOUNT STOPLAMP (CHMSL)	1141	REMOVE CHMSL (SEE SECTION 10)
CORNERING LAMP	1156	REMOVE COVER OVER HEADLAMP AND REMOVE SOCKET
COURTESY LAMPS		
FLOOR – LH	564	PULL FROM SOCKET IN LOWER SOUND INSULATOR
FLOOR – RH	564	(SEE SECTION 8C)
REAR COURTESY/ READ	168	REMOVE SCREW BY COAT HOOK COVER, SLIDE ASSEMBLY FROM HEADLINER
FRONT COURTESY/ READ	168	REMOVE TRIM PLATE
FRONT FOG LAMP	886	REACH INSIDE BUMPER
GLOVE BOX ILLUMINATION	194	OPEN GLOVE BOX, REMOVE LENS
HEADLAMP COMPOSITE	9005HB3	REMOVE HEADLAMP ASSEMBLY (SEE SECTION 10)
– HI BEAM	9006HB4	REMOVE HEADLAMP ASSEMBLY (SEE SECTION 10)
– LO BEAM	H4	REMOVE HEADLAMP ASSEMBLY (SEE SECTION 10)
– EXPORT	194	REMOVE HEADLAMP ASSEMBLY (SEE SECTION 10)
HEADLAMP SWITCH	BQ245–36210A	REMOVE HEADLAMP SWITCH FROM IP (SEE SECTION 8C)
ILLUMINATION ENTRY LOCK CYLINDER	192	REMOVE DOOR LOCK CYLINDER (SEE SECTION 10)
INSTRUMENT PANEL TELLTALES	194	REMOVE INSTRUMENT PANEL CLUSTER (SEE SECTION 8C)
LICENSE PLATE ILLUMINATION	194	REMOVE LICENSE PLATE ASSEMBLY (SEE SECTION 10)
PARK /TURN/ LAMP (FRONT)	2057	REMOVE LAMP ASSEMBLY (SEE SECTION 10)
PARK/STOP/TURN (REAR)	2057	PULL BACK TRUNK TRIM, REMOVE LAMP ASSEMBLY
PRNDL ILLUMINATION	194	REMOVE FRONT CONSOLE (SEE SECTION 8C)
REAR BLOWER SWITCH	BQ245–35003A	REMOVE SWITCH LEVER HANDLE AND COVER PLATE
REAR FOG/ BACK–UP LIGHT (EXPORT)	P21/5W	(SEE SECTION 10)
STOP/TAIL/TURN SIGNAL (EXPORT)	P21/5W	(SEE SECTION 10)
SIDE MARKER LAMP	194	REACH BEHIND BUMPER
TRUNK ILLUMINATION	561	OPEN TRUNK LID
UNDERHOOD LAMP	561	RAISE HOOD
VANITY MIRROR ILLUMINATION	7065	REMOVE LENS FROM BRACKET

84206158

Light bulb application chart—1992–93 Eldorado and Seville

BULB USAGE AND REPLACEMENT CHART		
BULB	TRADE #	TO ACCESS BULB
ASHTRAY ILLUMINATION	1445	REMOVE FRONT CONSOLE/ASHTRAY
BACKUP LAMP	2057	REMOVE LICENSE PLATE ASSEMBLY
CENTER HIGH MOUNT STOPLAMP (CHMSL)	1141	REMOVE CHMSL
CORNERING LAMP	1156	REMOVE COVER OVER HEADLAMP AND REMOVE SOCKET
COURTESY LAMPS		
FLOOR – LH	564	PULL FROM SOCKET IN LOWER SOUND INSULATOR
FLOOR – RH	564	
REAR COURTESY/ READ	168	REMOVE SCREW BY COAT HOOK COVER, SLIDE ASSEMBLY FROM HEADLINER
FRONT COURTESY/ READ	168	REMOVE TRIM PLATE
FRONT FOG LAMP	886	REACH INSIDE BUMPER
GLOVE BOX ILLUMINATION	194	OPEN GLOVE BOX, REMOVE LENS
HEADLAMP COMPOSITE	9005HB3	REMOVE HEADLAMP ASSEMBLY
– HI BEAM	9006HB4	REMOVE HEADLAMP ASSEMBLY
– LO BEAM	H4	REMOVE HEADLAMP ASSEMBLY
– EXPORT	194	REMOVE HEADLAMP ASSEMBLY
HEADLAMP SWITCH	BQ245–36210A	REMOVE HEADLAMP SWITCH FROM IP
ILLUMINATION ENTRY LOCK CYLINDER	192	REMOVE DOOR LOCK CYLINDER
INSTRUMENT PANEL TELLTALES	194	REMOVE INSTRUMENT PANEL CLUSTER
LICENSE PLATE ILLUMINATION	194	REMOVE LICENSE PLATE ASSEMBLY
PARK /TURN/ LAMP (FRONT)	2057	REMOVE LAMP ASSEMBLY
PARK/STOP/TURN (REAR)	2057	PULL BACK TRUNK TRIM, REMOVE LAMP ASSEMBLY
PRNDL ILLUMINATION	194	REMOVE FRONT CONSOLE
REAR BLOWER SWITCH	BQ245–35003A	REMOVE SWITCH LEVER HANDLE AND COVER PLATE
REAR FOG/ BACK–UP LIGHT (EXPORT)	P21/5W	
STOP/TAIL/TURN SIGNAL (EXPORT)	P21/5W	
SIDE MARKER LAMP	194	REACH BEHIND BUMPER
TRUNK ILLUMINATION	561	OPEN TRUNK LID
UNDERHOOD LAMP	561	RAISE HOOD
VANITY MIRROR ILLUMINATION	7065	REMOVE LENS FROM BRACKET

91046G25

Light bulb application chart—1994 Deville, Deville Concours, Eldorado and Seville

BULB CHART

DESCRIPTION	BULB NO.
Ash Tray Illumination	1445
Backup Lights	2057
Cornering Light	1156 DC7
Courtesy Reading Light	168
Fog Light	886
Glove Compartment Light	194
Headlights Composite	
-Inner High Beam	9005 HB3
-Outer Low Beam	9006 HB4
-Export Bulb	114
Illumination Entry Lock Lamp	192
Instrument Panel Illumination	194
Instrument Panel Telltales	194
License Plate Light	194
Park and Turn Signal	2357 NA

91046G26

Light bulb application chart—1995 Deville, Deville Concours and Eldorado

BULB CHART

Description	Bulb No.
Ashtray Illumination	1445
Backup Lamps	1156
Cornering Lamp	1156
Courtesy Reading Lamp	168
Fog Lamp	886
Glove Compartment Lamp	194
Headlamps Composite	
-Inner High Beam	9005
-Outer Low Beam	9006
-Export Bulb	H4
Illumination Entry Lock Lamp	192
Instrument Panel Illumination	194
Instrument Panel Telltales	194
License Plate Lamp	194
Park and Turn Signal	2357 NA
Rear Fog/Back-Up Lamp (Export)	P21/5W
Front Fender Side Turn Signal (Export)	WSW
Side Marker Lamps	194 NA
Stop/Tail/Turn Signal	2057
Stop/Tail/Turn Signal (Export)	P21/5W
Trunk Lamp	1003
Underhood Lamp	561
Vanity Mirror Illumination	124

91046G27

Light bulb application chart—1995 Seville

BULB USAGE	TRADE NO
Ashtray Illumination	1445
Backup Lamp	2057
Center High Mount Stoplamp (CHMSL)	1141
Cornering Lamp	1156
Floor Courtesy Lamps	564
Rear Courtesy/Reading	168
Front Courtesy/Reading	168
Front Fog Lamp	886
Instrument Panel Compartment	194
Headlamp	9005HB3
- HI Beam	9006HB4
- LO Beam	H4
- Export	194
Headlamp Switch	BQ245-36210A
Instrument Panel Telltales	194
License Plate Lamp	194
Park/Turn/Lamp (Front)	2057
Park/Stop/Turn(Rear)	2057
Rear Blower Switch	BQ245-35003A
Rear Fog/Back-Up Lamp (Export)	P21/5W
Stop/Tail/Turn Signal (Export)	P21/5W
Side Marker Lamp	194
Rear Compartment Lamp	561
Underhood Lamp	561
Vanity Mirror Illumination	7065

91046G28

Light bulb application chart—1996 Deville, Deville Concours, Eldorado and Seville

BULB USAGE - Exterior Lighting	TRADE NO
Backup	2057
Cornering	1141
Center High-Mounted Stoplamp	1156
Headlamp-High Beam	9005
Headlamp-Low Beam	9006
Headlamp-Export	194
Headlamp Switch	BQ245-36210A
Front Fog Lamp	886
Front Side Markers	194
Front Park/Turn	2057
License	194
Rear Compartment	561
Rear Fog Lamp-Export	P21/5W
Rear Park/Stop/Turn/	2057
Rear Side Marker	194
Rear Stop/Tail/Turn-Export	P21/5W
Underhood Lamp	561

BULB USAGE - Interior Lighting	TRADE NO
Ashtray	1445
Floor Courtesy	564
Front and Rear Reading	168
IP Compartment	194
Rear Blower Switch	BQ245-35003A
Sunshade Vanities	7065

91046G29

Light bulb application chart—1997–98 Deville, Deville Concours and Eldorado

Application	Number
Ashtray	161
Back-Up	2057
Cornering	1156
Courtesy/Reading	168
Fog	886
Glove Compartment	194
Headlamps Composite	
Inner High Beam	9005
Outer Low Beam	9006
Illumination Entry Lock	192
Instrument Panel Illumination	194
Instrument Panel Telltales	194
License Plate	194
Park and Turn Signal	2357 NA
Sidemarker	194
Stop/Tail/Turn Signal	2057
Trunk	561
Underhood	561
Vanity Mirror	124

91046G30

Light bulb application chart—1997–98 Seville

TRAILER WIRING

Wiring the vehicle for towing is fairly easy. There are a number of good wiring kits available and these should be used, rather than trying to design your own.

All trailers will need brake lights and turn signals as well as tail lights and side marker lights. Most areas require extra marker lights for overwide trailers. Also, most areas have recently required back-up lights for trailers, and most trailer manufacturers have been building trailers with back-up lights for several years.

Additionally, some Class I, most Class II and just about all Class III and IV trailers will have electric brakes. Add to this number an accessories wire, to operate trailer internal equipment or to charge the trailer's battery, and you can have as many as seven wires in the harness.

Determine the equipment on your trailer and buy the wiring kit necessary. The kit will contain all the wires needed, plus a plug adapter set which includes the female plug, mounted on the bumper or hitch, and the male plug, wired into, or plugged into the trailer harness.

When installing the kit, follow the manufacturer's instructions. The color coding of the wires is usually standard throughout the industry. One point to note: some domestic vehicles, and most imported vehicles, have separate turn signals. On most domestic vehicles, the brake lights and rear turn signals operate with the same bulb. For those vehicles without separate turn signals, you can purchase an isolation unit so that the brake lights won't blink whenever the turn signals are operated.

One, final point, the best kits are those with a spring loaded cover on the vehicle mounted socket. This cover prevents dirt and moisture from corroding the terminals. Never let the vehicle socket hang loosely; always mount it securely to the bumper or hitch.

CIRCUIT PROTECTION

The wiring circuits in your vehicle are protected from short circuits by a combination of fuses and circuit breakers. This greatly reduces the chance of fires caused by electrical problems.

Look at the silver-colored band inside the fuse. If the band is broken or melted, replace the fuse. Be sure you replace a bad fuse with a new one of the identical size and rating.

If you ever have a problem on the road and don't have a spare fuse, you can borrow one that has the same amperage. Pick some feature of your vehicle that you can get along without—like the radio or cigarette lighter— and use its fuse, if it is the correct amperage. Replace it as soon as you can.

There are three fuse blocks in most late model Cadillacs: the engine compartment fuse block, the MaxiFuse relay center and the rear compartment fuse block.

Fuses

♦ See Figure 167

Fuses are used to protect the electrical circuits in the vehicle. If there is an excessive amount of current flowing through a circuit, the element within the fuse will melt, stopping the current flow.

All Devilles and Fleetwoods are equipped with a fuse block located under the left-hand side of the instrument panel. In addition, 1991–93 Deville and Fleetwood are equipped with a fuse block located in the rear of the engine compartment. The fuse block is located in the glove box behind an access panel

on Eldorado and Seville. There are 2 fuse blocks on 1992–98 Eldorado and Seville, one located in the left-hand side of the engine compartment, on the wheelwell and the other is located on the side of the trunk.

REPLACEMENT

To determine if a fuse is blown, remove it from the fuse block and examine the fuse element for a break. If the element is broken, replace the fuse with one of equal current rating.

✳✳ CAUTION

Always replace a fuse with one that is the same type and current rating. Replacing a fuse with a fuse of a higher current rating may cause a vehicle fire and result in personal injury and vehicle damage.

BLADE FUSE COLOR CODING	
AMPERE RATING	HOUSING COLOR
4	Pink
5	Tan
10	Red
15	Light Blue
20	Yellow
25	Natural
30	Light Green

91046G21

Fig. 167 The ampere rating of a blade type fuse can also be determined by its color code

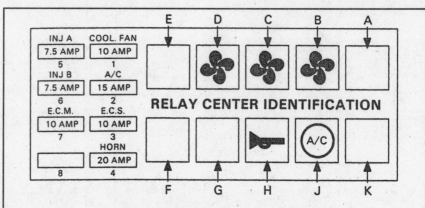

RELAY CENTER IDENTIFICATION

UNDERHOOD RELAY CENTER

1. **COOLANT FAN (10 AMP FUSE)**
   –A/C COMPRESSOR CLUTCH
   –BODY COMPUTER MODULE
   –LOW REFRIGERANT SWITCH
   –COOLANT FAN RELAYS
2. **A/C (15 AMP FUSE)**
   –A/C COMPRESSOR CLUTCH
3. **ECS (10 AMP FUSE)**
   –EMISSION CONTROL SYSTEM
4. **HORN (20 AMP FUSE)**
5. **INJ A (7.5 AMP FUSE)**
   –FUEL INJECTORS 2, 3, 5 AND 8
6. **INJ B (7.5 AMP FUSE)**
   –FUEL INJECTORS 1, 4, 6 AND 7
7. **ECM (10 AMP FUSE)**
   –ENGINE CONTROL MODULE
   –PASS KEY DECODER MODULE
8. **NOT USED**

A. NOT USED
B. COOLANT FAN RELAY
C. COOLANT FAN RELAY
D. COOLANT FAN RELAY
E. NOT USED
F. NOT USED
G. DAY TIME RUNNING LIGHTS
   (CANADIAN CAR ONLY)
H. HORN RELAY
J. A/C COMP. CLUTCH RELAY
K. NOT USED

91046G55

Engine compartment relay center locations—1990–91 Seville and Eldorado

Fuse panel:

ELC EXH 10A — 1	ELC COMP 20A — 6	RADIO 10A — 11	STOP/HAZ 20A — 16	LO-BEAM 10A BRKR — 21
BODY 20A — 2	BLOWER FDBK 5A — 7	WIPERS 25A — 12	RAD-PWR 10A — 17	HI-BEAM 20A BRKR — 22
ANT 10A — 3	CRUISE 3A — 8	DECK LID 15A — 13	IGN I-ISO 10A — 18	SEATS 30A BRKR — 23
CIGAR 20A — 4	HVAC 7.5A — 9	BCM 15A — 14	AIR BAGS 15A — 19	RAP 30A BRKR — 24
CPS 15A — 5	BCM 3A — 10	TAIL LPS 15A — 15	DEFOG 30A — 20	— 25

1. **ELC EXH** (10 AMP FUSE)
   - ELECTRONIC LEVEL CONTROL
2. **BODY** (20 AMP FUSE)
   - AUTOMATIC DOOR LOCKS
   - OUTSIDE POWER MIRRORS
   - LEFT AND RIGHT QUARTER READING/COURTESY LIGHTS
   - TRUNK LIGHT
   - FOOTWELL COURTESY LIGHTS
   - VANITY MIRRORS ILLUMINATION
   - OVERHEAD READING/ COURTESY LIGHTS
   - DOOR LOCKS FIBER OPTIC LIGHT
   - DOOR COURTESY AND WARNING LIGHTS
   - POWER DOOR LOCKS
3. **ANT** (10 AMP FUSE)
   - POWER ANTENNA
4. **CIGAR** (20 AMP FUSE)
   - CHIME MODULE
   - CONSOLE CIGAR LIGHTER
   - REAR ARMREST CIGAR LIGHT
   - LEFT AND RIGHT SEATS CONTOUR SWITCH
   - LEFT AND RIGHT SEAT LUMBAR SWITCH
5. **CPS** (15 AMP FUSE)
   - CENTRAL POWER SUPPLY
6. **ELC COMP** (20 AMP FUSE)
   - ELECTRONIC LEVEL CONTROL COMPRESSOR
7. **BLOWER FDBK** (5 AMP FUSE)
   - BLOWER MOTOR
8. **CRUISE** (3 AMP FUSE)
   - CRUISE CONTROL

- INSTRUMENT PANEL CLUSTER
- BATTERY NO CHARGE INDICATOR
9. **HVAC** (7.5 AMP FUSE)
   - HEATER AND AIR CONDITIONING
   - ELECTRONIC LEVEL CONTROL
   - REAR DEFOGGER
   - DAYTIME RUNNING LIGHTS
10. **BCM** (3 AMP FUSE)
    - BODY COMPUTER MODULE
11. **RADIO** (10 AMP FUSE)
    - RADIO
    - RETAINED ACCESSORY POWER
12. **WIPERS** (25 AMP FUSE)
    - WIPER/WASHERS
13. **DECK LID** (15 AMP FUSE)
    - TRUNK RELEASE
14. **BCM PWR** (10 AMP FUSE)
    - COURTESY LIGHT RELAY
    - RETAINED ACCESSORY POWER
    - HI/LO BEAM HEADLIGHTS
    - TWILIGHT SENTINEL
15. **TAIL LPS** (15 AMP FUSE)
    - TWILIGHT PARK LIGHT
    - ENGINE COMPARTMENT LIGHT
    - SIDE MARKER LIGHTS
    - FT PARK/TURN LIGHTS
    - INSTRUMENT PANEL CLUSTER
    - TAIL LIGHTS
    - LICENSE PLATE LIGHT
16. **STOP/HAZ** (20 AMP FUSE)
    - STOP LIGHT

- TURN SIGNAL ALERT MODULE
- TURN/HAZARD MODULE
17. **RDO-PWR** (10 AMP FUSE)
    - RADIO
18. **IGN 1-ISO** (10 AMP FUSE)
    - TURN/HAZARD MODULE
    - INFORMATION CENTER
    - BODY COMPUTER MODULE
    - TRANSAXLE POSITION SWITCH
    - AUTOMATIC DOOR LOCKS
    - FUEL GAGE
19. **SIR** (15 AMP FUSE)
    - DIAGNOSTIC ENERGY RESERVE MODULE (DERM)
20. **DEFOG** (30 AMP FUSE)
    - OUTSIDE HEATED MIRRORS
    - REAR DEFOGGER
21. **LO BEAM** (10 AMP CIRCUIT BREAKER)
    - DAYTIME RUNNING LIGHTS
    - LO BEAM HEADLIGHTS
22. **HI BEAM** (20 AMP CIRCUIT BREAKER)
23. **SEATS** (30 AMP CIRCUIT BREAKER)
    - POWER DOOR LOCKS
    - POWER SEAT RECLINER SWITCH
    - LUMBAR SWITCH
    - POWER SEAT SWITCH
24. **RAP** (30 AMP CIRCUIT BREAKER)
    - RETAINED ACCESSORY POWER
    - TRUNK RELEASE
    - ASTRO ROOF
    - RIGHT POWER SEAT
    - POWER WINDOWS

91046G54

Interior fuse center locations—1990–91 Seville and Eldorado

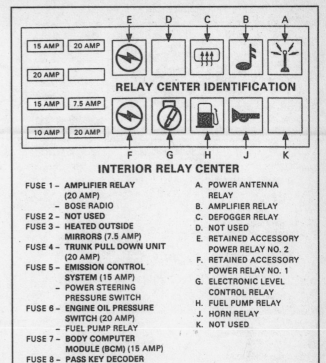

E	D	C	B	A
15 AMP	20 AMP			
20 AMP				

RELAY CENTER IDENTIFICATION

| 15 AMP | 7.5 AMP | | | |
| 10 AMP | 20 AMP | | | |

| F | G | H | J | K |

INTERIOR RELAY CENTER

FUSE 1 – **AMPLIFIER RELAY** (20 AMP)
- BOSE RADIO
FUSE 2 – **NOT USED**
FUSE 3 – **HEATED OUTSIDE MIRRORS** (7.5 AMP)
FUSE 4 – **TRUNK PULL DOWN UNIT** (20 AMP)
FUSE 5 – **EMISSION CONTROL SYSTEM** (15 AMP)
- POWER STEERING PRESSURE SWITCH
FUSE 6 – **ENGINE OIL PRESSURE SWITCH** (20 AMP)
- FUEL PUMP RELAY
FUSE 7 – **BODY COMPUTER MODULE (BCM)** (15 AMP)
FUSE 8 – **PASS KEY DECODER MODULE** (10 AMP)
- ELECTRONIC CONTROL MODULE

A. POWER ANTENNA RELAY
B. AMPLIFIER RELAY
C. DEFOGGER RELAY
D. NOT USED
E. RETAINED ACCESSORY POWER RELAY NO. 2
F. RETAINED ACCESSORY POWER RELAY NO. 1
G. ELECTRONIC LEVEL CONTROL RELAY
H. FUEL PUMP RELAY
J. HORN RELAY
K. NOT USED

91046G51

Engine compartment fuse center locations—1990–91 Deville and Fleetwood

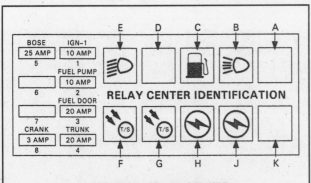

E	D	C	B	A
BOSE 25 AMP — 5	IGN-1 10 AMP — 1			
— 6	FUEL PUMP 10 AMP — 2			
— 7	FUEL DOOR 20 AMP — 3			
CRANK 3 AMP — 8	TRUNK 20 AMP — 4			

RELAY CENTER IDENTIFICATION

| F | G | H | J | K |

INTERIOR RELAY CENTER

1. **IGN-1** (15 AMP FUSE)
   - AUTOMATIC DAY/NIGHT MIRROR
   - BRAKE SWITCH
   - CHIME MODULE
   - THEFT DETERRENT
2. **FUEL PUMP** (10 AMP FUSE)
   - ENGINE CONTROL MODULE
   - FUEL PUMP
3. **FUEL DOOR** (20 AMP FUSE)
   - FUEL DOOR RELEASE
   - GLOVE BOX LIGHT
4. **TRUNK PULL-DN** (20 AMP FUSE)
   - TRUNK LID AUTOMATIC PULL DOWN UNIT
5. **BOSE** (25 AMP FUSE)
   - DELCO/BOSE RADIO SYSTEM
6. **NOT USED**
7. **NOT USED**

8. **CRANK** (3 AMP FUSE)
   - DIAGNOSTIC/ENERGY CONTROL MODULE
   - BODY COMPUTER MODULE
   - ELECTRONIC BRAKE CONTROL MODULE

A. NOT USED
B. HI BEAM RELAY
C. FUEL PUMP RELAY
D. TWILIGHT CRANK RELAY
E. LOW BEAM RELAY
F. TWILIGHT PARK LIGHT RELAY
G. TWILIGHT HEADLIGHT RELAY
H. RETAINED ACCESSORY POWER RELAY 1
J. RETAINED ACCESSORY POWER RELAY 2
K. NOT USED

91046G55

Interior relay center locations—1990–91 Seville and Eldorado

Fuse panel:

5A — 1	5A — 6	20A — 11	20A — 16	10A — 21
20A — 2	20A — 7	20A — 12	15A — 17	10A — 22
10A — 3	10A — 8	20A — 13	— 18	30A — 23
3A — 3	5A — 9	20A — 14	20A — 19	30A — 24
25A — 5	5A — 10	20A — 15	20A — 20	7.5A — 25

1 – **CRANK** (5 AMP)
   - DIAGNOSTIC/ENERGY RESERVE MODULE
2 – **SPARE/VAC PP** (20 AMP)
   - VACUUM ASSISTED BRAKES
   - VACUUM MOTOR
3 – **SUPINFL REST** (10 AMP)
   - SUPPLEMENTAL INFLATABLE RESTRAINT SYSTEM
4 – **RADIO** (10 AMP)
   - RADIO MUTE MODULE
   - BODY COMPUTER
5 – **WINDSHIELD WIPE/WASH** (25 AMP)
6 – **COOLING FAN RELAYS** (5 AMP)
   - ENGINE COOLING FAN
7 – **A/C** (25 AMP)
   - AIR CONDITIONING
   - REAR DEFOGGER
   - BODY COMPUTER MODULE
   - ELECTRONIC CLIMATE CONTROL PROGRAMMER
   - FUEL DATA CENTER
   - CLIMATE CONTROL PANEL
   - ELECTRONIC HEIGHT SENSOR
   - INSTRUMENT PANEL
   - HEATED WINDSHIELD CONTROL MODULE
8 – **ANTI–LOCK BRAKE–CONTROL** (5 AMP)
   - ELECTRONIC BRAKE CONTROL MODULE
9 – **ANTI–LOCK BRAKE–PUMP** (5 AMP)
   - HYDRAULIC PUMP RELAY
10 – **BLANK**
11 – **CHIME/CIGARETTE LIGHTER/ RADIO/POWER ANTENNA** (20 AMP)
   - TRUNK LIGHT
   - HORN
   - POWER ANTENNA
   - FRONT CIGAR LIGHTER
   - LEFT HAND INFORMATION CENTER
   - GLOVE COMPARTMENT LIGHT
   - FUEL DOOR RELEASE SWITCH
   - MULTIFUNCTION CHIME MODULE

- RADIO
12 – **AUTO LEVEL CONTROL** (20 AMP)
   - ELECTRONIC LEVEL CONTROL
13 – **BRAKE & HAZARD LPS** (20 AMP)
   - BRAKE LIGHTS
   - HAZARD FLASHER
14 – **PARK LAMPS** (20 AMP)
   - LICENSE PLATE LIGHT
   - TWILIGHT SENTINEL
   - DAYTIME RUNNING LIGHTS (CANADIAN)
   - HEADLIGHT SWITCH
   - INSTRUMENT CLUSTER
15 – **CTSY LP/POWER MIRROR** (20 AMP)
   - POWER DOOR LOCKS
   - ILLUMINATED ENTRY TIMER
   - DOME MAP LIGHTS AND GARAGE DOOR OPENER
   - COURTESY READING LIGHTS
   - BOTH FRONT AND REAR DOOR COURTESY AND RED WARNING LIGHTS
   - RIGHT AND LEFT VANITY MIRROR
   - REAR DOORS OR PANELS (COUPE) CIGAR LIGHTER
   - LEFT FRONT DOOR LOCK FIBER OPTIC LIGHT
   - OUTSIDE MIRROR CONTROL
16 – **GAUGES/DR LOCK/ILL ENT** (20 AMP)
   - LEFT AND RIGHT INFORMATION CENTERS
   - INSTRUMENT PANEL
   - MULTIFUNCTION CHIME MODULE
   - AUTOMATIC DOOR LOCK CONTROLLER
   - BODY COMPUTER MODULE
   - SEAT MEMORY MODULE
   - FUEL TANK SENDING UNIT
   - THEFT DETERRANT CONTROLLER
   - ILLUMINATED ENTRY TIMER
   - ELECTRO CHROMIC MIRROR
   - LT AND RT SEAT CONTROLS (SIXTY SPECIAL ONLY)

- DIAGNOSTIC ENERGY RESERVE MODULE (DERM)
17 – **ENGINE CONTROL MODULE** (15 AMP)
   - ELECTRONIC CONTROL MODULE
   - PASS KEY DECODER MODULE
   - VISCOVS CONVERTER CLUTCH BRAKE SWITCH
   - STARTER ENABLE RELAY
   - ELECTRONIC CONTROL MODULE (ECM)
18 – **BLANK**
19 – **TURN SIGNAL/BACK UP LPS** (20 AMP)
   - TURN SIGNAL FLASHER
   - TURN/HAZARD SWITCH
   - BACKUP LIGHTS
20 – **RR COMPT** (20 AMP)
   - TRUNK RELEASE
21 – **INJECTOR** (10 AMP)
   - FUEL INJECTOR NO. 1
   - FUEL INJECTOR NO. 5
   - FUEL INJECTOR NO. 8
   - FUEL INJECTOR NO. 3
22 – **INJECTOR** (10 AMP)
   - FUEL INJECTOR NO. 1
   - FUEL INJECTOR NO. 7
   - FUEL INJECTOR NO. 4
   - FUEL INJECTOR NO. 6
CIRCUIT BREAKER 23 – **POWER WINDOW/SUN ROOF** (30 AMP)
   - EXPRESS DOWN WINDOW
   - POWER WINDOW SWITCHES
   - ASTROROOF
   - EXPRESS ASTROROOF ACTUATOR ASSEMBLY
CIRCUIT BREAKER 24 – **LOCK MTR/ SEATS/RR DEFOGGER** (30 AMP)
   - POWER SEATS
   - REAR DEFOGGER
   - SEAT MEMORY MODULE
   - LEFT AND RIGHT POWER SEAT RECLINER
   - POWER SEATS
   - TRUNK PULL DOWN UNIT
   - RT AND LT SEAT CONTROL (SIXTY SPECIAL)
25 – **INSTRUMENT PANEL LAMPS** (7.5 AMP)
   - INSTRUMENT PANEL LIGHTS

91046G52

Interior fuse center locations—1990–91 Deville and Fleetwood

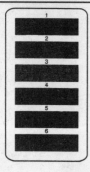
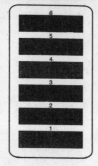

LH MAXI® FUSE BLOCK

FUSE 1 (50 AMP)
- RETAINED ACCESSORY POWER (RADIO/WIPERS)
- STARTER
- TRUNK COMP. FUSE A11
- ENGINE COMP. FUSES A1, A3, A5, A7, A9, A11, A13

FUSE 2 (60 AMP)
- U.S.A./CANADA Z49/SAUDI
- TRUNK COMP. FUSES C1, C3, C5, C7, C9, C11
- ROAD SENSING SUSPENSION

FUSE 2 EXPORT EXCEPT SAUDI (60 AMP)
- ROAD SENSING SUSPENSION
- REAR FOG LIGHT (EXPORT)
- TRUNK COMP. FUSES C1, C3, C5, C7, C9, C11, C13

CIRCUIT BREAKER 3 (30 AMP)
- FUEL DOOR RELEASE
- TRUNK RELEASE
- LEFT AND RIGHT POWER SEAT
- LEFT AND RIGHT LUMBAR CONTROL
- KEYLESS ENTRY MODULE
- POWER DOOR LOCKS
- HORNS

FUSE 4 (30 AMP)
- POWERTRAIN CONTROL MODULE (PCM)
- ELECTRONIC CLIMATE CONTROL
- RAP/ILLUMINATED ENTRY MODULE
- INSTRUMENT PANEL CLUSTER
- PASSKey® DECODER MODULE
- THEFT DETERRENT

FUSE 5 (60 AMP)
- LEFT AND RIGHT HEATED SEATS
- ELECTRONIC LEVEL CONTROL (ELC)
- TRUNK LID PULL DOWN
- POWER ANTENNA
- REAR DEFOGGER
- LEFT AND RIGHT MIRROR DEFOGGERS

FUSE 6 (60 AMP)
- RETAINED ACCESSORY POWER (SUNROOF/POWER WINDOWS)
- ENGINE COMP. FUSES C7, D1, D3, D5
- TRUNK COMP. FUSES A1, A3, A5, A7

RH MAXI® FUSE BLOCK

FUSE 1 (40 AMP)
- TURN/HAZ STOP LP
- PARK LIGHTS

FUSE 2 (30 AMP)
- DELCO-BOSE® SPEAKERS
- RADIO CONTROL HEAD
- REMOTE RADIO RECEIVER

CIRCUIT BREAKER 3 (30 AMP)
- FLASH TO PASS FEATURE
- DAYTIME RUNNING LIGHT (DRL)
- HEADLIGHTS

FUSE 4 (40 AMP) HAVAC BLOWER
- HVAC POWER MODULE
- A/C COMPRESSOR

FUSE 5 (50 AMP) ABS
- ANTILOCK BRAKE PRESSURE VALVE

FUSE 6 (50 AMP) COOLING FANS
- COOLING FANS

91046G49

Engine compartment fuse center locations—1992–93 Seville and Eldorado

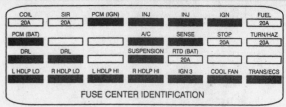

FUSE CENTER IDENTIFICATION

ENGINE COMPARTMENT FUSE BLOCK

COIL 20A
- 4.9L DISTRIBUTOR
- 4.6L IGNITION CONTROL MODULE

SIR 20A
- DIAGNOSTIC ENERGY RESERVE MODULE (DERM) SIR (AIR BAG)
- ARMING SENSOR

PCM (IGN) 10A
- POWERTRAIN CONTROL MODULE (PCM)
- PASSKey® DECODER MODULE

INJ 10A
- FUEL INJECTORS 1, 4, 6, 7

INJ 10A
- FUEL INJECTORS 2, 3, 5, 8

IGN 10A
- A/C COMPRESSOR
- ELECTROCHROMIC MIRROR
- INSTRUMENT PANEL CLUSTER
- DIAGNOSTIC ENERGY RESERVE MODULE (DERM) SIR (AIR BAG)
- KEYLESS ENTRY MODULE
- CORNERING LIGHTS
- CHIME MODULE
- TWILIGHT SENTINEL/DRL MODULE
- BACKUP LIGHTS
- BRAKE TRANSMISSION SHIFT INTERLOCK

FUEL 20A
- FUEL PUMP
- POWERTRAIN CONTROL MODULE

PCM (BAT) 10A
- POWERTRAIN CONTROL MODULE (PCM)

A/C 10A
- A/C COMPRESSOR

HTD W/S 10A
- HEATED WINDSHIELD

STOP LP 20A
- STOP LIGHTS

TURN/HAZ 20A
- HAZARD LIGHTS
- TURN SIGNAL LIGHTS

DRL 10A (CANADA)
- DAYTIME RUNNING LIGHTS

DRL 10A (CANADA)
- DAYTIME RUNNING LIGHTS

SUSPENSION 10A
- ROAD SENSING SUSPENSION (NORTHSTAR)
- SPEED SENSITIVE SUSPENSION (4.9L)

RTD (BAT) 20A
- ROAD SENSING SUSPENSION

L HDLP LO 10A (EXPORT)
- LEFT HEADLAMP LOW BEAM

R HDLP LO 10A (EXPORT)
- RT HEADLAMP LOW BEAM

L HDLP HI 10A (EXPORT)
- LEFT HEADLAMP HIGH BEAM

R HDLP HI (EXPORT)
- RIGHT HEADLAMP HIGH BEAM

IGN 3 10A
- HEATED WINDSHIELD
- HEATER AND A/C PROGRAMMER
- ELECT. LEVEL CONTROL (ELC)
- DEFOGGER RELAY "D"
- CRUISE CONTROL
- POWERTRAIN CONTROL MODULE

COOLING FAN 10A
- COOLING FANS
- POWERTRAIN CONTROL MODULE (4.6L)
- FRONT AND REAR HEATED OXYGEN SENSOR (4.6L)

TRANS/ECS 10A
- EXHAUST GAS RECIRCULATION (EGR) SOLENOID
- POWERTRAIN CONTROL MODULE (PCM)
- AUTOMATIC TRANSAXLE
- EVAPORATIVE EMISSION CONTROL SOLENOID
- OVERSPEED ALERT MODULE (EXPORT)
- POWER STEERING PRESSURE SWITCH

91046G50

Interior fuse center locations—1992–93 Seville and Eldorado

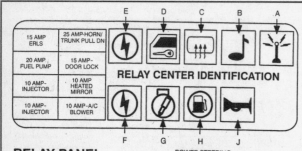

RELAY CENTER IDENTIFICATION

RELAY PANEL

25 AMP - HORN/TRUNK PULL DN
- HORN RELAY
- PULL DOWN UNIT

15 AMP DOOR LOCK
- DOOR LOCK SWITCHES
- OUTSIDE MIRROR CONTROL SWITCH
- LT AND RT REAR CIGAR LIGHTS
- KEYLESS ENTRY
- TRUNK LID RELEASE
- AUTOMATIC DOOR LOCKS
- ILLUMINATED ENTRY
- LT AND RT REAR DOOR LOCK SWITCHES
- LT AND RT REAR DOOR COURTESY LIGHTS

10 AMP HEATED MIRROR

10 AMP A/C PROGRAMMER

15 AMP ERLS
- A/C COMPRESSOR CONTROL RELAY
- VISCOVS CONVERTER CLUTCH BRAKE SWITCH
- EGR SOLENOID
- VAPOR CANISTER PURGE SOLENOID

- POWER STEERING PRESSURE SWITCH

20 AMP FUEL PUMP
- FUEL PUMP RELAY
- ENGINE OIL PRESSURE SWITCH

10 AMP INJECTOR
- FUEL INJECTORS 2, 3, 5 AND 8

10 AMP INJECTOR
- FUEL INJECTORS 1, 4, 6 AND 7

RELAYS
A. ANTENNA RELAY
B. BOSE RELAY (IF EQUIPPED)
C. DEFOGGER RELAY
D. WINDOW LOCKOUT RELAY
E. RETAINED ACCESSORY POWER RELAY NO. 2
F. RETAINED ACCESSORY POWER RELAY NO. 1
G. ELECTRONIC LEVEL CONTROL (ELC)
H. FUEL PUMP RELAY
J. HORN RELAY

91046G48

Engine compartment fuse center locations—1992–93 Deville and 1992 Fleetwood

1– 10 AMP - CRANK
- DIAG. ENERGY RESERVE MODULE
- STARTER ENABLE RELAY
2– 10 AMP - SPARE
3– 15 AMP - SPARE
4– 10 AMP - RADIO
- RADIO
- BODY COMPUTER MODULE
5– 25 AMP - WSHIELD WIPE/WASH
- WIPER/WASHER SWITCH
6– 10 AMP - COOLING FAN RELAYS
- HIGH SPEED COOLANT FAN
- LOW SPEED COOLANT FAN
7– 20 AMP - AIR CONDITIONING
- A/C COMPRESSOR RELAY
- BODY COMPUTER MODULE
- ELECTRONIC CLIMATE CONTROL
- CRUISE CONTROL SWITCH
- ELEC. CLIMATE CTRL PROG.
- ELEC. HEIGHT SENSOR
- FUEL DATA CENTER
- HEATED W/S CONTROL MODULE
- INSTRUMENT CLUSTER
- REAR DEFOGGER RELAY
- WINDOW LOCKOUT SWITCH
8– 10 AMP - ANTI-LOCK BRAKE-CONTR
* 20 AMP - VAC PUMP (H.D. CHASSIS ONLY)
- ELEC. BRAKE CONTROL MODULE
- BRAKE PRESSURE MODULE
- MAIN RELAY
9– BLANK
10– BLANK
11– 20 AMP - CHIME/CIG LTR/RADIO/PWR ANT
- POWER ANT. RELAY
- FRONT CIGAR LIGHTER
- LEFT HAND INFO. CENTER
- GLOVE COMPARTMENT LIGHT
- MULTIFUNCTION CHIME MODULE
- RADIO

12– 20 AMP - AUTO LEVEL CONTROL
- ELEC. COMPRESSOR
- ELEC. HEIGHT SENSOR
- ELEC. RELAY
13– 20 AMP - BRAKE & HAZARD LPS
- BRAKE LIGHT SWITCH
- HAZARD FLASHER
14– 20 AMP - PARK LAMPS
- INSTRUMENT CLUSTER
- LIGHT SWITCH
- TWILIGHT SENTINEL/DAYTIME RUNNING LIGHTS MODULE
15– 15 AMP - CTSY LP/PWR MIRROR
- DOME/MAP LIGHTS AND GARAGE DOOR OPENER
- FRONT DOOR LOCK FIBER OPTIC LIGHTS
- FRONT/REAR DOOR WARNING LIGHTS
- FRONT/FLEET VANITY MIRROR LIGHTS
- FRONT/REAR/QTR PANEL COURTESY/READING LIGHTS
- TRUNK LIGHT
- LT POWER SEAT SWITCH
16– 15 AMP - GAUGES/DR LOCK/ILL ENT
- AUTO. DAY/NIGHT MIRROR
- AUTO. DOOR LOCK MODULE
- BODY COMPUTER MODULE
- COMPUTER CONTROLLED RIDE MODULE
- DIAG. ENERGY RESERVE MODULE
- FUEL TANK UNIT
- ILLUMINATED ENTRY
- INSTRUMENT CLUSTER
- POWER SEATS
- KEYLESS ENTRY
- L & R 60 SPECIAL SEAT CTRLS
- MULTIFUNCTION CHIME MODULE
- RIGHT SIDE INFO. CENTER
- SEAT MEMORY MODULE
- THEFT DETERRENT MODULE

17– 15 AMP - ENGINE CTRL MOD
- POWER CONTROL MODULE
- PASS KEY DECODER MODULE
18– 10 AMP - SUP INFL REST
- DIAGNOSTIC/ENERGY RESERVE MODULE (DERM)
- DUAL SENSOR
19– 20 AMP - TURN SIGN/BACK UP LPS
- NEUTRAL SAFETY BACKUP SW
- TURN FLASHER
- TURN/HAZARD SWITCH
20– 20 AMP - SPARE
21– 20 AMP - SPARE
22– 20 AMP - TRUNK REL/FUEL FILLER
- TRUNK LID RELEASE SWITCH
- FUEL DOOR RELEASE SWITCH
23– 30 AMP CB – PWR WDO/SUN ROOF
- ASTROROOF CONTROL MODULE
- EXPRESS DOWN WINDOW MODULE
- POWER WINDOW SWITCHES AND LOCKOUT RELAY
24– 30 AMP CB – DR LKS/RR DEFOG
- DOOR LOCK RELAY
- LEFT & RIGHT SIDE RECLINER SWITCHES
- LEFT & RIGHT SEAT SWITCHES
- L & R 60 SPECIAL SEAT CTRL SW.
- REAR DEFOGGER
- SEAT MEMORY MODULE
- KEYLESS ENTRY
25– 10 AMP - INST PANEL LAMPS
- ASHTRAY LAMP
- BODY COMPUTER MODULE
- ENGINE COMPARTMENT LIGHT
- I/P AND SWITCH BACK LIGHTS
- RADIO DISPLAY DIMMING INPUT

91046G47

Interior fuse center locations—1992–93 Deville and 1992 Fleetwood

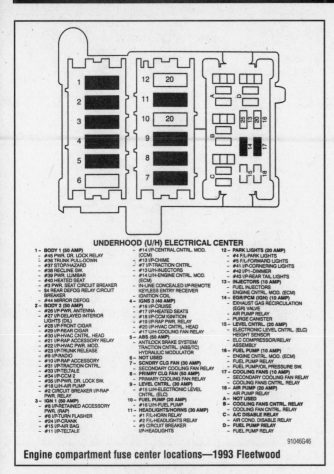

UNDERHOOD (U/H) ELECTRICAL CENTER

1 – BODY 1 (50 AMP)
 - #45 PWR. DR. LOCK RELAY
 - #36 TRUNK PULL-DOWN
 - #37 STOP/HAZARD
 - #38 RECLINE SW.
 - #39 PWR. LUMBAR
 - #40 HEATED SEAT
 - #3 PWR. SEAT CIRCUIT BREAKER
 - 54 REAR DEFOG RELAY CIRCUIT BREAKER
 - #44 MIRROR DEFOG
2 – BODY 2 (50 AMP)
 - #28 I/P-PWR. ANTENNA
 - #27 I/P-DELAYED INTERIOR LIGHTS (DIL)
 - #28 I/P-FRONT CIGAR
 - #29 I/P-REAR CIGAR
 - #30 I/P-RAP CNTRL. HEAD
 - #21 I/P-RAP ACCESSORY RELAY
 - #2 I/P-HVAC PWR. MOD.
 - #23 I/P-TRUNK RELEASE
 - #9 I/P-RADIO
 - #10 I/P-RAP ACCESSORY
 - #31 I/P-TRACTION CNTRL.
 - #33 I/P-TELTALE
 - #34 I/P-RAP CN 2
 - #35 I/P-PWR. DR. LOCK SW.
 - #18 U/H-AIR PUMP
 - #2 CIRCUIT BREAKER I/P-RAP PWR. RELAY
3 – IGN 1 (50 AMP)
 - #8 I/P-RETAINED ACCESSORY PWR. (RAP)
 - #1 I/P-TURN FLASHER
 - #24 I/P-CRANK
 - #15 I/P-AIR BAG
 - #11 I/P-TELTALE

 - #14 I/P-CENTRAL CNTRL. MOD. (CCM)
 - #13 I/P-CHIME
 - #7 I/P-TRACTION CNTRL.
 - #13 U/H-INJECTORS
 - #14 U/H-ENGINE CNTRL. MOD. (ECM)
 - IN-LINE CONCEALED I/P-REMOTE KEYLESS ENTRY RECEIVER
 - IGNITION COIL
4 – IGNS 3 (40 AMP)
 - #16 I/P-CRUISE
 - #17 I/P-HEATED SEATS
 - #18 I/P-CCM IGNITION
 - #19 I/P-RAP PWR. RELAY
 - #20 I/P-HVAC CNTRL. HEAD
 - #17 U/H-COOLING FAN RELAY
5 – ABS (30 AMP)
 - ANTILOCK BRAKE SYSTEM/TRACTION CNTRL. (ABS/TC) HYDRAULIC MODULATOR ASSEMBLY
6 – NOT USED
7 – SCNDRY CLG FAN (30 AMP)
 - SECONDARY COOLING FAN RELAY
 - PRIMARY CLG FAN (30 AMP)
 - PRIMARY COOLING FAN RELAY
9 – LEVEL CNTRL. (30 AMP)
 - #15 U/H-ELECTRONIC LEVEL CNTRL. (ELC)
10 – FUEL PUMP (20 AMP)
 - #16 U/H-FUEL PUMP RELAY
11 – HEADLIGHTS/HORNS (30 AMP)
 - #1 F/L-HORN RELAY
 - #2 F/L-HEADLIGHTS RELAY
 - #5 CIRCUIT BREAKER I/P-HEADLIGHTS

12 – PARK LIGHTS (20 AMP)
 - #4 F/L-PARK LIGHTS
 - #5 F/L-FORWARD LIGHTS
 - #41 I/P-CORNERING LIGHTS
 - #42 I/P1-DIMMER
 - #43 I/P-REAR TAIL LIGHTS
13 – INJECTORS (10 AMP)
 - FUEL INJECTORS
 - ENGINE CNTRL. MOD. (ECM)
14 – EGR/PCM (IGN) (10 AMP)
 - EXHAUST GAS RECIRCULATION (EGR) VALVE
 - AIR PUMP RELAY
 - PURGE CANISTER
15 – LEVEL CNTRL. (20 AMP)
 - ELECTRONIC LEVEL CNTRL. (ELC) HEIGHT SENSOR
 - ELC COMPRESSOR/RELAY ASSEMBLY
16 – FUEL PUMP (10 AMP)
 - ENGINE CNTRL. MOD. (ECM)
 - FUEL PUMP/OIL PRESSURE SW.
17 – COOLING FANS (10 AMP)
 - SECONDARY COOLING FAN RELAY
 - COOLING FANS CNTRL. RELAY
18 – AIR PUMP (20 AMP)
 - AIR PUMP RELAY
A – NOT USED
B – COOLING FANS CNTRL. RELAY
 - COOLING FANS CNTRL. RELAY
C – A/C DISABLE RELAY
 - AIR COND. DISABLE RELAY
D – FUEL PUMP RELAY
 - FUEL PUMP RELAY

91046G46

Engine compartment fuse center locations—1993 Fleetwood

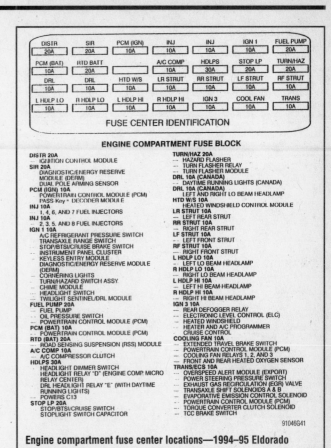

FUSE CENTER IDENTIFICATION

DISTR 20A	SIR 20A	PCM (IGN) 10A	INJ 10A	INJ 10A	IGN 1 10A	FUEL PUMP 20A
PCM (BAT) 10A	RTD BATT 20A		A/C COMP 10A	HDLPS 30A	STOP LP 20A	TURN/HAZ 20A
DRL 10A	DRL 10A	HTD W/S 10A	LR STRUT 10A	RR STRUT 10A	LF STRUT 10A	RF STRUT 10A
L HDLP LO 10A	R HDLP LO 10A	L HDLP HI 10A	R HDLP HI 10A	IGN 3 10A	COOL FAN 10A	TRANS 10A

ENGINE COMPARTMENT FUSE BLOCK

DISTR 20A
 - IGNITION CONTROL MODULE
SIR 20A
 - DIAGNOSTIC/ENERGY RESERVE MODULE (DERM)
 - DUAL POLE ARMING SENSOR
PCM (IGN) 10A
 - POWERTRAIN CONTROL MODULE (PCM)
 - PASS Key™ DECODER MODULE
INJ 10A
 - 1, 4, 6, AND 7 FUEL INJECTORS
INJ 10A
 - 2, 3, 5, AND 8 FUEL INJECTORS
IGN 1 10A
 - A/C REFRIGERANT PRESSURE SWITCH
 - TRANSAXLE RANGE SWITCH
 - STOP/BTSI/CRUISE BRAKE SWITCH
 - INSTRUMENT PANEL CLUSTER
 - KEYLESS ENTRY MODULE
 - DIAGNOSTIC/ENERGY RESERVE MODULE (DERM)
 - CORNERING LIGHTS
 - TURN/HAZARD SWITCH ASSY.
 - CHIME MODULE
 - HEADLIGHT SWITCH
 - TWILIGHT SENTINEL/DRL MODULE
FUEL PUMP 20A
 - FUEL PUMP
 - OIL PRESSURE SWITCH
 - POWERTRAIN CONTROL MODULE (PCM)
PCM (BAT) 10A
 - POWERTRAIN CONTROL MODULE (PCM)
RTD (BAT) 20A
 - ROAD SENSING SUSPENSION (RSS) MODULE
A/C COMP 10A
 - A/C COMPRESSOR CLUTCH
HDLPS 30A
 - HEADLIGHT DIMMER SWITCH
 - HEADLIGHT RELAY "D" (ENGINE COMP. MICRO RELAY CENTER)
 - DRL HEADLIGHT RELAY "E" (WITH DAYTIME RUNNING LIGHTS)
 - POWERS C13
STOP LP 20A
 - STOP/BTSI/CRUISE SWITCH
 - STOPLIGHT SWITCH CAPACITOR

TURN/HAZ 20A
 - HAZARD FLASHER
 - TURN FLASHER RELAY
 - TURN FLASHER MODULE
DRL 10A (CANADA)
 - DAYTIME RUNNING LIGHTS (CANADA)
DRL 10A (CANADA)
 - LEFT AND RIGHT LO BEAM HEADLAMP
HTD W/S 10A
 - HEATED WINDSHIELD CONTROL MODULE
LR STRUT 10A
 - LEFT REAR STRUT
RR STRUT 10A
 - RIGHT REAR STRUT
LF STRUT 10A
 - LEFT FRONT STRUT
RF STRUT 10A
 - RIGHT FRONT STRUT
L HDLP LO 10A
 - LEFT LO BEAM HEADLAMP
R HDLP LO 10A
 - RIGHT LO BEAM HEADLAMP
L HDLP HI 10A
 - LEFT HI BEAM HEADLAMP
R HDLP HI 10A
 - RIGHT HI BEAM HEADLAMP
IGN 3 10A
 - REAR DEFOGGER RELAY
 - ELECTRONIC LEVEL CONTROL (ELC)
 - HEATED WINDSHIELD
 - HEATER AND A/C PROGRAMMER
 - CRUISE CONTROL
COOLING FAN 10A
 - EXTENDED TRAVEL BRAKE SWITCH
 - POWERTRAIN CONTROL MODULE (PCM)
 - COOLING FAN RELAYS 1, 2, AND 3
 - FRONT AND REAR HEATED OXYGEN SENSOR
TRANS/ECS 10A
 - OVERSPEED ALERT MODULE (EXPORT)
 - POWER STEERING PRESSURE SWITCH
 - EXHAUST GAS RECIRCULATION (EGR) VALVE
 - TRANSAXLE SHIFT SOLENOIDS A & B
 - EVAPORATIVE EMISSION CONTROL SOLENOID
 - POWERTRAIN CONTROL MODULE (PCM)
 - TORQUE CONVERTER CLUTCH SOLENOID
 - TCC BRAKE SWITCH

91046G41

Engine compartment fuse center locations—1994–95 Eldorado

INSTRUMENT PANEL (I/P) FUSE BLOCK

1-5 – NOT USED
6 – T/SIG (15 AMP)
 - PARK/NEUTRAL AND BACKUP LAMP SWITCH
 - ELECTRIC TURN FLASHER
7 – ABS (10 AMP)
 - ELECTRONIC BRAKE CNTRL. MOD. (EBCM)
 - RAP WPR (25 AMP)
 - RETAINED ACCESSORY PWR. (RAP)
9 – RADIO (10 AMP)
 - RADIO RECEIVER
10 – WIPER (25 AMP)
 - WINDSHIELD WIPER/WASHER
11 – I/P INDC./TELLTALE (10 AMP)
 - DIAGNOSTIC ENERGY RESERVE MOD. (DERM)
 - LOW COOLANT MOD.
 - INSTRUMENT PANEL CLUSTER INDICATORS
12 – NOT USED
13 – CHIME (10 AMP)
 - CHIME MOD.
 - SPEED SENSOR BUFFER MOD.
 - TORQUE CONVERTER CLUTCH (TCC) DISABLE RELAY
 - AUTO. DAY/NIGHT MIRROR
 - REAR DEFOGGER RELAY
14 – CCM (10 AMP)
 - CENTRAL CNTRL. MOD. (CCM)
 - THROTTLE POSITION (TP) SENSOR MOD.
 - ELECTRONIC LEVEL CNTRL. (ELC)
15 – AIR BAG (10 AMP)
 - DUAL POLE ARMING SENSOR
16 – CRUISE (10 AMP)
 - GENERATOR
 - CRUISE CNTRL.
17 – HTD ST (10 AMP)
 - DRIVER HEATED SEAT
 - PASSENGER HEATED SEAT
18 – CCM IGN (10 AMP)
 - CENTRAL CNTRL. MOD. (CCM)
 - INSTRUMENT CLUSTER:

 - REMOTE KEYLESS ENTRY/UNIVERSAL THEFT DETERRENT RECEIVER
19 – RAP PWR (10 AMP)
 - RETAINED ACCESSORY PWR. (RAP)
20 – HVAC (40 AMP)
 - HVAC SOLENOID MOD.
 - INSTRUMENT CLUSTER
 - HVAC CNTRL. HEAD
21 – RAP BATT (25 AMP)
 - RETAINED ACCESSORY PWR. (RAP)
22 – HVAC (25 AMP)
 - HVAC PWR. MOD.
23 – TRK REL (10 AMP)
 - TRUNK LID RELEASE SW.
24 – STARTER (10 AMP)
 - STARTER ENABLE REALY
 - DIAGNOSTIC ENERGY RESERVE MOD. (DERM)
25 – RAP ANT (10 AMP)
 - SIDE VIEW MIRROR DEFOGGERS
26 – PWR ANT (20 AMP)
 - PWR. ANTENNA
27 – D/INT LPS (15 AMP)
 - DELAYED INTERIOR LIGHTS (DIL)
28 – FRT CIG (10 AMP)
 - FRONT CIGAR LIGHTER
29 – RR CIG (20 AMP)
 - REAR CIGAR LIGHTERS
30 – STOP LPS (20 AMP)
 - BRAKE TRANSMISSION SHIFT INTERLOCK (BTSI)/STOP LIGHT BRAKE SW.
31 – ABS (25 AMP)
 - ELECTRONIC BRAKE AND/TRACTION CNTRL. MOD.
32 – NOT USED
33 – CLUSTER (10 AMP)
 - CHIME MOD.
 - INSTRUMENT CLUSTER:
 - LOW ENGINE OIL MOD.
 - HEADLIGHT SW.
 - RADIO RECEIVER
34 – CCM (10 AMP)
 - CENTRAL CNTRL. MOD. (CCM)
35 – PWR LK (10 AMP)
 - PWR. DOOR LOCKS

 - PWR. MIRRORS
 - PWR. LUMBAR SEATS
36 – TRK DOWN (15 AMP)
 - TRUNK LID PULL-DOWN UNIT
37 – HZRD LP (20 AMP)
 - HAZARD WARNING FLASHER
38 – PWR RECL (15 AMP)
 - DRIVER SEAT RECLINE SW.
 - PASSENGER SEAT RECLINE SW.
39 – PWR LUMB (20 AMP)
 - PWR. LUMBAR SEAT MOTOR CNTRL. MOD.
40 – HTD ST (15 AMP)
 - DRIVER'S AND PASSENGER HEATED SEAT CNTRL. MOD. RELAY
41 – CORNR LP (10 AMP)
 - INSTRUMENT CLUSTER:
 - RADIO CNTRL. HEAD
 - CORNERING LIGHTS
42 – INT DIM (10 AMP)
 - HEADLIGHT SWITCH
 - INTERIOR LIGHTS
 - DIMMING
43 – RR T/LPS (10 AMP)
 - REAT TAIL LIGHTS
 - REAR SIDE MARKER LIGHTS
 - LICENSE LAMP
44 – STOP LPS (20 AMP)
 - PWR. SEAT (20 AMP)
45 – PWR LK (20 AMP)
 - PWR. DOOR LOCK RELAY
C/B 1 – NOT USED
C/B 2 – RAP PWR (30 AMP)
 - RETAINED ACCESSORY PWR. (RAP) RELAY
C/B 3 – PWR ST (25 AMP)
 - DRIVER'S PWR. SEAT SW.
 - PASSENGER PWR. SEAT SW.
C/B 4 – RR DEFG (30 AMP)
 - REAR DEFOGGER REALY
C/B 5 – HDG (30 AMP)
 - HEADLIGHT RELAY
 - DAYTIME RUNNING LIGHTS (DRL)

91046G45

Interior fuse center locations—1993 Fleetwood

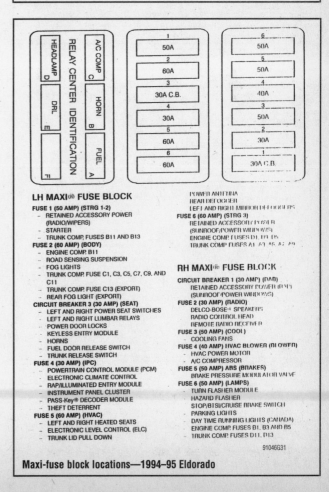

RELAY CENTER IDENTIFICATION

HEADLAMP D	1 – 50A
DRL E	2 – 60A
A/C COMP C	3 – 30A C.B.
HORN B	4 – 30A
FUEL A	5 – 60A
	6 – 60A

6 – 50A
5 – 50A
4 – 40A
3 – 50A
2 – 30A
1 – 30A C.B.

LH MAXI® FUSE BLOCK

FUSE 1 (50 AMP) (STRG 1-2)
 - RETAINED ACCESSORY POWER (RADIO/WIPERS)
 - STARTER
 - TRUNK COMP. FUSES B11 AND B13
FUSE 2 (60 AMP) (BODY)
 - ENGINE COMP. B11
 - ROAD SENSING SUSPENSION
 - FOG LIGHTS
 - TRUNK COMP. FUSE C1, C3, C5, C7, C9, AND C11
 - TRUNK COMP. FUSE C13 (EXPORT)
 - REAR FOG LIGHT (EXPORT)
CIRCUIT BREAKER 3 (30 AMP) (SEAT)
 - LEFT AND RIGHT POWER SEAT SWITCHES
 - LEFT AND RIGHT LUMBAR RELAYS
 - POWER DOOR LOCKS
 - KEYLESS ENTRY MODULE
 - HORNS
 - FUEL DOOR RELEASE SWITCH
 - TRUNK RELEASE SWITCH
FUSE 4 (30 AMP) (IPC)
 - POWERTRAIN CONTROL MODULE (PCM)
 - ELECTRONIC CLIMATE CONTROL
 - RAP/ILLUMINATED ENTRY MODULE
 - INSTRUMENT PANEL CLUSTER
 - PASS-Key® DECODER MODULE
 - THEFT DETERRENT
FUSE 5 (60 AMP) (HVAC)
 - LEFT AND RIGHT HEATED SEATS
 - ELECTRONIC LEVEL CONTROL (ELC)
 - TRUNK LID PULL DOWN

 - POWER ANTENNA
 - REAR DEFOGGER
 - LEFT AND RIGHT MIRROR DEFOGGERS
FUSE 6 (60 AMP) (STRG 3)
 - RETAINED ACCESSORY POWER (SUNROOF/POWER WINDOWS)
 - ENGINE COMP. FUSES D1, D3, D5
 - TRUNK COMP. FUSES A1, A3, A5, A7, A9

RH MAXI® FUSE BLOCK

CIRCUIT BREAKER 1 (30 AMP) (DAB)
 - RETAINED ACCESSORY POWER (RAP) (SUNROOF/POWER WINDOWS)
FUSE 2 (30 AMP) (RADIO)
 - DELCO-BOSE® SPEAKERS
 - RADIO CONTROL HEAD
 - REMOTE RADIO RECEIVER
FUSE 3 (50 AMP) (COOL)
 - COOLING FANS
FUSE 4 (40 AMP) HVAC BLOWER (BLOWER)
 - HVAC POWER MOTOR
 - A/C COMPRESSOR
FUSE 5 (50 AMP) ABS (BRAKES)
 - BRAKE PRESSURE MODULATOR VALVE
FUSE 6 (50 AMP) (LAMPS)
 - TURN FLASHER MODULE
 - HAZARD FLASHER
 - STOP/BTSI/CRUISE BRAKE SWITCH
 - PARKING LIGHTS
 - DAY TIME RUNNING LIGHTS (CANADA)
 - ENGINE COMP. FUSES B1, B3 AND B5
 - TRUNK COMP. FUSES D11, D13

91046G31

Maxi-fuse block locations—1994–95 Eldorado

TRUNK COMPARTMENT FUSE BLOCK

CRANK	IGN 1	HDLP WASH	SUSP	IPC (IGN)	CNSL SW	ABS
10A	10A	30A	10A	10A	10A	10A
WIPER	RAD (IGN)	R DEFOG	HTD MIRR	IPC (BATT)	THEFT	HVAC/DABIE
30A	10A	20A	10A	10A	10A	10A
REAR FOG	FOG LP	CNSL FAN	CIGAR	BODY 2	BODY 1	READ LP
10A	10A	10A	20A	10A	10A	10A
L PRK LP	R PRK LP	RAD (BAT)	ANT/TRK PLD	ELC	R HTD SEAT	L HTD SEAT
10A	10A	10A	20A	30A	10A	10A

CRANK (10 AMP)
- RAP/ILLUMINATED ENTRY MODULE
- DIAGNOSTIC/ENERGY RESERVE MODULE (DERM)
- TRANSAXLE RANGE SWITCH (NSSS)

IGN 1 (10 AMP)
- FUEL LEVER SENSOR
- ELECTROCHROMIC MIRROR
- RAP/ILLUMINATED ENTRY MODULE
- THEFT DETERRENT MODULE
- KEYLESS ENTRY MODULE
- TURN FLASHER RELAY "F" TRUNK COMP.
- MICRO RELAY CENTER
- CATALYTIC CONVERTER ALARM MODULE (EXPORT)

HDLP WASH (30 AMP) EXPORT ONLY
- HEADLIGHT WASHER MODULE

SUSP (10 AMP)
- ROAD SENSING SUSPENSION (RSS) MODULE

IPC (IGN) (10 AMP)
- INSTRUMENT PANEL CLUSTER

CNSL SW (10 AMP)
- REAR BLOWER RELAY "E"
- CONSOLE SWITCH

ABS (10 AMP)
- ELECTRONIC BRAKE AND TRACTION CONTROL MODULE (EBTCM)

WIPER (30 AMP)
- WIPER/WASHER SWITCH

RAD (IGN) (10 AMP)
- REMOTE RADIO RECEIVER

R DEFOG (20 AMP)
- REAR DEFOGGER

HTD MIRR (10 AMP)
- LT AND RT OUTSIDE MIRROR DEFOGGERS

IPC (BATT) (10 AMP)
- INSTRUMENT PANEL CLUSTER

THEFT (10 AMP)
- PASS-Key® DECODER MODULE
- THEFT DETERRENT RELAY "D" (TRUNK COMP RELAY CENTER)
- THEFT DETERRENT MODULE

HVAC/DABIE (10 AMP)
- HEATER AND A/C PROGRAMMER
- RAP/ILLUMINATED ENTRY MODULE

REAR FOG (10 AMP)
- REAR FOG LIGHT RELAY A (EXPORT)

FOG LP (10 AMP)
- FOG LIGHT RELAYS A AND F

CNSL FAN (10AMP)
- REAR BLOWER MOTOR
- REAR BLOWER RELAY

CIGAR (20 AMP)
- LT AND RT REAR CIGARETTE LIGHTERS (SEVILLE ONLY)
- FRONT CIGARETTE LIGHTER
- CHIME MODULE

BODY 2 (10 AMP)
- POWER MIRROR SWITCH
- RAP RELAY
- LOCK-OUT INHIBIT RELAY "B" (TRUNK COMP. 1 MICRO RELAY CENTER)
- PANEL LIGHTS INHIBIT RELAY "F" (TRUNK COMP. 3 MICRO RELAY CENTER)
- COURTESY LIGHTS RELAY "C" (TRUNK COMP 2 MICRO RELAY CENTER)
- RAP RELAY "E" (TRUNK COMP. 2 MICRO RELAY CENTER)
- KEYLESS ENTRY MODULE
- TRUNK LAMP
- SEAT BELT RETRACTOR SOLENOIDS (ELDORADO ONLY)

BODY 1 (10 AMP)
- FRONT DOOR LOCK SWITCHES
- GLOVE BOX LAMP
- LT AND RT FOOTWELL COURTESY LAMPS
- HEADLIGHT SWITCH

READ LP (10 AMP)
- LT AND RT FRONT HEADER LAMP
- LT AND RT VANITY MIRROR
- GARAGE DOOR OPENER
- LT AND RT REAR HEADER LAMPS

L PRK LP (10 AMP)
- LT REAR TAIL/STOP/TURN LAMPS
- LT FRONT PARK/TURN LAMPS
- FRONT AND REAR LEFT SIDE MARKER LAMPS
- RADIO CONTROL HEAD
- HEADLIGHT SWITCH
- INSTRUMENT PANEL CLUSTER

R PRK LP (10 AMP)
- RT TAIL/STOP TURN LAMPS
- RT FRONT AND REAR SIDE MARKER LAMPS
- RT FRONT PARK AND TURN LAMPS
- ENGINE COMP. LAMP
- LICENSE PLATE LAMPS

RAD (BAT) (10 AMP)
- RADIO

ANT/TRK PLD (20 AMP)
- TRUNK LID PULL DOWN MOTOR
- POWER ANTENNA

ELC (30 AMP)
- ELECTRONIC LEVEL CONTROL (ELC)

R HTD SEAT (10 AMP)
- PASSENGERS HEATED SEAT

L HTD SEAT (10 AMP)
- DRIVER'S HEATED SEAT

91046G32

Trunk compartment fuse panel locations—1994–95 Eldorado

FUSE CENTER IDENTIFICATION

DISTR	SIR	PCM (IGN)	INJ	INJ	IGN 1	FUEL PUMP
20A	20A	10A	10A	10A	10A	20A
PCM (BAT)	RTD BATT		A/C COMP	HDLPS	STOP LP	TURN/HAZ
10A	20A		10A	30A	20A	20A
DRL	DRL	HTD W/S	LR STRUT	RR STRUT	LF STRUT	RF STRUT
10A	10A	10A	10A	10A	10A	10A
L HDLP LO	R HDLP LO	L HDLP HI	R HDLP HI	IGN 3	COOL FAN	TRANS
10A	10A	10A	10A	10A	10A	10A

ENGINE COMPARTMENT FUSE BLOCK

DISTR 20A
- IGNITION CONTROL MODULE

SIR 20A
- DIAGNOSTIC/ENERGY RESERVE MODULE (DERM)
- DUAL POLE ARMING SENSOR

PCM (IGN) 10A
- POWERTRAIN CONTROL MODULE (PCM)
- PASS-Key® DECODER MODULE

INJ 10A
- 1, 4, 6, AND 7 FUEL INJECTORS

INJ 10A
- 2, 3, 5, AND 8 FUEL INJECTORS

IGN 1 10A
- A/C REFRIGERANT PRESSURE SWITCH
- TRANSAXLE RANGE SWITCH
- STOP/BTSI/CRUISE BRAKE SWITCH
- INSTRUMENT PANEL CLUSTER
- KEYLESS ENTRY MODULE
- DIAGNOSTIC/ENERGY RESERVE MODULE (DERM)
- CORNERING LIGHTS
- TURN/HAZARD SWITCH ASSY.
- CHIME MODULE
- HEADLIGHT SWITCH
- TWILIGHT SENTINEL/DRL MODULE

FUEL PUMP 20A
- FUEL PUMP
- OIL PRESSURE SWITCH
- POWERTRAIN CONTROL MODULE (PCM)

PCM (BAT) 10A
- POWERTRAIN CONTROL MODULE (PCM)

RTD (BAT) 20A
- ROAD SENSING SUSPENSION (RSS) MODULE

A/C COMP 10A
- A/C COMPRESSOR CLUTCH

HDLPS 30A
- HEADLIGHT DIMMER SWITCH
- HEADLIGHT RELAY "D" (ENGINE COMP. MICRO RELAY CENTER)
- DRL HEADLIGHT RELAY "E" (WITH DAYTIME RUNNING LIGHTS)
- POWERS C13

STOP LP 20A
- STOP/BTSI/CRUISE SWITCH
- STOPLIGHT SWITCH CAPACITOR

TURN/HAZ 20A
- HAZARD FLASHER
- TURN FLASHER RELAY
- TURN FLASHER MODULE

DRL 10A (CANADA)
- DAYTIME RUNNING LIGHTS (CANADA)

DRL 10A (CANADA)
- LEFT AND RIGHT LO BEAM HEADLAMP

HTD W/S 10A
- HEATED WINDSHIELD CONTROL MODULE

LR STRUT 10A
- LEFT REAR STRUT

RR STRUT 10A
- RIGHT REAR STRUT

LF STRUT 10A
- LEFT FRONT STRUT

RF STRUT 10A
- RIGHT FRONT STRUT

L HDLP LO 10A
- LEFT LO BEAM HEADLAMP

R HDLP LO 10A
- RIGHT LO BEAM HEADLAMP

L HDLP HI 10A
- LEFT HI BEAM HEADLAMP

R HDLP HI 10A
- RIGHT HI BEAM HEADLAMP

IGN 3 10A
- REAR DEFOGGER RELAY
- ELECTRONIC LEVEL CONTROL (ELC)
- HEATED WINDSHIELD
- HEATER AND A/C PROGRAMMER
- CRUISE CONTROL

COOLING FAN 10A
- EXTENDED TRAVEL BRAKE SWITCH
- POWERTRAIN CONTROL MODULE (PCM)
- COOLING FAN RELAYS 1, 2, AND 3
- FRONT AND REAR HEATED OXYGEN SENSOR

TRANS/ECS 10A
- OVERSPEED ALERT MODULE (EXPORT)
- POWER STEERING PRESSURE SWITCH
- EXHAUST GAS RECIRCULATION (EGR) VALVE
- TRANSAXLE SHIFT SOLENOIDS A & B
- EVAPORATIVE EMISSION CONTROL SOLENOID
- POWERTRAIN CONTROL MODULE (PCM)
- TORQUE CONVERTER CLUTCH SOLENOID
- TCC BRAKE SWITCH

91046G42

Engine compartment fuse center locations—1994–95 Deville and Concours Deville

DEVILLE TRUNK COMPARTMENT FUSE BLOCK

CRANK	IGN 1	HDLP WASH		IPC (IGN)	RTD	ABS
10A	10A	30A		10A	10A	10A
WIPER	RAD (IGN)	R DEFOG	HTD MIRR	IPC (BATT)	THEFT	HVAC/DABIE
30A	10A	20A	10A	10A	10A	10A
RADIO (AMP)	TRAILER	ANT	CIGAR	BODY 2	BODY 1	READ LP
30A	20A	10A	20A	10A	10A	10A
L PRK LP	R PRK LP	RAD (BAT)	TRUNK PLD	ELC	R HTD SEAT	L HTD SEAT
10A	10A	10A	20A	30A	10A	10A

CRANK (10 AMP)
- RAP ILLUMINATED ENTRY MODULE
- DIAGNOSTIC ENERGY RESERVE MODULE (DERM)
- TRANSAXLE RANGE SWITCH (NSSS)

IGN 1 (10 AMP)
- TRUNK-FUEL DOOR RELEASE INHIBIT RELAY "E"
- FUEL LEVER SENSOR
- ELECTROCHROMIC MIRROR
- RAP/ILLUMINATED ENTRY MODULE
- THEFT DETERRENT MODULE
- KEYLESS ENTRY MODULE
- TURN FLASHER RELAY "F" TRUNK COMP
- MICRO RELAY CENTER

HDLP WASH (30 AMP) EXPORT ONLY
- NOT EQUIPPED

IPC (IGN) (10 AMP)
- INSTRUMENT PANEL CLUSTER

RTD SUSP (10 AMP)
- SPEED SENSITIVE SUSPENSION
- ENGINE COMP. MICRO RELAY CENTER
- RSS DAMPER RELAY "F"

ABS (10 AMP)
- ELECTRONIC BRAKE AND TRACTION CONTROL MODULE (EBTCM)

WIPER (30 AMP)
- WIPER WASHER SWITCH

RAD (IGN) (10 AMP)
- REMOTE RADIO RECEIVER

R DEFOG (20 AMP)
- REAR DEFOGGER

HTD MIRR (10 AMP)
- LT AND RT OUTSIDE MIRROR DEFOGGERS

IPC (BATT) (10 AMP)
- INSTRUMENT PANEL CLUSTER

THEFT (10 AMP)
- PASS-Key DECODER MODULE
- THEFT DETERRENT RELAY "D" TRUNK COMP RELAY CENTER
- THEFT DETERRENT MODULE

HVAC DABIE (10 AMP)
- HEATER AND A C PROGRAMMER
- RAP/ILLUMINATED ENTRY MODULE

RADIO (30 AMP)
- ACTIVE AUDIO AMPLIFIER

TRAILER (20 AMP)
- NOT EQUIPPED

ANT (10 AMP)
- ANTENNA MOTOR

CIGAR (20 AMP)
- LT AND RT REAR CIGARETTE LIGHTERS
- FRONT CIGARETTE LIGHTER
- CHIME MODULE

BODY 2 (10 AMP)
- POWER MIRROR SWITCH
- RAP RELAY
- LOCK-OUT INHIBIT RELAY "A" (TRUNK COMP 1 MICRO RELAY CENTER)
- COURTESY LIGHTS RELAY "C" (TRUNK COMP 2 MICRO RELAY CENTER)
- RAP RELAY "E" (TRUNK COMP. 2 MICRO RELAY CENTER)
- KEYLESS ENTRY MODULE
- TRUNK LAMP

BODY 1 (10 AMP)
- FRONT DOOR LOCK SWITCHES
- FRONT DOOR COURTESY LAMP
- GLOVE BOX LAMP
- HEADLIGHT SWITCH

READ LP (10 AMP)
- LT AND RT FRONT HEADER LAMP
- GARAGE DOOR OPENER
- LT AND RT REAR HEADER LAMPS

L PRK LP (10 AMP)
- LT REAR TAIL/STOP/TURN LAMPS
- LT FRONT PARK/TURN LAMPS
- FRONT AND REAR LEFT SIDE MARKER LAMPS
- RT REAR MARKER LAMP
- HEADLIGHT SWITCH
- INSTRUMENT PANEL CLUSTER

R PRK LP (10 AMP)
- RADIO CONTROL HEAD
- RT TAIL/STOP TURN LAMPS
- RT FRONT AND REAR SIDE MARKER LAMPS
- RT FRONT PARK AND TURN LAMPS
- ENGINE COMP LAMP
- LICENSE PLATE LAMPS

RAD (BAT) (10 AMP)
- RADIO

TRUNK PLD (20 AMP)
- TRUNK LID PULL DOWN MOTOR

ELC (30 AMP)
- ELECTRONIC LEVEL CONTROL (ELC)

R HTD SEAT (10 AMP)
- PASSENGERS HEATED SEAT

L HTD SEAT (10 AMP)
- DRIVER'S HEATED SEAT

91046G33

Trunk compartment fuse panel locations—1994–95 Deville and Concours Deville

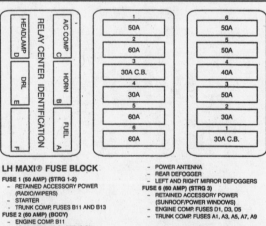

LH MAXI® FUSE BLOCK

FUSE 1 (50 AMP) (STRG 1-2)
- RETAINED ACCESSORY POWER (RADIO/WIPERS)
- STARTER
- TRUNK COMP. FUSES B11 AND B13

FUSE 2 (60 AMP) (BODY)
- ENGINE COMP. B11
- ROAD SENSING SUSPENSION
- FOG LIGHTS
- TRUNK COMP. FUSE C1, C3, C5, C7, C9, AND C11
- TRUNK COMP. FUSE C13 (EXPORT)
- REAR FOG LIGHT (EXPORT)

CIRCUIT BREAKER 3 (30 AMP) (SEAT)
- LEFT AND RIGHT POWER SEAT SWITCHES
- LEFT AND RIGHT LUMBAR RELAYS
- POWER DOOR LOCKS
- KEYLESS ENTRY MODULE
- HORNS
- FUEL DOOR RELEASE SWITCH
- TRUNK RELEASE SWITCH

FUSE 4 (30 AMP) (IPC)
- POWERTRAIN CONTROL MODULE (PCM)
- ELECTRONIC CLIMATE CONTROL
- RAP/ILLUMINATED ENTRY MODULE
- INSTRUMENT PANEL CLUSTER
- PASS-Key® DECODER MODULE
- THEFT DETERRENT

FUSE 5 (60 AMP) (HVAC)
- LEFT AND RIGHT HEATED SEATS
- ELECTRONIC LEVEL CONTROL (ELC)
- TRUNK LID PULL DOWN

- POWER ANTENNA
- REAR DEFOGGER
- LEFT AND RIGHT MIRROR DEFOGGERS

FUSE 6 (60 AMP) (STRG 3)
- RETAINED ACCESSORY POWER (SUNROOF/POWER WINDOWS)
- ENGINE COMP. FUSES D1, D3, D5
- TRUNK COMP. FUSES A1, A3, A5, A7, A9

RH MAXI® FUSE BLOCK

CIRCUIT BREAKER 1 (30 AMP) (DAB)
- RETAINED ACCESSORY POWER (RAP) (SUNROOF/POWER WINDOWS)

FUSE 2 (30 AMP) (RADIO)
- DELCO-BOSE® SPEAKERS
- RADIO CONTROL HEAD
- REMOTE RADIO RECEIVER

FUSE 3 (30 AMP) (COOL)
- COOLING FANS

FUSE 4 (40 AMP) HVAC BLOWER (BLOWER)
- HVAC POWER MOTOR
- A/C COMPRESSOR

FUSE 5 (50 AMP) ABS (BRAKES)
- BRAKE PRESSURE MODULATOR VALVE

FUSE 6 (50 AMP) (LAMPS)
- TURN FLASHER MODULE
- HAZARD FLASHER
- STOP/BTSI/CRUISE BRAKE SWITCH
- PARKING LIGHTS
- DAY TIME RUNNING LIGHTS (CANADA)
- ENGINE COMP. FUSES B1, B3 AND B5
- TRUNK COMP. FUSES D1, D13

91046G34

Maxi fuse block locations—1994–95 Deville and Concours Deville

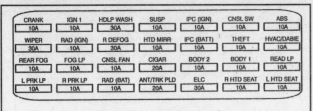

CRANK 10A	IGN 1 10A	HDLP WASH 30A	SUSP 10A	IPC (IGN) 10A	CNSL SW 10A	ABS 10A
WIPER 30A	RAD (IGN) 10A	R DEFOG 30A	HTD MIRR 10A	IPC (BATT) 10A	THEFT 10A	HVAC/DABIE 10A
REAR FOG 10A	FOG LP 10A	CNSL FAN 10A	CIGAR 20A	BODY 2 10A	BODY 1 10A	READ LP 10A
L PRK LP 10A	R PRK LP 10A	RAD (BAT) 10A	ANT/TRK PLD 20A	ELC 30A	R HTD SEAT 10A	L HTD SEAT 10A

TRUNK COMPARTMENT FUSE BLOCK

CRANK (10 AMP)
- RAP/ILLUMINATED ENTRY MODULE
- DIAGNOSTIC/ENERGY RESERVE MODULE (DERM)
- TRANSAXLE RANGE SWITCH (NSSS)

IGN 1 (10 AMP)
- FUEL LEVER SENSOR
- ELECTROCHROMIC MIRROR
- RAP/ILLUMINATED ENTRY MODULE
- THEFT DETERRENT MODULE
- KEYLESS ENTRY MODULE
- TURN FLASHER RELAY "F" TRUNK COMP. MICRO RELAY CENTER
- CATALYTIC CONVERTER ALARM MODULE (EXPORT)

HDLP WASH (30 AMP) EXPORT ONLY
- HEADLIGHT WASHER MODULE

SUSP (10 AMP)
- ROAD SENSING SUSPENSION (RSS) MODULE

IPC (IGN) (10 AMP)
- INSTRUMENT PANEL CLUSTER

CNSL SW (10 AMP)
- REAR BLOWER RELAY "E"
- CONSOLE SWITCH

ABS (10 AMP)
- ELECTRONIC BRAKE AND TRACTION CONTROL MODULE (EBTCM)

WIPER (30 AMP)
- WIPER/WASHER SWITCH

RAD (IGN) (10 AMP)
- REMOTE RADIO RECEIVER

R DEFOG (30 AMP)
- REAR DEFOGGER

HTD MIRR (10 AMP)
- LT AND RT OUTSIDE MIRROR DEFOGGERS

IPC (BATT) (10 AMP)
- INSTRUMENT PANEL CLUSTER

THEFT (10 AMP)
- PASS-Key® DECODER MODULE
- THEFT DETERRENT RELAY "D" (TRUNK COMP. RELAY CENTER)
- THEFT DETERRENT MODULE

HVAC/DABIE (10 AMP)
- HEATER AND A/C PROGRAMMER
- RAP/ILLUMINATED ENTRY MODULE

REAR FOG (10 AMP)
- REAR FOG LIGHT RELAY A (EXPORT)

FOG LP (10 AMP)
- FOG LIGHT RELAYS A AND F

CNSL FAN (10AMP)
- REAR BLOWER MOTOR
- REAR BLOWER RELAY

CIGAR (20 AMP)
- LT AND RT REAR CIGARETTE LIGHTERS (SEVILLE ONLY)
- FRONT CIGARETTE LIGHTER
- CHIME MODULE

BODY 2 (10 AMP)
- POWER MIRROR SWITCH
- RAP RELAY
- LOCK-OUT INHIBIT RELAY "B" (TRUNK COMP. 1 MICRO RELAY CENTER)
- PANEL LIGHTS INHIBIT RELAY "F" (TRUNK COMP 3 MICRO RELAY CENTER) (EXPORT)
- COURTESY LIGHTS RELAY "C" (TRUNK COMP. 2 MICRO RELAY CENTER)
- RAP RELAY "E" (TRUNK COMP. 2 MICRO RELAY CENTER)
- KEYLESS ENTRY MODULE
- TRUNK LAMP
- SEAT BELT RETRACTOR SOLENOIDS (ELDORADO ONLY)

BODY 1 (10 AMP)
- REAR DOOR LOCK SWITCHES (SEVILLE ONLY)
- FRONT DOOR LOCK SWITCHES
- GLOVE BOX LAMP
- LT AND RT FOOTWELL COURTESY LAMPS
- HEADLIGHT SWITCH

READ LP (10 AMP)
- LT AND RT FRONT HEADER LAMP
- LT AND RT VANITY LAMPS
- GARAGE DOOR OPENER
- LT AND RT REAR HEADER LAMPS

L PRK LP (10 AMP)
- LT REAR TAIL/STOP/TURN LAMPS
- LT FRONT PARK/TURN LAMPS
- FRONT AND REAR LEFT SIDE MARKER LAMPS
- RADIO CONTROL HEAD
- HEADLIGHT SWITCH
- INSTRUMENT PANEL CLUSTER

R PRK LP (10 AMP)
- RT TAIL/STOP/TURN LAMPS
- RT FRONT AND REAR SIDE MARKER LAMPS
- RT FRONT PARK AND TURN LAMPS
- ENGINE COMP. LAMP
- LICENSE PLATE LAMPS

RAD (BAT) (10 AMP)
- RADIO

ANT/TRK PLD (20 AMP)
- TRUNK LID PULL DOWN MOTOR
- POWER ANTENNA

ELC (30 AMP)
- ELECTRONIC LEVEL CONTROL (ELC)

R HTD SEAT (10 AMP)
- PASSENGERS HEATED SEAT

L HTD SEAT (10 AMP)
- DRIVER'S HEATED SEAT

91046G35

Trunk compartment fuse panel locations—1994–95 Seville

DISTR 20A	SIR 20A	PCM (IGN) 10A	INJ 10A	INJ 10A	IGN 1 10A	FUEL PUMP 20A
PCM (BAT) 10A	RTD BATT 10A	A/C COMP 10A	HDLPS 30A	STOP LP 20A	TURN/HAZ 20A	
DRL 10A	DRL 10A	HTD W/S 10A	LR STRUT 10A	RR STRUT 10A	LF STRUT 10A	RF STRUT 10A
L HDLP LO 10A	R HDLP LO 10A	L HDLP HI 10A	R HDLP HI 10A	IGN 3 10A	COOL FAN 10A	TRANS 10A

FUSE CENTER IDENTIFICATION

ENGINE COMPARTMENT FUSE BLOCK

DISTR 20A
- IGNITION CONTROL MODULE

SIR 20A
- DIAGNOSTIC/ENERGY RESERVE MODULE (DERM)
- DUAL POLE ARMING SENSOR

PCM (IGN) 10A
- POWERTRAIN CONTROL MODULE (PCM)
- PASS-Key® DECODER MODULE

INJ 10A
- 1, 4, 6, AND 7 FUEL INJECTORS

INJ 10A
- 2, 3, 5, AND 8 FUEL INJECTORS

IGN 1 10A
- A/C REFRIGERANT PRESSURE SWITCH
- TRANSAXLE RANGE SWITCH
- STOP/BTSI/CRUISE BRAKE SWITCH
- INSTRUMENT PANEL CLUSTER
- KEYLESS ENTRY MODULE
- DIAGNOSTIC/ENERGY RESERVE MODULE (DERM)
- CORNERING LIGHTS
- TURN/HAZARD SWITCH ASSY.
- CHIME MODULE
- HEADLIGHT SWITCH
- TWILIGHT SENTINEL/DRL MODULE

FUEL PUMP 20A
- FUEL PUMP
- OIL PRESSURE SWITCH
- POWERTRAIN CONTROL MODULE (PCM)

PCM (BAT) 10A
- POWERTRAIN CONTROL MODULE (PCM)

RTD (BAT) 10A
- ROAD SENSING SUSPENSION (RSS) MODULE

A/C COMP 10A
- A/C COMPRESSOR CLUTCH

HDLPS 30A
- HEADLIGHT DIMMER SWITCH
- HEADLIGHT RELAY "D" (ENGINE COMP. MICRO RELAY CENTER)
- DRL HEADLIGHT RELAY "E" (WITH DAYTIME RUNNING LIGHTS)
- POWERS C13

STOP LP 20A
- STOP/BTSI/CRUISE SWITCH
- STOPLIGHT SWITCH CAPACITOR

TURN/HAZ 20A
- HAZARD FLASHER
- TURN FLASHER RELAY
- TURN FLASHER MODULE

DRL 10A (CANADA)
- DAYTIME RUNNING LIGHTS (CANADA)

DRL 10A (CANADA)
- LEFT AND RIGHT LO BEAM HEADLAMP

HTD W/S 10A
- HEATED WINDSHIELD CONTROL MODULE

L HDLP LO 10A
- LEFT LO BEAM HEADLAMP

R HDLP LO 10A
- RIGHT LO BEAM HEADLAMP

L HDLP HI 10A
- LEFT HI BEAM HEADLAMP

R HDLP HI 10A
- RIGHT HI BEAM HEADLAMP

IGN 3 10A
- REAR DEFOGGER RELAY
- ELECTRONIC LEVEL CONTROL (ELC)
- HEATED WINDSHIELD
- HEATER AND A/C PROGRAMMER
- CRUISE CONTROL

COOLING FAN 10A
- EXTENDED TRAVEL BRAKE SWITCH
- POWERTRAIN CONTROL MODULE (PCM)
- COOLING FAN RELAYS 1, 2, AND 3
- FRONT AND REAR HEATED OXYGEN SENSOR

TRANS/ECS 10A
- OVERSPEED ALERT MODULE (EXPORT)
- POWER STEERING PRESSURE SWITCH
- EXHAUST GAS RECIRCULATION (EGR) VALVE
- TRANSAXLE SHIFT SOLENOIDS A & B
- EVAPORATIVE EMISSION CONTROL SOLENOID
- POWERTRAIN CONTROL MODULE (PCM)
- TORQUE CONVERTER CLUTCH SOLENOID
- TCC BRAKE SWITCH

91046G43

Engine compartment fuse center locations—1994–95 Seville

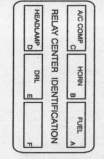

RELAY CENTER IDENTIFICATION			1 50A	6 50A
HEADLAMP D / E / F	A/C COMP C / HORN B / FUEL A	DRL	2 60A	5 50A
			3 30A C.B.	4 40A
			4 30A	3 50A
			5 60A	2 30A
			6 60A	1 30A C.B.

LH MAXI® FUSE BLOCK

FUSE 1 (50 AMP) (STRG 1-2)
- RETAINED ACCESSORY POWER (RADIO/WIPERS)
- STARTER
- TRUNK COMP. FUSES B11 AND B13

FUSE 2 (60 AMP) (BODY)
- ENGINE COMP. B11
- ROAD SENSING SUSPENSION
- FOG LIGHTS
- TRUNK COMP. FUSE C1, C3, C5, C7, C9, AND C11
- TRUNK COMP. FUSE C13 (EXPORT)
- REAR FOG LIGHT (EXPORT)

CIRCUIT BREAKER 3 (30 AMP) (SEAT)
- LEFT AND RIGHT POWER SEAT SWITCHES
- LEFT AND RIGHT LUMBAR RELAYS
- POWER DOOR LOCKS
- KEYLESS ENTRY MODULE
- HORNS
- FUEL DOOR RELEASE SWITCH
- TRUNK RELEASE SWITCH

FUSE 4 (30 AMP) (IPC)
- POWERTRAIN CONTROL MODULE (PCM)
- ELECTRONIC CLIMATE CONTROL
- RAP/ILLUMINATED ENTRY MODULE
- INSTRUMENT PANEL CLUSTER
- PASS-Key® DECODER MODULE
- THEFT DETERRENT

FUSE 5 (60 AMP) (HVAC)
- LEFT AND RIGHT HEATED SEATS
- ELECTRONIC LEVEL CONTROL (ELC)
- TRUNK LID PULL DOWN

- POWER ANTENNA
- REAR DEFOGGER
- LEFT AND RIGHT MIRROR DEFOGGERS

FUSE 6 (60 AMP) (STRG 3)
- RETAINED ACCESSORY POWER (SUNROOF/POWER WINDOWS)
- ENGINE COMP. FUSES D1, D3, D5
- TRUNK COMP. FUSES A1, A3, A5, A7, A9

RH MAXI® FUSE BLOCK

CIRCUIT BREAKER 1 (30 AMP) (DAB)
- RETAINED ACCESSORY POWER (RAP) (SUNROOF/POWER WINDOWS)

FUSE 2 (30 AMP) (RADIO)
- DELCO-BOSE® SPEAKERS
- RADIO CONTROL HEAD
- REMOTE RADIO RECEIVER

FUSE 3 (50 AMP) (COOL)
- COOLING FANS

FUSE 4 (40 AMP) HVAC BLOWER (BLOWER)
- HVAC POWER MOTOR
- A/C COMPRESSOR

FUSE 5 (50 AMP) ABS (BRAKES)
- BRAKE PRESSURE MODULATOR VALVE

FUSE 6 (50 AMP) (LAMPS)
- TURN FLASHER MODULE
- HAZARD FLASHER
- STOP/BTSI/CRUISE BRAKE SWITCH
- PARKING LIGHTS
- DAY TIME RUNNING LIGHTS (CANADA)
- ENGINE COMP. FUSES B1, B3 AND B5
- TRUNK COMP. FUSES D11, D13

91046G36

Maxi fuse block locations—1994–95 Seville

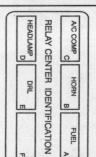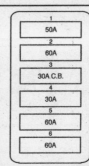

RELAY CENTER IDENTIFICATION			1 50A	6 50A
HEADLAMP D / E / F	A/C COMP C / HORN B / FUEL A	DRL	2 60A	5 50A
			3 30A C.B.	4 40A
			4 30A	3 50A
			5 60A	2 30A
			6 60A	1 30A C.B.

LH MAXI® FUSE BLOCK

FUSE 1 (50 AMP) (STRG 1-2)
- RETAINED ACCESSORY POWER (RADIO/WIPERS)
- STARTER
- TRUNK COMP. FUSES B11 AND B13

FUSE 2 (60 AMP) (BODY)
- ENGINE COMP. B11
- ROAD SENSING SUSPENSION
- FOG LIGHTS
- TRUNK COMP. FUSE C1, C3, C5, C7, C9, AND C11
- TRUNK COMP. FUSE C13 (EXPORT)
- REAR FOG LIGHT (EXPORT)

CIRCUIT BREAKER 3 (30 AMP) (SEAT)
- LEFT AND RIGHT POWER SEAT SWITCHES
- LEFT AND RIGHT LUMBAR RELAYS
- POWER DOOR LOCKS
- KEYLESS ENTRY MODULE
- HORNS
- FUEL DOOR RELEASE SWITCH
- TRUNK RELEASE SWITCH

FUSE 4 (30 AMP) (IPC)
- POWERTRAIN CONTROL MODULE (PCM)
- ELECTRONIC CLIMATE CONTROL
- RAP/ILLUMINATED ENTRY MODULE
- INSTRUMENT PANEL CLUSTER
- PASS-Key® DECODER MODULE
- THEFT DETERRENT

FUSE 5 (60 AMP) (HVAC)
- LEFT AND RIGHT HEATED SEATS
- ELECTRONIC LEVEL CONTROL (ELC)
- TRUNK LID PULL DOWN

- POWER ANTENNA
- REAR DEFOGGER
- LEFT AND RIGHT MIRROR DEFOGGERS

FUSE 6 (60 AMP) (STRG 3)
- RETAINED ACCESSORY POWER (SUNROOF/POWER WINDOWS)
- ENGINE COMP. FUSES D1, D3, D5
- TRUNK COMP. FUSES A1, A3, A5, A7, A9

RH MAXI® FUSE BLOCK

CIRCUIT BREAKER 1 (30 AMP) (DAB)
- RETAINED ACCESSORY POWER (RAP) (SUNROOF/POWER WINDOWS)

FUSE 2 (30 AMP) (RADIO)
- DELCO-BOSE® SPEAKERS
- RADIO CONTROL HEAD
- REMOTE RADIO RECEIVER

FUSE 3 (50 AMP) (COOL)
- COOLING FANS

FUSE 4 (40 AMP) HVAC BLOWER (BLOWER)
- HVAC POWER MOTOR
- A/C COMPRESSOR

FUSE 5 (50 AMP) ABS (BRAKES)
- BRAKE PRESSURE MODULATOR VALVE

FUSE 6 (50 AMP) (LAMPS)
- TURN FLASHER MODULE
- HAZARD FLASHER
- STOP/BTSI/CRUISE BRAKE SWITCH
- PARKING LIGHTS
- DAY TIME RUNNING LIGHTS (CANADA)
- ENGINE COMP. FUSES B1, B3 AND B5
- TRUNK COMP. FUSES D11, D13

91046G36

Engine compartment fuse center locations—1994–95 Eldorado

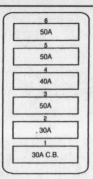

LH MAXI® FUSE BLOCK

FUSE 1 (50 AMP) (STRG 1-2)
RETAINED ACCESSORY POWER
(RADIO,WIPERS)
STARTER
TRUNK COMP. FUSES B11 AND B13

FUSE 2 (60 AMP) (BODY)
ENGINE COMP. B11
ROAD SENSING SUSPENSION
FOG LIGHTS
TRUNK COMP. FUSE C1, C3, C5, C7, C9, AND C11
TRUNK COMP. FUSE C13 (EXPORT)
REAR FOG LIGHT (EXPORT)

CIRCUIT BREAKER 3 (30 AMP) (SEAT)
LEFT AND RIGHT POWER SEAT SWITCHES
LEFT AND RIGHT LUMBAR RELAYS
POWER DOOR LOCKS
KEYLESS ENTRY MODULE
HORNS
FUEL DOOR RELEASE SWITCH
TRUNK RELEASE SWITCH

FUSE 4 (30 AMP) (IPC)
POWERTRAIN CONTROL MODULE (PCM)
ELECTRONIC CLIMATE CONTROL
RAP/ILLUMINATED ENTRY MODULE
INSTRUMENT PANEL CLUSTER
PASS-Key² DECODER MODULE
THEFT DETERRENT

FUSE 5 (60 AMP) (HVAC)
LEFT AND RIGHT HEATED SEATS
ELECTRONIC LEVEL CONTROL (ELC)
TRUNK LID PULL DOWN

- POWER ANTENNA
- REAR DEFOGGER
- LEFT AND RIGHT MIRROR DEFOGGERS

FUSE 6 (60 AMP) (STRG 3)
RETAINED ACCESSORY POWER
(SUNROOF/POWER WINDOWS)
ENGINE COMP. FUSES D1, D3, D5
TRUNK COMP. FUSES A1, A3, A5, A7, A9

RH MAXI® FUSE BLOCK

CIRCUIT BREAKER 1 (30 AMP) (DAB)
RETAINED ACCESSORY POWER (RAP)
(SUNROOF/POWER WINDOWS)

FUSE 2 (30 AMP) (RADIO)
DELCO-BOSE® SPEAKERS
RADIO CONTROL HEAD
REMOTE RADIO RECEIVER

FUSE 3 (50 AMP) (COOL)
COOLING FANS

FUSE 4 (40 AMP) HVAC BLOWER (BLOWER)
HVAC POWER MOTOR
A/C COMPRESSOR

FUSE 5 (50 AMP) ABS (BRAKES)
BRAKE PRESSURE MODULATOR VALVE

FUSE 6 (50 AMP) (LAMPS)
- TURN FLASHER MODULE
- HAZARD FLASHER
- STOP/BTSI/CRUISE BRAKE SWITCH
- PARKING LIGHTS
- DAY TIME RUNNING LIGHTS (CANADA)
- ENGINE COMP. FUSES B1, B3 AND B5
- TRUNK COMP. FUSES D11, D13

91046G38

Maxi fuse block locations—1994–95 Eldorado

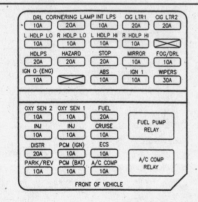

A/C COMP (10 A) ....
ABS Fuse (10 A) ....
CIG LTR1 Fuse (20 A) ....
CIG LTR2 Fuse (20 A) ....
CORNERING LAMP Fuse (10 A) ....
CRUISE Fuse (10 A) ....
DISTR Fuse (20 A) ....
DRL Fuse (10 A) ....
ECS Fuse (10 A) ....
FOG/DRL Fuse (10 A) ....
FUEL Fuse (20 A) ....
HAZARD Fuse (20 A) ....
HDLPS Fuse (20 A) ....
IGN 0 (ENG) Fuse (10 A) ....
IGN 1 Fuse (10 A) ....

J Fuse (10 A) ....
INJ Fuse (10 A) ....
INT LPS Fuse (10 A) ....
L HDLP HI Fuse (10 A) ....
L HDLP LO Fuse (10 A) ....
MIRROR Fuse (10 A) ....
OXY SEN 1 Fuse (10 A) ....
OXY SEN 2 Fuse (10 A) ....
PARK/REV Fuse (10 A) ....
PCM (BAT) Fuse (10 A) ....
PCM (IGN) Fuse (10 A) ....
R HDLP HI Fuse (10 A) ....
R HDLP LO Fuse (10 A) ....
STOP Fuse (20 A) ....
WIPERS Fuse (30 A) ....

91046G39

Engine compartment fuse center locations—1996–98 Deville, Concours Deville, Eldorado and Seville

Rear Compartment Fuse Block

FUSE	USAGE
CRANK	RAP/Illuminated Entry Module; Sensing & Diagnostic Module; Transaxle Range Switch (NSSS)
IGN 1	Fuel Lever Sensor; Electrochromic Mirror; RAP/Illuminated Entry Module; Theft Deterrent Module; Keyless Entry Module; Turn Flasher Relay "F" Trunk Comp. Micro Relay Center; Catalytic Converter Alarm Module (Export)
HDLP/WASH	Headlamp Washer Module (Export Only)
SUSP	Road Sensing Suspension (RSS) Module
IPC (IGN)	Instrument Panel Cluster
CNSL SW	Rear Blower Relay "E"; Console Switch
ABS	Electronic Brake and Traction Control Module (EBTCM)
WIPER	Wiper/Washer Switch
RAD (IGN)	Remote Radio Receiver
R DEFOG	Rear Defogger
HTD MIRR	Left and Right Outside Mirror Defoggers
IPC (BATT)	Instrument Panel Cluster
THEFT	PASS-Key®II Decoder Module; Theft Deterrent Relay "D" (Trunk Comp. Relay Center); Theft Deterrent Module
HVAC/DABIE	Heater and A/C Programmer; RAP/Illuminated Entry Module
REAR FOG	Rear Fog Lamp Relay A (Export)
FOG LP	Fog Lamp Relays A and F
CNSL FAN	Rear Blower Motor; Rear Blower Relay
CIGAR	Front Cigarette Lighter; Chime Module
BODY 2	Power Mirror Switch; RAP Relay; Lock-Out Inhibit Relay "B" (Trunk Comp. 1 Micro Relay Center); Panel Lights Inhibit Relay "F" (Trunk Comp. 3 Micro Relay Center)(Export); Courtesy Lamps Relay "C" (Trunk Comp. 2 Micro Relay Center); RAP Relay "E" (Trunk Comp. 2 Micro Relay Center); Keyless Entry Module; Trunk Lamp; Seat Belt Retractor Solenoids
BODY 1	Front Door Lock Switches; Glove Box Lamp; Left and Right Footwell Courtesy Lamps; Headlamp Switch
READ LP	Left and Right Front Header Lamp; Left and Right Vanity Mirror; Garage Door Opener; Left and Right Rear Header Lamps
L PRK LP	Left Rear Tail/Stop/Turn Lamps; Left Front Park/Turn Lamps; Front and Rear Left Side Marker Lamps; Radio Control Head; Headlamp Switch; Instrument Panel Cluster
R PRK LP	Right Tail/Stop/Turn Lamps; Right Front and Rear Side Marker Lamps; Right Front Park and Turn Lamps; Engine Comp. Lamp; License Plate Lamps
RAD (BAT)	Radio
ANT/TRK PLD	Trunk Lid Pull Down Motor; Power Antenna
ELC	Electronic Level Control (ELC)
R HTD SEAT	Passengers Heated Seat
L HTD SEAT	Driver's Heated Seat

91046G44

Trunk compartment fuse panel locations—1994–95 Eldorado

TRUNK COMPARTMENT FUSE BLOCK

ACC Fuse (10 A) ....
AMP Fuse (30 A) ....
ANTENNA Fuse (20 A) ....
BATT Fuse (10 A) ....
CLUSTER Fuse (20 A) ....
COMFORT Fuse (10 A) ....
CONSOLE Fuse (10 A) ....
CONVENC Fuse (20 A) ....
ELC Fuse (10 A) ....
HDLP WASH Fuse (30 A) ....
HTD BACKLT Fuse (30 A) ....
HTD MIR Fuse (10 A) ....
HTD SEAT L Fuse (10 A) ....
HTD SEAT R Fuse (10 A) ....

IGN 0-BODY Fuse (10 A) ....
IGN 0-BODY Fuse (10 A) (DEVILLE) ....
LT PARK Fuse (10 A) ....
PULL DOWN Fuse (20 A) ....
PZM Fuse (10 A) ....
RADIO/PHONE Fuse (10 A) ....
RLY IGN 1 Fuse (10 A) ....
RT PARK Fuse (10 A) ....
RSS Fuse (10 A) ....
RSS Fuse (10 A) ....
RSS Fuse (10 A) ....
SIR Fuse (20 A) ....
TURN Fuse (20 A) ....

91046G40

Trunk compartment fuse panel locations—1996–98 Deville, Concours Deville, Eldorado and Seville

Fusible Links

Fuse links are used to protect the main wiring harness and selected branches from complete burnout, should a short circuit or electrical overload occur. A fuse link is a short length of insulated wire, integral with the engine compartment wiring harness. It is several wire gauges smaller than the circuit it protects and generally located in-line directly from the positive terminal of the battery.

Production fuse links are color coded as follows:
- Gray: 12 gauge
- Dark Green: 14 gauge
- Black: 16 gauge
- Brown: 18 gauge
- Dark Blue: 20 gauge

When a heavy current flows, such as when a booster battery is connected incorrectly or when a short to ground occurs in the wiring harness, the fuse link burns out and protects the alternator or wiring.

A burned out fuse link may have bare wire ends protruding from the insulation, or it may have only expanded or bubbled insulation with illegible identification. When it is hard to determine if the fuse link is burned out, perform the continuity test:

1. Make sure the battery is okay, then turn on the headlights or an accessory. If the headlights or accessory do not work, the fuse link is probably burned out.

2. If equipped with more than one fuse link, use the same procedure as in Step 1 to test each link separately.

3. To test the fuse link that protects the alternator, make sure the battery is okay, then check with a voltmeter for voltage at the BAT terminal of the alternator. No voltage indicates that the fuse link is probably burned out.

REPLACEMENT

When replacing a fuse link, always make sure the replacement fuse link is a duplicate of the one removed with respect to gauge, length and insulation. Original equipment and original equipment specification replacement fuse links have insulation that is flame proof. Do not fabricate a fuse link from ordinary wire because the insulation may not be flame proof.

If a circuit protected by a fuse link becomes inoperative, inspect for a blown fuse link. If the fuse link wire insulation is burned or opened, disconnect the feed as close as possible behind the splice in the harness. If the damaged fuse link is between 2 splices (weld points in the harness), cut out the damaged portion as close as possible to the weld points.

Replace the fuse link as follows:

1. To service a 2-link group when only one link has blown and the other link is not damaged, proceed as follows:

   a. Disconnect the negative battery cable.

   b. Cut out the blown fusible link (2 places).

   c. Position the correct eyelet type service fusible link with the bare end to the correct size wire connector and crimp to the wire ends.

   d. Heat the splice insulation until the tubing shrinks and adhesive flows from each end of the connector.

   e. Connect the negative battery cable.

2. To service a fuse link in a multi-feed or single circuit, proceed as follows:

   a. Disconnect the negative battery cable.

   b. Determine which circuit is damaged, its location, and the cause of the open fuse link. If the damaged fuse link is one of 3 fed by a common number 10 or 12 gauge feed wire, determine the specific affected circuit.

   c. Cut the damaged fuse link from the wiring harness and discard. If the fuse link is one of 3 circuits fed by a single feed wire, cut it out of the harness at each splice end and discard.

   d. Obtain the proper fuse link and butt connectors for attaching the fuse link to the harness.

   e. Strip 5/16 in. (7.6 mm) of insulation from the wire ends and insert into the proper size wire connector. Crimp and heat the splice insulation until the tubing shrinks and adhesive flows from each end of the connector.

   f. To replace a fuse link on a single circuit in a harness, cut out the damaged portion. Strip approximately 1/2 in. (12.7 mm) of insulation from the 2 wire ends and attach the correct size fuse link to each wire end with the proper gauge wire connectors. Crimp and heat the splice insulation until the tubing shrinks and adhesive flows from each end of the connector.

   g. Connect the negative battery cable.

3. To service a fuse link with an eyelet terminal on one end, such as the charging circuit, proceed as follows:

   a. Disconnect the negative battery cable.

   b. Cut off the fuse link behind the weld, strip approximately 1/2 in. (12.7 mm) of insulation from the cut end, and attach the appropriate new eyelet fuse link to the cut stripped wire with the proper size connector.

   c. Crimp and heat the splice insulation until the tubing shrinks and adhesive flows from each end of the connector.

   d. Connect the negative battery cable.

➡ Do not mistake a resistor wire for a fuse link. The resistor wire is generally longer and has print stating "Resistor—do not cut or splice." When attaching a No. 16, 18 or 20 gauge fuse link to a heavy gauge wire, always double the stripped wire end of the fuse link before inserting and crimping it into the wire connector for positive wire retention.

Circuit Breakers

A circuit breaker is a protective device designed to open the circuit when a current load is in excess of the circuit breaker's rating. If there is a short or other type of overload in the circuit, the excessive current will open the circuit between the circuit breaker terminals.

RESETTING AND/OR REPLACEMENT

The headlights are protected by a circuit breaker in the headlight switch. If the circuit breaker opens, the headlights will either flash on and off, or stay off altogether. The circuit breaker resets automatically after the overload is removed.

The windshield wipers are protected by a circuit breaker. If the motor overheats, the circuit breaker will open, remaining off until the motor cools or the overload is removed. A common cause of wiper motor overheating is wiper operation in heavy snow.

Circuit breakers in the fuse block are used to protect the power windows and other power accessories.

Flashers

REPLACEMENT

Deville, Eldorado, Fleetwood, and Seville

▶ See Figures 168 and 169

➡ All vehicles except 1990–91 Eldorado and Seville are equipped with separate turn signal and hazard flashers, which are located under the instrument panel in the steering column area. 1990–91 Eldorado and Seville are equipped with a turn signal/hazard module located behind the center of the instrument panel.

1. Remove the necessary sound insulator panel(s) from under the instrument panel.

2. Remove the flasher from the retaining clip and detach the wiring connector.

To install:

3. Attach the wiring connector to the new flasher and install the flasher in the retaining clip.

4. Install the sound insulator panel(s).

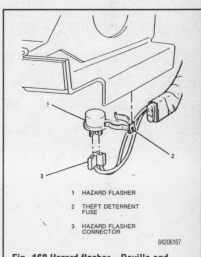

1	HAZARD FLASHER
2	THEFT DETERRENT FUSE
3	HAZARD FLASHER CONNECTOR

84206167

Fig. 168 Hazard flasher—Deville and Fleetwood

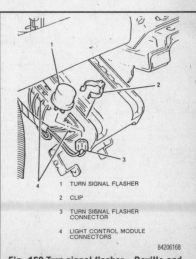

1	TURN SIGNAL FLASHER
2	CLIP
3	TURN SIGNAL FLASHER CONNECTOR
4	LIGHT CONTROL MODULE CONNECTORS

84206168

Fig. 169 Turn signal flasher—Deville and Fleetwood

WIRING DIAGRAMS

INDEX OF WIRING DIAGRAMS

91046W01

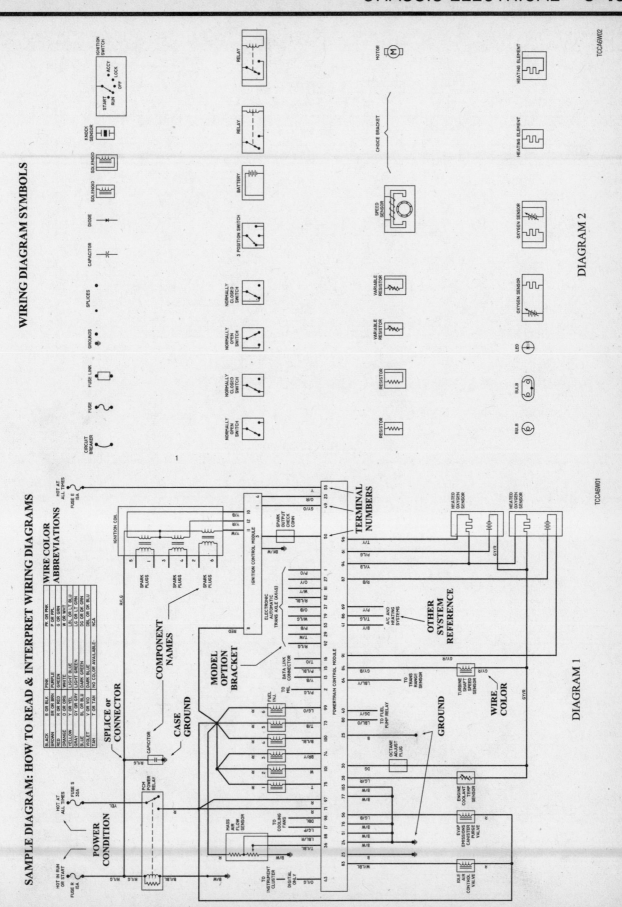

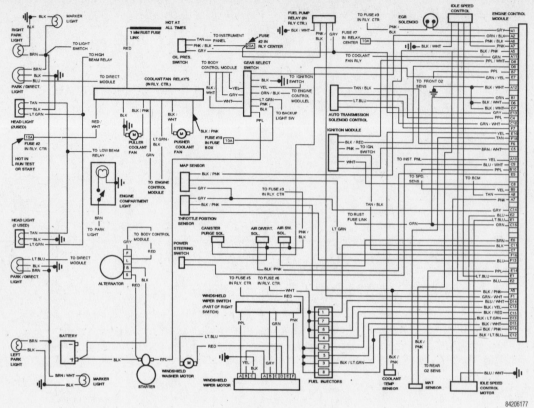

DIAGRAM 3

84206177

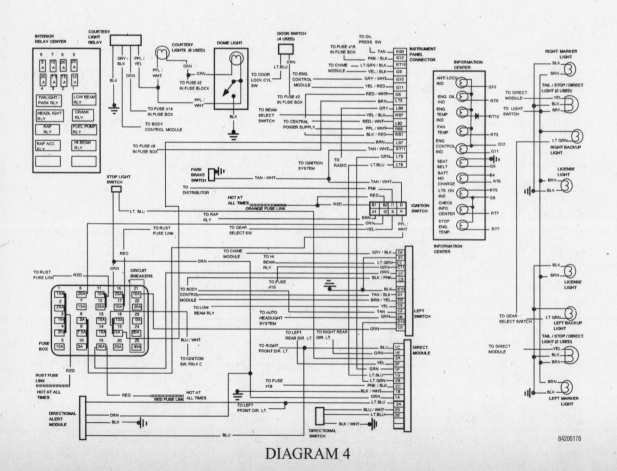

DIAGRAM 4

84206178

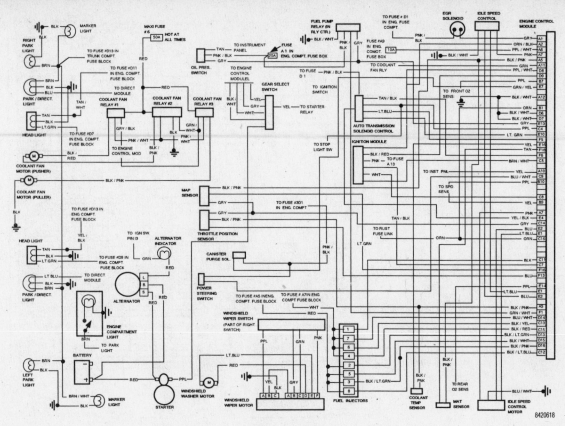

DIAGRAM 5

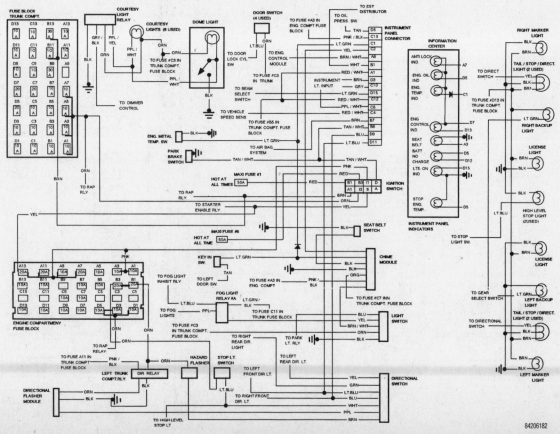

DIAGRAM 6

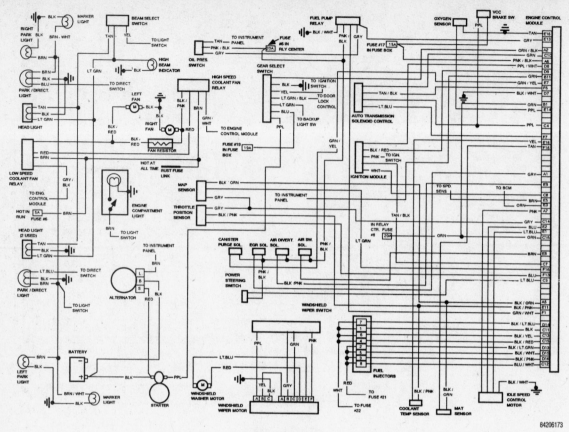

DIAGRAM 7

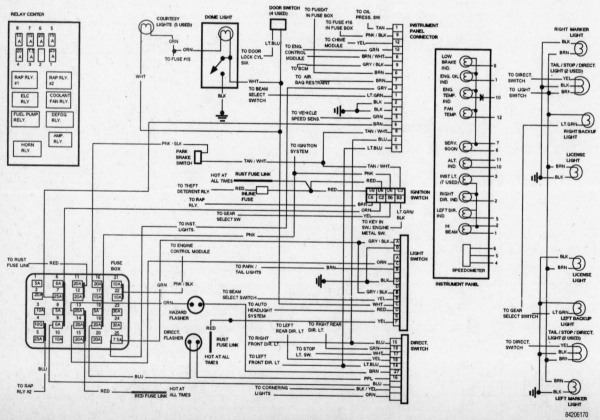

DIAGRAM 8

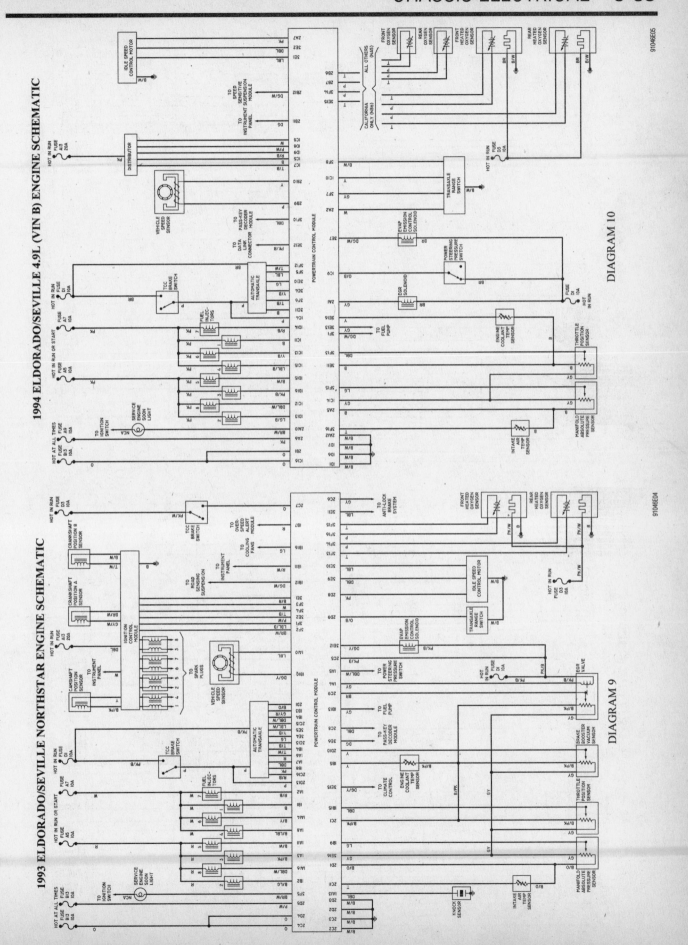

1994 ELDORADO/SEVILLE 4.9L (VIN B) ENGINE SCHEMATIC

DIAGRAM 10

1993 ELDORADO/SEVILLE NORTHSTAR ENGINE SCHEMATIC

DIAGRAM 9

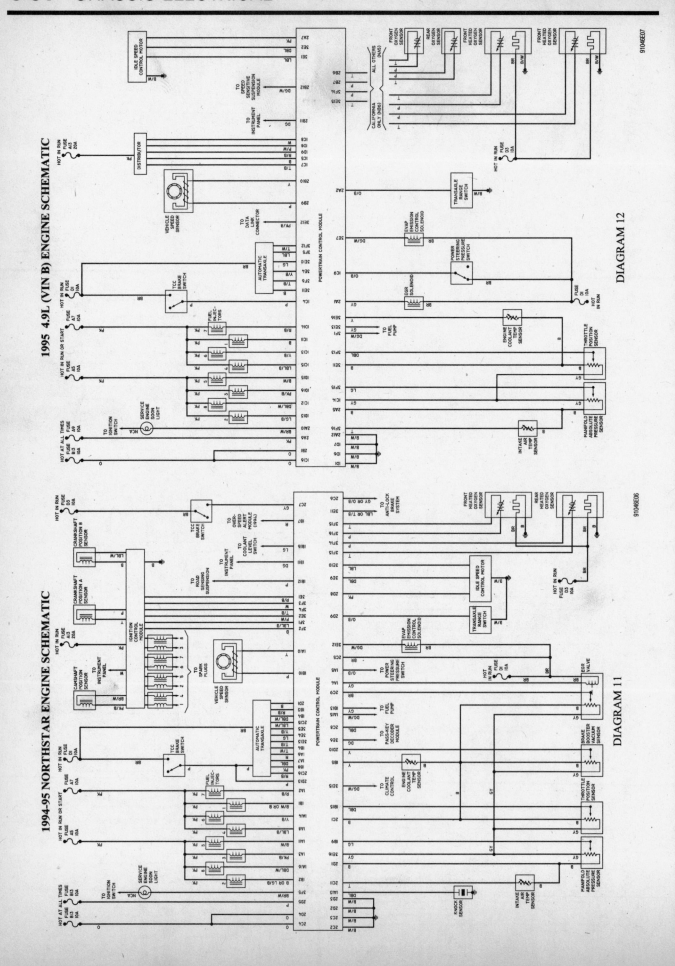

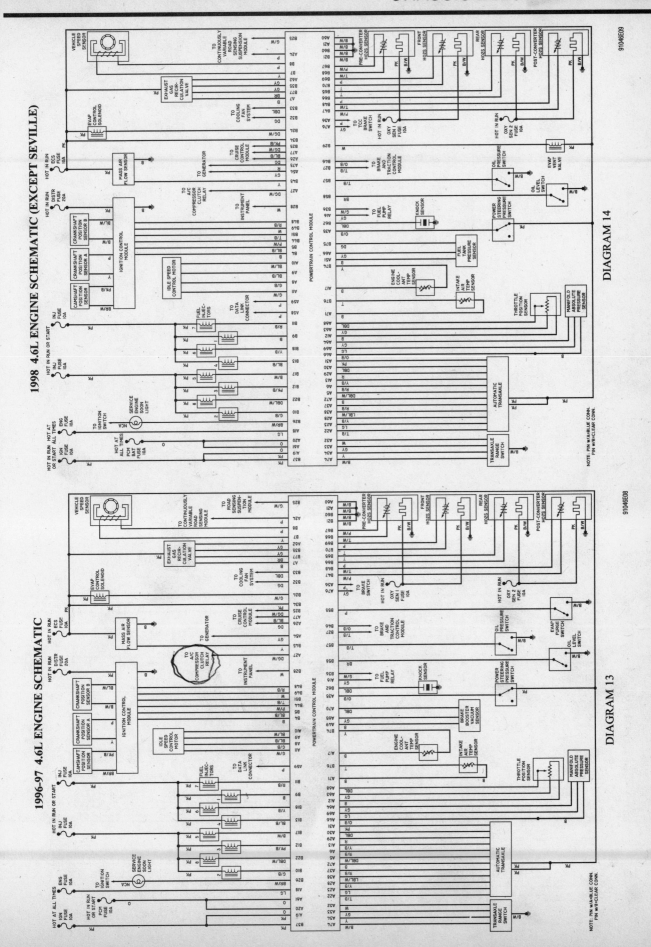

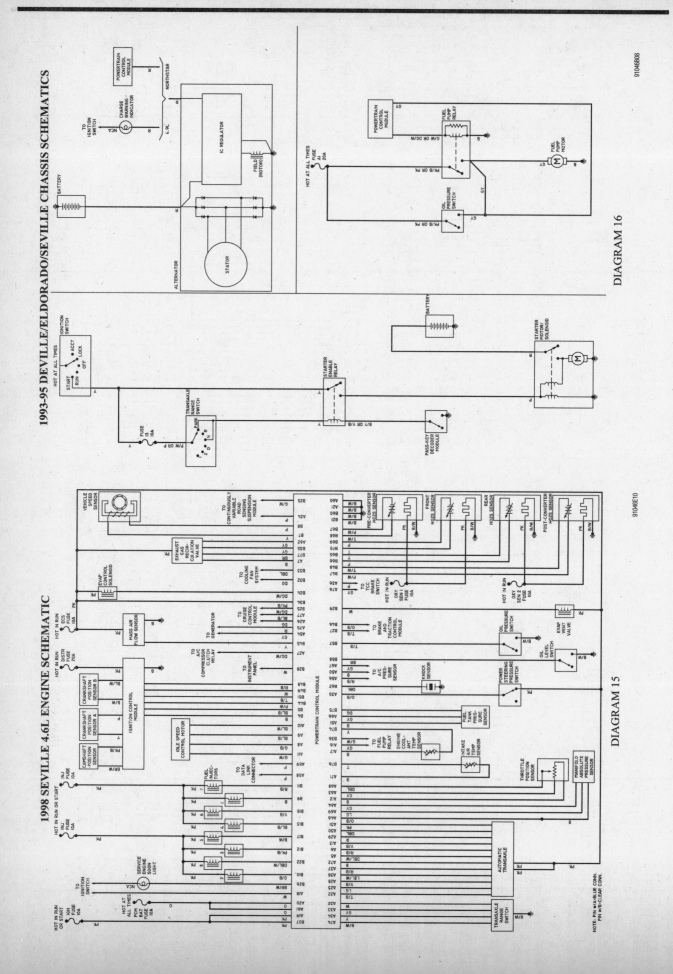

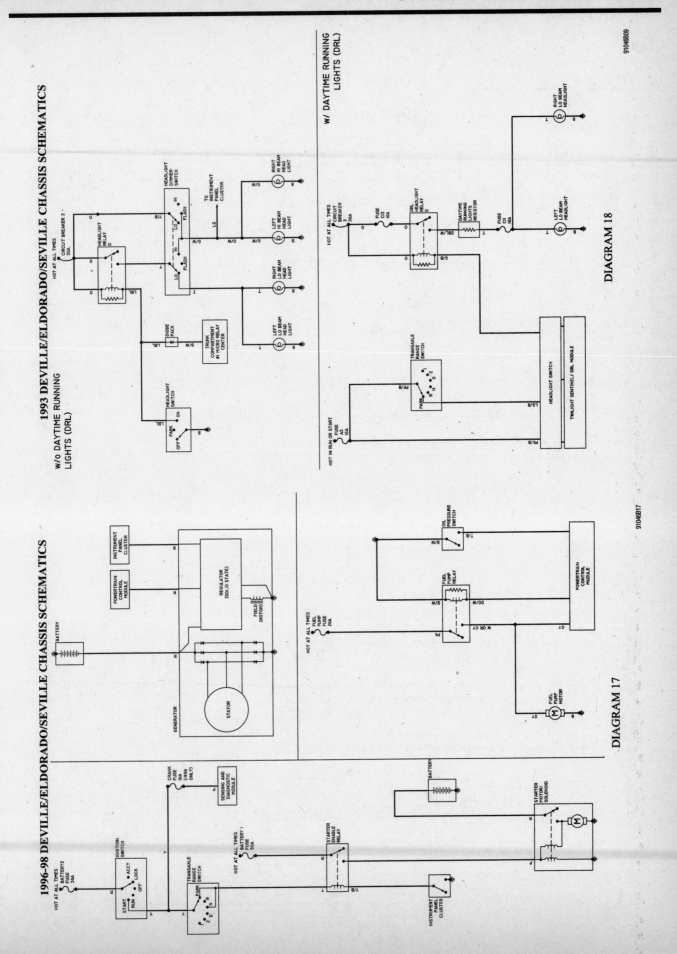

1993 DEVILLE/ELDORADO/SEVILLE CHASSIS SCHEMATICS

w/o DAYTIME RUNNING LIGHTS (DRL)

w/ DAYTIME RUNNING LIGHTS (DRL)

DIAGRAM 18

1996-98 DEVILLE/ELDORADO/SEVILLE CHASSIS SCHEMATICS

DIAGRAM 17

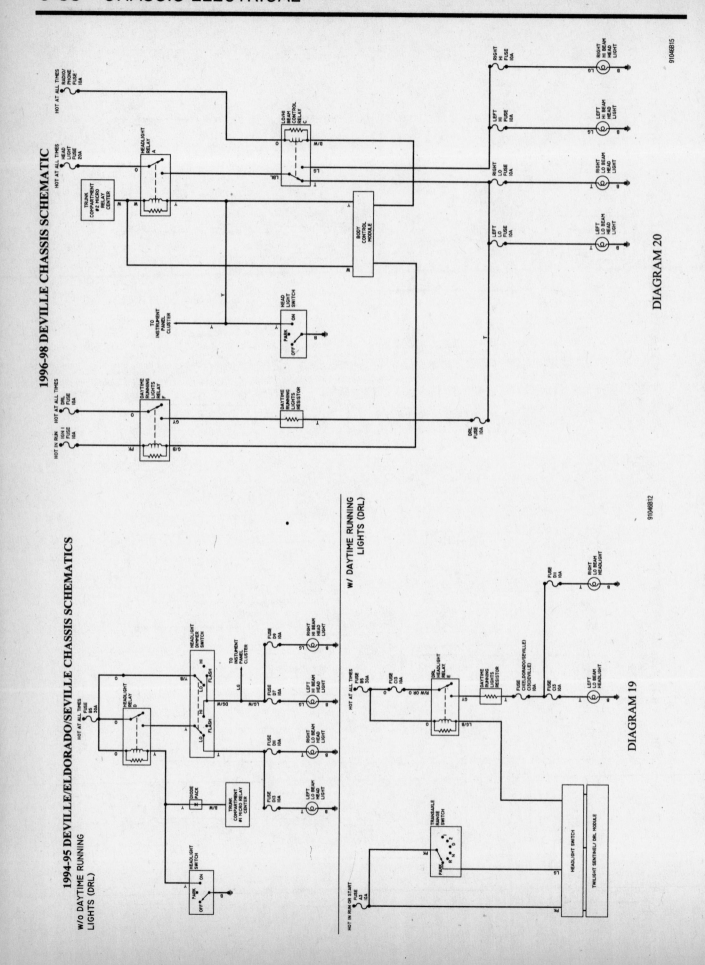

1996-98 DEVILLE CHASSIS SCHEMATIC

DIAGRAM 20

1994-95 DEVILLE/ELDORADO/SEVILLE CHASSIS SCHEMATICS

w/o DAYTIME RUNNING LIGHTS (DRL)

w/ DAYTIME RUNNING LIGHTS (DRL)

DIAGRAM 19

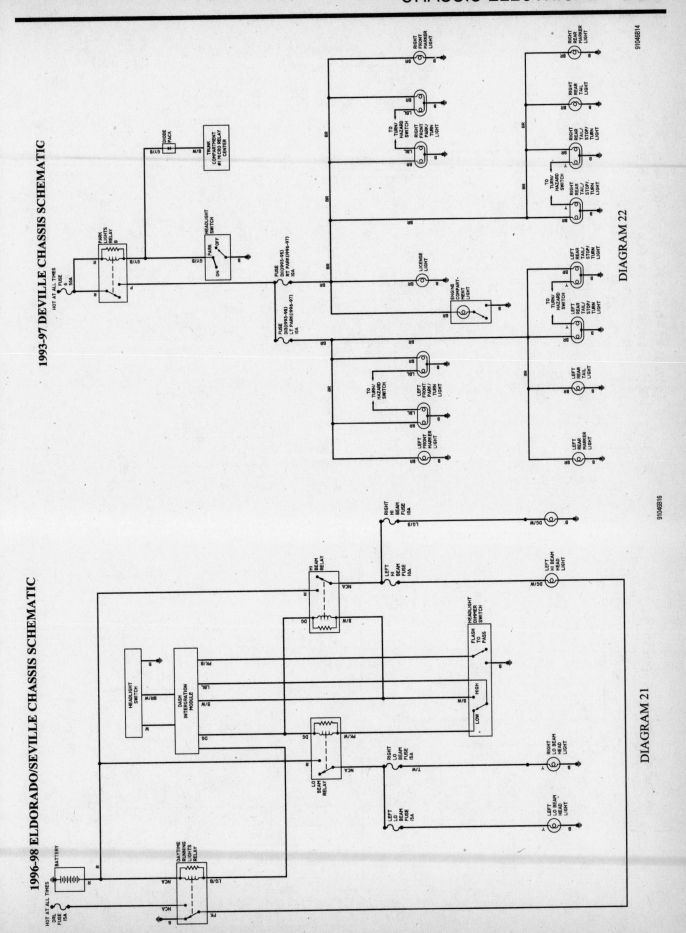

1993-97 DEVILLE CHASSIS SCHEMATIC

DIAGRAM 22

9104B14

1996-98 ELDORADO/SEVILLE CHASSIS SCHEMATIC

DIAGRAM 21

9104B16

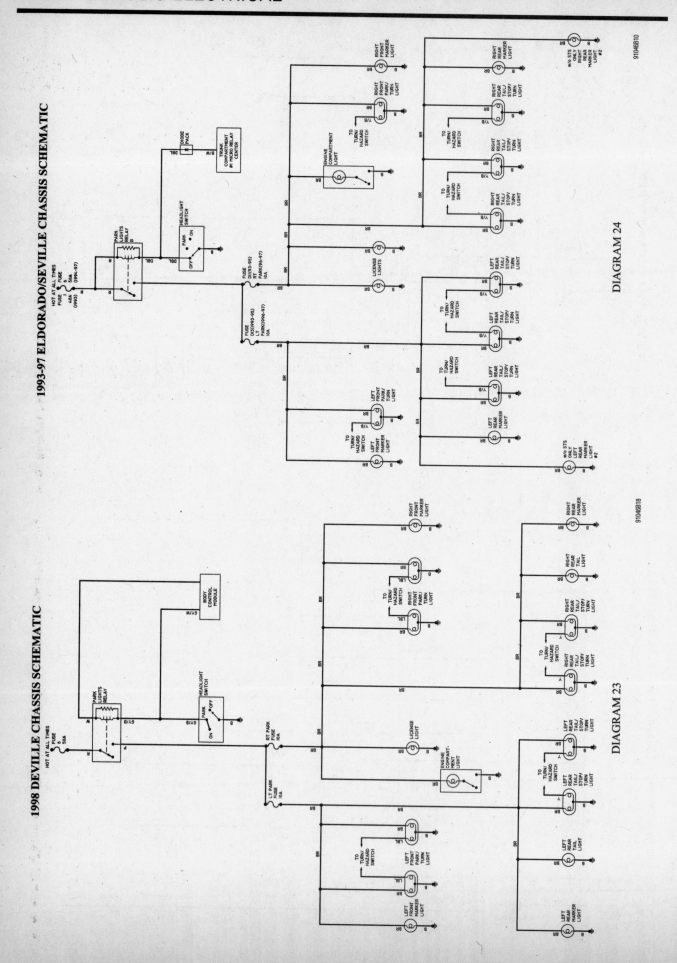

1993-97 ELDORADO/SEVILLE CHASSIS SCHEMATIC

DIAGRAM 24

9104GB10

1998 DEVILLE CHASSIS SCHEMATIC

DIAGRAM 23

9104GB18

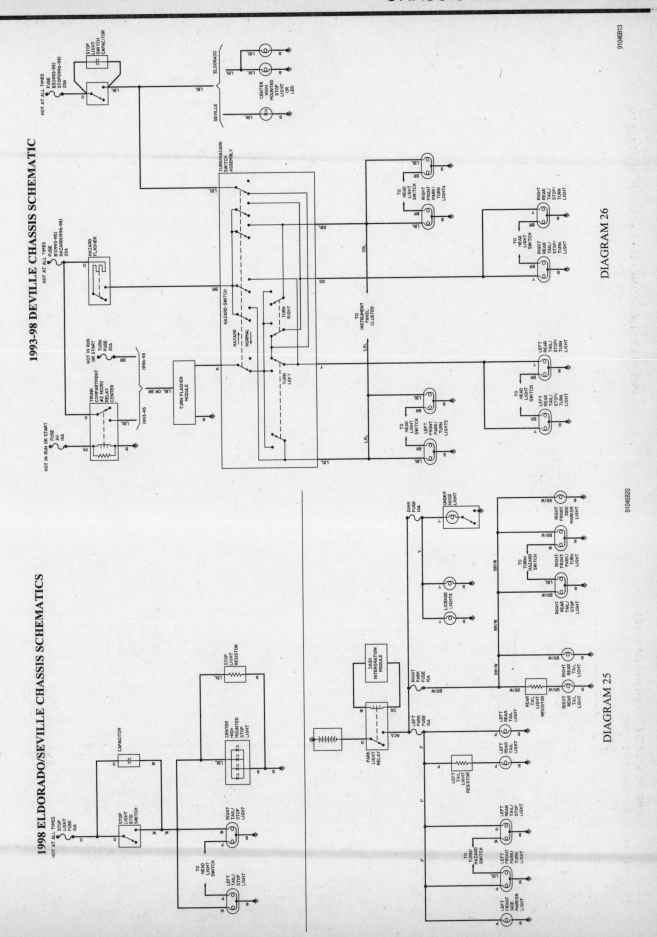

1993-98 DEVILLE CHASSIS SCHEMATIC

DIAGRAM 26

1998 ELDORADO/SEVILLE CHASSIS SCHEMATICS

DIAGRAM 25

1998 SEVILLE CHASSIS SCHEMATIC

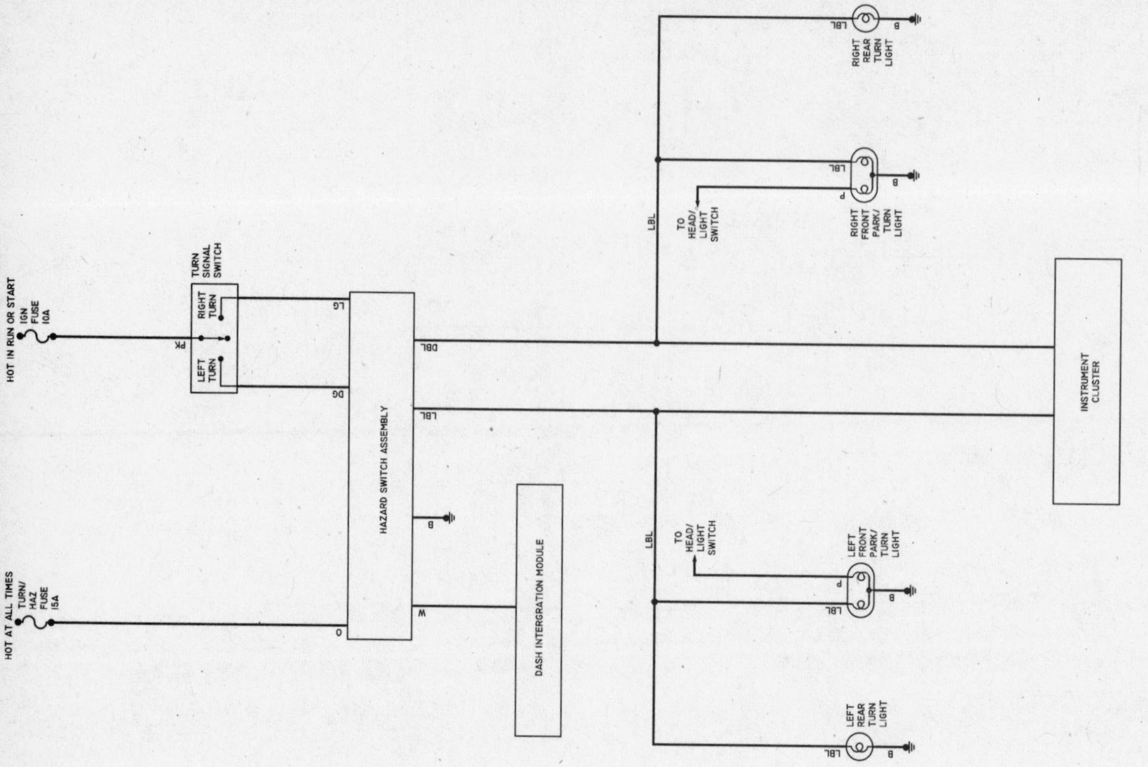

DIAGRAM 28

91046B21

1993-98 ELDORADO/93-97 SEVILLE CHASSIS SCHEMATIC

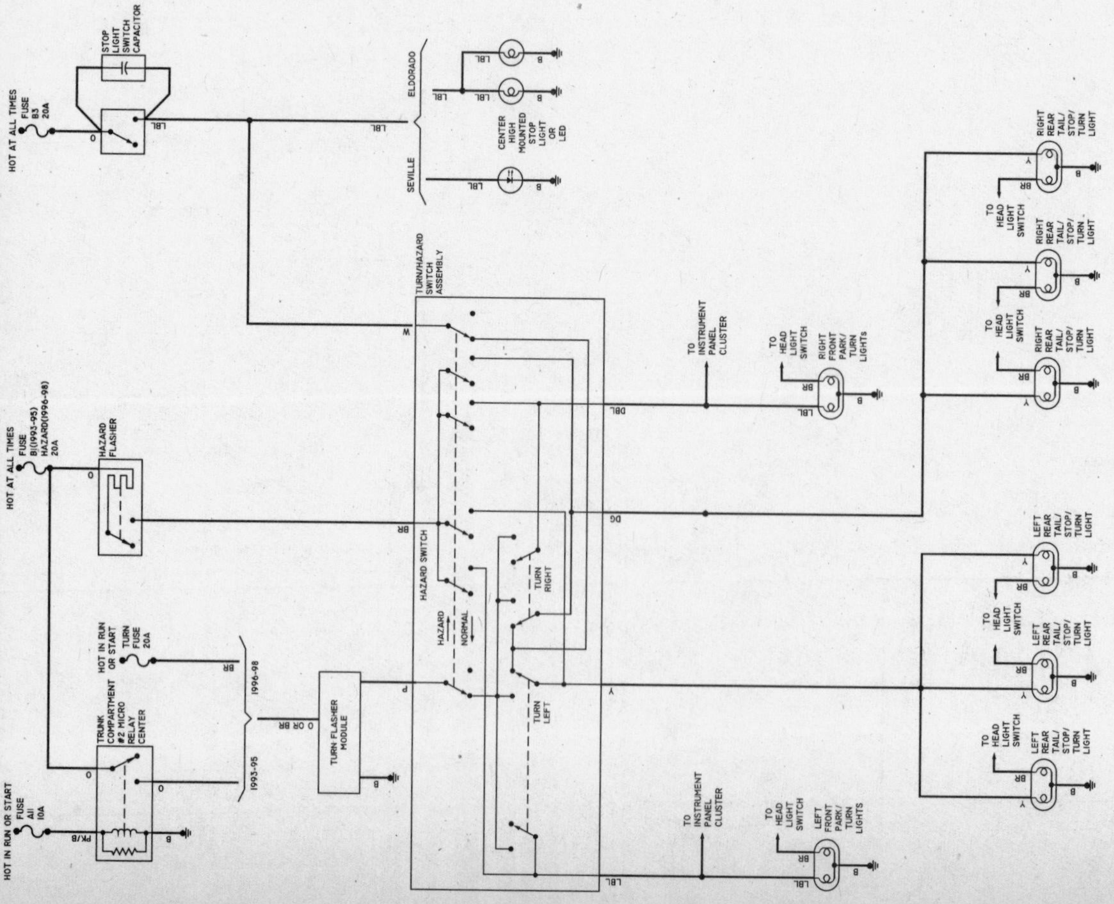

DIAGRAM 27

91046B11

1993-98 DEVILLE/ELDORADO/SEVILLE CHASSIS SCHEMATICS

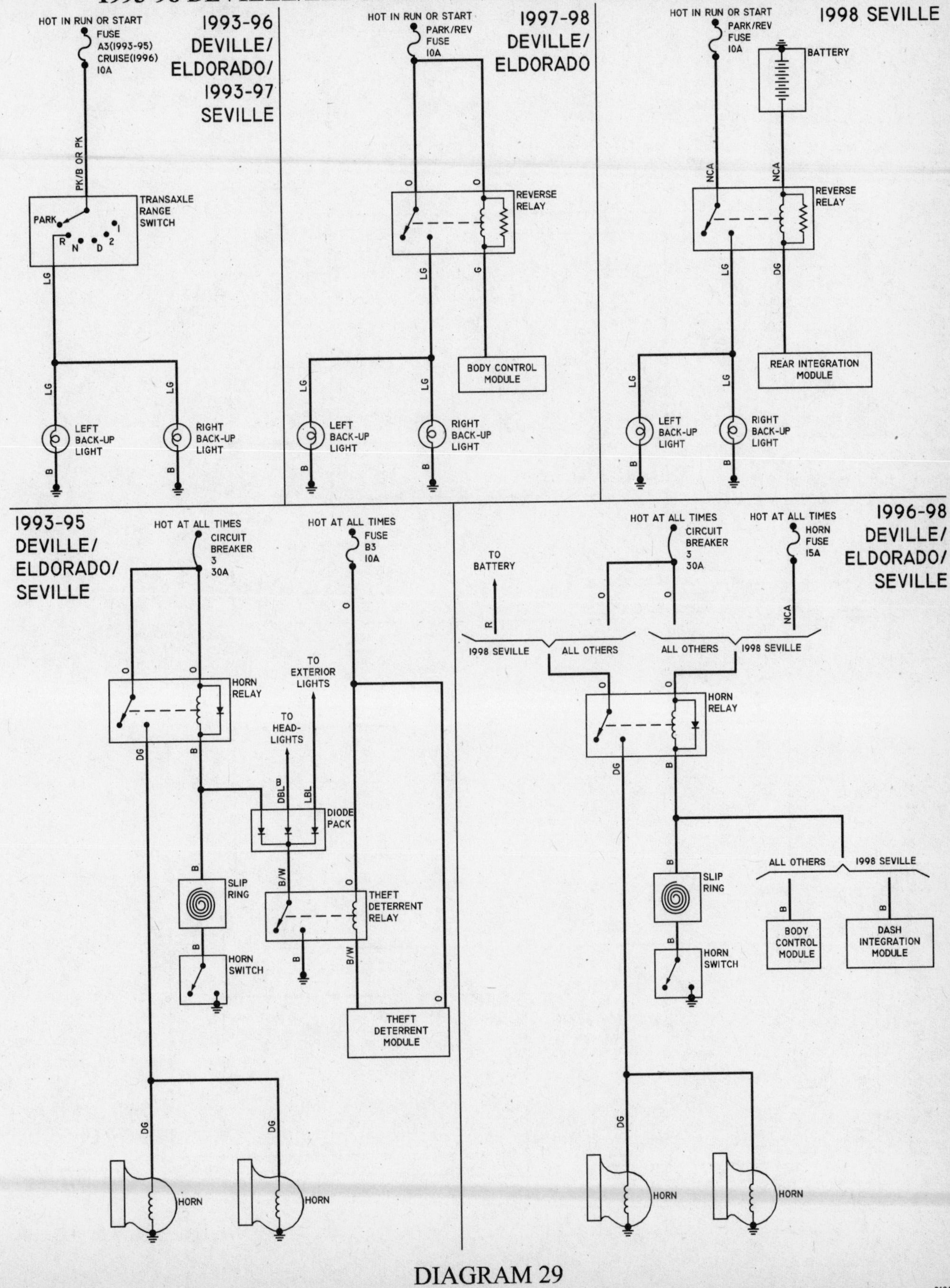

DIAGRAM 29

91046B06

1993-98 DEVILLE/ELDORADO/SEVILLE CHASSIS SCHEMATICS

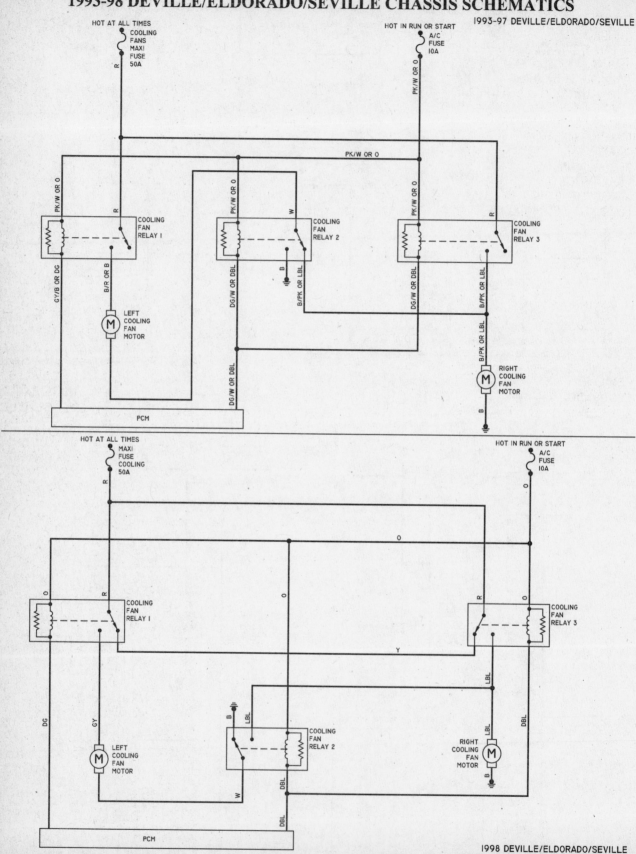

DIAGRAM 30

91046B07

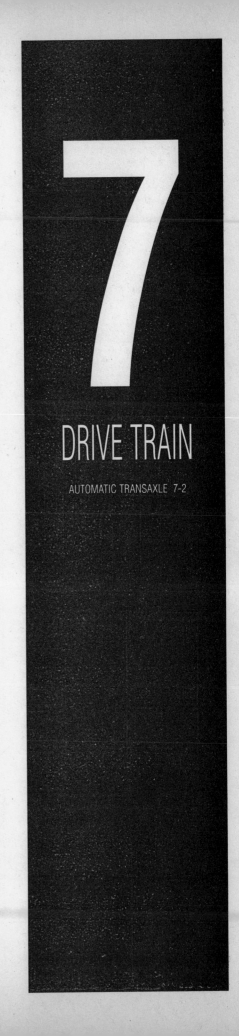

7

DRIVE TRAIN

AUTOMATIC TRANSAXLE 7-2

AUTOMATIC TRANSAXLE

Identification

All 1990 vehicles are equipped with the 4T60 four-speed automatic overdrive transaxle. All 1991–93 vehicles with the 4.9L engine are equipped with the 4T60-E four-speed automatic overdrive transaxle. The 4T60-E is a more advanced version of the 4T60, and features electronic shift control timing by the Powertrain Control Module (PCM). All 1993 and later vehicles with the 4.6L engine are equipped with the 4T80-E four-speed automatic overdrive transaxle. The 4T80-E was developed as an integral part of the Northstar powertrain. It features an electronically controlled torque converter as well as electronic shift control.

Fluid Pan

REMOVAL & INSTALLATION

4T60 and 4T60-E Transaxle

▶ **See Figures 1 thru 13**

1. Raise and safely support the vehicle.
2. Place a suitable drain pan under the transaxle fluid pan.

3. Remove the retaining bolts at the front and sides of the fluid pan.
4. Loosen the rear fluid pan bolts approximately four turns.
5. Pry the fluid pan loose with a small prybar (if necessary) and allow the fluid to drain.

✳✳ WARNING

Be careful not to damage the fluid pan and transaxle case mating surfaces, as damage may result in fluid leaks.

6. Remove the remaining bolts and the fluid pan and gasket.
7. Remove the transaxle screen/filter. The lip ring seal pressed into the case should be removed only if replacement is necessary.
8. Inspect the fluid pan and screen for foreign material, such as metal particles, clutch facing material, rubber particles, or engine coolant. If necessary, determine and correct the source of the contamination.

To install:

9. Clean all gasket-mating surfaces. Clean the fluid pan and screen in solvent and allow them to dry. Inspect the fluid pan flange for distortion and straighten, if necessary.

➡ **The transaxle case and fluid pan flanges must be clean, dry, and free of any oil film prior to fluid pan and gasket installation, or leakage may result. Inspect the washers on the fluid pan bolts before reuse, as shown in Fig. 3.**

10. Install the screen, using a new filter. The filter uses a lip ring seal pressed into the case. The seal should be removed only if replacement is necessary.
11. Install the fluid pan, using a new gasket. Tighten the bolts to 10 ft. lbs. (13 Nm) on 1990 vehicles or 12–13 ft. lbs. (16–17 Nm) on 1991–93 vehicles.
12. Lower the vehicle.
13. Fill the transaxle with six qts. of DEXRON III® transmission fluid.
14. Place the gearshift lever in **P**. Start the engine and let it idle; do not race the engine.
15. Check the fluid level and correct as required. Check the fluid pan for leaks.

4T80-E Transaxle

▶ **See Figures 14, 15 and 16**

➡ **The 4T80-E transaxle has a filter under the side cover that requires service only during a complete transaxle overhaul. However, the**

Fig. 1 Transaxle fluid pan and filter—1990 4T60 transaxle

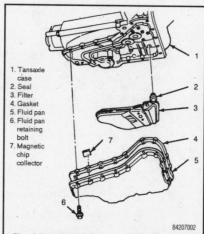

1. Tansaxle case
2. Seal
3. Filter
4. Gasket
5. Fluid pan
6. Fluid pan retaining bolt
7. Magnetic chip collector

Fig. 2 Transaxle fluid pan and filter—1991–93 vehicles with 4T60-E transaxle

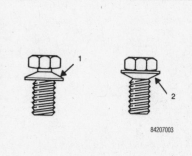

Fig. 3 If the washers on the fluid pan bolts look the same as on bolt No. 1, the bolts can be reused. If the washers look like the one on bolts No. 2, the bolts should not be reused

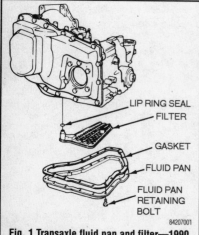

Fig. 4 Loosen the bolts on the transaxle pan

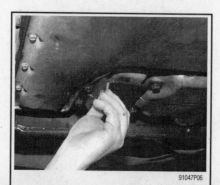

Fig. 5 Remove a select number of bolts to allow the pan to tilt

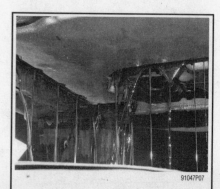

Fig. 6 Allow the fluid to drain before removing the pan completely

Fig. 7 Remove the scavenger screen from the transaxle

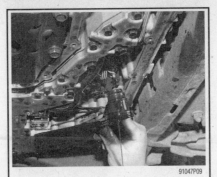

Fig. 8 Be careful when removing the filter, fluid will drain out

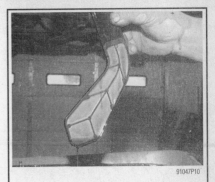

Fig. 9 The scavenger screen can be cleaned

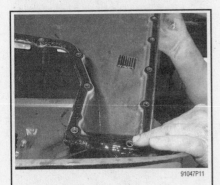

Fig. 10 Remove the gasket on the transaxle pan

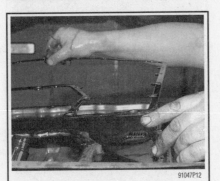

Fig. 11 The gasket on this application is reusable, but not all are like this

Fig. 12 Thoroughly clean the transaxle pan gasket surfaces

Fig. 13 This magnet is built into the pan. Clean it well before reinstalling the pan

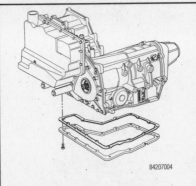

Fig. 14 Transaxle fluid pan and seal—4T80-E transaxle

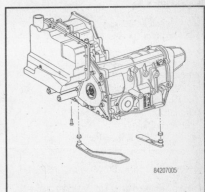

Fig. 15 Transaxle scavenger screens and drain plug—4T80-E transaxle

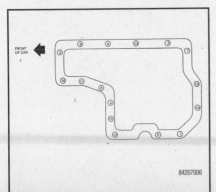

Fig. 16 Transaxle fluid pan retaining bolt torque sequence—4T80-E transaxle

scavenging screens under the bottom pan must be cleaned whenever the transaxle fluid is changed.

1. Raise and safely support the vehicle.
2. Place a suitable drain pan under the transaxle fluid pan.
3. Loosen the bottom fluid pan bolts in the reverse order of the torque sequence and drain the fluid from the pan.
4. Remove the drain plug in the case.

➡Removing the bottom fluid pan will only partially drain the transaxle fluid. The remaining fluid is held in the side cover and torque converter. Removing the drain plug in the case after bottom fluid pan removal will drain the fluid from the side cover.

5. Remove the retaining bolts, fluid pan, and seal. Discard the seal.
6. Remove the left and right scavenger screens.
7. Inspect the scavenger screen lip seals in the transaxle case for nicks or cuts and replace, if damaged. Inspect the scavenger screens for cuts in the screen or a cracked housing; replace if necessary.
8. Check the fluid pan and transaxle case for dents or nicks in the sealing surface that could cause leaks. Inspect the fluid pan bolts for damaged threads and replace, if necessary.

To install:
9. Clean the scavenger screens and fluid pan in solvent and allow drying. Clean the fluid pan retaining bolts and the tapped holes in the transaxle case.

➡The fluid pan and case sealing surfaces must be clean and dry for proper sealing. The retaining bolts and tapped holes must be clean and dry to maintain proper bolt torque.

10. Install the drain plug in the case and tighten to 6–10 ft. lbs. (8–14 Nm).

11. Install the left and right scavenger screens.

12. Install the bottom fluid pan using a new seal. Install the fluid pan retaining bolts finger-tight.

13. Tighten the fluid pan bolts in 3 steps. First, tighten the bolts, in sequence, to 27 inch lbs. (3 Nm). Then tighten the bolts, in sequence, to 53 inch lbs. (6 Nm). Finally, tighten the bolts, in sequence, to 106 inch lbs. (12 Nm).

14. Lower the vehicle. Add the proper quantity of DEXRON III® transmission fluid to the transaxle.

15. Make sure the transaxle is in **P**, then start the engine. With a cold powertrain, engine coolant temperature below 90°F (32°C), the fluid level should be in the 'Cold' range on the dipstick.

16. When the powertrain is at normal operating temperature, engine coolant temperature 180–200°F (82–93°C), the fluid level should be in the 'Hot' crosshatched range on the dipstick.

Neutral Safety Switch

➡The neutral safety switch incorporates the back-up light switch.

REMOVAL & INSTALLATION

4T60 and 4T60-E Transaxles

▶ See Figure 17

1. Disconnect the negative battery cable.
2. On 1992–93 Eldorado and Seville, remove the air cleaner housing and duct.
3. Remove the shift linkage, electrical connector and vacuum hose.
4. Remove the attaching nut and the shift lever.
5. Remove the fuel line bracket and bolt.
6. Remove the retaining bolts and the switch.

To install:

7. Installation is the reverse of the removal procedure. Adjust the switch and tighten the retaining bolts to 20 ft. lbs. (27 Nm).

4T80-E Transaxle

▶ See Figures 18 and 19

1. Disconnect the negative battery cable.
2. Remove the air cleaner duct and housing.

Fig. 18 Shift control cable adjustment— 4T80-E transaxle

1. Transaxle
2. Neutral safety switch
3. Manual shaft lever
4. Transaxle manual shaft
5. Nut
6. Bolt
7. Service gauge pin
8. Engine wiring harness

Fig. 19 Neutral safety switch installation—4T80-E transaxle

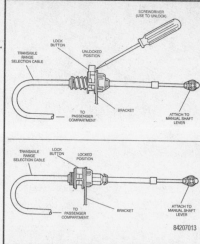

TIGHTEN FIRST

1. Transaxle
2. Transaxle manual shaft
3. Neutral safety switch
4. Service adjustment slot
5. Service gauge pin
6. Bolt

Fig. 17 Neutral safety switch installation—4T60 and 4T60-E transaxles

3. Remove the control cable at the lever on the transaxle manual shaft.

4. Remove the control cable bracket and cable on the transaxle.

5. Remove the retaining nut and transaxle manual shaft lever.

6. Detach the electrical connector and hose.

7. Remove the retaining bolts and the neutral safety switch.

To install:

8. Installation is the reverse of the removal procedure. Adjust the switch and tighten the retaining bolts to 106 inch lbs. (12 Nm).

9. Tighten the manual shaft lever retaining nut to 15 ft. lbs. (20 Nm).

✱✱ CAUTION

The neutral safety switch must be adjusted so that the engine will start in PARK or NEUTRAL only. Personal injury may result if the engine can be started in a drive position.

10. Loosen the neutral safety switch retaining bolts.

11. Rotate the transaxle manual shaft to the NEUTRAL position.

12. Rotate the switch until a 3/32 in. (2.34 mm) gauge pin can be inserted in the adjustment hole.

13. Tighten the switch retaining bolts to 20 ft. lbs. (27 Nm) on 4T60 and 4T60-E transaxles or 106 inch lbs. (12 Nm) on 4T80-E transaxle.

PNP Switch Replacement

REMOVAL & INSTALLATION

➡Special tool J 41545 may be required to perform this procedure.

4T80-E Late Models

▶ See Figures 20, 21, 22 and 23

1. Set the parking brake.
2. Set the gear selector to the neutral **N**.
3. Remove the electrical connector.
4. Remove the cable and the lever.
5. Remove the park/neutral position switch.

To install:

6. Verify that the transmission still is in the neutral **N** position. If the position has moved, rotate the shaft clockwise from park **P** through reverse **R**

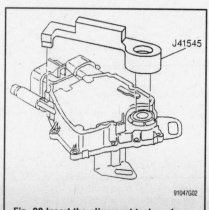

Fig. 20 Insert the alignment tool as shown

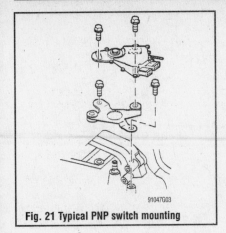

Fig. 21 Typical PNP switch mounting

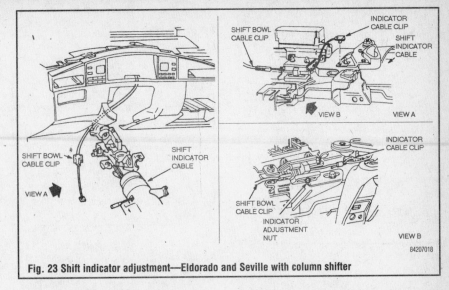

Fig. 23 Shift indicator adjustment—Eldorado and Seville with column shifter

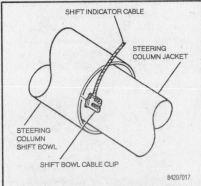

Fig. 22 Shift indicator adjustment—Deville and Fleetwood

into neutral **N**. Be careful not to damage the shaft flats, corners, or threads.

• New replacement park/neutral position switches already are pinned in the neutral **N** position.

• When installing a park/neutral position switch with a sheared pin, insert the alignment tool into the 2 slots on the switch in the area of the transmission shaft.

• Rotate the tool until rear leg on the tool falls into the slot on the switch near the hose.

• Verify that the tool is seated properly in all 3 slots.

• Remove the tool.

7. Check for a cracked carrier if either of the following conditions exist:

   a. The pin is sheared.
   b. You are installing the original switch.

To install:

➡️**After the park/neutral switch installation, verify that the engine starts only in P or N. If the engine starts in any other position, readjust the park/neutral position switch.**

➡️**Check the shifter for normal freedom of movement.**

8. Install the park/neutral position switch.

   a. Align the flats in the park/neutral position switch with the transmission manual shaft flats.

   b. Press the park/neutral position switch onto the shaft. Fully seat the switch against the transmission.

9. Install the bolts loosely.

10. With the alignment tool, verify the alignment of the switch before tightening the bolts.

11. Tighten the bolts to 18 ft. lbs. (25 Nm).

12. Remove the alignment tool.

13. Install the cable and the lever.

14. Install the linkage retaining nut and tighten to 15 ft. lbs. (20 Nm).

15. Attach the electrical connectors.

Automatic Transaxle Assembly

REMOVAL & INSTALLATION

4T60 and 4T60-E

▶ **See Figures 24 thru 30**

1. Disconnect the negative battery cable.

2. Remove the air cleaner. Disconnect the throttle valve cable and remove the throttle valve cable/engine cooler line bracket.

3. Remove the exhaust crossover pipe.

4. Disconnect the shift linkage, shift cable, and bracket. It is not necessary to remove the cable from the bracket.

5. Label and detach the electrical connectors for the converter clutch, cruise control servo, and neutral safety switch.

6. Remove the upper transaxle-to-engine bolts and studs in positions 2, 3, 4, and 5, as shown in the illustration.

7. Disconnect the vacuum line at the vacuum modulator, where applicable.

8. Support the engine with engine support tool J-28467 or equivalent. The engine should be supported in its normal position; it is not necessary to actually raise the engine.

9. Raise and safely support the vehicle. Remove the front wheel and tire assemblies.

10. Disconnect both ball joints from the steering knuckles.

11. Remove the halfshafts from the transaxle.

12. Remove the stabilizer bolt from the left control arm. Remove the left stabilizer-to-cradle clamp.

13. Remove the left engine and A/C splash shields. Remove the left No. 1 insulator cover and the wire harness cover.

14. Remove the vacuum pump assembly from

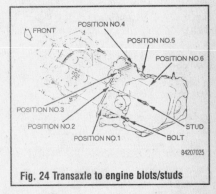

Fig. 24 Transaxle to engine blots/studs

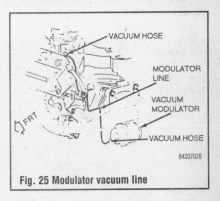

Fig. 25 Modulator vacuum line

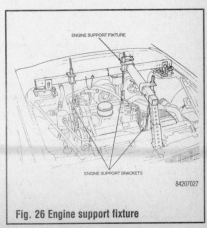

Fig. 26 Engine support fixture

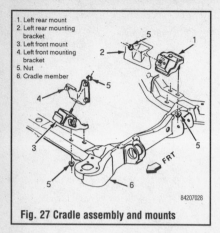

1. Left rear mount
2. Left rear mounting bracket
3. Left front mount
4. Left front mounting bracket
5. Nut
6. Cradle member

Fig. 27 Cradle assembly and mounts

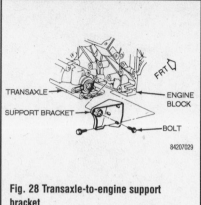

Fig. 28 Transaxle-to-engine support bracket

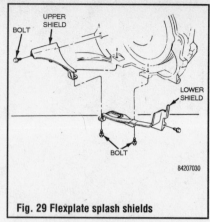

Fig. 29 Flexplate splash shields

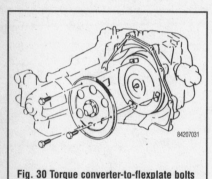

Fig. 30 Torque converter-to-flexplate bolts

the left cradle and support. Detach the vehicle speed sensor connector.

15. Disconnect the right and left front engine and transaxle mount-to-cradle attachments. Remove the left No. 1 cradle insulator bolt and left cradle assembly.

16. Disconnect the oil cooler lines and bracket at the transaxle. Remove the transaxle-to-engine support bracket.

17. Remove the right rear mount-to-transaxle bracket and the left rear transaxle mount-to-transaxle attachments.

18. Remove the flexplate splash shields, then remove the torque converter-to-flexplate bolts.

19. Position a suitable jack under the transaxle.

20. Remove the transaxle-to-engine bolt from position 1.

21. Working through the right wheelwell, use a 3 foot extension and socket to remove the transaxle-to-engine bolt from position 6.

22. Remove the transaxle from the vehicle.

To install:

23. Position the transaxle in the vehicle and install the lower transaxle-to-engine bolts/studs. Tighten the bolts/studs to 55 ft. lbs. (75 Nm).

➡**Studs must be installed in positions 2 and 3. Bolts must be installed in positions 1, 4, 5, and 6. Refer to the proper illustration for positions.**

24. Install the torque converter-to-flexplate bolts and tighten to 46 ft. lbs. (63 Nm). Install the flexplate splash shields.

25. Connect the oil cooler lines and bracket at the transaxle. Tighten the bracket mounting bolts to 40 ft. lbs. (55 Nm) and the oil cooler line fitting nuts to 15 ft. lbs. (21 Nm).

26. Install the right and left rear transaxle mount

attachments. Tighten the mounting bracket-to-transaxle bolts to 40 ft. lbs. (55 Nm) and the nuts to 23 ft. lbs. (31 Nm).

27. Install the transaxle-to-engine support bracket and tighten the bolts to 37 ft. lbs. (50 Nm).

28. Install the cradle assembly, No. 1 insulator bolt, and the right and left front cradle-to-cradle attachments. Tighten the insulator bolt and cradle bolts to 74 ft. lbs. (100 Nm).

➡**Before tightening the No. 1 insulator bolt, make sure the cradle and body are properly aligned, via the 10 mm locating holes in the body and cradle near the No. 1 insulator.**

29. Install the stabilizer bolt to the left control arm and the stabilizer cradle clamp.

30. Install the halfshafts.

31. Connect the lower ball joints to the steering knuckles.

32. Install the right and left front transaxle mount-to-cradle attachments. Tighten the nuts to 23 ft. lbs. (31 Nm).

33. Install the vacuum pump assembly to the left cradle.

34. Install the left engine and A/C splash shields and the No. 1 insulator cover.

35. Install the wire harness cover to the cradle. Attach the vehicle speed sensor connector.

36. Connect the vacuum line at the modulator.

37. Install the wheel and tire assemblies and lower the vehicle. Remove the engine support fixture.

38. Install the remaining transaxle-to-engine bolts and tighten to 55 ft. lbs. (75 Nm).

39. Attach the remaining electrical connectors. Connect the shift linkage at the transaxle and tighten the nuts and bolts to 18 ft. lbs. (24 Nm).

40. Install the exhaust crossover pipe.

41. Connect the throttle valve cable and install the cable and engine cooler line bracket.

42. Install the air cleaner and connect the negative battery cable.

43. Fill the transaxle with the proper type and quantity of fluid. Adjust the throttle valve cable and the shift linkage.

44. Road test the vehicle.

4T80-E Transaxle

◆ See Figures 31 thru 39

1. Disconnect the negative battery cable.

2. Remove the headlight housing upper filler panel and diagonal brace.

3. Remove the air cleaner assembly.

4. Disconnect the shift control cable and bracket at the transaxle.

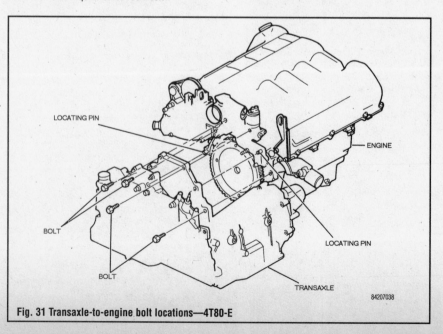

Fig. 31 Transaxle-to-engine bolt locations—4T80-E

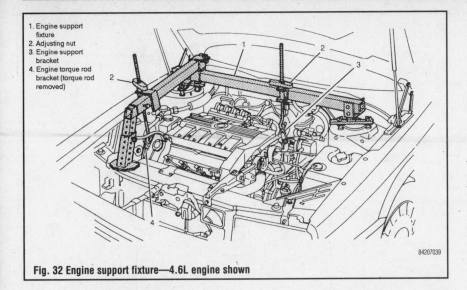

1. Engine support fixture
2. Adjusting nut
3. Engine support bracket
4. Engine torque rod bracket (torque rod removed)

84207039

Fig. 32 Engine support fixture—4.6L engine shown

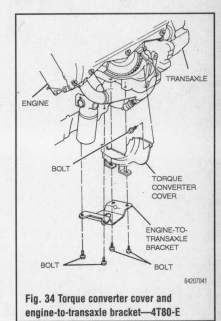

1. Transaxle
2. Radiator
3. Frame
4. Oil return line
5. Oil sending line
6. Fitting
7. Fitting
8. Nut

FRONT OF CAR

FRONT OF CAR

FRONT OF CAR

84207040

Fig. 33 Transaxle cooler lines and fittings—4T80-E

12. Disconnect both front suspension position sensors from the lower control arms and position aside.

13. Remove both stabilizer links from the struts.

14. Remove the tie rod end cotter pins and nuts. Separate the tie rod ends from the steering knuckles.

15. Remove the lower ball joint cotter pins and nuts. Separate the lower ball joints from the steering knuckles.

16. Remove the halfshafts.

17. Remove the power steering filter at the cradle and the A/C splash shield from the frame.

18. Remove the ABS modulator from the bracket and support. Remove the engine oil pan-to-transaxle bracket.

19. Remove the torque converter cover, then remove the torque converter-to-flexplate bolts. Prior to bolt removal, mark the torque converter position in relation to the flexplate so they can be reassembled in the same position.

20. Remove the powertrain mount nuts from the cradle.

21. Rotate the intermediate steering shaft until the steering gear stub shaft clamp bolt is accessible from the left wheelwell. Remove the clamp bolt and disconnect the intermediate steering shaft from the steering gear.

TRANSAXLE

ENGINE

BOLT

TORQUE CONVERTER COVER

ENGINE-TO-TRANSAXLE BRACKET

BOLT

BOLT

84207041

Fig. 34 Torque converter cover and engine-to-transaxle bracket—4T80-E

5. Remove the torque struts.

6. Disconnect the oil cooler lines at the cooler and the oil sending line at the transaxle.

7. Remove the 2 upper transaxle-to-engine bolts.

8. Disconnect the power steering return hose at the auxiliary cooler. Plug the cooler and return hose to prevent leakage.

9. Support the engine with engine support fixture J-28467 or equivalent, as shown. Tighten the wing nuts several turns to take the weight of the powertrain off the mounts and frame.

10. Raise and safely support the vehicle. Remove the front wheel and tire assemblies.

11. Remove the splash shields from both front wheelwells.

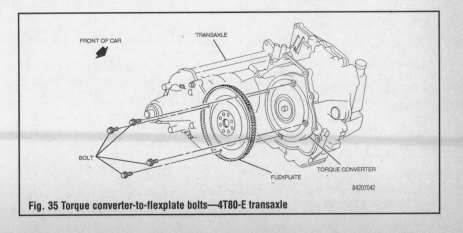

FRONT OF CAR

TRANSAXLE

BOLT

FLEXPLATE

TORQUE CONVERTER

84207042

Fig. 35 Torque converter-to-flexplate bolts—4T80-E transaxle

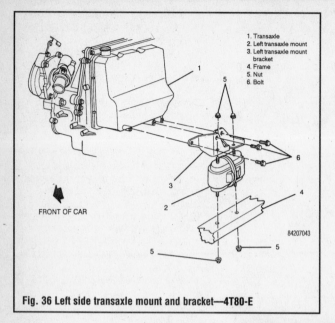

1. Transaxle
2. Left transaxle mount
3. Left transaxle mount bracket
4. Frame
5. Nut
6. Bolt

84207043

Fig. 36 Left side transaxle mount and bracket—4T80-E

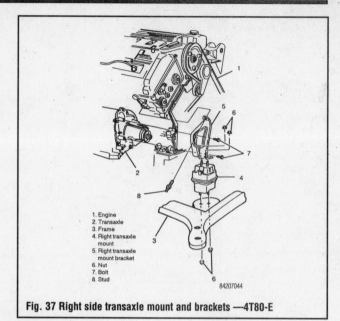

1. Engine
2. Transaxle
3. Frame
4. Right transaxle mount
5. Right transaxle mount bracket
6. Nut
7. Bolt
8. Stud

84207044

Fig. 37 Right side transaxle mount and brackets —4T80-E

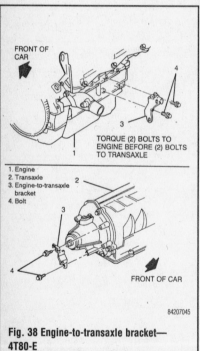

FRONT OF CAR

TORQUE (2) BOLTS TO ENGINE BEFORE (2) BOLTS TO TRANSAXLE

1. Engine
2. Transaxle
3. Engine-to-transaxle bracket
4. Bolt

FRONT OF CAR

84207045

Fig. 38 Engine-to-transaxle bracket—4T80-E

91047P03

Fig. 39 When replacing the transaxle, this support should be replaced also. This one has deteriorated because of a fluid leak

✶✶ CAUTION

If the intermediate steering shaft is not disconnected from the steering gear stub shaft, damage to the steering gear and/or intermediate shaft may result. This damage can cause loss of steering control that could result in personal injury.

✶✶ WARNING

Do not turn the steering wheel or move the position of the steering gear once the intermediate steering shaft is disconnected, as this will lose the center of the air bag coil in the steering column. If the air bag coil loses its center, it may be damaged during vehicle operation.

22. Remove the electrical harness and connector from the front of the cradle.

23. Support the rear of the cradle with a suitable jack, then remove the 4 rear cradle bolts.

24. Lower the jack a few inches to gain access to the power steering gear heat shield and return line fitting. Remove the heat shield and disconnect the return line. Plug the line and the opening in the gear to prevent fluid leakage.

25. Detach the power steering electrical connector.

26. Raise the jack and reinstall one rear cradle bolt on each side finger tight to support the cradle. Remove the jack.

27. Support the frame with a suitable jack and remove the 6 frame mount bolts. Lower the frame and/or raise the vehicle with the steering gear attached.

28. Label and detach the electrical connectors to the transaxle, vehicle speed sensor, and ground. Remove the transaxle harness from the transaxle clip.

29. Remove the fuel line bundle from the transaxle.

30. Remove the left and right transaxle mount and bracket from the transaxle.

31. Support the transaxle with a suitable jack.

32. Remove the engine-to-transaxle heat shield and bracket and the remaining transaxle-to-engine bolts. Lower the transaxle.

33. Remove the manual shaft linkage and neutral safety switch. Remove the vehicle speed sensor and oil return line.

To install:

34. Install the oil return line and the vehicle speed sensor.

35. Install the neutral safety switch and tighten the bolts to 106 inch lbs. (12 Nm).

36. Install the manual shaft linkage and tighten the manual shaft nut to 15 ft. lbs. (20 Nm).

37. Raise the transaxle into position and install the 2 lower transaxle-to-engine bolts. Tighten to 35 ft. lbs. (47 Nm).

38. Install the engine-to-transaxle bracket and heat shield. Tighten the bolts to 35 ft. lbs. (47 Nm).

39. Remove the transaxle jack.

40. Install the right and left transaxle bracket and mount to the transaxle. Tighten the bolts and nuts to 35 ft. lbs. (47 Nm).

41. Install the fuel line bundle to the transaxle.

42. Attach the electrical connectors to the transaxle, vehicle speed sensor, and ground. Install the transaxle harness to the transaxle clip.

43. Raise the frame and/or lower the vehicle while locating the engine and transaxle mount studs into the frame, harnesses at the cradle, and frame mount boltholes to the underbody.

44. Install 2 front and 2 rear cradle bolts finger-tight to support the cradle, then remove the cradle support.

45. Support the rear of the cradle with a suitable jack and remove the 2 rear cradle bolts.

46. Lower the jack a few inches to gain access to the power steering gear. Connect the hose at the steering gear and tighten the fitting to 20 ft. lbs. (27 Nm). Attach the power steering gear electrical connector and install the steering gear heat shield.

47. Raise the cradle with the jack. Install the 6 frame mount bolts beginning with the No. 2 mount bolt into the body, followed by the No. 1 mount bolt into the body, followed by the remaining frame mount bolts. Tighten the bolts to 74 ft. lbs. (100 Nm).

48. Install the electrical harness to the front of the cradle.

49. Connect the intermediate steering shaft to the steering gear and install the clamp bolt. Tighten the bolt to 35 ft. lbs. (47 Nm).

✳✳ WARNING

Do not turn the steering wheel or move the position of the steering gear once the intermediate steering shaft is disconnected, as this will lose the center of the air bag coil in the steering column. If the air bag coil loses its center, it may be damaged during vehicle operation.

50. Install the left and right transaxle mount nuts and right engine mount nuts at the frame. Tighten the nuts to 35 ft. lbs. (47 Nm).

51. Align the flexplate and torque converter using the marks made during the removal procedure. Install the flexplate-to-converter bolts and tighten to 35 ft. lbs. (47 Nm).

52. Install the torque converter cover and tighten the bolts to 106 inch lbs. (12 Nm).

53. Install the engine oil pan-to-transaxle bracket and tighten the bolts to 35 ft. lbs. (47 Nm).

54. Install the ABS modulator to the bracket and install the A/C splash shield at the frame.

55. Install the halfshafts. Tighten the halfshaft nuts to 110 ft. lbs. (145 Nm).

56. Install the lower ball joints into the steering knuckles and install the nuts. Tighten the ball joint nuts to 84 inch lbs. (10 Nm), then an additional 120 degrees.

➡**A minimum torque of 37 ft. lbs. (50 Nm) must be obtained when tightening the nuts. If the minimum torque is not obtained, inspect for stripped threads. If the threads are okay, replace the ball joint and knuckle.**

57. Install new cotter pins after the ball joint nuts have been torqued. If necessary, turn the nuts up to an additional 60°

to allow for installation of the cotter pins. NEVER loosen the nut to allow for cotter pin installation.

58. Install the tie rod ends into the steering knuckles and install the nuts. Tighten the nuts to 7.5 ft. lbs. (10 Nm), then an additional ⅓ turn (2 flats).

➡**A minimum torque of 33 ft. lbs. (45 Nm) must be obtained when tightening the nuts. If the minimum torque is not obtained, inspect for stripped threads. If the threads are okay, replace the tie rod end and knuckle.**

59. Install new cotter pins after the tie rod ends have been torqued. If necessary, align the slots in the nuts to the cotter pin holes by tightening the nuts. NEVER loosen the nut to allow for cotter pin installation.

60. Connect the stabilizer links to the struts and tighten the nuts to 49 ft. lbs. (65 Nm).

61. Install both front suspension position sensors to the lower control arms.

62. Install the power steering filter to the cradle and install the splash shields in the wheelwells.

63. Install the wheel and tire assemblies and lower the vehicle. Remove the engine support fixture.

64. Connect the power steering hose at the auxiliary cooler.

65. Install the remaining transaxle-to-engine bolts and tighten to 35 ft. lbs. (47 Nm).

66. Flush the transaxle oil cooler using flushing tool J-35944 and flushing solution J-35944-20. The transaxle oil cooler and lines should be flushed before the oil cooler lines are connected to the transaxle.

67. Connect the transaxle oil cooler lines to the transaxle. Start the fittings by hand and tighten them finger-tight, then tighten the fittings to 16 ft. lbs. (22 Nm).

68. Install the torque struts.

69. Adjust the neutral safety switch.

70. Install the shift control cable and bracket to the transaxle and tighten the bracket bolts to 106 inch lbs. (12 Nm). Adjust the shift control cable.

71. Install the air cleaner assembly. Install the headlight housing upper filler panel and diagonal brace.

72. Connect the negative battery cable.

73. Fill the transaxle with the proper type and quantity of transaxle fluid. Bleed the power steering system.

74. Check the front suspension alignment and adjust as necessary.

ADJUSTMENTS

1. The Powertrain Control Module (PCM) maintains 3 types of transaxle adapt parameters which are used to modify transaxle line pressure. The line pressure is modified to maintain shift quality regardless of wear or tolerance variations within the transaxle. Whenever the transaxle is replaced, the transaxle adapts must be reset as follows:

a. Turn the ignition key **ON**. Enter the self-diagnostic system.

b. Select Powertrain Control Module (PCM) override PS13 (TP SENSOR LEARN).

c. Press the WARMER button. The Driver Information Center (DIC) should display 09, indicating that the Garage Shift Adapt value has been reset.

d. Select PCM override PS14 (TRAN ADAPT).

e. Press the COOLER button. The DIC should display 90, indicating the Upshift Adapt value has been reset.

f. Press the WARMER button. The DIC should display 09, indicating the Steady State Adapt value has been reset.

2. The PCM maintains a value for transaxle oil life. This value indicates the percentage of oil life remaining and is calculated based on transaxle temperature and speed. When the vehicle is new, the transaxle oil life value is 100%. As the vehicle operates, the percentage will decrease. Whenever the transaxle is replaced, the transaxle oil life indicator should be reset to 100% as follows:

a. Turn the ignition key **ON**, but leave the engine **OFF**.

b. Press and hold the **OFF** and REAR DEFOG buttons on the DIC until the message TRANSAXLE OIL LIFE RESET is displayed on the DIC.

Throttle Linkage

◢ **See Figures 40, 41, 42 and 43**

1. After installation of the cable to the transaxle, engine bracket and cable actuating lever, check to make sure that the cable slider is in the 'zero' or fully retracted position. If it is not, proceed as follows:

a. Make sure the engine is **OFF**.

b. Depress and hold down the metal readjust tab at the engine end of the TV cable.

c. Move the slider until it stops against the fitting.

d. Release the readjustment tab.

e. Rotate the throttle lever to its 'full travel' position (wide-open throttle).

➡**Adjustment of the TV cable must be made by rotating the throttle lever at the throttle body. Do not use the accelerator pedal to rotate the throttle lever.**

2. The slider must move (ratchet) toward the lever when the lever is rotated to its 'full travel' position.

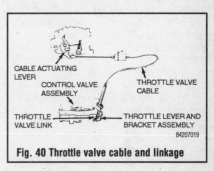

Fig. 40 Throttle valve cable and linkage

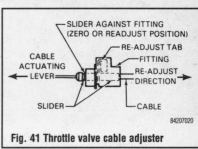

Fig. 41 Throttle valve cable adjuster

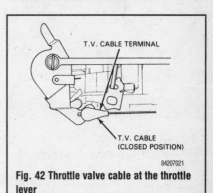

Fig. 42 Throttle valve cable at the throttle lever

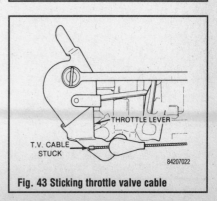

Fig. 43 Sticking throttle valve cable

Halfshafts

REMOVAL & INSTALLATION

▶ See Figures 44, 45, 46, 47 and 48

※※ WARNING

Be careful not to over-extend the inboard CV-joint. When either end of the halfshaft is disconnected, over-extension of the joint could result in separation of internal components and possible joint failure. Use CV-joint boot protectors any time service is performed on or near the halfshafts. If these precautions are not taken, boot or interior joint damage may result, with possible eventual joint failure.

1. Raise and safely support the vehicle.
2. Remove the wheel and tire assembly.
3. Install modified boot protector J-34754 or equivalent, on the outer CV-joint.
4. Insert a drift punch into the caliper and rotor to prevent the rotor from turning, then remove the hub nut.
5. Disconnect the stabilizer link, if necessary.
6. Remove the ball joint cotter pin and nut. Loosen the ball joint in the knuckle using a suitable ball joint tool, being careful not to damage the ball joint and grease seal. If removing the right halfshaft, turn the wheel to the left; if removing the left halfshaft, turn the wheel to the right.
7. Using a prybar between the suspension

Fig. 44 Use a long breaker bar to loosen the hubnut while the vehicle is still on the ground

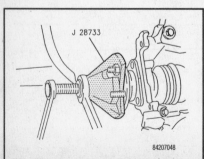

Fig. 45 Removing the halfshaft from the hub

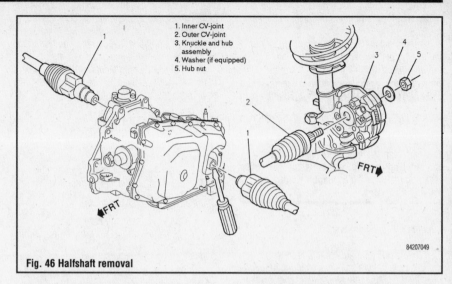

1. Inner CV-joint
2. Outer CV-joint
3. Knuckle and hub assembly
4. Washer (if equipped)
5. Hub nut

Fig. 46 Halfshaft removal

support and the lower control arm, separate the ball joint from the steering knuckle.
8. Partially install the hub nut to protect the threads, then remove the halfshaft from the hub using tool J-28733 or equivalent. Move the strut and knuckle rearward.
9. Separate the halfshaft from the transaxle using a suitable prybar and a wood block fulcrum to protect the transaxle case.

※※ WARNING

If equipped with anti-lock brakes, be careful not to damage the toothed sensor ring on

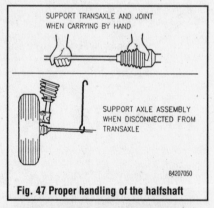

SUPPORT TRANSAXLE AND JOINT WHEN CARRYING BY HAND

SUPPORT AXLE ASSEMBLY WHEN DISCONNECTED FROM TRANSAXLE

Fig. 47 Proper handling of the halfshaft

Fig. 48 Make sure you tighten the hub nut using a torque wrench while the vehicle is on the ground

the halfshaft or the wheel speed sensor on the steering knuckle.

To install:
10. If installing the right side halfshaft, install tool J-37292-A or equivalent, so it can be pulled out after the halfshaft is installed.
11. Install the halfshaft into the transaxle by placing a small prybar into the groove on the inner CV-joint housing and tapping until seated. Verify that the halfshaft snapring is seated by grasping the inner CV-joint housing and pulling outward. DO NOT PULL ON THE HALFSHAFT.
12. Install the halfshaft into the hub and bearing assembly. Loosely install a new hub nut (and washer, if equipped).
13. Connect the ball joint to the steering knuckle and install the nut.
14. On Deville and Fleetwood, tighten the ball joint nut to 88 inch lbs. (10 Nm), then tighten to 41 ft. lbs. (55 Nm) minimum. Install a new cotter pin. If it is necessary to align the slot in the nut, tighten the nut (up to one more flats).
15. On Eldorado and Seville, tighten the ball joint nut to 84 inch lbs. (10 Nm), then an additional 120 degrees. A minimum torque of 37 ft. lbs. (50 Nm) must be obtained when tightening the nut. If the minimum torque is not obtained, inspect for stripped threads. If the threads are okay, replace the ball joint and knuckle. Install a new cotter pin after the ball joint nut has been torqued. If necessary, turn the nut up to an additional 60 degrees (one flat) to allow for installation of the cotter pin. NEVER loosen the nut to allow for cotter pin installation.
16. Insert a drift punch into the caliper and rotor to prevent the rotor from turning. On 1990–91 vehicles, tighten the hub nut to 185 ft. lbs. (251 Nm). On 1992–up vehicles, tighten the hub nut to 110 ft. lbs. (145 Nm), except on Deville and Fleetwood equipped with J55 brake option, in which case the torque is 130 ft. lbs. (177 Nm).
17. Connect the stabilizer link, if removed.
18. Remove the boot protector.
19. If tool J-37292-A or equivalent, was installed, remove it by pulling in line with the handle. Make sure it is completely removed and no pieces are left inside the transaxle.
20. Install the wheel and tire assembly and lower the vehicle.

Description Of Usage	Thread Size	N·m	Lb. Ft.	Lb. In.
Case Side Cover to Channel Plate (Nut)	M6X1.0	8 N·m		71 Lb. In.
Modulator to Case Oil Pan to Case	M8X1.25X20	24 N·m	18 Lb. Ft.	
Side Cover to Channel Plate Bolt	M6X1.0X21.3	11 N·m		98 Lb. In.
Scavenging Scoop to Case	M8X1.25X20	8 N·m		71 Lb. In.
Oil Pan to Case	M6X1.0X18	17 N·m		151 Lb. In.
Speed Sensor to Case Extension	M8X1.25X16	11 N·m		98 Lb. In.
Case Extension to Case	M10X1.5X35	36 N·m	27 Lb. Ft.	
Forward Servo to Case	M6X1.0X20	10 N·m		89 Lb. In.
2-1 Servo to Case	M8X1.25X25	24 N·m	18 Lb. Ft.	
Accumulator Housing to Case	M6X1.0X28	11 N·m		98 Lb. In.
Oil Pump to Valve Body	M8X1.25X30	24 N·m	18 Lb. Ft.	
Oil Pump Cover to Pump Body	M8X1.25X20	24 N·m	18 Lb. Ft.	
Oil Pump to Valve Body	M6X1.0X45	11 N·m		98 Lb. In.
Oil Pump to Channel Plate	M8X1.25X95	24 N·m	18 Lb. Ft.	
Oil Pump to Channel Plate	M6X1.0X85	11 N·m		98 Lb. In.
Pressure Switch	1/8 - 27	11 N·m		98 Lb. In.
Air Bleed Plug to Pump	1/16 - 27	8 N·m		72 Lb. In.
Channel Plate to Driven Sprocket Support	M8X1.25X45	24 N·m	18 Lb. Ft.	
Channel Plate to Case	M8X1.25X50	24 N·m	18 Lb. Ft.	
Channel Plate to Case	M8X1.25X30	24 N·m	18 Lb. Ft.	
Manual Detent to Channel Plate	M6X1.0X20	11 N·m		98 Lb. In.
Valve Body to Channel Plate	M8X1.25X70	24 N·m	18 Lb. Ft.	
Valve Body to Channel Plate	M6X1.0X35	11 N·m		98 Lb. In.
Valve Body to Channel Plate	M6X1.0X45	11 N·m		98 Lb. In.
Valve Body to Channel Plate	M6X1.0X55	11 N·m		98 Lb. In.
Valve Body to Case	M8X1.25X85	24 N·m	18 Lb. Ft.	
Valve Body To Driven Sprocket Support	M8X1.25X90	24 N·m	18 Lb. Ft.	
Manual Shaft to Inside Detent Lever (Nut)	M10X1.5	32 N·m	24 Lb. Ft.	
Drive Sprocket to Case (Torx)	M8X1.25X23.5	24 N·m	18 Lb. Ft.	
Cooler Line Ball Check Assembly	3/8 - 18	52 N·m	39 Lb. Ft.	

91047G20

4T60 and 4T60-E Transaxle torque specifications

Application	N·m	Lb Ft	Lb In
Stud, case cover to case (45)	20-27	15-20	—
Bolt, case cover to case (46)	20-27	15-20	—
Stud, case cover to case (47)	27-31	20-23	—
Bolt, case cover to driven sprocket support (48)	20-27	15-20	—
Stud, case cover to case (49)	27-31	20-23	—
Bolt, case cover to case (50)	27-31	20-23	—
Stud, case cover to case (67)	27-31	20-23	—
Bolt, scavenge pump cover to scavenge pump body (226)	11-13	8-9.5	—
Bolt, pump assembly to case (229)	11-13	8-9.5	—
Bolt, pump assembly to case (231)	11-13	8-9.5	—
Bolt, pump assembly to case cover (232)	11-13	8-9.5	—
Bolt, pump assembly to case cover (233)	11-13	8-9.5	—
Bolt, secondary pump to case cover (234)	11-13	8-9.5	—
Bolt, secondary pump to case cover (235)	11-13	8-9.5	—
Bolt, secondary pump to case (331)	11-13	8-9.5	—

4T80-E Transaxle torque specifications (1 of 2)

Application	N·m	Lb Ft	Lb In
Bolt, pressure control solenoid bracket to UCVB (15)	11-13	8-9.5	—
Bolt, UCVB to case (229)	11-13	8-9.5	—
Bolt, UCVB to case cover (329)	11-13	8-9.5	—
Bolt, UCVB to case cover (330)	11-13	8-9.5	—
Bolt, UCVB to case (331)	11-13	8-9.5	—
Bolt, UCVB to driven sprocket support (331)	11-13	8-9.5	—
Temperature sensor (350)	3.4	—	30
Bolt, channel plate to case (534)	8-14	6-10	—
Bolt, oil transfer plate to case (534)	8-14	6-10	—
Nut, channel plate to case (955)	8-14	6-10	—
Bolt, channel plate to case (958)	8-14	6-10	—
Bolt, channel plate to LCVB (534)	8-14	6-10	—
Bolt, channel plate to accumulator housing (534)	8-14	6-10	—
Bolt, accumulator housing to channel plate (534)	8-14	6-10	—
Bolt, LCVB to channel plate (938)	8-14	6-10	—
Bolt, spacer plate support to channel plate (939)	8-14	6-10	—
Bolt, LCVB to channel plate (940)	8-14	6-10	—
Bolt, LCVB to channel plate (941)	8-14	6-10	—
Bolt, accumulator housing to channel plate (951)	8-14	6-10	—
Bolt, accumulator housing to channel plate (952)	8-14	6-10	—
Bolt, accumulator housing to channel plate (954)	8-14	6-10	—
Bolt, accumulator housing cover (956)	8-14	6-10	—
Bolt, side cover to case cover (28)	50-55	37-40	—
Bolt, side cover to case cover (32)	20-27	15-20	—
Stud, side cover to case cover (66)	50-55	37-40	—
Bolt, bottom pan to case (62)	10-12	8-9	—
Stud, case extension to case (127)	50-55	37-40	—
Bolt, case extension to case (128)	50-55	37-40	—
Bolt, case extension to case (129)	20-27	15-20	—
Bolt, differential to final drive carrier (119)	70-76	52-56	—
Cooler connector, return (case) (3)	25-29	19-21	—
Stud, case to forward clutch support (5)	25-27	19-20	—
Plug, oil drain-bottom pan to case cover (8)	8-14	6-10	—
Bolt, scavenge tube to case (15)	8-14	6-10	—
Bolt, input speed sensor to case (15)	11-13	8-9.5	—
Nut, manual shaft to detent lever (18)	27-34	20-25	—
Bolt, detent lever and roller assembly (26)	8-14	6-10	—
Cooler connector to cooler (case cover) (38)	20-27	15-20	—
Plug, oil test - #40 TORX (case cover) (40)	18-26	13.5-19	—
Bolt, speed sensor to case extension (131)	8-14	6-10	—
Bolt, drive sprocket support to case (404)	11-13	8-9.5	—
Bolt, servo cover to case (534)	8-14	6-10	—

4T80-E Transaxle torque specifications (2 of 2)

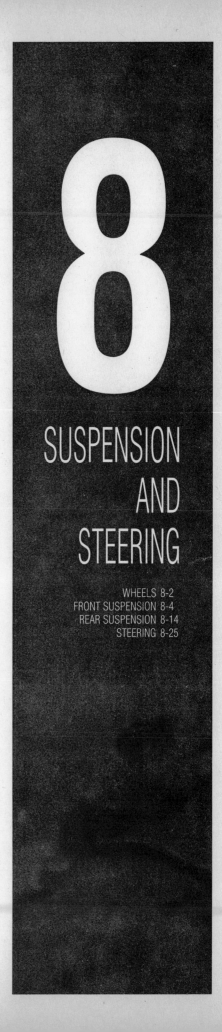

8

SUSPENSION AND STEERING

WHEELS

Wheels

REMOVAL & INSTALLATION

♦ **See Figures 1, 2, 3, 4 and 5**

1. Place the shift lever in **P** and apply the parking brake. Chock the wheels at the opposite end of the vehicle.

2. If removing a rear wheel and the vehicle is equipped with fender skirts, remove the fender skirt as follows:

   a. Push the handle, located inside the fender skirt, up and inward, and then pull it down.

   b. Pull the fender skirt toward you and remove it from the vehicle. Place the fender skirt aside, being careful not to damage the paint and trim.

3. If equipped with wheel covers, use the special wrench supplied with the car to pry off the small center cover and remove the anti-theft wheel nut. Remove the wheel cover.

4. If equipped with aluminum wheels, use the flat end of the lug wrench supplied with the car to carefully pry off the center cover. Be careful not to damage the wheel or cover.

5. Loosen, but do not remove the wheel lug nuts.

6. Raise and safely support the vehicle.

❄ CAUTION

If any service other than wheel removal & installation is to be performed, if the wheel will be removed from the vehicle for any length of time, or IF YOU ARE GOING TO CRAWL UNDER THE VEHICLE FOR ANY REASON, THE VEHICLE MUST BE SUPPORTED WITH JACKSTANDS.

7. Remove the lug nuts and remove the wheel. If the wheel is difficult to remove because of corrosion or a tight fit between the wheel center hole and hub or rotor, proceed as follows:

   a. Reinstall the lug nuts finger-tight, then loosen each nut 2 turns.

   b. Lower the vehicle.

   c. Rock the vehicle from side to side as hard as possible, using your body weight (and that of an assistants, if necessary) to loosen the wheel.

   d. If the wheel will still not come loose, start the engine and rock the vehicle from **D** to **R**, moving the vehicle several feet in each direction. Apply quick, hard jabs on the brake pedal to loosen the wheel.

   e. Stop the engine. Raise and safely support the vehicle. Remove the lug nuts and the wheel.

❄ WARNING

Never use heat to loosen a tight wheel, as the wheel and/or wheel bearings may become damaged. Never hammer on the wheel to loosen it, however, slight tapping on the tire sidewall with a rubber mallet is acceptable.

8. Inspect the wheel and hub mating surfaces. If necessary, use a scraper or wire brush to remove any dirt or corrosion.

To install:

9. Install the wheel on the hub. Install the lug nuts, tightening them until the wheel is fully seated.

10. Lower the vehicle. Tighten the lug nuts to 100 ft. lbs. (140 Nm), using the sequence shown in the accompanying figure.

11. If equipped with aluminum wheels, carefully install the center cover.

12. If equipped with wheel covers, install the wheelcover by hand, being careful to line up the tire valve stem with the hole in the wheelcover. Install the anti-theft wheel nut and the center cover.

13. If equipped, install the fender skirt as follows:

   a. Pull the fender skirt handle down.

   b. Align the locator pins and insert them into the holes.

   c. Push the handle up and lock it in place.

   d. Push the bottom part of the fender skirt into place by hand.

INSPECTION

Inspect the tires for lacerations, puncture marks, nails and other sharp objects. Repair or replace as necessary. Also check the tires for treadwear and air pressure.

Check the wheel assemblies for dents, cracks, rust and metal fatigue. Repair or replace as necessary.

Fig. 1 Reach inside the fender skirt to grab the hidden rod

Fig. 2 Pull the rod down to release the fender skirt

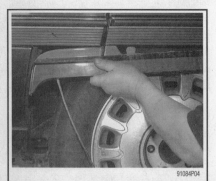

Fig. 3 Hold the fender skirt, the rod will release the front of the skirt

Fig. 4 Pull the fender skirt forward and out of the slot to remove it

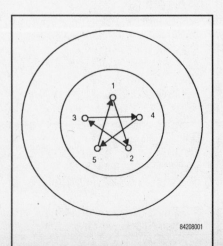

Fig. 5 Lug nut tightening sequence

Wheel Lug Studs

REMOVAL & INSTALLATION

With Disc Brakes

▶ See Figures 6, 7 and 8

1. Raise and support the appropriate end of the vehicle safely using jackstands, then remove the wheel.

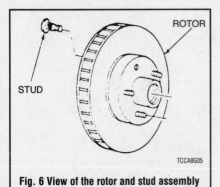

Fig. 6 View of the rotor and stud assembly

2. Remove the brake pads and caliper. Support the caliper aside using wire or a coat hanger.
3. Remove the outer wheel bearing and lift off the rotor.
4. Properly support the rotor using press bars, then drive the stud out using an arbor press.

➡️**If a press is not available, CAREFULLY drive the old stud out using a blunt drift. MAKE SURE the rotor is properly and evenly supported or it may be damaged.**

To install:

5. Clean the stud hole with a wire brush and start the new stud with a hammer and drift pin. Do not use any lubricant or thread sealer.
6. Finish installing the stud with the press.

➡️**If a press is not available, start the lug stud through the bore in the hub, then position about 4 flat washers over the stud and thread the lug nut. Hold the hub/rotor while tightening the lug nut, and the stud should be drawn into position. MAKE SURE THE STUD IS FULLY SEATED, then remove the lug nut and washers.**

7. Install the rotor and adjust the wheel bearings.
8. Install the brake caliper and pads.

9. Install the wheel, then remove the jackstands and carefully lower the vehicle.
10. Tighten the lug nuts to the proper torque.

With Drum Brakes

▶ See Figures 9, 10 and 11

1. Raise the vehicle and safely support it with jackstands, then remove the wheel.
2. Remove the brake drum.
3. If necessary to provide clearance, remove the brake shoes.
4. Using a large C-clamp and socket, press the stud from the axle flange.
5. Coat the serrated part of the stud with liquid soap and place it into the hole.

To install:

6. Position about 4 flat washers over the stud and thread the lug nut. Hold the flange while tightening the lug nut, and the stud should be drawn into position. MAKE SURE THE STUD IS FULLY SEATED, then remove the lug nut and washers.
7. If applicable, install the brake shoes.
8. Install the brake drum.
9. Install the wheel, then remove the jackstands and carefully lower the vehicle.
10. Tighten the lug nuts to the proper torque.

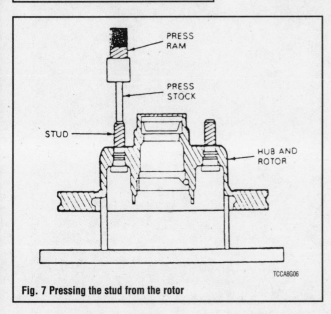

Fig. 7 Pressing the stud from the rotor

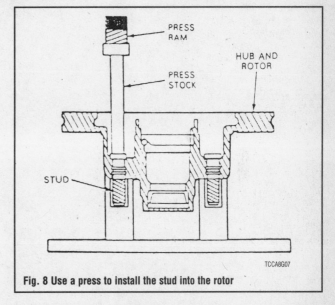

Fig. 8 Use a press to install the stud into the rotor

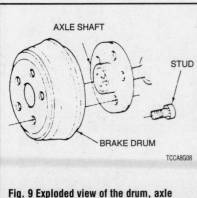

Fig. 9 Exploded view of the drum, axle flange and stud

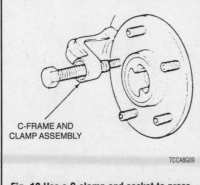

Fig. 10 Use a C-clamp and socket to press out the stud

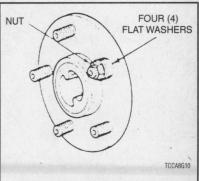

Fig. 11 Force the stud onto the axle flange using washers and a lug nut

FRONT SUSPENSION

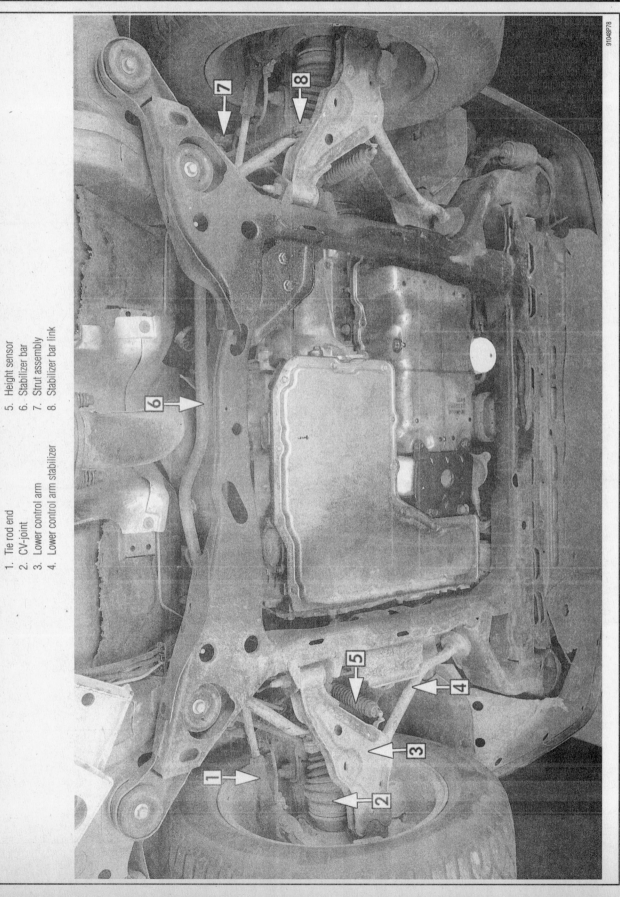

FRONT SUSPENSION COMPONENT LOCATIONS—DEVILLE CONCOURS

1. Tie rod end
2. CV-joint
3. Lower control arm
4. Lower control arm stabilizer
5. Height sensor
6. Stabilizer bar
7. Strut assembly
8. Stabilizer bar link

91048P78

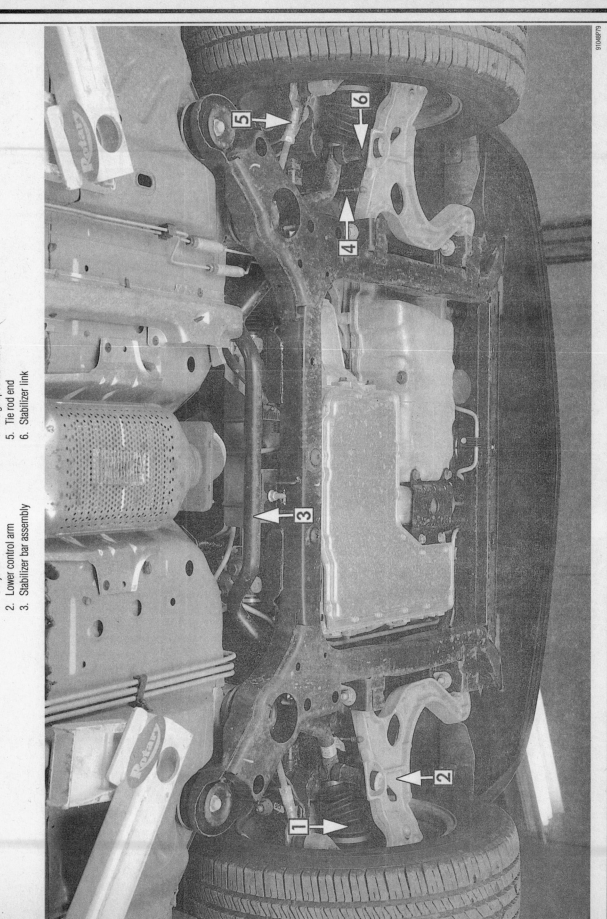

FRONT SUSPENSION COMPONENT LOCATIONS—SEVILLE TOURING SEDAN (STS)

1. CV-joint
2. Lower control arm
3. Stabilizer bar assembly
4. Height position sensor
5. Tie rod end
6. Stabilizer link

9104BP79

MacPherson Struts

REMOVAL & INSTALLATION

◆ See Figures 12 thru 20

1. Disconnect the negative battery cable.
2. Raise and safely support the vehicle. The vehicle must be supported by the frame with the control arms hanging free.
3. Remove the wheel and tire assembly.
4. On Eldorado and Seville, detach the electrical connector from the top of the strut, if equipped.
5. On Deville and Fleetwood, loosen the strut housing tie bar through bolts at each end of the bar.
6. On Eldorado and Seville with 4.6L engine, remove the road sensing suspension position sensor from the lower control arm.
7. Remove the nuts attaching the top of the strut to the body.
8. On Deville and Fleetwood equipped with anti-lock brakes, disconnect the wheel speed sensor and remove the sensor bracket from the strut.
9. On Eldorado and Seville, remove the stabilizer link from the strut.
10. Remove the brake line bracket from the strut.
11. Remove the strut-to-knuckle bolts and remove the strut. Support the knuckle with wire. The knuckle must be supported to prevent damage to the ball joint and/or halfshaft.

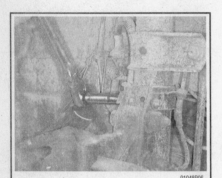

Fig. 12 Loosen the strut housing tie bar bolts

Fig. 13 Unbolt the strut mounted brake bracket

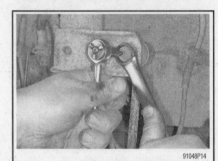

Fig. 14 When unbolting the stabilizer link, hold the retaining nut with a wrench, and drive the stud through it, using a driver and ratchet

Fig. 15 Matchmark the upper strut control nuts

Fig. 16 Loosen the upper mounting nuts

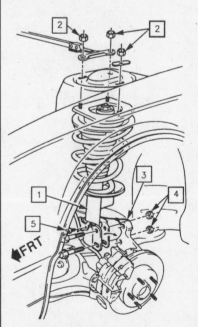

1. Strut
2. Strut-to-body nuts
3. Support the knuckle after strut is removed
4. Strut-to-knuckle nut
5. Brake line bracket bolt

Fig. 17 Remove the strut-to-knuckle bolts

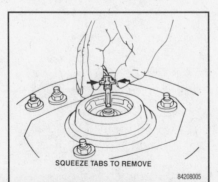

SQUEEZE TABS TO REMOVE

Fig. 18 Detaching the electrical connector at the top of the strut—electronically controlled suspension

Fig. 19 MacPherson strut installation—Deville and Fleetwood

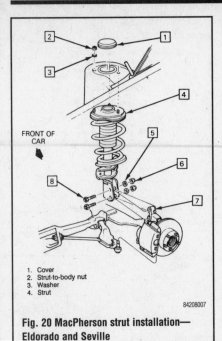

1. Cover
2. Strut-to-body nut
3. Washer
4. Strut

84208007

Fig. 20 MacPherson strut installation—Eldorado and Seville

To install:

12. Attach the strut to the knuckle with the bolts and nuts.

13. Attach the strut to the body with the nuts. On Deville and Fleetwood, position the washer and tie bar prior to installing the strut-to-body nuts.

14. Install the brake line bracket to the strut.

15. On Eldorado and Seville, connect the stabilizer link to the strut.

16. On Deville and Fleetwood with anti-lock brakes, install the wheel speed sensor bracket and connect the sensor

17. On Eldorado and Seville, install the road sensing suspension sensor to the lower control arm.

a. Connect the electrical connector at the top of the strut, if equipped.

18. Tighten as follows: Strut-to-knuckle bolts: 140 ft. lbs. (190 Nm) Strut-to-body nuts: 18 ft. lbs. (24 Nm) Stabilizer link nuts: 48 ft. lbs. (65 Nm) Tie bar through bolts: 20 ft. lbs. (27 Nm)

19. Install the wheel and tire assembly and lower the vehicle. Check and adjust the front wheel alignment.

OVERHAUL

▶ **See Figures 21 thru 26**

✳✳ WARNING

Be careful not to scratch or crack the coating on the coil spring, as damage may cause premature spring failure.

1. Mount the strut assembly in strut compressor tool J-34013 or equivalent.

2. Turn the compressor forcing screw until the spring compresses slightly.

3. Use a T-50 Torx® bit to keep the strut shaft from turning, then remove the nut on the top of the strut shaft.

4. Loosen the compressor screw while guiding the strut shaft out of the assembly. Continue loosening the compressor screw until the strut and spring can be removed.

To install:

5. Mount the strut in the strut compressor tool. Use clamping tool J-34013-20 or equivalent, to hold the strut shaft in place.

6. Install the spring over the strut. The flat on the upper spring seat must face out from the centerline of the vehicle, or when mounted in the strut compressor, the spring seat must face the same direction as the steering knuckle mounting flange.

➥ **If the bearing was removed from the upper spring seat, it must be reinstalled in the spring seat in the same position before attaching to the strut mount.**

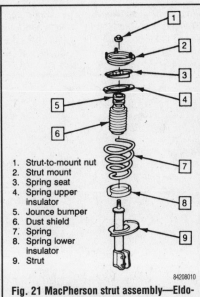

1. Strut-to-mount nut
2. Strut mount
3. Spring seat
4. Spring upper insulator
5. Jounce bumper
6. Dust shield
7. Spring
8. Spring lower insulator
9. Strut

84208010

Fig. 21 MacPherson strut assembly—Eldorado and Seville

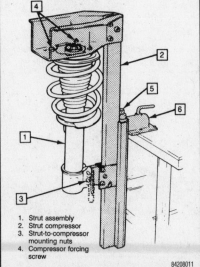

1. Strut assembly
2. Strut compressor
3. Strut-to-compressor mounting nuts
4. Compressor forcing screw

84208011

Fig. 22 Mount the strut in the strut compressor

7. Turn the compressor screw to compress the spring, while guiding the strut shaft through the top of the strut assembly. If necessary, use tool J-34013-38 or equivalent, to guide the shaft.

8. When the strut shaft threads are visible through the top of the strut assembly, install the washer and nut.

9. Remove clamping tool J-34013-20 from the strut shaft.

10. Tighten the strut shaft nut to 55 ft. lbs. (75 Nm) while holding the strut shaft with a T-50 Torx® bit.

11. Remove the strut assembly from the compressor tool.

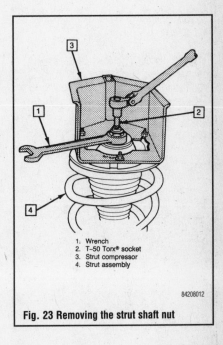

1. Wrench
2. T-50 Torx® socket
3. Strut compressor
4. Strut assembly

84208012

Fig. 23 Removing the strut shaft nut

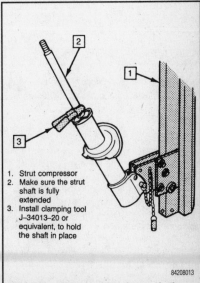

1. Strut compressor
2. Make sure the strut shaft is fully extended
3. Install clamping tool J-34013-20 or equivalent, to hold the shaft in place

84208013

Fig. 24 Installing the strut damper in the strut compressor

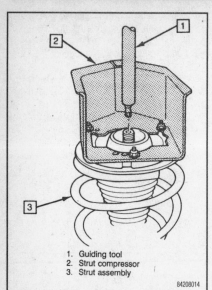

1. Guiding tool
2. Strut compressor
3. Strut assembly

84208014

Fig. 25 If necessary, use tool J-34013-38 or equivalent, to guide the strut shaft

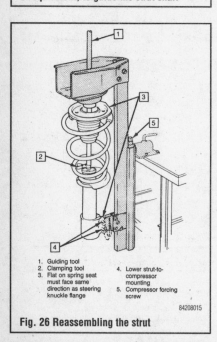

1. Guiding tool
2. Clamping tool
3. Flat on spring seat must face same direction as steering knuckle flange
4. Lower strut-to-compressor mounting
5. Compressor forcing screw

84208015

Fig. 26 Reassembling the strut

Lower Ball Joint

INSPECTION

Replace the lower ball joint if there is any looseness in the joint or if the ball joint seal is damaged. Inspect the ball joint as follows:

1. Raise and safely support the vehicle, allowing the front suspension to hang free.
2. Have an assistant grasp the tire at the top and bottom and move the top of the tire in and out. Check for any vertical movement of the knuckle relative to the lower control arm. If there is any movement, replace the ball joint.
3. Check the ball stud tightness in the knuckle boss by shaking the wheel and feeling for movement of the stud end or castellated nut at the

knuckle boss. Check the torque of the castellated nut—a loose nut can indicate a bent stud or an enlarged hole in the knuckle boss. Replace a worn or damaged ball joint and/or knuckle.

4. If the ball stud is disconnected from the knuckle and looseness is detected, or if the ball stud can be twisted in it's socket using finger pressure, replace the ball joint.

REMOVAL & INSTALLATION

▶ **See Figures 27, 28, 29, 30 and 31**

1. Raise and safely support the vehicle, allowing the front suspension to hang free.
2. Remove the wheel and tire assembly.

⁑⁑ WARNING

Be careful when working in the area of the CV-joint boot. Damage to the boot could result in eventual CV-joint failure. If necessary, install CV-joint boot protector tool J-34754 or equivalent, to protect the boot.

3. On Eldorado and Seville with 4.6L engine, remove the road sensing suspension position sensor from the lower control arm.
4. Remove the cotter pin and nut from the ball joint stud. Use ball joint separator tool J-36226 or equivalent, on Deville and Fleetwood or ball joint separator tool J-35315 or equivalent, on Eldorado

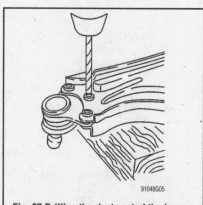

91048G05

Fig. 27 Drilling the rivets out of the lower control arm

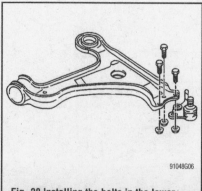

91048G06

Fig. 28 Installing the bolts in the lower control arm

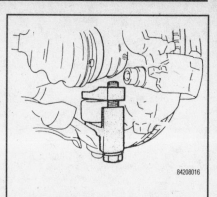

84208016

Fig. 29 Separating the ball joint from the steering knuckle

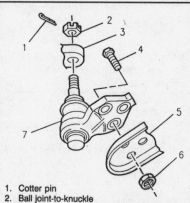

1. Cotter pin
2. Ball joint-to-knuckle nut
3. Steering knuckle
4. Ball joint-to-control arm bolts
5. Lower control arm
6. Ball joint-to-control arm nuts
7. Lower ball joint

84208017

Fig. 30 Lower ball joint installation— Deville and Fleetwood

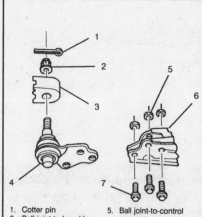

1. Cotter pin
2. Ball joint-to-knuckle nut
3. Steering knuckle
4. Lower ball joint
5. Ball joint-to-control arm nuts
6. Lower control arm
7. Ball joint-to-control arm bolts

84208018

Fig. 31 Lower ball joint installation—Eldorado and Seville

and Seville, to separate the ball joint from the steering knuckle.

5. On Deville and Fleetwood, loosen the stabilizer bar link nut.

 a. Drill out the 3 rivets retaining the ball joint to the lower control arm and remove the ball joint.

➡Recommended drill bit is ½ inch (13 mm).

To install:

6. Attach the new ball joint to the lower control arm with 3 mounting bolts and nuts.

 a. On Deville and Fleetwood, the bolts must be installed from the top of the control arm.

 b. On Eldorado and Seville, the bolts must be installed from the bottom of the control arm.

 c. Tighten the nuts to 50 ft. lbs. (68 Nm).

 d. Tighten the nuts to 26 ft. lbs. (35 Nm).

7. On Deville and Fleetwood, tighten the stabilizer bar link nut to 13 ft. lbs. (17 Nm).

8. Connect the ball joint to the steering knuckle and install the castellated nut.

9. On Deville and Fleetwood, tighten the ball joint nut to 88 inch lbs. (10 Nm). Then tighten the nut an additional 120°, during which a tighten of 41 ft. lbs. (55 Nm) must be obtained.

10. On Eldorado and Seville, tighten the ball joint nut to 84 inch lbs. (10 Nm). Then tighten the nut an additional 120°, during which a minimum torque of 37 ft. lbs. (50 Nm) must be obtained. If the minimum torque is not obtained, check for stripped threads. If the threads are okay, replace the ball joint and knuckle.

11. Install a new cotter pin. If the cotter pin cannot be installed because the hole in the stud does not align with a nut castellation, tighten the nut up to an additional 60°

to allow for installation. NEVER loosen the nut to provide for cotter pin installation.

12. On Eldorado and Seville with 4.6L engine, install the road sensing suspension position sensor to the lower control arm.

13. If necessary, remove the CV-joint boot protector tool.

14. Install the wheel and tire assembly and lower the vehicle.

Sway Bar

REMOVAL & INSTALLATION

Deville and Fleetwood

◆ See Figures 32, 33 and 34

1. Raise and safely support the vehicle, allowing the front suspension to hang free.

2. Remove the wheel and tire assemblies.

✳ WARNING

Be careful when working in the area of the CV-joint boots. Damage to the boots could result in eventual CV-joint failure. If necessary, install CV-joint boot protector tools J-34754 or equivalent, to protect the boots.

3. Remove the stabilizer bar link bolts from the lower control arms.

4. Remove the stabilizer bar bushing brackets from the frame.

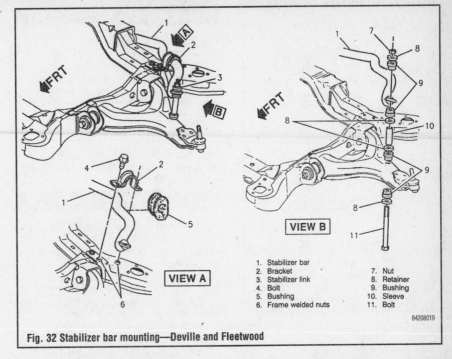

Fig. 32 Stabilizer bar mounting—Deville and Fleetwood

1. Stabilizer bar	7. Nut
2. Bracket	8. Retainer
3. Stabilizer link	9. Bushing
4. Bolt	10. Sleeve
5. Bushing	11. Bolt
6. Frame welded nuts	

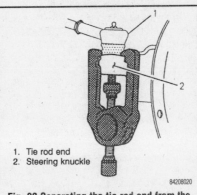

Fig. 33 Separating the tie rod end from the steering knuckle

1. Tie rod end
2. Steering knuckle

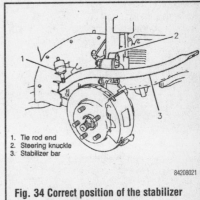

Fig. 34 Correct position of the stabilizer bar for removal or installation

1. Tie rod end
2. Steering knuckle
3. Stabilizer bar

5. Remove the cotter pins and nuts from the tie rod ends. Use separator tool J-24319-01 or equivalent, to separate the tie rod ends from the steering knuckles.

6. Disconnect the exhaust pipe from the exhaust manifold.

7. Turn the passenger side strut all the way to the right.

8. Slide the stabilizer bar over the steering knuckle and pull down until the stabilizer bar clears the frame. Remove the stabilizer bar.

To install:

9. Slide the stabilizer bar over the steering knuckle, raise it over the frame, and slide it into position. Loosely install the mount bushings, brackets and bolts.

10. Loosely install the stabilizer bar link components to the lower control arms.

11. Connect the tie rod ends to the steering knuckles. Install the tie rod end nuts and tighten to 35 ft. lbs. (48 Nm). Install new cotter pins. If a cotter pin cannot be installed because the hole in the stud does not align with a nut castellation, tighten

the nut up to a maximum of 52 ft. lbs. (70 Nm) to allow for installation. NEVER loosen the nut to provide for cotter pin installation.

12. Tighten the stabilizer bar bracket bolts to 35 ft. lbs. (48 Nm).

13. Tighten the stabilizer bar link bolt nuts to 13 ft. lbs. (17 Nm).

14. Connect the exhaust pipe to the manifold. Tighten the bolts to 15 ft. lbs. (20 Nm) on 1990–91 vehicles or 18 ft. lbs. (25 Nm) on 1992–93 vehicles.

15. If necessary, remove the CV-joint boot protector tools.

16. Install the wheel and tire assemblies and lower the vehicle.

Eldorado and Seville

◆ See Figure 35

1. Raise and safely support the vehicle, allowing the front suspension to hang free.

2. Remove the wheel and tire assembly from the right side of the vehicle.

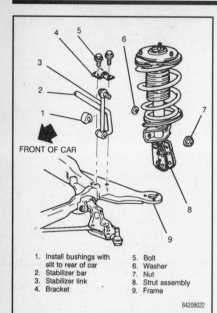

1. Install bushings with slit to rear of car
2. Stabilizer bar
3. Stabilizer link
4. Bracket
5. Bolt
6. Washer
7. Nut
8. Strut assembly
9. Frame

84208022

Fig. 35 Stabilizer bar mounting—Eldorado and Seville

3. On vehicles with 4.6L engine, remove the road sensing suspension position sensor from the lower control arm.

4. Remove the stabilizer links. Use pliers or a Torx® bit, as required, to keep the ball stud from turning while loosening the nut.

5. Remove the bracket bolts, brackets and bushings.

6. Disconnect the exhaust pipe from the manifold.

7. Remove the stabilizer bar.

To install:

8. Position the stabilizer bar in the vehicle.

9. Connect the exhaust pipe to the manifold.

10. Install the bushings with the slits to the rear of the vehicle. Install the brackets and loosely install the mounting bolts.

11. Install the stabilizer links.

12. Tighten the bracket bolts to 35 ft. lbs. (47 Nm). Tighten the stabilizer link nuts to 48 ft. lbs. (65 Nm), using pliers, or a Torx® bit to keep the ball stud from turning.

13. On vehicles with 4.6L engine, install the road sensing suspension position sensor to the lower control arm.

14. Install the right side wheel and tire assembly and lower the vehicle.

Lower Control Arm

REMOVAL & INSTALLATION

Deville and Fleetwood

▶ **See Figure 36**

1. Raise and safely support the vehicle, allowing the front suspension to hang free.

2. Remove the wheel and tire assembly.

⁂ WARNING

Be careful when working in the area of the CV-joint boot. Damage to the boot could result in eventual CV-joint failure. If necessary, install CV-joint boot protector tool J-34754 or equivalent, to protect the boot.

3. Remove the stabilizer bar-to-control arm bolt.

4. Remove the cotter pin and nut from the ball joint stud. Use ball joint separator tool J-36226 or equivalents, to separate the ball joint from the steering knuckle.

⁂ WARNING

When working near the halfshafts, be careful not to overextend the inner CV-joints. If the joint is overextended, the internal components may separate resulting in joint failure.

5. Remove the control arm mounting bolts and remove the control arm from the frame.

To install:

6. Position the control arm to the frame and install the mounting bolts, washers and nuts. Do not tighten the mounting nuts at this time.

7. Connect the stabilizer bar to the lower control arm and tighten the link nut to 13 ft. lbs. (17 Nm).

8. Connect the ball joint to the steering knuckle and install the castellated nut. Tighten the ball joint nut to 88 inch lbs. (10 Nm). Then tighten the nut an additional 120°, during which a torque of 41 ft. lbs. (55 Nm) must be obtained.

9. Install a new cotter pin in the ball joint stud. If the cotter pin cannot be installed because the hole in the stud does not align with a nut castellation, tighten the nut up to an additional 60° to allow for installation. NEVER loosen the nut to provide for cotter pin installation.

10. If necessary, remove the CV-joint boot protector tools.

11. Install the wheel and tire assembly and lower the vehicle.

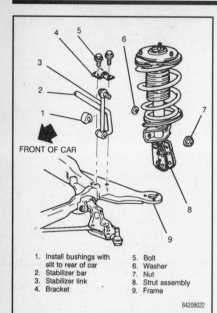

◀FRT

1. Nut
2. Control arm
3. Control arm mounted bushing
4. Frame mounted bushing
5. Washer
6. Nut

84208023

Fig. 36 Lower control arm installation—Deville and Fleetwood

---

12. When the weight of the vehicle is supported by the lower control arms, tighten the front mounting nut to 140 ft. lbs. (190 Nm), then the rear mounting nut to 91 ft. lbs. (123 Nm).

13. Check the front wheel alignment.

Eldorado and Seville

▶ **See Figure 37**

1. Raise and safely support the vehicle, allowing the front suspension to hang free.

2. Remove the wheel and tire assembly.

⁂ WARNING

When working near the halfshafts, be careful not to overextend the inner CV-joints. If the joint is overextended, the internal components may separate resulting in joint failure. Be careful when working in the area of the CV-joint boot. Damage to the boot could result in eventual CV-joint failure. If necessary, install CV-joint boot protector tool J-34754 or equivalent, to protect the boot.

3. On vehicles with 4.6L engine, remove the road sensing suspension position sensor from the lower control arm.

4. Remove the cotter pin and castellated nut from the lower ball joint stud. Use ball joint separator tool J-35315 or equivalents, to separate the ball joint from the steering knuckle.

5. Remove the control arm bushing bolt and brake reaction rod nut, retainer, and insulator. Remove the control arm.

To install:

6. Position the control arm to the frame and install the bushing bolt and brake reaction rod nut, retainer, and insulator. Do not tighten at this time.

7. Connect the ball joint to the steering knuckle and install the castellated nut. Tighten the ball joint nut to 84 inch lbs. (10 Nm). Then tighten the nut an additional 120°, during which a minimum torque of 37 ft. lbs. (50 Nm) must be obtained. If the minimum torque is not obtained, check for stripped threads. If the threads are okay, replace the ball joint and knuckle.

8. Install a new cotter pin in the ball joint stud. If the cotter pin cannot be installed because the hole in the stud does not align with a nut castellation, tighten the nut up to an additional 60° to allow for installation. NEVER loosen the nut to provide for cotter pin installation.

9. On 1993–98 vehicles with 4.6L engine, install the road sensing suspension position sensor to the lower control arm.

10. Install the tire and wheel assembly and lower the vehicle.

11. When the weight of the vehicle is supported by the lower control arms, tighten the control arm bushing bolt to 103 ft. lbs. (140 Nm) or nut to 91 ft. lbs. (123 Nm). Tighten the brake reaction rod nut to 58 ft. lbs. (78 Nm).

12. Check the front wheel alignment.

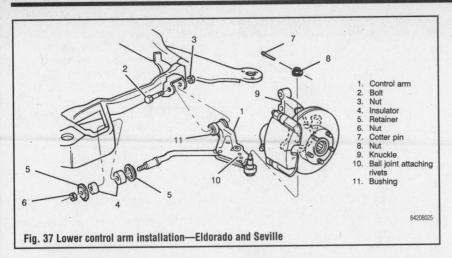

1. Control arm
2. Bolt
3. Nut
4. Insulator
5. Retainer
6. Nut
7. Cotter pin
8. Nut
9. Knuckle
10. Ball joint attaching rivets
11. Bushing

Fig. 37 Lower control arm installation—Eldorado and Seville

CONTROL ARM BUSHING REPLACEMENT

Deville and Fleetwood

FRAME-MOUNTED BUSHING

▶ See Figures 38 and 39

1. Remove the control arm from the vehicle.
2. Insert bolt, washer, and bearing assembly J-21474-19 or equivalent, through bushing driver J-21474-13 or equivalent, and position the small end facing the bushing.
3. Place bushing receiver J-21474-5 or equivalent, on the front of the bushing.
4. Tighten the bolt until the bushing is driven out of the frame, then remove the bushing driver tool.

To install:

5. Insert bolt, washer, and bearing assembly J-21474-19 or equivalent, through bushing receiver J-21474-5 or equivalent, with the large end facing the bushing.
6. Position the large end of bushing driver J-21474-13 or equivalent, facing the bushing.
7. Thread on nut J-21474-18 or equivalent.
8. Tighten bolt J-21474-19 or equivalent, until the bushing is fully seated.
9. Remove the bushing driver tool and reinstall the control arm.

CONTROL ARM-MOUNTED BUSHING

▶ See Figures 40 and 41

1. Remove the control arm from the vehicle.
2. Remove the bushing from the control arm by tapping down the flare with a hammer and punch.

To install:

3. Insert bolt, washer, and bearing assembly J-21474-19 or equivalent, through bushing driver J-21474-13 or equivalent, and position the small end facing the bushing.
4. Position flaring tool J-23915 or equivalent, with the small flare facing the bushing.
5. Install the nut J-21474-18 and tighten until a 45° flare is obtained and the bushing is secure in the control arm.
6. Install the control arm on the vehicle.

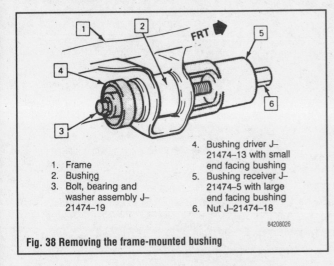

1. Frame
2. Bushing
3. Bolt, bearing and washer assembly J-21474-19
4. Bushing driver J-21474-13 with small end facing bushing
5. Bushing receiver J-21474-5 with large end facing bushing
6. Nut J-21474-18

Fig. 38 Removing the frame-mounted bushing

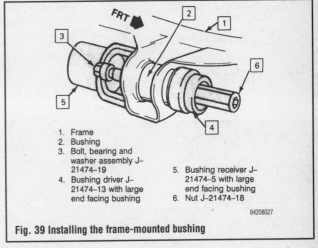

1. Frame
2. Bushing
3. Bolt, bearing and washer assembly J-21474-19
4. Bushing driver J-21474-13 with large end facing bushing
5. Bushing receiver J-21474-5 with large end facing bushing
6. Nut J-21474-18

Fig. 39 Installing the frame-mounted bushing

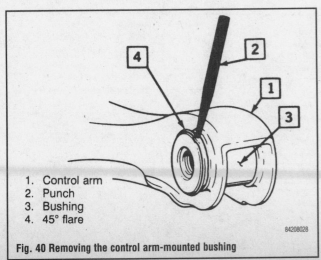

1. Control arm
2. Punch
3. Bushing
4. 45° flare

Fig. 40 Removing the control arm-mounted bushing

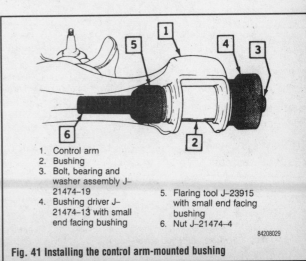

1. Control arm
2. Bushing
3. Bolt, bearing and washer assembly J-21474-19
4. Bushing driver J-21474-13 with small end facing bushing
5. Flaring tool J-23915 with small end facing bushing
6. Nut J-21474-4

Fig. 41 Installing the control arm-mounted bushing

Eldorado and Seville

♦ **See Figures 42 and 43**

1. Remove the lower control arm.
2. Position the control arm in a press with tools J-35561-1 and J-35561-2 or equivalents.
3. Press out the control arm bushing.

To install:

4. Lubricate a new bushing with a suitable rubber lubricant.
5. Position the control arm and bushing in a press with tools J-35561-1, J-35561-2 and J-35561-3 or equivalents, as shown in Fig. 43.
6. Press in the new control arm bushing.
7. Reinstall the control arm.

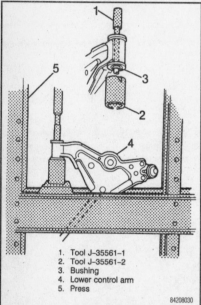

1. Tool J-35561-1
2. Tool J-35561-2
3. Bushing
4. Lower control arm
5. Press

84208030

Fig. 42 Removing the control arm bushing—Eldorado and Seville

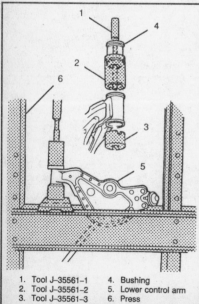

1. Tool J-35561-1	4. Bushing
2. Tool J-35561-2	5. Lower control arm
3. Tool J-35561-3	6. Press

84208031

Fig. 43 Installing the control arm bushing—Eldorado and Seville

Knuckle and Spindle

REMOVAL & INSTALLATION

Deville, Eldorado, Fleetwood and Seville

1. Raise and safely support the vehicle, allowing the front suspension to hang free.
2. Remove the wheel and tire assembly.

✷✷ WARNING

When working near the halfshafts, be careful not to overextend the inner CV-joints. If the joint is overextended, the internal components may separate resulting in joint failure. Be careful when working in the area of the CV-joint boot. Damage to the boot could result in eventual CV-joint failure. If necessary, install CV-joint boot protector tool J-34754 or equivalent, to protect the boot.

3. Remove the hub and bearing assembly.
4. Remove the cotter pin and nut from the tie rod end. Use separator tool J-24319-01 or equivalent, to separate the tie rod end from the steering knuckle.
5. Remove the cotter pin and nut from the ball joint stud. Use ball joint separator tool J-36226 or equivalent, on Deville and Fleetwood; or ball joint separator tool J-35315 or equivalent, on Eldorado and Seville, to separate the ball joint from the steering knuckle.
6. If necessary, disconnect the anti-lock brake wheel speed sensor, if equipped.
7. Remove the strut-to-knuckle bolts and remove the knuckle.

To install:

8. Position the knuckle and install the strut-to-knuckle bolts. Tighten the strut-to-knuckle bolts to 140 ft. lbs. (190 Nm).
9. If necessary, connect the anti-lock brake wheel speed sensor. If the sensor was removed on Eldorado and Seville, anti-corrosion compound must be applied to the sensor before assembly.
10. Connect the ball joint to the steering knuckle and install the castellated nut.
11. On Deville and Fleetwood, tighten the ball joint nut to 88 inch lbs. (10 Nm). Then tighten the nut an additional 120°, during which a torque of 41 ft. lbs. (55 Nm) must be obtained.
12. On Eldorado and Seville, tighten the ball joint nut to 84 inch lbs. (10 Nm). Then tighten the nut an additional 120°, during which a minimum torque of 37 ft. lbs. (50 Nm) must be obtained. If the minimum torque is not obtained, check for stripped threads. If the threads are okay, replace the ball joint and knuckle.
13. Install a new cotter pin. If the cotter pin cannot be installed because the hole in the stud does not align with a nut castellation, tighten the nut up to an additional 60° to allow for installation. NEVER loosen the nut to provide for cotter pin installation.
14. Connect the tie rod end to the steering knuckle. Install the tie rod end nut and tighten to 35 ft. lbs. (48 Nm). Install a new cotter pin. If the cotter pin cannot be installed because the hole in the stud does not align with a nut castellation, tighten the nut up to a maximum of 52 ft. lbs. (70 Nm) to allow for installation. NEVER loosen the nut to provide for cotter pin installation.
15. Install the hub and bearing assembly.
16. Install the wheel and tire assembly and lower the vehicle. Check the front wheel alignment.

Front Hub and Bearing

REMOVAL & INSTALLATION

Deville, Eldorado, Fleetwood and Seville

♦ **See Figures 44, 45, 46 and 47**

1. Raise and safely support the vehicle, allowing the front suspension to hang free.
2. Remove the wheel and tire assembly.

✷✷ WARNING

Be careful when working in the area of the CV-joint boot. Damage to the boot could result in eventual CV-joint failure. If necessary, install CV-joint boot protector tool J-34754 or equivalent, to protect the boot.

3. Clean the halfshaft threads of all dirt and lubricant. Insert a drift punch through the caliper and into the rotor to keep the rotor from turning, then remove the hub nut and washer, if equipped.
4. Remove the caliper without disconnecting the brake hose. Suspend the caliper from the coil spring with wire; do not let it hang by the brake hose.
5. Remove the disc brake rotor.
6. If equipped, detach the anti-lock brake wheel speed sensor connector.
7. Remove the hub and bearing assembly retaining bolts and the dust shield.
8. Use tool J-28733-A or equivalent, to separate the hub and bearing assembly from the halfshaft.

To install:

9. Apply a light coating of grease to the knuckle bore. Install the new hub and bearing assembly. Draw the hub and bearing assembly onto the halfshaft with a new hub nut.
10. Install the dust shield and the hub and bearing assembly retaining bolts. Tighten to 70 ft. lbs. (95 Nm).
11. If equipped, attach the anti-lock brake wheel speed sensor connector.
12. Install the disc brake rotor and caliper.
13. Insert a drift punch into the caliper and rotor to prevent the rotor from turning. On 1990–91 vehi-

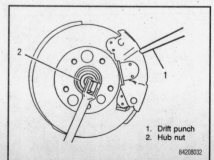

1. Drift punch
2. Hub nut

84208032

Fig. 44 Removing/installing the hub nut

cles, tighten the hub nut to 185 ft. lbs. (251 Nm). On 1992–98 vehicles, tighten the hub nut to 110 ft. lbs. (145 Nm), except on Deville and Fleetwood equipped with J55 brake option, in which case the torque is 130 ft. lbs. (177 Nm).

14. Install the wheel and tire assembly and lower the vehicle.

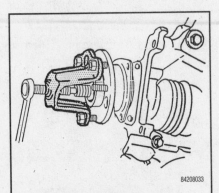

Fig. 45 Separating the hub and bearing assembly from the halfshaft

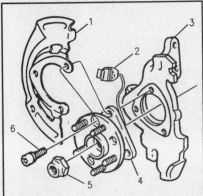

1. Dust shield
2. Wheel speed sensor connector
3. Steering knuckle
4. Hub and bearing assembly
5. Hub nut
6. Retaining bolt

Fig. 46 Hub and bearing assembly and related components—Deville and Fleetwood

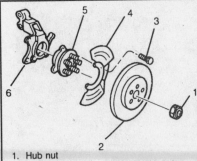

1. Hub nut
2. Disc brake rotor
3. Retaining bolt
4. Dust shield
5. Hub and bearing assembly
6. Steering knuckle

Fig. 47 Hub and bearing assembly and related components—Eldorado and Seville

Wheel Alignment

If the tires are worn unevenly, if the vehicle is not stable on the highway or if the handling seems uneven in spirited driving, the wheel alignment should be checked. If an alignment problem is suspected, first check for improper tire inflation and other possible causes. These can be worn suspension or steering components, accident damage or even unmatched tires. If any worn or damaged components are found, they must be replaced before the wheels can be properly aligned. Wheel alignment requires very expensive equipment and involves minute adjustments which must be accurate; it should only be performed by a trained technician. Take your vehicle to a properly equipped shop.

Following is a description of the alignment angles which are adjustable on most vehicles and how they affect vehicle handling. Although these angles can apply to both the front and rear wheels, usually only the front suspension is adjustable.

CASTER

▶ See Figure 48

Looking at a vehicle from the side, caster angle describes the steering axis rather than a wheel angle. The steering knuckle is attached to a control arm or strut at the top and a control arm at the bottom. The wheel pivots around the line between these points to steer the vehicle. When the upper point is tilted back,

this is described as positive caster. Having a positive caster tends to make the wheels self-centering, increasing directional stability. Excessive positive caster makes the wheels hard to steer, while an uneven caster will cause a pull to one side. Overloading the vehicle or sagging rear springs will affect caster, as will raising the rear of the vehicle. If the rear of the vehicle is lower than normal, the caster becomes more positive.

CAMBER

▶ See Figure 49

Looking from the front of the vehicle, camber is the inward or outward tilt of the top of wheels. When the tops of the wheels are tilted in, this is negative camber; if they are tilted out, it is positive. In a turn, a slight amount of negative camber helps maximize contact of the tire with the road. However, too much negative camber compromises straight-line stability, increases bump steer and torque steer.

TOE

▶ See Figure 50

Looking down at the wheels from above the vehicle, toe angle is the distance between the front of the wheels, relative to the distance between the back of the wheels. If the wheels are closer at the front, they are said to be toed-in or to have negative toe. A small amount of negative toe enhances directional stability and provides a smoother ride on the highway.

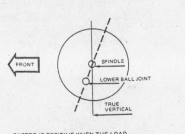

Fig. 48 Caster affects straight-line stability. Caster wheels used on shopping carts, for example, employ positive caster

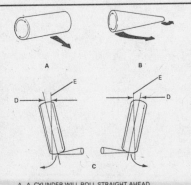

A A CYLINDER WILL ROLL STRAIGHT AHEAD
B A CONE WILL ROLL IN A CIRCLE TOWARD THE SMALL END
C TIRE CONTACTS THE ROAD SURFACE
D POSITIVE CAMBER ANGLE
E VERTICAL

Fig. 49 Camber influences tire contact with the road

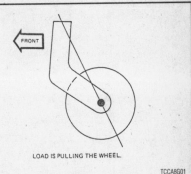

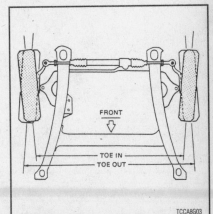

Fig. 50 With toe-in, the distance between the wheels is closer at the front than at the rear

REAR SUSPENSION

REAR SUSPENSION COMPONENT LOCATIONS—DEVILLE CONCOURS

1. Rear suspension support
2. Lower control arm
3. Spring
4. Upper control arm
5. Shock absorber
6. Stabilizer bar
7. Toe link
8. Parking brake adjuster

REAR SUSPENSION COMPONENT LOCATIONS—SEVILLE TOURING SEDAN (STS)

1. Rear suspension cradle
2. Rear alignment adjuster eccentrics
3. Lower control arm
4. Stabilizer link
5. Stabilizer bar
6. Tie rod end
7. Spring
8. Air adjustable shock absorber
9. Upper control arm

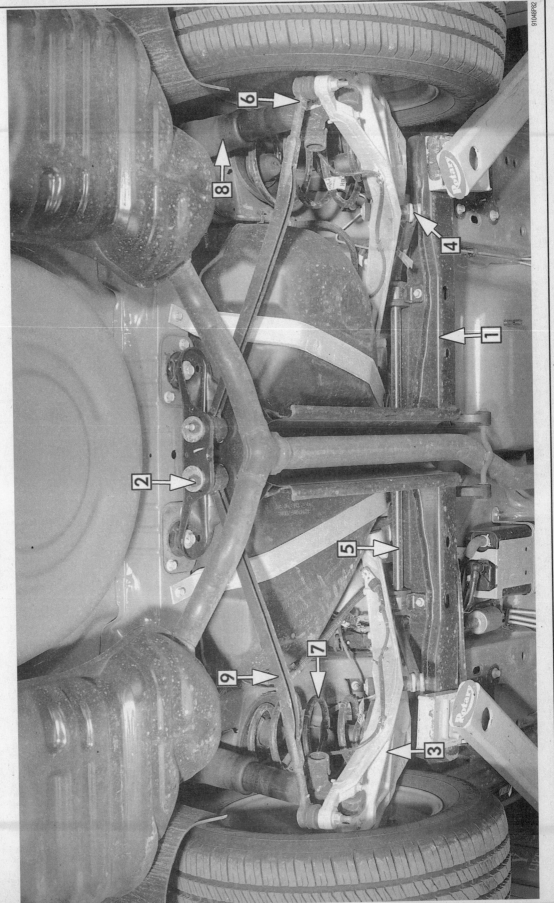

The late model Deville, Eldorado, Fleetwood, and Seville uses an independent short/long arm rear suspension. All the rear suspension components are mounted on a suspension support that is attached to the body at four points and is fully isolated with bushings and insulators to minimize road noise. Each rear wheel is connected to the suspension support through the suspension knuckle using and upper and lower control arm and toe link.

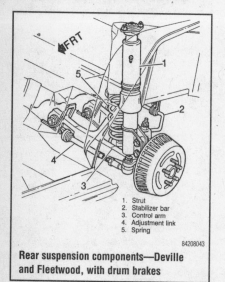

1. Strut
2. Stabilizer bar
3. Control arm
4. Adjustment link
5. Spring

84208043

Rear suspension components—Deville and Fleetwood, with drum brakes

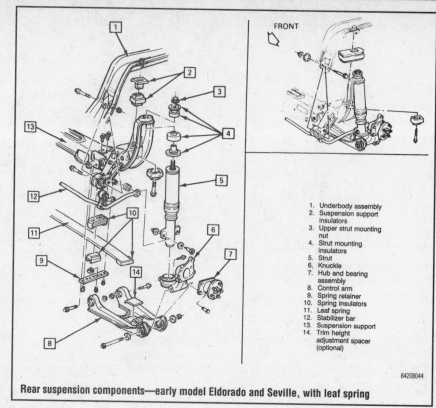

1. Underbody assembly
2. Suspension support insulators
3. Upper strut mounting nut
4. Strut mounting insulators
5. Strut
6. Knuckle
7. Hub and bearing assembly
8. Control arm
9. Spring retainer
10. Spring insulators
11. Leaf spring
12. Stabilizer bar
13. Suspension support
14. Trim height adjustment spacer (optional)

84208044

Rear suspension components—early model Eldorado and Seville, with leaf spring

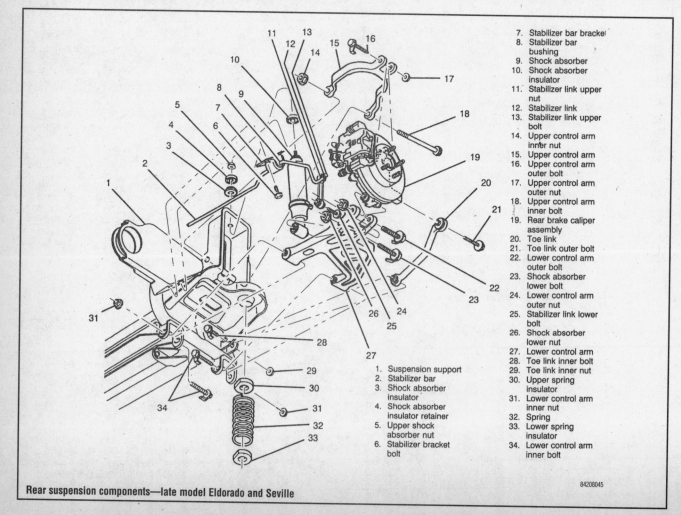

1. Suspension support
2. Stabilizer bar
3. Shock absorber insulator
4. Shock absorber insulator retainer
5. Upper shock absorber nut
6. Stabilizer bracket bolt
7. Stabilizer bar bracket
8. Stabilizer bar bushing
9. Shock absorber
10. Shock absorber insulator
11. Stabilizer link upper nut
12. Stabilizer link
13. Stabilizer link upper bolt
14. Upper control arm inner nut
15. Upper control arm
16. Upper control arm outer bolt
17. Upper control arm outer nut
18. Upper control arm inner bolt
19. Rear brake caliper assembly
20. Toe link
21. Toe link outer bolt
22. Lower control arm outer bolt
23. Shock absorber lower bolt
24. Lower control arm outer nut
25. Stabilizer link lower bolt
26. Shock absorber lower nut
27. Lower control arm
28. Toe link inner bolt
29. Toe link inner nut
30. Upper spring insulator
31. Lower control arm inner nut
32. Spring
33. Lower spring insulator
34. Lower control arm inner bolt

84208045

Rear suspension components—late model Eldorado and Seville

Coil Springs

REMOVAL & INSTALLATION

Deville and Fleetwood

▶ **See Figures 51, 52, 53 and 54**

1. Raise and safely support the vehicle so that the control arm hangs free.
2. Remove the wheel and tire assembly.
3. Remove the height sensor link from the right control arm and/or the parking brake cable-retaining clip from the left control arm.
4. Remove the rear stabilizer bar from the bracket on the knuckle.
5. Position tool J-23028-01 or equivalent, to cradle the control arm bushings. Secure the tool to a suitable jack.

✳ CAUTION

Tool J-23028-01 must be secured to a jack or personal injury may result.

6. Raise the jack to remove the tension from the control arm bolts.

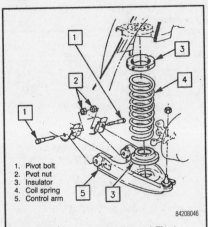

1. Pivot bolt
2. Pvot nut
3. Insulator
4. Coil spring
5. Control arm

84208046

Fig. 51 Coil spring—Deville and Fleetwood

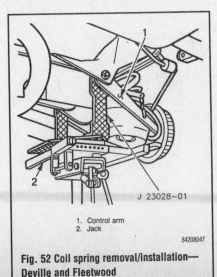

1. Control arm
2. Jack

J 23028-01

84208047

Fig. 52 Coil spring removal/installation—Deville and Fleetwood

7. As a safety measure, place a chain around the spring and through the control arm.
8. Remove the pivot bolt, nut and washer, if equipped, from the rear of the control arm.
9. Slowly maneuver the jack to relieve tension in the front control arm pivot bolt. Remove the pivot bolt, nut and washer, if equipped, from the front of the control arm.
10. Lower the jack, allowing the control arm to pivot downward. When all compression is removed from the spring, remove the safety chain, spring, and insulators.

➡ **Do not apply force to the control arm and/or ball joint to remove the spring. The spring can be removed easily with proper maneuvering.**

To install:

11. Inspect the spring insulators and replace them if they are cut or torn. If the vehicle has been driven more than 50,000 miles, replace the insulators regardless of condition.
12. Snap the upper insulator onto the spring. Install the lower insulator and spring in the vehicle; refer to Figs. 53 and 54 for proper spring positioning.
13. Using tool J-23028-01 or equivalent, mounted on a suitable jack, raise the control arm into position.
14. Slowly maneuver the jack until the front and rear control arm pivot bolts and nuts can be installed.
15. Connect the rear stabilizer bar to the knuckle bracket with the link.
16. Install the height sensor link to the right control arm and/or the parking brake cable retaining clip to the left control arm.
17. Install the wheel and tire assembly and lower the vehicle.

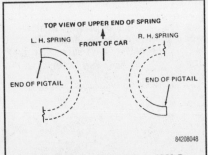

TOP VIEW OF UPPER END OF SPRING

L. H. SPRING   FRONT OF CAR   R. H. SPRING

END OF PIGTAIL   END OF PIGTAIL

84208048

Fig. 53 Coil spring positioning—1990 Deville and Fleetwood

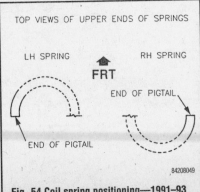

TOP VIEWS OF UPPER ENDS OF SPRINGS

LH SPRING   RH SPRING

FRT

END OF PIGTAIL

END OF PIGTAIL

84208049

Fig. 54 Coil spring positioning—1991–93 Deville and Fleetwood

18. When the vehicle is resting on its wheels, tighten the control arm nuts to 85 ft. lbs. (115 Nm) and the stabilizer bar link bolt to 13 ft. lbs. (17 Nm).

✳ WARNING

The control arm nuts must be tightened with the vehicle unsupported and resting on its wheels at normal trim height. If not, ride and handling may be adversely affected.

Eldorado and Seville

1. Raise and safely support the vehicle so that the control arm hangs free.
2. Remove the wheel and tire assembly.
3. Support the inner end of the lower control arm with a suitable jack. Position the jack to securely hold the control arm.
4. Disconnect the stabilizer bar and shock absorber from the lower control arm.
5. Remove the inner lower control arm nuts and bolts, then slowly lower the control arm to relieve the spring pressure.
6. Pull the lower control arm down and remove the coil spring.

To install:

7. Install the coil spring and insulators.

➡ **To ensure the spring is installed in the proper position, rest the spring (without insulators) on a flat surface prior to installation. The spring will stand up straight when resting on its lower end, but will lean or tip over when resting on its top end.**

8. Raise the inner end of the lower control arm with the jack to slightly compress the coil spring. Install the inner lower control arm nuts and bolts.
9. Connect the shock absorber and stabilizer link to the lower control arm.
10. Position the jack under the outer end of the lower control arm. Raise the jack until the suspension is in the normal ride height position.
11. With the suspension in the normal ride height position, tighten the stabilizer link lower nut to 44 ft. lbs. (60 Nm), the shock absorber lower nut to 75 ft. lbs. (102 Nm) and the lower control arm inner nuts to 75 ft. lbs. (102 Nm).

➡ **The inner control arm nuts must be tightened with the suspension in the normal ride height position to reduce wind up in the bushings.**

12. Install the wheel and tire assembly and lower the vehicle. Check the rear wheel alignment.

Leaf Spring

REMOVAL & INSTALLATION

Eldorado and Seville

1990–92 MODELS

▶ **See Figures 55 and 56**

➡ **Leaf spring removal requires disassembly of either the left or right suspension while leaving the other side intact. The spring can be removed from either side of the vehicle.**

1. Raise and safely support the vehicle.
2. Remove the wheel and tire assembly.
3. If disassembling the left control arm, disconnect the electronic level control height sensor link.
4. If equipped with a stabilizer bar, remove the stabilizer bar mounting bolt at the strut.
5. Reinstall 2 lug nuts to hold the disc brake rotor on the hub and bearing assembly.
6. Remove the rear brake caliper as follows:
   a. Loosen the parking brake cable at the adjuster.
   b. Lift up on the end of the cable spring to free the end of the cable from the lever.
   c. Remove the bolt and washer attaching the cable support bracket to the caliper.
   d. Remove the caliper mounting bracket bolts and suspend the caliper in the wheelwell with wire. Do not disconnect the brake hose or allow the caliper to hang by the brake hose.
7. Loosen, but do not remove, the knuckle pivot bolt on the outer end of the control arm. Support the outer end of the control arm with a suitable jack or jackstand to slightly compress the spring.

✳✳ CAUTION

The jack/jackstand must be strong enough to support the weight of the vehicle. It must also be securely positioned or personal injury may result.

8. Detach the strut electrical connector and remove the mounting nut, retainer and upper insulator. Slowly lower the jack or remove the jackstand to relieve the spring pressure.
9. Compress the strut by hand and remove the lower insulator. Detach the wheel speed sensor connector.
10. Remove the inner control arm nuts. Support the knuckle and control arm, then remove the inner control arm bolts and remove the control arm, knuckle, strut, hub and bearing and rotor from the vehicle as an assembly.
11. Place a jackstand under the outer end of the spring.

✳✳ CAUTION

The jackstand must be strong enough to support the weight of the vehicle. It must also be securely positioned or personal injury may result.

12. Lower the vehicle so that the vehicle weight loads the spring downward on the jackstand. Remove the 3 spring retainer bolts, retainer, and lower insulator from the retainer nearest the supported end of the spring.
13. Slowly raise the vehicle, allowing the spring to deflect downward until the spring no longer exerts force on the jackstand. Remove the jackstand.
14. Remove the spring retainer bolts, retainer and lower insulator from the retainer on the other side of the vehicle.
15. Remove the spring from the rear suspension support on the disassembled side of the vehicle. Remove the upper spring insulators, as required.
   To install:
16. Inspect the spring insulators, insulator locating pads, retainers and the control arm contact pads on the ends of the spring for cuts, cracks, tears, or other damage and replace as necessary.
17. Install the previously removed spring insulators. When installing the upper inner insulators, the molded arrow on the insulator must point toward the centerline of the car. Tighten the upper outer insulator nuts to 21 ft. lbs. (28 Nm).
18. Install the spring in the suspension support through the disassembled side of the vehicle.

✳✳ WARNING

The outer insulator locating bands must be centered on the spring insulators when the spring is positioned in the suspension support. Vehicle handling may be impaired if the spring is not positioned correctly.

19. Install the lower insulator and spring retainer on the side of the vehicle that was not disassembled. Place a jackstand under the free end of the spring.
20. Lower the vehicle, allowing the vehicle weight to load the spring and deflect the free end of the spring into position in the suspension support.
21. Install the lower insulator and spring retainer and on the disassembled side of the vehicle. Tighten the spring retainer bolts to 21 ft. lbs. (28 Nm).
22. Raise the vehicle and remove the jackstand.
23. Position the control arm, knuckle, strut, hub and bearing and rotor assembly in the suspension support. Install the inner control arm bolts and nuts but do not tighten at this time.
24. Attach the wheel speed sensor connector.
25. Install the lower strut insulator and position the strut in the suspension support assembly.
26. Position a jack or jackstand under the outer end of the lower control arm to slightly compress the spring.

✳✳ CAUTION

The jack/jackstand must be strong enough to support the weight of the vehicle. It must also be securely positioned or personal injury may result.

27. Install the upper strut insulator, retainer, and nut. Tighten the upper strut nut to 65 ft. lbs. (88 Nm), the knuckle pivot bolt to 59 ft. lbs. (80 Nm) and the inner control arm bolts to 66 ft. lbs. (90 Nm).
28. Attach the electrical connector at the top of the strut. Remove the jack or jackstand.
29. If equipped, install the stabilizer bar mounting bolt and tighten to 43 ft. lbs. (58 Nm).
30. Remove the 2 lug nuts that were installed to retain the rotor.
31. Install the caliper with new mounting bracket bolts. Tighten the mounting bracket bolts to 83 ft. lbs. (113 Nm). Install the parking brake cable

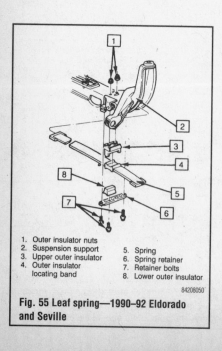

1. Outer insulator nuts
2. Suspension support
3. Upper outer insulator
4. Outer insulator locating band
5. Spring
6. Spring retainer
7. Retainer bolts
8. Lower outer insulator

84208050

Fig. 55 Leaf spring—1990–92 Eldorado and Seville

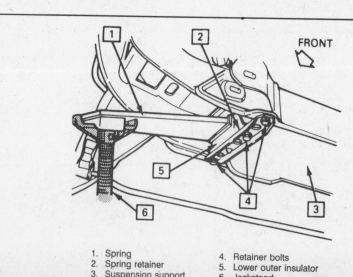

1. Spring
2. Spring retainer
3. Suspension support
4. Retainer bolts
5. Lower outer insulator
6. Jackstand

84208051

Fig. 56 Removing the leaf spring—1990–92 Eldorado and Seville

support bracket and tighten the bolt to 32 ft. lbs. (43 Nm).

32. Lift up on the end of the cable spring clip and work the end of the parking brake cable into the notch on the lever. Adjust the parking brake.

33. If assembling the left side of the suspension, connect the electronic level control height sensor link.

34. Install the wheel and tire assembly and lower the vehicle. Check the rear wheel alignment.

Shock Absorbers

REMOVAL & INSTALLATION

Deville and Fleetwood

♦ See Figures 57, 58 and 59

✳✳ CAUTION

The control arm must be supported with a suitable jack to prevent the coil spring from forcing the control arm downward, causing component damage and possible bodily injury.

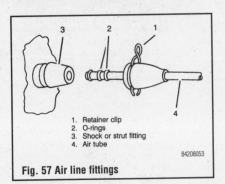

1. Retainer clip
2. O-rings
3. Shock or strut fitting
4. Air tube

84208053

Fig. 57 Air line fittings

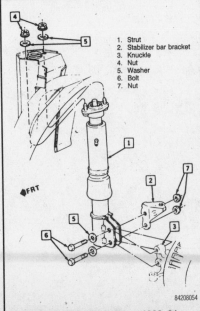

1. Strut
2. Stabilizer bar bracket
3. Knuckle
4. Nut
5. Washer
6. Bolt
7. Nut

84208054

Fig. 58 Air strut installation—1990-91 Deville and Fleetwood

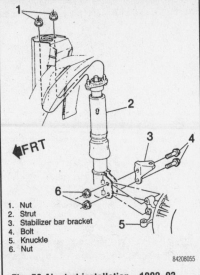

1. Nut
2. Strut
3. Stabilizer bar bracket
4. Bolt
5. Knuckle
6. Nut

84208055

Fig. 59 Air strut installation—1992-93 Deville and Fleetwood

✳✳ WARNING

To prevent ball joint damage, the knuckle must be restrained after the strut-to-knuckle bolts have been removed.

1. Raise and safely support the vehicle.
2. Remove the wheel and tire assembly.
3. Remove the trunk side cover.
4. Disconnect the electronic level control air line from the strut as follows:

    a. Clean the connector and surrounding area to prevent dirt from entering the system.

    b. Squeeze the spring clip to release the connector.

5. If equipped, detach the Computer Command Ride electrical connector.

6. Remove the strut tower mounting nuts from inside the trunk.

7. Remove the bolts, washers and nuts from the knuckle and stabilizer bar bracket and remove the strut.

To install:

8. Position the strut in the vehicle and install the upper mounting nuts.

➡**If equipped with Computer Command Ride, make sure the strut wiring is upright and centered on the strut mount when positioning the strut. After the strut is installed, make sure the wiring is upright and clear of the spacer plate to tower interface.**

9. Install the strut-to-knuckle and stabilizer bar bracket bolts, washers and nuts. On 1992-93 vehicles, the bolts must be installed in the direction shown in Fig. 59.

10. Moisten the air line O-rings with petroleum jelly or equivalent lubricant, and push the air line and connector fully into the fitting.

11. If equipped with Computer Command Ride, attach the electrical connector to the harness.

12. Tighten the strut tower mounting nuts to 19 ft. lbs. (25 Nm) and the strut-to-knuckle nuts to 140 ft. lbs. (190 Nm).

13. Install the trunk side cover.

14. Lightly pressurize the electronic level control system by momentarily grounding the compressor test lead in the engine compartment. This must be done before lowering the vehicle.

15. Install the wheel and tire assembly and lower the vehicle. Check the rear wheel alignment.

1990-92 Eldorado and Seville

♦ See Figure 60

1. Raise and safely support the vehicle.
2. Remove the wheel and tire assembly.
3. If equipped with 4.6L engine, detach the shock absorber electrical connector from the rear suspension support.
4. Support the lower control arm with a suitable jack to relieve the spring load.
5. Remove the shock absorber lower mounting nut and bolt.
6. If equipped with 4.9L engine, detach the electrical connector from the top of the shock absorber.
7. Disconnect the air line from the shock absorber as follows:

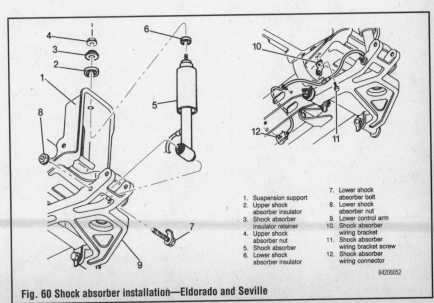

1. Suspension support
2. Upper shock absorber insulator
3. Shock absorber insulator retainer
4. Upper shock absorber nut
5. Shock absorber
6. Lower shock absorber insulator
7. Lower shock absorber bolt
8. Lower shock absorber nut
9. Lower control arm
10. Shock absorber wiring bracket
11. Shock absorber wiring bracket screw
12. Shock absorber wiring connector

84208052

Fig. 60 Shock absorber installation—Eldorado and Seville

a. Clean the connector and surrounding area to prevent dirt from entering the system.

b. Rotate the spring clip 90° to release the connector lock and pull the connector from the fitting.

8. Remove the upper mounting nut, retainer, and insulator. Compress the shock absorber by hand and remove it through the upper control arm.

To install:

9. Inspect the upper and lower shock absorber insulators for cuts, cracks, tears or other damage and replace as necessary.

10. Position the top of the shock absorber with the insulator attached in the suspension support. Install the upper shock absorber insulator, retainer, and nut.

11. Moisten the air line O-rings with petroleum jelly or equivalent lubricant, rotate the spring retainer to the engaged position and push the air line and connector fully into the fitting.

12. Install the shock absorber lower mounting nut and bolt. Tighten the upper shock absorber nut to 55 ft. lbs. (75 Nm) and the lower shock absorber nut to 75 ft. lbs. (102 Nm).

13. Attach the electrical connector at the top of the shock absorber, if equipped with 4.9L engine. Attach the shock absorber electrical connector to the rear suspension support, if equipped with 4.6L engine.

14. Install the wheel and tire assembly and lower the vehicle.

1993–98 Eldorado and Seville

◆ **See Figures 61 and 62**

1. Raise and safely support the vehicle.
2. Remove the wheel and tire assembly.
3. Disconnect the electronic level control height sensor link if removing the left strut.

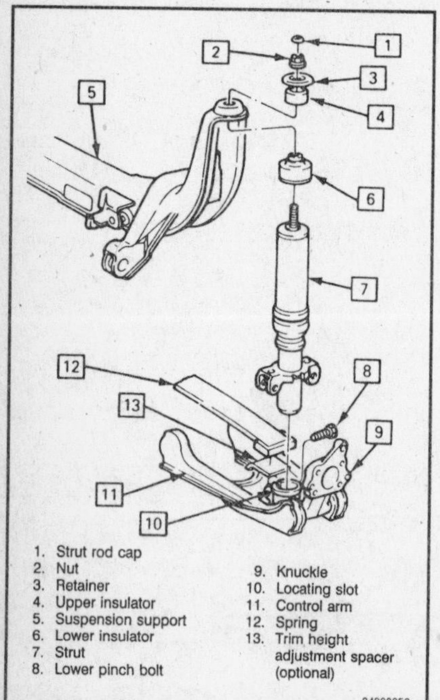

4. Install 2 lug nuts to hold the rotor on the hub and bearing assembly.

5. If equipped with a stabilizer bar, remove the mounting bolt at the strut.

6. Remove the rear brake caliper as follows:

a. Loosen the parking brake cable at the adjuster.

b. Lift up on the end of the cable spring to free the end of the cable from the lever.

c. Remove the bolt and washer attaching the cable support bracket to the caliper.

d. Remove the caliper mounting bracket bolts and suspend the caliper in the wheelwell with wire. Do not disconnect the brake hose or allow the caliper to hang by the brake hose.

7. Loosen, but do not remove, the knuckle pivot bolt on the outer end of the control arm. Support the outer end of the control arm with a suitable jack or jackstand to slightly compress the spring.

> ※ **CAUTION**
>
> **The jack/jackstand must be strong enough to support the weight of the vehicle. It must also be securely positioned or personal injury may result.**

8. If equipped, detach the Computer Command Ride electrical connector at the top of the strut.

9. Disconnect the air line from the strut as follows:

a. Clean the connector and surrounding area to prevent dirt from entering the system.

b. Rotate the spring clip 90° to release the connector lock and pull the connector from the fitting.

10. Remove the upper strut rod cap, mounting nut, retainer, and insulator. Slowly lower the jack or remove the jackstand to relieve the spring pressure.

11. Compress the strut by hand and remove the lower insulator. Rotate the strut and knuckle assembly outward by pivoting on the knuckle pivot bolt.

12. Remove the knuckle pinch bolt and remove the strut from the knuckle.

To install:

13. Inspect the upper and lower strut insulators for cuts, cracks, tears or other damage and replace as necessary.

14. Position the strut so it is fully seated in the knuckle with the tang on the strut bottomed in the knuckle slot. Install the knuckle pinch bolt and tighten to 40 ft. lbs. (55 Nm).

15. Install the lower insulator on the strut and position the strut rod in the suspension support.

16. Position a jack or jackstand under the outer end of the lower control arm to slightly compress the spring.

> ※※ **CAUTION**
>
> **The jack/jackstand must be strong enough to support the weight of the vehicle. It must also be securely positioned or personal injury may result.**

17. Install the upper strut insulator, retainer, and nut. Tighten the upper strut nut to 65 ft. lbs. (88 Nm) and the knuckle pivot bolt to 59 ft. (80 Nm). Remove the jack or jackstand.

18. Moisten the air line O-rings with petroleum jelly or equivalent lubricant, rotate the spring retainer to the engaged position and push the air line and connector fully into the fitting.

19. If equipped, attach the Computer Command Ride electrical connector of the top of the strut.

20. If equipped with a stabilizer bar, install the mounting bolt and tighten to 43 ft. lbs. (58 Nm).

21. Install the caliper with new mounting bracket bolts. Tighten the mounting bracket bolts to 83 ft. lbs. (113 Nm). Install the parking brake cable support bracket and tighten the bolt to 32 ft. lbs. (43 Nm).

22. Lift up on the end of the cable spring clip and work the end of the parking brake cable into the notch on the lever. Adjust the parking brake.

23. If installing the left strut, connect the electronic level control height sensor link.

24. Remove the 2 lug nuts that were installed to retain the rotor.

25. Install the wheel and tire assembly and lower the vehicle.

TESTING

◆ **See Figure 63**

The purpose of the shock absorber is simply to limit the motion of the spring during compression and rebound cycles. If the vehicle is not equipped with these motion dampers, the up and down motion would multiply until the vehicle was alternately trying to leap off the ground and to pound itself into the pavement.

Contrary to popular rumor, the shocks do not affect the ride height of the vehicle. This is controlled by other suspension components such as springs and tires. Worn shock absorbers can affect handling; if the front of the vehicle is rising or falling excessively, the "footprint" of the tires changes on the pavement and steering is affected.

The simplest test of the shock absorber is simply push down on one corner of the unladen vehicle and release it. Observe the motion of the body as it is released. In most cases, it will come up beyond it

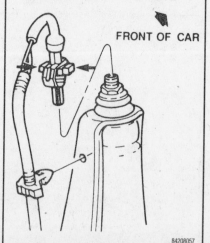

1. Strut rod cap
2. Nut
3. Retainer
4. Upper insulator
5. Suspension support
6. Lower insulator
7. Strut
8. Lower pinch bolt
9. Knuckle
10. Locating slot
11. Control arm
12. Spring
13. Trim height adjustment spacer (optional)

84206056

Fig. 61 Strut installation—Eldorado and Seville

SQUEEZE TABS TO REMOVE

FRONT OF CAR

84208057

Fig. 62 Detaching the Computer Command Ride electrical connector

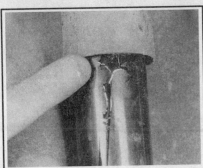

Fig. 63 When fluid is seeping out of the shock absorber, it's time to replace it

original rest position, dip back below it and settle quickly to rest. This shows that the damper is controlling the spring action. Any tendency to excessive pitch (up-and-down) motion or failure to return to rest within 2-3 cycles is a sign of poor function within the shock absorber. Oil-filled shocks may have a light film of oil around the seal, resulting from normal breathing and air exchange. This should NOT be taken as a sign of failure, but any sign of thick or running oil definitely indicates failure. Gas filled shocks may also show some film at the shaft; if the gas has leaked out, the shock will have almost no resistance to motion.

While each shock absorber can be replaced individually, it is recommended that they be changed as a pair (both front or both rear) to maintain equal response on both sides of the vehicle. Chances are quite good that if one has failed, its mate is weak also.

Air-adjustable shock absorbers should be stroked before testing. When stored horizontally, an air pocket can form in the pressure chamber. An air pocket can also form when the shock is off the vehicle if it is not continuously held with the top end up.

To remove air from the pressure chamber, extend the shock absorber in a vertical position with the top end up, then collapse the shock absorber in a vertical position with the top end down. Repeat this procedure 5 times to make sure the air is purged from the pressure chamber.

Test the shock absorber as follows:
1. Clamp the shock absorber in a vise with the shock absorber upright, top end up. Do not clamp on the reservoir tube.
2. Pump the shock absorber by hand at various rates of speed and note the resistance.
3. Rebound resistance normally is stronger than compression resistance by about 2 to 1. The resistance should be smooth and constant for each stroking rate.
4. Compare the shock absorber with one that is known to be good.
5. It is normal to hear a hissing noise from the shock absorber. The following symptoms are abnormal and indicate replacement is necessary:
   a. A skip or lag at reversal near mid-stroke.
   b. A seize, except at either extreme end of travel.
   c. A noise, such as a grunt or squeal, after completing one full stroke in both directions.
   d. A clicking noise at fast reversal.

Control Arms/Links

REMOVAL & INSTALLATION

1990–93 Deville and Fleetwood

♦ See Figure 64

1. Raise and safely support the vehicle.
2. Remove the wheel and tire assembly.
3. Remove the height sensor link from the right control arm and/or the parking brake cable retaining clip from the left control arm.
4. Remove the suspension adjustment link retaining nut and separate the link assembly from the control arm.
5. Remove the coil spring.
6. Remove the cotter pin and nut from the ball joint stud. Turn the nut over and install with the flat portion facing upward. Do not tighten the nut.
7. Use tool J-34505 or equivalent, on 1990 vehicles or tool J-36226 or equivalent, on 1991–93 vehicles, to separate the knuckle from the ball joint. Remove the nut from the ball joint stud.
8. Remove the control arm.

To install:

9. Position the control arm ball joint stud in the knuckle and install a new nut.
10. On 1990–91 vehicles, tighten the nut to 88 inch lbs. (10 Nm), then tighten an additional ⅔ turn.
11. On 1992–93 vehicles, tighten the nut to 88 inch lbs. (10 Nm), then tighten an additional 4 flats of the nut; the torque should be 40 ft. lbs. (55 Nm) minimum. On 1992–93 vehicles with heavy duty chassis and RPO J55 brake option, tighten the nut 2½ flats; the torque should be 99 ft. lbs. (135 Nm) minimum.

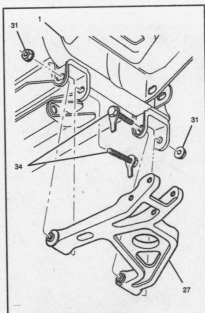

1	SUSPENSION SUPPORT
27	LOWER CONTROL ARM
31	NUT, LOWER CONTROL ARM INNER - 102 N•m (75 LBS. FT.)
34	BOLT, LOWER CONTROL ARM INNER

91048G28

Fig. 64 The lower control arm mounting

➡️ It may be necessary to partially load the ball joint to keep the ball stud from rotating while the nut is tightened.

12. Install a new cotter pin. If the hole in the ball stud does not align with the slot in the nut, tighten the nut to allow cotter pin installation. NEVER loosen the nut to align the hole and the slot.
13. Install the coil spring.
14. Attach the adjustment link to the control arm with the nut. Tighten the nut to 63 ft. lbs. (85 Nm).
15. Install the height sensor link to the right control arm and/or the parking brake cable retaining clip to the left control arm.
16. Install the wheel and tire assembly and lower the vehicle.
17. After the vehicle has been lowered and is resting on the wheels at normal trim height, tighten the control arm nuts to 85 ft. lbs. (115 Nm) and the stabilizer bar link bolt to 13 ft. lbs. (17 Nm).

✱✱ WARNING

The control arm nuts must be tightened with the wheels on the ground and the vehicle at normal trim height. Failure to do so may adversely affect ride and handling.

18. Lubricate the ball joint and inner link joint with suitable chassis lubricant.

1990–92 Eldorado and Seville

♦ See Figure 65

1. Raise and safely support the vehicle.
2. Remove the wheel and tire assembly.
3. If disassembling the left control arm, disconnect the electronic level control height sensor link.
4. If equipped with a stabilizer bar, remove the stabilizer bar mounting bolt at the strut.
5. Reinstall 2 lug nuts to hold the disc brake rotor on the hub and bearing assembly.
6. Remove the rear brake caliper as follows:
   a. Loosen the parking brake cable at the adjuster.
   b. Lift up on the end of the cable spring to free the end of the cable from the lever.
   c. Remove the bolt and washer attaching the cable support bracket to the caliper.
   d. Remove the caliper mounting bracket bolts and suspend the caliper in the wheelwell with wire. Do not disconnect the brake hose or allow the caliper to hang by the brake hose.
7. Loosen, but do not remove, the knuckle pivot bolt on the outer end of the control arm. Support the outer end of the control arm with a suitable jack or jackstand to slightly compress the spring.

✱✱ CAUTION

The jack/jackstand must be strong enough to support the weight of the vehicle. It must also be securely positioned or personal injury may result.

8. Detach the strut electrical connector and remove the mounting nut, retainer and upper insulator. Slowly lower the jack or remove the jackstand to relieve the spring pressure.
9. Compress the strut by hand and remove the

lower insulator. Detach the wheel speed sensor connector.

10. While supporting the knuckle, remove the knuckle pivot bolt and remove the knuckle, strut, hub and bearing and rotor from the vehicle as an assembly.

11. Remove both inner control arm bolts and remove the control arm from the vehicle.

To install:

12. Position the control arm in the vehicle and install both inner control arm bolts. Do not tighten the bolts at this time.

13. Position the assembled knuckle, strut, hub and bearing and rotor assembly in the control arm and install the knuckle pivot bolt. Do not tighten the bolt at this time.

14. Attach the wheel speed sensor connector.

15. Install the lower strut insulator and position the strut in the suspension support assembly.

16. Position a jack or jackstand under the outer end of the lower control arm to slightly compress the spring.

✷✷ CAUTION

The jack/jackstand must be strong enough to support the weight of the vehicle. It must also be securely positioned or personal injury may result.

17. Install the upper strut insulator, retainer, and nut. Tighten the upper strut nut to 65 ft. lbs. (88 Nm), the knuckle pivot bolt to 59 ft. lbs. (80 Nm), and the inner control arm bolts to 66 ft. lbs. (90 Nm).

18. Attach the electrical connector at the top of the strut. Remove the jack or jackstand.

19. If equipped, install the stabilizer bar mounting bolt and tighten to 43 ft. lbs. (58 Nm).

20. Remove the 2 lug nuts that were installed to retain the rotor.

21. Install the caliper with new mounting bracket bolts. Tighten the mounting bracket bolts to 83 ft. lbs. (113 Nm). Install the parking brake cable support bracket and tighten the bolt to 32 ft. lbs. (43 Nm).

22. Lift up on the end of the cable spring clip and work the end of the parking brake cable into the notch on the lever. Adjust the parking brake.

23. If installing the left control arm, connect the electronic level control height sensor link.

24. Install the wheel and tire assembly and lower the vehicle. Check the rear wheel alignment.

1993–98 Eldorado and Seville

LOWER CONTROL ARM

▶ **See Figure 66**

1. Raise and safely support the vehicle so that the control arm hangs free.

2. Remove the wheel and tire assembly.

3. Support the inner end of the lower control arm with a suitable jack. Position the jack to securely hold the control arm.

4. Disconnect the stabilizer bar and shock absorber from the lower control arm.

5. Remove the inner lower control arm nuts and bolts, then slowly lower the control arm to relieve the spring pressure.

6. Pull the lower control arm down and remove the coil spring.

7. Remove the lower control arm outer bolt and remove the lower control arm.

To install:

8. Position the lower control arm in the vehicle and install the outer bolt and nut. Tighten the nut to 75 ft. lbs. (102 Nm).

9. Install the coil spring and insulators.

➡**To ensure the spring is installed in the proper position, rest the spring (without insulators) on a flat surface prior to installation. The spring will stand up straight when resting on its lower end, but will lean or tip over when resting on its top end.**

10. Raise the inner end of the lower control arm with the jack to slightly compress the coil spring. Install the inner lower control arm nuts and bolts.

11. Connect the shock absorber and stabilizer link to the lower control arm.

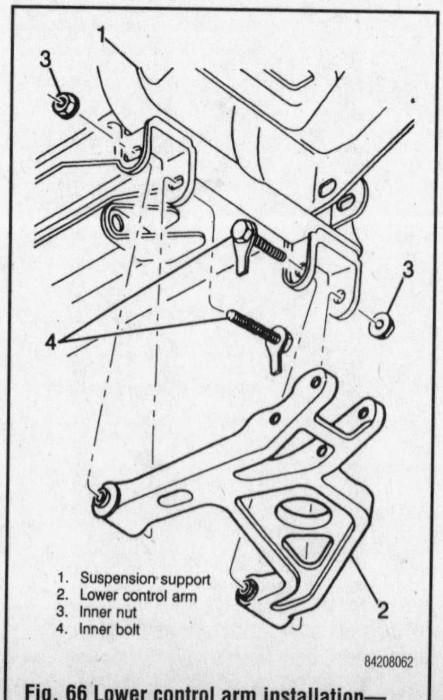

12. Position the jack under the outer end of the lower control arm. Raise the jack until the suspension is in the normal ride height position.

13. With the suspension in the normal ride height position, tighten the stabilizer link lower nut to 44 ft. lbs. (60 Nm), the shock absorber lower nut to 75 ft. lbs. (102 Nm) and the lower control arm inner nuts to 75 ft. lbs. (102 Nm).

➡**The inner control arm nuts must be tightened with the suspension in the normal ride height position to reduce wind up in the bushings.**

14. Install the wheel and tire assembly and lower the vehicle. Check the rear wheel alignment.

UPPER CONTROL ARM

▶ **See Figure 67**

1. Raise and safely support the vehicle.

2. Remove the wheel and tire assembly.

3. If equipped with 4.9L engine, remove the electronic level control height sensor link.

4. If equipped with 4.6L engine, remove the road sensing suspension position sensor and bracket from the shock tower.

5. Remove the inner and outer control arm bolts. Raise the control arm up over the shock tower and remove it from the vehicle.

To install:

6. Lower the control arm over the shock tower and position it in the vehicle. Install the inner and outer control arm bolts.

7. Position a suitable jack under the outer end of the lower control arm. Raise the suspension with the jack until it is in the normal ride height position, then tighten the upper control arm inner and outer nuts to 42 ft. lbs. (57 Nm).

✷✷ WARNING

The inner control arm nuts must be tightened with the suspension in the normal ride height position to reduce wind up in the bushings.

8. If equipped with 4.6L engine, install the road sensing suspension position sensor and bracket to the shock tower.

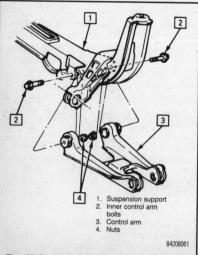

1. Suspension support
2. Inner control arm bolts
3. Control arm
4. Nuts

84208061

Fig. 65 Control arm installation—1990–92 Eldorado and Seville

1. Suspension support
2. Lower control arm
3. Inner nut
4. Inner bolt

84208062

Fig. 66 Lower control arm installation—1993–98 Eldorado and Seville

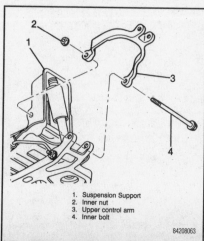

1. Suspension Support
2. Inner nut
3. Upper control arm
4. Inner bolt

84208063

Fig. 67 Upper control arm installation—1993–98 Eldorado and Seville

9. If equipped with 4.9L engine, install the electronic level control height sensor link.

10. Install the wheel and tire assembly and lower the vehicle.

1994–98 Deville

LOWER CONTROL ARM

▶ See Figure 68

1. Raise and safely support the vehicle securely.

2. Remove the tire and wheel assembly.

3. Support the inboard end of the lower control arm with a transmission jack. Position the brackets on the jack to securely hold the control arm.

4. Disconnect the stabilizer link lower attachment.

5. Unbolt the shock absorber lower attachment.

6. Remove the inboard lower control arm bolts and nuts.

7. Slowly lower transmission jack to relieve spring pressure.

8. Pull the lower control arm down to remove the spring.

9. Remove the lower control arm outboard bolt and the control arm.

To install:

10. Position the control arm in the vehicle and install the outboard control arm bolt and nut.

    a. Tighten the lower control arm outer nut to 75 ft. lbs. (102 Nm).

11. Install the spring and insulators.

➡**To insure proper orientation of the spring, rest the spring (without insulators) on a flat**

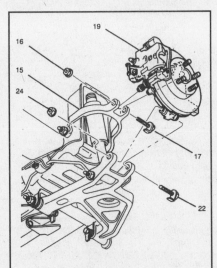

15 UPPER CONTROL ARM
16 BOLT, UPPER CONTROL ARM OUTER
17 NUT, UPPER CONTROL ARM OUTER - 57 N•m (42 LBS. FT.)
19 REAR BRAKE CALIPER ASSEMBLY
22 BOLT, LOWER CONTROL ARM OUTER
24 NUT, LOWER CONTROL ARM OUTER - 102 N•m (75 LBS. FT.)

91048G29

Fig. 68 This diagram of the rear suspension shows the removal of the steering knuckle to access the upper and lower control arms

surface. The spring will stand up straight when resting on its lower end, but will lean or tip when resting on its top end.

12. Raise the transmission jack under the inboard end of the lower control arm to slightly compress the spring.

13. Insert the inboard lower control arm bolts and nuts.

14. Attach the shock absorber lower attachment.

15. Install the stabilizer link lower attachment.

16. Remove the transmission jack and place it under outboard end of the lower control arm to bring the suspension to its design position. Inner control arm nuts must be tightened in the design position to reduce wind up in the bushings.

    a. Tighten the stabilizer link lower nut to 44 ft. lbs. (60 Nm).

    b. Tighten the shock absorber lower nut to 75 ft. lbs. (102 Nm).

    c. Tighten the lower control arm inner nuts to 75 ft. lbs. (102 Nm).

17. Install the wheel and tire.

➡**A rear wheel alignment is necessary whenever the inner lower control arm fasteners have been loosened.**

UPPER CONTROL ARM

1. Raise and safely support the vehicle securely.

2. Remove the wheel and tire assembly.

3. Disconnect the electronic level control height sensor link, on the vehicles with the 4.9L engine.

4. Disconnect the road sensing suspension position sensor and bracket from the shock tower on the vehicles with the 4.6L engine.

5. Remove the inner and outer control arm bolts.

6. Lift the control arm up over the shock tower to remove it from the vehicle.

To install:

7. Place the control arm over the shock tower to install it in the vehicle.

8. Install the inner and outer control arm bolts. Place a screw jack under the outboard end of the lower control arm to bring the suspension to design position. The inner control arm nuts must be tightened in the design position to reduce wind up in the bushings.

    a. Tighten the upper control arm inner and outer nuts to 42 ft. lbs. (57 Nm).

9. Connect the road sensing suspension position sensor bracket and sensor on the vehicles with the 4.6L engine.

10. Connect the electronic level control height sensor link on the vehicles with the 4.9L engine.

11. Install the wheel and tire assembly.

12. Lower the vehicle.

Sway Bar

REMOVAL & INSTALLATION

Deville and Fleetwood

1. Raise and safely support the vehicle.

2. Remove the rear wheel and tire assemblies.

3. Remove the stabilizer bar link bolt, nut, retainer and bushings from the stabilizer bar bracket.

4. Remove the link bolt and bend the open end of the link downward.

5. Remove the stabilizer bar and bushings.

To install:

6. Install the stabilizer bar and bushings. Install the bushing into the link with the slit facing the rear of the vehicle.

7. Bend the link upward to close around the bushing and install the link bolt.

8. Install the link bushings, retainers, support bolt and nut.

9. Tighten the link nut to 13 ft. lbs. (17 Nm) and the link bolt to 37 ft. lbs. (50 Nm) on 1990–91 vehicles or 17 ft. lbs. (23 Nm) on 1992–98 vehicles.

Eldorado and Seville

1990–92 MODELS

▶ See Figure 69

➡**It is easier to remove and install the stabilizer bar with the vehicle on the ground and supported by the wheels. If it is necessary to raise the vehicle for stabilizer bar removal & installation, use drive-on ramps or support the control arms as far outboard as possible with jacks.**

1. Raise and safely support the vehicle.

2. Remove the stabilizer bar attaching nut and bolt at the strut.

3. Remove the stabilizer link bolt and nut at the suspension support.

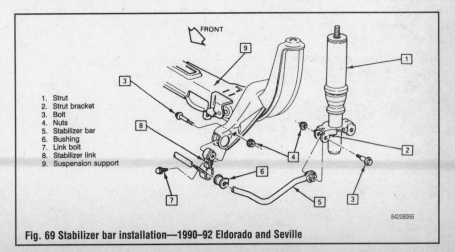

1. Strut
2. Strut bracket
3. Bolt
4. Nuts
5. Stabilizer bar
6. Bushing
7. Link bolt
8. Stabilizer link
9. Suspension support

84208066

Fig. 69 Stabilizer bar installation—1990–92 Eldorado and Seville

4. Remove the stabilizer bar from the vehicle. Remove the stabilizer link and bushings, if required.

To install:

5. Inspect the bushings for cuts, cracks or tears and replace as necessary.

6. Install the bushings and links on the stabilizer bar.

7. Position the stabilizer bar in the vehicle and install the bolts and nuts at the suspension support and strut.

8. Tighten the link bolt and stabilizer mounting nuts to 43 ft. lbs. (58 Nm).

1993–98 MODELS

▶ See Figure 70

1. Raise and safely support the vehicle.

2. Remove the rear wheel and tire assemblies.

3. Remove the stabilizer link lower bolt and upper nut on both sides of the vehicle.

4. Remove the stabilizer brackets and remove the bushings from the stabilizer bar.

5. Lower and support the exhaust system at the rear of the vehicle.

6. Remove the stabilizer bar.

To install:

7. Position the stabilizer bar in the vehicle.

8. Raise the exhaust system into position and secure.

9. Position the bushings on the stabilizer bar and install the brackets.

10. Install the link upper nuts and lower bolts. Tighten the upper link nut to 38 ft. lbs. (52 Nm) and the lower link bolt to 44 ft. lbs. (60 Nm).

11. Tighten the stabilizer bracket bolt to 44 ft. lbs. (60 Nm).

12. Install the wheel and tire assembly and lower the vehicle.

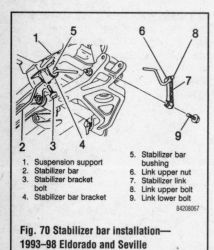

1. Suspension support
2. Stabilizer bar
3. Stabilizer bracket bolt
4. Stabilizer bar bracket
5. Stabilizer bar bushing
6. Link upper nut
7. Stabilizer link
8. Link upper bolt
9. Link lower bolt

84208067

Fig. 70 Stabilizer bar installation— 1993–98 Eldorado and Seville

Hub & Bearings

REMOVAL & INSTALLATION

Deville and Fleetwood

1990–93 MODELS

▶ See Figure 71

1. Raise and safely support the vehicle.

2. Remove the wheel and tire assembly.

3. Remove the brake drum.

4. Remove the retaining bolts and remove the hub and bearing assembly from the axle. If equipped with anti-lock brakes, be careful working around the sensor wires; disconnect them as needed.

❊❊ WARNING

The bolts that attach the hub and bearing also support the brake assembly. When the bolts are removed, the brake assembly must be supported with wire or other means. Do not let the brake assembly hang by the brake line or anti-lock brake electrical wire.

To install:

5. Install the hub and bearing assembly with the retaining bolts. Tighten the bolts to 52 ft. lbs. (70 Nm).

6. Reconnect the anti-lock brake sensor wire, as necessary.

7. Install the brake drum.

8. Install the wheel and tire assembly and lower the vehicle.

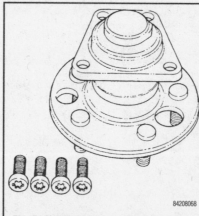

84208068

Fig. 71 Hub and bearing assembly—Deville and Fleetwood

Eldorado and Seville

1990–92 MODELS

1. Raise and safely support the vehicle.

2. Remove the wheel and tire assembly.

3. Remove the rear brake caliper as follows:

   a. Loosen the parking brake cable at the adjuster.

   b. Lift up on the end of the cable spring to free the end of the cable from the lever.

   c. Remove the bolt and washer attaching the cable support bracket to the caliper.

   d. Remove the caliper mounting bracket bolts and suspend the caliper in the wheelwell with wire. Do not disconnect the brake hose or allow the caliper to hang by the brake hose.

4. If equipped, remove and discard the disc brake rotor retainers. Remove the disc brake rotor.

5. Remove the hub mounting bolts and remove the hub and bearing assembly.

To install:

6. Position the hub and bearing assembly on the knuckle and install the mounting bolts. Tighten to 52 ft. lbs. (70 Nm).

7. Install the disc brake rotor.

8. Install the caliper with new mounting bracket bolts. Tighten the mounting bracket bolts to 83 ft. lbs. (113 Nm). Install the parking brake cable support bracket and tighten the bolt to 32 ft. lbs. (43 Nm).

9. Lift up on the end of the cable spring clip and work the end of the parking brake cable into the notch on the lever. Adjust the parking brake.

10. Install the wheel and tire assembly and lower the vehicle.

1993–98 Eldorado and Seville, and 1994–98 Deville

1. Raise and safely support the vehicle.

2. Remove the wheel and tire assembly.

3. Remove the parking brake cable bracket from the knuckle.

4. Remove and discard the caliper mounting bracket bolts. Remove the caliper and suspend it in the wheelwell with wire. Do not disconnect the brake hose or allow the caliper to hang by the brake hose.

5. Remove the disc brake rotor.

6. Remove the hub mounting bolts and remove the hub and bearing assembly.

To install:

7. Install the hub and bearing assembly and tighten the mounting bolts to 52 ft. lbs. (70 Nm).

8. Install the disc brake rotor.

9. Install the caliper with new mounting bracket bolts. Tighten the mounting bracket bolts to 83 ft. lbs. (113 Nm). Install the parking brake cable bracket and tighten the bolt to 32 ft. lbs. (43 Nm).

10. Install the wheel and tire assembly and lower the vehicle.

STEERING

Steering Wheel

REMOVAL & INSTALLATION

✳✳ CAUTION

Some models covered by this manual may be equipped with a Supplemental Restraint System (SRS), which uses an air bag. Whenever working near any of the SRS components, such as the impact sensors, the air bag module, steering column, and instrument panel disable the SRS.

Deville, Eldorado, Seville and Fleetwood—Early Models

◆ **See Figures 72, 73 and 74**

1. Disable the SIR system as follows:
   a. Disconnect the negative battery cable.
   b. Turn the ignition switch **OFF**.
   c. Remove the SIR fuse. On 1990 Deville and Fleetwood, remove SIR fuse No. 3 from the fuse panel. On 1991–93 Deville and Fleetwood, remove SIR fuse No. 18 from the fuse panel. On 1990–91 Eldorado and Seville, remove SIR fuse No. 19 from the fuse panel. On 1992–93 Eldorado and Seville, remove SIR fuse No. A11 from the engine compartment fuse panel.
   d. On Deville and Fleetwood, remove the left lower sound insulator. On Eldorado and Seville, remove the left side sound insulator.
   e. Remove the Connector Position Assurance (CPA) and detach the yellow 2-way connector at the base of the steering column.

2. Remove the bolts/screws from the back of the steering wheel and remove the inflator module.

3. Remove the horn contact by pushing slightly and twisting counterclockwise. Detach the electrical connectors from the inflator module.

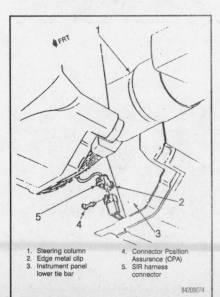

1. Steering column
2. Edge metal clip
3. Instrument panel lower tie bar
4. Connector Position Assurance (CPA)
5. SIR harness connector

84208074

Fig. 72 Yellow 2-way SIR harness connector and CPA

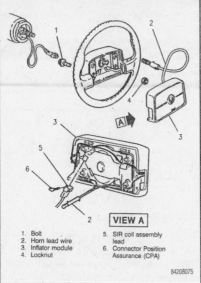

1. Bolt
2. Horn lead wire
3. Inflator module
4. Locknut
5. SIR coil assembly lead
6. Connector Position Assurance (CPA)

VIEW A

84208075

Fig. 73 Inflator module and steering wheel removal/installation

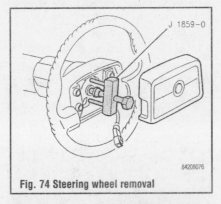

J 1859–0

84208076

Fig. 74 Steering wheel removal

✳✳ CAUTION

When carrying a live inflator module, make sure that the bag and trim cover are pointed away from you. Never carry the inflator module by the wires or connector on the underside of the module. In case of accidental deployment, the bag will then deploy with minimal chance of injury. When placing a live inflator module on a bench or other surface, always face the bag and trim cover up, away from the surface.

4. Remove the steering column shaft nut. If not already marked, mark the steering wheel and steering column shaft to ensure proper alignment during installation.

5. Remove the steering wheel using steering wheel puller J-1859-03 or equivalent.

To install:

6. Feed the SIR coil assembly lead through the slot in the steering wheel. Align the mark on the steering wheel with the mark on the steering column shaft and install the steering wheel.

7. Install the steering column shaft nut and tighten to 30 ft. lbs. (41 Nm).

8. Install the horn contact to the steering column.

9. Attach the electrical connectors to the inflator module. Position the inflator module on the steering wheel taking care to ensure no wires are pinched.

10. Install the inflator module retaining bolts/screws and tighten to 27 inch lbs. (3 Nm).

11. Enable the SIR system as follows:
    a. Connect the yellow 2-way connector at the base of the steering column and install the CPA.
    b. On Deville and Fleetwood, install the left lower sound insulator. On Eldorado and Seville, install the left side sound insulator.
    c. Install the SIR fuse.
    d. Connect the negative battery cable.
    e. Turn the ignition switch to **RUN**. Verify that the "INFLATABLE RESTRAINT" indicator light flashes 7–9 and then remains OFF. If the light does not function as specified, there is a fault in the SIR system.

Seville—Late Models

◆ **See Figures 75, 76 and 77**

➡**Some special tools may be necessary to perform this repair procedure.**

They include: J 1859-A, J42578

1. Disable the supplemental inflatable restraint system.

2. Insert a flat-bladed tool into one of the four openings in the back of the steering wheel.

3. Turn the tool counterclockwise to disengage the wire from the slot in the inflator module.

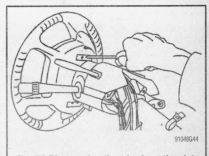

91048G44

Fig. 75 Disengaging the wire from the slot in the inflator module

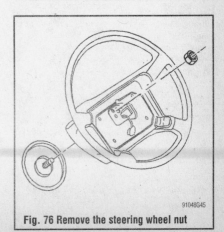

91048G45

Fig. 76 Remove the steering wheel nut

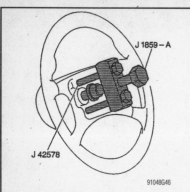

Fig. 77 These special tools are used to pull the steering wheel

4. Pull the driver inflator module gently away from the steering wheel.

5. Repeat the same steps for the three other holes.

➡Note the driver inflator wire routing positions, the redundant control routing positions, and the horn wire routing positions for the correct re-assembly.

6. Remove the connector position assurance (CPA) and driver inflator module electrical connector.

7. Remove the horn grounded lead from the threaded hole in the steering wheel.

8. Rotate the horn contact lead counterclockwise ¼ turn.

9. Remove the horn contact lead from the steering column cm tower.

10. Remove the inflatable restraint steering wheel module.

11. Remove the nut on the steering column shaft.

12. Using special tool J 1859-A and J 42578 separate the steering wheel from the steering shaft.

13. Remove the steering wheel.

To install:

14. Feed the wiring through the steering wheel.

15. Align the steering wheel with the mark on the steering shaft.

16. Install the nut for the steering wheel and tighten to 30 ft. lbs. (41 Nm).

17. Connect the horn ground lead into the tower left threaded hole in the steering wheel.

18. Connect the horn contact lead into the steering column cam tower.

19. Rotate the horn contact turn ¼ turn clockwise to lock.

20. Attach the inflator module electrical connector and CPA.

✳✳ CAUTION

Route the driver inflator wires, the redundant control wires, and the horn wires correctly.

21. Align the driver inflator module fasteners to the steering column fastener holes.

22. Push the driver inflator module firmly into the steering column to ensure the fasteners engage.

23. Enable the SIR system.

Deville and Eldorado—Late Models

▶ **See Figures 78 thru 84**

➡Some special tools may be necessary to perform this repair procedure, including J 1859-03 or equivalent steering wheel puller.

➡Rotating the steering wheel so that the access holes on the backside of the steering wheel are at the 12 and 6 o'clock positions will allow tool access and reduce the potential of marring the steering column.

1. Disable the SIR system.

2. Loosen the four screws from the back of the steering wheel until they are disengaged from the inflator module.

3. Remove the inflatable restraint steering wheel module form the steering wheel.

4. Disconnect the horn contact by pushing slightly and twisting counterclockwise.

5. Unplug the connector position assurance (CPA) and coil assembly connector from the inflator module.

6. Remove the steering column shaft nut.

7. Using the special tool J 1859-03, pull the steering wheel.

To install:

8. Feed the coil assembly lead through slot in the steering wheel.

9. Attach the steering wheel to the column shaft in the proper position.

10. Tighten the column shaft nut to 30 ft. lbs. (41 Nm).

11. Ensure the ignition switch is in the **OFF** position.

12. Attach the horn contact to the steering column.

13. Connect the coil assembly and the CPA to the inflator module.

14. Install the inflator module to the steering wheel securing it with the four screws.

15. Align the inflatable restraint steering wheel module to the steering wheel taking precautions so that no wires at the back of the inflator module get pinched during assembly. Tighten the bolts to 27 inch lbs. (3 Nm).

16. Enable the SIR system.

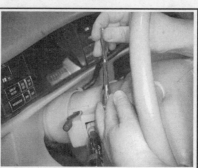

Fig. 78 Loosening the module retaining module . . .

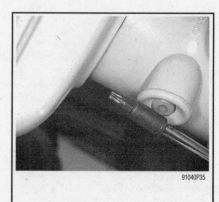

Fig. 79 . . . requires a Torx® head driver

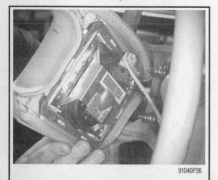

Fig. 80 Gently disengage the module from the wheel

Fig. 81 Remove the Connector Position Assurance (CPA) clip

Fig. 82 Detach the module electrical connector

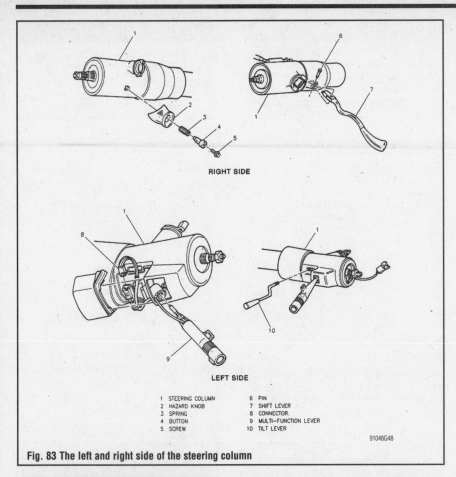

1	STEERING COLUMN	6	PIN
2	HAZARD KNOB	7	SHIFT LEVER
3	SPRING	8	CONNECTOR
4	BUTTON	9	MULTI-FUNCTION LEVER
5	SCREW	10	TILT LEVER

91048G48

Fig. 83 The left and right side of the steering column

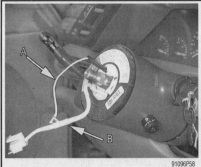

91096P58

Fig. 84 View of the horn lead (A) and inflator module electrical connector (B)—typical view

Turn Signal Switch

REMOVAL & INSTALLATION

✱✱ CAUTION

Some models covered by this manual may be equipped with a Supplemental Restraint System (SRS), which uses an air bag. Whenever working near any of the SRS components, such as the impact sensors, the air bag module, steering column, and instrument panel disable the SRS.

Deville, Eldorado, Seville and Fleetwood— Early Models

▶ **See Figures 85 thru 93**

1. Disable the SIR system.
   a. On Deville and Fleetwood, remove the left lower sound insulator. On Eldorado and Seville, remove the left side sound insulator.
   b. Remove the Connector Position Assurance (CPA) and detach the yellow 2-way connector at the base of the steering column.
   c. Remove the steering wheel.
   d. Make sure the ignition switch is in the **LOCK** position to prevent the SIR coil assembly from going off-center.
2. Remove the SIR coil assembly retaining ring and the coil assembly. Allow the coil to hang freely.

✱✱ WARNING

The SIR coil assembly will become off-center if the steering column is separated from the steering gear and is allowed to rotate or if the centering spring is pushed down, letting the hub rotate while the coil is removed from the column.

3. Remove the wave washer.
4. Use tool J-23653-C or equivalents, to depress the shaft lock, then remove and discard the shaft lock retaining ring.
5. Remove the shaft lock.
6. Remove the turn signal canceling cam assembly.

7. Remove the upper bearing spring, upper bearing inner race seat and inner race.
8. Move the turn signal switch to the RIGHT TURN position.
9. On Deville, Fleetwood, and 1990 Eldorado, and Seville, remove the multi-function turn signal lever as follows:
   a. Make sure the lever is in the **OFF** position.
   b. Remove the access cover from the steering column housing.
   c. Detach the cruise control wiring connector. Note the position of the connector when installed in the column.
   d. Pull the lever straight out of the turn signal switch.
10. On Eldorado and Seville, remove the multi-function turn signal lever as follows:
   a. On 1992–93 vehicles, slide the connector cover toward the front of the vehicle.
   b. Unplug the electrical connector. On 1991 vehicles, note the position of the connector when installed in the column.
   c. Push the lever straight in, rotate clockwise ¼ turn and pull the lever out of the switch.
11. On Deville, Fleetwood, and Eldorado and Seville, remove the screw, button, spring, and hazard warning switch knob.
12. On Deville and Fleetwood, remove the one signal switch arm retaining screw. On Eldorado and Seville, remove the 2 signal switch arm retaining screws. Remove the signal switch arm.
13. Remove the turn signal switch retaining screws.
14. Remove the wiring protector and detach the turn signal switch connector.
15. Gently pull the wire harness through the column and remove the turn signal switch.

To install:

16. Route the turn signal switch wire harness through the column and attach the electrical connector. Install the wiring connector.
17. Position the turn signal switch and install the retaining screws. Tighten the screws to 30 inch lbs. (3.4 Nm).
18. If equipped, install the signal switch arm and tighten the retaining screw(s) to 20 inch lbs. (2.3 Nm).
19. If removed, install the hazard warning switch knob, spring, button, and screw.
20. On 1991–93 Eldorado and Seville, install the multi-function turn signal lever as follows:
   a. Route the harness and attach the electrical connector.
   b. Push the lever straight in and rotate counterclockwise ¼ turn to lock into position.

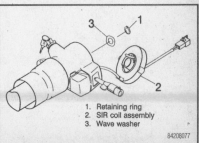

1. Retaining ring
2. SIR coil assembly
3. Wave washer

84208077

Fig. 85 Removing the SIR coil assembly

c. On 1992–93 vehicles, reposition the connector cover.

21. On Deville, Fleetwood, and 1990 Eldorado and Seville, install the multi-function turn signal lever as follows:

a. Make sure the lever is in the **OFF** position.

b. Push the lever into the turn signal switch.

c. Connect the cruise control wiring connector.

d. Install the access cover to the steering column housing.

22. Install the inner race, upper bearing inner race seat, and upper bearing spring.

23. Install the turn signal canceling cam assembly and lubricate with suitable grease.

24. Position the shaft lock. Use tool J-23653-C or equivalents, to depress the shaft lock, then install a new shaft lock retaining ring. The ring must be firmly seated in the groove on the shaft.

25. Install the wave washer.

26. If the SIR coil is off-center, proceed as follows:

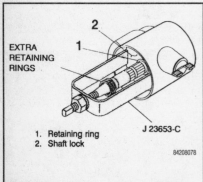

EXTRA RETAINING RINGS

1. Retaining ring
2. Shaft lock

J 23653-C

84208078

Fig. 86 Removing the shaft lock retaining ring

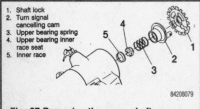

1. Shaft lock
2. Turn signal cancelling cam
3. Upper bearing spring
4. Upper bearing inner race seat
5. Inner race

84208079

Fig. 87 Removing the upper shaft components

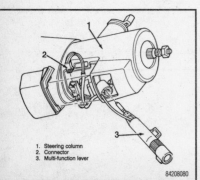

1. Steering column
2. Connector
3. Multi-function lever

84208080

Fig. 88 Removing the multi-function turn signal lever—1992–93 Eldorado and Seville shown, others similar

a. On early Deville, Fleetwood, Eldorado, and Seville, set the steering shaft so that the block teeth on the upper steering shaft are at the 12 o'clock and 6 o'clock positions. The alignment mark at the end of the shaft should be at the 12 o'clock position and the vehicle wheels straight ahead. Turn the ignition switch to the **LOCK** position.

b. On late model Deville, Fleetwood, Eldorado, and Seville, set the steering shaft so that the block tooth on the upper steering shaft is at the 12 o'clock position. The vehicle wheels should be straight ahead. Turn the ignition switch to the **LOCK** position.

c. Remove the SIR coil assembly.

d. Hold the coil assembly with the clear bottom up to see the coil ribbon. There are 2 different types of coils: one rotates clockwise and the other rotates counterclockwise.

e. While holding the coil assembly, depress the spring lock to rotate the hub in the direction of the arrow until it stops. The coil ribbon should be wound up snug against the center hub.

f. Rotate the coil hub in the opposite direction approximately 2½ turns. Release the spring lock between the locking tabs in front of the arrow.

➡ If a new SIR coil assembly is being installed, assemble the pre-centered coil assembly to the steering column. Remove the centering tab and dispose.

27. Install the SIR coil assembly, using the horn tower on the canceling cam assembly and the projection on the housing cover for alignment.

28. Install the coil assembly retaining ring. The ring must be firmly seated in the groove on the shaft.

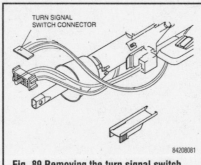

TURN SIGNAL SWITCH CONNECTOR

84208081

Fig. 89 Removing the turn signal switch

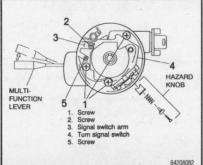

MULTI-FUNCTION LEVER

HAZARD KNOB

1. Screw
2. Screw
3. Signal switch arm
4. Turn signal switch
5. Screw

84208082

Fig. 90 Turn signal switch installed—1992–93 Eldorado and Seville shown, others similar

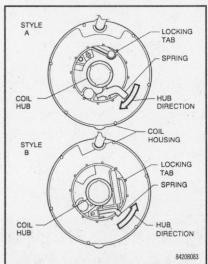

29. Install the steering wheel.

30. Enable the SIR system as follows:

a. Connect the yellow 2-way connector at the base of the steering column and install the CPA.

b. On Deville and Fleetwood, install the left lower sound insulator. On Eldorado and Seville, install the left side sound insulator.

c. Install the SIR fuse.

d. Connect the negative battery cable.

e. Turn the ignition switch to **RUN**. Verify

STYLE A

LOCKING TAB

SPRING

COIL HUB

HUB DIRECTION

COIL HOUSING

STYLE B

LOCKING TAB

SPRING

COIL HUB

HUB DIRECTION

84208083

Fig. 91 Centering the SIR coil assembly

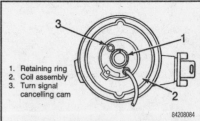

1. Retaining ring
2. Coil assembly
3. Turn signal cancelling cam

84208084

Fig. 92 SIR coil assembly installed—1990 Deville and Fleetwood, and 1990–91 Eldorado and Seville

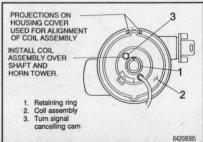

PROJECTIONS ON HOUSING COVER USED FOR ALIGNMENT OF COIL ASSEMBLY

INSTALL COIL ASSEMBLY OVER SHAFT AND HORN TOWER.

1. Retaining ring
2. Coil assembly
3. Turn signal cancelling cam

84208085

Fig. 93 SIR coil assembly installed—1991–93 Deville and Fleetwood, and 1992–93 Eldorado and Seville

that the "INFLATABLE RESTRAINT" indicator light flashes 7–9 times and then remains OFF. If the light does not function as specified, there is a fault in the SIR system.

Deville, Eldorado and Fleetwood—Late Models

♦ See Figures 94, 95 and 96

1. Disable the SIR system.
2. Remove the inflator module and the steering wheel.
3. Disconnect the negative battery cable.
4. Remove the coil assembly retaining ring. Remove the SIR coil assembly and allow it to hang freely.
5. Remove the wave washer.
6. Install special tool J 23653-C to push down the shaft lock and remove the shaft lock-bearing retainer.
7. Remove the shaft lock, the special tool, the turn signal canceling cam assembly, and the upper bearing spring.
8. Remove the upper bearing inner race seat, and the inner race.
9. Move the turn signal to the "RIGHT TURN" position.
10. Remove the multi-function lever and hazard knob assembly.
11. Carefully take out the 2 screws and the signal switch arm.
12. Remove the turn signal switch screws.
13. Detach the turn signal switch connector from the bulkhead connector.
14. Remove the wiring protector, and gently pull the wire harness through the steering column to remove the turn signal switch.

To install:

15. Feed the turn signal switch assembly wire harness through the steering column.
16. Attact the switch connector to the bulkhead connector.
17. Install the turn signal switch assembly an tighten the screws to 31 inch lbs. (3.5 Nm).
18. Replace the switch arm and tighten the two screws. Tighten the top screw to 27 inch lbs. (3 Nm). Tighten the bottom screw to 22 inch lbs. (2.5 Nm).
19. Install the Hazard knob assembly and multi-function lever.
20. Install the inner race, upper bearing inner race seat, and upper bearing spring. Lubricate the canceling cam assembly and install it.

21. Temporaily install the special tool J 23653-C and push down the shaft lock until it is possible to install a new shaft lock bearing retainer. Ensure the bearing retainer is firmly seated in the groove on the shaft.

➡ Set the steering shaft so that block tooth on the upper steering shaft is at the 12 o'clock position, the wheels on the vehicle should be straight ahead, then set the ignition switch to the "LOCK" position, to ensure no damage will occur to the coil.

22. Install the wave washer.

☀ WARNING

The SIR coil assembly wires must be kept tight with no slack while installing the SIR coil assembly. Failure to do so may cause wires to be kinked near the shaft lock area and cut when the steering wheel is turned.

23. Ensure that coil assembly hub is centered.
24. Pull the wire tight while positioning the SIR coil to the steering shaft.
25. Align the opening in the coil with the horn tower and "locating bump" between the two tabs on the housing cover.
26. Seat the coil assembly into the steering column. Attach the coil assembly retaining ring. Ensure the ring is firmly seated in the groove on the shaft.

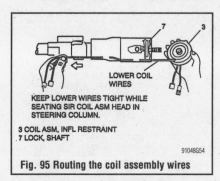

Fig. 95 Routing the coil assembly wires

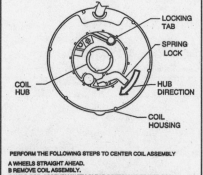

Fig. 96 Centering the coil assembly

☀ WARNING

Gently pull the lower coil assembly, turn signal and pivot and pulse wires t remove any wire kinks that may be inside the steering column assembly. Failure to do so may cause damage to the wire harness.

27. Install the wiring protector.
28. Install the remaining components in the reverse order of the removal procedure.

Seville

♦ See Figures 97 and 98

➡ Some special tools may be necessary to perform this repair procedure.

They include: J 41352 and J 42640

1. Disconnect the negative battery cable.
2. Disable the SIR system.
3. Remove the steering wheel.
4. Remove the knee bolster.
5. Remove the two nuts (1) securing the steering column.
6. Lower the column, remove the tilt handle lever.
7. Remove the upper and lower shroud.
8. Remove the two wire harness straps. Remove one wire harness strap from the steering column tilt head assembly.
9. Remove the wire harness assembly from the wire harness strap.

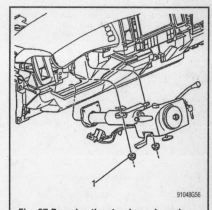

Fig. 97 Dropping the steering column by removing the two nuts

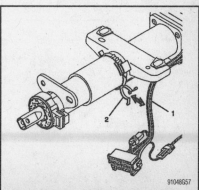

Fig. 98 Disengaging the wire harness (1) from its strap (2)

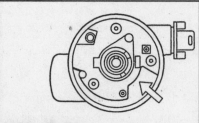

Fig. 94 Wire harness route through the column shown here

Ignition Switch

❋❋ CAUTION

When performing service around Supplemental Inflatable Restraint (SIR) system components or wiring, the SIR system must be disabled. Failure to do so could result in possible air bag deployment, personal injury, or unneeded SIR system repairs.

REMOVAL & INSTALLATION

Deville and Fleetwood

▶ **See Figures 99 thru 109**

1. Disable the SIR system as follows:
   a. Turn the ignition switch **OFF**.
   b. Disconnect the negative battery cable.
   c. Remove the SIR fuse. On 1990 vehicles, remove SIR fuse No. 3 from the fuse panel. On 1991–93 vehicles, remove SIR fuse No. 18 from the fuse panel.
   d. Remove the left lower sound insulator.
   e. Remove the Connector Position Assurance (CPA) and detach the yellow 2-way connector at the base of the steering column.
2. Lower and support the steering column.
3. Remove the screw and washer retaining the ignition switch and dimmer switch. Remove the ground wire from the mounting stud.
4. Remove the dimmer switch from the rod.
5. Remove the dimmer and ignition switch mounting stud.
6. Remove the ignition switch from the ignition switch actuator.
7. Remove the wire harness strap, if equipped.
8. Detach the necessary electrical connectors.

To install:

9. Attach the electrical connectors.
10. Move the ignition switch slider to the extreme right position, then move it one detent to the left to the **OFF-LOCK** position.

➡**The ignition switch must be installed with the switch in the OFF-LOCK position. A new ignition switch will be pinned in the OFF-LOCK position. Remove the plastic pin after the switch is installed on the column. Failure to do so may cause switch damage.**

11. Install the ignition switch with the mounting stud. Tighten the stud to 35 inch lbs. (4 Nm).
12. Install the dimmer switch and install the ground wire to the stud. Install the nut and screw finger-tight.
13. Adjust the dimmer switch as follows:
   a. Place a 3⁄32 in. drill bit in the hole on the switch to limit travel.

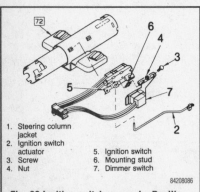

1. Steering column jacket
2. Ignition switch actuator
3. Screw
4. Nut
5. Ignition switch
6. Mounting stud
7. Dimmer switch

84208086

Fig. 99 Ignition switch removal—Deville and Fleetwood

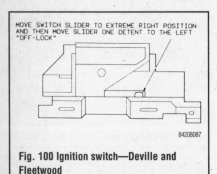

MOVE SWITCH SLIDER TO EXTREME RIGHT POSITION AND THEN MOVE SLIDER ONE DETENT TO THE LEFT "OFF-LOCK"

84208087

Fig. 100 Ignition switch—Deville and Fleetwood

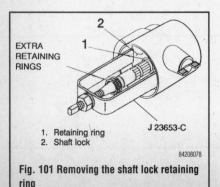

EXTRA RETAINING RINGS

1. Retaining ring
2. Shaft lock

J 23653-C

84208078

Fig. 101 Removing the shaft lock retaining ring

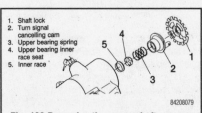

1. Shaft lock
2. Turn signal cancelling cam
3. Upper bearing spring
4. Upper bearing inner race seat
5. Inner race

84208079

Fig. 102 Removing the upper shaft components

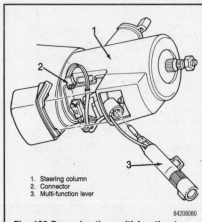

1. Steering column
2. Connector
3. Multi-function lever

84208080

Fig. 103 Removing the multi-function turn signal lever—1992–93 Eldorado and Seville shown, others similar

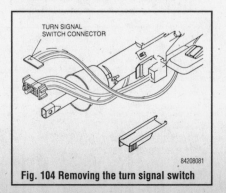

TURN SIGNAL SWITCH CONNECTOR

84208081

Fig. 104 Removing the turn signal switch

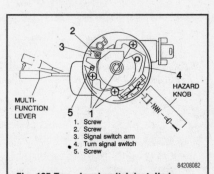

MULTI-FUNCTION LEVER

HAZARD KNOB

1. Screw
2. Screw
3. Signal switch arm
4. Turn signal switch
5. Screw

84208082

Fig. 105 Turn signal switch installed—1992–93 Eldorado and Seville shown, others similar

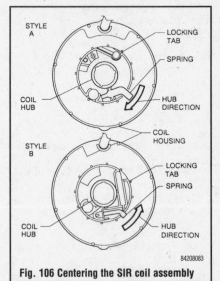

STYLE A

LOCKING TAB
SPRING
COIL HUB
HUB DIRECTION
COIL HOUSING

STYLE B

LOCKING TAB
SPRING
COIL HUB
HUB DIRECTION

84208083

Fig. 106 Centering the SIR coil assembly

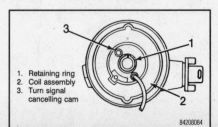

1. Retaining ring
2. Coil assembly
3. Turn signal cancelling cam

84208084

Fig. 107 SIR coil assembly installed—early model Deville and Fleetwood, Eldorado and Seville

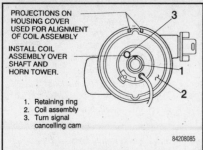

1. Retaining ring
2. Coil assembly
3. Turn signal cancelling cam

84208085

Fig. 108 SIR coil assembly installed—Deville, Fleetwood, Eldorado and Seville

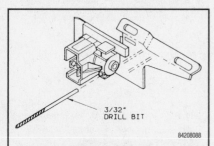

3/32" DRILL BIT

84208088

Fig. 109 Adjusting the dimmer switch—Deville and Fleetwood

b. Position the switch on the column and push against the dimmer switch rod to remove all lash.

c. Remove the drill bit and tighten the nut and screw to 35 inch lbs. (4 Nm).

14. Raise the column into position and secure.

15. Enable the SIR system as follows:

a. Connect the yellow 2-way connector at the base of the steering column and install the CPA.

b. Install the left lower sound insulator.

c. Install the SIR fuse.

d. Connect the negative battery cable.

e. Turn the ignition switch to **RUN**. Verify that the "INFLATABLE RESTRAINT" indicator light flashes 7–9 times and then remains OFF. If the light does not function as specified, there is a fault in the SIR system.

Eldorado and Seville—Early Models

1. Disable the SIR system as follows:

a. Turn the ignition switch **OFF**.

b. Disconnect the negative battery cable.

c. Remove SIR fuse No. 19 from the fuse panel.

d. Remove the left side sound insulator.

e. Remove the Connector Position Assurance (CPA) and detach the yellow 2-way connector at the base of the steering column.

2. Remove the 2 screws and the center trim plate.

3. Remove the 5 screws and the knee bolster.

4. Remove the 4 screws and the instrument panel steering column reinforcement plate.

5. Remove the ignition switch wiring protector and the ignition switch retaining screws.

6. Detach the ignition and turn signal switch column harness connectors from the instrument panel harness.

7. Detach the turn signal switch connector from the column harness. Remove the ignition switch.

To install:

8. Move the ignition switch slider to the extreme right position, then move it one detent to the left to the **OFF-LOCK** position. Install the ignition switch and secure with the retaining screws.

➡ **The ignition switch must be installed with the switch in the OFF-LOCK position. A new ignition switch will be pinned in the OFF-LOCK position. Remove the plastic pin after the switch is installed on the column. Failure to do so may cause switch damage.**

9. Attach the turn signal switch connector to the column harness and attach the ignition and turn signal switch column harness connectors to the instrument panel harness.

10. Install the ignition switch wiring protector.

11. Install the steering column reinforcement plate and secure with the 4 screws.

12. Install the knee bolster and secure with the 5 screws.

13. Install the center trim plate and secure with the 2 screws.

14. Enable the SIR system as follows:

a. Connect the yellow 2-way connector at the base of the steering column and install the CPA.

b. Install the left side sound insulator.

c. Install the SIR fuse.

d. Connect the negative battery cable.

e. Turn the ignition switch to **RUN**. Verify that the "INFLATABLE RESTRAINT" indicator light flashes 7–9 and then remains OFF. If the light does not function as specified, there is a fault in the SIR system.

Eldorado and Seville—Late Models

1. Disable the SIR system as follows:

a. Turn the ignition switch **OFF**.

b. Disconnect the negative battery cable.

c. On 1991 Eldorado and Seville, remove SIR fuse No. 19 from the fuse panel. On 1992–93 Eldorado and Seville, remove SIR fuse No. A11 from the engine compartment fuse panel.

d. Remove the left side sound insulator.

e. Remove the Connector Position Assurance (CPA) and detach the yellow 2-way connector at the base of the steering column.

2. Remove the knee bolster and instrument panel steering column reinforcement plate.

✳✳ WARNING

The steering column should never be supported by only the lower support bracket alone. Damage to the column lower bearing adapter could result.

3. Remove the 2 bolts or bolt and nut and the lower support bracket. Remove the 2 bolts and the upper column support from the instrument panel. Lower the steering column and let it rest on the driver seat.

4. Remove the ignition switch wiring protector and the ignition switch retaining screw and nut.

5. Detach the ignition and turn signal switch column harness connectors from the instrument panel harness.

6. Detach the turn signal switch connector from the column harness. Remove the ignition switch.

To install:

7. Move the ignition switch slider to the extreme right position, then move it one detent to the left to the **OFF-LOCK** position. Install the ignition switch and secure with the retaining screws.

➡ **The ignition switch must be installed with the switch in the OFF-LOCK position. A new ignition switch will be pinned in the OFF-LOCK position. Remove the plastic pin after the switch is installed on the column. Failure to do so may cause switch damage.**

8. Attach the turn signal switch connector to the column harness and attach the ignition and turn signal switch column harness connectors to the instrument panel harness.

9. Install the ignition switch wiring protector.

10. Raise the steering column to the support bracket. Install the 2 bolts to the upper support bracket and the bolt and nut or 2 bolts to the lower support bracket. Do not tighten at this time.

11. Align the steering column to the instrument panel opening. A small shim (wedge) placed between the instrument panel column support bracket and the column can be used to hold the column in place while tightening the support bolts. Tighten the upper and lower column support bolts (and nut, if equipped) to 20 ft. lbs. (27 Nm).

12. Install the instrument panel steering column reinforcement plate and knee bolster.

13. Enable the SIR system as follows:

a. Connect the yellow 2-way connector at the base of the steering column and install the CPA.

b. Install the left side sound insulator.

c. Install the SIR fuse.

d. Connect the negative battery cable.

e. Turn the ignition switch to **RUN**. Verify that the "INFLATABLE RESTRAINT" indicator light flashes 7–9 and then remains OFF. If the light does not function as specified, there is a fault in the SIR system.

Ignition Lock Cylinder

✳✳ CAUTION

When performing service around Supplemental Inflatable Restraint (SIR) system components or wiring, the SIR system must be disabled. Failure to do so could result in possible air bag deployment, personal injury, or unneeded SIR system repairs.

REMOVAL & INSTALLATION

Deville, Fleetwood, Eldorado and Seville

▶ See Figures 110 thru 115

1. Disable the SIR system as follows:

a. Disconnect the negative battery cable.

b. Turn the ignition switch **OFF**.

c. Remove the SIR fuse. On 1990 Deville and Fleetwood, remove SIR fuse No. 3 from the fuse panel. On 1991–93 Deville and Fleetwood, remove SIR fuse No. 18 from the fuse panel. On 1990–91 Eldorado and Seville, remove SIR fuse No. 19 from the fuse panel. On 1992–93 Eldorado and Seville, remove SIR fuse No. All from the engine compartment fuse panel.

d. On Deville and Fleetwood, remove the left lower sound insulator. On Eldorado and Seville, remove the left side sound insulator.

e. Remove the Connector Position Assurance (CPA) and detach the yellow 2-way connector at the base of the steering column.

2. Remove the steering wheel and the turn signal switch. When removing the turn signal switch, allow the switch to hang freely; do not detach the electric connectors.

3. Remove the key from the lock cylinder.

4. Remove the buzzer switch assembly.

5. Reinsert the key in the lock cylinder and turn the key to the **LOCK** position.

6. Remove the lock retaining screw. If not equipped with pass key lock cylinder, remove the lock cylinder.

7. On 1990–91 Eldorado and Seville equipped with pass key lock cylinder, remove the lock cylinder as follows:

a. Detach the terminal connector.

b. Remove the retaining clip from the housing cover and the wiring protector.

c. Attach a length of mechanics wire to the terminal connector to aid in reassembly.

d. Gently pull the wire through the bracket and column housing and remove the lock cylinder.

8. On 1991–93 Deville and Fleetwood and 1992–93 Eldorado and Seville equipped with pass key lock cylinder, remove the lock cylinder as follows:

a. Detach the pivot and pulse switch connector from the bulkhead connector and remove the 13-way secondary lock.

b. Remove the 2 terminals of the pass key wire harness from cavities 12 and 13 of the switch connector.

c. Remove the wiring protector.

d. Attach a length of mechanics wire to the terminal to aid in reassembly.

e. Remove the retaining clip from the housing cover and gently pull the wire harness through the column. Remove the lock cylinder.

To install:

❄ WARNING

If equipped with pass key lock cylinder, route the wire from the lock cylinder as shown in Figs. 114 or 115, and snap the retaining clip in the hole in the housing. Failure to route the wire properly may result in component damage or malfunction of the pass key lock cylinder.

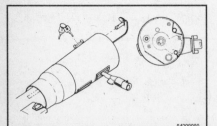

Fig. 110 Removing the buzzer switch—1990–91 Eldorado and Seville shown, others similar

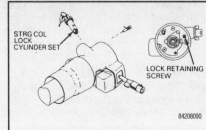

Fig. 111 Ignition lock cylinder removal—without pass key lock cylinder

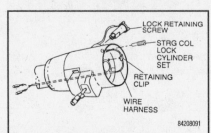

Fig. 112 Ignition lock cylinder removal—with pass key lock cylinder

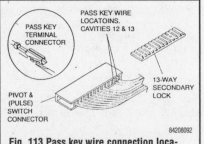

Fig. 113 Pass key wire connection locations—1991–93 Deville and Fleetwood, and 1992–93 Eldorado and Seville

9. Install the lock cylinder.

10. On 1990–91 Eldorado and Seville equipped with pass key lock cylinder, proceed as follows:

a. Connect the mechanics wire to the terminal connector and gently feed the lock cylinder wire through the column housing.

b. Snap the clip into the hole in the housing.

c. Make sure the wires are not interfered with by the normal travel of the switch actuator rack and lock cylinder sector gear.

d. Gently pull the lock cylinder wire at the base of the column to remove any wire kinks that may be inside the column assembly.

e. Connect the pass key connector to the vehicle harness.

11. On Deville, Fleetwood, Eldorado and Seville equipped with pass key lock cylinder, proceed as follows:

a. Route the wire terminal through the column and snap the retaining clip into the hole in the housing.

b. Connect the 2 terminal of the pass key wire harness to cavities 12 and 13 of the pivot and pulse switch connector.

c. Install the 13-way secondary lock.

d. Connect the switch connector to the bulkhead connector.

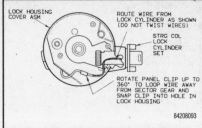

Fig. 114 Pass key wire harness routing—1990–91 Eldorado and Seville

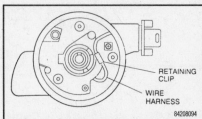

Fig. 115 Pass key wire harness routing—1991–93 Deville and Fleetwood, and 1992–93 Eldorado and Seville

12. Install the lock retaining screw and tighten to 22 inch lbs. (2.5 Nm).

13. On 1990 Deville and Fleetwood and 1990–91 Eldorado and Seville, turn the ignition key to the **RUN** position. On all other vehicles, remove the key.

14. Install the buzzer switch assembly.

15. If the key was removed, reinstall it and make sure it is in the **LOCK** position.

16. Install the turn signal switch and steering wheel.

17. Enable the SIR system as follows:

a. Connect the yellow 2-way connector at the base of the steering column and install the CPA.

b. On Deville and Fleetwood, install the left lower sound insulator. On Eldorado and Seville, install the left side sound insulator.

c. Install the SIR fuse.

d. Connect the negative battery cable.

e. Turn the ignition switch to **RUN**. Verify that the "INFLATABLE RESTRAINT" indicator light flashes 7–9 times and then remains OFF. If the light does not function as specified, there is a fault in the SIR system.

Steering Linkage

REMOVAL & INSTALLATION

Outer Tie Rod

▶ **See Figure 116**

1. Raise and safely support the vehicle.

2. Remove the wheel and tire assembly.

3. Remove the cotter pin and nut from the tie rod ball stud.

4. Loosen the jam nut on the inner tie rod.

5. Separate the outer tie rod from the steering knuckle using tool J-24319-01 or equivalent.

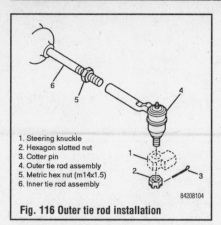

1. Steering knuckle
2. Hexagon slotted nut
3. Cotter pin
4. Outer tie rod assembly
5. Metric hex nut (m14x1.5)
6. Inner tie rod assembly

84208104

Fig. 116 Outer tie rod installation

6. Mark the position of the outer tie rod on the inner tie rod. Remove the outer tie rod from the inner tie rod.

➡Counting the number of turns (revolutions) necessary to remove the outer tie rod and then duplicating that number will aid in re-assembly to the original position.

To install:

7. Thread the outer tie rod onto the inner tie rod to the position marked during the removal procedure. This will approximate the original toe setting.

8. Connect the outer tie rod to the steering knuckle and install the nut. Tighten the nut to 35 ft. lbs. (47 Nm).

9. Install a new cotter pin. If the cotter pin cannot be installed because the hole in the stud does not align, tighten the nut to the next slot, up to a maximum of 52 ft. lbs. (70 Nm) to allow for installation. NEVER loosen the nut to provide for cotter pin installation.

10. Install the wheel and tire assembly and lower the vehicle. Adjust the toe setting by turning the inner tie rod.

➡Make sure the rack and pinion boot is not twisted during toe adjustment.

11. After the toe is set, tighten the jam nut against the outer tie rod to 40 ft. lbs. (54 Nm).

Inner Tie Rod

1. Remove the rack and pinion assembly from the vehicle.
2. Remove the outer tie rod.
3. Remove the jam nut from the inner tie rod.
4. Remove the tie rod end clamp. Remove the boot clamp using side cutters.
5. Mark the location of the breather tube on the steering gear before removing the tube or rack and pinion boot.
6. Remove the rack and pinion boot and breather tube.
7. Remove the shock dampener from the inner tie rod and slide it back on the rack.

✳ WARNING

The rack must be held during removal of the inner tie rod to prevent rack damage.

8. Place a wrench on the flat of the rack assembly and another wrench on the flats of the inner tie rod housing. Rotate the housing counterclockwise until the inner tie rod separates from the rack.

To install:

✳ WARNING

The rack must be held during inner tie rod installation to prevent internal gear damage.

9. Install the shock dampener onto the rack.

10. Position the inner tie rod on the rack. Place a wrench on the flat of the rack assembly and another wrench on the flats of the inner tie rod housing. Tighten the inner tie rod to 74 ft. lbs. (100 Nm).

➡Make sure the tie rod rocks freely in the housing before staking the inner tie rod assembly to the rack.

11. Support the rack and housing of the inner tie rod and stake both sides of the inner tie rod housing to the flats on the rack, as shown in Fig. 116. Check both stakes by inserting a 0.010 in. (0.25mm) feeler gauge between the rack and tie rod housing. The feeler gauge must not pass between the rack and housing stake.

12. Slide the shock dampener over the inner tie rod housing until it engages.

13. Install a new boot clamp onto the rack and pinion boot.

14. Apply grease to the inner tie rod and gear assembly prior to boot installation, then install the boot onto the inner tie rod assembly.

15. Make sure the breather tube is aligned with the mark made during removal the molded nipple of the boot is aligned with the tube.

16. Install the boot onto the gear assembly until it is seated in the gear assembly groove.

➡The boot must not be twisted or out of shape in any way. If the boot is not shaped properly, adjust by hand before installing the boot clamp.

17. Install the boot clamp onto the boot using tool J-22610 or equivalent, and crimp. Install the tie rod end and clamp on the boot using pliers.

18. Install the outer tie rod and install the rack and pinion assembly in the vehicle.

Power Steering Gear

REMOVAL & INSTALLATION

Deville and Fleetwood—Early Models

▶ See Figure 117

1. Raise and safely support the vehicle.
2. Remove both front wheel and tire assemblies.

✳ WARNING

The front wheels must be in the straight-ahead position and the steering column in the LOCK position before disconnecting the steering column or intermediate shaft from the steering gear. Failure to do so will cause the coil assembly in the steering column to become off-center, which will cause damage to the coil assembly.

3. Detach the intermediate shaft lower connection.

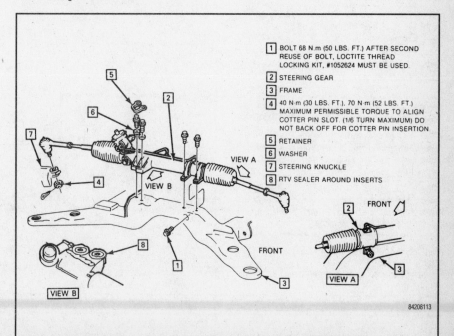

1 BOLT 68 N.m (50 LBS. FT.) AFTER SECOND REUSE OF BOLT, LOCTITE THREAD LOCKING KIT, #1052624 MUST BE USED.
2 STEERING GEAR
3 FRAME
4 40 N.m (30 LBS. FT.), 70 N.m (52 LBS. FT.) MAXIMUM PERMISSIBLE TORQUE TO ALIGN COTTER PIN SLOT. (1/6 TURN MAXIMUM) DO NOT BACK OFF FOR COTTER PIN INSERTION.
5 RETAINER
6 WASHER
7 STEERING KNUCKLE
8 RTV SEALER AROUND INSERTS

VIEW A
VIEW B
FRONT
FRONT

84208113

Fig. 117 Rack and pinion assembly installation—early model Deville and Fleetwood

※ CAUTION

Failure to disconnect the intermediate shaft from the rack and pinion stub shaft can result in damage to the steering gear and/or intermediate shaft. This damage can cause loss of steering control, which could result in personal injury.

4. Disconnect both tie rod ends from the steering knuckles.
5. Remove the line retainer.
6. Disconnect the outlet and pressure lines.
7. Remove the 5 rack and pinion mounting bolts and remove the rack and pinion assembly by sliding it out to the side.

To install:

8. Position the rack and pinion assembly and install the 5 mounting bolts. Tighten to 50 ft. lbs. (68 Nm).
9. Connect the outlet and pressure lines to the rack and pinion assembly and tighten the fittings to 20 ft. lbs. (27 Nm).
10. Install the line retainer.
11. Connect the tie rod ends to the steering knuckles.
12. Connect the intermediate shaft coupling and tighten the bolt to 30 ft. lbs. (50 Nm).
13. Install the wheel and tire assemblies and lower the vehicle.
14. Fill and bleed the power steering system.

Deville and Fleetwood—Late Models

▶ See Figure 118

1. Raise and safely support the vehicle.
2. Remove the front wheel and tire assemblies.

※ CAUTION

Failure to disconnect the intermediate shaft from the rack and pinion stub shaft can result in damage to the steering gear and/or intermediate shaft. This damage can cause loss of steering control, which could result in personal injury.

※ WARNING

The front wheels must be in the straight-ahead position and the steering column in the LOCK position before disconnecting the steering column or intermediate shaft from the steering gear. Failure to do so will cause the coil assembly in the steering column to become off-center, which will cause damage to the coil assembly.

3. Detach the intermediate shaft lower connection.
4. Disconnect both tie rod ends from the steering knuckles.
5. Remove the line retainer.
6. Detach the pressure switch electrical connection. If equipped with speed sensitive steering, detach the electrical connection at the control valve and manifold.
7. Disconnect the power steering pressure and

return lines. If equipped with speed sensitive steering, remove the filter as needed for access.
8. Support the body with jackstands to allow lowering of the frame.
9. Loosen the front frame bolts. Remove the rear frame bolts and lower the rear of the frame about 3 in. (76 mm).

※ WARNING

Do not lower the rear of the frame too far, as damage to the engine components nearest to the cowl may result.

10. Remove the rack and pinion mounting bolts and remove the rack and pinion assembly through the left wheel opening.

To install:

11. Install the rack and pinion assembly through the left wheel opening and position it in the vehicle.
12. Raise the rear of the frame and tighten the frame bolts to 76 ft. lbs. (103 Nm). Remove the jackstands.
13. Install the 2 washers and 5 rack and pinion mounting bolts. Loctite® thread locking kit No. 1052624 or equivalent must be used. Tighten the bolts to 50 ft. lbs. (68 Nm), in the sequence shown.
14. Connect the power steering pressure and return lines (including the filter on speed sensitive steering systems, if removed) and tighten the connections to 20 ft. lbs. (27 Nm).
15. Attach the pressure switch electrical connector. If equipped with speed sensitive steering, also make the electrical connections at the control valve and manifold.
16. Install the line retainer.
17. Connect the tie rod ends to the steering knuckles.
18. Connect the intermediate shaft lower coupling and tighten the bolt to 35 ft. lbs. (47 Nm).
19. Install the front wheel and tire assemblies and lower the vehicle.
20. Fill and bleed the power steering system.

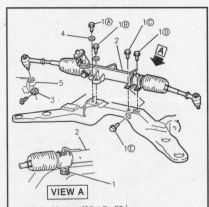

VIEW A

1 BOLT; 68 N·m (50 LB. FT.).
   TIGHTEN IN SEQUENCE A THRU E.
2 STEERING GEAR
3 NUT; 47 N·m (35 LB. FT.). MAXIMUM
   PERMISSIBLE TORQUE TO ALIGN COTTER
   PIN SLOT IS 70 N·m (52 LB. FT.).
4 WASHER
5 STEERING KNUCKLE

84208114

Fig. 118 Rack and pinion assembly installation—late model Deville and Fleetwood

Eldorado and Seville—Early Models

▶ See Figure 119

1. Raise and safely support the vehicle.
2. Remove the front wheel and tire assemblies.

※ CAUTION

Failure to disconnect the intermediate shaft from the rack and pinion stub shaft can result in damage to the steering gear and/or intermediate shaft. This damage can cause loss of steering control, which could result in personal injury.

※ WARNING

The front wheels must be in the straight-ahead position and the steering column in the LOCK position before disconnecting the steering column or intermediate shaft from the steering gear. Failure to do so will cause the coil assembly in the steering column to become off-center, which will cause damage to the coil assembly.

3. Disconnect the intermediate shaft lower coupling.
4. Remove the heat shield.
5. Disconnect both tie rod ends from the steering knuckles.
6. Support the rear of the frame with a jack.

※ WARNING

The frame must be properly supported before partial lowering. The frame should not be lowered any further than needed to gain access to the steering gear.

7. Loosen the rear body mount bolts and slowly lower the rear of the frame.
8. Remove the line retainer.
9. Disconnect the power steering pressure and return lines.
10. Detach the pressure switch connector.
11. Remove the 5 rack and pinion mounting bolts and remove the rack and pinion assembly by sliding it out to the side.

To install:

12. Position the rack and pinion assembly and install the 5 mounting bolts. Tighten to 50 ft. lbs. (68 Nm).
13. Connect the return and pressure lines to the rack and pinion assembly and tighten the fittings to 20 ft. lbs. (27 Nm).
14. Install the line retainer.
15. Raise the frame into position and tighten the body mount bolts to 76 ft. lbs. (103 Nm).
16. Connect the tie rod ends to the steering knuckles.
17. Connect the intermediate shaft lower coupling and tighten the bolt to 35 ft. lbs. (47 Nm).
18. Attach the pressure switch connector and install the heat shield.
19. Install the front wheel and tire assemblies and lower the vehicle.
20. Fill and bleed the power steering system.

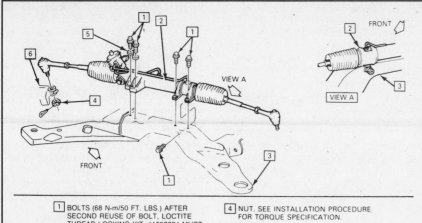

1. BOLTS (68 N·m/50 FT. LBS.) AFTER SECOND REUSE OF BOLT, LOCTITE THREAD LOCKING KIT, #1052624 MUST BE USED.
2. STEERING GEAR
3. FRAME
4. NUT. SEE INSTALLATION PROCEDURE FOR TORQUE SPECIFICATION.
5. WASHER
6. STEERING KNUCKLE

84208115

Fig. 119 Rack and pinion assembly installation—Eldorado and Seville

Eldorado and Seville—Late Models

▶ See Figure 120

> **❊❊ CAUTION**
>
> **Failure to disconnect the intermediate shaft from the rack and pinion stub shaft can result in damage to the steering gear and/or intermediate shaft. This damage can cause loss of steering control which could result in personal injury.**

> **❊❊ WARNING**
>
> **The front wheels must be in the straight-ahead position and the steering column in the LOCK position before disconnecting the steering column or intermediate shaft from the steering gear. Failure to do so will cause the coil assembly in the steering col-umn to become off-center, which will cause damage to the coil assembly.**

1. Disconnect the intermediate shaft lower coupling.
2. Raise and safely support the vehicle.
3. Remove the front wheel and tire assemblies.
4. If equipped with 4.6L engine, disconnect the road sensing suspension position sensor.
5. Disconnect both tie rod ends from the steering knuckles.
6. If equipped with 4.6L engine, disconnect the exhaust pipe at the catalytic converter.
7. Support the rear of the frame with a jack.

> **❊❊ WARNING**
>
> **The frame must be properly supported before partial lowering. The frame should not be lowered any further than needed to gain access to the steering gear.**

8. Loosen the rear body mount bolts and slowly lower the rear of the frame.
9. Remove the heat shield and the plastic line retainer.
10. Disconnect the power steering pressure and return lines.
11. Detach the speed sensitive steering solenoid valve connector.
12. Remove the 5 rack and pinion mounting bolts and remove the rack and pinion assembly by sliding it out to the side.

To install:

13. Position the rack and pinion assembly and install the 5 mounting bolts. Tighten to 50 ft. lbs. (68 Nm).
14. Attach the speed sensitive steering solenoid valve connector.
15. Connect the return and pressure lines to the rack and pinion assembly and tighten the fittings to 20 ft. lbs. (27 Nm).
16. Install the plastic line retainer and the heat shield.
17. Raise the frame into position and tighten the body mount bolts to 76 ft. lbs. (103 Nm).
18. If equipped with 4.6L engine, connect the exhaust pipe at the catalytic converter.
19. Connect the tie rod ends to the steering knuckles.
20. If equipped, connect the road sensing suspension position sensor.
21. Install the left front wheel and tire assembly and lower the vehicle.
22. Connect the intermediate shaft lower coupling and tighten the bolt to 35 ft. lbs. (47 Nm).
23. Fill and bleed the power steering system.

Power Steering Pump

REMOVAL & INSTALLATION

Deville and Fleetwood—Early Models

▶ See Figures 121, 122 and 123

1. Remove the serpentine drive belt.
2. Remove the power steering fluid from the reservoir.
3. Remove the reservoir mounting bolts and remove the reservoir from the vehicle by disengaging the reservoir tubes from the adapter.
4. Remove the belt tensioner.
5. Remove the power steering pump pulley using tool J-29785-A or equivalent. Hold the body of the tool with a wrench and turn the bolt into the body of the tool to remove the pulley from the shaft.
6. Remove the pressure line fitting from the pump.
7. Remove the pump mounting bolts.
8. Use a small prybar to disengage the return line adapter clip from the adapter.
9. Disengage the adapter from the pump inlet. Make sure the O-ring is removed from the inlet port.
10. Remove the adapter from the return line.

To install:

11. Inspect all adapter O-rings for proper positioning or damage. Replace any cut or damaged O-rings.
12. Insert the return line adapter clip on the adapter at the return line port. Make sure that the beveled edges of the clip are facing outward.

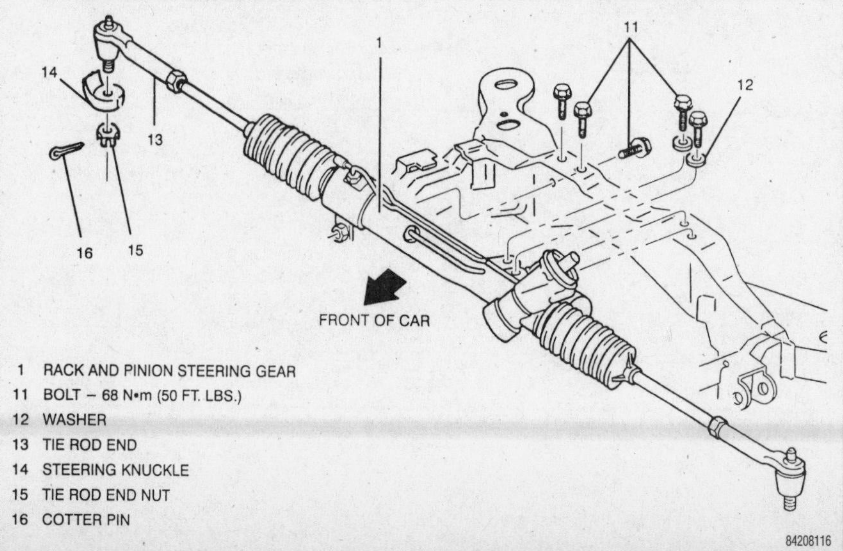

---

1   RACK AND PINION STEERING GEAR
11 BOLT – 68 N·m (50 FT. LBS.)
12 WASHER
13 TIE ROD END
14 STEERING KNUCKLE
15 TIE ROD END NUT
16 COTTER PIN

84208116

Fig. 120 Rack and pinion assembly installation—late model Eldorado and Seville

13. Position the adapter on the pump, inserting the pump inlet tube until fully seated.

14. Position the pump in the vehicle while inserting the return line into the adapter port. Make sure that the line is fully seated and is retained by the adapter clip.

15. Install the pump mounting bolts but do not tighten at this time.

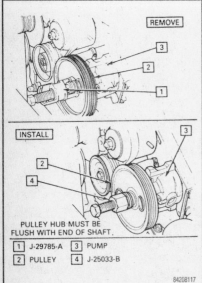

Fig. 121 Power steering pump pulley removal & installation—Deville and Fleetwood

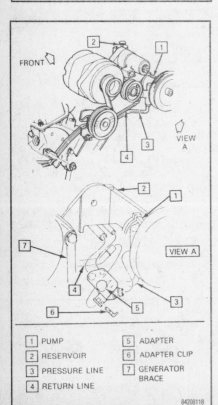

Fig. 122 Power steering pump lines and adapter—early model Deville and Fleetwood

16. Install the pressure line fitting to the pump.

17. Tighten the pump mounting bolts to 18 ft. lbs. (25 Nm) and the pressure line fitting to 20 ft. lbs. (27 Nm).

18. Press the pulley onto the pump shaft using tool J-25033-B or equivalent. The face of the pulley hub must be flush with the pump shaft.

19. Position the belt tensioner mounting bolt in the vehicle.

20. Install the reservoir by carefully inserting the reservoir tubes into the adapter ports. Use a rocking motion to fully seat the tubes in the adapter. Install the reservoir mounting bolts.

21. Install the belt tensioner and tighten the mounting nut to 55 ft. lbs. (75 Nm).

22. Install the serpentine drive belt.

23. Fill and bleed the power steering system.

Deville and Fleetwood—Late Models

♦ **See Figure 123**

1. Remove the pump drive belt.

2. Remove the belt tensioner, if necessary for access.

3. Remove the power steering pump pulley using tool J-29785-A or equivalent. Hold the body of the tool with a wrench and turn the bolt into the body of the tool to remove the pulley from the shaft.

4. Remove the pressure line fitting from the pump. Remove the return line from the adapter using tool J-36391 or equivalent.

5. Remove the pump mounting bolts and the pump adapter assembly.

6. Disengage the adapter from the pump inlet. Make sure the pump O-ring is removed from the inlet port.

To install:

7. Inspect all adapter O-rings for proper positioning or damage. Replace any cut or damaged O-rings.

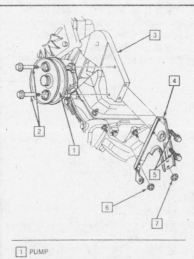

Fig. 123 Power steering pump mounting—late model Deville and Fleetwood

8. Position the adapter on the pump, inserting the pump inlet tube until fully seated.

9. Position the pump on the vehicle while inserting the adapter into the reservoir. The reservoir tubes do not need to be fully seated.

10. Insert the return pipe into the adapter port, making sure it is fully seated.

11. Install the pump mounting bolts but do not tighten at this time.

12. Install the pressure line fitting to the pump.

13. Tighten the pump mounting bolts to 18 ft. lbs. (25 Nm) and the pressure line fitting to 20 ft. lbs. (27 Nm).

14. Press the pulley onto the pump shaft using tool J-25033-B or equivalent. The face of the pulley hub must be flush with the pump shaft.

15. Install the belt tensioner, if removed, and tighten the mounting nut to 55 ft. lbs. (75 Nm).

16. Install the pump drive belt.

17. Fill and bleed the power steering system.

Eldorado and Seville

4.5L ENGINE

♦ **See Figures 124, 125 and 126**

1. Remove the pump drive belt.

2. Remove the belt tensioner, if necessary for access.

3. Remove the pump mounting bolts, then move the pump just enough for the pulley remover to access the shaft.

4. Remove the power steering pump pulley using tool J-29785-A or equivalent. Hold the body of the tool with a wrench and turn the bolt into the body of the tool to remove the pulley from the shaft.

5. Reinstall the pump and mounting bolts. Tighten the bolts just enough to hold the pump in place for disconnecting the power steering pressure hose from the pump.

6. Remove the pressure hose from the pump.

7. Remove the pump adapter, if necessary. Remove the return line from the adapter using tool J-36391 or equivalent. If the adapter is removed from the pump, make sure the pump O-ring is removed from the inlet port.

To install:

8. Inspect all adapter O-rings for proper positioning or damage. Replace any cut or damaged O-rings.

9. With a new O-ring in place, position the adapter on the pump, inserting the pump inlet tube until fully seated.

10. Loosely connect the pressure hose to the pump, but do not tighten the fitting at this time.

11. Press the pulley onto the pump shaft using tool J-25033-B or equivalent. The face of the pulley hub must be flush with the pump shaft.

12. Position the pump on the vehicle, mating adapter to reservoir. The reservoir tubes do not need to be fully seated. Insert the return pipe into the adapter port, making sure it is fully seated.

13. Install the pump mounting bolts and tighten to 18 ft. lbs. (25 Nm). Tighten the pressure line fitting to 20 ft. lbs. (27 Nm).

14. Install the belt tensioner and the pump drive belt.

15. Fill and bleed the power steering system.

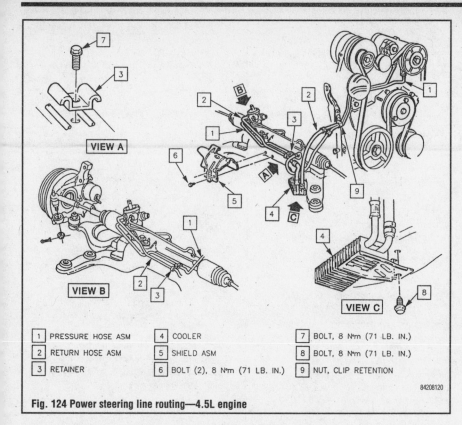

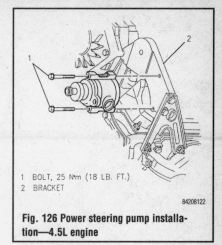

Fig. 124 Power steering line routing—4.5L engine

1	PRESSURE HOSE ASM	4	COOLER	7	BOLT, 8 N·m (71 LB. IN.)
2	RETURN HOSE ASM	5	SHIELD ASM	8	BOLT, 8 N·m (71 LB. IN.)
3	RETAINER	6	BOLT (2), 8 N·m (71 LB. IN.)	9	NUT, CLIP RETENTION

84208120

Fig. 124 Power steering line routing—4.5L engine

1	BOLT, 25 N·m (18 LB. FT.)
2	BRACKET

84208122

Fig. 126 Power steering pump installation—4.5L engine

4.6L ENGINE

♦ See Figure 127

1. Remove the serpentine drive belt.
2. Remove the power steering fluid from the reservoir.
3. Disconnect the return line from the reservoir and the pressure line from the pump.
4. Remove the pump mounting bolt, remove the pump, reservoir, pulley, and bracket assembly from the vehicle.
5. Remove the pump and reservoir from the bracket.
6. Remove the retaining clips that attach the reservoir to the pump.
7. Remove the pulley from the pump as follows:

   a. If not equipped with center hub, remove the pulley using 3-jaw puller J-25031 and tool J-38343-4 or equivalents. Make sure that the puller is properly aligned to the pump shaft.

   b. If equipped with center hub, remove the pulley using tool J-25034-B or equivalent. Hold the body of the tool with a wrench and turn the bolt into the body of the tool to remove the pulley from the shaft.

To install:

8. Install the pulley to the pump as follows:

   a. If not equipped with center hub, install the pulley using tools J-36015 and J-39391 or equivalents. The face of the pulley hub must be flush with the pump shaft.

✳✳ WARNING

Do not use an arbor press to install the pulley.

   b. If equipped with center hub, use installation tool J-25033-B or equivalent, to install the pulley.

9. Attach the reservoir to the pump with the retaining clips.
10. Install the pump and reservoir to the bracket and tighten the pump-to-bracket bolts to 18 ft. lbs. (24 Nm).
11. Position the pump, reservoir, pulley, and bracket assembly in the vehicle. Install the pump-to-engine mounting bolt and tighten to 35 ft. lbs. (47 Nm).
12. Connect the pressure line to the pump and tighten the fitting to 20 ft. lbs. (27 Nm).

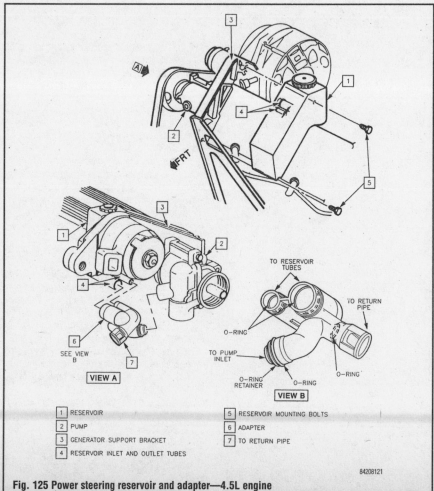

1	RESERVOIR	5	RESERVOIR MOUNTING BOLTS
2	PUMP	6	ADAPTER
3	GENERATOR SUPPORT BRACKET	7	TO RETURN PIPE
4	RESERVOIR INLET AND OUTLET TUBES		

84208121

Fig. 125 Power steering reservoir and adapter—4.5L engine

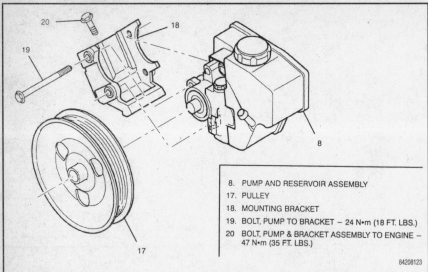

8. PUMP AND RESERVOIR ASSEMBLY
17. PULLEY
18. MOUNTING BRACKET
19. BOLT, PUMP TO BRACKET — 24 N•m (18 FT. LBS.)
20. BOLT, PUMP & BRACKET ASSEMBLY TO ENGINE — 47 N•m (35 FT. LBS.)

84208123

Fig. 127 Power steering pump mounting—1992–98 Eldorado and Seville with 4.6L engine

13. Connect the return line to the reservoir.
14. Install the serpentine drive belt.
15. Fill and bleed the power steering system.

4.9L ENGINE

▶ **See Figures 128 and 129**

1. Disconnect the negative battery cable.
2. Remove the serpentine drive belt.
3. Remove the pump pulley using removal tool J-25034-B or equivalent.
4. Disconnect the pressure line at the pump.
5. Remove the pump mounting bolts.
6. Remove the adapter from the pump as follows:

   a. Remove the power steering fluid from the reservoir.

   b. Remove the pressure line retainer nut on the engine block to ease removal of the return line.

   c. Remove the return line from the adapter using tool J-36391 or equivalent.

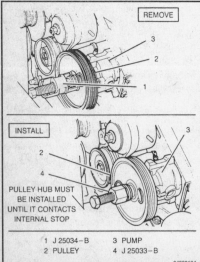

REMOVE

INSTALL

PULLEY HUB MUST
BE INSTALLED
UNTIL IT CONTACTS
INTERNAL STOP

1 J 25034–B   3 PUMP
2 PULLEY   4 J 25033–B

84208124

Fig. 128 Power steering pump pulley removal & installation—1991–93 Eldorado and Seville with 4.9L engine

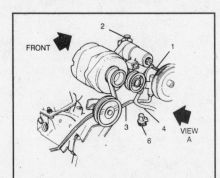

FRONT

VIEW A

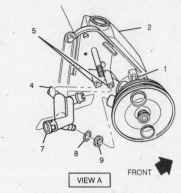

VIEW A

FRONT

BELT TENSIONER REMOVED

1 PUMP
2 RESERVOIR
3 PRESSURE PIPE (TO GEAR)
4 RETURN PIPE (FROM COOLER)
5 RESERVOIR TUBES
6 J 36391 QUICK DISCONNECT TOOL
7 ADAPTER
8 5/8" O–RING
9 SEAL PROTECTOR

84208126

Fig. 129 Power steering pump mounting— Eldorado and Seville with 4.9L engine

d. Reposition the pump to disengage the adapter from the pump inlet.

e. Disengage the return line from the adapter and remove the adapter from the reservoir tubes.

To install:

7. Inspect all adapter O-rings for proper positioning or damage. Replace any cut or damaged O-rings.

8. Make sure that all O-rings are properly positioned on the adapter, including the pump port O-ring and seal protector.

9. Lubricate all adapter ports with petroleum jelly.

10. Install the adapter on the return line.

11. Position the pump so the adapter pump inlet tube is positioned in the pump inlet. Be extremely careful to prevent seal damage.

12. Install the adapter on the reservoir tubes.

13. Install the pump mounting bolts and tighten to 18 ft. lbs. (24 Nm).

14. Install the retainer nut on the block.

15. Connect the pressure line at the pump.

16. Install the pulley using installation tool J-25033-B.

➡**On 1990 vehicles the pulley hub must be flush with the end of the shaft. On 1991–93 vehicles, the pulley hub is installed until it contacts the internal stop.**

17. Install the serpentine drive belt.
18. Fill and bleed the power steering system.

BLEEDING

If the power steering hydraulic system has been serviced, an accurate fluid level reading cannot be obtained unless air is bled from the system. The air in the fluid may cause pump cavitation noise and may cause pump damage over a period. Bleed the air from the system as follows:

1. The engine must be OFF. Raise and safely support the front of the vehicle just so the front wheels are off the ground.

2. Turn the front wheel all the way to the left.

3. Add power steering fluid to the FULL COLD mark on the fluid level indicator. Leave the capstick removed from the reservoir.

4. Bleed the air from the system by turning the wheels from side-to-side without hitting the stops. Keep the fluid level at the FULL COLD mark and check its color. Fluid with air in it has a light tan appearance.

5. Repeat Step 4 about 12 times. If the engine had been started before the bleeding procedure was begun, repeat Step 4 about 20 times with the engine OFF.

6. Return the wheel to the center position and lower the vehicle to the ground.

7. Install the capstick on the reservoir and start the engine. With the engine idling, recheck the fluid level. If necessary, add fluid to bring the level to the FULL COLD mark.

8. Road test the vehicle to make sure the steering functions normally and is free from noise.

9. Check for fluid leaks at all power steering system connection points.

10. Recheck the fluid level. The fluid level should be at the HOT mark after the system has stabilized at its normal operating temperature.

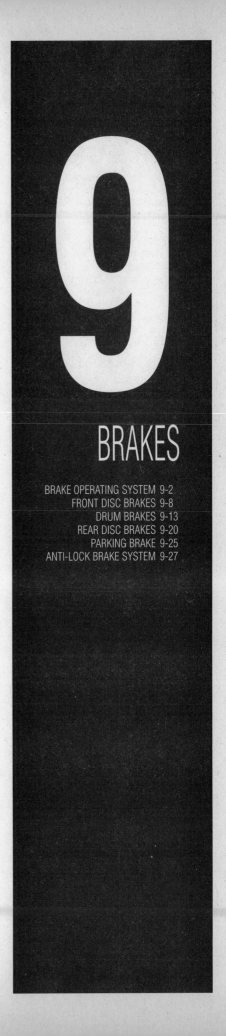

9

BRAKES

BRAKE OPERATING SYSTEM

Basic Operating Principles

Hydraulic systems are used to actuate the brakes of all modern automobiles. The system transports the power required to force the frictional surfaces of the braking system together from the pedal to the individual brake units at each wheel. A hydraulic system is used for two reasons.

First, fluid under pressure can be carried to all parts of an automobile by small pipes and flexible hoses without taking up a significant amount of room or posing routing problems.

Second, a great mechanical advantage can be given to the brake pedal end of the system, and the foot pressure required to actuate the brakes can be reduced by making the surface area of the master cylinder pistons smaller than that of any of the pistons in the wheel cylinders or calipers.

The master cylinder consists of a fluid reservoir along with a double cylinder and piston assembly. Double type master cylinders are designed to separate the front and rear braking systems hydraulically in case of a leak. The master cylinder coverts mechanical motion from the pedal into hydraulic pressure within the lines. This pressure is translated back into mechanical motion at the wheels by either the wheel cylinder (drum brakes) or the caliper (disc brakes).

Steel lines carry the brake fluid to a point on the vehicle's frame near each of the vehicle's wheels. The fluid is then carried to the calipers and wheel cylinders by flexible tubes in order to allow for suspension and steering movements.

In drum brake systems, each wheel cylinder contains two pistons, one at either end, which push outward in opposite directions and force the brake shoe into contact with the drum.

In disc brake systems, the cylinders are part of the calipers. At least one cylinder in each caliper is used to force the brake pads against the disc.

All pistons employ some type of seal, usually made of rubber, to minimize fluid leakage. A rubber dust boot seals the outer end of the cylinder against dust and dirt. The boot fits around the outer end of the piston on disc brake calipers, and around the brake actuating rod on wheel cylinders.

The hydraulic system operates as follows: When at rest, the entire system, from the piston(s) in the master cylinder to those in the wheel cylinders or calipers, is full of brake fluid. Upon application of the brake pedal, fluid trapped in front of the master cylinder piston(s) is forced through the lines to the wheel cylinders. Here, it forces the pistons outward, in the case of drum brakes, and inward toward the disc, in the case of disc brakes. The motion of the pistons is opposed by return springs mounted outside the cylinders in drum brakes, and by spring seals, in disc brakes.

Upon release of the brake pedal, a spring located inside the master cylinder immediately returns the master cylinder pistons to the normal position. The pistons contain check valves and the master cylinder has compensating ports drilled in it. These are uncovered as the pistons reach their normal position. The piston check valves allow fluid to flow toward the wheel cylinders or calipers as the pistons withdraw. Then, as the return springs force the brake pads or shoes into the released position, the excess fluid reservoir through the compensating ports. It is during the time the pedal is in the released position

that any fluid that has leaked out of the system will be replaced through the compensating ports.

Dual circuit master cylinders employ two pistons, located one behind the other, in the same cylinder. The primary piston is actuated directly by mechanical linkage from the brake pedal through the power booster. The secondary piston is actuated by fluid trapped between the two pistons. If a leak develops in front of the secondary piston, it moves forward until it bottoms against the front of the master cylinder, and the fluid trapped between the pistons will operate the rear brakes. If the rear brakes develop a leak, the primary piston will move forward until direct contact with the secondary piston takes place, and it will force the secondary piston to actuate the front brakes. In either case, the brake pedal moves farther when the brakes are applied, and less braking power is available.

All dual circuit systems use a switch to warn the driver when only half of the brake system is operational. This switch is usually located in a valve body which is mounted on the firewall or the frame below the master cylinder. A hydraulic piston receives pressure from both circuits, each circuit's pressure being applied to one end of the piston. When the pressures are in balance, the piston remains stationary. When one circuit has a leak, however, the greater pressure in that circuit during application of the brakes will push the piston to one side, closing the switch and activating the brake warning light.

In disc brake systems, this valve body also contains a metering valve and, in some cases, a proportioning valve. The metering valve keeps pressure from traveling to the disc brakes on the front wheels until the brake shoes on the rear wheels have contacted the drums, ensuring that the front brakes will never be used alone. The proportioning valve controls the pressure to the rear brakes to lessen the chance of rear wheel lock-up during very hard braking.

Warning lights may be tested by depressing the brake pedal and holding it while opening one of the wheel cylinder bleeder screws. If this does not cause the light to go on, substitute a new lamp, make continuity checks, and, finally, replace the switch as necessary.

The hydraulic system may be checked for leaks by applying pressure to the pedal gradually and steadily. If the pedal sinks very slowly to the floor, the system has a leak. This is not to be confused with a springy or spongy feel due to the compression of air within the lines. If the system leaks, there will be a gradual change in the position of the pedal with a constant pressure.

Check for leaks along all lines and at wheel cylinders. If no external leaks are apparent, the problem is inside the master cylinder.

DISC BRAKES

Instead of the traditional expanding brakes that press outward against a circular drum, disc brake systems utilize a disc (rotor) with brake pads positioned on either side of it. An easily-seen analogy is the hand brake arrangement on a bicycle. The pads squeeze onto the rim of the bike wheel, slowing its motion. Automobile disc brakes use the identical principle but apply the braking effort to a separate disc instead of the wheel.

The disc (rotor) is a casting, usually equipped with cooling fins between the two braking surfaces. This enables air to circulate between the braking surfaces making them less sensitive to heat buildup and more resistant to fade. Dirt and water do not drastically affect braking action since contaminants are thrown off by the centrifugal action of the rotor or scraped off the by the pads. Also, the equal clamping action of the two brake pads tends to ensure uniform, straight line stops. Disc brakes are inherently self-adjusting. There are three general types of disc brake:

- A fixed caliper.
- A floating caliper.
- A sliding caliper.

The fixed caliper design uses two pistons mounted on either side of the rotor (in each side of the caliper). The caliper is mounted rigidly and does not move.

The sliding and floating designs are quite similar. In fact, these two types are often lumped together. In both designs, the pad on the inside of the rotor is moved into contact with the rotor by hydraulic force. The caliper, which is not held in a fixed position, moves slightly, bringing the outside pad into contact with the rotor. There are various methods of attaching floating calipers. Some pivot at the bottom or top, and some slide on mounting bolts. In any event, the end result is the same.

DRUM BRAKES

Drum brakes employ two brake shoes mounted on a stationary backing plate. These shoes are positioned inside a circular drum which rotates with the wheel assembly. The shoes are held in place by springs. This allows them to slide toward the drums (when they are applied) while keeping the linings and drums in alignment. The shoes are actuated by a wheel cylinder which is mounted at the top of the backing plate. When the brakes are applied, hydraulic pressure forces the wheel cylinder's actuating links outward. Since these links bear directly against the top of the brake shoes, the tops of the shoes are then forced against the inner side of the drum. This action forces the bottoms of the two shoes to contact the brake drum by rotating the entire assembly slightly (known as servo action). When pressure within the wheel cylinder is relaxed, return springs pull the shoes back away from the drum.

Most modern drum brakes are designed to self-adjust themselves during application when the vehicle is moving in reverse. This motion causes both shoes to rotate very slightly with the drum, rocking an adjusting lever, thereby causing rotation of the adjusting screw. Some drum brake systems are designed to self-adjust during application whenever the brakes are applied. This on-board adjustment system reduces the need for maintenance adjustments and keeps both the brake function and pedal feel satisfactory.

POWER BOOSTERS

Virtually all modern vehicles use a vacuum assisted power brake system to multiply the braking force and reduce pedal effort. Since vacuum is always available when the engine is operating, the system is simple and efficient. A vacuum diaphragm is located on the front of the master cylinder and assists the driver in applying the brakes, reducing both the effort and travel he must put into moving the brake pedal.

The vacuum diaphragm housing is normally connected to the intake manifold by a vacuum hose. A check valve is placed at the point where the hose enters the diaphragm housing, so that during periods of low manifold vacuum brakes assist will not be lost.

Depressing the brake pedal closes off the vacuum source and allows atmospheric pressure to enter on one side of the diaphragm. This causes the master cylinder pistons to move and apply the brakes. When the brake pedal is released, vacuum is applied to both sides of the diaphragm and springs return the diaphragm and master cylinder pistons to the released position.

If the vacuum supply fails, the brake pedal rod will contact the end of the master cylinder actuator rod and the system will apply the brakes without any power assistance. The driver will notice that much higher pedal effort is needed to stop the car and that the pedal feels harder than usual.

Vacuum Leak Test

1. Operate the engine at idle without touching the brake pedal for at least one minute.
2. Turn off the engine and wait one minute.
3. Test for the presence of assist vacuum by depressing the brake pedal and releasing it several times. If vacuum is present in the system, light application will produce less and less pedal travel. If there is no vacuum, air is leaking into the system.

System Operation Test

1. With the engine **OFF**, pump the brake pedal until the supply vacuum is entirely gone.
2. Put light, steady pressure on the brake pedal.
3. Start the engine and let it idle. If the system is operating correctly, the brake pedal should fall toward the floor if the constant pressure is maintained.

Power brake systems may be tested for hydraulic leaks just as ordinary systems are tested.

Brake Light Switch

REMOVAL & INSTALLATION

▶ **See Figures 1, 2 and 3**

➡ **When installing the brake pedal switches it is very important that the brake pedal remain in the full up or at rest position, or damage to the brake system and/or switch misadjustment may occur**

1. Disconnect the negative battery cable.
2. Remove the necessary instrument panel sound insulators, to gain access to the switch.
3. Detach the electrical connector(s) from the switch.
4. If equipped, disconnect the vacuum hose from the switch.
5. Remove the brake light switch.
6. On Deville, twist the switch counter clockwise to remove

To install:

7. Installation is the reversal of the removal procedure. Adjust the switch as necessary.

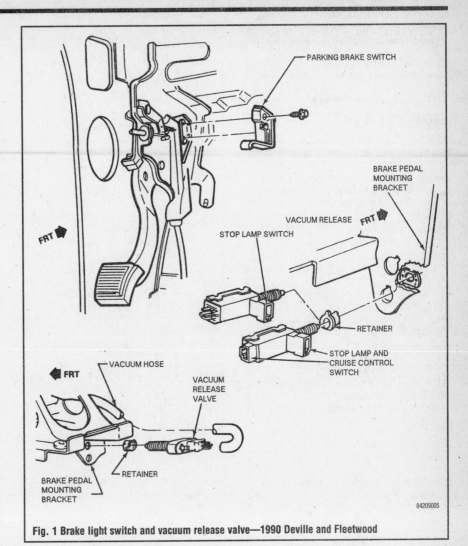

Fig. 1 Brake light switch and vacuum release valve—1990 Deville and Fleetwood

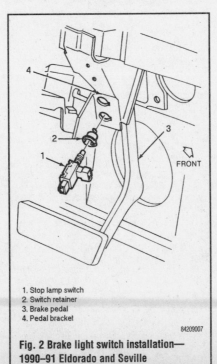

1. Stop lamp switch
2. Switch retainer
3. Brake pedal
4. Pedal bracket

84209007

Fig. 2 Brake light switch installation— 1990–91 Eldorado and Seville

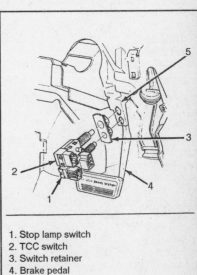

1. Stop lamp switch
2. TCC switch
3. Switch retainer
4. Brake pedal
5. Pedal bracket

84209008

Fig. 3 Brake light switch installation— 1992–98 Eldorado and Seville

Master Cylinder

REMOVAL & INSTALLATION

1990–93 Deville and Fleetwood

▶ See Figures 4, 5, 6 and 7

1. Disconnect the negative battery cable.
2. Using a syringe, remove as much brake fluid as possible from the master cylinder reservoir before removing.
   a. Dispose of brake fluid. DO NOT reuse.
   b. Reinstall the reservoir cap before proceeding.
3. Detach the electrical connector from the fluid level sensor switch.

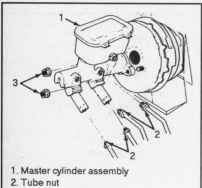

1. Master cylinder assembly
2. Tube nut
3. Nut

84209013

Fig. 4 Master cylinder installation—1990 models

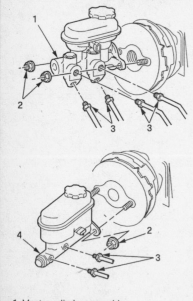

1. Master cylinder assembly
2. Nut, 27 N·m (20 lb.ft.)
3. Brake pipe, 15 N·m (133 lb.in.)
4. Master cylinder, antilock brake system

84209014

Fig. 5 Master cylinder installation—Deville and Fleetwood

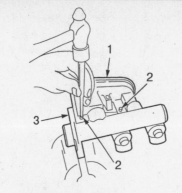

1. Reservoir assembly
2. Spring pin
3. Cylinder body

84209015

Fig. 6 Removing the master cylinder reservoir—Deville and Fleetwood

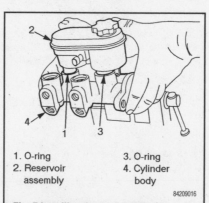

1. O-ring
2. Reservoir assembly
3. O-ring
4. Cylinder body

84209016

Fig. 7 Installing the master cylinder reservoir—Deville and Fleetwood

4. Disconnect the brake lines from the master cylinder and proportioning valves. Plug the lines and master cylinder and proportioning valve ports to prevent fluid loss.
5. Remove the master cylinder mounting nuts and remove the master cylinder.
To install:
6. Position the master cylinder on the power brake booster and install the mounting nuts. Tighten to 20 ft. lbs. (27 Nm).
7. Connect the brake lines and tighten the fittings to 11 ft. lbs. (15 Nm).
8. Connect the electrical connector to the fluid level sensor switch and connect the negative battery cable.
9. Fill the master cylinder and bleed the brake system.

1990–91 Eldorado and Seville

▶ See Figure 8

1. Disconnect the negative battery cable.
2. Detach the electrical connector from the fluid level sensor switch.
3. Disconnect the brake lines from the master cylinder and proportioning valves. Plug the lines and master cylinder and proportioning valve ports to prevent fluid loss.

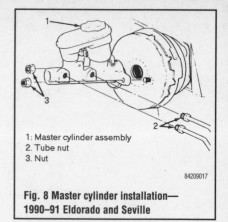

1. Master cylinder assembly
2. Tube nut
3. Nut

84209017

Fig. 8 Master cylinder installation—1990–91 Eldorado and Seville

4. Remove the master cylinder mounting nuts and remove the master cylinder.
To install:
5. Position the master cylinder on the power brake booster and install the mounting nuts. Tighten to 20 ft. lbs. (27 Nm).
6. Connect the brake lines. Tighten the brake line-to-proportioning valve fittings to 11 ft. lbs. (15 Nm) and the brake line-to-master cylinder fittings to 24 ft. lbs. (32 Nm).
7. Connect the electrical connector to the fluid level sensor switch and connect the negative battery cable.
8. Fill the master cylinder and bleed the brake system.

1992–98 Eldorado and Seville; 1994–98 Deville

▶ See Figure 9

This brake master cylinder is a composite design (plastic reservoir and aluminum body) to be used in a diagonally split system (one front and one diagonally opposite front and rear brake served by the primary piston, and the opposite front and rear brakes served by the secondary piston). It incorporates the functions of a standard dual master cylinder; in addition, it has a fluid level sensor switch and front reservoir access for use with Traction control.

1. Disconnect the negative battery cable.
2. Detach the electrical connector from the fluid level sensor.
3. Using a syringe, remove as much brake fluid as possible from the master cylinder reservoir before removing.
4. If equipped with anti-lock brakes, drain the brake fluid from the master cylinder reservoir, then disconnect, and plug the reservoir hose.
   a. Dispose of brake fluid. DO NOT reuse.
   b. Reinstall the reservoir cap before proceeding.
5. Detach the electrical connector from the fluid level sensor switch.
6. Disconnect the brake lines from the master cylinder. Plug the lines and master cylinder ports to prevent fluid loss.
7. Remove the master cylinder mounting nuts and remove the master cylinder.
8. If the vehicle is equipped with anti-lock brakes and the master cylinder is being replaced, remove the master cylinder reservoir as follows:
   a. Clamp the mounting flange on the master

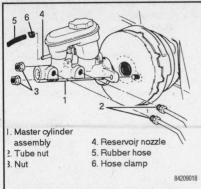

Fig. 9 Master cylinder installation—Eldo-rado and Seville

1. Master cylinder assembly
2. Tube nut
3. Nut
4. Reservoir nozzle
5. Rubber hose
6. Hose clamp

84209018

cylinder body in a vise. Do not clamp on the master cylinder body.

b. Tap back the spring pins until they are clear of the reservoir. Be careful not to damage the reservoir or master cylinder.

c. Remove the reservoir and the reservoir seals. Inspect the reservoir for cracks or deformities and replace as necessary.

To install:

9. If the vehicle is equipped with anti-lock brakes and the master cylinder is being replaced, install the master cylinder reservoir as follows:

a. Clean the reservoir with clean denatured alcohol and dry with unlubricated compressed air.

b. Lubricate new seals and the reservoir bayonets with clean brake fluid.

c. Install the seals on the master cylinder, making sure they are fully seated.

d. Install the reservoir onto the master cylinder by pressing straight down by hand until the pin holes are aligned.

e. Tap in the pins to retain the reservoir, being careful not to damage the reservoir or master cylinder.

10. Position the master cylinder on the power brake booster and install the mounting nuts. Tighten to 20 ft. lbs. (27 Nm).

11. Connect the brake lines and tighten the fittings to 11 ft. lbs. (15 Nm).

12. If equipped with anti-lock brakes, connect the reservoir hose.

13. Connect the electrical connector to the fluid level sensor and connect the negative battery cable.

14. Fill the master cylinder and bleed the brake system.

Power Brake Booster

The power brake booster is a tandem vacuum suspended unit. In a normal operating mode, with the service brakes in the released position, the tandem vacuum suspended booster operates with vacuum on both sides of its diaphragms. When the brakes are applied, air at atmospheric pressure is admitted to one side of each diaphragm to provide the power assist. When the brakes are released, the atmospheric air is shut off from one side of each diaphragm. The air is then drawn from the booster through the power brake booster vacuum check

valve to the vacuum source. The internal components of the booster are non-serviceable and non-interchangeable.

REMOVAL & INSTALLATION

▶ **See Figures 10, 11, 12 and 13**

1. Disconnect the negative battery cable.
2. Disconnect the booster vacuum hose from the vacuum check valve.
3. Remove the master cylinder mounting nuts. Remove the master cylinder from the booster without disconnecting the brake lines.

➡**Move the master cylinder forward just enough to clear the studs on the booster. This will flex the brake lines slightly; be careful not to bend or distort the brake lines.**

4. Working under the instrument panel, remove the acoustical barrier from the booster studs, if equipped.
5. Remove the booster mounting nuts.
6. Disengage the booster pushrod from the brake pedal. Tilt the entire booster slightly to work the pushrod off the pedal clevis pin without

putting unnecessary side pressure on the pushrod.

7. Remove the booster assembly from the vehicle. Remove the gasket if necessary.

To install:

8. If necessary, install the gasket to the booster.
9. Position the booster in the vehicle.
10. Connect the booster pushrod to the brake pedal. Tilt the entire booster slightly to work the pushrod onto the pedal clevis pin without putting unnecessary side pressure on the pushrod.
11. Install the booster mounting nuts. Tighten the nuts to 15 ft. lbs. (21 Nm) on Deville and Fleetwood or 20 ft. lbs. (27 Nm) on Eldorado and Seville.
12. If equipped, install the acoustical barrier onto the booster studs under the instrument panel.
13. Install the master cylinder to the booster and tighten the mounting nuts to 20 ft. lbs. (27 Nm).
14. Connect the booster vacuum hose to the vacuum check valve.
15. Connect the negative battery cable.

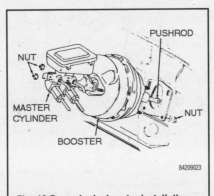

Fig. 10 Power brake booster installation—1990 models

84209023

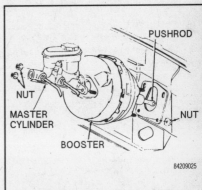

Fig. 12 Power brake booster installation—1992–98 Eldorado and Seville

84209025

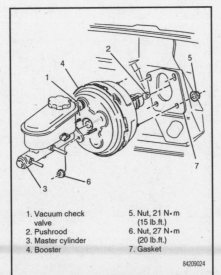

1. Vacuum check valve
2. Pushrod
3. Master cylinder
4. Booster
5. Nut, 21 N·m (15 lb.ft.)
6. Nut, 27 N·m (20 lb.ft.)
7. Gasket

84209024

Fig. 11 Power brake booster installation—1991–93 Deville and Fleetwood

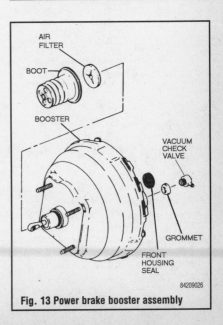

Fig. 13 Power brake booster assembly

84209026

Proportioning Valve

The brake proportioning valves improve front-to-rear brake balance under severe brake application. Severe brake application transfers part of the vehicle rear weight to the front wheels. The resulting decrease in weight at the rear wheels can cause reduced braking efficiency and rear wheel lockup. The valves limit the pressure to the rear brakes to reduce the tendency for reduced brake efficiency.

REMOVAL & INSTALLATION

Without Anti-Lock brakes

1990 VEHICLES

♦ See Figure 14

1. Disconnect the negative battery cable.
2. Disconnect the brake lines from the proportioning valves. Plug the lines to prevent fluid loss.
3. Remove the proportioning valve and O-rings from the master cylinder.

To install:

4. Lubricate new O-rings and the external proportioning valve threads with clean brake fluid. Install the new O-rings on the proportioning valves.
5. Install the proportioning valves on the master cylinder and tighten to 24 ft. lbs. (31 Nm).
6. Connect the brake lines to the proportioning valves and tighten the fittings to 11 ft. lbs. (15 Nm).
7. Connect the negative battery cable. Bleed the brake system.

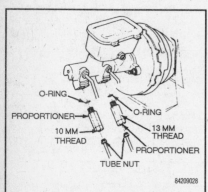

Fig. 14 Proportioning valve installation—1990 vehicles without anti-lock brakes

1991–93 DEVILLE AND FLEETWOOD

1. Remove the master cylinder from the vehicle.
2. Clamp the mounting flange on the master cylinder body in a vise. Do not clamp on the master cylinder body.
3. Tap back the spring pins until they are clear of the master cylinder reservoir. Be careful not to damage the reservoir or master cylinder.
4. Remove the reservoir and the reservoir seals. Inspect the reservoir for cracks or deformities and replace as necessary.
5. Remove the proportioning valve caps, O-rings, and springs.
6. Using needle nose pliers, remove the proportioning valve pistons.

7. Remove the seals from the pistons. Inspect the proportioning valve pistons for corrosion and deformities and replace as necessary.
8. Clean all parts in clean denatured alcohol and dry with unlubricated compressed air.

To install:

9. Lubricate new O-rings and proportioning valve seals as well as the stems of the proportioning valve pistons with silicone grease.
10. Install the new seals (seal lips facing upward toward the cap) on the proportioning valve pistons.
11. Install the proportioning valve pistons, seals, and springs into the master cylinder body.
12. Install the new O-rings in the grooves in the proportioning valve caps. Install the proportioning valve caps in the master cylinder and tighten to 20 ft. lbs. (27 Nm).
13. Lubricate new O-rings and the master cylinder reservoir bayonets with clean brake fluid.
14. Install the O-rings on the master cylinder, making sure they are fully seated.
15. Install the reservoir onto the master cylinder by pressing straight down by hand until the pinholes are aligned.
16. Tap in the pins to retain the reservoir, being careful not to damage the reservoir or master cylinder.
17. Install the master cylinder on the vehicle and bleed the brake system.

With Anti-Lock brakes

1990 MODELS

✳✳ CAUTION

The hydraulic system contains brake fluid at extremely high pressure. It is mandatory that the system be depressurized before disconnecting any hoses, lines or fittings, or personal injury may result.

1. Depressurize the hydraulic accumulator. The following procedure should be used:
2. With the ignition **OFF**, pressure switch disconnected, pump motor disconnected or the negative battery cable disconnected, pump the brake pedal a minimum of 25 times using at least 50 lbs. of pedal force each time. A definite change in pedal feel will occur when the accumulator is discharged.
3. When a definite increase in pedal effort is felt, stroke the pedal a few additional times to remove hydraulic pressure from the system.
4. Raise and safely support the vehicle.
5. Disconnect the brake lines from the proportioning valve. Plug the lines to prevent fluid loss.
6. Remove the proportioning valve.

To install:

7. Install the proportioning valve and connect the brake lines.
8. Tighten the brake line fittings to 11 ft. lbs. (15 Nm).
9. Lower the vehicle.
10. Fill the fluid reservoir and bleed the brake system.

1991–98 MODELS

♦ See Figures 15 and 16

1. Raise and safely support the vehicle.
2. Clean the proportioning valve and brake line connections to make sure the system will not be contaminated during servicing.
3. Disconnect the brake lines from the proportioning valve. Plug the lines to prevent fluid loss.
4. Remove the proportioning valve.

To install:

5. Install the proportioning valve and connect the brake lines. Tighten the brake line fittings to 11 ft. lbs. (15 Nm).
6. Lower the vehicle.
7. Fill the fluid reservoir and bleed the brake system.

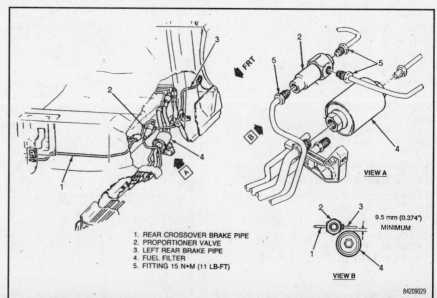

1. REAR CROSSOVER BRAKE PIPE
2. PROPORTIONER VALVE
3. LEFT REAR BRAKE PIPE
4. FUEL FILTER
5. FITTING 15 N•M (11 LB-FT)

Fig. 15 Proportioning valve—Deville and Fleetwood with anti-lock brakes, Eldorado and Seville with anti-lock brakes similar

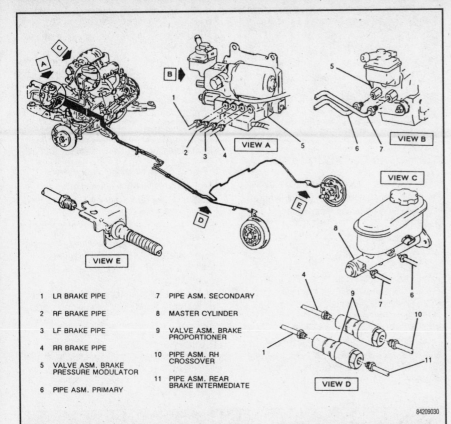

1 LR BRAKE PIPE

2 RF BRAKE PIPE

3 LF BRAKE PIPE

4 RR BRAKE PIPE

5 VALVE ASM. BRAKE PRESSURE MODULATOR

6 PIPE ASM. PRIMARY

7 PIPE ASM. SECONDARY

8 MASTER CYLINDER

9 VALVE ASM. BRAKE PROPORTIONER

10 PIPE ASM. RH CROSSOVER

11 PIPE ASM. REAR BRAKE INTERMEDIATE

84209030

Fig. 16 Proportioner valve and brake line connections—1991–93 Deville and Fleetwood with anti-lock brakes

Bleeding The Brake System

BRAKE BLEEDING

▶ **See Figures 17 thru 23**

When any part of the hydraulic system has been disconnected for repair or replacement, air may get into the lines and cause spongy pedal action (because air can be compressed and brake fluid cannot). To correct this condition, it is necessary to bleed the hydraulic system so to be sure all air is purged.

When bleeding the brake system, bleed one brake cylinder at a time, beginning at the cylinder with the longest hydraulic line (farthest from the master cylinder) first. ALWAYS Keep the master cylinder reservoir filled with brake fluid during the bleeding operation. Never use brake fluid that has been drained from the hydraulic system, no matter how clean it is.

The primary and secondary hydraulic brake systems are separate and are bled independently. During the bleeding operation, do not allow the reservoir to run dry. Keep the master cylinder reservoir filled with brake fluid.

On 1990 models equipped with the Teves Mk II ABS system the hydraulic accumulator must be depressurized before bleeding the brakes.

➡The ABS pump/motor assembly will keep the accumulator charged to a pressure between approximately 2000 and 2600 psi any time the ignition is in the RUN position. The pump/motor cannot operate if the ignition is OFF or if a battery cable is disconnected. Detaching the pressure switch connector or the pump motor connector from the hydraulic unit will also prevent the pump from operating. Unless otherwise specified, the hydraulic accumulator should be depressurized before working on any portion of the hydraulic system.

1. On 1990 models equipped with the Teves Mk II ABS system, depressurize the ABS accumulator using the following procedure:

a. With the ignition **OFF**, pressure switch disconnected, pump motor disconnected or the negative battery cable disconnected, pump the brake pedal a minimum of 25 times using at least 50 lbs. of pedal force each time. A definite change in pedal feel will occur when the accumulator is discharged.

b. When a definite increase in pedal effort is felt, stroke the pedal a few additional times

91149P13

Fig. 17 The bleed screw for the rear drum brakes is located on the rear of the backing plate, just above the brake line

91149P01

Fig. 18 Remove the protective rubber cap for the bleed screw

91149P11

Fig. 19 Attach a hose connected to a bottle with a small amount of brake fluid in it to the bleed screw

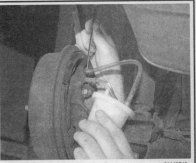

91149P12

Fig. 20 Slowly open the bleed screw and have an assistant depress the brake pedal while observing the hose for bubbles

Fig. 21 Remove the protective rubber cap for the bleed screw on the front brake caliper

Fig. 22 Attach a hose connected to a bottle with a small amount of brake fluid in it to the bleed screw on the brake caliper

Fig. 23 Slowly open the bleed screw on the brake caliper and have an assistant depress the brake pedal while observing the hose for bubbles

to remove all hydraulic pressure from the system.

2. Clean all dirt from around the master cylinder fill cap, remove the cap and fill the master cylinder with brake fluid until the level is within ¼ in. (6mm) of the top edge of the reservoir.

3. Clean the bleeder screws at all 4 wheels. The bleeder screws are located on the back of the brake backing plate (drum brakes) and on the top of the brake calipers (disc brakes).

Bleed the system in the following sequence:
- Right rear
- Left front
- Left rear
- Right front

4. Attach a length of rubber hose over the bleeder screw and place the other end of the hose in a glass jar, submerged in brake fluid.

5. Open the bleeder screw ½–¾ turn. Have an assistant slowly depress the brake pedal.

6. Close the bleeder screw and tell your assistant to allow the brake pedal to return slowly. Continue this process to purge all air from the system.

7. When bubbles cease to appear at the end of the bleeder hose, close the bleeder screw and remove the hose. Tighten the bleeder screw to the proper torque:

8. Check the master cylinder fluid level and add fluid accordingly. Do this after bleeding each wheel.

9. Repeat the bleeding operation at the remaining 3 wheels.

10. Fill the master cylinder reservoir to the proper level.

FRONT DISC BRAKES

Brake Pads

REMOVAL & INSTALLATION

♦ See Figures 24 thru 30

✳✳ CAUTION

Older brake pads or shoes may contain asbestos, which has been determined to be cancer causing agent. Never clean the brake surfaces with compressed air! Avoid inhaling any dust from any brake surface! When cleaning brake surfaces, use a commercially available brake cleaning fluid.

➡ Disc brake pads must be replaced in axle sets only.

1. Use a syringe or similar tool to remove ⅔ of the brake fluid from the master cylinder reservoir.

2. Raise and safely support the vehicle.

3. Remove the wheel and tire assembly, then reinstall 2 lug nuts to retain the disc brake rotor.

4. Remove the disc brake caliper from the mounting bracket, but do not disconnect the brake hose from the caliper. Suspend the caliper with wire from the coil spring.

✳✳ WARNING

Do not let the caliper hang from the brake hose. The hose may become damaged, causing possible brake failure.

Fig. 24 Remove the locating pins and . . .

Fig. 25 . . . remove the caliper from the knuckle

Fig. 26 Remove the outer pad from the caliper by releasing the clip

Fig. 27 The caliper piston can be depressed using a special tool, such as this one from Lisle®. If a tool like this is not available, a C-clamp works well also. Make sure you leave the inner pad in while doing this

Fig. 28 Remove the inner pad from the caliper

Fig. 29 Use mechanic's wire or a similar device to support the caliper out of the way

Fig. 30 A coating of Disc Brake Quiet or equivalent silencer should be applied to the backs of the new pads

5. Use a small prybar to disengage the buttons on the outboard disc brake pad from the holes in the caliper housing. Remove the outboard disc brake pad.

6. Remove the inboard disc brake pad.

7. Inspect the disc brake rotor and machine or replace, as necessary.

To install:

8. Wipe the outside surface of the caliper piston boot clean using denatured alcohol.

9. Using a C-clamp, bottom the caliper piston into the caliper bore. Tighten the clamp slowly, and be careful not to damage the piston or piston boot. After bottoming the piston, use a small plastic or wood tool to lift the inner edge of the boot next to the piston and press out any trapped air; the boot must lay flat.

10. Install the inboard disc brake pad by snapping the retainer spring into the piston. Make sure the pad lays flat against the piston and does not touch the boot. If the pad contacts the boot, remove the pad and reseat or reposition the boot.

11. Install the outboard disc brake pad. Position the pad so that the wear sensor is at the trailing edge of the pad during forward wheel rotation on all except 1990 Deville and Fleetwood. On 1990 Deville and Fleetwood, position the pad so that the wear sensor is at the leading edge of the pad during for-

ward wheel rotation. The back of the pad must lay flat against the caliper.

12. Install the disc brake caliper.

13. Install the wheel and tire assembly and lower the vehicle.

14. Apply the brake pedal several times to position the caliper piston and seat the brake pads in the caliper.

15. Check the brake fluid level in the master cylinder and add fluid as necessary.

INSPECTION

▶ **See Figures 31, 32 and 33**

Inspect the disc brake pads every 6000 miles and any time the wheels are removed. Check both ends of the outer pad by looking in at each end of the caliper. These points are where the highest rate of wear normally occurs. Check the inner pad by looking down through the hole in the top of the caliper. When any lining thickness is worn to within 1⁄32 in. (0.76mm) of the backing plate or rivet, the pads must be replaced in axle sets. Some inner pads have a thermal layer against the backing plate, integrally molded with the lining; don't confuse this extra layer with uneven inboard-outboard lining wear.

The outer disc brake pad is also equipped with a wear sensor. When the lining is worn, the sensor contacts the disc brake rotor and produces a warning noise, indicating that disc brake pad replacement is necessary.

Brake Caliper

REMOVAL & INSTALLATION

1990 Deville and Fleetwood

▶ **See Figures 34, 35, 36 and 37**

1. If equipped with anti-lock brakes, depressurize the hydraulic accumulator. Refer to Teves Mk II Anti-Lock Brake System.

✳✳ CAUTION

The hydraulic system contains brake fluid at extremely high pressure. It is mandatory that the system be depressurized before disconnecting any hoses, lines or fittings, or personal injury may result.

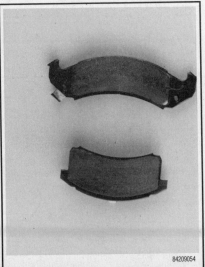

Fig. 31 View of the disc brake pads from a 1992 Deville. Note the wear sensor on the trailing edge of the outboard pad

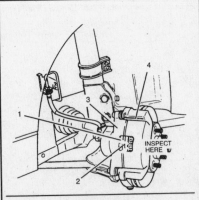

1 INBOARD LINING
2 ROTOR
3 CALIPER
4 CALIPER MOUNTING BRACKET

Fig. 32 Front disc brake pad inspection

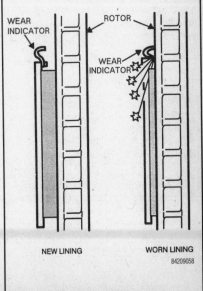

Fig. 33 Disc brake pad wear sensor

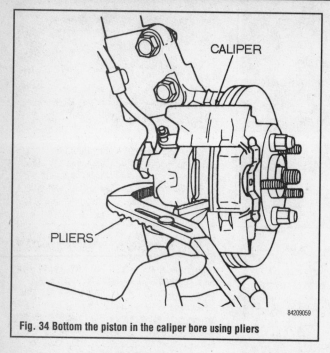

Fig. 34 Bottom the piston in the caliper bore using pliers

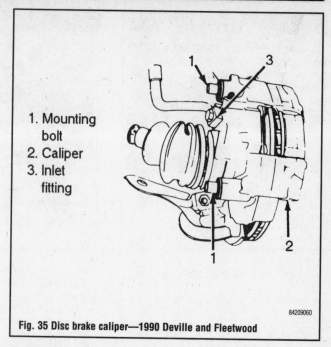

1. Mounting bolt
2. Caliper
3. Inlet fitting

Fig. 35 Disc brake caliper—1990 Deville and Fleetwood

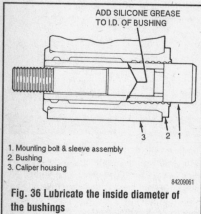

ADD SILICONE GREASE TO I.D. OF BUSHING

1. Mounting bolt & sleeve assembly
2. Bushing
3. Caliper housing

Fig. 36 Lubricate the inside diameter of the bushings

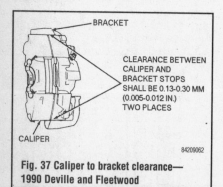

BRACKET

CLEARANCE BETWEEN CALIPER AND BRACKET STOPS SHALL BE 0.13-0.30 MM (0.005-0.012 IN.) TWO PLACES

CALIPER

Fig. 37 Caliper to bracket clearance— 1990 Deville and Fleetwood

2. Use a syringe or similar tool to remove ⅔ of the brake fluid from the master cylinder reservoir.

3. Raise and safely support the vehicle.

4. Remove the wheel and tire assembly, then reinstall 2 lug nuts to retain the disc brake rotor.

5. Position suitable pliers over the inboard brake pad and the inboard caliper housing to bottom the piston in the caliper.

6. If the caliper is to be removed from the vehicle, remove the bolt attaching the brake hose to

the caliper. Discard the gaskets. Plug the openings in the caliper and brake hose to prevent fluid loss.

7. Remove the caliper mounting bolt and sleeve assemblies, then remove the caliper from the rotor and mounting bracket. If only the brake pads are being replaced, suspend the caliper with wire from the coil spring.

※※ WARNING

Do not let the caliper hang from the brake hose. The hose may become damaged, causing possible brake failure.

To install:

8. Inspect the mounting bolt and sleeve assemblies for corrosion and the bushings for cuts and nicks. Replace parts as necessary; do not try to polish away corrosion.

9. Coat the inside diameter of the bushings with silicone grease, then install the caliper over the rotor in the mounting bracket.

10. Install the mounting bolt and sleeve assemblies and tighten to 38 ft. lbs. (51 Nm).

11. Measure the clearance between the caliper and the bracket stops, it should be 0.005–0.012 in. (0.13–0.30mm). If the clearance is not as specified, remove the caliper and file the ends of the bracket stops until the proper clearance is obtained.

12. Connect the brake hose to the caliper with the attaching bolt, using new gaskets. Tighten the bolt to 33 ft. lbs. (45 Nm).

13. Bleed the brake system.

14. Install the wheel and tire assembly and lower the vehicle.

15. Check the brake fluid level in the master cylinder and add fluid as necessary.

1990–91 Eldorado and Seville

♦ See Figures 38 and 39

1. On 1990 vehicles with anti-lock brakes, depressurize the hydraulic accumulator. Refer to Teves Mk II Anti-Lock Brake System.

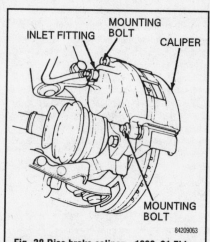

INLET FITTING   MOUNTING BOLT   CALIPER

MOUNTING BOLT

Fig. 38 Disc brake caliper—1990-91 Eldorado and Seville

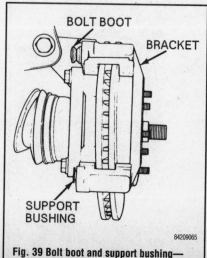

BOLT BOOT

BRACKET

SUPPORT BUSHING

Fig. 39 Bolt boot and support bushing— 1990-91 Eldorado and Seville

The hydraulic system contains brake fluid at extremely high pressure. It is mandatory that the system be depressurized before disconnecting any hoses, lines or fittings, or personal injury may result.

2. Use a syringe or similar tool to remove ⅔ of the brake fluid from the master cylinder reservoir.

3. Raise and safely support the vehicle.

4. Remove the wheel and tire assembly, then reinstall 2 lug nuts to retain the disc brake rotor.

5. If the caliper is to be removed from the vehicle, remove the bolt attaching the brake hose to the caliper. Discard the gaskets. Plug the openings in the caliper and brake hose to prevent fluid loss.

6. Remove the caliper mounting bolts, then remove the caliper from the rotor and mounting bracket. If only the brake pads are being replaced, suspend the caliper with wire from the coil spring.

⁂ WARNING

Do not let the caliper hang from the brake hose. The hose may become damaged, causing possible brake failure.

To install:

7. Inspect the bolt boots and mounting bracket support bushings for cuts, tears or deterioration and replace as necessary. Inspect the mounting bolts for corrosion and replace them and the bushings if any is found; do not try to polish away corrosion.

8. Position the caliper over the rotor in the mounting bracket, making sure the bolt boots are in place.

9. Lubricate the shaft of the mounting bolts with silicone grease. Install the bolts and tighten to 63 ft. lbs. (85 Nm).

10. Position the brake hose on the disc brake caliper. Connect the hose to the caliper using the attaching bolt and 2 new gaskets. Tighten the bolt to 32 ft. lbs. (44 Nm).

11. Bleed the brake system.

12. Install the wheel and tire assembly and lower the vehicle.

13. Check the brake fluid level in the master cylinder and add fluid as necessary.

1991–93 Deville and Fleetwood; 1992–98 Eldorado and Seville

▶ **See Figure 37**

1. Use a syringe or similar tool to remove ⅔ of the brake fluid from the master cylinder reservoir.

2. Raise and safely support the vehicle.

3. Remove the wheel and tire assembly, then reinstall 2 lug nuts to retain the disc brake rotor.

4. If the caliper is to be removed from the vehicle, remove the bolt attaching the brake hose to the caliper. Discard the gaskets. Plug the openings in the caliper and brake hose to prevent fluid loss.

5. Install a large C-clamp over the top of the caliper housing and against the back of the outboard pad. Slowly tighten the C-clamp until the piston is pushed into the caliper far enough to slide the caliper off the rotor.

6. Remove the caliper mounting bolts and sleeves, then remove the caliper. If only the brake pads are being replaced, suspend the caliper with wire from the coil spring.

⁂ WARNING

Do not let the caliper hang from the brake hose. The hose may become damaged, causing possible brake failure.

To install:

7. Inspect the mounting bolt and sleeve assemblies for corrosion and the bushings for cuts and nicks. Replace parts as necessary; do not try to polish away corrosion.

8. Coat the inside diameter of the bushings with silicone grease.

9. Install the mounting bolt and sleeve assemblies through the bushings using hand pressure only. If greater than hand force is required or mechanical assistance is needed, remove the mounting bolt and sleeve assemblies along with the bushings.

10. Inspect the mounting bores for corrosion. If there is any corrosion, remove it using a 1 in. wheel cylinder honing brush. Clean the mounting bores with clean denatured alcohol, replace the bushings and lubricate.

11. Install the caliper over the rotor in the mounting bracket. Tighten the mounting bolts to 38 ft. lbs. (51 Nm).

12. Position the brake hose on the disc brake caliper. Connect the hose to the caliper using the attaching bolt and 2 new gaskets. Tighten the bolt to 32 ft. lbs. (44 Nm).

13. Bleed the brake system.

14. Install the wheel and tire assembly and lower the vehicle.

15. Check the brake fluid level in the master cylinder and add fluid as necessary.

OVERHAUL

▶ **See Figures 40 thru 47**

➡Some vehicles may be equipped dual piston calipers. The procedure to overhaul the caliper is essentially the same with the exception of multiple pistons, O-rings and dust boots.

1. Remove the caliper from the vehicle and place on a clean workbench.

⁂ CAUTION

NEVER place your fingers in front of the pistons in an attempt to catch or protect the pistons when applying compressed air. This could result in personal injury!

➡Depending upon the vehicle, there are two different ways to remove the piston from the caliper. Refer to the brake pad replacement procedure to make sure you have the correct procedure for your vehicle.

2. The first method is as follows:
   a. Stuff a shop towel or a block of wood into the caliper to catch the piston.
   b. Remove the caliper piston using compressed air applied into the caliper inlet hole. Inspect the piston for scoring, nicks, corrosion and/or worn or damaged chrome plating. The piston must be replaced if any of these conditions are found.

3. For the second method, you must rotate the piston to retract it from the caliper.

4. If equipped, remove the anti-rattle clip.

5. Use a prytool to remove the caliper boot, being careful not to scratch the housing bore.

6. Remove the piston seals from the groove in the caliper bore.

7. Carefully loosen the brake bleeder valve cap and valve from the caliper housing.

8. Inspect the caliper bores, pistons and mounting threads for scoring or excessive wear.

9. Use crocus cloth to polish out light corrosion from the piston and bore.

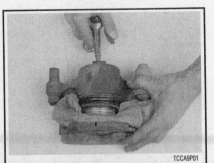

Fig. 40 For some types of calipers, use compressed air to drive the piston out of the caliper, but make sure to keep your fingers clear

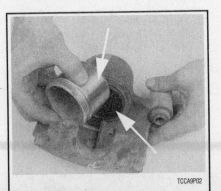

Fig. 41 Withdraw the piston from the caliper bore

Fig. 42 On some vehicles, you must remove the anti-rattle clip

Fig. 43 Use a prytool to carefully pry around the edge of the boot . . .

Fig. 44 . . . then remove the boot from the caliper housing, taking care not to score or damage the bore

Fig. 45 Use extreme caution when removing the piston seal; DO NOT scratch the caliper bore

Fig. 46 Use the proper size driving tool and a mallet to properly seal the boots in the caliper housing

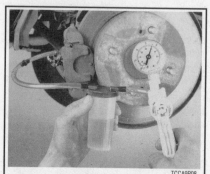

Fig. 47 There are tools, such as this Mighty-Vac, available to assist in proper brake system bleeding

10. Clean all parts with denatured alcohol and dry with compressed air.

To assemble:

11. Lubricate and install the bleeder valve and cap.

12. Install the new seals into the caliper bore grooves, making sure they are not twisted.

13. Lubricate the piston bore.

14. Install the pistons and boots into the bores of the calipers and push to the bottom of the bores.

15. Use a suitable driving tool to seat the boots in the housing.

16. Install the caliper in the vehicle.

17. Install the wheel and tire assembly, then carefully lower the vehicle.

18. Properly bleed the brake system.

Brake Disc (Rotor)

REMOVAL & INSTALLATION

▶ **See Figures 42, 43, 48, 49 and 50**

1. Raise and safely support the vehicle.

2. Remove the wheel and tire assembly.

3. Remove the brake caliper and suspend it with wire from the coil spring; do not let the caliper hang from the brake hose.

4. On 1990–91 Eldorado and Seville, remove the caliper mounting bracket mounting bolts and the mounting bracket.

5. If equipped, remove the retainers from the wheel studs and discard; they do not have to be reinstalled.

6. Remove the disc brake rotor. Inspect the rotor and machine or replace, as necessary.

To install:

7. Install the disc brake rotor over the wheel studs and hub assembly.

8. On 1990–91 Eldorado and Seville, install the caliper mounting bracket using new mounting bolts. Tighten the bolts to 83 ft. lbs. (112 Nm).

9. Install the brake caliper.

10. Install the wheel and tire assembly and lower the vehicle.

INSPECTION

Inspect the rotor surface finish for discoloration due to overheating, excessive glazing or scoring. If the rotor is discolored or glazed, it must be machined. Light scoring of the rotor surface not exceeding a depth of 0.050 in. (1.2mm), which may result from normal use, is not detrimental to brake operation and refinishing is usually not necessary. Heavier scoring must be removed by refinishing, being careful to observe the minimum thickness specification.

Inspect the rotor for thickness variation. Excessive thickness variation can cause brake pedal pulsation or roughness during brake applications. Check thickness variation by measuring the rotor thickness using a micrometer at a minimum of 4 points around the circumference of the rotor. All measurements should be made at the same distance from the edge of the rotor. A rotor that varies more than 0.0005 in. (0.013mm) must be machined, being careful to observe the minimum thickness specification.

Fig. 48 If the rotor is stuck onto the hub, a few taps with a soft-faced hammer can help to free it

Fig. 49 Grasp the rotor and pull it . . .

Fig. 50 . . . off of the hub and knuckle assembly

Inspect the rotor for excessive lateral runout. Excessive lateral, or side-to-side, runout of the rotor surface may cause vehicle vibration during braking. However, the vibration may not be felt through the brake pedal. Inspect for lateral runout as follows:

1. Remove the wheel and tire assembly and reinstall the wheel lug nuts to hold the rotor on the hub and bearing assembly.

2. Attach a dial indicator to the steering knuckle or caliper mounting bracket. Position the indicator foot so it contacts the rotor surface approximately ½–1 in. from the rotor edge.

3. Zero the dial indicator. Move the rotor one complete revolution and check the total indicated runout.

4. If runout is excessive, in some instances it can be corrected by indexing the rotor on the hub one or two wheel stud positions from the original position.

5. If the lateral runout cannot be corrected by indexing, check the hub and bearing assembly for excessive lateral runout or looseness. If the hub and bearing lateral runout exceeds 0.0015 in. (0.040mm) on Deville and Fleetwood, 0.004 in. (0.10mm) on 1990–91 Eldorado and Seville, or 0.002 in. (0.06mm) on 1992–98 Eldorado and Seville, replace the hub and bearing assembly and recheck rotor lateral runout.

6. If the lateral runout still exceeds specification, machine the rotor, being careful to observe the minimum thickness specification.

DRUM BRAKES

Brake Drums

REMOVAL & INSTALLATION

▶ **See Figures 51, 52 and 53**

❊❊ CAUTION

Older brake pads or shoes may contain asbestos, which has been determined to be cancer causing agent. Never clean the brake surfaces with compressed air! Avoid inhaling any dust from any brake surface! When cleaning brake surfaces, use a commercially available brake cleaning fluid.

1. Raise and safely support the vehicle.
2. Remove the wheel and tire assembly.
3. If equipped, remove the retainers from the wheel studs and discard; they do not have to be reinstalled.
4. Remove the brake drum. If the drum is difficult to remove, proceed as follows:

    a. Make sure the parking brake is released.

    b. Back off the parking brake cable adjustment.

    c. On 1990 through early 1992 vehicles, remove the access hole plug from the backing plate. On 1992–93 vehicles equipped with a knockout slug in the drum, use a hammer and a metal punch to bend in the backing plate knock-out slug.

    d. Insert a suitable tool through the hole and press in to push the parking brake lever off its stop. This will allow the brake shoes to retract slightly.

    e. Apply a small amount of penetrating oil around the drum pilot hole. Use a rubber mallet to tap gently on the outer rim of the drum and/or around the inner drum diameter by the spindle. Be careful not to deform the drum through the use of excessive force.

➥**After a drum having a metal knockout slug has been removed from the vehicle, remove the slug using pliers or vise grips. Install a rubber access hole plug into the hole to prevent dirt or contamination from entering the drum brake assembly.**

5. Inspect the brake drum and machine or replace, as necessary.

To install:

6. Adjust the brake shoes and install the brake drum.

7. Install the wheel and tire assembly and lower the vehicle.

INSPECTION

Inspect the brake drums for cracks, scores, deep grooves, out-of-round and taper. Replace any drum that is cracked; it is unsafe for further use. Do not attempt to weld a cracked drum.

Smooth up any light scores. Normal, light scoring of drum surfaces not exceeding a depth of ¹⁄₁₆ in. (1.5mm) is not detrimental to brake operation. Heavy or extensive scoring will cause excessive brake shoe wear, and it may be necessary to machine the drum. When machining the drum, observe the maximum machine diameter specification.

If the brake shoes are slightly worn (but still usable) and the drum is grooved, polish the drum with fine emery cloth; do not machine it. Eliminating all drum grooves and smoothing the lining ridges would require removing too much metal and lining, while if left alone, the grooves and ridges match and satisfactory service can be obtained. However, if the brake shoes are to be replaced, a grooved drum must be machined. A grooved drum will wear a new brake shoe, resulting in improper brake performance.

An out-of-round or tapered drum prevents accurate brake shoe adjustment, and could possibly wear other brake parts due to its eccentric action. An out-of-round drum can also cause severe and irregular tire tread wear, as well as a pulsating brake pedal. Check for out-of-round and taper by measuring the inside diameter of the drum at several points using an inside micrometer. Take measurements at the open and closed edges of the machined surface and at right angles to each other. Machine the drum to correct out-of-round and taper, being careful to observe the maximum machine diameter specification.

Brake Shoes

INSPECTION

❊❊ CAUTION

Older brake pads or shoes may contain asbestos, which has been determined to be cancer causing agent. Never clean the brake surfaces with compressed air! Avoid inhaling any dust from any brake surface! When cleaning brake surfaces, use a commercially available brake cleaning fluid.

Fig. 51 If equipped, remove the retainers from the wheel studs and discard; they do not have to be reinstalled

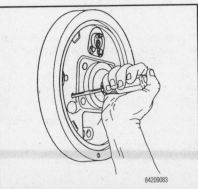

Fig. 52 Moving the parking brake lever off its stop

Fig. 53 Removing the brake drum

Inspect the brake shoes every 6000 miles and any time the wheels are removed. When any lining thickness is worn to within 1/32 in. (0.76mm) of the backing plate or rivet, the shoes must be replaced in axle sets.

REMOVAL & INSTALLATION

❋❋ CAUTION

Older brake pads or shoes may contain asbestos, which has been determined to be cancer causing agent. Never clean the brake surfaces with compressed air! Avoid inhaling any dust from any brake surface! When cleaning brake surfaces, use a commercially available brake cleaning fluid.

1990–91 Deville and Fleetwood

♦ **See Figures 54, 55 and 56**

1. Raise and safely support the vehicle.
2. Remove the wheel and tire assembly.
3. Remove the brake drum.
4. Remove the actuator spring, using suitable pliers.
5. Remove the upper return spring, using brake tool J-8057 or equivalent.
6. Remove the spring connecting link, adjuster actuator and spring washer.
7. Remove the brake shoe hold-down springs and pins using a suitable brake tool or pliers.
8. Disconnect the parking brake cable and remove the brake shoes.
9. Remove the adjusting screw assembly and lower return spring.
10. Remove the retaining ring, pin, spring washer and parking brake lever from the brake shoe.
11. Inspect all parts for wear, over-stress and discoloration from heat and replace as necessary. Inspect the wheel cylinder for leakage and the wheel cylinder dust boots for cuts or tears; replace the entire wheel cylinder if any damage is found.
12. Disassemble the adjuster screw assembly and clean the threads with a wire brush. Wash all components in clean denatured alcohol and allow to dry. Apply suitable brake lubricant to the adjuster screw threads, inside diameter of the socket and the socket face. Inspect the adjuster screw threads for smooth rotation over the full length.
   To install:
13. Install the parking brake lever on the brake shoe with the spring washer (concave side against the lever), pin and retaining ring.
14. Install the adjuster pin in the other brake shoe so that the pin projects 0.275–0.283 in. (7.0–7.2mm) from the side of the shoe web where the adjuster actuator is installed.
15. Assemble the adjuster screw assembly, making sure the spring clip is installed in the same position from where it was removed.
16. Install the lower return spring between the brake shoes.

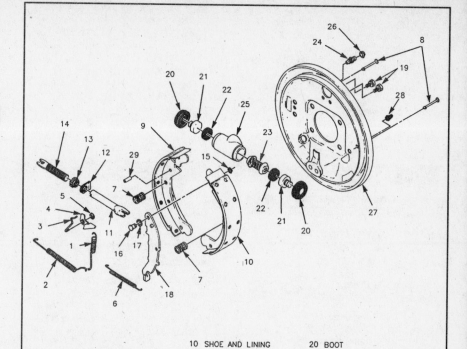

1	ACTUATOR SPRING	10	SHOE AND LINING	20	BOOT
2	UPPER RETURN SPRING	11	ADJUSTER SOCKET	21	PISTON
3	SPRING CONNECTING LINK	12	SPRING CLIP	22	SEAL
4	ADJUSTER ACTUATOR	13	ADJUSTER NUT	23	SPRING ASSEMBLY
5	SPRING WASHER	14	ADJUSTER SCREW	24	BLEEDER VALVE
6	LOWER RETURN SPRING	15	RETAINING RING	25	WHEEL CYLINDER
7	HOLD–DOWN SPRING ASSEMBLY	16	PIN	26	BLEEDER VALVE CAP
8	HOLD–DOWN PIN	17	SPRING WASHER	27	BACKING PLATE ASSEMBLY
9	ADJUSTER SHOE AND LINING	18	PARK BRAKE LEVER	28	ACCESS HOLE PLUG
		19	SCREW AND LOCKWASHER	29	ADJUSTER PIN

84209085

Fig. 54 Drum brake assembly—1990–91 Deville and Fleetwood

❋❋ WARNING

Do not over-stretch the lower return spring; it will be damaged if the extended length is greater than 3.88 in. (98.6mm).

17. Connect the parking brake cable and install the brake shoes with the hold pins and springs. The lower return spring should be positioned under the anchor plate.

➡**The adjuster brake shoe is the one in which the adjuster pin was installed in the shoe web. The adjuster brake shoe is to the front of the vehicle on the left-hand brake assembly and to the rear of the vehicle on the right-hand brake assembly.**

18. Install the adjuster screw assembly between the brake shoes on the backing plate. Make sure the adjuster screw engages the notch in the adjuster shoe and the spring clip points towards the backing plate.

19. Install the spring washer with the concave side against the web of the adjuster brake shoe.
20. Install the adjuster actuator so its top leg engages the notch in the adjuster screw.
21. Install the spring connecting link and hold in place.
22. Insert the angled hook end of the upper return spring through the parking brake lever and brake shoe. Grasp the long, straight section of the spring using brake tool J-8057 or equivalent, pull the spring straight across, then down to hook into the crook on the spring connecting link.

❋❋ WARNING

Do not over-stretch the upper return spring. The spring will be damaged if extended greater than 5.49 in. (139.5mm).

23. Install the actuator spring, using suitable pliers.

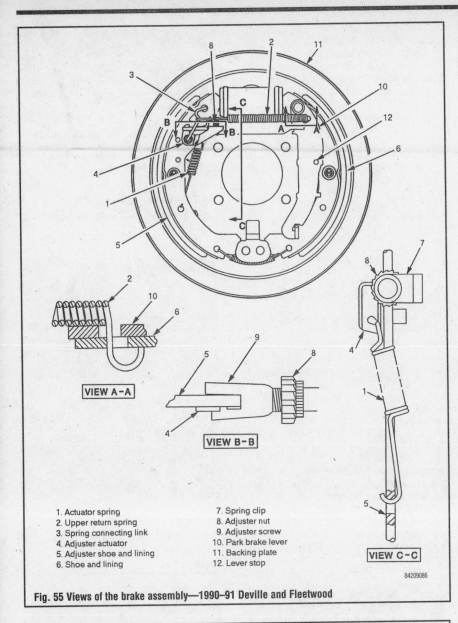

1. Actuator spring
2. Upper return spring
3. Spring connecting link
4. Adjuster actuator
5. Adjuster shoe and lining
6. Shoe and lining
7. Spring clip
8. Adjuster nut
9. Adjuster screw
10. Park brake lever
11. Backing plate
12. Lever stop

84209086

Fig. 55 Views of the brake assembly—1990–91 Deville and Fleetwood

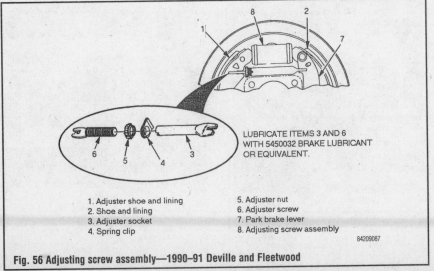

1. Adjuster shoe and lining
2. Shoe and lining
3. Adjuster socket
4. Spring clip
5. Adjuster nut
6. Adjuster screw
7. Park brake lever
8. Adjusting screw assembly

LUBRICATE ITEMS 3 AND 6
WITH 5450032 BRAKE LUBRICANT
OR EQUIVALENT.

84209087

Fig. 56 Adjusting screw assembly—1990–91 Deville and Fleetwood

❋❋ WARNING

Do not over-stretch the actuator spring. The spring will be damaged if extended greater than 3.27 in. (83mm).

24. Make sure the parking brake lever is on its stop and the brake shoes are properly centered on the wheel cylinder pistons.

25. Adjust the brakes and install the brake drum.

26. Install the wheel and tire assembly and lower the vehicle. Check the parking brake adjustment.

1992–93 Deville and Fleetwood

♦ **See Figures 57 thru 67**

1. Raise and safely support the vehicle.
2. Remove the wheel and tire assembly.
3. Remove the brake drum.
4. Remove the loop end of the actuator spring from the adjuster actuator, then disconnect the other end of the spring from the parking brake shoe web.
5. Pry the end of the retractor spring from the hole in the adjuster brake shoe web.

❋❋ CAUTION

Keep your fingers away from the retractor spring to prevent them from being pinched between the spring and shoe web or spring and backing plate.

❋❋ WARNING

When removing the retractor spring from either brake shoe, do not overstretch it. Overstretching reduces the spring's effectiveness.

6. Pry the end of the retractor spring toward the axle until the spring snaps down off the shoe web onto the backing plate.

7. Remove the adjuster brake shoe, adjuster actuator and adjusting screw assembly.

8. Remove the parking brake lever from the parking brake shoe. Do not remove the parking brake cable from the lever unless the lever is to be replaced.

9. Pry the end of the retractor spring from the hole in the parking brake shoe web.

❋❋ CAUTION

Keep your fingers away from the retractor spring to prevent them from being pinched between the spring and shoe web or spring and backing plate.

10. Pry the end of the retractor spring toward the axle until the spring snaps down off the shoe web onto the backing plate.

11. Remove the parking brake shoe.

12. Remove the retractor spring from the backing plate. If only the brake shoes are being replaced, the retractor spring does not have to be removed.

13. Clean all parts in clean denatured alcohol.

14. Inspect all parts for wear, over-stress and discoloration from heat and replace as necessary. Inspect the wheel cylinder for leakage and wheel cylinder dust boots for cuts or tears; replace the entire wheel cylinder if any damage is found.

15. Disassemble the adjuster screw assembly

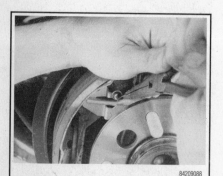

Fig. 57 Removing the actuator spring from the adjuster actuator—1992–93 Deville and Fleetwood

Fig. 58 Removing the actuator spring from the brake shoe web—1992–93 Deville and Fleetwood

Fig. 59 Prying the end of the retractor spring from the hole in the adjuster brake shoe web—1992–93 Deville and Fleetwood

and clean the threads with a wire brush. Wash all components in clean denatured alcohol and allow to dry. Apply suitable brake lubricant to the adjuster screw threads, inside diameter of the socket and the socket face. Inspect the adjuster screw threads for smooth rotation over the full length.

To install:

16. Lubricate the 6 raised brake shoe pads on the backing plate and the anchor surfaces on the backing plate that contact the lower ends of the brake shoes with suitable brake lubricant.

17. If the retractor spring was removed, reinstall it, hooking the center spring section under the tab on the anchor.

18. Position the parking brake shoe on the backing plate. Using a suitable brake tool, pull the end of the retractor spring up to rest on the web of the brake shoe. Pull the end of the spring over until it snaps into the slot in the brake shoe.

19. Install the parking brake lever to the parking brake shoe. Connect the parking brake cable to the lever, if disconnected.

20. Assemble the adjusting screw assembly.

21. Engage the pivot nut of the adjusting screw assembly with the web of the parking brake shoe and the parking brake lever. Position the adjuster brake shoe so that the shoe web engages the deep slot in the adjuster socket.

22. Using a suitable brake tool, pull the end of the retractor spring up to rest on the web of the adjuster brake shoe. Pull the end of the spring over until it snaps into the slot in the brake shoe.

23. Lubricate the tab and pivot point on the adjuster actuator with suitable brake lubricant. Using a suitable tool, spread the brake shoes while working the adjuster actuator into position.

24. Engage the U-shaped end of the actuator spring in the hole in the web of the parking brake shoe. Using a suitable tool, stretch the spring and engage the loop end over the tab on the adjuster actuator.

Fig. 60 Removing the adjuster brake shoe and adjuster actuator—1992–93 Deville and Fleetwood

Fig. 61 Removing the adjusting screw assembly—1992–93 Deville and Fleetwood

Fig. 62 Prying the end of the retractor spring from the hole in the parking brake shoe web—1992–93 Deville and Fleetwood

Fig. 63 Removing the retractor spring—1992–93 Deville and Fleetwood

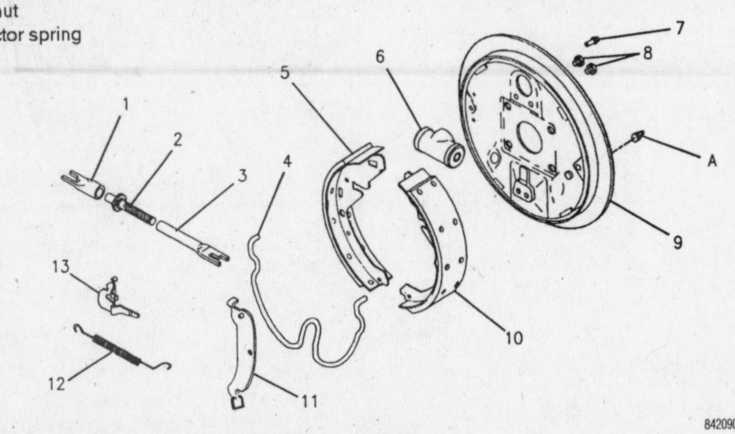

A. Access hole plug.
   Not part of assembly
   on 1993 vehicles.
   Service only item.
1. Adjuster socket
2. Adjuster screw
3. Pivot nut
4. Retractor spring

5. Adjuster shoe and lining
6. Wheel cylinder
7. Bleeder valve
8. Bolt
9. Backing plate

10. Park brake shoe and lining
11. Park brake lever
12. Actuator Spring
13. Adjuster actuator

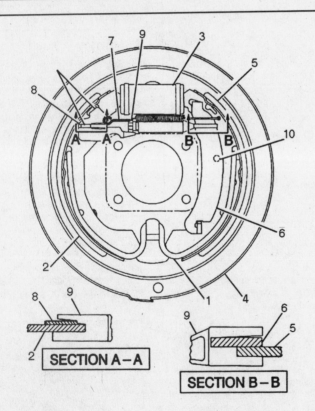

Fig. 64 Drum brake assembly—1992–93 Deville and Fleetwood

1. Retractor spring
2. Adjuster shoe and lining
3. Wheel cylinder
4. Backing plate
5. Park brake shoe
   and lining

6. Park brake lever
7. Actuator spring
8. Adjuster actuator
9. Adjusting screw
   assembly
10. Lever stop

SECTION A–A

SECTION B–B

Fig. 65 Brake component views—1992–93 Deville and Fleetwood

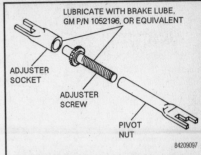

LUBRICATE WITH BRAKE LUBE,
GM P/N 1052196, OR EQUIVALENT

ADJUSTER
SOCKET

ADJUSTER
SCREW

PIVOT
NUT

Fig. 66 Adjusting screw assembly components—1992–93 Deville and Fleetwood

Fig. 67 Lubricate the 6 raised brake shoe
pads on the backing plate with suitable
brake lubricant

25. . Check the following to make sure the
adjuster actuator is positioned and functioning .
properly:
   a. Adjuster actuator pivot in shoe web slot.
   b. Notch in adjuster actuator is on step in
adjusting screw notch.
   c. Arm of adjuster actuator is resting freely
on star wheel teeth of adjuster screw, not trapped
under teeth in a downward angle.
   d. Position a suitable brake tool between the
upper ends of the brake shoes. Spread the
shoes and watch for proper operation of the star
wheel.
26. Adjust the brakes and install the brake
drum.
27. Install the wheel and tire assembly and
lower the vehicle. Check the parking brake adjustment.

ADJUSTMENTS

▶ **See Figures 68 and 69**

1. Raise and safely support the vehicle.
2. Remove the rear wheel and tire assemblies.
3. Remove the brake drums.
4. Make sure the stops on the parking brake
levers are against the edge of the shoe web. If the
parking brake cable is holding the stops off of the
edge of the shoe web, loosen the parking brake
cable adjustment.
5. Measure the inside diameter of the brake
drum using tool J-21177-A or equivalent.
6. Turn the adjuster nut until the brake shoe
diameter is 0.050 in. (1.27mm) less than the inside
drum diameter for each rear wheel.
7. Install the brake drums and the wheel and
tire assemblies.

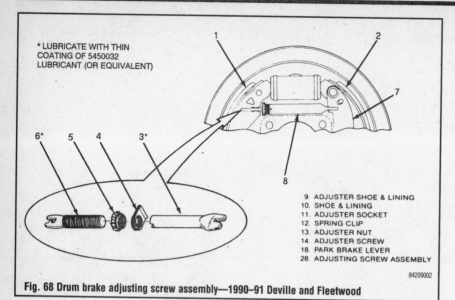

* LUBRICATE WITH THIN
COATING OF 5450032
LUBRICANT (OR EQUIVALENT)

9. ADJUSTER SHOE & LINING
10. SHOE & LINING
11. ADJUSTER SOCKET
12. SPRING CLIP
13. ADJUSTER NUT
14. ADJUSTER SCREW
18. PARK BRAKE LEVER
28. ADJUSTING SCREW ASSEMBLY

84209002

Fig. 68 Drum brake adjusting screw assembly—1990–91 Deville and Fleetwood

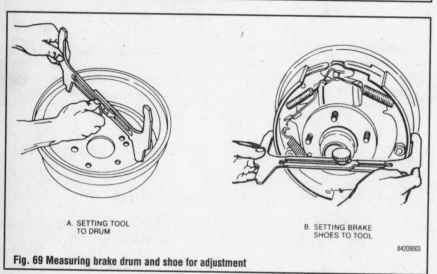

A. SETTING TOOL
TO DRUM

B. SETTING BRAKE
SHOES TO TOOL

84209003

Fig. 69 Measuring brake drum and shoe for adjustment

8. Lower the vehicle.

9. Apply and release the brake pedal 30–35 times using normal pedal force, pausing about one second between applications.

Wheel Cylinders

REMOVAL & INSTALLATION

♦ See Figure 70

1. On 1990 vehicles with anti-lock brakes, depressurize the hydraulic accumulator. Refer to Teves Mk II Anti-Lock Brake System.

✷✷✷ CAUTION

The hydraulic system contains brake fluid at extremely high pressure. It is mandatory that the system be depressurized before disconnecting any hoses, lines or fittings, or personal injury may result.

2. Raise and safely support the vehicle.

3. Remove the wheel and tire assembly and the brake drum.

4. Clean the area around the wheel cylinder inlet, pilot and bleeder valve.

5. Remove the brake shoes.

6. Remove the bleeder valve.

7. Disconnect the brake line from the wheel cylinder. Plug the opening in the line to prevent fluid loss.

8. Remove the wheel cylinder mounting bolts and the wheel cylinder.

9. Clean the old sealant from the backing plate where the wheel cylinder was removed. Clean the sealant from the wheel cylinder if it is to be reinstalled.

To install:

10. Apply Loctite® Master Gasket or equivalent, to the wheel cylinder shoulder face that contacts the backing plate.

11. Position the wheel cylinder and install the mounting bolts. Tighten the mounting bolts to 106 inch lbs. (12 Nm).

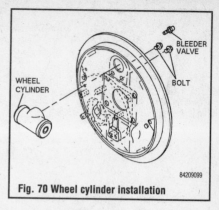

WHEEL
CYLINDER

BLEEDER
VALVE

BOLT

84209099

Fig. 70 Wheel cylinder installation

12. Connect the brake line to the wheel cylinder and tighten the fitting to 11 ft. lbs. (15 Nm).

13. Install the bleeder valve and tighten to 88 inch lbs. (10 Nm).

14. Install the brake shoes. Adjust the brake shoes and install the brake drum.

15. Bleed the brake system.

16. Install the wheel and tire assembly and lower the vehicle. Check the parking brake adjustment.

OVERHAUL

♦ See Figures 71 thru 80

Wheel cylinder overhaul kits may be available, but often at little or no savings over a reconditioned wheel cylinder. It often makes sense with these components to substitute a new or reconditioned part instead of attempting an overhaul.

If no replacement is available, or you would prefer to overhaul your wheel cylinders, the following procedure may be used. When rebuilding and installing wheel cylinders, avoid getting any contaminants into the system. Always use clean, new, high quality brake fluid. If dirty or improper fluid has been used, it will be necessary to drain the entire system, flush the system with proper brake fluid, replace all rubber components, then refill and bleed the system.

1. Remove the wheel cylinder from the vehicle and place on a clean workbench.

2. First remove and discard the old rubber boots, then withdraw the pistons. Piston cylinders

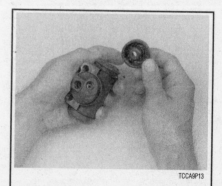

TCCA9P13

Fig. 71 Remove the outer boots from the wheel cylinder

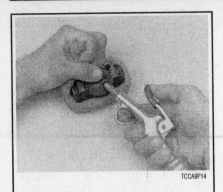

Fig. 72 Compressed air can be used to remove the pistons and seals

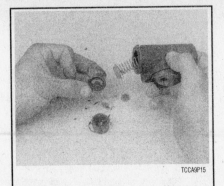

Fig. 73 Remove the pistons, cup seals and spring from the cylinder

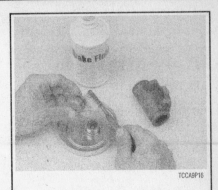

Fig. 74 Use brake fluid and a soft brush to clean the pistons . . .

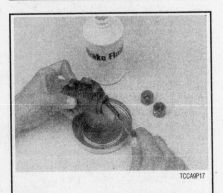

Fig. 75 . . . and the bore of the wheel cylinder

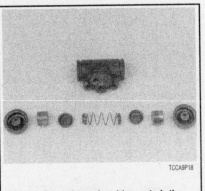

Fig. 76 Once cleaned and inspected, the wheel cylinder is ready for assembly

Fig. 77 Lubricate the cup seals with brake fluid

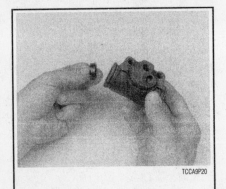

Fig. 78 Install the spring, then the cup seals in the bore

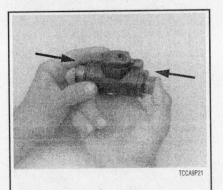

Fig. 79 Lightly lubricate the pistons, then install them

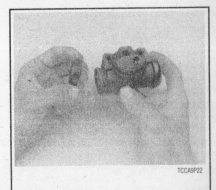

Fig. 80 The boots can now be installed over the wheel cylinder ends

are equipped with seals and a spring assembly, all located behind the pistons in the cylinder bore.

3. Remove the remaining inner components, seals and spring assembly. Compressed air may be useful in removing these components. If no compressed air is available, be VERY careful not to score the wheel cylinder bore when removing parts from it. Discard all components for which replacements were supplied in the rebuild kit.

4. Wash the cylinder and metal parts in denatured alcohol or clean brake fluid.

✳✳ WARNING

Never use a mineral-based solvent such as gasoline, kerosene or paint thinner for cleaning purposes. These solvents will swell rubber components and quickly deteriorate them.

5. Allow the parts to air dry or use compressed air. Do not use rags for cleaning, since lint will remain in the cylinder bore.

6. Inspect the piston and replace it if it shows scratches.

7. Lubricate the cylinder bore and seals using clean brake fluid.

8. Position the spring assembly.

9. Install the inner seals, then the pistons.

10. Insert the new boots into the counterbores by hand. Do not lubricate the boots.

11. Install the wheel cylinder.

REAR DISC BRAKES

Brake Pads

REMOVAL & INSTALLATION

1990–91 Eldorado and Seville

▶ See Figures 81 thru 86

1. Use a syringe or similar tool to remove ⅓ of the brake fluid from the master cylinder reservoir.
2. Raise and safely support the vehicle.
3. Remove the wheel and tire assembly, then reinstall 2 lug nuts to retain the disc brake rotor.
4. Remove the disc brake caliper from the rotor and mounting bracket, but do not disconnect the brake hose from the caliper. Suspend the caliper with wire from the strut.

> ❊❊ **WARNING**
>
> **Do not let the caliper hang from the brake hose. The hose may become damaged, causing possible brake failure.**

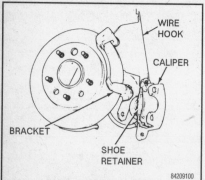

Fig. 81 Suspend the caliper with wire from the strut; do not let the caliper hang from the brake hose

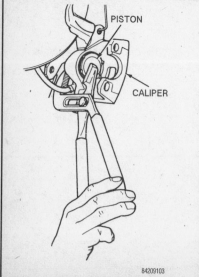

Fig. 84 Compressing the caliper piston— 1990–91 Eldorado and Seville

5. Remove the outboard disc brake pad by unsnapping the springs from the caliper holes.
6. Press in on the edge of the inboard disc brake pad from the open side of the caliper, and tilt outward to release the pad from the retainer.
7. Remove the bushings from the mounting bolt holes in the caliper mounting bracket.
8. Remove the 2-way check valve from the end of the caliper piston using a small prybar.

➡ **If evidence of leakage can be seen at the piston hole after the check valve is removed, replace the actuator and overhaul the caliper.**

To install:

9. Position suitable adjustable pliers over the caliper housing and piston surface, and bottom the caliper piston in the caliper bore. After the piston is

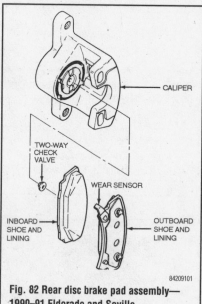

Fig. 82 Rear disc brake pad assembly— 1990–91 Eldorado and Seville

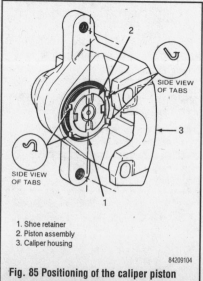

1. Shoe retainer
2. Piston assembly
3. Caliper housing

Fig. 85 Positioning of the caliper piston and disc brake pad retainer—1990–91 Eldorado and Seville

bottomed, lift the inner edge of the boot next to the piston and press out any trapped air. The boot must lay flat.

> ❊❊ **WARNING**
>
> **Do not let the pliers contact the actuator screw. Protect the piston so the surface will not be damaged.**

10. Lubricate new bushings with silicone grease and install them in the mounting bolt holes in the caliper mounting bracket.
11. Lubricate a new 2-way check valve and install it into the end of the caliper piston.
12. Install the inboard disc brake pad as follows:

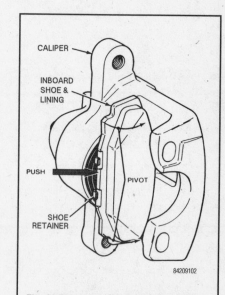

Fig. 83 Removing the inboard disc brake pad—1990–91 Eldorado and Seville

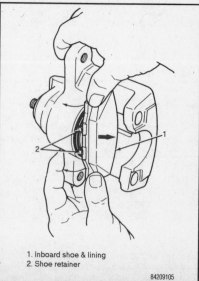

1. Inboard shoe & lining
2. Shoe retainer

Fig. 86 Installing the inboard disc brake pad—1990–91 Eldorado and Seville

a. Engage the inboard pad edge in the straight tabs on the retainer, press down and snap the pad under the S-shaped tabs. The back of the pad must lay flat against the caliper piston.

b. Make sure the pad retainer and piston are properly positioned. The tabs on the pad retainer are different; rotate the retainer if necessary.

c. The buttons on the back of the pad must engage the D-shaped notches in the piston. The piston will be properly aligned when the D-shaped notches are aligned with the caliper mounting bolt holes. Turn the piston with spanner wrench J-7624 or equivalent, if necessary.

13. Install the outboard disc brake pad with the wear sensor at the trailing edge of the pad during forward wheel rotation. Snap the pad springs fully into the caliper holes. The back of the pad must lay flat against the caliper.

14. Install the disc brake caliper.

15. Install the wheel and tire assembly and lower the vehicle.

16. Apply the brake pedal several times to seat the brake pads in the caliper.

17. Check the brake fluid level in the master cylinder and add fluid as necessary.

1992–98 Eldorado and Seville; 1994–98 Deville

▶ See Figures 87 thru 95

1. Use a syringe or similar tool to remove ⅔ of the brake fluid from the master cylinder reservoir.

2. Raise and safely support the vehicle.

3. Remove the wheel and tire assembly, then reinstall 2 lug nuts to retain the disc brake rotor.

4. Remove the bolt and washer attaching the cable support bracket to the caliper.

➡It is not necessary to disconnect the parking brake cable from the caliper parking brake lever or disconnect the brake hose unless the caliper is to be completely removed from the vehicle. Freeing the cable support bracket provides enough flexibility in the cable to pivot the caliper up and remove the disc brake pads.

5. Remove the sleeve bolt.

6. Pivot the caliper upward; do not completely remove the caliper.

7. Remove the disc brake pads and clips from the caliper mounting bracket.

To install:

8. Use a suitable tool in the caliper piston slots to turn the piston and thread it into the caliper. After bottoming the piston, lift the inner edge of the boot next to the piston and press out any trapped air. The boot must lay flat.

➡Make sure the slots in the end of the caliper piston are positioned as shown in the figure before pivoting the caliper down over the brake pads in the caliper support. Use a suitable tool in the piston slots to turn the piston as necessary.

9. Install 2 new pad clips in the caliper mounting bracket. New clips should always be used when replacing the disc brake pads.

10. Install the disc brake pads in the caliper

mounting bracket with the wear sensor on the outboard pad positioned downward at the leading edge of the rotor during forward wheel rotation. Hold the metal pad edge against the spring end of the clips in the caliper mounting bracket, then push the pad in toward the hub, bending the spring ends slightly, and engage the pad notches with the bracket abutments.

11. Pivot the caliper down over the disc brake pads, being careful not to damage the piston boot on the inboard pad. Compress the sleeve boot by hand as the caliper moves into position, to prevent boot damage.

➡After the caliper is in position, recheck the installation of the pad clips. If necessary, use a suitable tool to reseat or center the pad clips on the bracket abutments.

12. Install the sleeve bolt and tighten to 20 ft. lbs. (27 Nm).

13. Install the cable support bracket (with the cable attached) with the bolt and washer. Tighten the bolt to 32 ft. lbs. (43 Nm).

14. Install the wheel and tire assembly and lower the vehicle.

15. Apply the brake pedal several times to seat the brake pads against the rotor.

16. Check the brake fluid level in the master cylinder and add fluid as necessary.

INSPECTION

Refer to brake pad inspection under Front Disc Brakes.

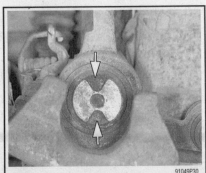

Fig. 87 Remove the locating pins

Fig. 88 The caliper may need a little gentle prying to help release it from the retaining bracket

Fig. 89 Once the caliper is free, remove it from the bracket and support it

Fig. 90 The caliper piston on the rear calipers requires a special tool to retract the piston

Fig. 91 A special adapter is needed with small prongs that insert into the indents on the caliper piston

Fig. 92 Place the adapter on the caliper tool and . . .

Fig. 93 . . . install the tool in the caliper

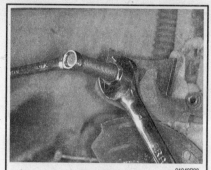

Fig. 94 While holding the nut, turn the forcing screw to rotate the caliper piston into the caliper until it bottoms out

Fig. 95 A coating of Disc Brake Quiet or equivalent silencer should be applied to the backs of the new pads

Brake Caliper

REMOVAL & INSTALLATION

1990–91 Eldorado and Seville

▶ See Figures 96, 97, 98 and 99

1. On 1990 vehicles with anti-lock brakes, depressurize the hydraulic accumulator. Refer to Teves Mk II Anti-Lock Brake System.

✸✸ CAUTION

The hydraulic system contains brake fluid at extremely high pressure. It is mandatory that the system be depressurized before disconnecting any hoses, lines or fittings, or personal injury may result.

2. Use a syringe or similar tool to remove ⅓ of the brake fluid from the master cylinder reservoir.

3. Raise and safely support the vehicle.

4. Remove the wheel and tire assembly, then reinstall 2 lug nuts to retain the disc brake rotor.

5. Loosen the tension on the parking brake cable at the equalizer.

6. Remove the retaining clip from the parking brake lever.

7. Remove the parking brake cable and return spring, then remove the damper from the return spring.

8. Hold the parking brake lever and remove the locknut.

9. Remove the parking brake lever, lever seal and antifriction washer, and check them for cuts, nicks and excessive wear. Replace any worn or damaged parts.

10. Bottom the piston into the caliper bore to provide clearance between the disc brake pads and rotor.

11. Reinstall the anti-friction washer, lever seal (sealing bead against housing), lever and nut.

12. If the caliper is to be removed from the vehicle, remove the bolt attaching the brake hose to the caliper. Discard the gaskets. Plug the openings in the caliper and brake hose to prevent fluid loss.

13. Remove the mounting bolts and remove the caliper from the rotor and mounting bracket. If only the disc brake pads are being replaced, suspend the caliper with wire from the strut.

✸✸ WARNING

Do not let the caliper hang from the brake hose. The hose may become damaged, causing possible brake failure.

To install:

14. Inspect the bolt boots and mounting bracket support bushings for cuts, tears or deterioration and replace as necessary. Inspect the mounting bolts for corrosion and replace them and the bushings if any is found; do not try to polish away corrosion.

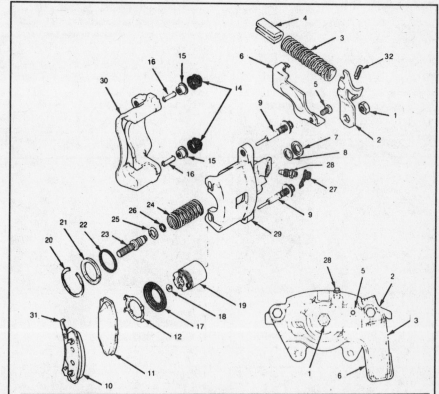

1	NUT	12	SHOE RETAINER	23	ACTUATOR SCREW
2	PARK BRAKE LEVER	14	BOLT BOOT	24	BALANCE SPRING & RETAINER
3	RETURN SPRING	15	SUPPORT BUSHING	25	THRUST WASHER
4	DAMPER	16	BUSHING	26	SHAFT SEAL
5	BOLT	17	CALIPER PISTON BOOT	27	CAP
6	BRACKET	18	TWO-WAY CHECK VALVE	28	BLEEDER VALVE
7	LEVER SEAL	19	PISTON ASSEMBLY	29	CALIPER HOUSING
8	ANTI-FRICTION WASHER	20	RETAINER	30	BRACKET
9	MOUNTING BOLT	21	PISTON LOCATOR	31	WEAR SENSOR
10	OUTBOARD SHOE & LINING	22	PISTON SEAL	32	RETAING CLIP
11	INBOARD SHOE & LINING				

Fig. 96 Rear disc brake caliper assembly—1990–91 Eldorado and Seville

15. Position the caliper over the rotor in the mounting bracket, making sure the bolt boots are in place.

16. Lubricate the shaft of the mounting bolts with silicone grease. Install the bolts and tighten to 63 ft. lbs. (85 Nm).

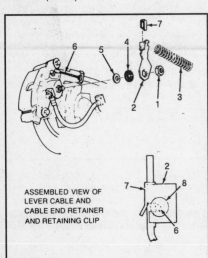

ASSEMBLED VIEW OF
LEVER CABLE AND
CABLE END RETAINER
AND RETAINING CLIP

1. Nut
2. Park brake lever
3. Return spring
4. Lever seal
5. Anti-friction
   washer
6. Parking brake
   cable
7. Retainer clip
8. Cable end
   retainer

84209111

Fig. 97 Parking brake cable-to-caliper attachment—1990–91 Eldorado and Seville

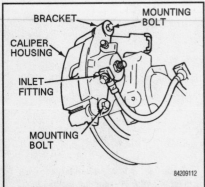

BRACKET
MOUNTING BOLT
CALIPER HOUSING
INLET FITTING
MOUNTING BOLT

84209112

Fig. 98 Caliper mounting—1990–91 Eldorado and Seville

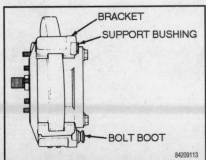

BRACKET
SUPPORT BUSHING
BOLT BOOT

84209113

Fig. 99 Bolt boot and support bushing—1990–91 Eldorado and Seville

17. Position the brake hose on the disc brake caliper. Connect the hose to the caliper using the attaching bolt and 2 new gaskets. Tighten the bolt to 32 ft. lbs. (44 Nm).

18. Disconnect the nut, parking brake lever, lever seal and anti-friction washer. Clean any contamination from the caliper surface in the area of the lever seal and around the actuator screw.

19. Install the anti-friction washer.

20. Lubricate the lever seal and install it with the sealing bead against the caliper housing.

21. Install the parking brake lever on the actuator screw hex with the lever pointing down.

22. Rotate the parking brake lever toward the front of the vehicle and hold in position. Install the nut and tighten to 35 ft. lbs. (48 Nm), then rotate the lever back against the stop on the caliper.

23. Install the damper and return spring.

24. Connect the parking brake cable. Install the retaining clip on the lever to keep the cable from sliding out of the slot in the lever.

25. Bleed the brake system.

26. Install the wheel and tire assembly and lower the vehicle. Check the parking brake adjustment.

1992–98 Eldorado and Seville

▶ See Figures 100 and 101

1. Raise and safely support the vehicle.

2. Remove the wheel and tire assembly.

3. If the caliper is to be removed from the vehicle, remove the bolt attaching the brake hose to the caliper. Discard the gaskets. Plug the openings in the caliper and brake hose to prevent fluid loss.

4. If the caliper is to be removed from the vehicle, lift up on the end of the parking brake cable spring to free the end of the cable from the parking brake lever.

5. Remove the bolt and washer attaching the cable support bracket to the caliper.

6. Remove the sleeve bolt, pivot the caliper up to clear the rotor and then slide it inboard off the pin sleeve.

7. If the caliper is being removed only for brake pad replacement or to provide access to the mounting bracket, rotor or other components, suspend the caliper with wire from the strut.

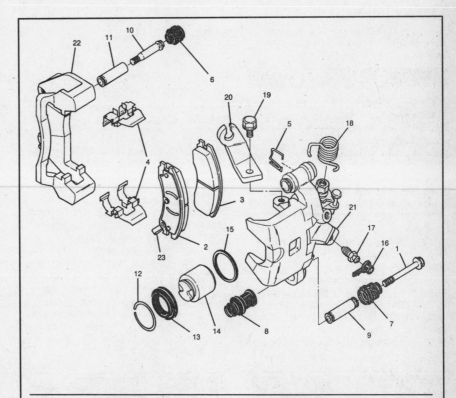

1	SLEEVE BOLT	13	PISTON BOOT
2	OUTBOARD SHOE & LINING	14	PISTON ASSEMBLY
3	INBOARD SHOE & LINING	15	PISTON SEAL
4	PAD CLIP	16	BLEEDER VALVE CAP
5	CABLE SPRING CLIP	17	BLEEDER VALVE
6	PIN BOOT	18	LEVER RETURN SPRING
7	BOLT BOOT	19	BOLT AND WASHER
8	SLEEVE BOLT	20	CABLE SUPPORT BRACKET
9	BOLT SLEEVE	21	CALIPER BODY ASSEMBLY
10	PIN BOLT	22	CALIPER SUPPORT
11	PIN SLEEVE	23	WEAR SENSOR
12	BOOT RING		

84209114

Fig. 100 Rear disc brake caliper assembly—1992–98 Eldorado and Seville

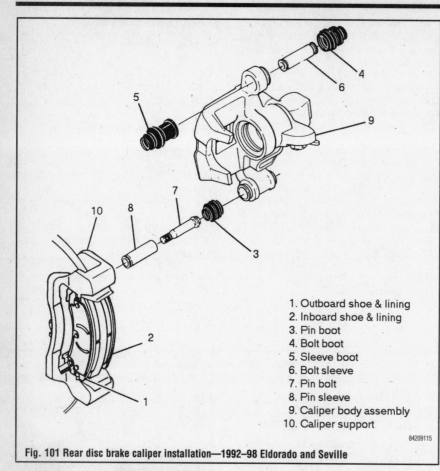

1. Outboard shoe & lining
2. Inboard shoe & lining
3. Pin boot
4. Bolt boot
5. Sleeve boot
6. Bolt sleeve
7. Pin bolt
8. Pin sleeve
9. Caliper body assembly
10. Caliper support

84209115

Fig. 101 Rear disc brake caliper installation—1992–98 Eldorado and Seville

✳ WARNING

Do not let the caliper hang from the brake hose. The hose may become damaged, causing possible brake failure.

To install:

8. Inspect the pin boot, bolt boot and sleeve boot for cuts, tears or deterioration and replace as necessary.

9. Inspect the bolt sleeve and pin sleeve for corrosion or damage. Pull the boots to gain access to the sleeves for inspection or replacement. Replace corroded or damaged sleeves; do not try to polish away corrosion.

10. If not replaced, remove the pin boot from the caliper and install the small end over the pin sleeve (installed on caliper support) until the boot seats in the pin groove. This prevents cutting the pin boot when sliding the caliper onto the pin sleeve.

11. Hold the caliper in the position it was removed and start it over the end of the pin sleeve. As the caliper approaches the pin boot, work the large end of the pin boot in the caliper groove, then push the caliper fully onto the pin.

12. Pivot the caliper down, being careful not to damage the piston boot on the inboard disc brake pad. Compress the sleeve boot by hand as the caliper moves into position to prevent boot damage.

13. After the caliper is in position, recheck the position of the pad clips. If necessary, use a small prybar to reseat or center the pad clips on the bracket abutments.

14. Install the sleeve bolt and tighten to 20 ft. lbs. (27 Nm).

15. Install the cable support bracket (with cable attached) with the bolt and washer and tighten to 32 ft. lbs. (43 Nm).

16. Lift up on the end of the cable spring clip and work the end of the parking brake cable into the notch in the lever.

17. Position the brake hose on the disc brake caliper. Connect the hose to the caliper using the attaching bolt and 2 new gaskets. Tighten the bolt to 32 ft. lbs. (44 Nm).

18. Bleed the brake system.

19. Install the wheel and tire assembly and lower the vehicle. Check the parking brake adjustment.

OVERHAUL

Refer to brake caliper overhaul under Front Disc Brakes.

Brake Disc (Rotor)

REMOVAL & INSTALLATION

▶ **See Figures 102, 103, 104 and 105**

1. Raise and safely support the vehicle.
2. Remove the wheel and tire assembly.
3. Remove the brake caliper and suspend it with wire from the strut; do not let the caliper hang from the brake hose.
4. On 1992–98 vehicles, remove the disc brake pads from the caliper mounting bracket.

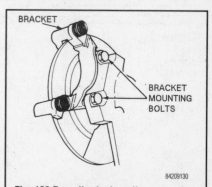

84209130

Fig. 102 Rear disc brake caliper mounting bracket—1990–91 Eldorado and Seville

91049P20

Fig. 103 Remove the caliper bracket bolts and pull the caliper and bracket off of the knuckle

91049P21

Fig. 104 Grasp the rotor and pull it off of the hub and knuckle assembly

91049P23

Fig. 105 Cleaning the hub off any rust build-up is a good idea before reinstalling the rotor

5. Remove the caliper mounting bracket mounting bolts and the mounting bracket.

6. If equipped, remove the retainers from the wheel studs and discard; they do not have to be reinstalled.

7. Remove the disc brake rotor. Inspect the rotor and machine or replace, as necessary.

To install:

8. Install the disc brake rotor over the wheel studs and hub assembly.

9. Install the caliper mounting bracket using new mounting bolts. Tighten the bolts to 83 ft. lbs. (112 Nm).

10. On 1992–98 vehicles, install the disc brake pads in the caliper mounting bracket.

11. Install the brake caliper.

12. Install the wheel and tire assembly and lower the vehicle.

INSPECTION

Refer to brake rotor inspection under Front Disc Brakes.

PARKING BRAKE

Cables

REMOVAL & INSTALLATION

1990–93 Deville and Fleetwood

▶ **See Figure 106**

FRONT CABLE

1. Raise and safely support the vehicle.
2. Loosen the adjuster.
3. Remove the cable from the adjuster.
4. Remove the cable retaining nut from the underbody of the vehicle.
5. Lower the vehicle and remove the cable from the lever assembly.

To install:

6. Attach the cable to the lever assembly.
7. Raise and safely support the vehicle.
8. Install the cable retaining nut and tighten to 22 ft. lbs. (30 Nm).
9. Attach the cable to the adjuster.
10. Adjust the parking brake cable and lower the vehicle.

INTERMEDIATE CABLE

1. Raise and safely support the vehicle.
2. Disconnect the cable from the adjuster.
3. On 1990–91 vehicles, proceed as follows:
   a. Remove the cable from the front bracket.
   b. Disconnect the cable from the clips and retainers.
   c. Disconnect the cable from the rear equalizer.
4. On 1992–93 vehicles, proceed as follows:
   a. Remove the clip from the brake line retainer and cable.
   b. Disconnect the cable from the rear equalizer.
   c. Remove the cable from the bracket and brake line retainers.

To install:

5. On 1990–91 vehicles, proceed as follows:
   a. Connect the cable to the rear equalizer.
   b. Attach the cable to the clips and retainers.
   c. Install the cable through the front bracket.
   d. Connect the cable to the adjuster.
   e. Adjust the parking brake cable and lower the vehicle.
6. On 1992–93 vehicles, proceed as follows:
   a. Snap the cable into the bracket.
   b. Install the cable through the top support hole in the vehicle underbody.
   c. Connect the cable to the rear equalizer.
   d. Install the clip around the cable and then to the brake line retainer. Tighten the bolt to 17 inch lbs. (3 Nm).
   e. Connect the cable to the adjuster.
   f. Adjust the parking brake cable.

g. Install the cable into the brake line retainers and lower the vehicle.

REAR CABLES

1. Raise and safely support the vehicle.
2. Back off the adjuster nut to release the cable tension.
3. Remove the wheel and tire assembly and the brake drum.

4. Disconnect the cable from the brake shoe parking brake lever.

5. Depress the conduit fitting retaining tangs and remove the conduit fitting from the backing plate.

6. If removing the left rear cable on 1990 vehicles, proceed as follows:
   a. Back off the equalizer nut and disconnect the cable from the equalizer.

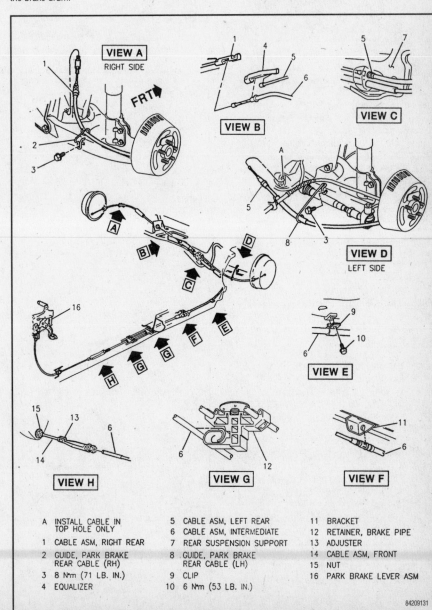

A	INSTALL CABLE IN TOP HOLE ONLY	5	CABLE ASM, LEFT REAR	11	BRACKET
1	CABLE ASM, RIGHT REAR	6	CABLE ASM, INTERMEDIATE	12	RETAINER, BRAKE PIPE
2	GUIDE, PARK BRAKE REAR CABLE (RH)	7	REAR SUSPENSION SUPPORT	13	ADJUSTER
		8	GUIDE, PARK BRAKE REAR CABLE (LH)	14	CABLE ASM, FRONT
3	8 N·m (71 LB. IN.)	9	CLIP	15	NUT
4	EQUALIZER	10	6 N·m (53 LB. IN.)	16	PARK BRAKE LEVER ASM

84209131

Fig. 106 Parking brake cables—1992–93 Deville and Fleetwood; 1990–91 models similar

b. Depress the conduit fitting retaining tangs and remove the conduit fitting from the axle bracket.

c. Remove the 2 attaching screws, then remove the conduit fitting from the underbody bracket.

7. If removing the right rear cable on 1990 vehicles, proceed as follows:

a. Disconnect the cable end button from the connector.

b. Depress the conduit fitting retaining tangs and remove the conduit fitting from the axle bracket.

8. On all other vehicles, remove the cable from the equalizer, the frame retaining hole and the rear parking brake guide.

To install:

9. If installing the right rear cable on 1990 vehicles, proceed as follows:

a. Install the conduit fitting retaining tangs and conduit fitting into the axle bracket.

b. Attach the cable end button to the connector.

10. If installing the left rear cable on 1990 vehicles, proceed as follows:

a. Install the conduit fitting retaining tangs and conduit fitting into the axle bracket.

b. Attach the left cable to the equalizer nut.

c. Install the conduit fitting to the underbody bracket and tighten the mounting screws to 84 inch lbs. (10 Nm).

11. On all other vehicles, install the cable through the rear parking brake guide and snap the cable into place in the retaining hole. Attach the cable to the equalizer.

12. Install the conduit fitting into the backing plate.

13. Attach the cable to the brake shoe parking brake lever.

14. Install the brake drum and the wheel and tire assembly.

15. Adjust the parking brake cable and lower the vehicle.

Eldorado and Seville; 1994–98 Deville

♦ **See Figure 107**

FRONT CABLE

1. Raise and safely support the vehicle.
2. Disconnect the front cable from the intermediate cable at the adjuster.
3. Disengage the cable housing retainer/nut at the point where the cable passes through the underbody.
4. Lower the vehicle.
5. Remove the left dash close-out panel/sound insulator.
6. Disconnect the cable from the pedal assembly and remove it from the vehicle.

To install:

7. Position the cable in the vehicle and attach it to the pedal assembly.
8. Install the close-out panel/sound insulator.
9. Raise and safely support the vehicle.
10. Connect the front cable to the intermediate cable at the adjuster.
11. Adjust the parking brake cable and lower the vehicle.

INTERMEDIATE CABLE

1. Raise and safely support the vehicle.
2. Disconnect the front cable from the intermediate cable at the adjuster.
3. Remove the adjuster from the intermediate cable.
4. Disconnect the left rear, right rear and intermediate cables at the equalizer.
5. Remove the intermediate cable from the vehicle.

To install:

6. Install the intermediate cable through the retainers as shown in the illustration.
7. Connect the intermediate and rear cables at the equalizer.
8. Install the adjuster at the forward end of intermediate cable.
9. Connect the intermediate cable to the front cable at the adjuster.
10. Adjust the parking brake cable and lower the vehicle.

REAR CABLES

1. Raise and safely support the vehicle.
2. Remove the wheel and tire assembly on the side of the vehicle from which the cable is being removed.
3. Loosen the cable at the adjuster.
4. Disconnect the left rear, right rear and intermediate cables at the equalizer.
5. Disengage the cable retainer from the rear suspension crossmember.
6. Remove the cable from the caliper. Remove the retainer clip from the lever and the cable from the lever slot, then disengage the cable retainer from the caliper bracket.
7. Remove the cable from the vehicle.

To install:

8. Install the cable in the retainers as shown in the illustration.
9. Install the cable in the caliper. Install the cable retainer in the caliper bracket: Position the cable in the lever slot and install the retainer clip on the lever.
10. Connect the intermediate and rear cables at the equalizer.
11. Adjust the parking brake cable.
12. Install the wheel and tire assembly and lower the vehicle.

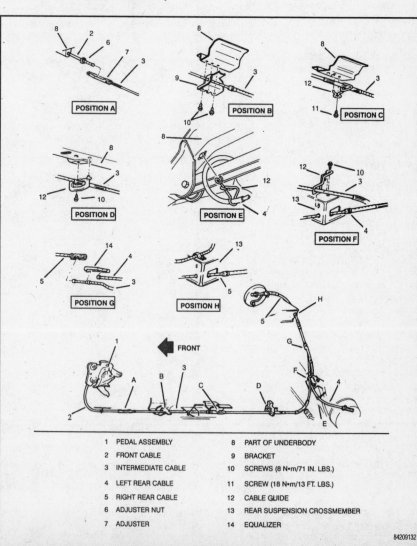

1	PEDAL ASSEMBLY	8	PART OF UNDERBODY
2	FRONT CABLE	9	BRACKET
3	INTERMEDIATE CABLE	10	SCREWS (8 N•m/71 IN. LBS.)
4	LEFT REAR CABLE	11	SCREW (18 N•m/13 FT. LBS.)
5	RIGHT REAR CABLE	12	CABLE GUIDE
6	ADJUSTER NUT	13	REAR SUSPENSION CROSSMEMBER
7	ADJUSTER	14	EQUALIZER

84209132

Fig. 107 Parking brake cables—Eldorado and Seville

ADJUSTMENT

Deville and Fleetwood

▶ **See Figures 106, 108 and 109**

1. Make sure the brake shoes are properly adjusted.

2. Apply and release the parking brake 6 times to 10 clicks, then release the parking brake pedal.

3. Check the parking brake pedal for full release by turning the ignition **ON** and checking the 'BRAKE' warning light. The light should be OFF. If

the light is ON and the brake appears to be released, operate the pedal release lever and pull downward on the front parking brake cable to remove slack from the assembly.

4. Raise and safely support the vehicle.

5. Remove the access hole plugs in the rear brake backing plates.

6. Adjust the parking brake cable until a ⅛ in. drill bit can be inserted through the access hole into the space between the shoeweb and the parking brake lever. The cable is adjusted properly when a ⅛ in. bit will fit into the space, but a ¼ in. bit will not.

7. Apply the parking brake to 4 clicks. The wheels should not move when you try to rotate them in a forward direction; they should drag or not move when you try to rotate them in a rearward direction.

8. Release the parking brake and check for free wheel rotation.

9. Install the access hole plugs and lower the vehicle.

Eldorado and Seville

▶ **See Figure 107**

1. Apply the service brake with a pedal force of approximately 150 lbs. and release.

2. Fully apply the parking brake using approximately 125 lbs. pedal force and release. Apply and release the parking brake in the same manner, 2 more times.

3. Check the parking brake pedal for full release by turning the ignition ON and checking the 'BRAKE' warning light. The light should be OFF. If the light is ON and the brake appears to be released, operate the pedal release lever and pull downward on the front parking brake cable to remove slack from the pedal assembly.

4. Raise and safely support the vehicle.

5. Check the parking brake levers on the rear calipers. The levers should be against the stops on the caliper. If the levers are not against the stops, check for binding in the rear cables and/or loosen the cables at the adjuster until both levers are against their stops.

6. Tighten the parking brake cable at the adjuster until either the left or right lever begins to move off of stop. Then loosen the adjuster until the lever is again resting on the stop. Both levers should now be resting on the stops.

7. Operate the parking brake several times to check the adjustment. A firm pedal feel should be obtained by pumping the pedal less than 3½ full strokes on 1990–91 vehicles or depressing the pedal less than one full stroke on 1992–98 vehicles.

8. Inspect the caliper levers. Both levers must be resting on the stops after adjustment of the parking brake.

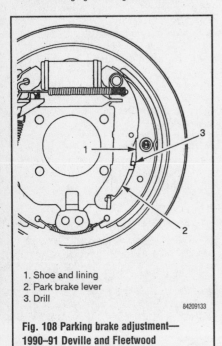

1. Shoe and lining
2. Park brake lever
3. Drill

84209133

Fig. 108 Parking brake adjustment— 1990–91 Deville and Fleetwood

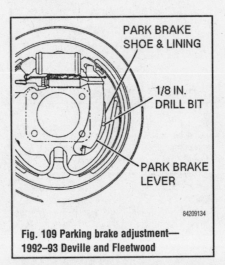

PARK BRAKE SHOE & LINING

1/8 IN. DRILL BIT

PARK BRAKE LEVER

84209134

Fig. 109 Parking brake adjustment— 1992–93 Deville and Fleetwood

ANTI-LOCK BRAKE SYSTEM

General Information

The Anti-lock Brake System (ABS) is an electronically operated, all wheel brake control system. Major components include the vacuum power brake booster, master cylinder, the wheel speed sensors, Hydraulic Control Unit (HCU), control module, a relay, and the pressure control valves.

The system is designed to retard wheel lockup during periods of high wheel slip when braking. Retarding wheel lockup is accomplished by modulating fluid pressure to the wheel brake units. When the control module detects a variation in voltage across the wheel speed sensors, the ABS is activated. The control module opens and closes various valves located inside the HCU. These valves, called dump and isolation valves, modulate the hydraulic pressure to the wheels by applying and venting the pressure to the brake fluid circuits.

TEVES MK II

▶ **See Figures 110 and 111**

The Teves Mk II Anti-lock Brake System (ABS) is only used on all 1990 vehicles. The system uses a combination of wheel speed sensors and a micro-

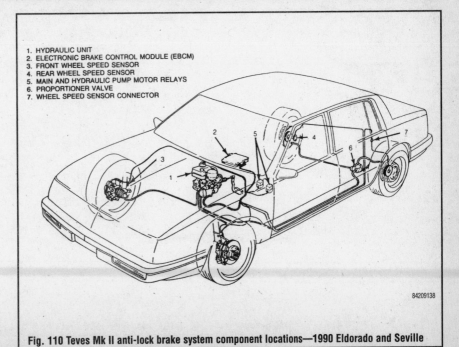

1. HYDRAULIC UNIT
2. ELECTRONIC BRAKE CONTROL MODULE (EBCM)
3. FRONT WHEEL SPEED SENSOR
4. REAR WHEEL SPEED SENSOR
5. MAIN AND HYDRAULIC PUMP MOTOR RELAYS
6. PROPORTIONER VALVE
7. WHEEL SPEED SENSOR CONNECTOR

84209138

Fig. 110 Teves Mk II anti-lock brake system component locations—1990 Eldorado and Seville

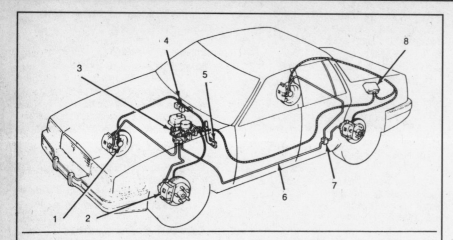

1	WHEEL SPEED SENSOR AND TOOTHED SENSOR RING (ONE AT EACH WHEEL)	5	PEDAL
2	CALIPER (ONE AT EACH WHEEL)	6	REAR BRAKE PIPE
3	HYDRAULIC UNIT	7	PROPORTIONER/TEE
4	RELAY BRACKET	8	ELECTRONIC BRAKE CONTROL MODULE (EBCM)

84209139

Fig. 111 Teves Mk II anti-lock brake system component locations—1990 Deville and Fleetwood

processor to determine impending wheel lock-up and adjust the brake pressure to maintain the best braking. The Teves Mk II system components include a Electronic Brake Control Module (EBCM), a separate control relay, hydraulic control unit (HCU), and 4 wheel speed sensors (one at each wheel).

TEVES MK IV

▶ **See Figure 112**

The Teves Mk IV anti-lock brake system is used on 1991–93 Deville and Fleetwood. Some vehicles are equipped with a Traction Control System (TCS) in addition to ABS. The TCS prevents the wheels from spinning excessively during acceleration or when turning corners at higher speeds. The TCS also prevents wheel slip on slippery surfaces, allowing improved acceleration ability and vehicle stability. The ABS and TCS are both part of the same hydraulic and electrical system. Both systems use many of the same components; a problem in either system usually will disable the other system until it is repaired.

The Teves Mk IV system components include a Electronic Brake Control Module (EBCM), a pressure modulator valve (also know as the Hydraulic

control unit-HCU), and 4 wheel speed sensors—one on each wheel.

BOSCH ANTI-LOCK BRAKE SYSTEM

▶ **See Figure 113**

The Bosch Anti-lock Brake System (ABS) is used on 1991–98 Eldorado and Seville, and 1994–98 Deville. Some vehicles are equipped with a Traction Control System (TCS) in addition to ABS. The TCS prevents the wheels from spinning excessively during acceleration or when turning corners at higher speeds. The TCS also prevents wheel slip on slippery surfaces, allowing improved acceleration ability and vehicle stability. The ABS and TCS are both part of the same hydraulic and electrical system. Both systems use many of the same components; a problem in either system usually will disable the other system until it is repaired.

The Bosch system components include a Electronic Brake Control Module (EBCM) on non-TCS vehicles or the Electronic Brake and Traction Control Module (EBTCM) on TCS equipped vehicles, a hydraulic modulator (also know as the Hydraulic control unit-HCU), and 4 wheel speed sensors- one on each wheel.

PRECAUTIONS

- Certain components within the ABS system are not intended to be serviced or repaired individually.
- Do not use rubber hoses or other parts not specifically specified for and ABS system. When using repair kits, replace all parts included in the kit. Partial or incorrect repair may lead to functional problems and require the replacement of components.
- Lubricate rubber parts with clean, fresh brake fluid to ease assembly. Do not use shop air to clean parts; damage to rubber components may result.
- Use only DOT 3 brake fluid from an unopened container.
- If any hydraulic component or line is removed or replaced, it may be necessary to bleed the entire system.
- A clean repair area is essential. Always clean the reservoir and cap thoroughly before removing the cap. The slightest amount of dirt in the fluid may plug an orifice and impair the system function. Perform repairs after components have been thoroughly cleaned; use only denatured alcohol to clean components. Do not allow ABS components to come into contact with any substance containing mineral oil; this includes used shop rags.
- The Anti-Lock control unit is a microprocessor similar to other computer units in the vehicle. Ensure that the ignition switch is **OFF** before removing or installing controller harnesses. Avoid static electricity discharge at or near the controller.
- If any arc welding is to be done on the vehicle, the control unit should be unplugged before welding operations begin.

1 FRONT WHEEL SPEED SENSOR

2 ABS RELAYS

3 ELECTRONIC BRAKE CONTROL MODULE (EBCM)

4 REAR WHEEL SPEED SENSOR

5 PROPORTIONER VALVES

6 BRAKE PIPE HARNESS FROM PMV ASSEMBLY

7 PRESSURE MODULATOR VALVE (PMV) ASSEMBLY

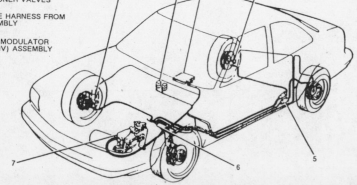

84209150

Fig. 112 Teves Mk IV ABS component locations—1991–93 Deville and Fleetwood

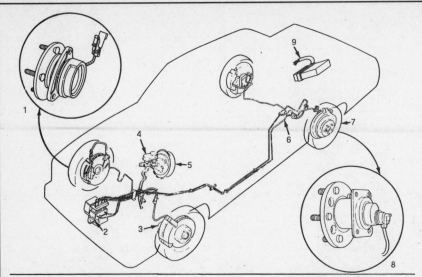

1 FRONT WHEEL SPEED SENSOR INTEGRAL WITH BEARING
2 HYDRAULIC MODULATOR
3 CALIPER
4 MASTER CYLINDER
5 VACUUM ASSIST POWER BRAKE BOOSTER
6 REAR BRAKE CIRCUIT PROPORTIONING VALVES
7 CALIPER
8 REAR WHEEL SPEED SENSOR INTEGRAL WITH BEARING
9 ELECTRONIC BRAKE CONTROL MODULE (EBCM)

84209161

Fig. 113 Bosch anti-lock brake system component locations—1991–92 Eldorado and Seville; 1993–98 vehicles similar

Trouble Codes

READING CODES

Teves Mk II

▶ See Figures 114, 115 and 116

Only certain ABS malfunctions will cause the EBCM to store diagnostic trouble codes. Failures causing a code will generally involve wheel speed sensors, main valve or the inlet and outlet valves. Conditions affecting the pump/motor assembly, the accumulator, pressure switch or fluid level sensor usually do not cause a code to set.

The EBCM will store trouble codes in a non-volatile memory. These codes remain in memory until erased through use of the correct procedure. The codes are NOT erased by disconnecting the EBCM, disconnecting the battery cable or turning off the ignition. Always be sure to clear the codes

from the memory after repairs are made. To read stored ABS trouble codes:

1. Turn ignition switch to **NO**. Allow the pump to charge the accumulator; if fully discharged, dash warning lights may stay on up to 30 seconds. If ANTI-LOCK warning light does not go off within 30 seconds, note it and go to Step 2.

2. Turn ignition switch to **OFF**.

3. Remove the cover from the ALDL connector. Enter the diagnostic mode by using a jumper wire to connect pins H and A or to connect pin H to body ground. The ALDL is located on the driver's side of the vehicle under the dash.

4. Turn the ignition switch to **RUN** and count the light flashes for the first digit of the first code. The ANTI-LOCK light should illuminate for 4 seconds before beginning to flash. If, after 4 seconds, the light turns off and stays off, no codes are stored.

5. The light will pause for 3 seconds between the first and second digits of the first code and then continue flashing. When counting flashes, count only the ON pulses.

6. When the EBCM is finished transmitting the second digit of the first code, the ANTI-LOCK light will remain on. This last, constant ON should not be counted as a flash. Record the 2-digit code.

7. Without turning the ignition switch **OFF**, disconnect the jumper from pin H and reconnect it. If an additional code is present, it will be displayed in similar fashion to the first. Record the second code.

8. Repeat the disconnection and reconnection of pin H without changing the ignition switch until no more codes are displayed. The system is capable of storing and displaying 7 codes; the ANTI-LOCK warning light will stay on continuously when all codes have been displayed.

9. After recording all codes, remove the jumper from the ALDL and replace the cover.

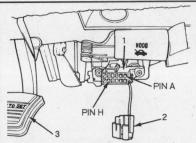

PIN A
PIN H
2
3
TO SET

PLACE JUMBER BETWEEN PINS A AND H (OR BETWEEN H AND GROUND) TO ENTER ABS DIAGNOSTIC MODE

1. ALDL connector
2. ALDL connector cover
3. Parking brake pedal

84209140

Fig. 114 ALDL connector location—1990 Eldorado and Seville; 1990 Deville and Fleetwood similar

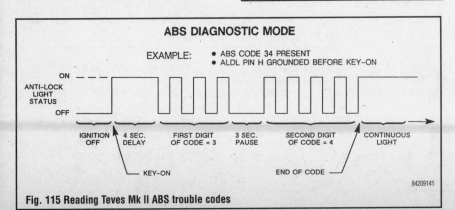

ABS DIAGNOSTIC MODE

EXAMPLE:
● ABS CODE 34 PRESENT
● ALDL PIN H GROUNDED BEFORE KEY-ON

ON
ANTI-LOCK LIGHT STATUS
OFF

IGNITION OFF | 4 SEC. DELAY | FIRST DIGIT OF CODE = 3 | 3 SEC. PAUSE | SECOND DIGIT OF CODE = 4 | CONTINUOUS LIGHT

KEY-ON   END OF CODE

84209141

Fig. 115 Reading Teves Mk II ABS trouble codes

ABS CODE	SYSTEM	ABS CODE	SYSTEM
11	EBCM	45	2 SENSOR (LF)
12	EBCM	46	2 SENSORS (RF)
21	MAIN VALVE	47	2 SENSORS (REAR)
22	LF INLET VALVE	48	3 SENSORS
23	LF OUTLET VALVE	51	LF OUTLET VALVE
24	RF INLET VALVE	52	RF OUTLET VALVE
25	RF OUTLET VALVE	53	REAR OUTLET VALVE
26	REAR INLET VALVE	54	REAR OUTLET VALVE
27	REAR OUTLET VALVE	55	LF WSS
31	LF WSS	56	RF WSS
32	RF WSS	57	RR WSS
33	RR WSS	58	LR WSS
34	LR WSS	61	EBCM LOOP CKT
35	LF WSS	71	LF OUTLET VALVE
36	RF WSS	72	RF OUTLET VALVE
37	RR WSS	73	REAR OUTLET VALVE
38	LR WSS	74	REAR OUTLET VALVE
41	LF WSS	75	LF WSS
42	RF WSS	76	RF WSS
43	RR WSS	77	RR WSS
44	LR WSS	78	LR WSS

84209142

Fig. 116 Teves Mk II ABS trouble codes

➡The ABS trouble codes are not specifically designated current or history codes. If the ANTI-LOCK light is on before entering the ABS diagnostic mode, at least 1 of the stored codes is current. It is impossible to tell which code is current. If the ANTI-LOCK light is off before entering the diagnostic mode, none of the codes are current.

Teves Mk IV

▶ See Figures 117 and 118

The EBCM monitors operating conditions for possible system malfunctions. Malfunctions are detected by comparing system conditions against standard operating limits. Evidence of a malfunction is stored in the computer memory in the form of a 2-digit numerical Diagnostic Trouble Code (DTC).

Trouble codes are accessed by connecting a bi-directional scan tool to the Assembly Line Diagnostic Link (ALDL) connector. Follow the scan tool manufacturer's instructions to read the trouble codes. After all codes have been read and repairs are completed, use the scan tool to clear the codes, then cycle the ignition switch.

'Current' or 'history' codes are not differentiated in the EBCM, however, if the amber ANTILOCK lamp is illuminated before entering the diagnostic mode, at least one DTC is current. If the amber ANTILOCK lamp is not illuminated before entering the diagnostic mode, no DTC is current. If more than one DTC is stored and the amber ANTILOCK lamp was illuminated before entering the diagnostic mode, it is impossible to determine between current and history trouble codes.

Bosch

1991–96 MODELS

▶ See Figures 119, 120, 121, 122 and 123

The EBCM/EBTCM can store several fault codes simultaneously. The order in which the codes are displayed may not indicate the order in which they occurred. If the ANTILOCK warning light is on before displaying the trouble codes, at least 1 of the codes is current, having occurred during the present ignition cycle.

If a scanning diagnostic tool is not available, the system may still be put in the diagnostic mode except when any of the current or hard faults involve the solenoid valves or pump motor. If one or more of the codes is/are Code 41, 45, 55, or 63, diagnostic display of the trouble codes cannot occur until the fault has been repaired. (Use of the scan tool eliminates this problem; all stored codes will display.)

To enter the diagnostic mode and have fault codes transmitted without the use of a scan tool:

1. Turn ignition switch **ON**. If the ANTILOCK warning light does not go out within 4 seconds, make a note of it and continue.

2. Turn ignition switch **OFF**. Remove the cover from the Assembly Line Diagnostic Link (ALDL) connector, located behind the left-hand side of the instrument panel, to the right of the parking brake.

3. Connect a jumper wire between pin H of the ALDL connector and body ground or connect pin H to pin A.

CODE	DESCRIPTION	CODE	DESCRIPTION
21	RF speed sensor circuit open	45	LF inlet valve circuit
22	RF speed sensor signal erratic	46	LF outlet valve circuit
23	RF wheel speed is 0 mph	47	LF speed sensor noisy
25	LF speed sensor circuit open	51	RR inlet valve circuit
26	LF speed sensor signal erratic	52	RR outlet valve circuit
27	LF wheel speed is 0 mph	53	RR speed sensor noisy
31	RR speed sensor circuit open	55	LR inlet valve circuit
32	RR speed sensor signal is erratic	56	LR outlet valve circuit
33	RR wheel speed is 0 mph	57	LR speed sensor noisy
35	LR speed sensor circuit open	61	Pump motor test fault
36	LR speed sensor signal erratic	62	Pump motor fault in ABS stop
37	LR wheel speed is 0 mph	71	EBCM problem
41	RF inlet valve circuit	72	VCC/antilock brake switch circuit.
42	RF outlet valve circuit	73	Fluid level switch circuit
43	RF speed sensor noisy		

84209152

Fig. 117 Teves Mk IV ABS trouble codes—1991 Deville and Fleetwood

DTC	DESCRIPTION	DTC	DESCRIPTION
21	RF speed sensor circuit open	44	LF isolation valve circuit
22	RF speed sensor signal erratic	45	LF inlet valve circuit
23	RF wheel speed is 0 mph	46	LF outlet valve circuit
25	LF speed sensor circuit open	48	RF isolation valve circuit
26	LF speed sensor signal erratic	51	RR inlet valve circuit
27	LF wheel speed is 0 mph	52	RR outlet valve circuit
31	RR speed sensor circuit open	55	LR inlet valve circuit
32	RR speed sensor signal is erratic	56	LR outlet valve circuit
33	RR wheel speed is 0 mph	61	Pump motor test fault
35	LR speed sensor circuit open	62	Pump motor fault in ABS stop
36	LR speed sensor signal erratic	71	EBCM problem
37	LR wheel speed is 0 mph	72	VCC/antilock brake switch circuit
41	RF inlet valve circuit	73	Fluid level switch circuit
42	RF outlet valve circuit	74	PMV pressure switch circuit

84209153

Fig. 118 Teves Mk IV ABS trouble codes—1992–93 Deville and Fleetwood

4. Turn the ignition switch **ON** and watch the ANTILOCK warning light. It should illuminate for 4 seconds and switch off, after which it will flash the stored codes.

5. The first code displayed will be Code 12. This is an initialization code and is not a fault code. It will be displayed as one flash followed by 2 flashes and a pause. Code 12 will be displayed 3 times in succession before fault codes are displayed.

6. Count the light flashes for any stored fault codes. Each stored code will be displayed 3 times before the next code is displayed. Record each code in writing. If no codes are stored, the readout of the Code 12 initialization sequence will begin again.

7. The code readout will repeat until the ground or jumper at the ALDL is removed. After recording all stored codes, disconnect the jumper from the ALDL and reinstall the cover.

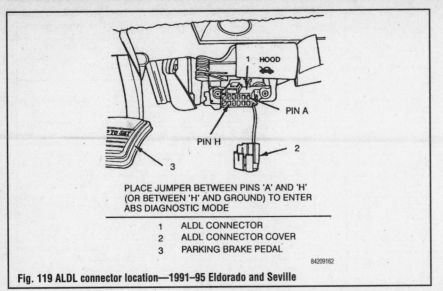

PLACE JUMPER BETWEEN PINS 'A' AND 'H'
(OR BETWEEN 'H' AND GROUND) TO ENTER
ABS DIAGNOSTIC MODE

1 ALDL CONNECTOR
2 ALDL CONNECTOR COVER
3 PARKING BRAKE PEDAL

84209162

Fig. 119 ALDL connector location—1991–95 Eldorado and Seville

FAULT CODE	DESCRIPTION
21	RF WHEEL SPEED SENSOR FAULT
22	RF WHEEL SPEED SENSOR FREQUENCY ERROR
23	RF WHEEL SPEED SENSOR CONTINUITY FAULT
25	LF WHEEL SPEED SENSOR FAULT
26	LF WHEEL SPEED SENSOR FREQUENCY ERROR
27	LF WHEEL SPEED SENSOR CONTINUITY FAULT
28	WHEEL SPEED SENSOR FREQUENCY ERROR
31	RR WHEEL SPEED SENSOR FAULT
32	RR WHEEL SPEED SENSOR FREQUENCY ERROR
33	RR WHEEL SPEED SENSOR CONTINUITY FAULT
35	LR WHEEL SPEED SENSOR FAULT
36	LR WHEEL SPEED SENSOR FREQUENCY ERROR
37	LR WHEEL SPEED SENSOR CONTINUITY FAULT
41	RF ABS VALVE SOLENOID FAULT
44	RF TCS PILOT VALVE FAULT
45	LF ABS VALVE SOLENOID FAULT
48	LF TCS PILOT VALVE FAULT
51	RR ABS VALVE SOLENOID FAULT
55	LR VALVE SOLENOID FAULT (TCS)
55	REAR VALVE SOLENOID FAULT (NON–TCS)
61	PUMP MOTOR OR PUMP MOTOR RELAY FAULT
63	VALVE RELAY CIRCUIT FAULT
67	BRAKE LIGHT SWITCH FAULT
71	EBTCM/EBCM INTERNAL FAULT
72	SERIAL DATA LINK FAULT
73	PCM–EBTCM/EBCM PWM SIGNAL FAULT (4.6L)
83	BRAKE FLUID LEVEL LOW

84209165

Fig. 122 Bosch ABS trouble codes— 1993–94 Eldorado and Seville

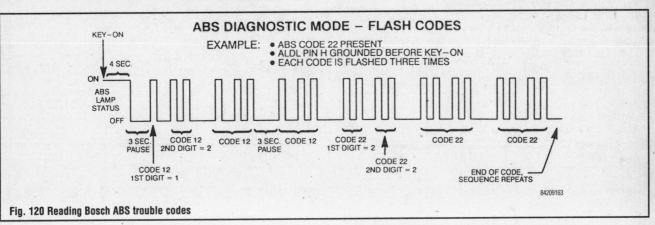

84209163

Fig. 120 Reading Bosch ABS trouble codes

ABS CODE	SYSTEM
21	RIGHT FRONT WHEEL SPEED SENSOR FAULT
22	RIGHT FRONT TOOTHED WHEEL FREQUENCY ERROR
25	LEFT FRONT WHEEL SPEED SENSOR FAULT
26	LEFT FRONT TOOTHED WHEEL FREQUENCY ERROR
31	RIGHT REAR WHEEL SPEED SENSOR FAULT
32	RIGHT REAR TOOTHED WHEEL FREQUENCY ERROR
35	LEFT REAR SPEED SENSOR FAULT
36	LEFT REAR TOOTHED WHEEL FREQUENCY ERROR
41	RIGHT FRONT SOLENOID VALVE FAULT
45	LEFT FRONT SOLENOID VALVE FAULT
55	REAR SOLENOID VALVE FAULT
61	MOTOR PUMP CIRCUIT FAULT
63	SOLENOID VALVE RELAY FAULT
71	ELECTRONIC BRAKE CONTROL MODULE FAULT
72	SERIAL DATA LINK FAULT (TECH 1 ERROR)

84209164

Fig. 121 Bosch ABS trouble codes—1991–92 Eldorado and Seville

DIAGNOSTIC TROUBLE CODE	DESCRIPTION
21	RF WHEEL SPEED SENSOR CIRCUIT MALFUNCTION
23	RF WHEEL SPEED SENSOR CIRCUIT CONTINUITY MALFUNCTION
25	LF WHEEL SPEED SENSOR CIRCUIT MALFUNCTION
27	LF WHEEL SPEED SENSOR CIRCUIT CONTINUITY MALFUNCTION
28	WHEEL SPEED SENSOR CIRCUIT FREQUENCY MALFUNCTION
31	RR WHEEL SPEED SENSOR CIRCUIT MALFUNCTION
33	RR WHEEL SPEED SENSOR CIRCUIT CONTINUITY MALFUNCTION
35	LR WHEEL SPEED SENSOR CIRCUIT MALFUNCTION
37	LR WHEEL SPEED SENSOR CIRCUIT CONTINUITY MALFUNCTION
41	RIGHT FRONT INLET VALVE SOLENOID MALFUNCTION
42	RIGHT FRONT OUTLET VALVE SOLENOID MALFUNCTION
43	RIGHT FRONT TCS PRIME VALVE SOLENOID MALFUNCTION
44	RIGHT FRONT TCS ISOLATION VALVE SOLENOID MALFUNCTION
45	LEFT FRONT INLET VALVE SOLENOID MALFUNCTION
46	LEFT FRONT OUTLET VALVE SOLENOID MALFUNCTION
47	LEFT FRONT TCS PRIME VALVE SOLENOID MALFUNCTION
48	LEFT FRONT TCS ISOLATION VALVE SOLENOID MALFUNCTION
51	RIGHT REAR INLET VALVE SOLENOID MALFUNCTION
52	RIGHT REAR OUTLET VALVE SOLENOID MALFUNCTION
55	LEFT REAR INLET VALVE SOLENOID MALFUNCTION
56	LEFT REAR OUTLET VALVE SOLENOID MALFUNCTION
61	BPM VALVE PUMP MOTOR MALFUNCTION
63	BPM VALVE POWER SUPPLY MALFUNCTION
67	TCC/BLS BRAKE SWITCH MALFUNCTION
71	EBTCM INTERNAL ERROR
72	IPC/SERIAL DATA LINE MALFUNCTION
73	PCM/EBTCM-TCS INTERFACE MALFUNCTION (4.6L ONLY)
77	PCM SERIAL DATA LINE MALFUNCTION
83	LOW BRAKE FLUID
84	PCM TRACTION CONTROL NOT ALLOWED (4.9L)
85	LOW VOLTAGE

91049G19

Fig. 123 Bosch ABS trouble codes—1995–96 Eldorado, Seville and Deville

DTC	DESCRIPTION
C1211	ABS Indicator Lamp Circuit Malfunction
C1214	Solenoid Valve Relay Contact or Coil Circuit Open
C1217	BPMV Pump Motor Relay Contact Circuit Open
C1221	LF Wheel Speed Sensor Input Signal = 0
C1222	RF Wheel Speed Sensor Input Signal = 0
C1223	LR Wheel Speed Sensor Input Signal = 0
C1224	RR Wheel Speed Sensor Input Signal = 0
C1225	LF - Excessive Wheel Speed Variation
C1226	RF - Excessive Wheel Speed Variation
C1227	LR - Excessive Wheel Speed Variation
C1228	RR - Excessive Wheel Speed Variation
C1232	LF Wheel Speed Sensor Circuit Open Or Shorted
C1233	RF Wheel Speed Sensor Circuit Open Or Shorted
C1234	LR Wheel Speed Sensor Circuit Open Or Shorted
C1235	RR Wheel Speed Sensor Circuit Open Or Shorted
C1236	Low System Voltage
C1237	High System Voltage
C1238	Brake Thermal Model Limit Exceeded
C1241	Magna Steer® Circuit Malfunction
C1242	BPMV Pump Motor Ground Circuit Open
C1243	BPMV Pump Motor Stalled
C1251	RSS Steering Sensor Data Malfunction
C1252	ICCS2 Data Link Left Malfunction
C1253	ICCS2 Data Link Right Malfunction
C1255 xx	EBTCM Internal Malfunction (ABS/TCS/ICCS Disabled)
C1256 xx	EBTCM Internal Malfunction
C1261	LF Hold Valve Solenoid Malfunction

91049G21

Fig. 124 Bosch ABS trouble codes—1997–98 Eldorado, Seville and Deville (1 of 2)

DTC	DESCRIPTION
C1262	LF Release Valve Solenoid Malfunction
C1263	RF Hold Valve Solenoid Malfunction
C1264	RF Release Valve Solenoid Malfunction
C1265	LR Hold Valve Solenoid Malfunction
C1266	LR Release Valve Solenoid Malfunction
C1267	RR Hold Valve Solenoid Malfunction
C1268	RR Release Valve Solenoid Malfunction
C1271	LF TCS Master Cylinder Isolation Valve Malfunction
C1272	LF TCS Prime Valve Malfunction
C1273	RF TCS Master Cylinder Isolation Valve Malfunction
C1274	RF TCS Prime Valve Malfunction
C1276	Delivered Torque Signal Circuit Malfunction
C1277	Requested Torque Signal Circuit Malfunction
C1278	TCS Temporarily Inhibited By PCM
C1281	Stabilitrak® Sensors Uncorrelated
C1282	Yaw Rate Sensor Bias Circuit Malfunction
C1283	Excessive Time to Center Steering
C1284	Lateral Accelerometer Sensor Self Test Malfunction
C1285	Lateral Accelerometer Sensor Circuit Malfunction
C1286	Steering/Lateral Accelerometer Sensor Bias Malfunction
C1287	Steering Sensor Rate Malfunction
C1288	Steering Sensor Circuit Malfunction
C1291	Open Brake Lamp Switch During Deceleration
C1293	DTC C1291 Set In Current Or Previous Ignition Cycle
C1294	Brake Lamp Switch Circuit Always Active
C1295	Brake Lamp Switch Circuit Open
C1297	PCM Indicated Brake Extended Travel Switch Failure
C1298	PCM Indicated Class 2 Serial Data Link Malfunction
U1016	Loss of PCM Communications
U1056	Loss of CVRSS Communications
U1255	Generic Loss of Communications
U1300	Class 2 Circuit Shorted to Ground
U1301	Class 2 Circuit Shorted to Battery+

91049G22

Fig. 125 Bosch ABS trouble codes—1997–98 Eldorado, Seville and Deville (2 of 2)

1997–98 MODELS

▶ See Figures 124 and 125

The codes must be retrieved using an OBD-II capatible scan tool linked through the 16-pin diagnostic connector under the instrument panel. Follow the scan tool manufacturer's instructions to retrieve the codes.

CLEARING CODES

Teves Mk II

Stored ABS trouble codes should not be cleared until all repairs are completed. The control module will not allow any codes to be cleared until all have been read. Drive the vehicle at a speed greater than 18 mph to clear ABS trouble codes.

Re-read the system; if codes are still present, not all codes were read previously or additional repair is needed.

Teves Mk IV

Use an appropriate scan tool to clear the trouble codes.

Bosch

1991–96 MODELS

The control module will not permit codes to be cleared until all have been read. Codes cannot be cleared by unplugging the module, disconnecting the battery or turning the ignition **OFF**. If using the Tech I diagnostic tool, codes may be cleared using the Clear Codes function of the tool.

To clear codes via the ALDL connector:
1. Turn the ignition switch **OFF**.
2. Ground pin H on the ALDL connector.
3. Turn the ignition switch **ON**.
4. Wait for codes to begin flashing.
5. Unground pin H for at least 1 second, then reconnect the ground. This must be done 3 times within 10 seconds.
6. Wait at least 15 seconds. Repeat Steps 1–4 of this procedure: confirm that code 12 is the only code being flashed. If not, either codes were not cleared properly or an ABS fault still exists.

Additionally, if the vehicle ignition is cycled a pre-determined number of times without a particular fault reappearing, the related fault code will be erased from the control module memory and the ignition cycle counter will reset to zero. The reset threshold is usually either 50 or 100 cycles, depending on the model and the system fault.

1997–98 MODELS

The codes must be cleared using an OBD-II capatible scan tool linked through the 16-pin diagnostic connector under the instrument panel.

Speed Sensors

REMOVAL & INSTALLATION

Front Sensor

1990 VEHICLES

▶ See Figures 126 and 127

1. Disconnect the negative battery cable.
2. Detach the sensor connector. Cut the wire retaining strap, if necessary.
3. Raise and safely support the vehicle. Remove the wheel and tire assembly.
4. On Eldorado and Seville, disengage the sensor cable grommet from the wheelwell pass-through hole.
5. Remove the sensor cable from the brackets/retainers.
6. Remove the sensor mounting bolt and remove the sensor.
7. Inspect the sensor face for accumulation of metallic particles, dirt, grease or other contaminants and clean as necessary. Make sure the sensor face shows no evidence of damage from toothed sensor ring contact.

To install:
8. Coat the sensor with anti-corrosion compound 1052856 or equivalent, where the sensor will contact the knuckle.
9. Install the sensor with the mounting bolt.

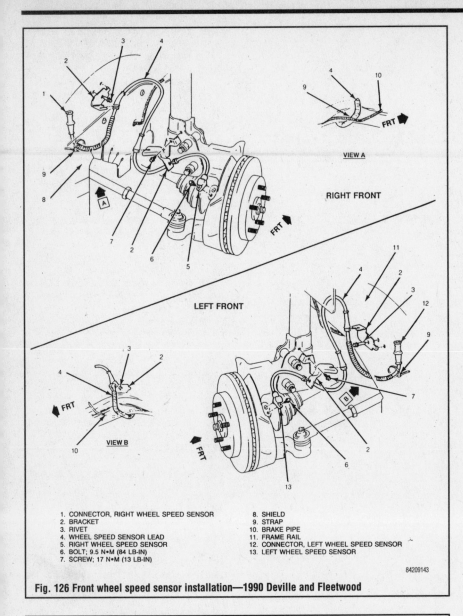

1. CONNECTOR, RIGHT WHEEL SPEED SENSOR
2. BRACKET
3. RIVET
4. WHEEL SPEED SENSOR LEAD
5. RIGHT WHEEL SPEED SENSOR
6. BOLT; 9.5 N•M (84 LB-IN)
7. SCREW; 17 N•M (13 LB-IN)
8. SHIELD
9. STRAP
10. BRAKE PIPE
11. FRAME RAIL
12. CONNECTOR, LEFT WHEEL SPEED SENSOR
13. LEFT WHEEL SPEED SENSOR

84209143

Fig. 126 Front wheel speed sensor installation—1990 Deville and Fleetwood

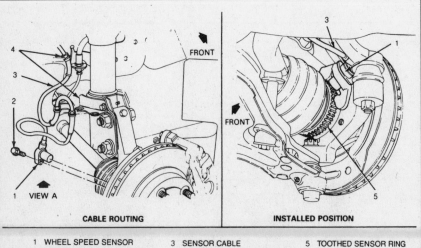

1 WHEEL SPEED SENSOR	3 SENSOR CABLE	5 TOOTHED SENSOR RING
2 SENSOR MOUNTING BOLT (12 N•m/106 LB. IN.) — 2 REQ'D	4 CABLE RETAINER BRACKETS	

84209144

Fig. 127 Front wheel speed sensor installation—1990 Eldorado and Seville

Tighten the bolt to 84 inch lbs. (9.5 Nm) on Deville and Fleetwood or 106 inch lbs. (12 Nm) on Eldorado and Seville.

10. Position and install the cable in the grommets, brackets and retainers, as necessary. The cable must be secure in the retainers and clear of moving parts. The cable must not be pulled too tight.

11. Connect the sensor to the wiring harness.

12. Install the wheel and tire assembly and lower the vehicle.

13. Connect the negative battery cable.

1991 DEVILLE AND FLEETWOOD

▶ See Figure 128

1. Disconnect the negative battery cable.

2. Working under the hood, detach the wheel speed sensor connector.

3. Cut the strap retaining the sensor cable.

4. Raise and safely support the vehicle.

5. Disconnect the sensor cable from the brackets.

6. Remove the retaining bolt and remove the sensor.

7. Inspect the sensor face for accumulation of metallic particles, dirt, grease or other contaminants and clean as necessary. Make sure the sensor face shows no evidence of damage from toothed sensor ring contact.

To install:

8. Coat the sensor with anti-corrosion compound 1052856 or equivalent, where the sensor will contact the knuckle.

9. Route the sensor cable and install the retainers. The cable must be secure in the retainers and clear of moving parts. The cable must not be pulled too tight.

10. Position the sensor in the knuckle and install the retaining bolt. Tighten the bolt to 84 inch lbs. (9.5 Nm).

11. Lower the vehicle.

12. Connect the sensor connector and install a new retaining strap.

13. Connect the negative battery cable.

1992–93 DEVILLE AND FLEETWOOD

▶ See Figures 129 and 130

1. Disconnect the negative battery cable.

2. Detach the sensor connector.

3. Remove the hub and bearing assembly. Clean all dirt from the sensor housing area.

4. Gently pry the slinger from the speed sensor assembly. Discard the used slinger.

5. Carefully pry the speed sensor from the bearing assembly. Do not allow dirt to enter the bearing when the sensor is removed. Do not add lubricant through the sensor opening; the bearing is permanently lubricated.

6. Inspect the bearing and sensor for any signs of rust or water intrusion; if such damage is found, replace the hub and bearing assembly. Do not clean the grease from the toothed sensor ring; grease does not affect operation of the sensor.

7. Use a clean, lint-free cloth to remove sealant from the outer diameter of the bearing hub.

To install:

8. Apply a sealant, 620 Loctite® or equivalent, to the groove in the outer diameter of the bearing hub.

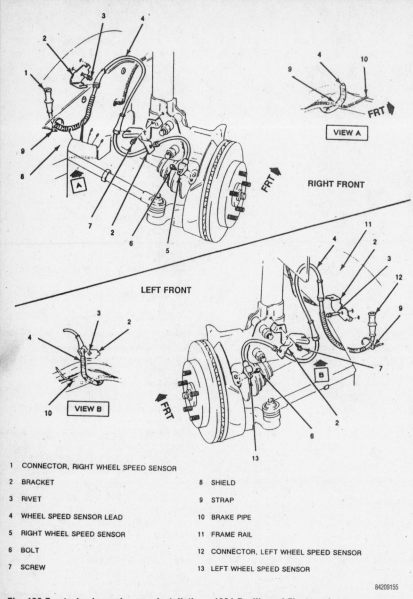

1	CONNECTOR, RIGHT WHEEL SPEED SENSOR		
2	BRACKET	8	SHIELD
3	RIVET	9	STRAP
4	WHEEL SPEED SENSOR LEAD	10	BRAKE PIPE
5	RIGHT WHEEL SPEED SENSOR	11	FRAME RAIL
6	BOLT	12	CONNECTOR, LEFT WHEEL SPEED SENSOR
7	SCREW	13	LEFT WHEEL SPEED SENSOR

84209155

Fig. 128 Front wheel speed sensor installation—1991 Deville and Fleetwood

9. Place the hub and bearing on tool J-38764–4 or equivalent, to prevent damage to the studs.

10. Install the sensor using a press and tool J-38764–1 or equivalent.

11. Install the hub and bearing assembly.

12. Connect the sensor wiring connector and connect the negative battery cable.

1991 ELDORADO AND SEVILLE

♦ See Figure 131

1. Disconnect the negative battery cable.

2. Detach the sensor connector at the strut tower.

3. Raise and safely support the vehicle.

4. Disengage the sensor cable grommet from the wheelwell pass-through hole and remove the sensor cable from the retainers.

5. Remove the sensor mounting bolt and remove the sensor from the vehicle.

6. Inspect the sensor face for accumulation of metallic particles, dirt, grease or other contaminants and clean as necessary.

To install:

7. Coat the sensor with anti-corrosion compound 1052856 or equivalent, where the sensor will contact the knuckle.

8. Route the sensor cable and install the retainers. The cable must be secure in the retainers and clear of moving parts. The cable must not be pulled too tight.

9. Position the sensor in the knuckle and install the retaining bolt. Tighten the bolt to 106 inch lbs. (12 Nm).

10. Lower the vehicle.

11. Connect the sensor connector and connect the negative battery cable.

1992–98 ELDORADO AND SEVILLE; 1994–98 DEVILLE

♦ See Figure 132

➡The front wheel speed sensors are integrated with the hub and bearing assembly. The sensor may be replaced and is serviced separately from the hub and bearing assembly. The sensor must be replaced whenever it is separated from the hub or bearing. Do not attempt to reuse the sensor once it is removed

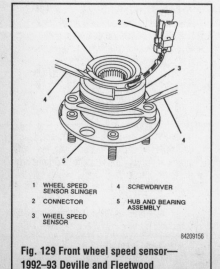

1	WHEEL SPEED SENSOR SLINGER	4	SCREWDRIVER
2	CONNECTOR	5	HUB AND BEARING ASSEMBLY
3	WHEEL SPEED SENSOR		

84209156

Fig. 129 Front wheel speed sensor— 1992–93 Deville and Fleetwood

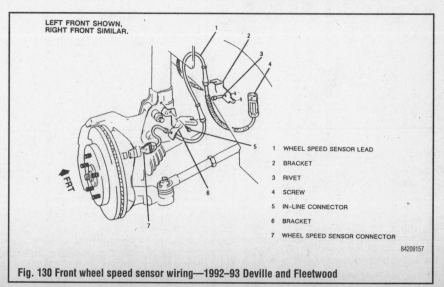

1	WHEEL SPEED SENSOR LEAD
2	BRACKET
3	RIVET
4	SCREW
5	IN-LINE CONNECTOR
6	BRACKET
7	WHEEL SPEED SENSOR CONNECTOR

84209157

Fig. 130 Front wheel speed sensor wiring—1992–93 Deville and Fleetwood

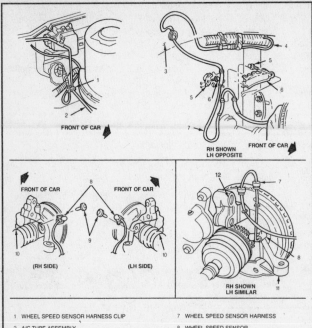

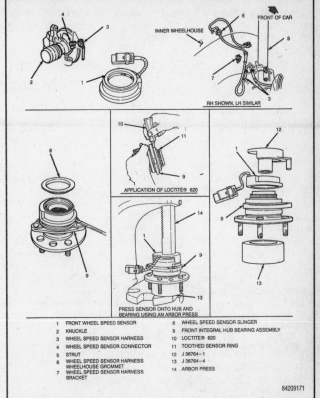

1 WHEEL SPEED SENSOR HARNESS CLIP	7 WHEEL SPEED SENSOR HARNESS
2 A/C TUBE ASSEMBLY	8 WHEEL SPEED SENSOR
3 LH/RH WHEEL HOUSE	9 WHEEL SPEED SENSOR MOUNTING BOLT
4 STRUT	10 DRIVE AXLE ASSEMBLY
5 WHEEL SPEED SENSOR BRACKET BOLT — 4 REQUIRED	11 KNUCKLE ASSEMBLY
6 WHEEL SPEED SENSOR BRACKET	12 TOOTHED WHEEL SPEED SENSOR RING

84209170

Fig. 131 Front wheel speed sensor installation—1991 Eldorado and Seville

1 FRONT WHEEL SPEED SENSOR	8 WHEEL SPEED SENSOR SLINGER
2 KNUCKLE	9 FRONT INTEGRAL HUB BEARING ASSEMBLY
3 WHEEL SPEED SENSOR HARNESS	10 LOCTITE® 620
4 WHEEL SPEED SENSOR CONNECTOR	11 TOOTHED SENSOR RING
5 STRUT	12 J 38764–1
6 WHEEL SPEED SENSOR HARNESS WHEELHOUSE GROMMET	13 J 38764–4
7 WHEEL SPEED SENSOR HARNESS BRACKET	14 ARBOR PRESS

84209171

Fig. 132 Front wheel speed sensor installation—1992–98 Eldorado and Seville

1. Disconnect the negative battery cable.
2. Detach the wheel speed sensor connector.
3. Remove the hub and bearing assembly.
4. Clean all dirt from the sensor housing area.
5. Gently pry the slinger from the speed sensor assembly. Discard the used slinger.
6. Carefully pry the speed sensor from the bearing assembly. Do not allow dirt to enter the bearing when the sensor is removed. Do not add lubricant through the sensor opening; the bearing is permanently lubricated.
7. Inspect the bearing and sensor for any signs of rust or water intrusion; if damage is found, replace the hub and bearing assembly. Do not clean the grease from the toothed sensor ring; grease does not affect operation of the sensor.
8. Use a clean, lint-free cloth to remove sealant from the outer diameter of the bearing hub.

To install:

9. Apply a sealant, 620 Loctite® or equivalent, to the groove in the outer diameter of the bearing hub.
10. Place the hub and bearing on tool J-38764–4 or equivalent, to prevent damage to the studs.
11. Install the sensor using a press and tool J-38764–1 or equivalent.
12. Install the hub and bearing assembly.
13. Connect the sensor wiring connector and make sure the connector is clipped to the dust shield on the knuckle.
14. Connect the negative battery cable.

Rear Sensor

1990 DEVILLE AND FLEETWOOD

▶ **See Figure 133**

1. Disconnect the negative battery cable.
2. Open the trunk and remove the side panel carpeting.
3. Detach the sensor connector, located forward of the shock tower.

4. Raise and safely support the vehicle.
5. Disconnect the sensor cable from the bracket.
6. Remove the bracket bolts and the sensor bolt.
7. Carefully raise the bracket while removing the sensor.
8. Remove the 2 screws holding the sensor retainer and remove the retainer.
9. Remove the sensor cable and sensor.

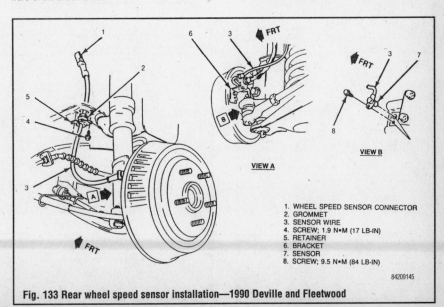

1. WHEEL SPEED SENSOR CONNECTOR
2. GROMMET
3. SENSOR WIRE
4. SCREW; 1.9 N•M (17 LB-IN)
5. RETAINER
6. BRACKET
7. SENSOR
8. SCREW; 9.5 N•M (84 LB-IN)

84209145

Fig. 133 Rear wheel speed sensor installation—1990 Deville and Fleetwood

10. Inspect the sensor face for accumulation of metallic particles, dirt, grease or other contaminants and clean as necessary. Make sure the sensor face shows no evidence of damage from toothed sensor ring contact.

To install:

11. Coat the sensor with anti-corrosion compound 1052856 or equivalent, where the sensor will contact the knuckle.

12. Route the sensor cable and install and retainers. The cable must be secure in the retainers and clear of moving parts. The cable must not be pulled too tight.

13. Carefully lift the bracket and install the sensor. Install the sensor bolt and tighten to 84 inch lbs. (9.5 Nm). Install the bracket bolts and tighten to 75 inch lbs. (8.5 Nm).

14. Install the sensor cable through the trunk opening.

15. Install the retainer with the 2 screws and tighten to 17 inch lbs. (1.9 Nm).

16. Lower the vehicle.

17. Connect the speed sensor to the harness and install the side panel carpeting. Connect the negative battery cable.

1990 ELDORADO AND SEVILLE

▶ **See Figure 134**

1. Disconnect the negative battery cable.
2. Raise and safely support the vehicle.
3. Detach the sensor connector and remove the sensor cable from the retainer brackets.
4. Remove the sensor mounting bolts and remove the sensor.
5. Inspect the sensor face for accumulation of metallic particles, dirt, grease or other contaminants and clean as necessary. Make sure the sensor face shows no evidence of damage from toothed sensor ring contact.

To install:

6. Coat the sensor with anti-corrosion compound 1052856 or equivalent, where the sensor will contact the knuckle. Position the sensor in the knuckle and install the mounting bolt. Tighten the bolt to 106 inch lbs. (12 Nm).

7. Install the sensor cable in the retainers. The cable must be secure in the retainers and clear of moving parts. The cable must not be pulled too tight.

8. Connect the sensor connector and lower the vehicle. Connect the negative battery cable.

1991–93 FLEETWOOD AND DEVILLE

▶ **See Figures 135 and 136**

1. Disconnect the negative battery cable.
2. Detach the wheel speed sensor connector.
3. Remove the hub and bearing assembly.
4. Clean the sensor housing of any dirt or debris.
5. Remove the screws holding the sensor and remove the sensor. Do not allow dirt to enter the bearing when the sensor is removed. Do not add lubricant through the sensor opening; the bearing is permanently lubricated.
6. Inspect the sensor ring and plate for any signs of contact or mechanical wear; if such dam-

age is found, replace the hub and bearing assembly. Do not clean the grease from the toothed sensor ring; grease does not affect operation of the sensor.

To install:

7. Inspect the O-ring for damage and replace if necessary.
8. Install the sensor with the screws. Tighten the screws to 33 inch lbs. (3.7 Nm).
9. Install the hub and bearing assembly.
10. Connect the sensor wiring connector and connect the negative battery cable.

1992–98 ELDORADO AND SEVILLE; 1994–98 DEVILLE

The rear wheel speed sensor is an integral part of the rear hub and bearing assembly and cannot be serviced separately. Should a sensor fail, the entire hub and bearing assembly must be replaced.

Control Module

REMOVAL & INSTALLATION

1990 Deville and Fleetwood

▶ **See Figure 137**

1. Disconnect the negative battery cable.
2. Remove the right sound insulator.
3. Slide the EBCM from the bracket and detach the harness connector.

To install:

4. Connect the harness connector.
5. Slide the EBCM into the bracket.
6. Install the right sound insulator.
7. Connect the negative battery cable.

1990 Eldorado and Seville

1. Disconnect the negative battery cable.
2. Open the trunk and remove the left trunk carpet trim.
3. Detach the harness connector.

Fig. 135 Rear wheel speed sensor— 1991–93 Deville and Fleetwood

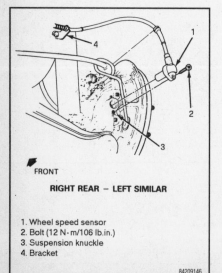

FRONT

RIGHT REAR – LEFT SIMILAR

1. Wheel speed sensor
2. Bolt (12 N·m/106 lb.in.)
3. Suspension knuckle
4. Bracket

84209146

Fig. 134 Rear wheel speed sensor installation—1990 Eldorado and Seville

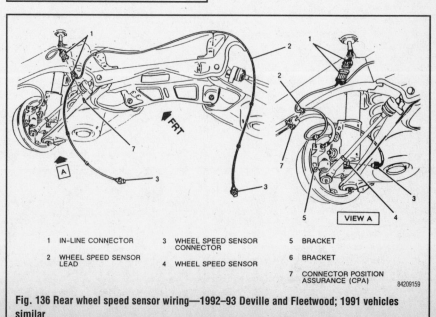

1	IN-LINE CONNECTOR	3	WHEEL SPEED SENSOR CONNECTOR	5	BRACKET
2	WHEEL SPEED SENSOR LEAD	4	WHEEL SPEED SENSOR	6	BRACKET
				7	CONNECTOR POSITION ASSURANCE (CPA)

84209159

Fig. 136 Rear wheel speed sensor wiring—1992–93 Deville and Fleetwood; 1991 vehicles similar

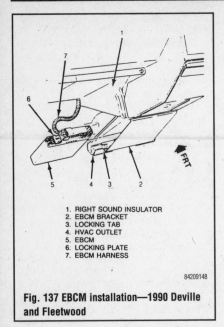

Fig. 137 EBCM installation—1990 Deville and Fleetwood

4. Remove the EBCM from the mounting bracket.
To install:
5. Attach the EBCM to the mounting bracket.
6. Connect the harness connector.
7. Install the left trunk carpet trim and close the trunk.
8. Connect the negative battery cable.

1991–93 Fleetwood and Deville

▶ See Figure 138

1. Disconnect the negative battery cable.
2. Remove the right and left sound insulators from the instrument panel.
3. Remove the floor outlet for the heating and cooling system.
4. Remove the EBCM retaining bolt and slide the unit toward the accelerator pedal.
5. Detach the harness connector and remove the EBCM.
To install:
6. Connect the wiring harness connector to the EBCM.
7. Slide the EBCM into its mounting bracket and install the retaining bolt. Tighten the bolt to 19 inch lbs. (2.2 Nm) on 1991 vehicles or 42 inch lbs. (4.7 Nm) on 1992–93 vehicles.
8. Install the floor outlet and the sound insulators.
9. Connect the negative battery cable.

1991–98 Eldorado and Seville; 1994–98 Deville

▶ See Figures 139 and 140

1. Disconnect the negative battery cable.
2. Open the trunk and remove the necessary carpeting to gain access to the EBCM/EBTCM.
3. Detach the harness connector from the EBCM/EBTCM.
4. Remove the EBCM/EBTCM from its mounting bracket.

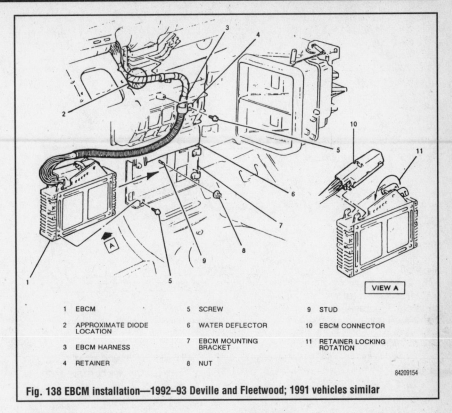

Fig. 138 EBCM installation—1992–93 Deville and Fleetwood; 1991 vehicles similar

1	EBCM	5	SCREW	9	STUD
2	APPROXIMATE DIODE LOCATION	6	WATER DEFLECTOR	10	EBCM CONNECTOR
3	EBCM HARNESS	7	EBCM MOUNTING BRACKET	11	RETAINER LOCKING ROTATION
4	RETAINER	8	NUT		

To install:
5. Secure the EBCM/EBTCM in its mounting bracket.
6. Connect the wiring harness connector. Make sure the connector is securely mated to the EBCM/EBTCM.
7. Reposition the carpet and close the trunk.
8. Connect the negative battery cable.

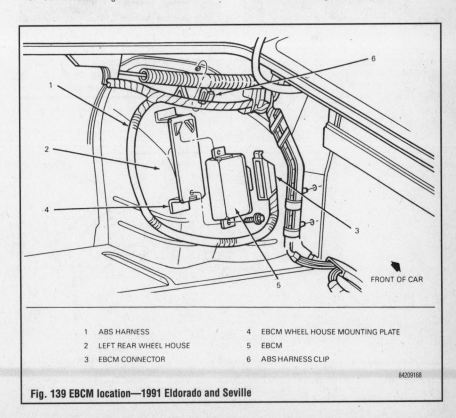

1	ABS HARNESS	4	EBCM WHEEL HOUSE MOUNTING PLATE
2	LEFT REAR WHEEL HOUSE	5	EBCM
3	EBCM CONNECTOR	6	ABS HARNESS CLIP

Fig. 139 EBCM location—1991 Eldorado and Seville

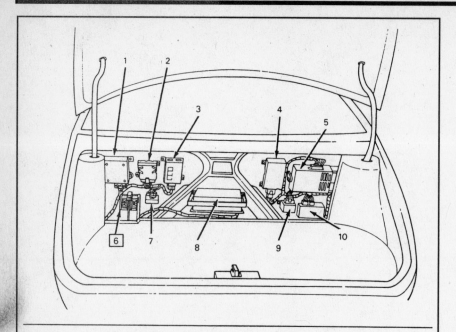

1	REMOTE KEYLESS ENTRY MODULE	6	RELAY CENTER
2	UNIVERSAL THEFT DETERRENT MODULE	7	POWER DOOR LOCK RELAY
3	HEATED WINDSHIELD CONTROL MODULE	8	ANTI-LOCK BRAKE CONTROL MODULE
4	PASS KEY MODULE	9	DELAYED ACCESSORY BUS MODULE
5	REMOTE RADIO CHASSIS	10	COMPUTER COMMAND RIDE MODULE

84209169

Fig. 140 EBCM location—1992 Eldorado and Seville; 1993–98 similar

Hydraulic Control Unit

REMOVAL & INSTALLATION

1990 Vehicles

▶ See Figure 141

1. Disconnect the negative battery cable.
2. Depressurize the hydraulic accumulator.

✳✳ CAUTION

The hydraulic accumulator contains brake fluid and nitrogen gas at extremely high pressures. It is mandatory that it be depressurized before disconnecting any brake lines, or personal injury may result.

3. Label and detach all electrical connections at the hydraulic unit.

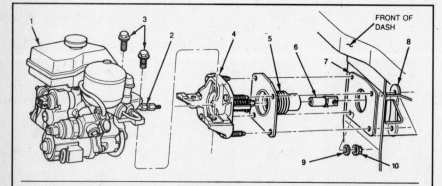

1	HYDRAULIC UNIT	5	RUBBER BOOT	9	WASHER - USED ON LOWER R.H. STUD ONLY
2	FRONT PUSHROD HALF	6	REAR PUSHROD HALF		
3	MOUNTING BOLTS (50 N·m/37 LB . FT.)	7	GASKET	10	NUTS - 4 REQ'D (20 N·m/15 LB.FT.)
4	PUSHROD BRACKET ASM.	8	REINFORCEMENT WASHER		

84209147

Fig. 141 Hydraulic unit installation—1990 Eldorado and Seville; 1990 Deville and Fleetwood similar

4. On Eldorado and Seville, remove the cross-car brace.

5. Remove the pump mounting bolt and move pump/motor assembly aside to allow access to the brake lines.

6. Using a backup wrench, disconnect the brake lines from the valve block.

7. Working inside the vehicle, disconnect the pushrod from the brake pedal. Push the dust boot forward, past the hex on the pushrod, and separate the pushrod into 2 sections by unscrewing it.

8. Remove the hydraulic unit mounting bolts at the pushrod bracket and remove the hydraulic unit from the vehicle. The front half of the pushrod will remain locked into the hydraulic unit.

To install:

9. Position the hydraulic unit in the vehicle and install new retaining bolts at the pushrod bracket. Tighten the bolts to 37 ft. lbs. (50 Nm).

10. From inside the vehicle, thread the pushrod halves together and tighten. Reposition the dust boot and connect the pushrod to the brake pedal.

11. Connect the brake lines to the valve block and tighten the fittings to 106 inch lbs. (12 Nm).

12. Position the pump/motor assembly on the hydraulic unit. Install the mounting bolt and tighten to 71 inch lbs. (8 Nm) on Deville and Fleetwood or 10 ft. lbs. (13 Nm) on Eldorado and Seville.

13. Install the cross-car brace, if removed.

14. Connect the electrical harness to the hydraulic unit.

15. Connect the negative battery cable.

16. Bleed the brake system.

1991–93 Deville and Fleetwood

▶ See Figure 142

1. Disconnect the negative battery cable.
2. Remove the air cleaner assembly.
3. Label and detach the wiring connectors at the PMV assembly. The connectors are for the fluid level switch, pump motor and valve block.
4. Loosen or reposition the clamp on the hose at the PMV reservoir.
5. Position a clean pan to catch any spilled fluid from the reservoir. Disconnect the hose from the reservoir and plug the hose with a ⅝-inch (15.5mm) diameter plug.
6. Disconnect the primary and secondary brake lines at the PMV.
7. Disconnect the 4 brake lines from the PMV assembly.
8. Raise and safely support the vehicle.
9. Remove the lower PMV assembly retaining bolt.
10. Lower the vehicle to the ground.
11. Remove the harness strap, if equipped.
12. Support the PMV assembly and remove the upper retaining bolts. Remove the assembly from the vehicle. If the unit is being replaced with another, the reservoir and bracket(s) must be transferred to the new assembly.

➡The PMV assembly is not serviceable. Do not attempt to disassemble any part of the unit.

To install:

13. Position the PMV assembly and install the upper retaining bolts. Tighten the bolts to 20 ft. lbs. (27 Nm).

14. Raise and safely support the vehicle. Install

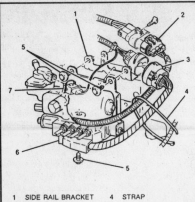

1	SIDE RAIL BRACKET	4	STRAP
2	PMV ASSEMBLY CONNECTOR C2	5	BOLT
3	PMV ASSEMBLY CONNECTOR C1	6	PMV ASSEMBLY
		7	PMV FLUID LEVEL SWITCH

84209160

Fig. 142 Pressure Modulator Valve (PMV) Assembly—1991–93 Deville and Fleetwood

the lower retaining bolt and tighten it to 20 ft. lbs. (27 Nm). Lower the vehicle.

15. Connect the 4 brake lines to the PMV. Tighten the fittings to 11 ft. lbs. (15 Nm).

16. Install the primary and secondary brake lines, tightening each fitting to 11 ft. lbs. (15 Nm).

17. Connect the hose to the PMV reservoir and secure the clamp.

18. Connect the electrical connectors to the PMV assembly; make certain each connector is squarely seated and firmly retained.

19. Install the air cleaner assembly.

20. Connect the negative battery cable.

21. Fill the brake fluid reservoir and bleed the brake system.

22. Clean any spilled brake fluid from the PMV assembly and surrounding area to prevent damage to other components or paintwork.

1991–92 Eldorado and Seville

▶ See Figure 143

1. Disconnect the negative battery cable.

2. Use a syringe or similar tool to remove the brake fluid from the master cylinder.

3. Remove the left front radiator brace and air cleaner intake hose.

4. Remove the modulator relay cover and detach the 12-way connector and modulator ground strap.

5. Label and disconnect the brake lines from the modulator. Plug the lines to prevent the entry of dirt and debris.

6. Remove the modulator mounting nuts and remove the modulator from the mounting bracket.

7. Remove the modulator mounting insulators and inspect them for damage. Replace as necessary.

To install:

8. Install the insulators on the modulator and install the modulator to the mounting bracket. Install the nuts and tighten to 8 ft. lbs. (11 Nm).

9. Connect the brake lines to the modulator and tighten the fittings to 9 ft. lbs. (12 Nm).

10. Connect the modulator connector and ground strap. Install the relay cover.

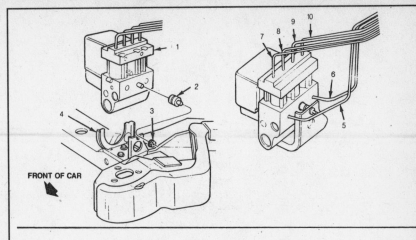

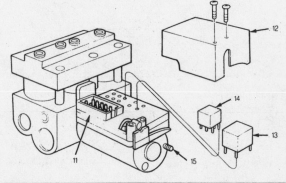

1	HYDRAULIC MODULATOR	9	LEFT REAR BRAKE LINE-TO LR WHEEL
2	MOUNTING INSULATOR — 3 REQUIRED	10	RIGHT FRONT BRAKE LINE-TO RF WHEEL
3	NUT — 3 REQUIRED	11	MODULATOR CONNECTOR
4	MOUNTING BRACKET	12	MODULATOR COVER AND SCREWS
5	FRONT HYDRAULIC CIRCUIT FROM MASTER CYLINDER	13	PUMP RELAY
6	REAR HYDRAULIC CIRCUIT FROM MASTER CYLINDER	14	SOLENOID VALVE RELAY
7	LEFT FRONT BRAKE LINE-TO LF WHEEL	15	MODULATOR GROUND CONNECTION
8	RIGHT REAR BRAKE LINE-TO-RR WHEEL		

84209166

Fig. 143 Hydraulic modulator—1991–92 Eldorado and Seville

11. Install the air intake hose and radiator brace.

12. Fill the master cylinder reservoir with brake fluid and bleed the brake system.

1993–98 Eldorado and Seville; 1994–98 Deville

▶ See Figure 144

1. Disconnect the negative battery cable.

2. Raise and safely support the vehicle.

3. Remove the left front wheel and tire assembly.

4. Support the front of the cradle with a suitable jack.

5. Disconnect the exhaust pipe from the catalytic converter.

6. Remove the left front wheelwell splash shields.

7. Label and disconnect the brake lines from the modulator. Plug the lines to prevent the entry of dirt and debris.

8. Disconnect the brake line bundle from the left-hand frame rail.

9. Remove the bolts from the No. 1 and No. 2 body mounts. Loosen the No. 3 body mounts.

10. Using the jack, slowly lower the front cradle about 4–5 inches.

11. Remove the BPM valve cover.

12. Pull out (do not remove) the locking mechanism on the outer side of the ABS/TCS wiring harness connector. When 2 clicks are heard, the connector is completely disengaged and can be removed from the BPM valve.

13. Remove the TCS prime pipe, if equipped.

14. Disconnect the BPM ground strap.

15. Remove the BPM mounting nuts and remove the BPM through the left front wheelwell.

To install:

16. Install the BPM through the left front wheelwell and position it on the mounting bracket. Install the mounting nuts and tighten to 86 inch lbs. (10 Nm).

17. Connect the ground strap.

18. Connect the ABS/TCS wiring harness connector and install the BPM valve cover.

19. Connect the brake lines to the BPM and tighten the fittings to 13 ft. lbs. (18 Nm).

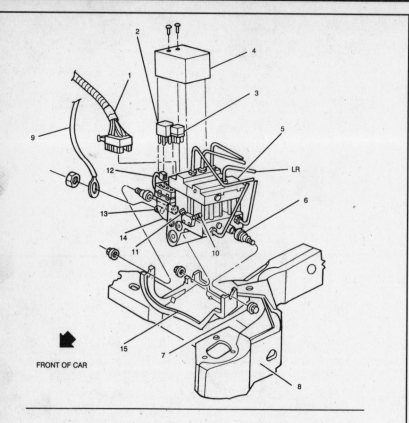

FRONT OF CAR

1	ABS VALVE HARNESS CONNECTOR	9	PUMP/MOTOR GROUND STOP
2	PUMP RELAY	10	TCS PRIME PIPE NOZZLE
3	VALVE RELAY	11	TCS PRIME PIPE BLEED SCREW
4	BPM VALVE COVER	12	PUMP/MOTOR POWER FEED
5	BRAKE PRESSURE MODULATOR VALVE (BPM)	13	PUMP/MOTOR GROUND STUD
6	BUSHING (3)	14	PUMP/MOTOR
7	MOUNTING NUT (3)	15	BPM VALVE MOUNTING BRACKET
8	FRAME		

84209167

Fig. 144 Brake Pressure Modulator—1993 Eldorado and Seville

⁂ CAUTION

Make sure the brake lines are connected to their proper locations. If the lines are switched by mistake (inlet vs. outlet), wheel lockup will occur and personal injury may result.

20. Connect the TCS prime pipe, if equipped.
21. Raise the front cradle into position with the jack (do not over raise). Install the body mount bolts and tighten to 50 ft. lbs. (68 Nm).
22. Connect the brake line bundle to the left-hand frame rail.
23. Install the left front wheelwell splash shields.
24. Connect the exhaust pipe to the catalytic converter and tighten the bolts to 9 ft. lbs. (12 Nm).
25. Install the wheel and tire assembly and lower the vehicle.
26. Connect the negative battery cable.
27. Fill the master cylinder reservoir with brake fluid and bleed the brake system.

Bleeding the ABS System

The ABS system is bled the same as the regular brake system. 1990 Models equipped with the Teves MkII system must have the hydraulic accumulator depressurized. Refer to the brake bleeding procedure.

BRAKE SPECIFICATIONS
All measurements in inches unless noted

Year	Model		Master Cylinder Bore	Brake Disc			Brake Drum Diameter						
				Original Thickness	Minimum Thickness	Maximum Runout	Original Inside Diameter	Max. Wear Limit	Maximum Machine Diameter				
1990	DeVille	F	0.937	1.043	0.957	0.004	—	—	—				
		R	—	—	—	—	8.860	8.909	8.800				
	Fleetwood	F	0.937	1.043	0.957	0.004	—	—	—	0.030	—		
		R	—	—	—	—	8.860	8.909	8.800	—	0.030	—	20
	Eldorado	F	①	1.035	0.956	0.004	—	—	—	0.030	—	—	38
		R	—	0.494	0.429	0.003	—	—	—	—	0.030	—	20
	Seville	F	①	1.035	0.956	0.004	—	—	—	0.030	—	—	38
		R	—	0.494	0.429	0.003	—	—	—	—	0.030	—	20
1991	DeVille	F	1.000	1.276	1.209	0.002	—	—	—	0.030	—	—	38
		R	—	—	—	—	8.860	8.909	8.800	—	0.030	—	20
	Fleetwood	F	1.000	1.276	1.209	0.002	—	—	—	0.030	—	—	38
		R	—	—	—	—	8.860	8.909	8.800	—	0.030	—	20
	Eldorado	F	①	1.035	0.956	0.004	—	—	—	0.030	—	—	38
		R	—	0.494	0.429	0.003	—	—	—	—	0.030	—	20
	Seville	F	①	1.035	0.956	0.004	—	—	—	0.030	—	—	38
		R	—	0.494	0.429	0.003	—	—	—	—	0.030	—	20
1992	DeVille	F	1.000	1.276	1.209	0.002	—	—	—	0.030	—	—	38
		R	—	—	—	—	8.860	8.909	8.800	—	0.030	—	20
	Fleetwood	F	1.000	1.276	1.209	0.002	—	—	—	0.030	—	—	38
		R	—	—	—	—	8.860	8.909	8.800	—	0.030	—	20
	Eldorado	F	1.000	1.268	1.209	0.002	—	—	—	0.030	—	—	38
		R	—	0.433	0.374	0.002	—	—	—	—	0.030	—	20
	Seville	F	1.000	1.268	1.209	0.002	—	—	—	0.030	—	—	38
		R	—	0.433	0.374	0.002	—	—	—	—	0.030	—	20
1993	DeVille	F	1.000	1.276	1.209	0.002	—	—	—	0.030	—	—	38
		R	—	—	—	—	8.860	8.909	8.800	—	0.030	—	20
	Fleetwood	F	1.000	1.276	1.209	0.002	—	—	—	0.030	—	—	38
		R	—	—	—	—	8.860	8.909	8.800	—	0.030	—	20
	Eldorado	F	1.000	1.268	1.209	0.002	—	—	—	0.030	—	—	38
		R	—	0.433	0.374	0.002	—	—	—	—	0.030	—	20
	Seville	F	1.000	1.268	1.209	0.002	—	—	—	0.030	—	—	38
		R	—	0.433	0.374	0.002	—	—	—	—	0.030	—	20
1994	DeVille	F	1.000	1.268	1.209	0.002	—	—	—	0.030	—	—	38
		R	—	0.433	0.374	0.002	—	—	—	—	0.030	—	20
	DeVille Concours	F	1.000	1.268	1.209	0.002	—	—	—	0.030	—	—	38
		R	—	0.433	0.374	0.002	—	—	—	—	0.030	—	20
	Eldorado	F	1.000	1.268	1.209	0.002	—	—	—	0.030	—	—	38
		R	—	0.433	0.374	0.002	—	—	—	—	0.030	—	20
	Seville	F	1.000	1.268	1.209	0.002	—	—	—	0.030	—	—	38
		R	—	0.433	0.374	0.002	—	—	—	—	0.030	—	20
1995	DeVille	F	1.000	1.268	1.209	0.002	—	—	—	0.030	—	—	38
		R	—	0.433	0.374	0.002	—	—	—	—	0.030	—	20
	DeVille Concours	F	1.000	1.268	1.209	0.002	—	—	—	0.030	—	—	38
		R	—	0.433	0.374	0.002	—	—	—	—	0.030	—	20
	Eldorado	F	1.000	1.268	1.209	0.002	—	—	—	0.030	—	—	38
		R	—	0.433	0.374	0.002	—	—	—	—	0.030	—	20
	Seville	F	1.000	1.268	1.209	0.002	—	—	—	0.030	—	—	38
		R	—	0.433	0.374	0.002	—	—	—	—	0.030	—	20

91049C01

BRAKE SPECIFICATIONS
All measurements in inches unless noted

Year	Model		Master Cylinder Bore	Brake Disc Original Thickness	Brake Disc Minimum Thickness	Brake Disc Maximum Runout	Brake Drum Diameter Original Inside Diameter	Brake Drum Diameter Max. Wear Limit	Brake Drum Diameter Maximum Machine Diameter	Minimum Lining Thickness Front	Minimum Lining Thickness Rear	Brake Caliper Bracket Bolts (ft. lbs.)	Brake Caliper Mounting Bolts (ft. lbs.)
1996	DeVille	F	1.000	1.268	1.209	0.002	—	—	—	0.030	—	—	38
		R	—	0.433	0.374	0.002	—	—	—	—	0.030	—	20
	DeVille Concours	F	1.000	1.268	1.209	0.002	—	—	—	0.030	—	—	38
		R	—	0.433	0.374	0.002	—	—	—	—	0.030	—	20
	Eldorado	F	1.000	1.268	1.209	0.002	—	—	—	0.030	—	—	38
		R	—	0.433	0.374	0.002	—	—	—	—	0.030	—	20
	Seville STS	F	1.000	1.268	1.209	0.002	—	—	—	0.030	—	—	38
		R	—	0.433	0.374	0.002	—	—	—	—	0.030	—	20
1997	DeVille	F	1.000	1.268	1.209	0.002	—	—	—	0.030	—	—	38
		R	—	0.433	0.374	0.002	—	—	—	—	0.030	—	20
	DeVille Concours	F	1.000	1.268	1.209	0.002	—	—	—	0.030	—	—	38
		R	—	0.433	0.374	0.002	—	—	—	—	0.030	—	20
	Eldorado	F	1.000	1.268	1.209	0.002	—	—	—	0.030	—	—	38
		R	—	0.433	0.374	0.002	—	—	—	—	0.030	—	20
	Seville STS	F	1.000	1.268	1.209	0.002	—	—	—	0.030	—	—	38
		R	—	0.433	0.374	0.002	—	—	—	—	0.030	—	20
1998	DeVille	F	1.000	1.268	1.209	0.002	—	—	—	0.030	—	—	38
		R	—	0.433	0.374	0.002	—	—	—	—	0.030	—	20
	DeVille Concours	F	1.000	1.268	1.209	0.002	—	—	—	0.030	—	—	38
		R	—	0.433	0.374	0.002	—	—	—	—	0.030	—	20
	Eldorado	F	1.000	1.268	1.209	0.002	—	—	—	0.030	—	—	38
		R	—	0.433	0.374	0.002	—	—	—	—	0.030	—	20
	Seville STS	F	1.000	1.268	1.209	0.002	—	—	—	0.030	—	—	38
		R	—	0.433	0.374	0.002	—	—	—	—	0.030	—	20

①Standard brake system: 1.126
Anti-lock brake system: 1.000

91049CR2

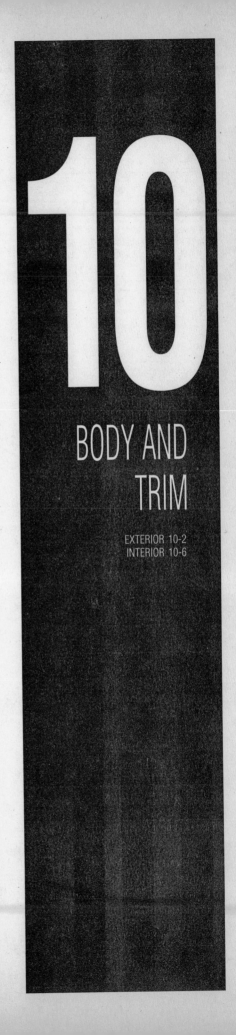

10

BODY AND TRIM

EXTERIOR

Doors

ADJUSTMENT

Adjust the door for proper door-to-body alignment and lock-to-striker engagement. Move the door up or down or in or out by loosening the nuts on the pillar side of the hinge and repositioning the door as needed. Move the door fore and aft by loosening the bolts on the door side of the hinge and repositioning the door as needed.

Hood

REMOVAL & INSTALLATION

◆ **See Figures 1, 2 and 3**

1. Scribe the locations of the hinges on the underside of the hood so the hood can be reinstalled in the same position.
2. Support the hood with the aid of an assistant.

3. Remove the nuts and bolts retaining the hood to the hinges and remove the gas spring clips.
4. Remove the hood from the vehicle with the aid of an assistant.

✳✳ WARNING

Position the hood on its side when it is removed from the vehicle, in order to prevent damage to the sheet metal.

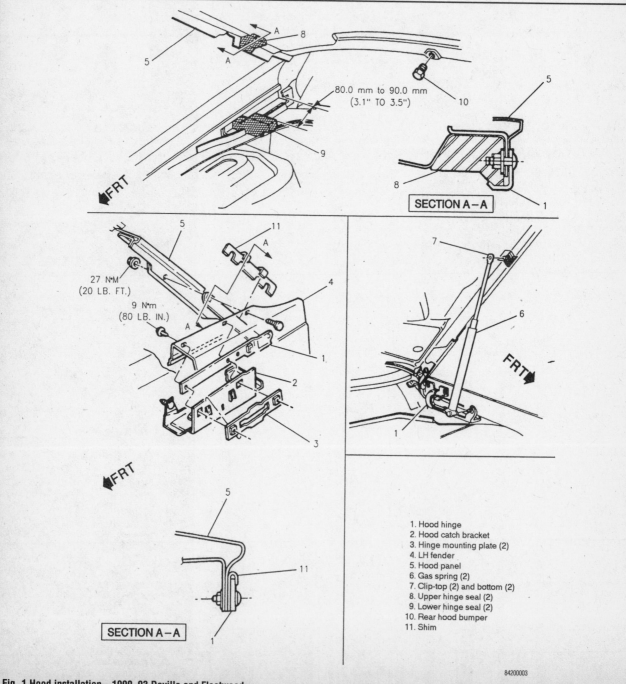

80.0 mm to 90.0 mm
(3.1" TO 3.5")

SECTION A–A

27 N•M
(20 LB. FT.)

9 N•m
(80 LB. IN.)

SECTION A–A

1. Hood hinge
2. Hood catch bracket
3. Hinge mounting plate (2)
4. LH fender
5. Hood panel
6. Gas spring (2)
7. Clip-top (2) and bottom (2)
8. Upper hinge seal (2)
9. Lower hinge seal (2)
10. Rear hood bumper
11. Shim

84200003

Fig. 1 Hood installation—1990–93 Deville and Fleetwood

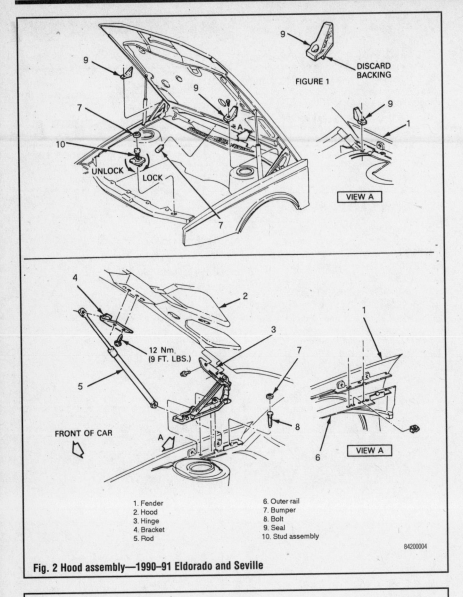

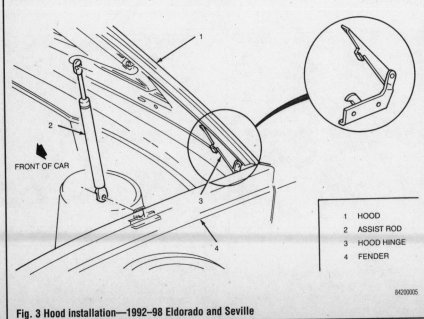

Fig. 2 Hood assembly—1990–91 Eldorado and Seville

1. Fender
2. Hood
3. Hinge
4. Bracket
5. Rod
6. Outer rail
7. Bumper
8. Bolt
9. Seal
10. Stud assembly

84200004

12 Nm
(9 FT. LBS.)

FRONT OF CAR

VIEW A

DISCARD BACKING

FIGURE 1

UNLOCK   LOCK

VIEW A

Fig. 3 Hood installation—1992–98 Eldorado and Seville

1 HOOD
2 ASSIST ROD
3 HOOD HINGE
4 FENDER

FRONT OF CAR

84200005

To install:

5. With the aid of an assistant, position the hood on the hinges, aligning the scribe marks that were made during the removal procedure.

6. Install the nuts, bolts and gas spring clips.

7. Check hood alignment and adjust, if necessary.

ALIGNMENT

▶ **See Figure 4**

Hood Panel

1. Loosen the hood attaching bolts at each hood hinge. The holes in the hinge are elongated for fore an aft hood adjustment.

2. When the hood is positioned properly, tighten the hinge-to-hood attaching bolts.

3. Adjust the rubber bumpers so the hood is flush with the fenders.

4. Adjust the hood latch mechanism.

5. After hood alignment, there must be sufficient load remaining on the hood stops to eliminate hood flutter. This can be obtained by lowering the primary latch an additional 1/8 inch.

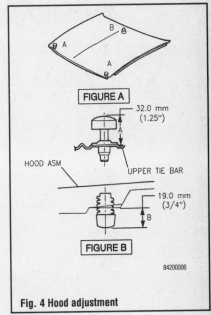

FIGURE A

32.0 mm
(1.25")

HOOD ASM

UPPER TIE BAR

19.0 mm
(3/4")

FIGURE B

84200006

Fig. 4 Hood adjustment

Hood Latch

The striker plate in the hood panel is large enough to allow normal fore and aft adjustment. Cross vehicle adjustment is provided at the hood lock mounting bracket to radiator support on Deville and Fleetwood or at the front end sheet metal support-to-radiator support tie bar on Eldorado and Seville. Up and down adjustment is provided by loosening the 2 screws securing the latch to the hood latch bracket or support.

When the hood latch mounting screws have been loosened or the hood adjustment changed, make sure that proper alignment has been obtained before tightening the mounting screws. Proper cross vehicle adjustment of the primary lock is achieved by slowly lowering the hood onto the lock with the attaching screws loose, then raising the hood and tightening the screws.

Trunk Lid

REMOVAL & INSTALLATION

▶ **See Figures 5, 6, 7 and 8**

1. Disconnect the negative battery cable.
2. Detach the electric lock release solenoid connector.
3. If equipped, detach the trunk lid courtesy light connector.
4. If equipped, detach the connector from the lock cylinder.
5. Tie a string to the wiring harness and pull the harness out of the trunk lid, leaving the string completely through the lid and hanging out.
6. Scribe the locations of the hinges on the trunk lid so the trunk lid can be reinstalled in the same position.
7. Support the trunk lid with the aid of an assistant.
8. Remove the trunk lid mounting bolts, then remove the trunk lid from the vehicle with the aid of an assistant.

To install:
9. With the aid of an assistant, position the trunk lid on the hinges, aligning the scribe marks that were made during the removal procedure.
10. Install the trunk lid mounting bolts.
11. Pull the wiring harness through the trunk lid using the string, then remove the string from the wiring harness.
12. Attach the necessary electrical connectors and connect the negative battery cable.
13. Check the trunk lid alignment and adjust, if necessary.

ALIGNMENT

▶ **See Figures 5, 6, 7 and 8**

1. Loosen the trunk lid mounting bolts and move the trunk lid, as necessary.
2. When the trunk lid is properly positioned within the body opening, tighten the mounting bolts.
3. To adjust the up and down alignment at the rear corners, turn the rubber bumpers to raise or lower the trunk lid.

Grille

REMOVAL & INSTALLATION

Deville and Fleetwood

1990 MODELS

1. Open the hood.
2. Remove the left and right headlamp filler panels.
3. Remove the 6 grille mounting screws and remove the grille.

To install:
4. Position the grille and install the mounting screws.
5. Install the headlamp filler panels.

1991–93 FLEETWOOD AND 1991–98 DEVILLE

▶ **See Figures 9 and 10**

1. Open the hood.
2. Remove the 5 screws attaching the grille to the grille support bracket.

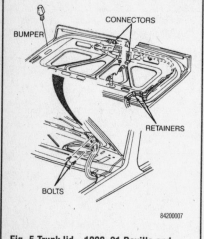

Fig. 5 Trunk lid—1990–91 Deville and Fleetwood

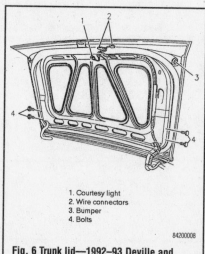

1. Courtesy light
2. Wire connectors
3. Bumper
4. Bolts

Fig. 6 Trunk lid—1992–93 Deville and Fleetwood

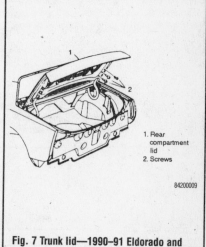

1. Rear compartment lid
2. Screws

Fig. 7 Trunk lid—1990–91 Eldorado and Seville

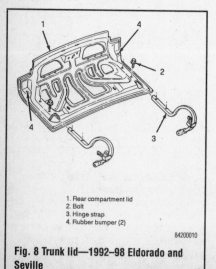

1. Rear compartment lid
2. Bolt
3. Hinge strap
4. Rubber bumper (2)

Fig. 8 Trunk lid—1992–98 Eldorado and Seville

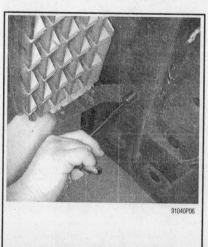

Fig. 9 Remove the grille retaining bolts from the top of the grille and . . .

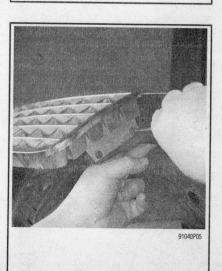

Fig. 10 . . . the side of the grille

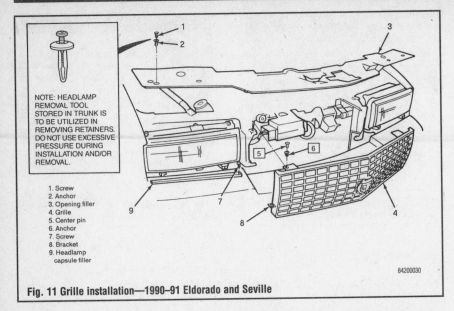

NOTE: HEADLAMP REMOVAL TOOL STORED IN TRUNK IS TO BE UTILIZED IN REMOVING RETAINERS. DO NOT USE EXCESSIVE PRESSURE DURING INSTALLATION AND/OR REMOVAL.

1. Screw
2. Anchor
3. Opening filler
4. Grille
5. Center pin
6. Anchor
7. Screw
8. Bracket
9. Headlamp capsule filler

84200030

Fig. 11 Grille installation—1990–91 Eldorado and Seville

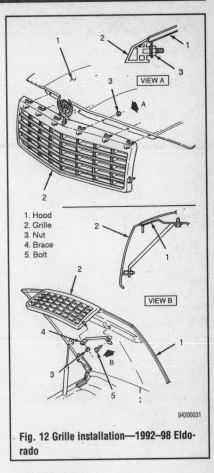

1. Hood
2. Grille
3. Nut
4. Brace
5. Bolt

84200031

Fig. 12 Grille installation—1992–98 Eldorado

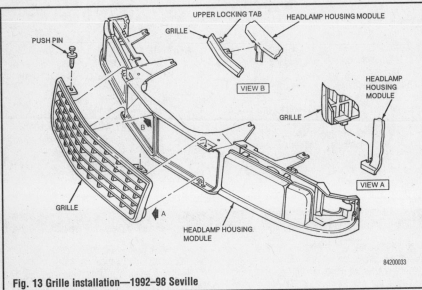

84200033

Fig. 13 Grille installation—1992–98 Seville

3. Remove the 4 nuts attaching the grille to the hood and remove the hood.

To install:

4. Position the grille to the hood and support bracket.

5. Install the nuts to the hood and the screws to the support bracket.

Eldorado and Seville

1990–91 MODELS

▶ **See Figure 11**

1. Open the hood.

2. Remove the 4 plastic screws and anchors securing the radiator/grille opening filler and remove the opening filler.

3. Remove the 2 plastic screws at each side of the grille securing the headlamp filler to the bracket.

4. Remove the 4 grille retainers. Pull the center pin out and remove with the anchor.

5. Remove the grille.

To install:

6. Position the grille and secure with the grille retainers. Push in the anchor and the center pin.

7. Install the 2 plastic screws at each side of the grille securing the headlamp filler to the bracket.

8. Position the radiator/grille opening filler and secure with the plastic anchors and screws.

1992–98 ELDORADO

▶ **See Figure 12**

1. Open the hood.

2. Remove the 2 bolts securing the secondary latch release lever and the 2 nuts securing the grille support brace.

3. Remove the 6 grille-to-hood nuts and remove the grille.

To install:

4. Position the grille and install the 6 nuts.

5. Install the 2 nuts securing the support brace and the 2 bolts securing the secondary latch release lever.

1992–98 SEVILLE

▶ **See Figure 13**

1. Open the hood.

2. Remove the 4 plastic rivets and unsnap the 2 clips securing the headlamp housing upper filler panel. Remove the filler panel.

3. Remove the 2 push pins and release the locking tabs.

4. Remove the grille.

To install:

5. Install the grille, making sure the retaining tabs engage the slots in the headlamp housing module.

6. Install the 2 push pins.

7. Install the headlamp housing upper filler panel. Snap the clips and install the plastic riv-ets.

Outside Mirrors

REMOVAL & INSTALLATION

▶ **See Figures 14, 15 and 16**

1. Disconnect the negative battery cable.

2. Remove the door trim panel.

3. Detach the wiring connector.

4. If necessary, remove the trim plate.

5. If necessary, remove the foam sound insulator.

6. Remove the 3 mounting nuts and the mirror. The black plastic cap under the door weatherstrip must be removed to access the forward nut.

Fig. 14 Detach the mirror wiring connector

Fig. 15 Remove the 3 mounting nuts while supporting the mirror and . . .

Fig. 16 . . . remove the mirror from the door

To install:

7. Position the mirror to the door and install the mounting nuts. Tighten to 54 inch lbs. (6 Nm).

8. Install the black plastic cap under the weatherstrip.

9. Attach the wiring connector.

10. If necessary, install the foam sound insulator.

11. If necessary, install the mirror trim plate.

12. Install the door trim panel.

13. Connect the negative battery cable.

Antenna

REPLACEMENT

1990–93 Deville and Fleetwood

1. Disconnect the negative battery cable.
2. Open the trunk and pull back the trunk liner.
3. Remove the antenna upper nut and bezel.

4. Remove the antenna bracket bolts.

5. Detach the wiring connector from the relay.

6. Disconnect the antenna cable and remove the antenna assembly.

To install:

7. Position the antenna assembly and connect the antenna cable.

8. Install the antenna bracket bolts.

9. Install the antenna bezel and upper nut.

10. Attach the wiring connector to the relay.

11. Reposition the trunk liner.

12. Connect the negative battery cable.

Eldorado and Seville; 1994–98 Deville

1. Disconnect the negative battery cable.

2. Open the trunk and remove the right-hand sound insulating panel.

3. Detach the antenna cable and detach the wiring connector from the relay.

4. Disconnect the ground strap from the body, if equipped.

5. On 1990–91 vehicles, use a suitable tool to remove the antenna mounting nut above the fender. Be careful not to strip the nut or slip and damage the paint.

6. Remove the nut from the mounting bracket to wheelwell weld flange and remove the antenna assembly.

To install:

7. Position the antenna assembly and install the nut through the mounting bracket to wheel-well.

8. On 1990–91 vehicles, install the antenna mounting nut above the fender.

9. Connect the ground strap, if equipped.

10. Attach the wiring connector to the antenna relay and connect the antenna cable.

11. Install the sound insulating panel.

12. Connect the negative battery cable.

INTERIOR

Instrument Panel and Pad

REMOVAL & INSTALLATION

✳✳ CAUTION

When performing service around Supplemental Inflatable Restraint (SIR) system components or wiring, the SIR system must be disabled. Failure to do so could result in possible air bag deployment, personal injury or unneeded SIR system repairs.

1990–93 Deville and Fleetwood

♦ See Figures 17, 18 and 19

1. Disconnect the negative battery cable.

2. Disable the Supplemental Inflatable Restraint (SIR) system.

3. Remove the push-on nuts and screws and remove the right, then left sound insulators.

4. Carefully pry the heating/air conditioning outlets from the upper trim pad.

5. Remove the upper trim pad retaining screws. One screw is found behind each outlet and 3 screws are accessed through the defroster outlet.

6. Remove the retaining screws, label and detach the wiring connectors from the switches and light, and remove the glove box module.

7. Remove 2 screws through the glove box opening.

8. Detach the in-vehicle temperature sensor wiring connector and aspirator tube.

9. Remove the solar sensor from the upper trim pad and remove the upper trim pad.

10. Snap out the upper steering column filler.

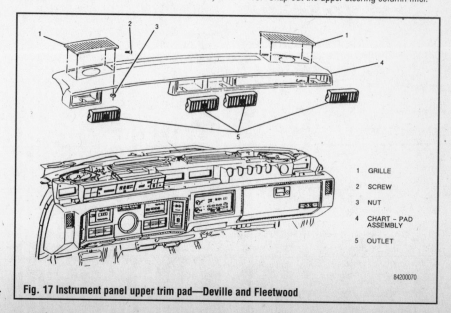

1	GRILLE
2	SCREW
3	NUT
4	CHART – PAD ASSEMBLY
5	OUTLET

Fig. 17 Instrument panel upper trim pad—Deville and Fleetwood

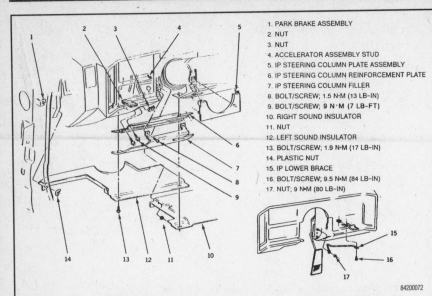

1. PARK BRAKE ASSEMBLY
2. NUT
3. NUT
4. ACCELERATOR ASSEMBLY STUD
5. IP STEERING COLUMN PLATE ASSEMBLY
6. IP STEERING COLUMN REINFORCEMENT PLATE
7. IP STEERING COLUMN FILLER
8. BOLT/SCREW; 1.5 N•M (13 LB-IN)
9. BOLT/SCREW; 9 N•M (7 LB-FT)
10. RIGHT SOUND INSULATOR
11. NUT
12. LEFT SOUND INSULATOR
13. BOLT/SCREW; 1.9 N•M (17 LB-IN)
14. PLASTIC NUT
15. IP LOWER BRACE
16. BOLT/SCREW; 9.5 N•M (84 LB-IN)
17. NUT; 9 N•M (80 LB-IN)

84200072

Fig. 18 Instrument panel steering column reinforcement plate and instrument panel lower brace—Deville and Fleetwood

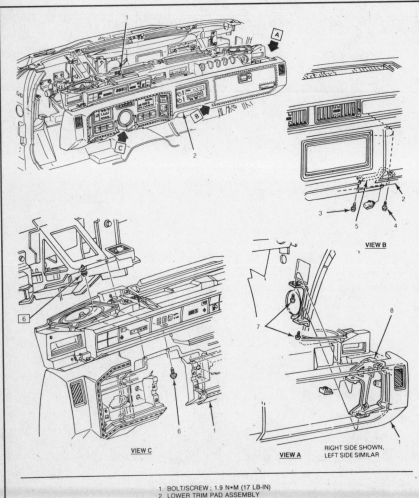

1. BOLT/SCREW; 1.9 N•M (17 LB-IN)
2. LOWER TRIM PAD ASSEMBLY
3. BOLT/SCREW; 9 N•M (7 LB-FT)
4. BOLT/SCREW; 12 N•M (9 LB-FT)
5. LOWER TRIM PAD SUPPORT
6. BOLT/SCREW; 12 N•M (106 LB-IN)
7. BOLT/SCREW; 9 N•M (7 LB-FT)
8. I/P OUTER BRACKET

VIEW B

VIEW C

VIEW A   RIGHT SIDE SHOWN, LEFT SIDE SIMILAR

84200073

Fig. 19 Instrument panel lower trim pad—Deville and Fleetwood

Remove the retaining screws and remove the lower steering column filler, then the steering column reinforcement plate.

11. Lower the steering column.

12. Remove the lower trim pad support.

13. Remove the nut from the accelerator pedal stud and the screw(s) from the instrument panel end of the instrument panel lower brace. Remove the instrument panel lower brace.

14. Remove the lower trim pad retaining screws. Label and detach the necessary wiring connectors.

15. Remove the lower trim pad with the aid of an assistant.

16. If necessary, disassemble the lower trim pad by removing the following components:
   a. Information centers
   b. Trim plates
   c. Headlamp switch
   d. Fuel data center
   e. Climate control panel
   f. Instrument cluster
   g. Radio
   h. Ashtray
   i. Warning/reminder chime module
   j. A/C ducts
   k. Instrument panel harness
   l. Knee bolster
   m. Headlamp switch bracket
   n. Instrument panel outer brackets
   o. Side window defogger outlets
   p. Clips and nuts

To install:

17. If necessary, assemble the lower trim pad by installing the following components:
   a. Clips and nuts
   b. Side window defogger outlets
   c. Instrument panel outer brackets
   d. Headlamp switch bracket
   e. Knee bolster
   f. Instrument panel harness
   g. A/C ducts
   h. Warning/reminder chime module
   i. Headlamp switch
   j. Radio
   k. Ashtray
   l. Information centers
   m. Climate control panel
   n. Fuel data center
   o. Instrument cluster
   p. Trim plates

18. Position the lower trim pad in the vehicle with the aid of an assistant.

19. Attach the wiring connectors and install the retaining screws.

20. Install the steering column.

21. Install the steering column reinforcement plate and tighten the screws to 17 inch lbs. (1.9 Nm).

22. Install the lower steering column filler and tighten the screws to 13 inch lbs. (1.5 Nm). Snap in the upper steering column filler.

23. Attach the in-vehicle temperature sensor wiring connector and aspirator tube. Install the solar sensor to the upper trim pad.

24. Position the upper trim pad and install the retaining screws. Install the outlets.

25. Attach the wiring connectors to the switches and light and position the glove box module. Install the retaining screws.

26. Install the instrument panel lower brace over the accelerator pedal stud and install the screw at

the instrument panel end of the brace. Tighten to 84 inch lbs. (9.5 Nm). Tighten the nut to the accelerator pedal stud to 84 inch lbs. (9.5 Nm).

27. Install the lower trim pad support.
28. Install the left, then right sound insulators.
29. Enable the SIR system.
30. Connect the negative battery cable.

Eldorado and Seville; 1994–98 Deville

1990–91 MODELS

▶ **See Figures 20, 21 and 22**

1. Disconnect the negative battery cable.
2. Disable the Supplemental Inflatable Restraint (SIR) system.
3. Remove the 3 screws and the center sound insulator.
4. Remove the 3 screws and 2 nuts retaining the right side sound insulator. Remove the courtesy lamp and remove the right side sound insulator.
5. Remove the 2 screws and the center trim plate.
6. Remove the 5 screws and the knee bolster.
7. Remove the 4 screws and the instrument panel steering column reinforcement plate.
8. Remove the steering column.
9. Remove the 3 screws and the Climate Control/Driver Information Center.
10. Remove the instrument cluster.
11. Remove the front console assembly.
12. Detach the dash-to-instrument panel interconnect.
13. Remove the 4 screws and the glove box unit. Pull the fuse panel up from the dash panel.
14. Label and detach the instrument panel wiring connectors.
15. Remove the instrument panel reinforcement brace.
16. Remove the 6 screws retaining the instrument panel. With the aid of an assistant, remove the instrument panel from the vehicle.

To install:

17. With the aid of an assistant, position the instrument panel in the vehicle. Install the retaining screws.
18. Install the instrument panel reinforcement brace.
19. Attach the instrument panel wiring connectors.
20. Push the glove box fuse panel into place in the dash panel. Install the glove box unit with the 4 screws.
21. Attach the dash-to-instrument panel interconnect.
22. Install the front console assembly.
23. Install the instrument cluster.
24. Install the Climate Control/Driver Information Center with the 3 screws.
25. Install the steering column.
26. Install the instrument panel steering column reinforcement plate with the 4 screws.
27. Install the knee bolster and the center trim panel.
28. Install the courtesy lamp to the right side sound insulator and install the sound insulator with the nuts and screws.
29. Install the center sound insulator.
30. Enable the SIR system.
31. Connect the negative battery cable.

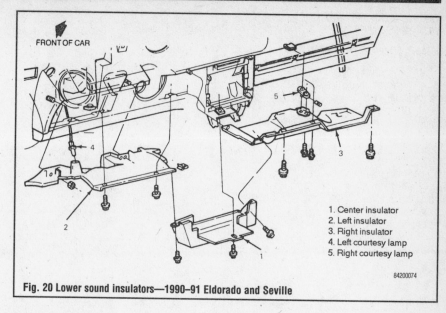

1. Center insulator
2. Left insulator
3. Right insulator
4. Left courtesy lamp
5. Right courtesy lamp

84200074

Fig. 20 Lower sound insulators—1990–91 Eldorado and Seville

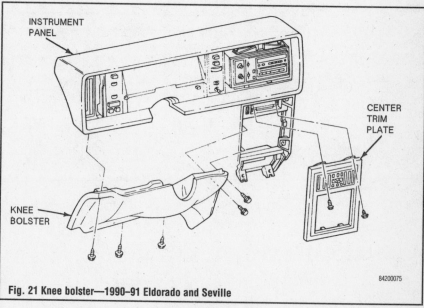

84200075

Fig. 21 Knee bolster—1990–91 Eldorado and Seville

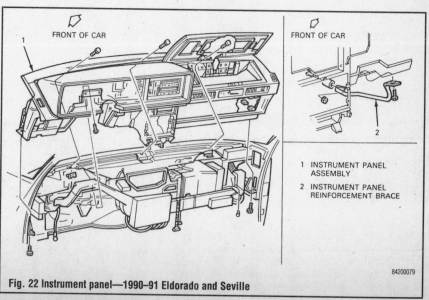

1. INSTRUMENT PANEL ASSEMBLY
2. INSTRUMENT PANEL REINFORCEMENT BRACE

84200079

Fig. 22 Instrument panel—1990–91 Eldorado and Seville

1992–98 ELDORADO AND SEVILLE; 1994–98 DEVILLE

▶ **See Figures 23, 24 and 25**

1. Disconnect the negative battery cable.
2. Disable the Supplemental Inflatable Restraint (SIR) system.
3. Carefully pry upward, using a small, flat-bladed tool, to remove the defroster grille.
4. Remove the Sunload and Headlamp Auto Control sensors from the defroster grille.
5. Working through the defroster grille opening, remove 3 upper trim panel retaining screws.
6. Remove the heater/air conditioning vents from the front of the instrument panel by releasing the tab on each side from inside the vent and pulling out.
7. Working through the vent openings, remove 4 upper trim panel retaining screws and remove the upper trim panel.
8. Remove the instrument cluster.
9. Remove the right and left A/C vent trim panels.
10. Open the trap door in the rear of the glove compartment and remove the passenger inflatable restraint wiring connector from the retaining clip on the rear of the glove compartment assembly.
11. Remove the 4 glove compartment-to-instrument panel retaining screws.
12. Pull the glove compartment assembly outward enough to access the wiring connectors for the glove compartment switches. Label and detach the wiring connectors.
13. Remove the glove compartment assembly from the instrument panel.
14. Remove the retaining screws and courtesy lamps from the right and left sound insulators and remove the sound insulators.
15. Remove the steering column opening filler trim by grasping at the front and rear edges and pulling downward.
16. Remove the 4 retaining bolts and the steering column opening bracket.
17. If equipped with full console, remove the console.
18. If equipped with mini console, remove the radio.
19. Remove the headlamp switch module.
20. Remove the 2 bolts and the hood latch release.
21. Move the driver's seat to its full rearward position.
22. Remove the steering column.
23. Remove the 8 instrument panel retaining screws, detach the wiring connector at each side of the instrument panel, and remove the shims at the lower mounting screws.
24. Remove the instrument panel with the aid of an assistant.

To install:

25. With the aid of an assistant, position the instrument panel in the vehicle.
26. Attach the wiring connector at each side of the instrument panel, install the shims and the 8 instrument panel retaining screws.
27. Install the steering column.
28. Install the hood latch release with the 2 bolts.
29. Install the headlamp switch module.
30. If equipped with mini console, install the radio.

31. If equipped, install the console.
32. Install the steering column opening bracket and the steering column opening filler trim.
33. Install the right and left sound insulators.
34. Position the glove compartment assembly and attach the wiring connectors to the switches.
35. Push the glove compartment into place and install the retaining screws.
36. Place the passenger inflatable restraint wiring connector on the retaining clip on the rear of the glove compartment assembly and close the trap door.
37. Install the right and left A/C vent trim panels.
38. Install the instrument cluster.
39. Position the upper trim panel on top of the instrument panel, making sure the sensors are through the trim panel.
40. Install the upper trim panel retaining screws through the heater/air conditioning vent openings.
41. Gently push the heater/air conditioning vents into place.
42. Install the upper trim panel retaining screws through the defroster grille opening.

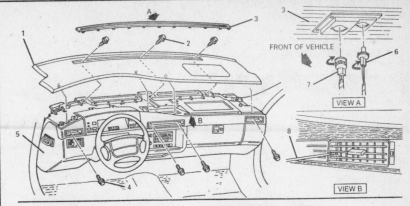

1	INSTRUMENT PANEL UPPER TRIM PANEL	5	INSTRUMENT PANEL CARRIER
2	SCREWS	6	SUNLOAD SENSOR
3	WINDSHIELD DEFROSTER GRILLE	7	HEADLAMP AUTO CONTROL AMBIENT LIGHT SENSOR
4	SCREWS	8	SMALL FLAT-BLADED TOOL

84200080

Fig. 23 Instrument panel upper trim panel—1992–98 Eldorado and Seville

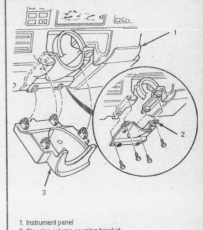

1. Instrument panel
2. Steering column opening bracket
3. Steering column opening filler trim

84200083

Fig. 24 Steering column opening bracket and filler trim—1992–98 Eldorado and Seville

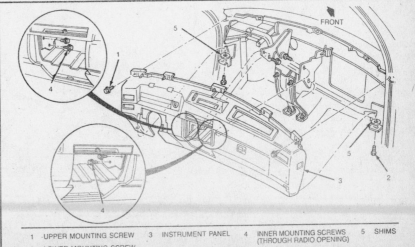

1 UPPER MOUNTING SCREW	3 INSTRUMENT PANEL	4 INNER MOUNTING SCREWS (THROUGH RADIO OPENING)	5 SHIMS
2 LOWER MOUNTING SCREW			

84200084

Fig. 25 Instrument panel—1992–98 Eldorado and Seville

43. Install the Sunload and Headlamp Auto Control sensors to the defroster grille.
44. Gently push the defroster grille into place.
45. Enable the SIR system.
46. Connect the negative battery cable.

Console

REMOVAL & INSTALLATION

1990 Deville and Fleetwood With 45/55 Split Seat

▶ See Figure 26

1. Disconnect the negative battery cable.
2. Remove the 4 mounting bolts.
3. Detach the wiring connector.
4. Remove the console.
To install:
5. Position the console in the vehicle and install the mounting bolts.

6. Attach the wiring connector.
7. Connect the negative battery cable.

1990–91 Eldorado and Seville Front Console

▶ See Figures 27, 28, 29 and 30

1. Disconnect the negative battery cable.
2. Remove the gearshift retaining clip and knob.
3. Remove the 2 retaining screws and remove the storage compartment assembly.
4. Pull the ashtray from the ashtray housing.
5. Detach the cigar lighter wiring connector.
6. Remove the retaining screw and the ashtray housing assembly.
7. Remove the 5 upper console retaining screws.
8. Disconnect the illumination bulbs and sockets and remove the upper console assembly.
9. Remove the retaining screw and 2 nuts retaining the lower console to the brackets.

10. Remove the 2 lower console-to-instrument panel retaining screws, the support rod and the lower console.
To install:
11. Install the lower console and support rod.
12. Install the 2 lower console-to-instrument panel retaining screws.
13. Install the screw and 2 nuts securing the lower console to the brackets.
14. Connect the bulbs and sockets to the upper console and install the upper console. Install the 5 upper-to-lower console retaining screws.
15. Install the ashtray housing and attach the cigar lighter wiring connector. Push the ashtray into the housing.
16. Install the storage compartment with the retaining screws.
17. Install the gearshift handle and retaining clip.
18. Connect the negative battery cable.

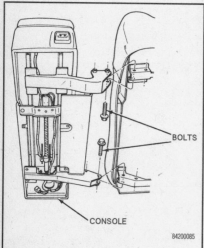

84200085

Fig. 26 Console—1990 Deville and Fleetwood with 45/55 split seat

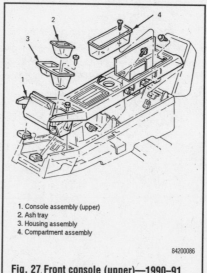

1. Console assembly (upper)
2. Ash tray
3. Housing assembly
4. Compartment assembly

84200086

Fig. 27 Front console (upper)—1990–91 Eldorado and Seville

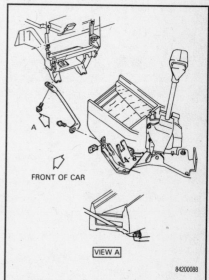

FRONT OF CAR

VIEW A

84200088

Fig. 28 Instrument panel support rod—1990–91 Eldorado and Seville

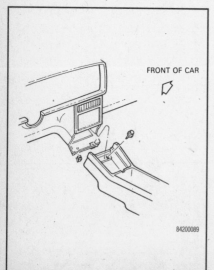

FRONT OF CAR

84200089

Fig. 29 Front console-to-instrument panel attachment—1990–91 Eldorado and Seville

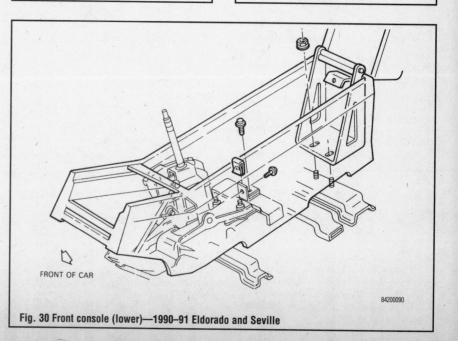

FRONT OF CAR

84200090

Fig. 30 Front console (lower)—1990–91 Eldorado and Seville

1990–91 Seville STS Rear Console

▶ **See Figure 31**

1. Disconnect the negative battery cable.
2. Open the upper and lower storage compartment doors. Remove the upper and lower storage compartment boxes by gently prying up and out of the console assembly.
3. Remove the 2 lower retaining bolts and 2 upper retaining screws.
4. Remove the 3 screws retaining the lumbar seat air pump and control assembly from the back of the upper console assembly.
5. Lift and remove the console assembly.

To install:

6. Position the console assembly in the vehicle.

7. Install the lumbar seat air pump and control assembly on the back of the upper console and secure with the 3 screws.
8. Install the console retaining screws and bolts.
9. Snap the upper and lower storage compartment boxes into place.
10. Connect the negative battery cable.

1992–98 Seville, Eldorado and 1994–98 Deville Full Console

▶ **See Figures 32 and 33**

1. Disconnect the negative battery cable.
2. Remove the storage compartment by pulling up and out.

3. Remove the gearshift handle retaining clip and handle.
4. Gently pull the console upper trim plate up and out.
5. Detach the wiring connector for the cigar lighter.
6. Remove the radio.
7. Remove the 4 console-to-instrument panel retaining screws.
8. Remove the gear selector trim plate, which is retained by clips, and the PRNDL illumination lamp socket.
9. Remove the 2 shifter plate upper mounting bolts and the 2 nuts retaining the shifter assembly to the floor.
10. Working through the storage compartment opening, remove the 2 console-to-floor retaining nuts.
11. Turn to release the console blower air supply duct.
12. Slide the console up, then label and detach the wiring connectors.
13. Slide the console back to clear the shifter and remove the console.

To install:

14. Position the console over the shifter and attach the wiring connectors.
15. Turn to push on the console blower air supply duct.
16. Working through the storage compartment opening, install the 2 console-to-floor retaining nuts.
17. Install the 2 shifter assembly-to-floor retaining nuts and the 2 shifter plate upper mounting bolts.
18. Install the PRNDL illumination lamp socket and gear selector trim plate.
19. Install the 4 console-to-instrument panel retaining screws.
20. Install the radio.
21. Attach the wiring connector for the cigar lighter and install the console upper trim plate.
22. Install the gearshift handle and retaining clip.
23. Install the storage compartment.
24. Connect the negative battery cable.

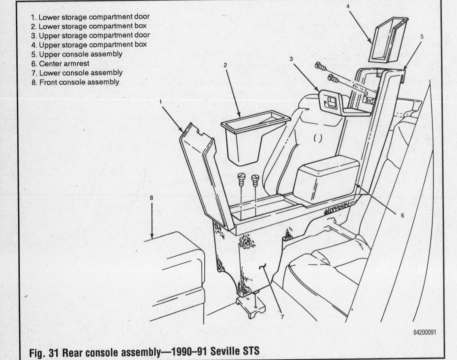

1. Lower storage compartment door
2. Lower storage compartment box
3. Upper storage compartment door
4. Upper storage compartment box
5. Upper console assembly
6. Center armrest
7. Lower console assembly
8. Front console assembly

84200091

Fig. 31 Rear console assembly—1990–91 Seville STS

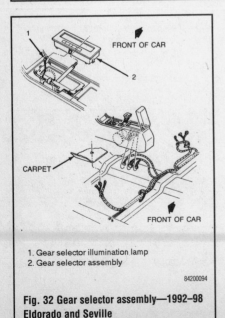

FRONT OF CAR

CARPET

FRONT OF CAR

1. Gear selector illumination lamp
2. Gear selector assembly

84200094

Fig. 32 Gear selector assembly—1992–98 Eldorado and Seville

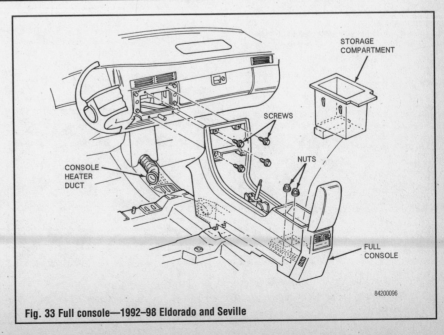

STORAGE COMPARTMENT

SCREWS

NUTS

CONSOLE HEATER DUCT

FULL CONSOLE

84200096

Fig. 33 Full console—1992–98 Eldorado and Seville

1992–98 Seville, Eldorado, And 1994–98 Deville Mini Console

1. Disconnect the negative battery cable.
2. Pull the storage compartment up and out.
3. Working through the storage compartment opening, remove the 2 retaining nuts.
4. Remove a console-to-floor retaining bolt from each side of the front of the console.
5. Label and detach the wiring connectors.
6. Remove the console.

To install:

7. Position the console in the vehicle and attach the wiring connectors.
8. Install a console-to-floor retaining bolt at each side of the front of the console.
9. Working through the storage compartment opening, install the 2 retaining nuts.
10. Install the storage compartment.
11. Connect the negative battery cable.

Door Panels

REMOVAL & INSTALLATION

Deville and Fleetwood

FRONT DOOR

♦ **See Figures 34 thru 45**

1. Disconnect the negative battery cable.
2. Insert a flat-bladed tool between the door panel and the rear edge of the power window switch plate to disengage the retainer from the panel.
3. Slide the power window switch plate forward, then label and detach the wiring connectors.
4. Remove the power door lock switch plate retaining screw. Remove the switch plate and detach the wiring connector.
5. Remove the pull handle retaining screws.
6. Using a thin-bladed tool, carefully pry the courtesy lamp lenses off. Remove the courtesy lamp bulb.
7. Pinch the courtesy lamp retainers and pull out the lamp socket holder. Detach the courtesy lamp wiring connector.
8. Remove the door panel retaining screws.
9. Using tool J-2459B or equivalent, disengage the door panel fasteners from the holes in the door. Detach any remaining wiring connectors and remove the door panel.

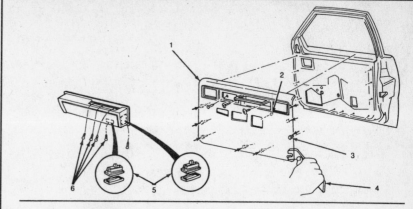

1	TRIM PANEL	4	TOOL J 2459B
2	RETAINER NUTS (ARMREST)	5	LENS ASSEMBLIES
3	TRIM PANEL RETAINERS	6	SCREWS (TRIM PANEL)

84200098

Fig. 34 Front door panel—1990–91 Deville and Fleetwood

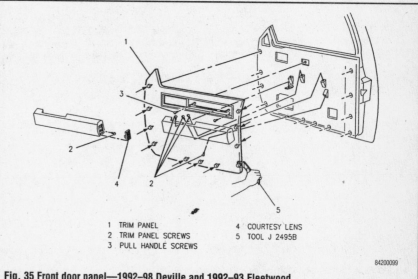

1	TRIM PANEL	4	COURTESY LENS
2	TRIM PANEL SCREWS	5	TOOL J 2495B
3	PULL HANDLE SCREWS		

84200099

Fig. 35 Front door panel—1992–98 Deville and 1992–93 Fleetwood

To install:

10. Position the door panel close to the door and attach the wiring connectors.
11. Align the door panel fasteners with the holes in the door. Push in on the door panel to install it to the door.
12. Install the door panel and pull handle retaining screws.
13. Install the courtesy lamps and switch plates.
14. Connect the negative battery cable.

91040P03

Fig. 36 Carefully pry up the power window switchplate and . . .

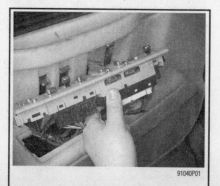

91040P01

Fig. 37 . . . gently remove it from the door panel

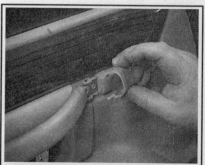

91040P50

Fig. 38 Remove the door pull strap retaining screw covers by gently prying them off

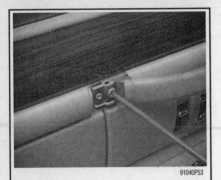

Fig. 39 Remove the door pull strap retaining screws

Fig. 40 Gently pull the inside door handle panel down and . . .

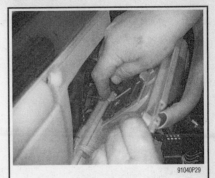

Fig. 41 . . . release the rod from the handle

Fig. 42 Carefully lift up the door panel to release the . . .

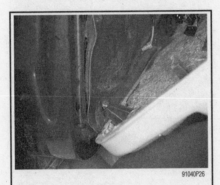

Fig. 43 . . . retaining pegs on the door panel

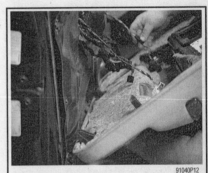

Fig. 44 Do not pull the panel too far away from the door, as some components still have a wiring harness connected

Fig. 45 Detach any necessary wiring connectors and remove the door panel from the vehicle

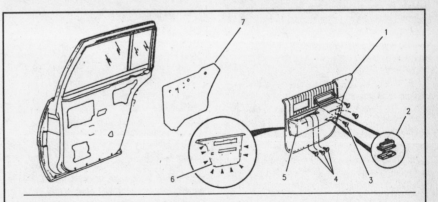

1 TRIM PANEL
2 LENS ASSEMBLIES
3 RETAINING SCREWS (TRIM PANEL)
4 RETAINING SCREWS
5 ARMREST
6 RETAINERS (TRIM PANEL)
7 WATER DEFLECTOR

84200102

Fig. 46 Rear door panel—Deville and Fleetwood

REAR DOOR

▶ See Figure 46

1. Disconnect the negative battery cable.
2. Using a thin-bladed tool, carefully pry the courtesy lamp lenses off. Remove the courtesy lamp bulb.
3. Pinch the courtesy lamp retainers and pull out the lamp socket holder. Detach the courtesy lamp wiring connector.
4. Insert a flat-bladed tool between the door panel and the rear edge of the power window switch plate to disengage the retainer from the panel.
5. Slide the power window switch plate forward, then label and detach the wiring connectors.
6. Remove the power door lock switch plate

retaining screw. Remove the switch plate and detach the wiring connector.
7. Remove the door panel retaining screws and the retaining screws under the pull handle.
8. Using tool J-2459B or equivalent, disengage the door panel fasteners from the holes in the door and remove the door panel.

To install:

9. Align the door panel fasteners with the holes in the door. Push in on the door panel to install it to the door.

10. Install the retaining screws under the pull handle and the door panel retaining screws.
11. Install the switch plates and courtesy lamp assemblies.
12. Connect the negative battery cable.

Eldorado and Seville

1990–91 FRONT DOOR

1. Disconnect the negative battery cable.
2. Insert a flat-bladed tool between the door

panel and the front edge of the power seat switch plate to disengage the retainer from the panel. Slide the switch plate forward and detach the wiring connectors.

3. Insert a flat-bladed tool between the door panel and the rear edge of the power window switch plate to disengage the retainer from the panel. Slide the switch plate rearward and detach the wiring connector.

4. On all except Seville STS, remove the cover plug and screw from the power door lock switch plate and remove the finishing cup. Remove the door lock switch plate retaining screw and detach the switch wiring connector.

5. On Eldorado, lift up on the pull handle and remove the 2 retaining screws. Push down on top of the handle, tip it out and up to remove it from the door panel.

6. On Seville, except STS, remove the pull strap covers by sliding them away from the pull strap. Remove the retaining screws and remove the pull strap.

7. On Seville STS, use 2 small flat-bladed tools to carefully pry and slide off the 2 pull strap covers. Remove the 2 screws at the pull strap, then remove the plug, screw and pull control blockout cover. Remove the pull strap panel and detach the wiring connector at the lock switch.

8. Remove the 2 door panel retaining screws at the rear edge of the door panel.

9. Using tool J-2459B or equivalent, disengage the door panel fasteners from the holes in the door. Label and detach the speaker, courtesy and warning lamp connectors and remove the door panel.

To install:

10. Position the door panel close to the door and attach the speaker, courtesy and warning lamp connectors.

11. Align the door panel fasteners with the holes in the door. Push in on the door panel to install it to the door.

12. Install the 2 door panel retaining screws at the rear edge of the door panel.

13. Install the pull handle or pull strap and the switch plates.

14. Connect the negative battery cable.

1990-91 REAR DOOR—SEVILLE ONLY

♦ See Figure 47

1. Disconnect the negative battery cable.

2. Using a flat-bladed tool, carefully push in and pull up the power window switch plate. Unscrew the knob and detach the wiring connector at the window switch and detach the wiring connector at the lighter. Remove the switch plate.

3. On all except STS, remove the pull strap covers by sliding them away from the pull strap. Remove the retaining screws and remove the pull strap.

4. On STS, use 2 small flat-bladed tools to carefully pry and slide off the 2 pull strap covers. Remove the 2 screws at the pull strap, then remove the plug, screw and pull control blockout cover. Remove the pull strap panel and detach the wiring connector at the lock switch.

5. Remove the door panel retaining screw at the rear edge of the door panel.

6. Using tool J-2459B or equivalent, disengage the door panel fasteners from the holes in the

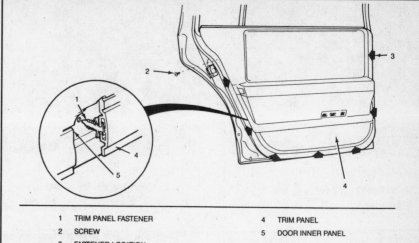

1	TRIM PANEL FASTENER		4	TRIM PANEL
2	SCREW		5	DOOR INNER PANEL
3	FASTENER LOCATION			

84200112

Fig. 47 Rear door panel—1990–91 Seville

door. Detach the courtesy and lamp connectors and remove the door panel.

To install:

7. Position the door panel close to the door and attach the courtesy lamp connectors.

8. Align the door panel fasteners with the holes in the door. Push in on the door panel to install it to the door.

9. Install the door panel retaining screw at the rear edge of the door panel.

10. Install the pull strap and the switch plates.

11. Connect the negative battery cable.

1992-98 ELDORADO

1. Disconnect the negative battery cable.

2. Remove the power window switch plate as follows:

   a. Use a 1/2 in. wide flat-bladed tool to pry up on the rear edge of the trim plate.

   b. Insert the blade 3/4 in. into the door trim to engage the retention clip. Press firmly toward the switch plate to disengage the clip.

   c. Pull the flat-bladed tool upward while pressing firmly toward the plate to pull the plate from the door panel.

➡**Before lifting the switch plate from the door panel, make sure the flat-bladed tool has fully disengaged the retention clip, or damage to the switch plate or clip may occur.**

   d. Label and detach the wiring connectors and remove the switch plate.

3. Carefully pull the power door lock switch trim plate from the door panel. Detach the wiring connector for the switch and remove the door lock switch.

4. Working through the switch plate opening, remove the door panel retaining screw.

5. Insert a flat-bladed tool between the upper rear corner of the carpet attached to the door panel. Disengage the fastener and fold back the carpet to expose the door panel retaining screw. Remove the screw.

6. Lift the door panel up and away from the door to disengage the hooks.

To install:

7. Position the door panel on the door. Align

the hooks to the holes in the door and push in and down on the door panel.

8. Install one screw through the switch plate opening and one screw under the carpet.

9. Fold the carpet flush to the trim panel and engage the fastener.

10. Install the door switches.

11. Connect the negative battery cable.

1992-98 SEVILLE

1. Disconnect the negative battery cable.

2. If removing the front door panel, remove the power window switch plate as follows:

   a. Use a 1/2 in. wide flat-bladed tool to pry up on the rear edge of the trim plate.

   b. Insert the blade 3/4 in. into the door trim to engage the retention clip. Press firmly toward the switch plate to disengage the clip.

   c. Pull the flat-bladed tool upward while pressing firmly toward the plate to pull the plate from the door panel.

➡**Before lifting the switch plate from the door panel, make sure the flat-bladed tool has fully disengaged the retention clip, or damage to the switch plate or clip may occur.**

   d. Label and detach the wiring connectors and remove the switch plate.

3. If removing the rear door panel, remove the power window switch plate as follows:

   a. Using a flat-bladed tool, carefully push in firmly and pull up to disengage the window switch/ash tray clip from the door panel.

   b. Label and detach the wiring connectors for the window switch and lighter.

   c. Remove the window switch/ash tray.

4. Carefully pull the power door lock switch trim plate from the door panel. Detach the wiring connectors for the switch and lamp and remove the door lock switch.

5. Remove one door panel retaining screw from the door lock switch plate area.

6. Insert a flat-bladed tool between the upper rear corner of the carpet attached to the door panel. Disengage the fastener and fold back the carpet to expose the door panel retaining screw. Remove the screw.

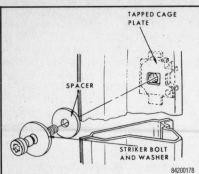

Fig. 48 Door lock striker—1990 Deville and Fleetwood, and 1990–91 Eldorado and Seville

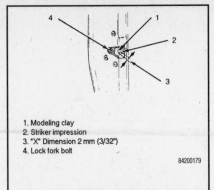

1. Modeling clay
2. Striker impression
3. "X" Dimension 2 mm (3/32")
4. Lock fork bolt

84200179

Fig. 49 Door lock-to-striker fore-and-aft adjustment—1990 Deville and Fleetwood

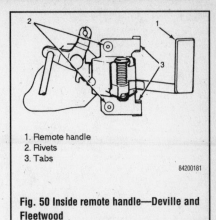

1. Remote handle
2. Rivets
3. Tabs

84200181

Fig. 50 Inside remote handle—Deville and Fleetwood

7. Lift the door panel up and out to disengage the door panel hooks from the holes in the door.

To install:

8. Position the door panel on the door. Align the hooks to the holes in the door and push in and down on the door panel.

9. Install the door panel retaining screws.

10. Fold the carpet flush to the trim panel and engage the fastener.

11. Install the door switches.

12. Connect the negative battery cable.

Door Locks

REMOVAL & INSTALLATION

1990 Deville and Fleetwood

LOCK STRIKER

▶ See Figures 48 and 49

1. Mark the position of the striker on the body lock pillar using a pencil.

2. Use tool J-23457, BT 7107 or equivalent, remove the lock striker.

To install:

3. Install the striker to the body using tool J-23457, BT 7107 or equivalent. Align the striker with the pencil marks and tighten the striker bolt to 42 ft. lbs. (55 Nm).

4. If striker adjustment is necessary, proceed as follows:

 a. Make sure the door is properly aligned.

 b. Apply modeling clay or body caulking compound to the lock bolt opening.

 c. Close the door just enough for the striker bolt to form an impression in the clay or caulking compound.

➡**Closing the door completely will make clay removal difficult.**

 d. The striker impression should be centered fore and aft. The minimum allowable measurement for dimension X is 3/32 in. (2mm). The maximum allowable measurement for dimension X is 5/32 in. (4mm). A 3/32 in. (2mm) spacer, part No. 4469196 or equivalent, can be used for alignment.

 e. If adjustment is necessary, insert tool J-23457, BT 7107 or equivalent, into the star-shaped recess in the head of the striker and loosen the striker bolt. Shift the striker as

required, then tighten the striker bolt to 42 ft. lbs. (55 Nm).

5. Touch up any exposed unpainted surface on the lock pillar next to the striker, if the striker is outside the pencil marks.

INSIDE REMOTE HANDLE

▶ See Figure 50

1. Remove the door panel.

2. Remove the water deflector.

3. Center punch each rivet, then drill out the rivets using a 3/8 in. (4.8mm) drill bit.

4. Slide the remote handle rearward to disengage the tabs on the handle from the slots in the door.

To install:

5. Place the tabs on the handle into the slots in the door and slide the handle forward.

6. Secure the remote handle using 3/16 in. peel type rivets.

7. Install the water deflector and door panel.

POWER DOOR LOCK ACTUATOR

1. Remove the door panel.

2. Remove the water deflector.

3. Disconnect the actuator linkage from the bell crank.

4. Use a 3/16 in. (4.8mm) drill bit to drill out the rivets retaining the actuator to the door.

5. Remove the actuator.

To install:

6. Attach the actuator to the door using 5/16 in. rivets.

7. Connect the actuator linkage to the bell crank.

8. Check for proper operation.

9. Install the water deflector and door panel.

DOOR LOCK ASSEMBLY

▶ See Figures 51, 52 and 53

1. Remove the door panel.

2. Remove the water deflector.

3. Disconnect all rods attached to the lock.

4. Remove the lock by straightening the tabs.

5. Remove the door ajar switch attaching screw.

6. Remove the door ajar switch by pushing down on the switch to disengage the lip on the switch from the lock.

To install:

➡**A new service lock will have a block-out plug installed. Do not operate the lock or remove the plug until the lock is installed and the rod is connected to the lock.**

7. Position the lip on the door ajar switch to the lock and push up on the switch. Install the attaching screw.

8. Position the lock on the door and bend the tabs over to secure.

9. Attach all rods that were disconnected in the removal procedure.

10. Remove the block-out plug, if necessary.

11. Install the water deflector and door panel.

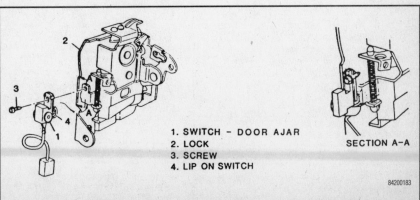

1. SWITCH – DOOR AJAR
2. LOCK
3. SCREW
4. LIP ON SWITCH

SECTION A-A

84200183

Fig. 51 Door lock assembly and door ajar switch—1990 Deville and Fleetwood, and 1990–91 Eldorado and Seville

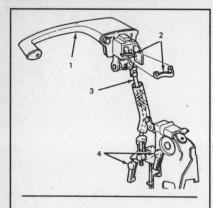

1. OUTSIDE HANDLE
2. BLOCK-OUT SPRING
3. OUTSIDE HANDLE TO LOCK ROD
4. BLOCK-OUT PLUG

84200184

Fig. 52 Door lock block-out spring and plug—1990 Deville and Fleetwood

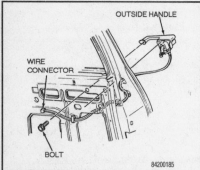

OUTSIDE HANDLE

WIRE CONNECTOR

BOLT

84200185

Fig. 53 Outside door handle installation—Deville and Fleetwood

OUTSIDE HANDLE

➡ The door glass must be in the full-up position for this procedure.

1. Remove the door panel.
2. Remove the water deflector.
3. Disconnect the rod from the outside handle.
4. Detach the wiring connector, if equipped.
5. Remove the retaining screws and remove the outside handle.

To install:

6. Install the outside handle and tighten the screws to 54 inch lbs. (7 Nm).
7. Attach the wiring connector, if equipped.
8. Connect the rod to the handle.
9. If installing a new service handle, remove the block-out spring.
10. Check the door lock system for proper operation.
11. Install the water deflector and door panel.

LOCK CYLINDER

♦ See Figure 54

➡ The door glass must be in the full-up position for this procedure.

1. Remove the door panel.
2. Remove the water deflector.

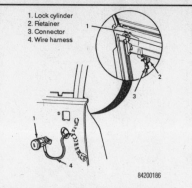

1. Lock cylinder
2. Retainer
3. Connector
4. Wire harness

84200186

Fig. 54 Door lock cylinder installation—Deville and Fleetwood

3. Disconnect the rod.
4. Detach the wiring connector, if equipped.
5. Detach or reposition any wiring harnesses that are in the way.
6. Use a flat-bladed tool to remove the lock cylinder retainer and remove the lock cylinder.

To install:

7. Install a gasket over the lock cylinder.
8. Install the lock cylinder, including any wiring harnesses that may be attached.
9. Install the lock cylinder retainer.
10. Attach the wiring connector, if equipped.
11. Connect or reposition any other wiring harnesses, as necessary.
12. Connect the rod.
13. Install the water deflector and door panel.

1991–93 Deville and Fleetwood

LOCK STRIKER

♦ See Figure 55

1. Mark the position of the striker on the body lock pillar using a pencil.
2. Remove the 2 striker bolts and the lock striker.

To install:

3. Position the lock striker on the lock pillar and install the striker bolts.
4. Align the striker with the pencil marks and tighten the bolts to 18 ft. lbs. (24 Nm).

5. If necessary, align the striker as follows:
   a. Loosen the striker bolts, then snug them so that the striker can still be moved.
   b. Hold the outside handle out and gently push the door against the body to be sure the striker allows a flush fit.
   c. Slowly open the door and tighten the striker bolts to 18 ft. lbs. (24 Nm).
   d. Touch up any exposed or unpainted surface on the lock pillar.

INSIDE REMOTE HANDLE

1. Remove the door panel.
2. Remove the water deflector.
3. Center punch each rivet, then drill out the rivets using a ³⁄₁₆ in. (4.8mm) drill bit.
4. Slide the remote handle rearward to disengage the tabs on the handle from the slots in the door.

To install:

5. Place the tabs on the handle into the slots in the door and slide the handle forward.
6. Secure the remote handle using ³⁄₁₆ in. peel type rivets.
7. Install the water deflector and door panel.

OUTSIDE HANDLE

➡ The door glass must be in the full-up position for this procedure.

1. Remove the door panel.
2. Remove the water deflector.
3. Disconnect the rod from the outside handle on 1991–92 vehicles or from the latch on 1993 vehicles.
4. Detach the wiring connector, if equipped.
5. Remove the retaining screws and remove the outside handle.

To install:

6. Install the outside handle and tighten the screws to 54 inch lbs. (7 Nm).
7. Attach the wiring connector, if equipped.
8. Connect the rod to the handle.
9. Remove the block-out spring, if equipped.
10. Check the door lock system for proper operation.
11. Install the water deflector and door panel.

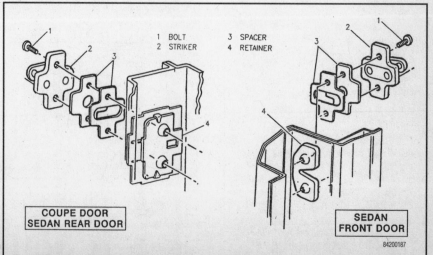

1. BOLT
2. STRIKER
3. SPACER
4. RETAINER

COUPE DOOR
SEDAN REAR DOOR

SEDAN FRONT DOOR

84200187

Fig. 55 Door lock striker—1991–93 Deville and Fleetwood

LOCK CYLINDER

➡ **The door glass must be in the full-up position for this procedure.**

1. Remove the door panel.
2. Remove the water deflector.
3. Disconnect the rod.
4. Detach the wiring connector, if equipped.
5. Detach or reposition any wiring harnesses that are in the way.
6. Use a flat-bladed tool to remove the lock cylinder retainer and remove the lock cylinder.

To install:

7. Install a gasket over the lock cylinder.
8. Install the lock cylinder, including any wiring harnesses that may be attached.
9. Install the lock cylinder retainer.
10. Attach the wiring connector, if equipped.
11. Connect or reposition any other wiring harnesses, as necessary.
12. Connect the rod.
13. Install the water deflector and door panel.

DOOR LOCK ACTUATOR—COUPE FRONT DOOR

▶ **See Figure 56**

1. Remove the door panel.
2. Remove the water deflector.
3. Detach the actuator harness.
4. Drill out the 2 rivets.
5. Disconnect the lock actuator linkage and remove the lock actuator.

To install:

6. Position the lock actuator and connect the linkage.
7. Install the actuator with 2 rivets.
8. Connect the actuator harness.
9. Install the water deflector and door panel.

DOOR LOCK ACTUATOR—SEDAN FRONT DOOR

▶ **See Figure 57**

1. Remove the door panel.
2. Remove the water deflector.
3. Drill out the 3 mounting plate-to-door rivets.
4. Detach the lock actuator harness.
5. Disconnect the lock actuator linkage.
6. Remove the mounting plate and actuator from the door.
7. Drill out the 2 actuator-to-mounting plate rivets and remove the actuator.

To install:

8. Install the actuator to the mounting plate with 2 rivets.
9. Position the mounting plate in the door.
10. Connect the lock actuator linkage and wiring harness.
11. Install 3 mounting plate-to-door rivets.
12. Install the water deflector and door panel.

DOOR LOCK ACTUATOR—REAR DOOR

▶ **See Figure 58**

1. Remove the door panel.
2. Remove the water deflector.
3. Drill out the rivet on the lock rod cover.
4. Drill out the 2 actuator rivets.
5. Detach the lock actuator harness.

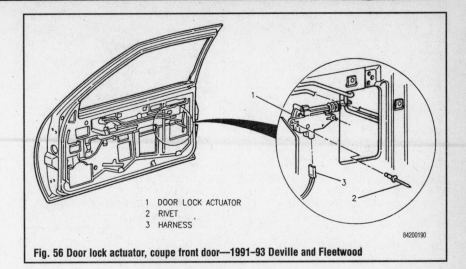

1 DOOR LOCK ACTUATOR
2 RIVET
3 HARNESS

84200190

Fig. 56 Door lock actuator, coupe front door—1991–93 Deville and Fleetwood

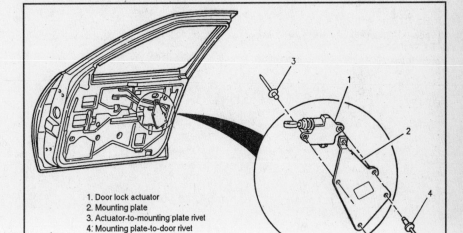

1. Door lock actuator
2. Mounting plate
3. Actuator-to-mounting plate rivet
4. Mounting plate-to-door rivet

84200191

Fig. 57 Door lock actuator, sedan front door—1991–93 Deville and Fleetwood

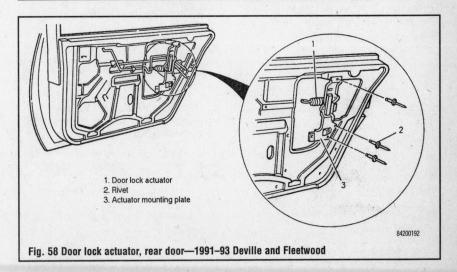

1. Door lock actuator
2. Rivet
3. Actuator mounting plate

84200192

Fig. 58 Door lock actuator, rear door—1991–93 Deville and Fleetwood

6. Disconnect the lock actuator linkage.
7. Remove the lock actuator.

To install:

8. Position the lock actuator and connect the linkage and wiring harness.

9. Install the 2 actuator rivets.
10. Install the rivet on the lock rod cover.
11. Install the water deflector and door panel.

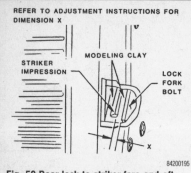

Fig. 59 Door lock-to-striker fore-and-aft adjustment—1990–91 Eldorado and Seville

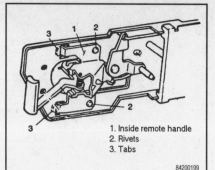

1. Inside remote handle
2. Rivets
3. Tabs

Fig. 60 Inside remote handle—1990–91 Eldorado and Seville

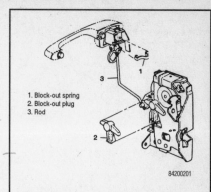

1. Block-out spring
2. Block-out plug
3. Rod

Fig. 61 Door lock block-out spring and plug—1990–91 Eldorado and Seville

1990–91 Eldorado and Seville

LOCK STRIKER

▶ See Figure 59

1. Mark the position of the striker on the body lock pillar using a pencil.
2. Use tool J-23457, BT 7107 or equivalent, remove the lock striker.

To install:

3. Install the striker to the body using tool J-23457, BT 7107 or equivalent. Align the striker with the pencil marks and tighten the striker bolt to 42 ft. lbs. (55 Nm).
4. If striker adjustment is necessary, proceed as follows:

   a. Make sure the door is properly aligned.
   b. Apply modeling clay or body caulking compound to the lock bolt opening.
   c. Close the door just enough for the striker bolt to form an impression in the clay or caulking compound.

➡**Closing the door completely will make clay removal difficult.**

   d. The striker impression should be centered fore and aft. The minimum allowable measurement for dimension X in is ³⁄₃₂ in. (2mm). The maximum allowable measurement for dimension X is ⁵⁄₃₂ in. (4mm). A ³⁄₃₂ in. (2mm) spacer, part No. 4469196 or equivalent, can be used for alignment.
   e. If adjustment is necessary, insert tool J-23457, BT 7107 or equivalent, into the star-shaped recess in the head of the striker and loosen the striker bolt. Shift the striker as required, then tighten the striker bolt to 42 ft. lbs. (55 Nm).

5. Touch up any exposed unpainted surface on the lock pillar next to the striker, if the striker is outside the pencil marks.

INSIDE REMOTE HANDLE

▶ See Figure 60

1. Remove the door panel.
2. Remove the water deflector.
3. Center punch each rivet, then drill out the rivets using a ³⁄₁₆ in. (4.8mm) drill bit.
4. Slide the remote handle rearward to disengage the tabs on the handle from the slots in module assembly.

To install:

5. Place the tabs on the handle into the slots in the module and slide the handle forward.
6. Secure the remote handle using ³⁄₁₆ in. peel type rivets.
7. Install the water deflector and door panel.

LOCK ACTUATOR

1. Remove the water deflector.
2. Remove the screws retaining the actuator to the lock module assembly and disengage the actuator from the bell crank.
3. Remove the actuator.

To install:

4. Connect the actuator to the bell crank and install the actuator retaining screws.
5. Install the water deflector and door panel.

LOCK ASSEMBLY

▶ See Figure 60

1. Remove the door panel.
2. Remove the water deflector.
3. Remove the lock module assembly.
4. Disconnect all rods attached to the lock.
5. Remove the lock by straightening the tabs.
6. Remove the door ajar switch attaching screw.
7. Remove the door ajar switch by pushing down on the switch to disengage the lip on the switch from the lock.

To install:

➡**A new service lock will have a block-out plug installed. Do not operate the lock or remove the plug until the lock is installed and the rod is connected to the lock.**

8. Position the lip on the door ajar switch to the lock and push up on the switch. Install the attaching screw.
9. Position the lock on the lock module and bend the tabs over to secure.
10. Attach all rods that were disconnected in the removal procedure.
11. Install the lock module assembly.
12. The block-out plug is used to adjust the outside handle. With the block-out plug in place, push the outside handle rod up and adjust the barrel nut to fit in the lock lever. Remove the block-out plug.
13. Install the water deflector and door panel.

OUTSIDE HANDLE

▶ See Figure 61

➡**The door glass must be in the full-up position for this procedure.**

1. Remove the door panel.
2. Remove the water deflector.
3. On Seville front door, remove the inner panel cam retaining screws and remove the inner panel cam by sliding off roller of regulator.
4. Disconnect the rod from the outside handle.
5. On Seville rear door, remove the lock module assembly.
6. Detach the wiring connector, if equipped.
7. Remove the retaining screws and the outside handle.

To install:

8. Install the outside handle and tighten the retaining screws to 48–60 inch lbs. (6–8 Nm).
9. Attach the wiring connector, if equipped.
10. On Seville rear door, install the lock module assembly.
11. Connect the rod to the handle.
12. If installing a new service handle, remove the block-out spring.
13. Inspect the door lock system for proper operation.
14. On Seville front door, install the inner panel cam locating over roller of regulator. Install the screws and tighten to 72–96 inch lbs. (9–12 Nm).
15. Install the water deflector and door panel.

LOCK CYLINDER

▶ See Figure 62

➡**The door glass must be in the full-up position for this procedure.**

1. Remove the door panel.
2. Remove the water deflector.
3. On Seville front door, remove the inner panel cam retaining screws and remove the inner panel cam by sliding off roller of regulator.
4. On Seville, use a ¼ in. (6.3mm) drill bit to drill out the rear run channel retainer rivet. Remove the rear run channel retainer by lifting up on the retainer to disengage the lower retainer from the upper channel.
5. Disconnect the rod.
6. Detach the wiring connector, if equipped.
7. Detach or reposition any wiring harnesses that are in the way.

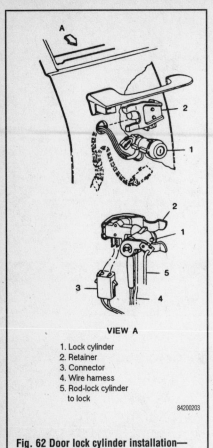

VIEW A

1. Lock cylinder
2. Retainer
3. Connector
4. Wire harness
5. Rod-lock cylinder
   to lock

84200203

Fig. 62 Door lock cylinder installation—1990–91 Eldorado and Seville

8. Use a flat-bladed tool to remove the lock cylinder retainer and remove the lock cylinder.

To install:

9. Install a gasket over the lock cylinder.
10. Install the lock cylinder, including any wiring harnesses that may be attached.
11. Install the lock cylinder retainer.
12. Attach the wiring connector, if equipped.
13. Connect or reposition any other wiring harnesses, as necessary.
14. Connect the rod.
15. On Seville, engage the tab on the rear run channel retainer with the slot in the upper channel. Secure with a new rivet.
16. On Seville front door, install the inner panel cam locating over roller of regulator. Install the screws and tighten to 72–96 inch lbs. (9–12 Nm).
17. Install the water deflector and door panel.

1992–98 Eldorado and Seville; 1994–98 Deville

LOCK STRIKER

▸ See Figures 63, 64 and 65

1. Mark the position of the striker on the body lock pillar using a pencil.
2. Remove the 2 striker bolts and the lock striker, spacer and washer.

To install:

3. Assemble the washer, spacer and striker.
4. Position the lock striker assembly on the lock pillar and install the striker bolts.

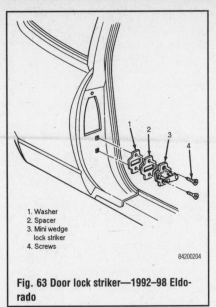

1. Washer
2. Spacer
3. Mini wedge
   lock striker
4. Screws

84200204

Fig. 63 Door lock striker—1992–98 Eldorado

5. Align the striker with the pencil marks and tighten the bolts to 18 ft. lbs. (24 Nm).
6. If necessary, align the striker as follows:

a. Loosen the striker bolts, then snug them so that the striker can still be moved. Place tool J-39346 or equivalent, over the striker.

b. Hold the outside handle out and gently push the door flush against the body to locate the striker.

c. Slowly open the door and tighten the striker bolts to 18 ft. lbs. (24 Nm).

d. Touch up any exposed or unpainted surface on the lock pillar.

7. Install the locating rivets using monobolt type rivets and monobolt rivet head in rivet gun.

➡ **The upper front and upper rear corner rivets are locating rivets. On Eldorado, install the front rivet first, then the rear rivet. On Seville rear door, install the locating rivet first, then working clockwise install the remaining rivets. On Seville front door, install the locating rivet, then the remaining rivets.**

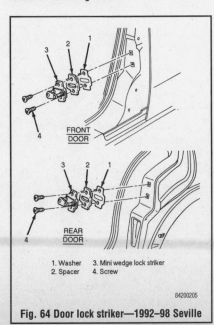

FRONT DOOR

REAR DOOR

1. Washer   3. Mini wedge lock striker
2. Spacer   4. Screw

84200205

Fig. 64 Door lock striker—1992–98 Seville

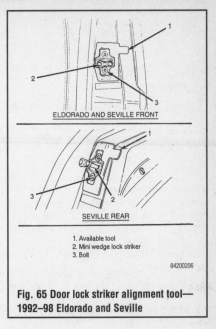

ELDORADO AND SEVILLE FRONT

SEVILLE REAR

1. Available tool
2. Mini wedge lock striker
3. Bolt

84200206

Fig. 65 Door lock striker alignment tool—1992–98 Eldorado and Seville

8. Install the remaining rivets.
9. Attach the wiring harness connectors.
10. On Eldorado, install the window sash bolts.
11. On Seville, install the rivets retaining the window to the sash.
12. Connect the outside handle and lock rods to the lock.
13. Install the water deflector and door panel.

INSIDE REMOTE HANDLE

▸ See Figure 66

1. Remove the door panel.
2. Remove the water deflector.
3. Center punch each rivet, then drill out the rivets using a 3/16 in. (4.8mm) drill bit.
4. Disengage the tabs on the handle from the slots in the module assembly.
5. Disconnect the lock rods from the handle.

To install:

6. Connect the lock rods to the handle.

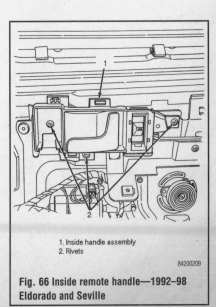

1. Inside handle assembly
2. Rivets

84200209

Fig. 66 Inside remote handle—1992–98 Eldorado and Seville

7. Place the tabs on the handle into the slots in the module.

8. Secure the remote handle using 3/16 in. peel type rivets.

9. Install the water deflector and door panel.

LOCK ACTUATOR

1. Remove the door panel.
2. Remove the water deflector.
3. Remove the lock assembly.
4. Remove the 2 Torx® screws retaining the actuator to the lock assembly and remove the actuator.

To install:

➡ Before installing the new actuator, the lock assembly must be in the full open position and the teeth on the lock switch (part of the actuator) must be pushed fully toward the actuator arm to prevent damage to the lock switch when the lock assembly is operated.

5. Release the lock assembly to be sure it is in the full open position. Do this by pushing up on the outside lock rod lever and then pulling on the inside lock handle lever.

6. Before placing the new actuator on the lock assembly, first position the plastic teeth of the lock switch. Push the teeth fully toward the actuator arm so they will mesh correctly with the teeth on the lock assembly when installed. Refer to appropriate illustration.

7. Make sure that the actuating arm rubber bumper is on the actuating arm. Install the actuating arm and bumper into the locking lever, align the lock switch teeth to the gear tooth fork bolt and align the screw holes.

8. Install the Torx® screws and tighten to 6–9 inch lbs. (0.64–1.05 Nm).

9. Manually operate the lock assembly by pushing inward on the fork bolt until it clicks into the fully closed position.

➡ The lock must operate to the fully closed position without any interference.

10. Attach the wiring connectors and test operation of the actuator and lock switch.

11. Install the lock assembly. Make sure the lock carrier is properly mounted and retained.

12. Install the water deflector and door panel.

LOCK ASSEMBLY

▶ See Figure 67

1. Remove the door panel.
2. Remove the water deflector.
3. Remove the lock rod shield from the module.
4. Disconnect the lock rods from the lock.
5. Detach the wiring connectors.
6. Remove the 3 retaining screws and the lock assembly.

To install:

7. Install the lock assembly and tighten the screws to 62 inch lbs. (7 Nm).

8. Attach the wiring connectors and the lock rods.

9. Install the lock rod shield.
10. Install the water deflector and door panel.

OUTSIDE HANDLE

▶ See Figure 68

➡ The door glass must be in the full-up position for this procedure.

1. Remove the door panel.
2. Remove the water deflector.
3. Disconnect the rod from the outside handle.
4. Remove the nut retaining the key cylinder but leave the cylinder in the door.
5. Detach the wiring connector.
6. Remove the 2 bolts and the outside handle.

To install:

7. Install the outside handle and tighten the bolts to 48–60 inch lbs. (6–8 Nm).

8. Install the nut retaining the key lock cylinder.

9. Attach the wiring connector and connect the rod to the handle.

10. Install the water deflector and door panel.

LOCK CYLINDER

▶ See Figure 69

➡ The door glass must be in the full-up position for this procedure.

1. Remove the door panel.
2. Remove the water deflector.
3. Disconnect the lock cylinder-to-lock rod.
4. Detach the wiring connector, if equipped.
5. Remove the retaining nut and the lock cylinder.

To install:

6. Install the lock cylinder, including any wiring harnesses that may be attached. Secure with the retaining nut.

7. Attach the wiring connector, if equipped.
8. Connect the lock cylinder-to-lock rod.
9. Install the water deflector and door panel.

Door Glass and Regulator

REMOVAL & INSTALLATION

1990–93 Deville and Fleetwood

FRONT DOOR GLASS

▶ See Figure 70

1. Remove the door panel.
2. Remove the water deflector.
3. Remove the door panel upper retainer.
4. Remove the inner belt sealing strip.
5. Remove the front run channel screws.
6. Pull the run channel to the bottom of the door.
7. Pop the guide free from the rear run channel.
8. Remove the glass from the outboard side.

To install:

9. Install the front run channel and screws, finger tight, to the door.

10. Lower the glass into the door from the outboard side of the door frame.

11. Install the front guide to the rear run channel.
12. Adjust the door glass.

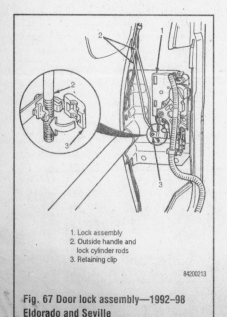

1. Lock assembly
2. Outside handle and lock cylinder rods
3. Retaining clip

84200213

Fig. 67 Door lock assembly—1992–98 Eldorado and Seville

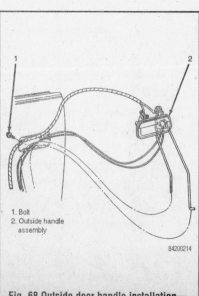

1. Bolt
2. Outside handle assembly

84200214

Fig. 68 Outside door handle installation—1992–98 Eldorado and Seville

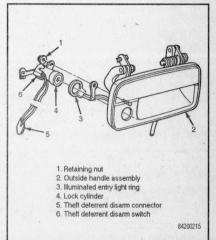

1. Retaining nut
2. Outside handle assembly
3. Illuminated entry light ring
4. Lock cylinder
5. Theft deterrent disarm connector
6. Theft deterrent disarm switch

84200215

Fig. 69 Door lock cylinder—1992–98 Eldorado and Seville

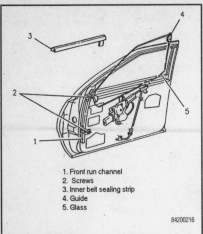

1. Front run channel
2. Screws
3. Inner belt sealing strip
4. Guide
5. Glass

84200216

Fig. 70 Front door glass installation—Deville and Fleetwood

13. Install the inner belt sealing strip and retainer.
14. Install the water deflector and door panel.

REAR DOOR GLASS

▶ **See Figure 71**

1. Remove the door panel.
2. Remove the water deflector.
3. Remove the sash bolts while supporting the glass.
4. Free the guide from the rear of the run channel.
5. Remove the vent glass retaining screws and remove the vent glass.
6. Remove the glass from the inboard side.

To install:

7. Install the glass from the inboard side.
8. Install the vent glass with the retaining screws.
9. Install the guide to the rear of the run channel.
10. Install the sash bolts.
11. Install the water deflector and door panel.

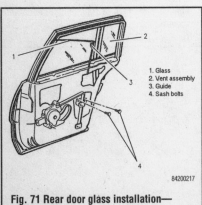

1. Glass
2. Vent assembly
3. Guide
4. Sash bolts

84200217

Fig. 71 Rear door glass installation— 1990–93 Deville and Fleetwood

FRONT DOOR WINDOW REGULATOR

▶ **See Figure 72**

1. Remove the door panel.
2. Remove the water deflector.
3. Center punch each regulator-to door inner

panel rivet, then drill out the rivets using a ¼ in. (6.3mm) drill bit.
4. Disconnect the lock actuator linkage.
5. Remove the regulator guide and block assembly from the lower sash channel by positioning the window half way down, and pushing the regulator forward. Once removed, tape the glass in the full up position.
6. Detach the wiring connector.
7. Remove the regulator through the access hole.
8. Drill out the module-to-door inner panel rivets.
9. Detach the wiring connector and remove the module.

To install:

10. Install the regulator through the access hole.
11. Install the guide and block assembly to the regulator.
12. Attach the wiring connector.

13. Attach the regulator to the door using ¼ in. (6.3mm) peel type rivets.
14. Attach the module to the door using ³⁄₁₆ in. (4.8mm) rivets.
15. Attach the wiring connectors.
16. Remove the tape and check window operation.
17. Install the water deflector and door panel.

REAR DOOR WINDOW REGULATOR

▶ **See Figure 73**

1. Remove the door panel.
2. Remove the water deflector.
3. Tape the window in the full up position.
4. Remove the 3 rivets to the trim panel armrest retainer bracket.
5. Use a ¼ in. (6.3mm) drill bit to drill out the regulator retaining rivets.

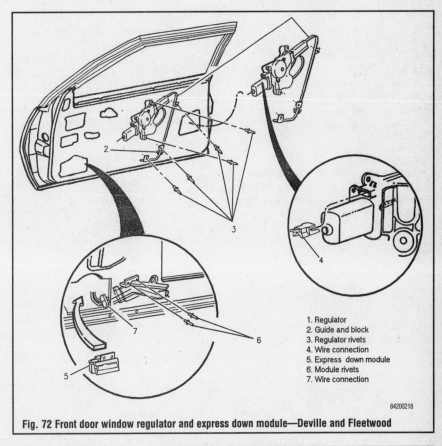

1. Regulator
2. Guide and block
3. Regulator rivets
4. Wire connection
5. Express down module
6. Module rivets
7. Wire connection

84200218

Fig. 72 Front door window regulator and express down module—Deville and Fleetwood

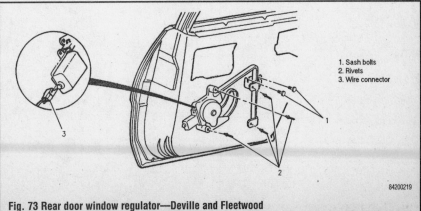

1. Sash bolts
2. Rivets
3. Wire connector

84200219

Fig. 73 Rear door window regulator—Deville and Fleetwood

6. Remove the sash bolts.

7. Detach the wiring connector and remove the regulator through the access hole. To install:

8. Install the regulator through the access hole.

9. Attach the wiring connector.

10. Install the sash bolts and tighten to 79 inch lbs. (9 Nm).

11. Install the 3 rivets to the trim panel armrest retainer bracket.

12. Attach the regulator to the door using ¼ in. (6.3mm) peel type rivets.

13. Remove the tape from the window and check for proper window operation.

14. Install the water deflector and door panel.

1990–91 Eldorado and Seville

DOOR GLASS—ELDORADO

▶ **See Figure 74**

➡ **The guides are bonded to the glass and are not serviceable. The removal and installation procedure must be followed to lessen the chance of damaging the guides.**

1. Remove the door panel.

2. Remove the sound absorber pad, if equipped, and water deflector.

3. Remove the door panel retainer.

4. Remove the inner belt sealing strip.

5. Remove the screws and the front run channel retainer.

6. Lower the glass to the bottom of the door, then slide the glass forward to disengage the rollers on the regulator from the glass sash channel and to disengage the guides on the glass from the rear run channel retainer.

7. Remove the glass from the door inboard of the door frame.

To install:

8. Install the glass to the door inboard of the door frame.

9. Move the glass to the bottom of the door, engaging the roller on the regulator to the glass sash channel. Slide the glass rearward and engage the rear guide on the glass to the rear run channel retainer.

10. Install the front run channel retainer and tighten the screws to 72–96 inch lbs. (9–12 Nm).

11. Install the inner belt sealing strip.

12. Install the door panel retainer.

13. Install the water deflector and, if equipped, sound absorber pad.

14. Install the door panel.

FRONT DOOR GLASS—SEVILLE

1. Remove the door panel.

2. Remove the sound absorber pad, if equipped, and water deflector.

3. Remove the door panel retainer.

4. Remove the inner belt sealing strip.

5. Remove the screws and the front run channel retainer.

6. Slide the glass forward, then rearward to disengage the rollers on the regulator from the glass sash channel.

7. Lift the glass up and outboard of the door frame.

To install:

8. Install the glass to the door from outboard of the door frame.

9. Connect the rollers on the regulator to the glass sash channel.

10. Install the front run channel retainer and tighten the screws to 72–96 inch lbs. (9–12 Nm).

11. Install the inner belt sealing strip.

12. Install the door panel retainer.

13. Install the water deflector and, if equipped, sound absorber pad.

14. Install the door panel.

REAR DOOR GLASS—SEVILLE

1. Remove the door panel.

2. Remove the sound absorber pad, if equipped, and water deflector.

3. Remove the door panel retainer.

4. Remove the inner belt sealing strip.

5. Remove the nuts and remove the glass inboard of the door frame.

To install:

6. Install the glass inboard of the door frame.

7. Align the sash on the glass to the guide block on the regulator.

8. Install the nuts and tighten to 72–96 inch lbs. (9–12 Nm).

9. Install the inner belt sealing strip.

10. Install the door panel retainer.

11. Install the water deflector and, if equipped, sound absorber pad.

12. Install the door panel.

FRONT DOOR WINDOW REGULATOR

▶ **See Figures 75 and 76**

➡ **Tape the glass in the full-up position.**

1. Remove the door panel.

2. Remove the sound absorber pad, if equipped, and water deflector.

3. On Seville, remove the inner panel cam by removing the screws and sliding the inner panel cam off roller of regulator.

4. Drill out the rivets using a ¼ in. (6.3mm) drill bit.

5. Detach the wiring connector from the regulator motor and remove the regulator.

❋❋ CAUTION

The regulator lift arm is under tension from the counterbalance spring and can cause personal injury if the sector gear is not locked in position.

To install:

6. Position the regulator to the door panel and attach the wiring connector.

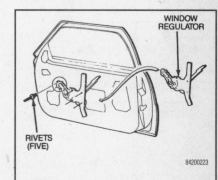

Fig. 75 Door window regulator—1990–91 Eldorado

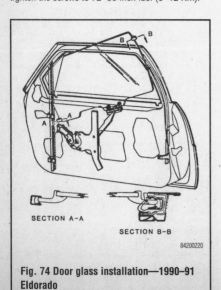

Fig. 74 Door glass installation—1990–91 Eldorado

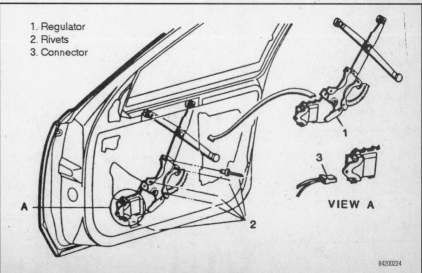

1. Regulator
2. Rivets
3. Connector

Fig. 76 Front door window regulator—1990–91 Seville

7. Attach the regulator using ¼ by ⅝ peel type rivets.

8. On Seville, position the inner panel cam over roller of regulator. Install the screws and tighten to 72–96 inch lbs. (9–12 Nm).

9. Install the water deflector and, if equipped, sound absorber pad.

10. Install the door panel.

REAR DOOR WINDOW REGULATOR

♦ See Figure 77

➥Tape the glass in the full-up position.

1. Remove the door panel.
2. Remove the sound absorber pad, if equipped, and water deflector.
3. Remove the lock module assembly.
4. Drill out the rivets using a ¼ in. (6.3mm) drill bit.

5. Detach the wiring connector from the regulator motor and remove the regulator.

To install:

6. Position the regulator to the door panel and attach the wiring connector.

7. Attach the regulator using ¼ by ⅝ peel type rivets.

8. Install the lock module assembly.

9. Install the water deflector and, if equipped, sound absorber pad.

10. Install the door panel.

1992–98 Eldorado and Seville; 1994–98 Deville

DOOR GLASS—ELDORADO

♦ See Figure 78

1. Remove the door panel.
2. Remove the water deflector. Note the position of the water deflector prior to removal, as it must be reinstalled in the same position to prevent water leaks.

3. Remove the inner belt sealing strip as follows:
   a. Remove the mirror.
   b. Remove the screw at mirror bucket end of the sealing strip.
   c. Remove the fasteners at the rear edge of the door.
   d. Lift upward to remove the sealing strip.

4. Loosen and allow the rear wedge to drop.
5. Remove the window guide blocks.
6. Position the window to gain access to the 3 window sash-to-regulator bolts.
7. Have an assistant hold the window, then remove the 3 window sash-to-regulator bolts.
8. Remove the window from the door.
9. Remove the run channel retaining bolts and lift both run channels up and out of the adjuster.

To install:

10. Place the window and run channels on a bench.
11. Place the guide blocks on the window and loosely secure with the bolts.
12. Place the run channels fully into the guide blocks and adjust the guide block parallelism to run channel. There should be a ½ in. (12mm) gap between the edge of the window and the run channel.
13. Set the guide block to the alignment mark on the guide block retainer as illustrated. Tighten the guide blocks.
14. Remove the screw and nut and remove the door lower molding and adjuster access plugs. Set the bevel adjusters to mid point (approximately 12 full revolutions from the full inward or outward travel stops). Leave the molding and adjuster access plugs off.
15. Install the run channels into the door.
16. Install the window into the door.
17. Install the 3 regulator-to-window sash bolts.
18. Install the inner belt sealing strip as follows:
   a. With the window in the up position, install the mirror bucket with the screws.
   b. Install the sealing strip hollow bulb over the mirror bucket bayonet. Make sure the joint is tight.
   c. Install the fasteners at the rear edge of the door.
   d. Push the sealing strip onto the flange and press down the entire length.

19. Raise the window until it is 1 in. (25mm) below full up, then tighten the front and rear upper run channel bolts to 97 inch lbs. (11 Nm).
20. Loosen the window up stops.
21. Check the window parallelism adjustment as follows:
   a. Raise the window to approximately ½ in. (12mm) below the full up position, checking the parallelism on the upstroke of window motion.
   b. The gap from the horizontal edge of the window to the weatherstrip should be even at the front and rear of the window.
   c. Adjust the parallelism by loosening and repositioning the inner cam bolts. Tighten the inner panel cam bolts to 97 inch lbs. (11 Nm).
22. Loosen the regulator-to-window sash channel bolts and position the window rearward just enough to relieve the pressure of the window to pillar post weatherstrip. Snug the sash channel bolts.

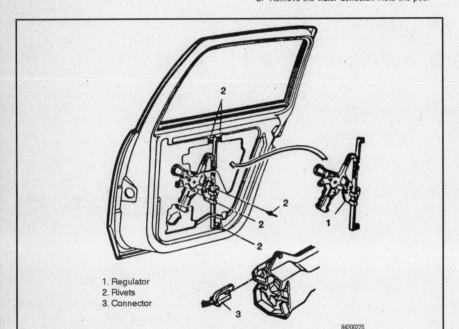

1. Regulator
2. Rivets
3. Connector

84200225

Fig. 77 Rear door window regulator—1990–91 Seville

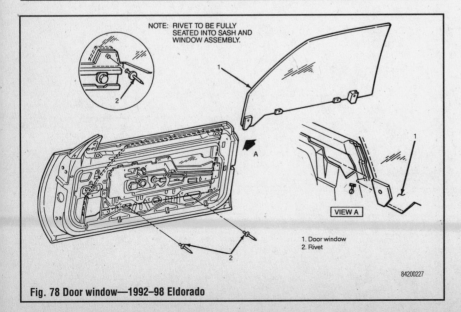

NOTE: RIVET TO BE FULLY SEATED INTO SASH AND WINDOW ASSEMBLY.

VIEW A

1. Door window
2. Rivet

84200227

Fig. 78 Door window—1992–98 Eldorado

23. Set the rear upstop so the window will pass just under the weatherstrip outer lip and 1mm below the blow out clip as the door is being closed. Set the front upstop to maintain parallelism. Both upstops should contact the guide blocks simultaneously.

24. Check window tip-in as follows:

a. With the door in the open position and the window in the full up position, move the door toward the closed position until the upper rear corner of the window contacts the weatherstrip.

b. The distance from the outer surface of the quarter panel to the door panel outer surface should not exceed 1⅛ in. (30mm).

c. If necessary, adjust the bevel gear adjusters which are accessed through the bottom of the door. The front and rear adjusters should be turned in equal amounts so that there is sufficient and/or even weatherstrip compression.

d. If the bevel gear adjuster travel is not sufficient to allow the adjustment needed, reposition the front and rear run channel guide blocks inward or outward, as required.

➡**High door closing effort can result if the window tip-in is adjusted too far inward. Door closing effort with the window lowered should increase only slightly with the window fully raised. The window should be cycled and the door closed several times to verify door window performance.**

25. Loosen the regulator-to-window sash channel bolts and position the window forward to achieve water/wind noise seal at the pillar post weatherstrip. Tighten the regulator-to-sash channel bolts to 97 inch lbs. (11 Nm).

➡**Moving the window forward too far will increase door closing effort and reduce window clearance to the blow out clip.**

26. With the window in the full up position, check for a smooth transition from bucket at mirror to window. Transition should be checked with slight outward pressure on the window or in the door closed position. Loosen the mirror attachment nuts and bucket attachment screws to reposition the bucket, as needed.

27. With the window still in the full up position, raise the rear wedge until it lightly contacts the rear edge of the window. Tighten the wedge attachment screw to 27 inch lbs. (3 Nm), using a thin flat-bladed tool in the adjustment slot to keep the wedge from rotating when tightened.

28. Install the window adjuster access plugs and the door lower molding.

29. Install the water deflector and door panel.

DOOR WINDOW—SEVILLE AND DEVILLE

▶ **See Figure 79**

1. Remove the door panel.
2. Remove the door speaker.
3. Remove the water deflector.
4. Lift upward to remove the inner belt sealing strip.
5. Remove the retaining bolt and the front run channel retainer.
6. Drill out the 2 regulator sash-to-window rivets and remove the window from the door.

To install:

7. Install the window to the door from outboard of the door frame.

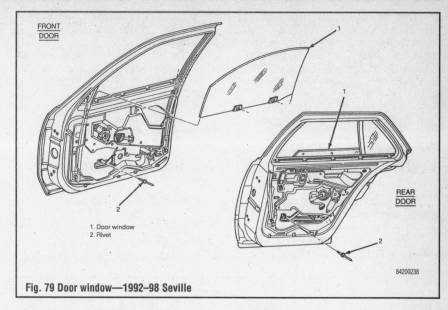

FRONT DOOR

REAR DOOR

1. Door window
2. Rivet

84200238

Fig. 79 Door window—1992–98 Seville

8. Install the rivets on the regulator-to-window sash channel.

9. Install the front run channel retainer and tighten the bolt to 72–96 inch lbs. (9–12 Nm).

10. Locate the front edge of the inner belt sealing strip over the door flange and press down the entire length of the sealing strip.

11. Install the water deflector.

12. Install the door speaker.

13. Install the door panel.

WINDOW REGULATOR

The window regulator is part of the door lock module; if replacement is necessary, refer to the door lock module removal and installation procedure.

Electric Window Motor

REMOVAL & INSTALLATION

1990–93 Deville and Fleetwood

▶ **See Figure 80**

1. Remove the window regulator.
2. Use a ³⁄₁₆ in. (4.8mm) drill to drill out the motor attaching rivets.
3. Remove the motor from the regulator.

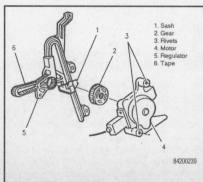

1. Sash
2. Gear
3. Rivets
4. Motor
5. Regulator
6. Tape

84200239

Fig. 80 Electric window motor—Deville and Fleetwood

To install:

4. Use ³⁄₁₆ in. rivets to attach the motor to the regulator.

5. Install the window regulator in the vehicle.

1990–91 Eldorado and Seville

FRONT DOOR

▶ **See Figure 81**

1. Remove the window regulator.

⁂ CAUTION

The following Step must be performed when the regulator is removed from the door. The regulator lift arms are under tension from the counterbalance spring and can cause serious injury if the motor is removed without locking the sector gear in position.

2. Drill a hole through the regulator sector gear and back plate and install a screw and nut to lock the sector gear in position. Do not drill the hole closer than ½ in. (13mm) to the edge of the sector gear or backplate.

3. Use a ³⁄₁₆ in. (4.8mm) drill to drill out the motor attaching rivets.

4. Remove the motor from the regulator.

To install:

5. Use ³⁄₁₆ in. rivets to attach the motor to the regulator.

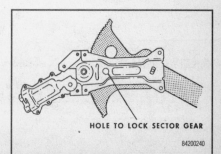

HOLE TO LOCK SECTOR GEAR

84200240

Fig. 81 Electric window motor, front door—1990–91 Eldorado and Seville

Fig. 82 Remove the 3 retaining nuts and . . .

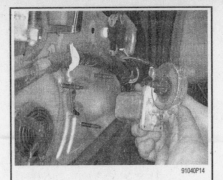

Fig. 83 . . . remove the motor from the window regulator

Fig. 84 Make sure the window motor splines engage the regulator

6. Remove the screw and nut locking the sector gear in a fixed position.

7. Install the window regulator in the vehicle.

REAR DOOR

1. Remove the window regulator.

2. Use a 3/16 in. (4.8mm) drill to drill out the motor attaching rivets.

3. Remove the motor from the regulator.

To install:

4. Use 3/16 in. rivets to attach the motor to the regulator.

5. Install the window regulator in the vehicle.

1992–98 Eldorado and Seville; 1994–98 Deville

▶ See Figures 82, 83 and 84

✳✳ CAUTION

If the motor must be removed with the window regulator out of the vehicle, tool J-38864 or equivalent, must be used to remove the counterbalance spring before the motor can be removed. The regulator lift arms are under tension from the counterbalance spring and can cause serious injury if the motor is removed without removing the spring.

1. Remove the door panel.

2. Remove the water deflector.

3. Detach the motor wiring connector.

4. Remove the 3 retaining nuts and the motor.

To install:

5. Install the motor and secure with the retaining nuts.

6. Attach the wiring connector.

7. Install the e water deflector.

8. Install the door panel.

Inside Rear View Mirror

REMOVAL & INSTALLATION

1990–93 Models

▶ See Figure 85

1. Carefully loosen the windshield garnish molding toward the driver's side of the vehicle, then

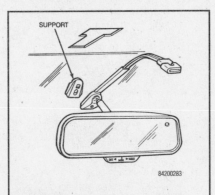

Fig. 85 Electrochromic mirror—except 1993–98 Eldorado and Seville

loosen the upper windshield pillar garnish molding along the left side of the windshield.

2. Expose the wire from behind the loose garnish molding.

3. Unplug the connector on the mirror stem and the one on the attaching wire harness.

4. Loosen the screw and remove the mirror from the mirror support.

To install:

5. With the wire harness supplied in the kit, plug the connector on the mirror stem and the one on the harness together. Place the mirror on the support and tighten the screw.

6. Starting just above the mirror, at the center of the vehicle, thread the wire harness over the windshield garnish molding and pull the wire toward you. Be sure enough wire is left going to the connectors and that the wire is not stretched tight.

7. Keeping the wire harness straight, carefully tuck the wire behind the loose garnish moldings.

✳✳ WARNING

Be careful not to stretch or pinch the wire. Do not use a sharp tool to force the wire under the molding as this could damage the wire and short the system. Position the protective wire tube under the molding, then carefully tighten the garnish moldings back to their original positions using extreme caution not to pinch or kink the wire harness.

1994–98 Models

ELECTROCHROMIC MIRROR

▶ See Figures 86, 87, 88 and 89

1. Detach the electrical connectors at the rear of the mirror.

2. Twist the mirror to one side and use one hand to support the edge of the mirror against the windshield.

3. Use the other hand to pull the mirror away from the windshield with a quick jerk.

To install:

4. Slide the mirror onto the mirror support. The

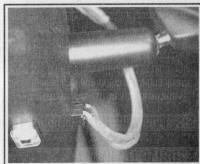

Fig. 86 Detach the connectors on the back of the rear view mirror

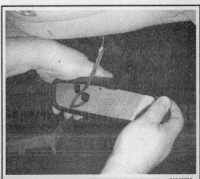

Fig. 87 Twist the mirror to one side and use one hand to support the edge of the mirror against the windshield

Fig. 88 Use the other hand to pull the mirror up and away from . . .

91040P32

Fig. 89 . . . the windshield with a quick jerk

91040P31

mirror is fully seated on the support when an audible "click" is heard.

5. Attach the electrical connectors.

CONVENTIONAL MIRROR

▶ See Figure 90

1. Remove the set screw retaining the mirror base to the mirror support.

2. Lift the mirror base from the support.

3. Remove the Torx® screw at the rear of the swivel arm.

To install:

4. Install the lock tooth washer and mirror base to the swivel arm.

5. Install the Torx® screw to the swivel arm and tighten until snug.

6. Install the mirror support and install the set screw.

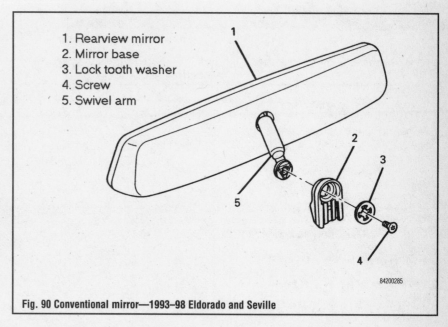

1. Rearview mirror
2. Mirror base
3. Lock tooth washer
4. Screw
5. Swivel arm

84200285

Fig. 90 Conventional mirror—1993–98 Eldorado and Seville

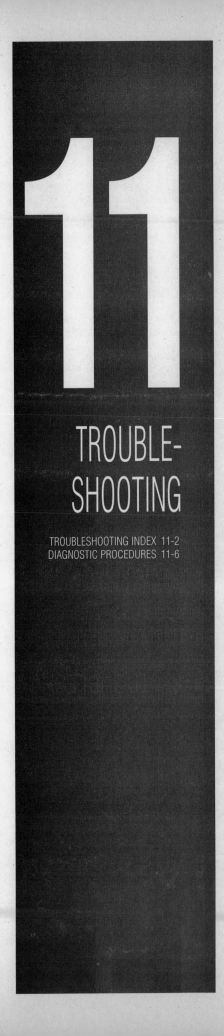

Condition	Section/Item Number

The following troubleshooting charts are divided into 7 sections covering engine, drive train, brakes, wheels/tires/steering/suspension, electrical accessories, instruments and gauges, and climate control. The first portion (or index) consists of a list of symptoms, along with section and item numbers. After selecting the appropriate condition, refer to the corresponding diagnostic procedure in the second portion's specified location.

INDEX

SECTION 1. ENGINE

A. Engine Starting Problems

Gasoline Engines

Engine turns over, but will not start	1-A, 1
Engine does not turn over when attempting to start	1-A, 2
Engine stalls immediately when started	1-A, 3
Starter motor spins, but does not engage	1-A, 4
Engine is difficult to start when cold	1-A, 5
Engine is difficult to start when hot	1-A, 6

B. Engine Running Conditions

Gasoline Engines

Engine runs poorly, hesitates	1-B, 1
Engine lacks power	1-B, 2
Engine has poor fuel economy	1-B, 3
Engine runs on (diesels) when turned off	1-B, 4
Engine knocks and pings during heavy acceleration, and on steep hills	1-B, 5
Engine accelerates but vehicle does not gain speed	1-B, 6

C. Engine Noises, Odors and Vibrations

Engine makes a knocking or pinging noise when accelerating	1-C, 1
Starter motor grinds when used	1-C, 2
Engine makes a screeching noise	1-C, 3
Engine makes a growling noise	1-C, 4
Engine makes a ticking or tapping noise	1-C, 5
Engine makes a heavy knocking noise	1-C, 6
Vehicle has a fuel odor when driven	1-C, 7
Vehicle has a rotten egg odor when driven	1-C, 8
Vehicle has a sweet odor when driven	1-C, 9
Engine vibrates when idling	1-C, 10
Engine vibrates during acceleration	1-C, 11

D. Engine Electrical System

Battery goes dead while driving	1-D, 1
Battery goes dead overnight	1-D, 2

E. Engine Cooling System

Engine overheats	1-E, 1
Engine loses coolant	1-E, 2
Engine temperature remains cold when driving	1-E, 3
Engine runs hot	1-E, 4

F. Engine Exhaust System

Exhaust rattles at idle speed	1-F, 1
Exhaust system vibrates when driving	1-F, 2
Exhaust system seems too low	1-F, 3
Exhaust seems loud	1-F, 4

Condition	Section/Item Number

SECTION 2. DRIVE TRAIN

A. Automatic Transmission

Transmission shifts erratically	2-A, 1
Transmission will not engage	2-A, 2
Transmission will not downshift during heavy acceleration	2-A, 3

G. Axles

Front Wheel Drive Vehicles

Front wheel makes a clicking noise	2-G, 1
Rear wheel makes a clicking noise	2-G, 2

H. Other Drive Train Conditions

Burning odor from center of vehicle when accelerating	2-H, 1; 2-C, 1; 3-A, 9
Engine accelerates, but vehicle does not gain speed	2-H, 2; 2-C, 1; 3-A, 9

SECTION 3. BRAKE SYSTEM

Brakes pedal pulsates or shimmies when pressed	3-A, 1
Brakes make a squealing noise	3-A, 2
Brakes make a grinding noise	3-A, 3
Vehicle pulls to one side during braking	3-A, 4
Brake pedal feels spongy or has excessive brake pedal travel	3-A, 5
Brake pedal feel is firm, but brakes lack sufficient stopping power or fade	3-A, 6
Vehicle has excessive front end dive or locks rear brakes too easily	3-A, 7
Brake pedal goes to floor when pressed and will not pump up	3-A, 8
Brakes make a burning odor	3-A, 9

SECTION 4. WHEELS, TIRES, STEERING AND SUSPENSION

A. Wheels and Wheel Bearings

Front Wheel Drive Vehicles

Front wheel or wheel bearing loose	4-A, 1
Rear wheel or wheel bearing loose	4-A, 2

B. Tires

Tires worn on inside tread	4-B, 1
Tires worn on outside tread	4-B, 2
Tires worn unevenly	4-B, 3

C. Steering

Excessive play in steering wheel	4-C, 1
Steering wheel shakes at cruising speeds	4-C, 2
Steering wheel shakes when braking	3-A, 1
Steering wheel becomes stiff when turned	4-C, 4

D. Suspension

Vehicle pulls to one side	4-D, 1
Vehicle is very bouncy over bumps	4-D, 2
Vehicle seems to lean excessively in turns	4-D, 3
Vehicle ride quality seems excessively harsh	4-D, 4
Vehicle seems low or leans to one side	4-D, 5

Condition	Section/Item Number

E. Driving Noises and Vibrations

Noises

Vehicle makes a clicking noise when driven	4-E, 1
Vehicle makes a clunking or knocking noise over bumps	4-E, 2
Vehicle makes a low pitched rumbling noise when driven	4-E, 3
Vehicle makes a squeaking noise over bumps	4-E, 4

Vibrations

Vehicle vibrates when driven	4-E, 5

SECTION 5. ELECTRICAL ACCESSORIES

A. Headlights

One headlight only works on high or low beam	5-A, 1
Headlight does not work on high or low beam	5-A, 2
Headlight(s) very dim	5-A, 3

B. Tail, Running and Side Marker Lights

Tail light, running light or side marker light inoperative	5-B, 1
Tail light, running light or side marker light works intermittently	5-B, 2
Tail light, running light or side marker light very dim	5-B, 3

C. Interior Lights

Interior light inoperative	5-C, 1
Interior light works intermittently	5-C, 2
Interior light very dim	5-C, 3

D. Brake Lights

One brake light inoperative	5-D, 1
Both brake lights inoperative	5-D, 2
One or both brake lights very dim	5-D, 3

E. Warning Lights

Ignition, Battery and Alternator Warning Lights, Check Engine Light, Anti-Lock Braking System (ABS) Light, Brake Warning Light, Oil Pressure Warning Light, and Parking Brake Warning Light

Warning light(s) remains on after the engine is started	5-E, 1
Warning light(s) flickers on and off when driving	5-E, 2
Warning light(s) inoperative with ignition on, and engine not started	5-E, 3

F. Turn Signal and 4-Way Hazard Lights

Turn signals or hazard lights come on, but do not flash	5-F, 1
Turn signals or hazard lights do not function on either side	5-F, 2
Turn signals or hazard lights only work on one side	5-F, 3
One signal light does not work	5-F, 4
Turn signals flash too slowly	5-F, 5
Turn signals flash too fast	5-F, 6
Four-way hazard flasher indicator light inoperative	5-F, 7
Turn signal indicator light(s) do not work in either direction	5-F, 8
One turn signal indicator light does not work	5-F, 9

G. Horn

Horn does not operate	5-G, 1
Horn has an unusual tone	5-G, 2

Condition	Section/Item Number

H. Windshield Wipers

Windshield wipers do not operate — 5-H, 1
Windshield wiper motor makes a humming noise, gets hot or blows fuses — 5-H, 2
Windshield wiper motor operates but one or both wipers fail to move — 5-H, 3
Windshield wipers will not park — 5-H, 4

SECTION 6. INSTRUMENTS AND GAUGES

A. Speedometer (Cable Operated)

Speedometer does not work — 6-A, 1
Speedometer needle fluctuates when driving at steady speeds — 6-A, 2
Speedometer works intermittently — 6-A, 3

B. Speedometer (Electronically Operated)

Speedometer does not work — 6-B, 1
Speedometer works intermittently — 6-B, 2

C. Fuel, Temperature and Oil Pressure Gauges

Gauge does not register — 6-C, 1
Gauge operates erratically — 6-C, 2
Gauge operates fully pegged — 6-C, 3

SECTION 7. CLIMATE CONTROL

A. Air Conditioner

No air coming from air conditioner vents — 7-A, 1
Air conditioner blows warm air — 7-A, 2
Water collects on the interior floor when the air conditioner is used — 7-A, 3
Air conditioner has a moldy odor when used — 7-A, 4

B. Heater

Blower motor does not operate — 7-B, 1
Heater blows cool air — 7-B, 2
Heater steams the windshield when used — 7-B, 3

1. ENGINE

1-A. Engine Starting Problems

Gasoline Engines

1. Engine turns over, but will not start

a. Check fuel level in fuel tank, add fuel if empty.
b. Check battery condition and state of charge. If voltage and load test below specification, charge or replace battery.
c. Check battery terminal and cable condition and tightness. Clean terminals and replace damaged, worn or corroded cables.
d. Check fuel delivery system. If fuel is not reaching the fuel injectors, check for a loose electrical connector or defective fuse, relay or fuel pump and replace as necessary.
e. Engine may have excessive wear or mechanical damage such as low cylinder cranking pressure, a broken camshaft drive system, insufficient valve clearance or bent valves.
f. Check for fuel contamination such as water in the fuel. During winter months, the water may freeze and cause a fuel restriction. Adding a fuel additive may help, however the fuel system may require draining and purging with fresh fuel.
g. Check for ignition system failure. Check for loose or shorted wires or damaged ignition system components. Check the spark plugs for excessive wear or incorrect electrode gap. If the problem is worse in wet weather, check for shorts between the spark plugs and the ignition coils.
h. Check the engine management system for a failed sensor or control module.

2. Engine does not turn over when attempting to start

a. Check the battery state of charge and condition. If the dash lights are not visible or very dim when turning the ignition key on, the battery has either failed internally or discharged, the battery cables are loose, excessively corroded or damaged, or the alternator has failed or internally shorted, discharging the battery. Charge or replace the battery, clean or replace the battery cables, and check the alternator output.
b. Check the operation of the neutral safety switch. On automatic transmission vehicles, try starting the vehicle in both Park and Neutral. On manual transmission vehicles, depress the clutch pedal and attempt to start. On some vehicles, these switches can be adjusted. Make sure the switches or wire connectors are not loose or damaged. Replace or adjust the switches as necessary.
c. Check the starter motor, starter solenoid or relay, and starter motor cables and wires. Check the ground from the engine to the chassis. Make sure the wires are not loose, damaged, or corroded. If battery voltage is present at the starter relay, try using a remote starter to start the vehicle for test purposes only. Replace any damaged or corroded cables, in addition to replacing any failed components.
d. Check the engine for seizure. If the engine has not been started for a long period of time, internal parts such as the rings may have rusted to the cylinder walls. The engine may have suffered internal damage, or could be hydro-locked from ingesting water. Remove the spark plugs and carefully attempt to rotate the engine using a suitable breaker bar and socket on the crankshaft pulley. If the engine is resistant to moving, or moves slightly and then binds, do not force the engine any further before determining the problem.

3. Engine stalls immediately when started

a. Check the ignition switch condition and operation. The electrical contacts in the run position may be worn or damaged. Try restarting the engine with all electrical accessories in the off position. Sometimes turning the key on an off will help in emergency situations, however once the switch has shown signs of failure, it should be replaced as soon as possible.
b. Check for loose, corroded, damaged or shorted wires for the ignition system and repair or replace.
c. Check for manifold vacuum leaks or vacuum hose leakage and repair or replace parts as necessary.

d. Measure the fuel pump delivery volume and pressure. Low fuel pump pressure can also be noticed as a lack of power when accelerating. Make sure the fuel pump lines are not restricted. The fuel pump output is not adjustable and requires fuel pump replacement to repair.
e. Check the engine fuel and ignition management system. Inspect the sensor wiring and electrical connectors. A dirty, loose or damaged sensor or control module wire can simulate a failed component.
f. Check the exhaust system for internal restrictions.

4. Starter motor spins, but does not engage

a. Check the starter motor for a seized or binding pinion gear.
b. Remove the flywheel inspection plate and check for a damaged ring gear.

5. Engine is difficult to start when cold

a. Check the battery condition, battery state of charge and starter motor current draw. Replace the battery if marginal and the starter motor if the current draw is beyond specification.
b. Check the battery cable condition. Clean the battery terminals and replace corroded or damaged cables.
c. Check the fuel system for proper operation. A fuel pump with insufficient fuel pressure or clogged injectors should be replaced.
d. Check the engine's tune-up status. Note the tune-up specifications and check for items such as severely worn spark plugs; adjust or replace as needed. On vehicles with manually adjusted valve clearances, check for tight valves and adjust to specification.
e. Check for a failed coolant temperature sensor, and replace if out of specification.
f. Check the operation of the engine management systems for fuel and ignition; repair or replace failed components as necessary.

6. Engine is difficult to start when hot

a. Check the air filter and air intake system. Replace the air filter if it is dirty or con-taminated. Check the fresh air intake system for restrictions or blockage.
b. Check for loose or deteriorated engine grounds and clean, tighten or replace as needed.
c. Check for needed maintenance. Inspect tune-up and service related items such as spark plugs and engine oil condition, and check the operation of the engine fuel and ignition management system.

1-B. Engine Running Conditions

Gasoline Engines

1. Engine runs poorly, hesitates

a. Check the engine ignition system operation and adjust if possible, or replace defective parts.
b. Check for restricted fuel injectors and replace as necessary.
c. Check the fuel pump output and delivery. Inspect fuel lines for restrictions. If the fuel pump pressure is below specification, replace the fuel pump.
d. Check the operation of the engine management system and repair as necessary.

2. Engine lacks power

a. Check the engine's tune-up status. Note the tune-up specifications and check for items such as severely worn spark plugs; adjust or replace as needed. On vehicles with manually adjusted valve clearances, check for tight valves and adjust to specification.
b. Check the air filter and air intake system. Replace the air filter if it is dirty or con-taminated. Check the fresh air intake system for restrictions or blockage.
c. Check the operation of the engine fuel and ignition management systems. Check the sensor operation and wiring. Check for low fuel pump pressure and repair or replace components as necessary.

d. Check the throttle linkage adjustments. Check to make sure the linkage is fully opening the throttle. Replace any worn or defective bushings or linkages.
e. Check for a restricted exhaust system. Check for bent or crimped exhaust pipes, or internally restricted mufflers or catalytic converters. Compare inlet and outlet temperatures for the converter or muffler. If the inlet is hot, but outlet cold, the component is restricted.
f. Check for a loose or defective knock sensor. A loose, improperly torqued or defective knock sensor will decrease spark advance and reduce power. Replace defective knock sensors and install using the recommended torque specification.
g. Check for engine mechanical conditions such as low compression, worn piston rings, worn valves, worn camshafts and related parts. An engine which has severe mechanical wear, or has suffered internal mechanical damage must be rebuilt or replaced to restore lost power.
h. Check the engine oil level for being overfilled. Adjust the engine's oil level, or change the engine oil and filter, and top off to the correct level.
i. Check for an intake manifold or vacuum hose leak. Replace leaking gaskets or worn vacuum hoses.
j. Check for dragging brakes and replace or repair as necessary.
k. Check tire air pressure and tire wear. Adjust the pressure to the recommended settings. Check the tire wear for possible alignment problems causing increased rolling resistance, decreased acceleration and increased fuel usage.
l. Check the octane rating of the fuel used during refilling, and use a higher octane rated fuel.

3. Poor fuel economy
a. Inspect the air filter and check for any air restrictions going into the air filter housing. Replace the air filter if it is dirty or contaminated.
b. Check the engine for tune-up and related adjustments. Replace worn ignition parts, check the engine ignition timing and fuel mixture, and set to specifications if possible.
c. Check the tire size, tire wear, alignment and tire pressure. Large tires create more rolling resistance, smaller tires require more engine speed to maintain a vehicle's road speed. Excessive tire wear can be caused by incorrect tire pressure, incorrect wheel alignment or a suspension problem. All of these conditions create increased rolling resistance, causing the engine to work harder to accelerate and maintain a vehicle's speed.
d. Inspect the brakes for binding or excessive drag. A sticking brake caliper, overly adjusted brake shoe, broken brake shoe return spring, or binding parking brake cable or linkage can create a significant drag, brake wear and loss of fuel economy. Check the brake system operation and repair as necessary.

4. Engine runs on (diesels) when turned off
a. Check for idle speed set too high and readjust to specification.
b. Check the operation of the idle control valve, and replace if defective.
c. Check the ignition timing and adjust to recommended settings. Check for defective sensors or related components and replace if defective.
d. Check for a vacuum leak at the intake manifold or vacuum hose and replace defective gaskets or hoses.
e. Check the engine for excessive carbon build-up in the combustion chamber. Use a recommended decarbonizing fuel additive or disassemble the cylinder head to remove the carbon.
f. Check the operation of the engine fuel management system and replace defective sensors or control units.
g. Check the engine operating temperature for overheating and repair as necessary.

5. Engine knocks and pings during heavy acceleration, and on steep hills
a. Check the octane rating of the fuel used during refilling, and use a higher octane rated fuel.
b. Check the ignition timing and adjust to recommended settings. Check for defective sensors or related components and replace if defective.
c. Check the engine for excessive carbon build-up in the combustion chamber. Use a recommended decarbonizing fuel additive or disassemble the cylinder head to remove the carbon.

d. Check the spark plugs for the correct type, electrode gap and heat range. Replace worn or damaged spark plugs. For severe or continuous high speed use, install a spark plug that is one heat range colder.
e. Check the operation of the engine fuel management system and replace defective sensors or control units.
f. Check for a restricted exhaust system. Check for bent or crimped exhaust pipes, or internally restricted mufflers or catalytic converters. Compare inlet and outlet temperatures for the converter or muffler. If the inlet is hot, but outlet cold, the component is restricted.

6. Engine accelerates, but vehicle does not gain speed
a. On manual transmission vehicles, check for causes of a slipping clutch. Refer to the clutch troubleshooting section for additional information.
b. On automatic transmission vehicles, check for a slipping transmission. Check the transmission fluid level and condition. If the fluid level is too high, adjust to the correct level. If the fluid level is low, top off using the recommended fluid type. If the fluid exhibits a burning odor, the transmission has been slipping internally. Changing the fluid and filter may help temporarily, however in this situation a transmission may require overhauling to ensure long-term reliability.

ENGINE PERFORMANCE TROUBLESHOOTING HINTS
When troubleshooting an engine running or performance condition, the mechanical condition of the engine should be determined before lengthy troubleshooting procedures are performed.

The engine fuel management systems in fuel injected vehicles rely on electronic sensors to provide information to the engine control unit for precise fuel metering. Unlike carburetors, which use the incoming air speed to draw fuel through the fuel metering jets in order to provide a proper fuel-to-air ratio, a fuel injection system provides a specific amount of fuel which is introduced by the fuel injectors into the intake manifold or intake port, based on the information provided by electronic sensors.

The sensors monitor the engine's operating temperature, ambient temperature and the amount of air entering the engine, engine speed and throttle position to provide information to the engine control unit, which, in turn, operates the fuel injectors by electrical pulses. The sensors provide information to the engine control unit using low voltage electrical signals. As a result, an unplugged sensor or a poor electrical contact could cause a poor running condition similar to a failed sensor.

When troubleshooting a fuel related engine condition on fuel injected vehicles, carefully inspect the wiring and electrical connectors to the related components. Make sure the electrical connectors are fully connected, clean and not physically damaged. If necessary, clean the electrical contacts using electrical contact cleaner. The use of cleaning agents not specifically designed for electrical contacts should not be used, as they could leave a surface film or damage the insulation of the wiring.

The engine electrical system provides the necessary electrical power to operate the vehicle's electrical accessories, electronic control units and sensors. Because engine management systems are sensitive to voltage changes, an alternator which over or undercharges could cause engine running problems or component failure. Most alternators utilize internal voltage regulators which cannot be adjusted and must be replaced individually or as a unit with the alternator.

Ignition systems may be controlled by, or linked to, the engine fuel management system. Similar to the fuel injection system, these ignition systems rely on electronic sensors for information to determine the optimum ignition timing for a given engine speed and load. Some ignition systems no longer allow the ignition timing to be adjusted. Feedback from low voltage electrical sensors provide information to the control unit to determine the amount of ignition advance. On these systems, if a failure occurs the failed component must be replaced. Before replacing suspected failed electrical components, carefully inspect the wiring and electrical connectors to the related components. Make sure the electrical connectors are fully connected, clean and not physically damaged. If necessary, clean the electrical contacts using electrical contact cleaner. The use of cleaning agents not specifically designed for electrical contacts should be avoided, as they could leave a surface film or damage the insulation of the wiring.

1-C. Engine Noises, Odors and Vibrations

1. Engine makes a knocking or pinging noise when accelerating
a. Check the octane rating of the fuel being used. Depending on the type of driving or driving conditions, it may be necessary to use a higher octane fuel.
b. Verify the ignition system settings and operation. Improperly adjusted ignition timing or a failed component, such as a knock sensor, may cause the ignition timing to advance excessively or prematurely. Check the ignition system operation and adjust, or replace components as needed.
c. Check the spark plug gap, heat range and condition. If the vehicle is operated in severe operating conditions or at continuous high speeds, use a colder heat range spark plug. Adjust the spark plug gap to the manufacturer's recommended specification and replace worn or damaged spark plugs.

2. Starter motor grinds when used
a. Examine the starter pinion gear and the engine ring gear for damage, and replace damaged parts.
b. Check the starter mounting bolts and housing. If the housing is cracked or damaged replace the starter motor and check the mounting bolts for tightness.

3. Engine makes a screeching noise
a. Check the accessory drive belts for looseness and adjust as necessary.
b. Check the accessory drive belt tensioners for seizing or excessive bearing noises and replace if loose, binding, or excessively noisy.
c. Check for a seizing water pump. The pump may not be leaking; however, the bearing may be faulty or the impeller loose and jammed. Replace the water pump.

4. Engine makes a growling noise
a. Check for a loose or failing water pump. Replace the pump and engine coolant.
b. Check the accessory drive belt tensioners for excessive bearing noises and replace if loose or excessively noisy.

5. Engine makes a ticking or tapping noise
a. On vehicles with hydraulic lash adjusters, check for low or dirty engine oil and top off or replace the engine oil and filter.
b. On vehicles with hydraulic lash adjusters, check for collapsed lifters and replace failed components.
c. On vehicles with hydraulic lash adjusters, check for low oil pressure caused by a restricted oil filter, worn engine oil pump, or oil pressure relief valve.
d. On vehicles with manually adjusted valves, check for excessive valve clearance or worn valve train parts. Adjust the valves to specification or replace worn and defective parts.
e. Check for a loose or improperly tensioned timing belt or timing chain and adjust or replace parts as necessary.
f. Check for a bent or sticking exhaust or intake valve. Remove the engine cylinder head to access and replace.

6. Engine makes a heavy knocking noise
a. Check for a loose crankshaft pulley or flywheel; replace and torque the mounting bolt(s) to specification.
b. Check for a bent connecting rod caused by a hydro-lock condition. Engine disassembly is necessary to inspect for damaged and needed replacement parts.
c. Check for excessive engine rod bearing wear or damage. This condition is also associated with low engine oil pressure and will require engine disassembly to inspect for damaged and needed replacement parts.

7. Vehicle has a fuel odor when driven
a. Check the fuel gauge level. If the fuel gauge registers full, it is possible that the odor is caused by being filled beyond capacity, or some spillage occurred during refueling. The odor should clear after driving an hour, or twenty miles, allowing the vapor canister to purge.
b. Check the fuel filler cap for looseness or seepage. Check the cap tightness and, if loose, properly secure. If seepage is noted, replace the filler cap.
c. Check for loose hose clamps, cracked or damaged fuel delivery and return lines, or leaking components or seals, and replace or repair as necessary.
d. Check the vehicle's fuel economy. If fuel consumption has increased due to a failed component, or if the fuel is not properly ignited due to an ignition related failure, the catalytic converter may become contaminated. This condition may also trigger the check engine warning light. Check the spark plugs for a dark, rich condition or verify the condition by testing the vehicle's emissions. Replace fuel fouled spark plugs, and test and replace failed components as necessary.

8. Vehicle has a rotten egg odor when driven
a. Check for a leaking intake gasket or vacuum leak causing a lean running condition. A lean mixture may result in increased exhaust temperatures, causing the catalytic converter to run hotter than normal. This condition may also trigger the check engine warning light. Check and repair the vacuum leaks as necessary.
b. Check the vehicle's alternator and battery condition. If the alternator is overcharging, the battery electrolyte can be boiled from the battery, and the battery casing may begin to crack, swell or bulge, damaging or shorting the battery internally. If this has occurred, neutralize the battery mounting area with a suitable baking soda and water mixture or equivalent, and replace the alternator or voltage regulator. Inspect, service, and load test the battery, and replace if necessary.

9. Vehicle has a sweet odor when driven
a. Check for an engine coolant leak caused by a seeping radiator cap, loose hose clamp, weeping cooling system seal, gasket or cooling system hose and replace or repair as needed.
b. Check for a coolant leak from the radiator, coolant reservoir, heater control valve or under the dashboard from the heater core, and replace the failed part as necessary.
c. Check the engine's exhaust for white smoke in addition to a sweet odor. The presence of white, steamy smoke with a sweet odor indicates coolant leaking into the combustion chamber. Possible causes include a failed head gasket, cracked engine block or cylinder head. Other symptoms of this condition include a white paste build-up on the inside of the oil filler cap, and softened, deformed or bulging radiator hoses.

10. Engine vibrates when idling
a. Check for loose, collapsed, or damaged engine or transmission mounts and repair or replace as necessary.
b. Check for loose or damaged engine covers or shields and secure or replace as necessary.

11. Engine vibrates during acceleration
a. Check for missing, loose or damaged exhaust system hangers and mounts; replace or repair as necessary.
b. Check the exhaust system routing and fit for adequate clearance or potential rubbing; repair or adjust as necessary.

1-D. Engine Electrical System

1. Battery goes dead while driving
a. Check the battery condition. Replace the battery if the battery will not hold a charge or fails a battery load test. If the battery loses fluid while driving, check for an overcharging condition. If the alternator is overcharging, replace the alternator or voltage regulator. (A voltage regulator is typically built into the alternator, necessitating alternator replacement or overhaul.)
b. Check the battery cable condition. Clean or replace corroded cables and clean the battery terminals.
c. Check the alternator and voltage regulator operation. If the charging system is over or undercharging, replace the alternator or voltage regulator, or both.
d. Inspect the wiring and wire connectors at the alternator for looseness, a missing ground or defective terminal, and repair as necessary.

e. Inspect the alternator drive belt tension, tensioners and condition. Properly tension the drive belt, replace weak or broken tensioners, and replace the drive belt if worn or cracked.

2. Battery goes dead overnight
a. Check the battery condition. Replace the battery if the battery will not hold a charge or fails a battery load test.
b. Check for a voltage draw, such as a trunk light, interior light or glove box light staying on. Check light switch position and operation, and replace if defective.
c. Check the alternator for an internally failed diode, and replace the alternator if defective.

1-E. Engine Cooling System

1. Engine overheats
a. Check the coolant level. Set the heater temperature to full hot and check for internal air pockets, bleed the cooling system and inspect for leakage. Top off the cooling system with the correct coolant mixture.
b. Pressure test the cooling system and radiator cap for leaks. Check for seepage caused by loose hose clamps, failed coolant hoses, and cooling system components such as the heater control valve, heater core, radiator, radiator cap, and water pump. Replace defective parts and fill the cooling system with the recommended coolant mixture.
c. On vehicles with electrically controlled cooling fans, check the cooling fan operation. Check for blown fuses or defective fan motors, temperature sensors and relays, and replace failed components.
d. Check for a coolant leak caused by a failed head gasket, or a porous water jacket casting in the cylinder head or engine block. Replace defective parts as necessary.
e. Check for an internally restricted radiator. Flush the radiator or replace if the blockage is too severe for flushing.
f. Check for a damaged water pump. If coolant circulation is poor, check for a loose water pump impeller. If the impeller is loose, replace the water pump.

2. Engine loses coolant
a. Pressure test the cooling system and radiator cap for leaks. Check for seepage caused by loose hose clamps, failed coolant hoses, and cooling system components such as the heater control valve, heater core, radiator, radiator cap, and water pump. Replace defective parts and fill the cooling system with the recommended coolant mixture.
b. Check for a coolant leak caused by a failed head gasket, or a porous water jacket casting in the cylinder head or engine block. Replace defective parts as necessary.

3. Engine temperature remains cold when driving
a. Check the thermostat operation. Replace the thermostat if it sticks in the open position.
b. On vehicles with electrically controlled cooling fans, check the cooling fan operation. Check for defective temperature sensors and stuck relays, and replace failed components.
c. Check temperature gauge operation if equipped to verify proper operation of the gauge. Check the sensors and wiring for defects, and repair or replace defective components.

4. Engine runs hot
a. Check for an internally restricted radiator. Flush the radiator or replace if the blockage is too severe for flushing.
b. Check for a loose or slipping water pump drive belt. Inspect the drive belt condition. Replace the belt if brittle, cracked or damaged. Check the pulley condition and properly tension the belt.
c. Check the cooling fan operation. Replace defective fan motors, sensors or relays as necessary.
d. Check temperature gauge operation if equipped to verify proper operation of the gauge. Check the sensors and wiring for defects, and repair or replace defective components.
e. Check the coolant level. Set the heater temperature to full hot, check for internal air pockets, bleed the cooling system and inspect for leakage. Top

off the cooling system with the correct coolant mixture. Once the engine is cool, recheck the fluid level and top off as needed.

NOTE: The engine cooling system can also be affected by an engine's mechanical condition. A failed head gasket or a porous casting in the engine block or cylinder head could cause a loss of coolant and result in engine overheating.

Some cooling systems rely on electrically driven cooling fans to cool the radiator and use electrical temperature sensors and relays to operate the cooling fan. When diagnosing these systems, check for blown fuses, damaged wires and verify that the electrical connections are fully connected, clean and not physically damaged. If necessary, clean the electrical contacts using electrical contact cleaner. The use of cleaning agents not specifically designed for electrical contacts could leave a film or damage the insulation of the wiring.

1-F. Engine Exhaust System

1. Exhaust rattles at idle speed
a. Check the engine and transmission mounts and replace mounts showing signs of damage or wear.
b. Check the exhaust hangers, brackets and mounts. Replace broken, missing or damaged mounts.
c. Check for internal damage to mufflers and catalytic converters. The broken pieces from the defective component may travel in the direction of the exhaust flow and collect and/or create a blockage in a component other than the one which failed, causing engine running and stalling problems. Another symptom of a restricted exhaust is low engine manifold vacuum. Remove the exhaust system and carefully remove any loose or broken pieces, then replace any failed or damaged parts as necessary.
d. Check the exhaust system clearance, routing and alignment. If the exhaust is making contact with the vehicle in any manner, loosen and reposition the exhaust system.

2. Exhaust system vibrates when driving
a. Check the exhaust hangers, brackets and mounts. Replace broken, missing or damaged mounts.
b. Check the exhaust system clearance, routing and alignment. If the exhaust is making contact with the vehicle in any manner, check for bent or damaged components and replace, then loosen and reposition the exhaust system.
c. Check for internal damage to mufflers and catalytic converters. The broken pieces from the defective component may travel in the direction of the exhaust flow and collect and/or create a blockage in a component other than the one which failed, causing engine running and stalling problems. Another symptom of a restricted exhaust is low engine manifold vacuum. Remove the exhaust system and carefully remove any loose or broken pieces, then replace any failed or damaged parts as necessary.

3. Exhaust system hangs too low
a. Check the exhaust hangers, brackets and mounts. Replace broken, missing or damaged mounts.
b. Check the exhaust routing and alignment. Check and replace bent or damaged components. If the exhaust is not routed properly, loosen and reposition the exhaust system.

4. Exhaust sounds loud
a. Check the system for looseness and leaks. Check the exhaust pipes, clamps, flange bolts and manifold fasteners for tightness. Check and replace any failed gaskets.
b. Check and replace exhaust silencers that have a loss of efficiency due to internally broken baffles or worn packing material.
c. Check for missing mufflers and silencers that have been replaced with straight pipes or with non-original equipment silencers.

NOTE: Exhaust system rattles, vibration and proper alignment should not be overlooked. Excessive vibration caused by collapsed engine mounts, damaged or missing exhaust hangers and misalignment may cause surface cracks and broken welds, creating exhaust leaks or internal damage to exhaust components such as the catalytic converter, creating a restriction to exhaust flow and loss of power.

2. DRIVE TRAIN

2-A. Automatic Transmission

1. Transmission shifts erratically

a. Check and if not within the recommended range, add or remove transmission fluid to obtain the correct fluid level. Always use the recommended fluid type when adding transmission fluid.

b. Check the fluid level condition. If the fluid has become contaminated, fatigued from excessive heat or exhibits a burning odor, change the transmission fluid and filter using the recommended type and amount of fluid. A fluid which exhibits a burning odor indicates that the transmission has been slipping internally and may require future repairs.

c. Check for an improperly installed transmission filter, or missing filter gasket, and repair as necessary.

d. Check for loose or leaking gaskets, pressure lines and fittings, and repair or replace as necessary.

e. Check for loose or disconnected shift and throttle linkages or vacuum hoses, and repair as necessary.

2. Transmission will not engage

a. Check the shift linkage for looseness, wear and proper adjustment, and repair as necessary.

b. Check for a loss of transmission fluid and top off as needed with the recommended fluid.

c. If the transmission does not engage with the shift linkage correctly installed and the proper fluid level, internal damage has likely occurred, requiring transmission removal and disassembly.

3. Transmission will not downshift during heavy acceleration

a. On computer controlled transmissions, check for failed sensors or control units and repair or replace defective components.

b. On vehicles with kickdown linkages or vacuum servos, check for proper linkage adjustment or leaking vacuum hoses or servo units.

NOTE: Many automatic transmissions use an electronic control module, electrical sensors and solenoids to control transmission shifting. When troubleshooting a vehicle with this type of system, be sure the electrical connectors are fully connected, clean and not physically damaged. If necessary, clean the electrical contacts using electrical contact cleaner. The use of cleaning agents not specifically designed for electrical contacts could leave a film or damage the insulation of the wiring.

2-G. Axles

Front Wheel Drive Vehicles

1. Front wheel makes a clicking noise

a. Check for debris such as a pebble, nail or glass in the tire or tire tread. Carefully remove the debris. Small rocks and pebbles rarely cause a puncture; however, a sharp object should be removed carefully at a facility capable of performing tire repairs.

b. Check for a loose, damaged or worn Constant Velocity (CV) joint and replace if defective.

2. Rear wheel makes a clicking noise

a. Check for debris such as a pebble, nail or glass in the tire or tire tread. Carefully remove the debris. Small rocks and pebbles rarely cause a puncture; however, a sharp object should be removed carefully at a facility capable of performing tire repairs.

2-H. Other Drive Train Conditions

1. Burning odor from center of vehicle when accelerating

a. Check for a seizing brake hydraulic component such as a brake caliper. Check the caliper piston for surface damage such as rust, and measure for out-of-round wear and caliper-to-piston clearance. For additional information on brake related odors, refer to section 3-A, condition number 9.

b. On vehicles with a manual transmission, check for a slipping clutch. For possible causes and additional information, refer to section 2-C, condition number 1.

c. On vehicles with an automatic transmission, check the fluid level and condition. Top off or change the fluid and filter using the recommended replacement parts, lubricant type and amount. If the odor persists, transmission removal and disassembly will be necessary.

2. Engine accelerates, but vehicle does not gain speed

a. On vehicles with a manual transmission, check for a slipping or damaged clutch. For possible causes and additional information refer to section 2-C, condition number 1.

b. On vehicles with an automatic transmission, check the fluid level and condition. Top off or change the fluid and filter using the recommended replacement parts, lubricant type and amount. If the slipping continues, transmission removal and disassembly will be necessary.

3. BRAKE SYSTEM

3-A. Brake System Troubleshooting

1. Brake pedal pulsates or shimmies when pressed

a. Check wheel lug nut torque and tighten evenly to specification.

b. Check the brake rotor for trueness and thickness variations. Replace the rotor if it is too thin, warped, or if the thickness varies beyond specification. Some rotors can be machined; consult the manufacturer's specifications and recommendations before using a machined brake rotor.

c. Check the brake caliper or caliper bracket mounting bolt torque and inspect for looseness. Torque the mounting bolts and inspect for wear or any looseness, including worn mounting brackets, bushings and sliding pins.

d. Check the wheel bearing for looseness. If the bearing is loose, adjust if possible, otherwise replace the bearing.

2. Brakes make a squealing noise

a. Check the brake rotor for the presence of a ridge on the outer edge; if present, remove the ridge or replace the brake rotor and brake pads.

b. Check for debris in the brake lining material, clean and reinstall.

c. Check the brake linings for wear and replace the brake linings if wear is approaching the lining wear limit.

d. Check the brake linings for glazing. Inspect the brake drum or rotor surface and replace, along with the brake linings, if the surface is not smooth or even.

e. Check the brake pad or shoe mounting areas for a lack of lubricant or the presence of surface rust. Clean and lubricate with a recommended high temperature brake grease.

3. Brakes make a grinding noise

a. Check the brake linings and brake surface areas for severe wear or damage. Replace worn or damaged parts.

b. Check for a seized or partially seized brake causing premature or uneven brake wear, excessive heat and brake rotor or drum damage. Replace defective parts and inspect the wheel bearing condition, which could have been damaged due to excessive heat.

4. Vehicle pulls to one side during braking

a. Check for air in the brake hydraulic system. Inspect the brake hydraulic seals, fluid lines and related components for fluid leaks. Remove the air from the brake system by bleeding the brakes. Be sure to use fresh brake fluid that meets the manufacturer's recommended standards.

b. Check for an internally restricted flexible brake hydraulic hose. Replace the hose and flush the brake system.

c. Check for a seizing brake hydraulic component such as a brake caliper. Check the caliper piston for surface damage such as rust, and measure for out-of-round wear and caliper-to-piston clearance. Overhaul or replace failed parts and flush the brake system.

d. Check the vehicle's alignment and inspect for suspension wear. Replace worn bushings, ball joints and set alignment to the manufacturer's specifications.

e. If the brake system uses drum brakes front or rear, check the brake adjustment. Inspect for seized adjusters and clean or replace, then properly adjust.

5. Brake pedal feels spongy or has excessive travel

a. Check the brake fluid level and condition. If the fluid is contaminated or has not been flushed every two years, clean the master cylinder reservoir, and bleed and flush the brakes using fresh brake fluid that meets the manufacturer's recommended standards.

b. Check for a weak or damaged flexible brake hydraulic hose. Replace the hose and flush the brake system.

c. If the brake system uses drum brakes front or rear, check the brake adjustment. Inspect for seized adjusters and clean or replace, then properly adjust.

6. Brake pedal feel is firm, but brakes lack sufficient stopping power or fade

a. Check the operation of the brake booster and brake booster check valve. Replace worn or failed parts.

b. Check brake linings and brake surface areas for glazing and replace worn or damaged parts.

c. Check for seized hydraulic parts and linkages, and clean or replace as needed.

7. Vehicle has excessive front end dive or locks rear brakes too easily

a. Check for worn, failed or seized brake proportioning valve and replace the valve.

b. Check for a seized, disconnected or missing spring or linkage for the brake proportioning valve. Replace missing parts or repair as necessary.

8. Brake pedal goes to floor when pressed and will not pump up

a. Check the brake hydraulic fluid level and inspect the fluid lines and seals

for leakage. Repair or replace leaking components, then bleed and flush the brake system using fresh brake fluid that meets the manufacturer's recommended standards.

b. Check the brake fluid level. Inspect the brake fluid level and brake hydraulic seals. If the fluid level is ok, and the brake hydraulic system is free of hydraulic leaks, replace the brake master cylinder, then bleed and flush the brake system using fresh brake fluid that meets the manufacturer's recommended standards.

9. Brakes produce a burning odor

a. Check for a seizing brake hydraulic component such as a brake caliper. Check the caliper piston for surface damage such as rust, and measure for out-of-round wear and caliper-to-piston clearance. Overhaul or replace failed parts and flush the brake system.

b. Check for an internally restricted flexible brake hydraulic hose. Replace the hose and flush the brake system.

c. Check the parking brake release mechanism, seized linkage or cable, and repair as necessary.

BRAKE PERFORMANCE TROUBLESHOOTING HINTS

Brake vibrations or pulsation can often be diagnosed on a safe and careful test drive. A brake vibration which is felt through the brake pedal while braking, but not felt in the steering wheel, is most likely caused by brake surface variations in the rear brakes. If both the brake pedal and steering wheel vibrate during braking, a surface variation in the front brakes, or both front and rear brakes, is very likely.

A brake pedal that pumps up with repeated use can be caused by air in the brake hydraulic system or, if the vehicle is equipped with rear drum brakes, the brake adjusters may be seized or out of adjustment. A quick test for brake adjustment on vehicles with rear drum brakes is to pump the brake pedal several times with the vehicle's engine not running and the parking brake released. Pump the brake pedal several times and continue to apply pressure to the brake pedal. With pressure being applied to the brake pedal, engage the parking brake. Release the brake pedal and quickly press the brake pedal again. If the brake pedal pumped up, the rear brakes are in need of adjustment. Do not compensate for the rear brake adjustment by adjusting the parking brake, this will cause premature brake lining wear.

To test a vacuum brake booster, pump the brake pedal several times with the vehicle's engine off. Apply pressure to the brake pedal and then start the engine. The brake pedal should move downward about one inch (25mm).

4. WHEELS, TIRES, STEERING AND SUSPENSION

4-A. Wheels and Wheel Bearings

1. Front wheel or wheel bearing loose

Front Wheel Drive Vehicles

a. Torque lug nuts and axle nuts to specification and recheck for looseness.

b. Wheel bearing worn or damaged. Replace wheel bearing.

c. Wheel bearing out of adjustment. Adjust wheel bearing to specification; if still loose, replace.

2. Rear wheel or wheel bearing loose

Front Wheel Drive Vehicles

a. Wheel bearing out of adjustment. Adjust wheel bearing to specification; if still loose, replace.

b. Torque lug nuts to specification and recheck for looseness.

c. Wheel bearing worn or damaged. Replace wheel bearing.

4-B. Tires

1. Tires worn on inside tread

a. Check alignment for a toed-out condition. Check and set tire pressures and properly adjust the toe.

b. Check for worn, damaged or defective suspension components. Replace defective parts and adjust the alignment.

2. Tires worn on outside tread

a. Check alignment for a toed-in condition. Check and set tire pressures and properly adjust the toe.

b. Check for worn, damaged or defective suspension components. Replace defective parts and adjust the alignment.

3. Tires worn unevenly

a. Check the tire pressure and tire balance. Replace worn or defective tires and check the alignment; adjust if necessary.

b. Check for worn shock absorbers. Replaced failed components, worn or defective tires and check the alignment; adjust if necessary.

c. Check the alignment settings. Check and set tire pressures and properly adjust the alignment to specification.

d. Check for worn, damaged or defective suspension components. Replace defective parts and adjust the alignment to specification.

4-C. Steering

1. Excessive play in steering wheel

a. Check the steering gear free-play adjustment and properly adjust to remove excessive play.

b. Check the steering linkage for worn, damaged or defective parts. Replace failed components and perform a front end alignment.

c. Check for a worn, damaged, or defective steering box, replace the steering gear and check the front end alignment.

2. Steering wheel shakes at cruising speeds

a. Check for a bent front wheel. Replace a damaged wheel and check the tire for possible internal damage.

b. Check for an unevenly worn front tire. Replace the tire, adjust tire pressure and balance.

c. Check the front tires for hidden internal damage. Tires which have encountered large pot holes or suffered other hard blows may have sustained internal damage and should be replaced immediately.

d. Check the front tires for an out-of-balance condition. Remove, spin balance and reinstall. Torque all the wheel bolts or lug nuts to the recommended specification.

e. Check for a loose wheel bearing. If possible, adjust the bearing, or replace the bearing if it is a non-adjustable bearing.

3. Steering wheel shakes when braking

a. Refer to section 3-A, condition number 1.

4. Steering wheel becomes stiff when turned

a. Check the steering wheel free-play adjustment and reset as needed.

b. Check for a damaged steering gear assembly. Replace the steering gear and perform a front end alignment.

c. Check for damaged or seized suspension components. Replace defective components and perform a front end alignment.

4-D. Suspension

1. Vehicle pulls to one side

a. Tire pressure uneven. Adjust tire pressure to recommended settings.

b. Tires worn unevenly. Replace tires and check alignment settings.

c. Alignment out of specification. Align front end and check thrust angle.

d. Check for a dragging brake and repair or replace as necessary.

2. Vehicle is very bouncy over bumps

a. Check for worn or leaking shock absorbers or strut assemblies and replace as necessary.

b. Check for seized shock absorbers or strut assemblies and replace as necessary.

NOTE: When one shock fails, it is recommended to replace front or rear units as pairs.

3. Vehicle leans excessively in turns

a. Check for worn or leaking shock absorbers or strut assemblies and replace as necessary.

b. Check for missing, damaged, or worn stabilizer links or bushings, and replace or install as necessary.

4. Vehicle ride quality seems excessively harsh

a. Check for seized shock absorbers or strut assemblies and replace as necessary.

b. Check for excessively high tire pressures and adjust pressures to vehicle recommendations.

5. Vehicle seems low or leans to one side

a. Check for a damaged, broken or weak spring. Replace defective parts and check for a needed alignment.

b. Check for seized shock absorbers or strut assemblies and replace as necessary.

c. Check for worn or leaking shock absorbers or strut assemblies and replace as necessary.

4-E. Driving Noises and Vibrations

Noises

1. Vehicle makes a clicking noises when driven

a. Check the noise to see if it varies with road speed. Verify if the noise is present when coasting or with steering or throttle input. If the clicking noise frequency changes with road speed and is not affected by steering or throttle input, check the tire treads for a stone, piece of glass, nail or another hard object imbedded into the tire or tire tread.

Stones rarely cause a tire puncture and are easily removed. Other objects may create an air leak when removed. Consider having these objects removed immediately at a facility equipped to repair tire punctures.

b. If the clicking noise varies with throttle input and steering, check for a worn Constant Velocity (CV-joint) joint, universal (U- joint) or flex joint.

2. Vehicle makes a clunking or knocking noise over bumps

a. A clunking noise over bumps is most often caused by excessive movement or clearance in a suspension component. Check the suspension for soft, cracked, damaged or worn bushings. Replace the bushings and check the vehicle's alignment.

b. Check for loose suspension mounting bolts. Check the tightness on subframe bolts, pivot bolts and suspension mounting bolts, and torque to specification.

c. Check the vehicle for a loose wheel bearing. Some wheel bearings can be adjusted for looseness, while others must be replaced if loose. Adjust or replace the bearings as recommended by the manufacturer.

d. Check the door latch adjustment. If the door is slightly loose, or the latch adjustment is not centered, the door assembly may create noises over bumps and rough surfaces. Properly adjust the door latches to secure the door.

3. Vehicle makes a low pitched rumbling noise when driven

a. A low pitched rumbling noise is usually caused by a drive train related bearing and is most often associated with a wheel bearing which has been damaged or worn. The damage can be caused by excessive brake temperatures or physical contact with a pot hole or curb. Sometimes the noise will vary when turning. Left hand turns increase the load on the vehicle's right side, and right turns load the left side. A failed front wheel bearing may also cause a slight steering wheel vibration when turning. A bearing which exhibits noise must be replaced.

b. Check the tire condition and balance. An internally damaged tire may cause failure symptoms similar to failed suspension parts. For diagnostic purposes, try a known good set of tires and replace defective tires.

4. Vehicle makes a squeaking noise over bumps

a. Check the vehicle's ball joints for wear, damaged or leaking boots. Replace a ball joint if it is loose, the boot is damaged and leaking, or the ball joint is binding. When replacing suspension parts, check the vehicle for alignment.

b. Check for seized or deteriorated bushings. Replace bushings that are worn or damaged and check the vehicle for alignment.

c. Check for the presence of sway bar or stabilizer bar bushings which wrap around the bar. Inspect the condition of the bushings and replace if worn or damaged. Remove the bushing bracket and apply a thin layer of suspension grease to the area where the bushings wrap around the bar and reinstall the bushing brackets.

Vibrations

5. Vehicle vibrates when driven

a. Check the road surface. Roads which have rough or uneven surfaces may cause unusual vibrations.

b. Check the tire condition and balance. An internally damaged tire may cause failure symptoms similar to failed suspension parts. For diagnostic purposes, try a known good set of tires and replace defective tires immediately.

c. Check for a worn Constant Velocity (CV-joint) joint, universal (U- joint) or flex joint and replace if loose, damaged or binding.

d. Check for a loose, bent, or out-of-balance axle or drive shaft. Replace damaged or failed components.

NOTE: Diagnosing failures related to wheels, tires, steering and the suspension system can often times be accomplished with a careful and thorough test drive. Bearing noises are isolated by noting whether the noises or symptoms vary when turning left or right, or occur while driving a straight line. During a left hand turn, the vehicle's weight shifts to the right, placing more force on the right side bearings, such that if a right side wheel bearing is worn or damaged, the noise or vibration should increase during light-to-heavy acceleration. Conversely, on right hand turns, the vehicle tends to lean to the left, loading the left side bearings.

Knocking noises in the suspension when the vehicle is driven over rough roads, railroad tracks and speed bumps indicate worn suspension components such as bushings, ball joints or tie rod ends, or a worn steering system.

5. ELECTRICAL ACCESSORIES

5-A. Headlights

1. One headlight only works on high or low beam
a. Check for battery voltage at headlight electrical connector. If battery voltage is present, replace the headlight assembly or bulb if available separately. If battery voltage is not present, refer to the headlight wiring diagram to troubleshoot.

2. Headlight does not work on high or low beam
a. Check for battery voltage and ground at headlight electrical connector. If battery voltage is present, check the headlight connector ground terminal for a proper ground. If battery voltage and ground are present at the headlight connector, replace the headlight assembly or bulb if available separately. If battery voltage or ground is not present, refer to the headlight wiring diagram to troubleshoot.
b. Check the headlight switch operation. Replace the switch if the switch is defective or operates intermittently.

3. Headlight(s) very dim
a. Check for battery voltage and ground at headlight electrical connector. If battery voltage is present, trace the ground circuit for the headlamp electrical connector, then clean and repair as necessary. If the voltage at the headlight electrical connector is significantly less than the voltage at the battery, refer to the headlight wiring diagram to troubleshoot and locate the voltage drop.

5-B. Tail, Running and Side Marker Lights

1. Tail light, running light or side marker light inoperative
a. Check for battery voltage and ground at light's electrical connector. If battery voltage is present, check the bulb socket and electrical connector ground terminal for a proper ground. If battery voltage and ground are present at the light connector, but not in the socket, clean the socket and the ground terminal connector. If battery voltage and ground are present in the bulb socket, replace the bulb. If battery voltage or ground is not present, refer to the wiring diagram to troubleshoot for an open circuit.
b. Check the light switch operation and replace if necessary.

2. Tail light, running light or side marker light works intermittently
a. Check the bulb for a damaged filament, and replace if damaged.
b Check the bulb and bulb socket for corrosion, and clean or replace the bulb and socket.
c. Check for loose, damaged or corroded wires and electrical terminals, and repair as necessary.
d. Check the light switch operation and replace if necessary.

3. Tail light, running light or side marker light very dim
a. Check the bulb and bulb socket for corrosion and clean or replace the bulb and socket.
b. Check for low voltage at the bulb socket positive terminal or a poor ground. If voltage is low, or the ground marginal, trace the wiring to, and check for loose, damaged or corroded wires and electrical terminals; repair as necessary.
c. Check the light switch operation and replace if necessary.

5-C. Interior Lights

1. Interior light inoperative
a. Verify the interior light switch location and position(s), and set the switch in the correct position.
b. Check for battery voltage and ground at the interior light bulb socket. If battery voltage and ground are present, replace the bulb. If voltage is not present, check the interior light fuse for battery voltage. If the fuse is missing, replace the fuse. If the fuse has blown, or if battery voltage is present, refer to the wiring diagram to troubleshoot the cause for an open or shorted circuit. If ground is not present, check the door switch contacts and clean or repair as necessary.

2. Interior light works intermittently
a. Check the bulb for a damaged filament, and replace if damaged.
b. Check the bulb and bulb socket for corrosion, and clean or replace the bulb and socket.
c. Check for loose, damaged or corroded wires and electrical terminals; repair as necessary.
d. Check the door and light switch operation, and replace if necessary.

3. Interior light very dim
a. Check the bulb and bulb socket for corrosion, and clean or replace the bulb and socket.
b. Check for low voltage at the bulb socket positive terminal or a poor ground. If voltage is low, or the ground marginal, trace the wiring to, and check for loose, damaged or corroded wires and electrical terminals; repair as necessary.
c. Check the door and light switch operation, and replace if necessary.

5-D. Brake Lights

1. One brake light inoperative
a. Press the brake pedal and check for battery voltage and ground at the brake light bulb socket. If present, replace the bulb. If either battery voltage or ground is not present, refer to the wiring diagram to troubleshoot.

2. Both brake lights inoperative
a. Press the brake pedal and check for battery voltage and ground at the brake light bulb socket. If present, replace both bulbs. If battery voltage is not present, check the brake light switch adjustment and adjust as necessary. If the brake light switch is properly adjusted, and battery voltage or the ground is not present at the bulb sockets, or at the bulb electrical connector with the brake pedal pressed, refer to the wiring diagram to troubleshoot the cause of an open circuit.

3. One or both brake lights very dim
a. Press the brake pedal and measure the voltage at the brake light bulb socket. If the measured voltage is close to the battery voltage, check for a poor ground caused by a loose, damaged, or corroded wire, terminal, bulb or bulb socket. If the ground is bolted to a painted surface, it may be necessary to remove the electrical connector and clean the mounting surface, so the connector mounts on bare metal. If battery voltage is low, check for a poor connection caused by either a faulty brake light switch, a loose, damaged, or corroded wire, terminal or electrical connector. Refer to the wiring diagram to troubleshoot the cause of a voltage drop.

5-E. Warning Lights

1. Warning light(s) stay on when the engine is started

Ignition, Battery or Alternator Warning Light
a. Check the alternator output and voltage regulator operation, and replace as necessary.
b. Check the warning light wiring for a shorted wire.

Check Engine Light
a. Check the engine for routine maintenance and tune-up status. Note the engine tune-up specifications and verify the spark plug, air filter and engine oil condition; replace and/or adjust items as necessary.

b. Check the fuel tank for low fuel level, causing an intermittent lean fuel mixture. Top off fuel tank and reset check engine light.

c. Check for a failed or disconnected engine fuel or ignition component, sensor or control unit and repair or replace as necessary.

d. Check the intake manifold and vacuum hoses for air leaks and repair as necessary.

e. Check the engine's mechanical condition for excessive oil consumption.

Anti-Lock Braking System (ABS) Light

a. Check the wheel sensors and sensor rings for debris, and clean as necessary.

b. Check the brake master cylinder for fluid leakage or seal failure and replace as necessary.

c. Check the ABS control unit, pump and proportioning valves for proper operation; replace as necessary.

d. Check the sensor wiring at the wheel sensors and the ABS control unit for a loose or shorted wire, and repair as necessary.

Brake Warning Light

a. Check the brake fluid level and check for possible leakage from the hydraulic lines and seals. Top off brake fluid and repair leakage as necessary.

b. Check the brake linings for wear and replace as necessary.

c. Check for a loose or shorted brake warning light sensor or wire, and replace or repair as necessary.

Oil Pressure Warning Light

a. Stop the engine immediately. Check the engine oil level and oil filter condition, and top off or change the oil as necessary.

b. Check the oil pressure sensor wire for being shorted to ground. Disconnect the wire from the oil pressure sensor and with the ignition in the ON position, but not running, the oil pressure light should not be working. If the light works with the wire disconnected, check the sensor wire for being shorted to ground. Check the wire routing to make sure the wire is not pinched and check for insulation damage. Repair or replace the wire as necessary and recheck before starting the engine.

c. Remove the oil pan and check for a clogged oil pick-up tube screen.

d. Check the oil pressure sensor operation by substituting a known good sensor.

e. Check the oil filter for internal restrictions or leaks, and replace as necessary.

WARNING: If the engine is operated with oil pressure below the manufacturer's specification, severe (and costly) engine damage could occur. Low oil pressure can be caused by excessive internal wear or damage to the engine bearings, oil pressure relief valve, oil pump or oil pump drive mechanism.

Before starting the engine, check for possible causes of rapid oil loss, such as leaking oil lines or a loose, damaged, restricted, or leaking oil filter or oil pressure sensor. If the engine oil level and condition are acceptable, measure the engine's oil pressure using a pressure gauge, or determine the cause for the oil pressure warning light to function when the engine is running, before operating the engine for an extended period of time. Another symptom of operating an engine with low oil pressure is the presence of severe knocking and tapping noises.

Parking Brake Warning Light

a. Check the brake release mechanism and verify the parking brake has been fully released.

b. Check the parking brake light switch for looseness or misalignment.

c. Check for a damaged switch or a loose or shorted brake light switch wire, and replace or repair as necessary.

2. Warning light(s) flickers on and off when driving

Ignition, Battery or Alternator Warning Light

a. Check the alternator output and voltage regulator operation. An intermittent condition may indicate worn brushes, an internal short, or a defective voltage regulator. Replace the alternator or failed component.

b. Check the warning light wiring for a shorted, pinched or damaged wire and repair as necessary.

Check Engine Light

a. Check the engine for required maintenance and tune-up status. Verify engine tune-up specifications, as well as spark plug, air filter and engine oil condition; replace and/or adjust items as necessary.

b. Check the fuel tank for low fuel level causing an intermittent lean fuel mixture. Top off fuel tank and reset check engine light.

c. Check for an intermittent failure or partially disconnected engine fuel and ignition component, sensor or control unit; repair or replace as necessary.

d. Check the intake manifold and vacuum hoses for air leaks, and repair as necessary.

e. Check the warning light wiring for a shorted, pinched or damaged wire and repair as necessary.

Anti-Lock Braking System (ABS) Light

a. Check the wheel sensors and sensor rings for debris, and clean as necessary.

b. Check the brake master cylinder for fluid leakage or seal failure and replace as necessary.

c. Check the ABS control unit, pump and proportioning valves for proper operation, and replace as necessary.

d. Check the sensor wiring at the wheel sensors and the ABS control unit for a loose or shorted wire and repair as necessary.

Brake Warning Light

a. Check the brake fluid level and check for possible leakage from the hydraulic lines and seals. Top off brake fluid and repair leakage as necessary.

b. Check the brake linings for wear and replace as necessary.

c. Check for a loose or shorted brake warning light sensor or wire, and replace or repair as necessary.

Oil Pressure Warning Light

a. Stop the engine immediately. Check the engine oil level and check for a sudden and rapid oil loss, such as a leaking oil line or oil pressure sensor, and repair or replace as necessary.

b. Check the oil pressure sensor operation by substituting a known good sensor.

c. Check the oil pressure sensor wire for being shorted to ground. Disconnect the wire from the oil pressure sensor and with the ignition in the ON position, but not running, the oil pressure light should not be working. If the light works with the wire disconnected, check the sensor wire for being shorted to ground. Check the wire routing to make sure the wire is not pinched and check for insulation damage. Repair or replace the wire as necessary and recheck before starting the engine.

d. Remove the oil pan and check for a clogged oil pick-up tube screen.

Parking Brake Warning Light

a. Check the brake release mechanism and verify the parking brake has been fully released.

b. Check the parking brake light switch for looseness or misalignment.

c. Check for a damaged switch or a loose or shorted brake light switch wire, and replace or repair as necessary.

3. Warning light(s) inoperative with ignition on, and engine not started

a. Check for a defective bulb by installing a known good bulb.

b. Check for a defective wire using the appropriate wiring diagram(s).

c. Check for a defective sending unit by removing and then grounding the wire at the sending unit. If the light comes on with the ignition on when grounding the wire, replace the sending unit.

5-F. Turn Signal and 4-Way Hazard Lights

1. Turn signals or hazard lights come on, but do not flash

a. Check for a defective flasher unit and replace as necessary.

2. Turn signals or hazard lights do not function on either side
a. Check the fuse and replace, if defective.
b. Check the flasher unit by substituting a known good flasher unit.
c. Check the turn signal electrical system for a defective component, open circuit, short circuit or poor ground.

3. Turn signals or hazard lights only work on one side
a. Check for failed bulbs and replace as necessary.
b. Check for poor grounds in both housings and repair as necessary.

4. One signal light does not work
a. Check for a failed bulb and replace as necessary.
b. Check for corrosion in the bulb socket, and clean and repair as necessary.
c. Check for a poor ground at the bulb socket, and clean and repair as necessary.

5. Turn signals flash too slowly
a. Check signal bulb(s) wattage and replace with lower wattage bulb(s).

6. Turn signals flash too fast
a. Check signal bulb(s) wattage and replace with higher wattage bulb(s).
b. Check for installation of the correct flasher unit and replace if incorrect.

7. Four-way hazard flasher indicator light inoperative
a. Verify that the exterior lights are functioning and, if so, replace indicator bulb.
b. Check the operation of the warning flasher switch and replace if defective.

8. Turn signal indicator light(s) do not work in either direction
a. Verify that the exterior lights are functioning and, if so, replace indicator bulb(s).
b. Check for a defective flasher unit by substituting a known good unit.

9. One turn signal indicator light does not work
a. Check for a defective bulb and replace as necessary.
b. Check for a defective flasher unit by substituting a known good unit.

5-G. Horn

1. Horn does not operate
a. Check for a defective fuse and replace as necessary.
b. Check for battery voltage and ground at horn electrical connections when pressing the horn switch. If voltage is present, replace the horn assembly.

If voltage or ground is not present, refer to Chassis Electrical coverage for additional troubleshooting techniques and circuit information.

2. Horn has an unusual tone
a. On single horn systems, replace the horn.
b. On dual horn systems, check the operation of the second horn. Dual horn systems have a high and low pitched horn. Unplug one horn at a time and recheck operation. Replace the horn which does not function.
c. Check for debris or condensation build-up in horn and verify the horn positioning. If the horn has a single opening, adjust the opening downward to allow for adequate drainage and to prevent debris build-up.

5-H. Windshield Wipers

1. Windshield wipers do not operate
a. Check fuse and replace as necessary.
b. Check switch operation and repair or replace as necessary.
c. Check for corroded, loose, disconnected or broken wires and clean or repair as necessary.
d. Check the ground circuit for the wiper switch or motor and repair as necessary.

2. Windshield wiper motor makes a humming noise, gets hot or blows fuses
a. Wiper motor damaged internally; replace the wiper motor.
b. Wiper linkage bent, damaged or seized. Repair or replace wiper linkage as necessary.

3. Windshield wiper motor operates, but one or both wipers fail to move
a. Windshield wiper motor linkage loose or disconnected. Repair or replace linkage as necessary.
b. Windshield wiper arms loose on wiper pivots. Secure wiper arm to pivot or replace both the wiper arm and pivot assembly.

4. Windshield wipers will not park
a. Check the wiper switch operation and verify that the switch properly interrupts the power supplied to the wiper motor.
b. If the wiper switch is functioning properly, the wiper motor parking circuit has failed. Replace the wiper motor assembly. Operate the wiper motor at least one time before installing the arms and blades to ensure correct positioning, then recheck using the highest wiper speed on a wet windshield to make sure the arms and blades do not contact the windshield trim.

6. INSTRUMENTS AND GAUGES

6-A. Speedometer (Cable Operated)

1. Speedometer does not work
a. Check and verify that the speedometer cable is properly seated into the speedometer assembly and the speedometer drive gear.
b. Check the speedometer cable for breakage or rounded-off cable ends where the cable seats into the speedometer drive gear and into the speedometer assembly. If damaged, broken or the cable ends are rounded off, replace the cable.
c. Check speedometer drive gear condition and replace as necessary.
d. Install a known good speedometer to test for proper operation. If the substituted speedometer functions properly, replace the speedometer assembly.

2. Speedometer needle fluctuates when driving at steady speeds.
a. Check speedometer cable routing or sheathing for sharp bends or kinks. Route cable to minimize sharp bends or kinks. If the sheathing has been damaged, replace the cable assembly.

b. Check the speedometer cable for adequate lubrication. Remove the cable, inspect for damage, clean, lubricate and reinstall. If the cable has been damaged, replace the cable.

3. Speedometer works intermittently
a. Check the cable and verify that the cable is fully installed and the fasteners are secure.
b. Check the cable ends for wear and rounding, and replace as necessary.

6-B. Speedometer (Electronically Operated)

1. Speedometer does not work
a. Check the speed sensor pickup and replace as necessary.
b. Check the wiring between the speed sensor and the speedometer for corroded terminals, loose connections or broken wires and clean or repair as necessary.
c. Install a known good speedometer to test for proper operation. If the substituted speedometer functions properly, replace the speedometer assembly.

2. Speedometer works intermittently

a. Check the wiring between the speed sensor and the speedometer for corroded terminals, loose connections or broken wires and clean or repair as necessary.
b. Check the speed sensor pickup and replace as necessary.

6-C. Fuel, Temperature and Oil Pressure Gauges

1. Gauge does not register

a. Check for a missing or blown fuse and replace as necessary.
b. Check for an open circuit in the gauge wiring. Repair wiring as necessary.
c. Gauge sending unit defective. Replace gauge sending unit.
d. Gauge or sending unit improperly installed. Verify installation and wiring, and repair as necessary.

2. Gauge operates erratically

a. Check for loose, shorted, damaged or corroded electrical connections or wiring and repair as necessary.
b. Check gauge sending units and replace as necessary.

3. Gauge operates fully pegged

a. Sending unit-to-gauge wire shorted to ground.
b. Sending unit defective; replace sending unit.
c. Gauge or sending unit not properly grounded.
d. Gauge or sending unit improperly installed. Verify installation and wiring, and repair as necessary.

7. CLIMATE CONTROL

7-A. Air Conditioner

1. No air coming from air conditioner vents

a. Check the air conditioner fuse and replace as necessary.
b. Air conditioner system discharged. Have the system evacuated, charged and leak tested by an MVAC certified technician, utilizing approved recovery/recycling equipment. Repair as necessary.
c. Air conditioner low pressure switch defective. Replace switch.
d. Air conditioner fan resistor pack defective. Replace resistor pack.
e. Loose connection, broken wiring or defective air conditioner relay in air conditioning electrical circuit. Repair wiring or replace relay as necessary.

2. Air conditioner blows warm air

a. Air conditioner system is discharged. Have the system evacuated, charged and leak tested by an MVAC certified technician, utilizing approved recovery/recycling equipment. Repair as necessary.
b. Air conditioner compressor clutch not engaging. Check compressor clutch wiring, electrical connections and compressor clutch, and repair or replace as necessary.

3. Water collects on the interior floor when the air conditioner is used

a. Air conditioner evaporator drain hose is blocked. Clear the drain hose where it exits the passenger compartment.
b. Air conditioner evaporator drain hose is disconnected. Secure the drain hose to the evaporator drainage tray under the dashboard.

4. Air conditioner has a moldy odor when used

a. The air conditioner evaporator drain hose is blocked or partially restricted, allowing condensation to build up around the evaporator and drainage tray. Clear the drain hose where it exits the passenger compartment.

7-B. Heater

1. Blower motor does not operate

a. Check blower motor fuse and replace as necessary.
b. Check blower motor wiring for loose, damaged or corroded contacts and repair as necessary.
c. Check blower motor switch and resistor pack for open circuits, and repair or replace as necessary.
d. Check blower motor for internal damage and repair or replace as necessary.

2. Heater blows cool air

a. Check the engine coolant level. If the coolant level is low, top off and bleed the air from the cooling system as necessary and check for coolant leaks.
b. Check engine coolant operating temperature. If coolant temperature is below specification, check for a damaged or stuck thermostat.
c. Check the heater control valve operation. Check the heater control valve cable or vacuum hose for proper installation. Move the heater temperature control from hot to cold several times and verify the operation of the heater control valve. With the engine at normal operating temperature and the heater temperature control in the full hot position, carefully feel the heater hose going into and exiting the control valve. If one heater hose is hot and the other is much cooler, replace the control valve.

3. Heater steams the windshield when used

a. Check for a loose cooling system hose clamp or leaking coolant hose near the engine firewall or under the dash area, and repair as necessary.
b. Check for the existence of a sweet odor and fluid dripping from the heater floor vents, indicating a failed or damaged heater core. Pressure test the cooling system with the heater set to the fully warm position and check for fluid leakage from the floor vents. If leakage is verified, remove and replace the heater core assembly.

NOTE: On some vehicles, the dashboard must be disassembled and removed to access the heater core.

GLOSSARY

AIR/FUEL RATIO: The ratio of air-to-gasoline by weight in the fuel mixture drawn into the engine.

AIR INJECTION: One method of reducing harmful exhaust emissions by injecting air into each of the exhaust ports of an engine. The fresh air entering the hot exhaust manifold causes any remaining fuel to be burned before it can exit the tailpipe.

ALTERNATOR: A device used for converting mechanical energy into electrical energy.

AMMETER: An instrument, calibrated in amperes, used to measure the flow of an electrical current in a circuit. Ammeters are always connected in series with the circuit being tested.

AMPERE: The rate of flow of electrical current present when one volt of electrical pressure is applied against one ohm of electrical resistance.

ANALOG COMPUTER: Any microprocessor that uses similar (analogous) electrical signals to make its calculations.

ARMATURE: A laminated, soft iron core wrapped by a wire that converts electrical energy to mechanical energy as in a motor or relay. When rotated in a magnetic field, it changes mechanical energy into electrical energy as in a generator.

ATMOSPHERIC PRESSURE: The pressure on the Earth's surface caused by the weight of the air in the atmosphere. At sea level, this pressure is 14.7 psi at 32°F (101 kPa at 0°C).

ATOMIZATION: The breaking down of a liquid into a fine mist that can be suspended in air.

AXIAL PLAY: Movement parallel to a shaft or bearing bore.

BACKFIRE: The sudden combustion of gases in the intake or exhaust system that results in a loud explosion.

BACKLASH: The clearance or play between two parts, such as meshed gears.

BACKPRESSURE: Restrictions in the exhaust system that slow the exit of exhaust gases from the combustion chamber.

BAKELITE: A heat resistant, plastic insulator material commonly used in printed circuit boards and transistorized components.

BALL BEARING: A bearing made up of hardened inner and outer races between which hardened steel balls roll.

BALLAST RESISTOR: A resistor in the primary ignition circuit that lowers voltage after the engine is started to reduce wear on ignition components.

BEARING: A friction reducing, supportive device usually located between a stationary part and a moving part.

BIMETAL TEMPERATURE SENSOR: Any sensor or switch made of two dissimilar types of metal that bend when heated or cooled due to the different expansion rates of the alloys. These types of sensors usually function as an on/off switch.

BLOWBY: Combustion gases, composed of water vapor and unburned fuel, that leak past the piston rings into the crankcase during normal engine operation. These gases are removed by the PCV system to prevent the buildup of harmful acids in the crankcase.

BRAKE PAD: A brake shoe and lining assembly used with disc brakes.

BRAKE SHOE: The backing for the brake lining. The term is, however, usually applied to the assembly of the brake backing and lining.

BUSHING: A liner, usually removable, for a bearing; an anti-friction liner used in place of a bearing.

CALIPER: A hydraulically activated device in a disc brake system, which is mounted straddling the brake rotor (disc). The caliper contains at least one piston and two brake pads. Hydraulic pressure on the piston(s) forces the pads against the rotor.

CAMSHAFT: A shaft in the engine on which are the lobes (cams) which operate the valves. The camshaft is driven by the crankshaft, via a belt, chain or gears, at one half the crankshaft speed.

CAPACITOR: A device which stores an electrical charge.

CARBON MONOXIDE (CO): A colorless, odorless gas given off as a normal byproduct of combustion. It is poisonous and extremely dangerous in confined areas, building up slowly to toxic levels without warning if adequate ventilation is not available.

CARBURETOR: A device, usually mounted on the intake manifold of an engine, which mixes the air and fuel in the proper proportion to allow even combustion.

CATALYTIC CONVERTER: A device installed in the exhaust system, like a muffler, that converts harmful byproducts of combustion into carbon dioxide and water vapor by means of a heat-producing chemical reaction.

CENTRIFUGAL ADVANCE: A mechanical method of advancing the spark timing by using flyweights in the distributor that react to centrifugal force generated by the distributor shaft rotation.

CHECK VALVE: Any one-way valve installed to permit the flow of air, fuel or vacuum in one direction only.

CHOKE: A device, usually a moveable valve, placed in the intake path of a carburetor to restrict the flow of air.

CIRCUIT: Any unbroken path through which an electrical current can flow. Also used to describe fuel flow in some instances.

CIRCUIT BREAKER: A switch which protects an electrical circuit from overload by opening the circuit when the current flow exceeds a predetermined level. Some circuit breakers must be reset manually, while most reset automatically.

COIL (IGNITION): A transformer in the ignition circuit which steps up the voltage provided to the spark plugs.

COMBINATION MANIFOLD: An assembly which includes both the intake and exhaust manifolds in one casting.

COMBINATION VALVE: A device used in some fuel systems that routes fuel vapors to a charcoal storage canister instead of venting them into the atmosphere. The valve relieves fuel tank pressure and allows fresh air into the tank as the fuel level drops to prevent a vapor lock situation.

COMPRESSION RATIO: The comparison of the total volume of the cylinder and combustion chamber with the piston at BDC and the piston at TDC.

CONDENSER: 1. An electrical device which acts to store an electrical charge, preventing voltage surges. 2. A radiator-like device in the air conditioning system in which refrigerant gas condenses into a liquid, giving off heat.

CONDUCTOR: Any material through which an electrical current can be transmitted easily.

CONTINUITY: Continuous or complete circuit. Can be checked with an ohmmeter.

COUNTERSHAFT: An intermediate shaft which is rotated by a mainshaft and transmits, in turn, that rotation to a working part.

CRANKCASE: The lower part of an engine in which the crankshaft and related parts operate.

CRANKSHAFT: The main driving shaft of an engine which receives reciprocating motion from the pistons and converts it to rotary motion.

CYLINDER: In an engine, the round hole in the engine block in which the piston(s) ride.

CYLINDER BLOCK: The main structural member of an engine in which is found the cylinders, crankshaft and other principal parts.

CYLINDER HEAD: The detachable portion of the engine, usually fastened to the top of the cylinder block and containing all or most of the combustion chambers. On overhead valve engines, it contains the valves and their operating parts. On overhead cam engines, it contains the camshaft as well.

DEAD CENTER: The extreme top or bottom of the piston stroke.

DETONATION: An unwanted explosion of the air/fuel mixture in the combustion chamber caused by excess heat and compression, advanced timing, or an overly lean mixture. Also referred to as "ping".

DIAPHRAGM: A thin, flexible wall separating two cavities, such as in a vacuum advance unit.

DIESELING: A condition in which hot spots in the combustion chamber cause the engine to run on after the key is turned off.

DIFFERENTIAL: A geared assembly which allows the transmission of motion between drive axles, giving one axle the ability to turn faster than the other.

DIODE: An electrical device that will allow current to flow in one direction only.

DISC BRAKE: A hydraulic braking assembly consisting of a brake disc, or rotor, mounted on an axle, and a caliper assembly containing, usually two brake pads which are activated by hydraulic pressure. The pads are forced against the sides of the disc, creating friction which slows the vehicle.

DISTRIBUTOR: A mechanically driven device on an engine which is responsible for electrically firing the spark plug at a predetermined point of the piston stroke.

DOWEL PIN: A pin, inserted in mating holes in two different parts allowing those parts to maintain a fixed relationship.

DRUM BRAKE: A braking system which consists of two brake shoes and one or two wheel cylinders, mounted on a fixed backing plate, and a brake drum, mounted on an axle, which revolves around the assembly.

DWELL: The rate, measured in degrees of shaft rotation, at which an electrical circuit cycles on and off.

ELECTRONIC CONTROL UNIT (ECU): Ignition module, module, amplifier or igniter. See Module for definition.

ELECTRONIC IGNITION: A system in which the timing and firing of the spark plugs is controlled by an electronic control unit, usually called a module. These systems have no points or condenser.

END-PLAY: The measured amount of axial movement in a shaft.

ENGINE: A device that converts heat into mechanical energy.

EXHAUST MANIFOLD: A set of cast passages or pipes which conduct exhaust gases from the engine.

FEELER GAUGE: A blade, usually metal, or precisely predetermined thickness, used to measure the clearance between two parts.

FIRING ORDER: The order in which combustion occurs in the cylinders of an engine. Also the order in which spark is distributed to the plugs by the distributor.

FLOODING: The presence of too much fuel in the intake manifold and combustion chamber which prevents the air/fuel mixture from firing, thereby causing a no-start situation.

FLYWHEEL: A disc shaped part bolted to the rear end of the crankshaft. Around the outer perimeter is affixed the ring gear. The starter drive engages the ring gear, turning the flywheel, which rotates the crankshaft, imparting the initial starting motion to the engine.

FOOT POUND (ft. lbs. or sometimes, ft.lb.): The amount of energy or work needed to raise an item weighing one pound, a distance of one foot.

FUSE: A protective device in a circuit which prevents circuit overload by breaking the circuit when a specific amperage is present. The device is constructed around a strip or wire of a lower amperage rating than the circuit it is designed to protect. When an amperage higher than that stamped on the fuse is present in the circuit, the strip or wire melts, opening the circuit.

GEAR RATIO: The ratio between the number of teeth on meshing gears.

GENERATOR: A device which converts mechanical energy into electrical energy.

HEAT RANGE: The measure of a spark plug's ability to dissipate heat from its firing end. The higher the heat range, the hotter the plug fires.

HUB: The center part of a wheel or gear.

HYDROCARBON (HC): Any chemical compound made up of hydrogen and carbon. A major pollutant formed by the engine as a byproduct of combustion.

HYDROMETER: An instrument used to measure the specific gravity of a solution.

INCH POUND (inch lbs.; sometimes in.lb. or in. lbs.): One twelfth of a foot pound.

INDUCTION: A means of transferring electrical energy in the form of a magnetic field. Principle used in the ignition coil to increase voltage.

INJECTOR: A device which receives metered fuel under relatively low pressure and is activated to inject the fuel into the engine under relatively high pressure at a predetermined time.

INPUT SHAFT: The shaft to which torque is applied, usually carrying the driving gear or gears.

INTAKE MANIFOLD: A casting of passages or pipes used to conduct air or a fuel/air mixture to the cylinders.

JOURNAL: The bearing surface within which a shaft operates.

KEY: A small block usually fitted in a notch between a shaft and a hub to prevent slippage of the two parts.

MANIFOLD: A casting of passages or set of pipes which connect the cylinders to an inlet or outlet source.

MANIFOLD VACUUM: Low pressure in an engine intake manifold formed just below the throttle plates. Manifold vacuum is highest at idle and drops under acceleration.

MASTER CYLINDER: The primary fluid pressurizing device in a hydraulic system. In automotive use, it is found in brake and hydraulic clutch systems and is pedal activated, either directly or, in a power brake system, through the power booster.

MODULE: Electronic control unit, amplifier or igniter of solid state or integrated design which controls the current flow in the ignition primary circuit based on input from the pick-up coil. When the module opens the primary circuit, high secondary voltage is induced in the coil.

NEEDLE BEARING: A bearing which consists of a number (usually a large number) of long, thin rollers.

OHM: (Ω) The unit used to measure the resistance of conductor-to-electrical flow. One ohm is the amount of resistance that limits current flow to one ampere in a circuit with one volt of pressure.

OHMMETER: An instrument used for measuring the resistance, in ohms, in an electrical circuit.

OUTPUT SHAFT: The shaft which transmits torque from a device, such as a transmission.

OVERDRIVE: A gear assembly which produces more shaft revolutions than that transmitted to it.

OVERHEAD CAMSHAFT (OHC): An engine configuration in which the camshaft is mounted on top of the cylinder head and operates the valve either directly or by means of rocker arms.

OVERHEAD VALVE (OHV): An engine configuration in which all of the valves are located in the cylinder head and the camshaft is located in the cylinder block. The camshaft operates the valves via lifters and pushrods.

OXIDES OF NITROGEN (NOx): Chemical compounds of nitrogen produced as a byproduct of combustion. They combine with hydrocarbons to produce smog.

OXYGEN SENSOR: Use with the feedback system to sense the presence of oxygen in the exhaust gas and signal the computer which can reference the voltage signal to an air/fuel ratio.

PINION: The smaller of two meshing gears.

PISTON RING: An open-ended ring with fits into a groove on the outer diameter of the piston. Its chief function is to form a seal between the piston and cylinder wall. Most automotive pistons have three rings: two for compression sealing; one for oil sealing.

PRELOAD: A predetermined load placed on a bearing during assembly or by adjustment.

PRIMARY CIRCUIT: the low voltage side of the ignition system which consists of the ignition switch, ballast resistor or resistance wire, bypass, coil, electronic control unit and pick-up coil as well as the connecting wires and harnesses.

PRESS FIT: The mating of two parts under pressure, due to the inner diameter of one being smaller than the outer diameter of the other, or vice versa; an interference fit.

RACE: The surface on the inner or outer ring of a bearing on which the balls, needles or rollers move.

REGULATOR: A device which maintains the amperage and/or voltage levels of a circuit at predetermined values.

RELAY: A switch which automatically opens and/or closes a circuit.

RESISTANCE: The opposition to the flow of current through a circuit or electrical device, and is measured in ohms. Resistance is equal to the voltage divided by the amperage.

RESISTOR: A device, usually made of wire, which offers a preset amount of resistance in an electrical circuit.

RING GEAR: The name given to a ring-shaped gear attached to a differential case, or affixed to a flywheel or as part of a planetary gear set.

ROLLER BEARING: A bearing made up of hardened inner and outer races between which hardened steel rollers move.

ROTOR: 1. The disc-shaped part of a disc brake assembly, upon which the brake pads bear; also called, brake disc. 2. The device mounted atop the distributor shaft, which passes current to the distributor cap tower contacts.

SECONDARY CIRCUIT: The high voltage side of the ignition system, usually above 20,000 volts. The secondary includes the ignition coil, coil wire, distributor cap and rotor, spark plug wires and spark plugs.

SENDING UNIT: A mechanical, electrical, hydraulic or electro-magnetic device which transmits information to a gauge.

SENSOR: Any device designed to measure engine operating conditions or ambient pressures and temperatures. Usually electronic in nature and designed to send a voltage signal to an on-board computer, some sensors may operate as a simple on/off switch or they may provide a variable voltage signal (like a potentiometer) as conditions or measured parameters change.

SHIM: Spacers of precise, predetermined thickness used between parts to establish a proper working relationship.

SLAVE CYLINDER: In automotive use, a device in the hydraulic clutch system which is activated by hydraulic force, disengaging the clutch.

SOLENOID: A coil used to produce a magnetic field, the effect of which is to produce work.

SPARK PLUG: A device screwed into the combustion chamber of a spark ignition engine. The basic construction is a conductive core inside of a ceramic insulator, mounted in an outer conductive base. An electrical charge from the spark plug wire travels along the conductive core and jumps a preset air gap to a grounding point or points at the end of the conductive base. The resultant spark ignites the fuel/air mixture in the combustion chamber.

SPLINES: Ridges machined or cast onto the outer diameter of a shaft or inner diameter of a bore to enable parts to mate without rotation.

TACHOMETER: A device used to measure the rotary speed of an engine, shaft, gear, etc., usually in rotations per minute.

THERMOSTAT: A valve, located in the cooling system of an engine, which is closed when cold and opens gradually in response to engine heating, controlling the temperature of the coolant and rate of coolant flow.

TOP DEAD CENTER (TDC): The point at which the piston reaches the top of its travel on the compression stroke.

TORQUE: The twisting force applied to an object.

TORQUE CONVERTER: A turbine used to transmit power from a driving member to a driven member via hydraulic action, providing changes in drive ratio and torque. In automotive use, it links the driveplate at the rear of the engine to the automatic transmission.

TRANSDUCER: A device used to change a force into an electrical signal.

TRANSISTOR: A semi-conductor component which can be actuated by a small voltage to perform an electrical switching function.

TUNE-UP: A regular maintenance function, usually associated with the replacement and adjustment of parts and components in the electrical and fuel systems of a vehicle for the purpose of attaining optimum performance.

TURBOCHARGER: An exhaust driven pump which compresses intake air and forces it into the combustion chambers at higher than atmospheric pressures. The increased air pressure allows more fuel to be burned and results in increased horsepower being produced.

VACUUM ADVANCE: A device which advances the ignition timing in response to increased engine vacuum.

VACUUM GAUGE: An instrument used to measure the presence of vacuum in a chamber.

VALVE: A device which control the pressure, direction of flow or rate of flow of a liquid or gas.

VALVE CLEARANCE: The measured gap between the end of the valve stem and the rocker arm, cam lobe or follower that activates the valve.

VISCOSITY: The rating of a liquid's internal resistance to flow.

VOLTMETER: An instrument used for measuring electrical force in units called volts. Voltmeters are always connected parallel with the circuit being tested.

WHEEL CYLINDER: Found in the automotive drum brake assembly, it is a device, actuated by hydraulic pressure, which, through internal pistons, pushes the brake shoes outward against the drums.

MASTER INDEX

PARA RESETEAR El servicio del
haceite se preciona El informacion
RESed se empuja el reston hasta
que salga el oil 100X100.

PARA LAS cherokee se abre el
swich. se preciona seeleet una ves
x luego set